THE HOUSE OF PERCY

THE HOUSE
OF PERCY

Honor, Melancholy, and Imagination
in a Southern Family

BERTRAM WYATT-BROWN

New York   *Oxford*

OXFORD UNIVERSITY PRESS

1994

Oxford University Press

Oxford   New York   Toronto
Delhi   Bombay   Calcutta   Madras   Karachi
Kuala Lumpur   Singapore   Hong Kong   Tokyo
Nairobi   Dar es Salaam   Cape Town
Melbourne   Auckland   Madrid

and associated companies in
Berlin   Ibadan

Library of Congress Cataloging-in-Publication Data
Wyatt-Brown, Bertram, 1932–
The house of Percy : honor, melancholy, and imagination
in a Southern family / Bertram Wyatt-Brown.
p. cm.   Includes bibliographical references (p.) and index.
ISBN 0-19-505626-4   1. Percy family.
2. Percy, Walker, 1916–   —Bibliography.
3. Percy, William Alexander, 1885–1942—Bibliography.
4. Dorsey, Sarah A. (Sarah Anne), 1829–1879—Bibliography.
5. Authors, American—Southern States—Biography.
6. Intellectuals—Southern States—Biography.
I. Title. CT274.P48W93   1994   929'.2'0973—dc20
93-20690

Frontispiece: "The Patriot," over the grave of Senator LeRoy Percy,
by Malvina Hoffman, commissioned by William Alexander Percy, 1930.
Photo by Bertram Wyatt-Brown

1 3 5 7 9 8 6 4 2

Printed in the United States of America
on acid-free paper

This book is dedicated to

ANNE MARBURY WYATT-BROWN

Preface

"Tragedy pursues the Percy family like Nemesis."

Harry Ball, a resident of Greenville[1]

At the moment, historians are wrestling with the nature of their craft, experimenting, unwisely some think, with forms of fiction and questioning the utility of seeking historical objectivity.[2] *The House of Percy* is straight history—without, I hope, much partisanship. The reader will find no made-up dialogues, no entries into undocumented thoughts, no distortions of chronology except the conventional rearrangements that literary structure seemed to require. Nonetheless, at the heart of the text lies the complicated issue of portrayal—the family's representation of itself versus the historian's representation of the family. Both, one must confess, are artifacts. Without doubt the Percys will not recognize themselves in this book. Besides, their version of past reality is more useful to them than mine would be. But, like an anthropologist seeking to describe village social structure or burial rites, the historian intrudes upon the scene, stirs up the dust, and becomes an unsettling force without so intending.

Such are the perils of biography for the relatives and friends of the subject, but hazards await the biographer, too. Only on the surface of things are these the best of times for writers in a genre which has enjoyed an astonishing revival in recent years. The lives of writers, thinkers and politicians have been subjected to thorough treatments that not only explore the psychology of their subjects but also the genealogical heritage to which their inspiration and their troubles may be traced. One thinks of such works as R. W. B. Lewis's narrative of the James family of Massachusetts; Jean Strouse's *Alice James;* Lynda Wagner-Martin's *Sylvia Plath;* and, in another field of creativity, Peter Gay on Sigmund Freud and Lawrence Friedman's history of the Menninger family and their psychoanalytic clinic. The list in Southern studies has been especially strong: Paul Nagel on the Lees of Virginia; James Klotter on the Breckinridges of Kentucky; Craig Simpson on Henry Wise; Drew Faust's James Henry Hammond; Darden

Pyron's Margaret Mitchell; Joel Williamson's study of William Faulkner and his lineage—to select just a handful.[3]

Despite these gleaming successes, biographers must be wary. Amid much praise, Diane Middlebrook's thoughtful life of Anne Sexton came under withering fire because she used taped recordings of sessions of Sexton's analysis, even though she did so with the cooperation and encouragement of Sexton's literary executor and the analyst involved.[4] From a less antagonistic point of view, questions of ethics and aesthetics also arise. If reticence was a cardinal principle governing generations of Percys, as it will later appear, should an outsider to their domain unearth facts that might cause pain to family members? Recognizing this difficulty, I have left out of the account living members of the Percy family as much as possible and rely to a great extent upon Jay Tolson's indispensable biography of Walker Percy and other sources already published. (An exception to this rule is a brief account that covers Walker Percy's months in Sewanee, Tennessee, at the close of World War II.) I trust that I do not overuse the darker colors in family portrayals but reveal the complex shadings that made the Percys human.[5]

Concerning the availability of historical sources, the chief problem in writing this work was not an overabundance of unsubstantiated rumors but a scarcity of materials about key figures. Some family members (notably Sarah Dorsey) deliberately had papers destroyed. Others allowed them to disappear. A family genealogist was exasperated with cousins who let crucial documents vanish without a trace. Fortunately, LeRoy Percy of Greenville, Mississippi, who heads the clan, did not follow his brother Walker Percy's advice and burn the entire family archive. The Percy papers, housed at the Mississippi Department of Archives and History, are an enormous, indispensable help, which earns LeRoy Percy the historian's permanent gratitude. However, they are by no means complete and cover well only a score or so of years.

The spottiness of the available data makes inevitable a certain unevenness in the narrative, especially of the internal, domestic aspect of family life. But for a number of Percys and relations, I simply could not find much relevant information, a lack which makes final judgments about some incidents and personalities hard to reach. Other chapters cover political affairs in the Percys' history not only because those accounts have meaning beyond the family itself but also because such areas are the only aspect of their lives which can be recaptured at all. Other sections rely chiefly upon novels or published work with few quotations from letters, since the Percy relations in question have left almost no other resource. Unlike fiction-writers, historians are limited to their evidence.

To make up for a sparsity of personal papers, I scoured the archives, libraries, and courthouses of the South, from Galveston and Hattiesburg to Nashville and Baltimore. Visits to Dublin historical archives, and to various libraries and a church in England, and to repositories in Maine,

Massachusetts, and Pennsylvania have brought to light invaluable items. Materials have arrived by mail from Kirkwall in the Orkneys, Edinburgh and Greenock in Scotland, and Wolfville and Halifax in Nova Scotia, not to mention a dozen places from Cincinnati to San Marino, California.

The unusual aspect of the investigation was tracking down the location of two compilations of chiefly late eighteenth-century documents and late nineteenth-century genealogical papers. The Thompson-Wright materials are located at two private homes in Baton Rouge, and the Longcope-Johansen papers are deposited in a farmhouse attic in Lee, Massachusetts. Having the chance to use these splendid collections, I found that they opened doors of fact and interpretive possibility without which this work would have been much the poorer. Likewise, the discovery and use of Sarah Dorsey materials in the vast Stanley family collection at the John Rylands Library at the University of Manchester, England, enriched the narrative of several chapters. Although I interviewed a considerable number of people, I err on the side of caution in using their remarks, not because they were personally untrustworthy but because they could usually testify only to rumors and perceptions, not to facts.

This family biography has been personally rewarding. Anyone studying the Percys must become impressed with the resilience and the pride of one of America's more accomplished and yet tragic families. As one of the Percys' neighbors in Greenville declared in a statement placed at the head of the Preface, Nemesis cruelly raked them down. Yet, there are lessons here for the millions in this country who have suffered the numbing effects of depression. The Percys provide for them hope in their many examples of fortitude, wit, and compassion. In the literary achievements of Will Percy and his adoptive son Walker, generations of readers will come to greater self-understanding and the stigma too long associated with the malady will ultimately disappear. Although a recent advertisement for a biography of Walker Percy describes them as "the Kennedy family of their time," a closer analogy is the Adamses of Massachusetts. That lineage provided the nation with two Presidents, John and John Quincy, as well as one of its greatest diplomats in Charles Francis and one of its finest historians and memorialists in Henry. Like the Percys, the Adams clan reached high goals in politics, economic power, and literary art while haunted by the tragedy of deep melancholy. Since this mental condition has so pronounced a genetic origin, they belong in the company of other extraordinary, dynamic families, the lineages that produced among their afflicted kindred such artistic geniuses as Samuel Johnson and James Boswell, Mary Wollstonecraft and Mary Percy Shelley, Samuel Taylor Coleridge, Lord Byron, Alfred, Lord Tennyson, Robert Schumann, the Jameses—Henry and William—Herman Melville, Virginia Woolf, and Ernest Hemingway.[6] In many respects, the Percys, though less well known, were the Southern counterparts of these brilliant, troubled family lines. As Robert Burton, the seventeenth-century writer, observed, "I need not therefore make any doubt of Melancholy, but that it is an hereditary disease," but one, it must be added, that transforms the "taint of blood," as the poet Tennyson called it, into the elixir of creativity. From the depths of sadness has arisen the paradox of their many and extraordinary contributions to the American spirit.[7]

Bertram Wyatt-Brown
Gainesville
February 1994

Acknowledgments

A book of this length and complexity could not have been written without the help of more people than I can acknowledge here. Foremost among the contributors were those who read the manuscript in its various stages and offered advice which greatly strengthened whatever coherence and concision it now has. My wife Anne Marbury Wyatt-Brown has been the most constant source of inspiration and critical comment as ideas emerged and chapters were created—sometimes to be wisely thrown away. A first-class scholar in her own right, she has a special gift of psychological insight which she applied effectively to understand the women whose lives are explored here. For that reason I dedicate this book to her as a form of celebration for over thirty years of love and intellectual companionship.

As one of the nation's most skillful editors, Anita Rutman gallantly slashed through a thicket of turgid phrases, overwritten details, and whole chapters that blocked the horizon. With the same zeal with which Daniel Webster eliminated the ranks of proconsuls in President Harrison's inaugural address in 1840, she cleared away the debris so that without her sensible criticisms *The House of Percy* would have been much longer, less coherent, and less readable. Her work made the task for Leona Capeless of Oxford University Press much easier, but she further strengthened the text with her acute insights. Sheldon Meyer of Oxford University Press has been a patient source of encouragement and a sensitive reader over the many years that it took to complete *The House of Percy*. Leona Capeless gave whatever final sheen and accuracy that the text may have, a service for which I am much in her debt.

As usual when reviewing my work, David Hackett Fischer of Brandeis University and another veteran in the Oxford UP pen, made invaluable suggestions about the structuring of the book. In the late summer, 1993, Susan Marbury, my brilliant sister-in-law, pointed out problems of flawed logic in the Prologue. Kieran Quinlan of the University of Alabama, Birmingham, wisely critiqued the Walker Percy chapters.

Patiently reading the entire manuscript, sometimes in successive versions of chapters, Lucas Myers of San Francisco and Otto Olsen of Gainesville were also instrumental, Lucas with regard to style, Otto in catching points of historical confusion. Jeffrey Adler and David Chalmers of the University of Florida, Larry Friedman of Indiana University, Henry M. McGiven of the University of South Alabama, Randolph Boehm of University Micro-films, James Cobb of the University of Tennessee, David Lewis of Auburn, and Jeff Norrell of Alabama were all most helpful, but much of the material they read had to be cut. Daniel Dupre of the University of North Carolina, Charlotte, shared with me his informative chapters on early Huntsville. William S. Coker of the University of West Florida, Jack Holmes, who later tragically killed himself, and Douglas Inglis of Seville, Spain, were indispensable for straightening out for me the tangled history of British and then Spanish West Florida. Dr. Paul McHugh, Director of the Phipps Psychiatric Clinic, the Johns Hopkins University Hospitals, Baltimore, was as helpful as his fine sense of professional discretion could permit.

I am most indebted to Mellie Johansen and Duncan Longcope of Corn-hilll Farm, Lee, Massachusetts, for their unstinting help. Without access to the genealogical papers relating to the early Percys and Robert Percy's descendants, the first and last parts of the book would have been much less rich in texture and factual content. The same grateful acknowledgment is due to Dr. and Mrs. O. M. Thompson and Mr. and Mrs. William H. Wright, Jr. of Baton Rouge. They generously permitted me to photocopy the papers, many of them, like the Cornhill Farm documents, dating from the eighteenth century. The materials had been gathered by their relation, John Hereford Percy, the family's most assiduous genealogist. Professor Robert Gilmore of Lafayette, Louisiana, lent me additional genealogical letters that added materially to the story.

As a fellow wayfarer through the Percy saga, Jay Tolson, editor of the *Wilson Quarterly* and author of the moving and perceptive biography, *Pilgrim in the Ruins: A Life of Walker Percy* (1992), has been a most coopera-tive and enlightening companion. We first encountered each other on par-allel intellectual trails at a meeting of the Organization of American Historians in Philadelphia, 1987, and my association with him has been one of the treasured aspects of this undertaking.

Over the last four years or so a number of graduate students assisted in collecting material, running down references, checking the notes and the quotations. Especially notable in this way were Timothy Huebner, Kimb-erly Hanger, Dan Kilbride, Andrew Frank, Stan Deaton, and Christopher Morris, all students at the University of Florida, current or past. In check-ing the sources, they may not have caught all the textual errors that accu-mulated like carbuncles, but what was inadvertently missed must remain the author's responsibility and not theirs. Brad Bond, a student of Profes-sor William J. Cooper at Louisiana State University, S. W. Taylor, Jim Cobb's student at the University of Tennessee, and a student of Nancy Tomes and Charles Rosenberg at the University of Pennsylvania all con-tributed to the work by looking up documents and forwarding copies.

Professional genealogists and others interested in Percy-related ancestry have also been helpful. Among them I offer special thanks to the well-informed Alma Carpenter of Natchez and Marianne Barrett of Gulfport, Mississippi; Mrs. Elizabeth Dart of St. Francisville, Louisiana; Sharon Dubeau of Agincourt, Canada; Mrs. A. C. H. Hallett of Pembroke, Bermuda; Michael Maclagan, Herald, the College of Arms, London; Mrs. William King Holland of Saint Louis; Russell S. Hall of Memphis, with his special interest in the Dahlgrens; retired Vanderbilt professor Herschel Gower with similar interests; F. James Dallett of Taconic, Connecticut, an expert on the Sigoignes and LaRoches; and Malcolm Bell of Savannah. Not least in helpfulness in tracking down fugitive clues were Arthur Ben and Betty Nick Chitty of Sewanee, Tennessee.

Several individuals were kind enough to permit interviews, but their reminiscences chiefly served as background and only occasionally if at all appear in the text itself. I mention in this connection, Cynthia Ware of New Orleans, Shelby Foote of Memphis, Billups Phinizy Percy of New Orleans, LeRoy Percy, the late Roberta Miller, Leon K. Koury, Clinton Bagley, all of Greenville; Mrs. Mildred Commodore and William Armstrong Percy III of Boston; Mr. and Mrs. Joseph Johnston and Betty Wright, who entertained me on a memorable fall weekend, 1989, at their historic summer residence, Bremo, on the James River; retired attorney Lee C. Bradley then aged 93 and since deceased, the late Mrs. Charles Allison, John and Louise Wrinkle, all of Birmingham, Alabama; Lady Thornton (Rosamond Myers) of Surry, England, Mary Shepherd Quintard Wyatt-Brown of Beaufort, South Carolina. Special notice must be accorded Charles Bell of Santa Fe, New Mexico, Professor Emeritus of St. John's College. He not only gave me a most fascinating interview in Montpelier, Vermont, in 1988 but also supplied me with some highly useful copies of papers from the Judge Bell family archives. Nor should my indebtedness to Walker Percy for two interviews be omitted.

Archivists and librarians on this side of the Atlantic as well in the British Isles uniformly met the ideals of their profession, answering inquiries promptly, volunteering additional information or bibliographical suggestions, and copying scores of documents. Outstanding among these highly proficient professionals are Anne Lipscomb of the Mississippi Department of Archives and History; Richard Schraeder and John White at the Southern Historical Collection, Wilson Library, University of North Carolina, Chapel Hill; Anne Armour, archivist, Jessie Ball DuPont Library, University of the South; Faye Phillips, Special Collections, Hill Memorial Library, Louisiana State University; James J. Holmberg, Archivist, the Filson Club, Louisville; Thomas Horrocks, Library, College of Physicians of Philadelphia; Mrs. L. E. Couperwhite, Greenock, Scotland; Carolyn Morris, Archivist, Pennsylvania Hospital Historic Library, Philadelphia; Alison Fraser, Archivist, Orkney Library, Kirkwall, Scotland. Canadian librarians were also a great resource: Carmon Carroll of the Public Archives of Nova Scotia; Patricia Belier of the University of New Brunswick; and Burton Glendenning of the New Brunswick Provincial Archives. I must also mention the staffs at the Rosenberg Library, Galveston; the Maine Historical Society, Portland; the Historical Society of Pennsylvania, Philadelphia; the Library of the University of Kentucky, Lexington; the Tennessee Historical Society and State Museum, Nashville; the Delaware Historical Society, Wilmington; the Manuscripts Division, Library of Congress and National Archives, Washington; the Public Records Office, Kew, London; and the John Rylands Library, University of Manchester.

Finally a succession of able secretaries somehow navigated successfully through the rocks and shoals of this project, contributing in many ways to its completion. I mention Debbie Webb, Joyce Phillips, Pat Ferguson, Cynthia Sain, and B. J. Clager, the last of whom helped immeasurably during the last stages of the enterprise. The Department of History has been favored with efficient, conscientious, and friendly staff members, most especially under the recent leadership of Kim Yocum and Betty Corwine.

Foremost among the institutions to furnish financial support and facilities was the National Humanities Center, Research Triangle Park. I am most especially grateful to its director, W. Robert Connor, and Kent Mullikin, his able assistant. They have assembled a remarkably congenial staff, including Wayne and Mary Donna Pond, Alan Tuttle, Sandra Copeland, Rebecca Vargha, Jean Houston, and too many others to name them all. During a wonderful year at that remarkable location in the wooded hills of North Carolina, I began the writing of this book. Doubtless heavenly authorities have already studied the management of the place as a model for a similar institution for scholars happily destined to commune together and write through eternity. The Center permitted me a crucial ten days in residence during the fall of 1993 to make the final cuts and revisions of the work. An appropriate seminar on "Solitude" that year brought together Stanley Chojnacki, Brenda Meehan-Waters, Richard Peterson, and Nikita Pokrovsky, whose brother, Anton Kumanov of Moscow, supplied me with the handsome sketch of Robert Percy.

I also heartily thank David P. Kennedy, president of the Earhart Foundation, Ann Arbor, Michigan, which provided indispensable financial support for the year at the NHC. Additionally, I received a National Endowment for the Humanities Senior Fellowship in 1985–86 when the ideas for this book were still being formed. I am particularly indebted to Richard J. Milbauer, late philanthropist of Tarpon Springs, Florida, who established the professorial chair of which I am the first occupant. His interest in the history of the Spanish borderlands of North America led, upon his suicide in 1981, to the bequest of a substantial endowment, managed by the University of Florida Foundation. The income supports graduate-student stipends, salary for a part-time secretary, and funds for travel and research, all of which expenditure, I hope, redounds to the honor of the benefactor.

A final word of appreciation must also be offered to the memory of Will Percy and Walker Percy. This book would not have been written had the guardian and his ward not expressed themselves with such force and perceptiveness. I regret that my study appears after Walker Percy's death. He understood the strengths and weaknesses of historical scholarship. After receipt of my manuscript article entitled, "Will, Walker and Honor Dying: The Percys and Literary Creativity," he, in reply, gently pointed to both its insights and its blind spots.* He died less than four months later. How instructive it would have been to have his reaction to *The House of Percy,* a more ambitious exploration of his family's heritage and significance.

B. W-B.

*Bertram Wyatt-Brown, "Will, Walker and Honor Dying: The Percys and Literary Creativity," in Winfred B. Moore, Jr. and Joseph F. Tripp, eds., *Looking South: Chapters in the Story of an American Region* (Westport, Conn.: Greenwood Press, 1989), 229–58; Walker Percy to the author, January 24, 1990, in author's possession.

Contents

PART FOUR

Fiction, Legend, and Lineage

THE HOUSE OF PERCY

PROLOGUE

The Brooding Knight

They outtalked thee, hissed thee, tore thee?
Better men fared thus before thee;
Fired their ringing shots and passed,
Hotly charged—and sank at last.
Charge once more then and be dumb!
Let the victors, when they come,
When the forts of folly fall,
Find thy body by the wall!

Matthew Arnold [1]

Across the road from St. James Episcopal Church in Greenville, Mississippi, lies its tree-shaded cemetery, green and quiet as a graveyard should be. Yet among the prosaic rows of headstones, urns, and slabs of gray and white an unexpected sight greets the visitor: a statue in burnished armor, marking the grave of Senator LeRoy Percy, 1861–1929. The standing figure gazes downward, its mailed hands resting on a great sword. The rugged face does not suggest joy or reflection, but defiance, grit, and, in no small measure, bitter melancholy. The sculptor intended no sentimental meditation. A Victorian artist of the Burne-Jones school would have fashioned a kneeling figure with a serene countenance turned toward the heavens in appeal for succor and blessing. But the maker of this work designed instead a statue that conveyed a credible human presence despite the incongruity of a medieval knight standing watch over land once traversed by Choctaws and cropped by slaves. Bearing the inscription PATRIOT, the warrior stands before a white marble stele; carved verses upon its back report his mood. The lines come from Matthew Arnold's poem "The Last Word" and are given above. In every aspect the monument reflected the family's claim to a noble English ancestry and cultural heritage.

After the Mississippi senator's death in 1929, his son William Alexander (Will) Percy, invited Malvina Hoffman of New York to visit Greenville and make the memorial, which was completed before the end of 1933.[2] Hoffman was familiar with the shrouded figure of Grief which Henry

3

Adams had commissioned in 1885 for the grave of his wife "Clover" Hooper from the sculptor Augustus Saint-Gaudens. Adams considered the statue in the Rock Creek Cemetery in Washington, D.C., an expression of his sorrow as well as of the enigma and uncertainty of human existence.[3] Like "Grief," the "Patriot" in the Greenville graveyard bears a broad symbolism, not only as an emblem for a distinguished Delta leader and benefactor but also for the history of one of the most remarkable and fascinating families in America. Throughout the generations, the Percys helped to create the Deep South—not just as slaveholding frontiersmen but as agents of change in the post-Civil War years. They belonged as much to the New South of heavy industry and plantation agribusiness as to the Old South of large-scale land speculation and cotton-growing. Walker Percy, their most recent public spokesman, considered himself a son of the newly emerging South, who thought himself freed from such shackles of the past as segregation, cross-burnings, and Confederate flag-waving. In their active pursuits, the Percy men usually kept up with the times in which they lived. Their occupations as planters, lawyers, physicians, militia officers, corporation lawyers, and bank directors complemented their energetic civic work—from establishing the first public library in Huntsville, Alabama, to leadership of relief work in the Mississippi Flood of 1927. No less important was their contribution to Southern letters in the twentieth century as well as in the nineteenth century. In the latter period, the Percys with lively ambitions were women who had extraordinary literary careers.

The statue is meant to convey the distinguished character of the Percys' past. Yet there is something incongruous about it. Will Percy might have followed convention and authorized a bust or full-length sculpture of the senator. In life his father had seemed the very model of a prominent statesman of the Progressive era—strong jaw, piercing gray eyes, noble brow, and iron-gray hair. Instead, his worshipful son sought something more arresting, more universal in meaning, like the Saint-Gaudens abstraction. The knight was meant to embody Will Percy's conception of his forebears and his wish that they all—not the senator alone—should be known. At the same time, the representation helped to obscure the individual, who became lost under the symbol.

Will Percy's requisition of the bronze cast was the first of two acts of commemoration. The second was the publication by Alfred Knopf in 1941 of his memoir, *Lanterns on the Levee: Recollections of a Planter's Son,* in which he once again expressed his sense of bereavement and his longing for vindication of the family's ideological defeats. No less than Henry Adams's renowned works, *Mont-Saint-Michel and Chartres* and *The Education,* the autobiography served to proclaim both a personal and a family credo. With wry humor and an elegant style, *Lanterns on the Levee* offered a tragic vision of past and future—what the late Melvin Bradford called the very heart of modern Southern literature—the exposition of an "elegiac wisdom." By that he meant an implied if not always explicit comparison of the present to earlier times and experiences, moments not necessarily morally better but more vital than the soulless here and now. William Faulkner's *The Sound and Fury,* Allen Tate's *The Fathers,* and Caroline Gordon's *Penhally*—these and many other works belong to this tradition. Varied though the approaches may be, they all stress the tragedy of dissolution and defeat. Yet in recompense for the struggle, the writers celebrate the toil and the joy of writing, the perpetuation of worthy purposes, the act of remembrance. This, too, was the message of *Lanterns on the Levee.*

Like some other notable works of art, both Will Percy's autobiography and Malvina Hoffman's monument have more meanings than their simple classical lines would suggest. My introduction to the family's complexity and fascination grew out of an invitation to speak at a special gathering in Athens, Georgia. In October 1985, I presented a paper at a symposium to celebrate the bicentennial of the founding of the state university. Numan V. Bartley, the organizer in the History Department, had suggested some reflections growing out of my previously published *Southern Honor: Ethics and Behavior in the Old South.*[4] Taking his advice, I divided the topic of heroes' honor in the Southern literary imagination into four discrete phases: honor as a social and literary assumption in the Revolutionary era; honor romanticized in the nineteenth century; honor uncovered and yet mourned during the middle years of the twentieth century—William Faulkner's generation; honor ridiculed or forgotten in more recent fiction. The literary history of the ethic was seen to parallel the steady decline of what Southerners once liked to call "chivalry" as the region, particularly after the Civil War, gradually became urbanized, secular, and undifferentiated from the rest of the country.

Having read Walker Percy's *Love in the Ruins* and *The Last Gentleman,* I discussed the novelist as a curiously transitional figure. Unlike his predecessor Faulkner, who had lamented the passing of honor but revealed its untamed character, Walker Percy had no tattered, second-hand memories of Civil War glory. He bristled at any suggestion that he belonged in the Faulknerian tradition at all.[5] Yet as Percy readily acknowledged himself, he too had been reared on the cult of noblesse oblige and gallantry, first in Birmingham where his father almost fought a duel with pistols in the mid-1920s and later in Greenville where, as a teenager, he was introduced to the romantic faith of Will Percy. With his great powers of conversation, "Uncle Will," as Walker and his two younger brothers called their cousin, regaled them with stories that amplified the luster of his stoic philosophy— the "broad-sword virtues" of manhood and valiance. (Will Percy, who was their father LeRoy Pratt Percy's first cousin, became the legal guardian and surrogate father for the boys in 1932 after the death of their parents.) Try as he might, Walker Percy could not forget that heritage. Having reached his middle age, the novelist could not burlesque the premises of the chivalric code as younger contemporary Southern writers in the 1960s and 1970s were beginning to do. Loyalty to family and particularly to Will Percy would have made such reaction feel like a base betrayal.

In view of Percy's ambivalence about the values of honor, his sponsorship of John Kennedy Toole's *Confederacy of Dunces* was most striking, as my paper at Athens, Georgia, pointed out. The work had been turned down by Alfred A. Knopf, Inc., publisher of Percy's first novel, *The Moviegoer,* which had appeared in 1961. Percy managed to have Louisiana State University Press produce Toole's manuscript posthumously, and it became a bestseller and winner of a Pulitzer Prize. *Confederacy of Dunces* is a picaresque, set in the working-class district of New Orleans. As Walker Percy put it in the foreword, Ignatius Reilly, the hero, is a "mad Oliver Hardy, a fat Don Quixote, a perverse Thomas Aquinas." Lurching, like the Sad Knight, from one lunatic adventure to the next, Reilly rolls his food cart, shaped like a hot-dog and looking like an oversized phallus, through the streets during Mardi Gras. In Percy's words, Toole's character Reilly is occupied in a "thunderous" war against not merely "the assorted excesses of modern times" but also the foundations of old Southern values and customs.[6]

How curious that the author of the prize-winning novel *The Moviegoer* and other works noted for their philosophical sophistication had associated himself with a comic novelist like Toole. Walker Percy himself was surprised at his positive reaction to the young writer's manic lampooning of the honor code that the Percys for generations had espoused. But even the least psychologically aware reader could perceive how close they really were. In their fiction both vented a rage that was masked by laughter. In their understanding of the world and its evils, Roman Catholicism greatly influenced both these authors. Behind the manic hilarity of Toole's fictional persona was an artist who was chronically depressed—a state of mind that involves repressed fury. Prompted by Toole's persistent mother, Percy had undertaken his rescue mission after the young writer killed himself in 1969.

My interest in the puzzling connection between an obscure novelist, a victim of suicide, and a widely read Southern author in whose novels the lure of self-destruction is a persistent theme led to an exploratory reading in the papers of Senator LeRoy Percy and his son, William Alexander Percy, at the state archives in Jackson, Mississippi. In the midst of that large collection of faded carbon copies of business letters, yellow newspaper clippings, and barely readable drafts of Will Percy's poems and sketches, I made the kind of discovery that alerts the historian as a brief shimmer in a muddy sieve catches the gold-miner's eye. The item was a note of a few lines from Martha Susan Phinizy, Walker Percy's mother. Written to Senator Percy, the letter concerned the mental health of LeRoy Pratt Percy, her husband and the senator's nephew and showed that

Walker Percy's engrossment with suicide had a highly personal basis and was not just a metaphor for the plight of modern man in a morally empty world. The manner of his father LeRoy's death had had an enormous effect upon his art and view of the world.

I had to consult the novelist himself but did not come to know Walker Percy well and paid only two visits to his lovely house, which overlooked an acid-brown tributary creek leading to the Bogue Falaya at Covington, Louisiana. Both appointments were memorable yet brief. On the first occasion at midday in June 1987, the weather was sunny and unusually mild and the living-room bright and airy. Comfortable sofas surrounded a television set whose screen was cheerfully animated but mercifully silent. It took little time to realize that the writer was prepared for what had become a ritual in dealing with interviewers. Like others I found him gracious, seemingly outgoing but clearly self-protective. In fact so automatic and deflective had his answers become to questions about Existentialism, the Meaning of Life, Alienation in Modern Society, Kierkegaard, and other philosophical issues for which his fiction was known, that ten years before in *Esquire* he had published a satire called "Questions They Never Asked Me." [7]

Perhaps to his surprise, my inquiries fell under that category. They concerned the role of suicide and depression in his work and in his family—matters seldom raised by others. In fact, Robert Coles, Professor of Psychiatry and Medical Humanities at Harvard, had written a book based upon extensive interviews with Walker Percy, but scarcely mentioned issues of death and depression.[8] My queries were brash and could have been off-putting, but he was tolerant and more forthcoming than I had any reason to expect. Our second meeting in the fall of 1988 was less successful. Perhaps the writer had grown concerned about anyone's searching into corners of Percy history that no one else—not even family members—had explored. Also, his health was declining. He died of cancer in May 1990. Nevertheless, after getting permission, I sent him the best two essays on *The Last Gentleman* composed by students in an honors class at the University of Florida, and he was generous enough to respond with remarks on their interpretations. His occasional correspondence with me was warm and showed a lively interest in my researches.

Originally I had expected to write a work centering on Will Percy and Walker Percy, but as my inquiries proceeded, I found myself thoroughly engaged in the family's history from its beginnings in America to the mid-1940s. What struck me so forcibly was the consistency of family values, problems, and pursuits over a two-hundred-year span but even more the family's heroic response to suffering, setbacks, and regional calamities. By reading the genealogical history published by John Hereford Percy in the 1940s, I discovered that one of Charles Percy's female descendants had written novels "of some note," a clue that led to the discovery of three more published female authors in the nineteenth century.[9] Further investigation disclosed that these women's publications, while largely conventional, unveiled their sensitivity to the world of art and their intention of finding in that milieu a way of handling creatively their own burdens and sorrows.

Other discoveries followed. At the suggestion of Manning Parsons of Baltimore, I reached by phone Barbara Keyser, a member of the Longcope family who eventually led me to Cornhill Farm, Lee, Massachusetts. In the attic of that summer cottage Duncan Longcope of Boston and his sister Mary Lee (Mellie) Johansen stored invaluable eighteenth-century Percy items inherited from their mother, Janet Dana Longcope. These records, along with another cache of eighteenth-century Percy papers that Dr. O. M. and Mrs. Thompson graciously allowed me to photocopy, made possible a reconstruction of Percy history across the Atlantic and in the Western Hemisphere that greatly deepens an appreciation for the family's diversity and record of adventure and achievement. In a land of new beginnings, Americans have always hailed change over the stasis of unending woe that they have traditionally identified with the Old World. But here was a family that honored its past in extraordinary fashion. Retaining old papers and planting a knight on the banks of the Mississippi announced that, "this family has proud roots that reach across the seas and the centuries. We mattered then, we matter now."

I decided not to write a book about Walker Percy. By then, too, I was aware that Jay Tolson had a head start on his elegant biography, *Pilgrim in the Ruins,* and that Patrick Samway had been at work on the author's life for a number of years. A title, "Walker Percy's Forebears," was considered but abandoned as too limiting. It did not seem appropriate to offer a purely descriptive narrative about one generation of Percys after another— "an annotated genealogy," as the genre has been labeled.[10] Rather, my studies had given rise to a broader set of concerns which called for an increasingly elaborate treatment of family history. Thus, the purpose became an exploration of a family's culture: a means to explain how the Percy dynasty has succeeded in retaining its social standing, wealth, set of habits, and steadfast principles over a lengthy span. The ways of meeting those problems that have troubled its inner life have been as consistent as the problems themselves. If nations, ethnic groups, and even small communities have distinctive ways of behaving and articulating ideas over great stretches of time, we should not be surprised if families act along similar lines. Records have been too spotty, however, to permit many studies covering so long a period, at least in America. Moreover, a preoccupation with the concept of individualism in American life challenges the idea that traits of character, intelligence, and other qualities can be linked by means of natural and environmental inheritance. *The House of Percy* deals with what biographer James Klotter has called a family's "internal process of change."[11]

In the American South, where a more conservative and family-centered

order persisted longer than elsewhere, similar examples of generational biography spring to mind—studies of the Randolphs, Lees, Butlers, and
Breckinridges, among the better known. This work does not differ in
method from these, but analysis of significant continuities in family life
is combined with narration, which is ordinarily given preference in such
publications.[12] Meantime, the new social history has concentrated on a
largely anonymous reconstruction of the masses. Such egalitarian researches cannot show how a set of values such as a sense of special rectitude can enable generations to sustain a family's distinctiveness. The annals
of the American Percys are unique, the family so different from others in
our national history, and their multiplicity of talents and of tragedies so
astonishing that one hesitates to call them representative and to designate
this study as a guide for new approaches to biography and cultural studies.
Nevertheless, I hope that this work will encourage an appreciation for
the ways American families transmit their special sense of identity and
challenge as well as accept the conventions and prescriptions of their
region.

The result of research which spanned the Atlantic and carried the author
from Portland, Maine, to Galveston, Texas, and many points in between,
was the discovery of three main threads in the Percys' historical tapestry.
They are specified in the subtitle—Honor, Melancholy, and Imagination—
but are named here as the ethic of honor, the "humour" of melancholy, to
borrow a term from the English Renaissance, and the role of invention and
myth-making. The last phrase widens the definition of imagination to include published narratives in prose and verse as well as informal family
story-telling. These three salient elements that helped to shape the destiny
of this family for almost two hundred years are almost indivisible, for each
element merges into the others.

With regard to the sentiment of honor, like most others of their country
and times, the Percys thought of themselves in terms of a masculine
ideal—aggressive, possibly rash, jealous of the family name, and protective
of its women. In societies in which honor matters, the community of families, not individual members, decides what is right or wrong, courageous
and cowardly, prudent or reckless. A soldierly character in Lope de Vega's
seventeenth-century honor play *Los Commendadores de Córdoba* exclaims,
"Honor is that which is contained in another; no man grants honor to
himself; rather, he receives it from others."[13] Such was also the character
of the Deep South, particularly in the nineteenth century. The Percys
sought that form of acclaim but, in keeping with the code itself, never
surrendered pride to the demands of an unheeding public. Inner strength,
which in part was derived from a strong sense of family identity, was a
prerequisite of honor, an ideal for which they productively strove.

In keeping with Hoffman's art in the Episcopal churchyard, the Percy's sense of honor found reinforcement in their surname, itself appreciated by the family as symbolic of chivalry. From the time of William the Conqueror, Percys had ruled Northumberland, a primitive English district on the Scottish border. A succession of earls and later dukes perpetuated a fortune in landed wealth that, apart from royalty itself, was scarcely equaled by any other noble family in Great Britain. The example of Henry Percy, the Harry Hotspur whom William Shakespeare immortalized, figured in the American Percy family lore. The name implies a connection with the noble English house, but incontrovertible proof of kinship has never been found. Grand as the possibility of such a genealogical link might be, it mattered little whether a blood relationship really existed. The American Percys assumed it and behaved accordingly. Because an honor claimed and genuinely grasped may become an honor acknowledged, their Southern contemporaries accepted the Percys' right to full respect. Fulfilling the role conferred legitimacy. Fantasy became fact.

The building of legend about the Percy name reinforced the stature of the family at the top of the social and political elite of the South in the nineteenth century, and the reach of the family extended beyond the Southern border. Some nineteenth- and early twentieth-century cousins married into Northern families and found that their assumptions of status, taste, and good breeding, as the phrase went, were quite compatible with the criteria prevailing in the salons of Boston, New York, Philadelphia, and London. By the late nineteenth century, some of these Percy-related women lived the kind of life portrayed in the novels of Henry James.

Class consciousness, based in part upon family pride, was very much a part of the family's cultural heritage, one more common in the United States than a powerful myth of classlessness in American society would acknowledge. Despite the progress of democratic principles in national history, the conservative ideals of honor and "good blood," though greatly eroded today, were once no less American than the egalitarian impulse.[14] A strong sense of honor has never been a part of official ideology in America, but it has a more significant place in our ways of thinking and acting than historians have recognized. The ethic complemented the Percys' sense of class. The first Percy was a dedicated Tory who hated Americans and came to admire the Spanish regime under which he throve. His descendants, however, were Federalist-leaning Jeffersonians, then anti-Jacksonian Whigs until secession, war, and so-called Redemption confirmed them as Democrats with distinctly mugwumpish and finally progressive Republican inclinations. Senator Percy's friendships with President Theodore Roosevelt and William Howard Taft were cases in point. The Percys never questioned the assumption that everyone had an allotted place in the scheme of things and that their own appointed position was among the ruling, propertied ranks.

Such views inspired a degree of imperiousness. Although they were never bigoted snobs and were much attracted to Jews, a people so many others in the Percys' social group despised, they were nonetheless exclusive by inclination. Except for a few cherished intimates, outsiders were not to be wholly admitted to the inner family circle. The Percys trusted, loved, and depended upon one another in a fashion that another scholar recently noted about early planter families of the Southwest generally.[15] As part of their credo, the family members felt a deep obligation to help one another, both immediate and rather distant kin, in times of tragedy and need, a custom that so many Southerners observed, whether rich or poor. But more exceptional in the Percys' family life was a faculty for close friend-ships. In generation after generation each allied himself or herself with a companion whose intellectual interests, social tastes, politics, and habits best matched his or her own. Sometimes these relationships became almost fraternal, as in the case of Thomas George Percy and John Williams Walker at the beginning of the nineteenth century or Walker Percy and his friend Shelby Foote, also a prominent writer. In other cases, the pairing joined the opposite sexes—Sarah Dorsey, novelist, and Jefferson Davis, ex-President of the Confederacy, and William Alexander Percy and Janet Dana Longcope, a distant cousin. In none of these instances were the rela-tionships sexual. Instead they betokened a meeting of minds and hearts but not without psychological complexities. These bondings might seem irrelevant to matters of honor, but the forming of enduring friendships of this kind was usually undertaken to help meet the exigencies of the code and, in earlier days especially, soften its harsh requirements. To make mat-ters clearer, the code must be more fully explained.

For the Percys as well as for many other Southerners, the concepts of honor were defined in terms of the Stoic philosophy of Epictetus and the Emperor Marcus Aurelius. As one literary critic has observed, Stoicism offered such influential Southerners as Thomas Jefferson and Robert E. Lee "a gospel of endurance rather than hope, enabled them to reconcile social dependency with personal independence, allowed the idea that God was not separate from this world, and confirmed their suspicion that what is happening now will happen over and over, whatever our passions."[16] Although pagan in character, Stoicism affected the outlook of even the most religious-minded of the Percys. Sarah Dorsey, a devout Episcopalian, found the philosophy an assistance in accepting with hardihood the perils and personal losses of the Civil War.

Similarly, Walker Percy, a Roman Catholic convert, criticized the Stoic approach because it offered no hope in the afterlife, but he found its em-phasis upon personal responsibility an antidote to the moral relativism and permissiveness of the modern age. Moreover, the novelist thought the Stoic tradition, planted so deeply in his family's past, was a much-neglected as-pect of Southern history in general. As he explained to a French television audience in 1986, among upper-class "Anglo-Saxon Southerners, particu-larly in the military caste, this Stoic tradition was as strong as the Christian tradition." In the same year he told Charlotte Hays, a reporter, that all through his upbringing he had heard such incantations as these: "behave like a gentleman, the Southern honor code, chivalry, grace about doing right, treating women with respect. If somebody insults you then fight. Aren't these the Roman stoic virtues?" A "tough, Roman, chivalric code," he argued, "was much more military than Christian." And he would not, he added, discredit these ideas, old-fashioned though they were. In fact, he sometimes found it easier in his fiction to deal with the principles of Aurelian honor than with Christianity because an indirect approach was less didactic. Moreover, Roman Stoicism served him as an effective counterfoil to the Protestant ethos to which Southerners gave their official commitment but which Percy found inherently deficient.[17]

The novelist had acquired his understanding of the Stoic tradition in Southern life from William Alexander Percy, an agnostic. Although formerly a Catholic "Uncle Will" stressed the imperatives of manly duty and gave him and Walker's younger brothers copies of Marcus Aurelius' *Meditations*. In Will's opinion, this work and the gospels, which he urged them to study for reasons of comparison, should be central to the educated Southerner's self-conception. Moreover, he suggested to them that in many respects, the two leading guides to human behavior in the Western world were basically compatible. Both Stoicism and Christianity proclaimed the balm of brotherhood. Will Percy, a veteran of World War I, often told them, that soldiers in the field could not survive without a sense of mutual trust. Stoics had given comradeship under arms a wider meaning, one comparable to the Christian doctrine of love. As the statue in the Greenville cemetery attested, Will Percy preferred the darker code to the hopeful one of Christianity, and his adopted son Walker, despite his religious convictions, could not escape its influence.

※ ※

The second element concerns the role that melancholy played in family life. Neither a sense of honor nor a fancy for myth-making and an impulse for the writing of fiction can be fully understood in the family biography without taking account of this complication. From the late eighteenth to the mid-twentieth century the propensity for melancholia touched each generation and did so with disconcerting randomness. In earlier times in the Western world, chronic depression or, what the ancients called "sadness without a cause," was situated in a context of personal discomfort and wretchedness more severe than what we in the prosperous West experience today. Living in an age of medical innovation, we forget that early deaths of loved ones made prolonged periods of mourning a comparatively frequent occurrence. Scarcely a nineteenth-century family existed that had not followed the casket of at least one or two infants and young children.

The Percys were not spared the misfortune of losing young ones. To make matters worse, the family was inclined toward early fatality. For almost a hundred and fifty years, male Percys were struck down prematurely in life either by psychological or purely somatic maladies. For six generations of male Percys, the average age at death was thirty-nine. (Since the 1940s, Percys have been living longer.) The family's troubles were compounded by an additional, more perplexing problem. From 1794 to 1929, in each generation save one, a member of the lineage took his own life. Under these conditions, survivors cannot help but wonder what they contributed by action or neglect to so horrifying a decision. The novelist Walker Percy's father and his grandfather died at their own hands. Especially for children whose inexperience makes them vulnerable, the reaction to a father's suicide could well lead to irremediable emotional damage. The Percys showed enviable strength of mind and character under these strains, yet repeated occurrences from one generation to another were almost bound to induce suspicions about one's own capacity to survive. Some, including Walker and his "Uncle Will" Percy, confessed to episodes of depression, though never to the point of tempting death.

Those Percys with problems of deep despair showed neither uniformity of symptoms nor equal degrees of severity. Only one, for instance, suffered from psychotic delusion that sometimes accompanies the most calamitous form of the illness. In the climactic state of a depressive incident, a victim of the disease may experience hallucinations of phantoms of one kind or another and hear insistent voices. Afflicted with sleeplessness and toxic reaction to alcohol or withdrawal from it, W. J. Cash, the North Carolina writer, in 1941 was certain that Nazi spies were outside his door whispering plans for his assassination. Likewise, in 1941, with threats of a German invasion that would lead to her Jewish husband Leonard's death in a Nazi camp, Virginia Woolf lamented, "I am always hearing voices, and I know I shan't get over it now . . . It is this madness." Less than a month later, she walked into the tidal river Ouse with a large stone in her pocket. In her last letter to Leonard Woolf she explained that she planned to reach exactly where she wished to be: "deep under the sea." [18] At the time of a raging war against Revolutionary France, Charles Percy, beset with similar worries of personal victimization by the enemy, followed a similar course in ending his life.

For other depressives, the disease does not involve psychotic delusions. Nevertheless, the agony can be so extreme that the individual feels as if an alien force has filled the mind, numbed the senses, stirred dull hatred of the self, others, and the world. Constance Fenimore Woolson, a popular nineteenth-century writer and friend of Henry James, denounced "this deadly enemy of mine [which] creeps in, and once in, he is master." She later flung herself fatally from a window of her villa in Venice. [19] The poet Sylvia Plath called the malady the "demon of negation" and "the groveling image of the fearful beast in myself." Winston Churchill, whose sufferings were acute, labeled it "the black dog," and Franz Kafka, sometimes tempted to suicide, thought of mice, of which he was deathly afraid, as a metaphor for the invasiveness of despair. Twentieth-century Percys would use similar expressions. For them as well as for many others so afflicted, depression had to be fought "minute by minute" with "a stoic face" and a posture of "irony," as Plath reminded herself in her journal. "I cannot ignore this murderous self; it's there. I smell it and feel it, but will not give it my name. When it says you shall not sleep . . . I shall go on anyway, knocking its nose in." [20] Brave, sad words.

When a depressive found defenses weakening and committed suicide, the traditional response in Western societies has been severe. In Tudor and Stuart England it was called "an offence against God, against the king, and against Nature." Self-dissolution could bring not only disgrace upon surviving kin but confiscation of property, sometimes reducing the mighty to pauperism. The coroner would order that a wooden stake be hammered through the corpse to prevent its rising from the grave. Clergy did not attend the burial; no prayers for the departed were permitted at the site. Prejudice against suicide dated back to pre-Christian times. Even in ancient Rome and Greece, what Walker Percy sometimes called "the Roman option" was less often tolerated than later opinion would fancy. Aristotle, Pythagoras, and Socrates all condemned it, though some Stoic and Epicurean philosophers found a few, carefully restricted justifications for self-destruction—as protest against tyranny or rationale against a life of relentless pain. [21] Even as recently as 1990, the wife of a suicide spoke bitterly of how she had "to avoid the subject" owing to "the mark society puts on the survivors." [22] The Southern novelist William Styron has explained that "the age-old stigma" will persist until a better understanding of its causes arises. Most of those "who do away with themselves," Styron argues, "do not do it because of any frailty, and rarely out of impulse, but because they are in the grip of an illness that causes almost unimaginable pain." [23] The victim gropes with a frightening experience of lost self-mastery, a dark hollowness, and an inner paralysis that deepens a sense of self-disgust. Melancholy, declares a recent literary critic, is "both multiple and unitary, heavy and evanescent, fog that nevertheless constitutes a wall, mud that entraps, a long sounding of the horn that is 'full.' " Physical distress—headaches, blurred vision, tremors and spasms, stomach and eating disorders, partial paralysis of limbs or face as well as the disorienting effects of insomnia—may also accompany the mental ailment. As a result, the nullity of death seems the only salvation.

What can explain these circumstances? Three major theories might seem applicable: the somatic, the psychological, and the cultural. The first of these is the biological, a biochemical predisposition in some families toward depression and suicidal impulses. [24] The late nineteenth- and early twentieth-century German psychiatrist Emil Kraepelin was the father of this approach and long dominated the treatment of depression, until Sigmund Freud's psychoanalytic approach gained adherents. Kraepelin believed that depression had physical more than psychological causes. He advocated the removal of patients from the stresses of home and family and admission to a facility for the mentally ill, with rest and warm baths as the principal remedies. Not until after the Second World War were the neurological aspects of depression made much clearer. Scientists learned that, if imbalanced, serotonin and other compounds affecting the neural functioning of the brain can have devastating effects on temperament. Nowadays, various anti-depressants, when administered in proper doses, and carefully controlled shock treatments, offer hope that the Percys discussed here could not have had. Some, though not all, victims often respond effectively to psychoanalytic therapy, especially if combined with monitored administrations of drugs.[25] A physician by training, Walker Percy himself believed that a chemical dysfunction, perhaps carried in the family genes, accounted for the despairing moods that sometimes came upon him as they had upon his forebears. But whatever the source of the family pain, the subject was something that he and many others earlier in the line brooded over and strove with tenacity to overcome.[26]

The second approach, which until recently held almost exclusive sway, is the psychological. In 1917, in his ground-breaking essay, "Mourning and Melancholia," Sigmund Freud introduced the concept of injurious mourning, a repressed anger against the lost object—a father or some other significant figure—as the explanation for melancholia. The normal process of mourning involves an actual loss of someone beloved, Freud argued, but the pathological mourner cannot name the reasons for a sense of inanition and hopelessness.[27] Writing during the horrors and bloodshed of the Great War and preoccupied by thoughts of his own death, Freud recognized that the loss being lamented in the depressive state of mind could be both personal and social—a sense of general impoverishment in a world of grim ordeal, hatred, and death on the one hand and individual deprivation and inability to love on the other. At the heart of the matter was the depressive's sense of *moral* rather than physical or even social inferiority, a fear of shame that compounds the misery that the illness generates.[28] Freud offered no remedy whatsoever for the condition, not even psychoanalysis. He concluded somewhat lamely that the condition diminished in the course of time more or less on its own. Yet even as a means to understand melancholia, the Freudian approach is at best only a partial explanation. Often its application places unfair culpability upon child-rearers. They are stigmatized for what could chiefly be attributed to biological factors or even external causes over which they could have little control.[29]

The third explanation for depression and suicide offers a sociological approach. Émile Durkheim, the French social scientist, in his study *Suicide* proposed that an interaction between culture and individual sensibilities produced the alienated personality. Durkheim argued that in industrial Protestant cultures, in which individuality was stressed, the isolate was likely to convert antipathy toward the world into a rage against the self. In Catholic countries, however, the sociologist proposed that a community of believers, assisted by the rituals and the ranked ecclesiastical order, helped the alienated to overcome thoughts of suicide.[30]

Striking as the Durkheimian explanation is, it seems to be mechanistic, predetermined, and so broad that the individual case becomes a mere statistic in a larger cultural pattern. Besides, the lower statistics for suicide in Catholic districts may simply indicate that the deed is likely to be translated into the euphemism of accidental death rather than correctly identified as in Protestant countries, where the stigma is less imposing. Persuasively, social historian Howard Kushner contends that none of these theories alone can explain suicidal depression. He suggests that an interplay of all three is necessary.[31]

In the case of the Percys, combining the psychological, medical, and cultural elements does not exhaust the possibilities, for no less significant was the historical factor that bound them to their regional culture. The Southern code of honor by which they lived made the struggle of life all the more trying. By its rubrics one was expected to live up to almost impossible standards of valor and manhood. The Percys called upon their young to meet exceedingly high expectations both in school and on the playground, in college, marriage, and money-making careers. Early indoctrination under pressure of this kind at times left even the most accomplished of them disappointed by their own performance.[32] Certainly that kind of inner tension might explain Walker Percy's rich appreciation of human absurdity. Humor is the antidote to high hopes unceremoniously dashed by the gods.

Physically, as well as mentally, attempts to reach great heights, regardless of the significance or pettiness of the goal, could be most taxing—hard living, hard gambling and drinking, hard hunting, with days spent idle in damp duck blinds and sweatily trekking through wilderness. The foolhardiness that some Percys showed was also mirrored in their attitude toward ordinary living—what Walker Percy called "everydayness." Unchallenged by the monotonous routines of life and eager to meet the martial ideals of their heritage, Percys often found political contest and war a way to stir the blood and assert the family's claim to honor. In the life of the family, the tradition of soldiering established expectations of manhood and bloody daring that peaceful circumstances thwarted.

To speak in general terms, a sense of inadequacy and dejection might arise when the warrior spirit had no legitimate outlet. Under that circumstance, the depressive dreads a loss of identity and in the male Percys' case, a separation from a cherished, martial role. In the mind of the depressive, war means escape from the allegedly emasculating demands of womankind and domestic peace, with the horror of sexual impotence a peril to be avoided. Perceptions of how honor, military life, and dejection can be related are found in a number of plays written in the Spanish

Golden Age and, of course, in Cervantes's epic of the Sad Knight of La Mancha, one of Walker Percy's favorite pieces of literature. More to the point, Shakespeare spoke to the issue in ways the American Percys readily grasped. The playwright has Lady Percy berate her husband, Hotspur, for cruelly forsaking her to embrace "thick-ey'd musing and curst melancholy." Instead of making love with her, he shouts in his sleep "Courage! to the field!" The warrior refuses Kate Percy's advice on the grounds that she is "yet a woman," a sex that men of valor need never take too seriously. Hotspur was bred for warfare, like a thoroughbred for racing, but when denied his role he could not function. He mutters, "This is no world to play with mammets [dolls] and to tilt with lips. We must have bloody noses and crack'd crowns."[33]

The long-observed relation of war and honor to depression intimates a purely male character to the illness. By convention, women are meant to weep, but men to agonize in a grander fashion. Throughout Western history, men's sense of affliction was considered a form of privileged suffering. On the other hand, women have been relegated to the duties of nursing the fatally ill, dressing the dead, and wailing by the graveside. If women fell victim to seemingly unpredictable moods of grieving, moral condemnation was the usual community response. The depression was attributed to an emotional fragility inherent in their sex. A sixteenth-century physician pointed out that women "are cruelly used and violently disturbed by it, for melancholia being more opposed to their temperament, it removes them from their natural constitution."[34] He was unaware, of course, that culture, not "natural constitution" might help to shape reactions of despair, but there may well have been differences in the way men and women in a rigidly separated sexual order of things responded to the adversity of the mental illness. The Percy family bears testimony to this cheerless division of labor, as it were. Some of the men killed themselves; none of the women did so. Indeed, in Western societies, although more subject to depression, females have traditionally been much less likely to kill themselves than have men.[35] A few women of the Percy bloodline were beset with mental problems. In the sole generation spared the tragedy of male suicide (early in the nineteenth century), a female member as well as one of her talented daughters surrendered to what alienists of the day identified as melancholia. (The surviving daughters, stricken by the number of tragedies in the family, were also deeply affected by depression. Yet they neither lost their reason nor contemplated suicide.) In both the nineteenth and the twentieth centuries, other Percy women were similarly affected.

Protective of family privacy, particularly for the sake of the women's standing, as they would have argued, the Percys were sensitive about a problem over which they had tragically so little control. One strategy was for the family to impose silence on the topic to avoid any stigma, but the matter must not rest there.[36] Evasion is a strategy with positive consequences. The literary Percys, both male and female, were denied the privilege of outspokenness on private matters by family and regional custom and personal preference, but they found in art the means to express the matter in other forms. Melancholia involves a hyperconsciousness of moral weakness—in oneself and in others—and that perspective, however warped or unfair, provides in those with high intelligence a special angle of vision, an ability to unite seemingly disparate ideas. Moreover, the depressive with uncommon abilities may gain special access to those primitive emotions and ideas that move us without our knowing. The very fact that depression and suicidal feelings held special meaning for men made it somehow ennobling. Even when melancholy took the form of alcoholism and other ruinous types of behavior, a "kind of romantic self-destructiveness" invested the afflicted family members with a special "masculinity," as Gerald O'Connor, a twentieth-century Irish-American recalled about his youthful reaction to boozy elders.[37]

For those with artistic skills, depression prompts a desire to crowd the empty canvas, fill the blank page, and create order to replace a sense of emptiness. Intimate thoughts that could not be whispered even into one's own mind, much less voiced for someone else to hear, are transcribed upon the yellow pad. The novelist Arthur Koestler depicted art and depression as an interrelationship based upon "a regression to earlier, more primitive levels in the mental hierarchy, while other processes continue simultaneously on the rational surface." Koestler, himself a suicide, maintained that "the capacity to regress, more or less at will, to the games of the underground, without losing contact with the surface, seems to be the essence of the poetic, and of any other form of creativity." Melancholy can even be thought to have a nurturing character. Writing, however, should not be considered an activity that necessarily provides the artist with complete self-confidence. Just as producing art may lessen the pangs of anxiety it can also increase them without ever serving as a form of mental therapy. Yet the very persistence of the suffering permits the writer to continue the adventure in the dominion of the mind.[38]

For at least a century, Western clinicians and social scientists have pondered the sources of creativity. That tradition, especially strong with regard to male activity, can be traced back as far as the era of ancient Greece. Aristotle asked, "Why is it that all men who have become outstanding in philosophy, poetry or the arts are melancholic, and some to such an extent that they are infected with the diseases arising from black bile, as the story of Heracles among the heroes tells?"[39] The philosopher does not mention women but endows the illness with the grandeur of male heroics. Nor have later investigators of the phenomenon examined the subject in a gender context. The attitude about male melancholia that Aristotle first displayed but still continues endows the male writer with a permission to explore the female aspects of his own psyche without loss of his sense of manhood. This addition to the storehouse of his experience and probe of feeling makes possible a heightened creative impulse. For women of intellect, however, that resource was largely unavailable until the twentieth century, when Virginia Woolf, Sylvia Plath and others could express an almost masculine rage and aggressiveness in poems and fiction. Belonging to an earlier day when women's self-expression was highly circumscribed, the Percy-related female writers could not reach the levels of art that their male successors in the family achieved. It would be too sweeping to claim that depression is so culture-bound that it becomes almost a prerequisite for masculine greatness and ingenuity, particularly in the arts, but the presence of melancholy in family culture may have a stimulating effect at least in part because we in the West have come to expect it.

In rising to the challenge that the malady poses, members of the Percy clan, both male and female, were no less resourceful than the many other artists, leaders, and intellectuals who have felt its grim effects. As the writer Nancy Mairs recently observed, the affliction creates a distance between the subject of art and the woes of its author, examining and interpreting pain without seeming to become its prey. To make her point, she quotes, the short-fiction author Andre DuBus: "After the dead are buried . . . after the physical pain of grief has become with time, a permanent wound in the soul, a sorrow that will last as long as the body does, after the horrors become nightmares and sudden daylight memories, then comes the transcendent and common bond of human suffering, and with that comes forgiveness, and with forgiveness comes love." [40] The expression of these sentiments—without guile or sentimentality—is the contribution of the literary Percys, most especially Will and Walker.

With reference to imagination, last of the themes, much has already been stated since the building of legend involved both the sentiment of honor and the life-taking and life-giving force of melancholy. Translating honor into myth was scarcely a peculiarity of the Percys alone. Story-telling and heeding the rules of honor have long been considered distinguishing features of the Southern past. Yet to some degree the pattern is more widespread than we are aware. As Northern writer Elizabeth Stone argues, the stories that family members tell to inspire, exculpate, blame, warn, and reassure the young and each other become "our first syntax, our first grammar, the foundation" upon which successive generations add their "own perceptions and modifications." [41] So it was in the Percy family but with a benefit denied most families—a powerful heritage of success and a gift of letters for dealing with pain. Through the course of generations, a surprising number of the Percys passed on to the next generation the capabilities and strategies for succeeding in politics, law, money-making, art, music, and, above all, literature.

The ethic of honor and the use of imagination were inseparable. Much of the literary work that the Percy women of the nineteenth century and the Percy men of the twentieth produced dealt with the duties that honor and gentility dictated under trying personal and social circumstances. Will Percy's codification of treasured stories in his memoir was chiefly designed to provide a record of how men and women ought to behave according to his Stoic code. *Lanterns on the Levee* was chiefly a tribute to the Percy mind, not its sense of history. Will Percy sought to explain the family to itself in order to perpetuate ideals of loyalty and obligation, but he did so without worrying very much about historical accuracy. He invested the work with his own vivid spirit, poignant insights, and sympathy for the underdog, characteristics to be found in other Percys with literary ingenuity as well.

Walker Percy's imaginative achievements, unlike his "Uncle Will's," were not based simply upon a defense of the old and antipathy for the new. He had deeper issues in mind, nor was he as autobiographical in approach. Nonetheless, his novels, as a sophisticated form of myth-making, exhibited many of the family's innermost values. For instance, with reference to Will Barrett, hero of *The Last Gentleman,* the narrator observes: "It was an honorable and violent family, but gradually the violence had been deflected and turned inward."[42] Walker Percy was reflecting on his own family history in writing those words. Sensitive to the internal and external calamities to which the family was subject, both Will and Walker Percy used their literary imaginations to gain some distance from threatening events and to construct, through myth-making and writing fiction, poetry and memoir, a livable world.

"Fable is fable, and history is history," declared a Southwestern historian in antebellum times, referring to the ways Indian-fighters could exaggerate their mettle.[43] Yet on that seemingly incontrovertible division, the Percys tax us at every juncture. The reader will find heroes of considerable stature among them, but none lacked failings. Yet imperfect as they were, to take them out of their regional context—a particularly unsophisticated, raw society of the Southwest—would make them appear far worse than they were by the only standards that they would recognize. Negotiating these biographical difficulties leads unavoidably to ambivalence in interpreting their lives and creates a sense of ill-focused duality about almost everything in this family's history. Just as we cannot know exactly what prompted the Percy's mental trials, so, too, it is not always easy to separate good deeds from bad, fancy from reality. If the family had to confront the darkest passions known to mankind, its members could also exhibit resilience, dignity, humor, and a discernment of human tragedy that made the suffering seem almost redemptive. If they were arrogant, they were also cognizant of democratic excesses and bravely spoke their minds against racist cruelties. If they sought gain in questionable ways as directors of banks, railroads, and coal companies or as business-minded plantation bosses, they were still more honest and forthright than most in their class and region. Moreover, they tried to construct a South freed from the ineptitude and anti-intellectuality of old agrarian custom. Thus, their complexity resists easy answers and parries every lunge of righteous indignation. If by repression of memories they sought to escape the past, they also used their history—caparisoned as legend—to inspire themselves. Indeed, for all their nostalgia for a time that never was, they were also forward-looking—a quality Malvina Hoffman's paladin does not convey. The paradoxes are striking. A warrior breed with traces of Borderland savagery about them, they stood apart from their less honor-conscious neighbors. They were Stoics in a time of Epicurean license, conservatives in a time of liberalism, Catholics (at least some of them) in a Protestant region, and aristocrats in a country devoted to democratic principles. And yet for all these differences they still represented the ideals of their region.

Even if such ironies could be simplified to embody moral lessons for our day, an essential riddle would still lie at the heart of the Percys' story. Who were they, after all? Will Percy liked to make fun of the family's ancestor and his dubious pedigree, but with the dualism which would be the family hallmark, the memorialist also told his friends his conviction that the Percys belonged to the noble line. In the Greenville cemetery, the tight-lipped knight with downcast eyes, however, could not embody the secret of family origins. For all their achievements, their glorification of battles fought and lost, their ruminations by means of fiction, memoir, poem, and genealogical tree, the Percys were never to discover from whom they had descended. That failure would always cast doubt upon the authenticity of claims to the nobility that the brooding knight was supposed to incarnate. The first chapter explains how that circumstance came about. It also begins the story of the way that the mystery constantly reinvigorated the family's aspirations, providing the stimulus to resist when great things needed to be done. The symbolism of a gloomy knight in a graveyard tells only part of a remarkable story.

PART ONE

The Early Male Percys

CHAPTER ONE

The Demons of Charles Percy

Charles Peerceys gost has Rizen and entered
your Mortal Body.

Curse by James Smith, yeoman, 1800[1]

The enigma of the Percy family began with Charles, its founder in the American Southwest, born in 1740 in some part of the British Isles, most probably southern Ireland. An enigmatic figure, he could be said to symbolize the ambiguity of Southern white origins. W. J. Cash, author of the classic *The Mind of the South,* took particular interest in him after reading William Alexander Percy's *Lanterns on the Levee.* Cash argued that Southerners had long overrated their noble lineage to create the impression of a refinement that belied their plain-folk origins. It gratified Jack Cash, hill-country son of a textile-mill operative, that Will Percy "has it in him to smile at the lordly legend of his ancestry." According to legend, Cash continued, the first Percy was possibly "the disinherited son of the mighty Percys of Northumberland," but all that really could be ascertained was his quaint distinction as "a bigamist."[2]

Whoever he was, this Percy knew very well how to cover his tracks, particularly in light of the problem Cash mentioned. In a recent study, the historian Bernard Bailyn uses William Dunbar, one of Charles Percy's neighbors in Mississippi, to illustrate "the strange forms of life" that sometimes materialized on the far-flung margins of the British Empire. In 1774, using a company of slaves that he had transported from Jamaica, Dunbar erected an ample residence, an indigo plantation, cattle ranch, hog farm, and timber operation producing over 100,000 barrel staves for the West Indian market. His later enterprises were situated near Natchez, and undoubtedly he entertained Charles Percy, since both were interested in intellectual matters and lived within easy reach.

Dunbar and Percy symbolized the odd mixture of classes and characters who peopled the southern rim of the continent. They were similar in their keen ambition and to reach their ends required a heavy extraction of labor from their slaves. No records have survived to chart Percy's management of his growing plantations, whereas Dunbar's daily log still exists. In it he recorded in 1777 his displeasure and mystification when a slave whom he had apprehended for alleged insurrectionary plotting succeeded in killing himself by leaping from his captors' boat and drowning. Dunbar was convinced that remorse had made the rebel "ashamed to look a master in the face against whom he could urge no plea to palliate his intended diabolical plan." In actuality, the perjured testimony of tortured fellow slaves had rendered his situation so hopeless that self-destruction seemed the only way to avoid a grislier death.[3]

Percy also faced a similar situation though he was much more terse in describing the circumstances. "I have lost poor Sambo," Charles Percy wrote his son Robert in 1792. "He jumt out of the Boat and was drowned in my sight and [resisted?] all our efforts to save him." He did not pause to speculate on the slave's motives or describe the circumstances. Among a number of suicidal slaves directly from Africa, death was often thought to be a means of reaching their distant homeland, but harsh conditions and loneliness under indifferent or cruel masters were reasons enough.[4]

Though similarly disposed toward the hands who worked to create their fortunes, Percy and Dunbar were very different in a most significant respect. The former claimed to be related to the Percys of Northumberland but could not, or at least chose not to, prove it. Dunbar, on the other hand, had clear bloodlines. In that period claims to high birth mattered. Even on the frontier, rank, credit, and moral reputation were often based upon the eminence that one's family possessed, particularly if one's demeanor and largesse seemed to bear out claims that might otherwise be questioned. Sometimes Southerners spoke of lineage as if a nursery were analogous to a stable. In recommending a young kinsman one South Carolinian wrote the governor of the state, "I know him very well. He comes from first rate Carolina stock and his breed is good." Without question Dunbar met that criterion. He was a younger son in the second marriage of Sir Archibald Dunbar of Morayshire, whose castle stood near Elgin. In America some contemporaries added "Sir" to his name, although the College of Heralds would not have recognized the presumption.[5]

On the other hand, about Charles Percy little can be unearthed—nothing of his place of birth and family origins. In establishing himself in the New World, young Dunbar had the benefit of capital supplied by his father. Percy did not. A safe guess would be, however, that he arrived in the Western world with few resources. The newcomer to America had undoubtedly absconded from the British Isles, where he left behind his first love. Time and haphazard London record-keeping have erased most evidence about Charles's Margaret, though it is known she lived in various parts of London for some years after her husband's disappearance. It is likely, however, that the couple's betrothal and wedding took place in Ireland, not the English capital—if a wedding actually ever occurred. When their first child Robert (to whom Charles had written about Sambo) was born on September 1, 1762, Percy was serving in the British army at Kilkenny, Ireland.[6]

From that point until Charles Percy's appearance on Western colonial shores, sometime in 1775 or 1776, his history cannot be sketched with much certainty. According to Robert Dow, a Scottish physician from New Orleans, who first met him on the Dutch island of St. Eustatius in the Leeward chain, Charles Percy had abandoned Margaret and then had taken up with another woman, possibly a Miss Burroughs, who lived in the Bermudas. The lady was most distressed to learn that Charles Percy had left a family in the British Isles. Dow explained that the news was alleged to have "precipitated her death." The wayfarer was free to move on.[7] (No record of a Bermuda marriage has survived.) Two of Dow's "principal friends" at St. Eustatius knew that Percy's "conduct was there known & disapproved of," and advised him not to remain in his company, but the pair continued their association anyhow. Percy had apparently reached St. Eustatius from North Carolina, where he claimed to have owned a plantation. (Although a John Peircey and a William Peircey owned land and slaves in Bertie County, no record of such a property owned by a Charles Percy can be located for that period.[8])

Although frequently battered by hurricanes, the Dutch colony was a major entrepôt for European supplies to the American Revolutionary forces. The population was a mixture of Frenchmen, Dutchmen, Spanish Jews, and Englishmen, most of whom were engaged in the trans-shipping business. Warehouses and even tents, hastily flung up, bulged to overflowing with military and civilian goods of all kinds. Seventy-five to eighty ships anchored daily in the harbor.[9] Percy had taken temporary residence on the island, but he and Dow saw greater opportunities in British West Florida and took passage for Pensacola, the provincial seat, arriving sometime between the middle of 1775 and early 1776.

Percy's reasons for choosing to settle in so vast a wilderness present no mystery. At this juncture, the British Crown had begun to quicken an effort to populate the lands acquired from Spain by conquest in the Seven Years' War. As an ally of the defeated French king, Spain had lost Cuba but, at the peace conference in Paris, 1763, had regained the rich sugar colony. In compensation, England received an enormous section of the continent. It stretched from the tip of the Florida peninsula to the eastern banks of the Mississippi. The new acquisition included scores of native American tribes. There were, however, no major European settlements or fortifications, save for St. Augustine, seat of the East Florida government, and, in the province of West Florida, the small fortifications of Pensacola, Mobile, and Baton Rouge.

To solidify its western boundary, in 1766 the British authorized the laying out of a town called Natchez. Lord Hillsborough's Proclamation Line of 1763 prohibited settlers from encroaching on native American lands. British West Florida, however, was not included in the ban, yet it grew only slowly. From its eastern border at the Appalachicola River to the Mississippi, scarcely a Spaniard remained and the French had vanished except at Mobile. With each change of government, the province had to reinvent itself, as it were. Seeking a place where few questions would be asked, Charles Percy fit those circumstances well.

Alarmed at the increasing rebelliousness of the eastern colonies of North America, authorities in London had given the succession of governors permission to offer veterans and persecuted Loyalists liberal grants with a suspension of quitrent for ten years. According to a recent historical account, the colony on its western border along the Mississippi could have quickly risen to great wealth and British expansion. Many obstacles—the inattention of the home government among them—emerged. The governors of West Florida did their best to encourage settlement, but one, as it happened, was more luckless than the rest. Governor John Eliot fell into a "fatal melancholy" and killed himself "in a violent apoplectic fit" in 1769. Despite these and other setbacks, however, the liberal policy for distributing land persisted.[10]

As a veteran of the Royal Army, Percy was eligible for a grant of "family land," and in 1777 Peter Chester, the current governor of British West Florida, and his Council at last awarded him 600 acres. The size of the grant suggested that he may have brought with him nine dependents, doubtlessly slaves, perhaps ones brought from North Carolina or from St. Eustatius.[11] The tract was located on the right bank of Bayou Sara, near a settlement later called St. Francisville, not far from the border that later separated the future American states of Mississippi and Louisiana. Soon he bought some 400 acres on Buffalo Creek for 300 pesos. In the fall of 1778, the planter acquired an additional 1000 acres of "bounty land" on Bayou Pierre as overdue compensation. According to his petition for the property he had "left the Province of North Carolina sometime in the month of July 1775 on account of the Rebellion." He claimed before Governor Chester at Pensacola that he had been compelled to abandon his plantation. His loyalty to the Crown had cost him, he pled, "near[ly] three thousand Pounds Sterling" and had since undergone other unspecified "Misfortunes" which were too "well known to your Excellency and the Board" to warrant "Recapitulation."[12] Was he embroidering the truth or was the omission from official documents the result of poor record-keeping? Was yet another wife or jilted lover left behind in North Carolina when he headed for St. Eustatius? No answer is now possible.

The record of Percy's presence in the colony can only be known by his applications for land. In 1779 Percy petitioned the governor for yet another tract. Later, through an American marriage, he acquired still more property near Opelousas, St. Landry Parish. There he raised large herds of cattle. At intervals he sold the livestock on the New Orleans market for the West Indian trade. Thus he eventually came to hold three plantations, one near St. Francisville (Louisiana) on Bayou Sara, which he called Abluses, another at Opelousas, and the third, his residence, which he called Northumberland House, on Buffalo Creek.[13] His area of chief concentration became the Buffalo Creek landholding. The property was located about six miles east of the Mississippi, not far from an old French redoubt whose name under British authority was Fort Panmure. It was fifteen or so miles below Natchez, in the future Mississippi county of Wilkinson.[14]

Despite the minimal requirements for legal possession, acquiring land was only a first step in the process of its development. The country itself was a wilderness, "a thicket of timber and cane in tangled masses," as pioneer John Hutchins recalled. The new settlers were surrounded by native Americans who made a practice of stealing such valuables as cattle and blankets and holding the pioneers' horses hostage for ransom money. Until a slaveholder's hands could clear enough acres to grow corn, no means of making bread existed. Years passed before Anthony Hutchins, a former English army officer and one of the earliest Englishmen to arrive, built the first grist mill in the Buffalo Creek area. Freighted up from New Orleans, flour cost $30 a barrel. A barrel of salt brought $20 and a pound of tea $12. Housing was crude and spare.[15]

Charles Percy suffered the same discomforts as other newcomers. Yet, like them, he overcame the privations to create a new order, first under British and then under Spanish rule. Although more complex and secretive than most of his farming neighbors, the adventurer was not as unique a settler as it might seem at first. Men of easy habits were attracted to places like West Florida and the Caribbean, where the rules of society seldom applied, particularly with regard to sexual relations. For instance, Alexander Hamilton, born on British-held Nevis and raised on Danish St. Croix, was the illegitimate son of a roguish fourth son of a Scottish laird in a collateral branch of a ducal line. Alexander's mother was a divorcée, who lived with James Hamilton until he deserted her in 1765 with the same abruptness that marked Charles Percy's flight to the New World some years later.[16] There was also another signal besides multiple marriages to reveal Charles's character: his role in the American Revolution.

⁂

The first North American Percy was always able to inspire trust and display the comportment of a responsible leader. Through successive governments, Charles Percy managed to present himself well without much self-revelation. In 1777, Peter Chester, governor of West Florida, appointed him one of the commissioners at Natchez, a post of some trust. Loyalties to remote European and American nations, however, counted little in the daily struggle to survive in that backwater. Percy's course during the American Revolution was governed less by patriotic sentiments toward one or another country than by opportunity. For the most part, the struggle for the vast hinterland was confined to skirmishes in Spanish Illinois and other northwestern districts. An adventurous ne'er-do-well named James Willing and some thirty companions floated down the Mississippi to invade the British-held region and despoil the plantations that belonged to Loyalists, to settle Willing's grudges in a region that he had left some years before insolvent and disgraced.[17] The Continentals' official assignment, however, was somewhat more legitimate: to swing the Southwest into the American orbit.

In early 1778, having set out from Pittsburgh, the raiders arrived in Natchez, then a relatively new village of some twenty log and frame houses. Willing boldly announced that the residents were prisoners of war and their possessions subject to military confiscation. Charles Percy managed to placate the invader by entertaining him at Buffalo Creek and thus saved his own plantation from a looting. Others not so canny were less lucky. Along with Luke Collins, Sr., his future father-in-law, and several others, Percy served on a delegation that offered terms of capitulation in hopes of preventing the spoliation of their property. The signers promised not to take up arms against the United States or to "aid, abet or in any wise give assistance to the enemies" thereof.[18]

In return, Willing pledged to respect the assets of the Natchez settlers, less for humanitarian than tactical reasons. His own force was small, and it also made sense not to arouse hostility toward the United States, although his activity in the matter undermined that position. For instance, he made an example of Anthony Hutchins's plantation not far from Percy's. Willing and his men took the outraged Englishman prisoner and carried off twenty-three slaves and Hutchins's valuables on the grounds that Hutchins was a Tory spy. Marching south from Natchez, Willing's men, joined by some eighty or more adventurers, caused much damage and misery, without achieving any gain at all. The "banditti," as they were soon called, sacked and burned dozens of vulnerable and isolated plantations between Natchez and Manchac, and thus turned the inhabitants permanently against the American cause. Willing foolishly squandered whatever good will the American cause might have previously enjoyed.[19]

When news reached them of Willing's atrocities, Charles Percy and the other Natchez planters felt released from their pledge of neutrality. Meanwhile Hutchins managed to escape from Willing's men and sent word to his Tory friends in Natchez that Willing was about to return for a more thorough campaign of plunder. Alarmed, the planters placed themselves under Charles Percy and Alexander McIntosh, both of whom claimed to have had considerable military experience. On April 15, 1778, about thirty Tories assembled at a place called White Cliffs, fifteen miles south of Natchez. Commanding their men to hide themselves along the cliffs, the two leaders awaited the arrival of Willing's boats coming up from New Orleans. In the ambush that followed, Reuben Harrison, the lieutenant in charge, and four other Continentals fell dead. Percy and McIntosh counted no losses on their side at all. The Mississippi River remained in English hands.

Reporting the victory at White Cliffs, Governor Chester wrote Lord Germain at the War Office that "these People behaved with great spirit & bravery, particularly Captn McIntosh and Charles Percy Esquire." Although he sympathized with the Loyalist cause, Percy was probably more concerned to defend his property in concert with the other Natchez planters. Chester, an energetic and competent leader, counted on Percy and his friends to guard the northwestern corner of British West Florida. Having no Redcoats to spare, he organized some 250 civilians of the Natchez district into five companies.[20]

Chester appointed Charles Percy to command one of the companies on the grounds that he was "formerly an Officer in the King's Army," as the governor reported to Lord Germain. If Charles Percy presented any papers to support his claim for holding a commission, they were not preserved, but probably the governor simply took his word of honor on the matter. Chester was satisfied that Percy had recently proved himself a loyal subject of the British Crown and certainly that was his general reputation, even among the Americans. Oliver Pollock, a leader of the Patriots in the Southwest, complained to General George Rogers Clark in the Northwestern theater of the Revolution, that Anthony Hutchins and Charles Percy were the two "rascals" who had "poisoned" the minds of their American neighbors against the United States.[21] Despite the honor conferred, Percy may never have accepted the command. If he did so, his tenure was very brief. Perhaps he had his own reasons for not resuming military service under King George. Besides, staying on the sidelines was by far the safest policy in the shifting course of events.

On May 18, 1779, the king of Spain, Carlos III, joined his nephew Louis XVI by declaring war on Great Britain, but unlike his kinsman, the Spanish Bourbon did not make alliance with the Americans.[22] Already deeply involved in assisting James Willing and resupplying the Americans, Gálvez, the Spanish commandant at New Orleans, quickly seized an opportunity in the late summer, 1779, to drive the British from Manchac, Baton Rouge, and Feliciana, the district that included Percy's Northumberland House and Bayou Sara plantations. Gálvez ordered Lt.-Col. Alexander Dickson, the British commander, to surrender the besieged fort at Baton Rouge and also Fort Panmure at Natchez, just to the west of Percy's place. Outmaneuvered, Dickson surrendered. Along with fifty-eight other British subjects, on October 4, 1779, Charles Percy thanked Dickson for his "generous and disinterested Attention to our Welfare in the Capitulation" of all the British forces at Baton Rouge, but the "brave" officers and men could take consolation in the fact that they were "in the Hands of a brave and generous Conqueror."[23] Stunned by Gálvez's rapid movements, the British authorities in West Florida were sorely provoked that planters like Percy had proved so dilatory and self-serving. Before the West Florida Council at Pensacola, General John Campbell lamented that Feliciana had fallen only because the settlers placed "gain and their private concerns" above "the general principles of national defense" which were "too generous and exalted for their conceptions." [24]

Thanks to Dickson's accommodating decision, Gálvez had won control of the Lower Mississippi Valley at very little cost. The victory enabled Spain to monopolize all trade on the Mississippi River from Spanish Illinois to the Gulf. With equal speed and effectiveness, in 1781, he and José Solano, vice admiral of the Spanish navy, combined forces and besieged Pensacola. Meantime, in April of that year, Anthony Hutchins and some Tories more active than Charles Percy had captured Fort Panmure from the Spanish garrison, but the victory was quickly suppressed when five Spanish barges, loaded with troops, appeared on the river. That surprise occurred just as news arrived that Pensacola had fallen to the Spanish. In none of these efforts was Charles Percy involved. Some months later there came the surrender at Yorktown, the Treaty of Paris, and recognition of Spain's reacquisition of the Floridas.[25]

Charles Percy adjusted to Spanish rule with an alacrity that Gálvez shrewdly encouraged among all the British colonials under his governance. For their part, Percy and his equally compliant English neighbors were solely interested in peace and welcomed the military protection the Spanish authorities could provide them against bandits, restive Indians, and American frontiersmen to the east. If British arms were no longer available, Spanish ones would do almost as well for checking American advances. Indeed, Oliver Pollock, the American agent in Spanish New Orleans, accused Percy, Hutchins, Francis Pousset, and some other Natchez planters, of being "Violent Royalists" who, in the event of American conquest, would dissemble and "ingratiate themselves" with false claims of a "Noble Defence" of American liberty.[26]

᠅ ᠅

Shortly after the Spanish occupation of Natchez, Percy began to court Susannah Collins, the daughter of Luke Collins, Sr. Leaving behind a trail of indebtedness in Hampshire County, Virginia, Major Collins had reason to seek new opportunities. He and a party of twelve had come down the Monongahela, Ohio, and Mississippi rivers in 1773 and established themselves in West Florida under the same liberal land policies that were making Percy a gentleman of substance. Collins's properties just north of Natchez grew until he became one of the richest men in the vicinity.[27] Charles Percy was forty years old when he married Collins's sixteen-year-old daughter in 1780; he had been forced to wait for Susannah to mature to that age before asking her father for her hand.

In the 1780s and early 90s, Charles and Susannah Percy had a total of seven children, one son and three daughters surviving to adulthood. Among the boys, the eldest was Charles; there followed Thomas George, June 4, 1786, the only heir by the Collins marriage to perpetuate the family name. The last two sons, Luke and William, both infants in 1794, died before the turn of the century. Born sometime in August 1781, Sarah was the eldest daughter and, as it happened, the unluckiest of the surviving offspring. Then came two other daughters: Susannah or Susan, born September 26, 1784, and Catherine, May 5, 1788. All the children were christened by the Spanish priest from Opelousas who made his rounds to Natchez every so often. Whether Charles Percy had been a Catholic during his years in Ireland cannot be known. Whatever his nominal affiliation may have been—Anglican or Roman—little interest in religion is found in the few surviving materials.[28]

At this point in their marriage Percy and his bride were only moderately well off, but a rich future for the family lay ahead. Twelve years later, he was very friendly with Baron Francisco Luis Hector de Carondelet, who was the Governor-General and Intendant of Louisiana and West Florida, and with Manuel Gayoso de Lemos, the district governor and lieutenant-colonel of troops at Natchez. He shipped, through the port at New Orleans, some 15,000 pounds of tobacco of such a quality, he boasted, that at the warehouse a consignment "passed the inspection with great applause." That same year he sold 150 head of cattle in New Orleans. Unfortunately, Charles Percy had completely fabricated this supposed triumph. The Spanish census reveals that he cropped no tobacco at all that year. In 1790 the Spanish authorities in Cuba had to face a ruinous glut on the market and, since trade in the crop was a government monopoly, orders went out not to buy any more from planters, and no tobacco was purchased as late as 1793. Why had Don Carlos made up the story of enormous sales; was it simply to impress his son?[29]

With greater accuracy Charles Percy reported his success with indigo, the dye most favored in the making of eighteenth-century cloth. The Spanish government encouraged its production with heavy subsidies. By 1792, the Northumberland House plantation and the one at Bayou Sara were producing over 6000 pounds and 500 pounds respectively, constituting one-seventh of the total crop in the district. Raising indigo required much capital, which Percy, like other early planters in the Southwest, had accumulated by means of profits from cattle sales.[30] The necessary pair of vats and other equipment alone cost 1000 or more dollars, not to mention the outlay for a sizable slave force. It was also a risky enterprise with wildly fluctuating prices. Still worse, preparation of the dye involved processes that attracted flies to the vats, poisoned the wells and streams so that cattle losses were also high, and, most serious of all, spread sickness and death among the slaves. But in favorable years a good harvest of indigo paid handsomely. In 1794, his indigo harvest was worth $1250, an impressive return at a time when production and prices had dropped throughout the Southwest by almost 70 percent.[31] Competition from Central America, where a superior product was raised, had drastically reduced the plantings.

To produce indigo and raise cattle, swine, and large crops of corn, Percy had a labor force of forty-seven slaves; he also began planting cotton.[32] The foundations for the economic boom in Natchez had been laid. The decline in the profitability of indigo was soon to be replaced by a turn to short-staple cotton. The town itself was beginning to look as cosmopolitan in population and appearance as some of the West Indian islands. In fact, a visitor at the turn of the eighteenth century thought it resembled St. Johns, Antigua. "The houses all with balconies and piazzas—some merchants' stores—several little shops kept by free mulattoes, and French and Spanish creoles—the great mixture of colour of the people in the streets" made it seem, he said, almost Caribbean—except for the presence of Indians and the low quality of the hotels and taverns, particularly at Natchez-under-the-Hill.[33]

Percy's official honors rose with the increase in his wealth, and he had time to visit with such friends as Robert Dow and Monsieur Vaudon, his agent in New Orleans, and with Hutchins and other notables in the Natchez neighborhood. In 1792, Percy was appointed a captain in the second company, fourth squadron of the Natchez Cavalry Militia and an alcalde, or local magistrate. The latter office entitled him to be called "Don Carlos," an honorific that Will Percy in *Lanterns on the Levee* was delighted to use. In addition, the alliance with the numerous Collinses—Luke Sr., Luke Jr., John, William, and Theophilus, into which family he had married—added to Charles Percy's social, economic, and political prominence.[34]

These advances did not, however, signify that domestic comfort had kept pace. Don Carlos Percy's Northumberland House was a dwelling rather typical for a pioneer plantation. He had so named it after the noble Percys' London seat at Charing Cross, a residence that covered as many city blocks as the Hanoverians' St. James's Palace nearby and was seated in a park that extended from present-day Trafalgar Square to the banks of the Thames. Percy's residence consisted of only three large rooms on one floor, and a surrounding veranda. Three beds were crowded into one chamber, presumably for the brood of children. Two more beds, for the parents, were placed in what was called the "sitting room."

The master's bedchamber also housed the library. Charles, whose bold hand and style of writing revealed eighteenth-century courtesy, was proud that he owned "50 Volumes of different Authors and the History of England." By family reputation, Charles was supposed to have been "an intellectual." In addition, he furnished the house with some chests, a silver coffee pot, a dozen teaspoons, and other items of use or worth. With the exception of a few places like of those of Governor Gayoso de Lemos, William Dunbar, Anthony Hutchins, and Richard Ellis, one could not expect to find more luxurious living so early in Natchez history. Profits, chiefly from cattle and tobacco, were moderate. House furnishings remained very simple. Rooms served many purposes and the verandas provided shelter for harnesses, tools, cattle brands, and other farm equipment. Nonetheless, Northumberland House obviously belonged to an owner of superior discernment, even if the house itself was a modest dwelling.[35]

꒜ ꒜

Successful though he was in weathering the depressed 1794 market, Charles had been showing signs of a growing derangement. In 1790 Lieutenant Robert Percy of the Royal Navy, his son by marriage to Margaret in the British Isles, had at last located his father after so many years' truancy. But the unexpected appearance of his son by itself was not enough to explain how Charles Percy plunged into a depressive state from which he was never to emerge. In fact, he was victim not of depression alone but psychosis as well—what the psychiatrist Emil Kraepelin was later to call *melancholia gravis* or "fantastic melancholia." Those so afflicted seize upon all the negative aspects of their lives and habits as part of their withdrawal from the world, and according to another authority, entertain "delusions of economic, bodily, and spiritual ruin." Indifference toward family members, loss of appetite, unrelenting insomnia, and loss of weight are also common characteristics of the illness. Charles Percy suffered from these symptoms. A neighbor reported to Robert Dow that Percy had been subject lately to much "bodily sickness."[36] Most alarming were Charles Percy's paranoid delusions that were all too typical of such cases. They reached a climax in 1794 even as his friends tried to reassure him that his worries were unwarranted. Percy voiced suspicions that enemies were coming to seize him, some from upriver, others from downriver. As often in such instances, a modicum of fact lay behind his fantasies. Throughout the post-Revolutionary era, conspiracies were rampant in the West. Spanish authorities encouraged them as they helped to prevent American aggression toward Mexico and other Spanish provinces. Baron de Carondelet, Gálvez's successor at New Orleans, steadfastly was withholding permission for Kentuckians to ship their crops through the Spanish port. With no other cheap access to transatlantic commerce, some Americans in Kentucky and Tennessee grew restive and plotted secession. Spain was most interested. In exchange, Daniel Clark, Jr., of Natchez later reported to Congress that "the trade of the Mississippi was to be rendered free, the port of New Orleans to be opened to them and a free commerce allowed in the productions of the new Government with Spain and her West India island."[37]

Clark owned over 3000 acres near Percy's property. He served as financial backer to the spendthrift General James Wilkinson, a flamboyant Kentucky secessionist, secretly on the Spanish payroll. Wilkinson's connection with the New Orleans authorities began as early as 1787.[38] Faced with bankruptcy and disappointed that he had lost out to George Rogers Clark in military rivalry, Wilkinson increased his pro-Spanish efforts in 1792 and 1793.

Meantime Daniel Clark, Sr., a leading Irish-born factor in New Orleans and uncle of Percy's neighbor, was serving as American consul in the Spanish port. Percy had never trusted him for some reason, writing in 1792 that Clark was "ungrateful" and not the man he supposed him to be. Having won the support of Thomas Paine, then in Paris, Daniel Clark, Sr., offered to serve as commandant in charge of a French force to conquer Spanish territories in the Southwest at the cost of £3000 sterling. Citizen Genêt, the French minister, lent assistance. The troops were to assemble in New York City and sail to New Orleans, then move upriver to secure that region. Still worse, Daniel Clark, Jr., Percy's neighbor, switched sides to join his uncle's schemes, aiding the new Revolutionary government of France, at war with Spain and England. Why Clark took so perilous a step is hard to guess, but these Irishmen may have linked themselves to the Jacobin cause in France because they saw an opportunity to strike at France's chief enemy, Great Britain. Percy had once called Daniel Clark, Jr., "a fine young fellow." At this point, however, the former Tory must have been greatly dismayed that his neighbor was proving to be a democratic radical subverting Spanish authority.[39]

The Clark-Genêt plot was plainly foolhardy. In that gossipy society it was hard to keep any secret for long. Spanish officials soon learned of it, and perhaps Percy himself informed his friend Governor Gayoso about activities and rumors in his neighborhood. In any event, the authorities in New Orleans collaborated with James Wilkinson to meet the French Jacobin foe. In return for his help in dispersing whatever force the Clarks could muster, Wilkinson was to receive over $6000 to be delivered by one Joseph Collins. Collins's partner on the trip was later murdered on the way to Wilkinson in Kentucky and the sum stolen from the pair. Collins, from Pascagoula, might have been related to the Luke Collins family.[40]

Such was the situation that faced Charles Percy: his neighbor Daniel Clark, Jr., was involved in perilous subversions with his uncle, and armies were supposedly readying their advances upon Natchez. Joseph Collins was spying for Spain's enemies, he might have imagined, and Percy might have thought that when and if Carondelet and Gayoso called into service his cavalry unit in Natchez, the citizen-troopers might betray the Crown and raise the tricolor of Jacobinism.[41]

Don Francis Pousset, a Buffalo Creek neighbor, had visited "poor Mr. Percy" in late January and found him "in very low spirits," fretting incoherently about what he fancied was to be bloody apocalypse. After receipt of a heartening letter from Governor Gayoso, Pousset hastened back to Northumberland House to announce that the French Revolutionary expedition against Natchez "had been disconcerted." Indeed, under the pressure of public exposure, the Clarks' project had been canceled before it had advanced very far at all. Somehow, the shrewd New Orleans merchant and his nephew managed to step back from the abyss and even to regain favor with the provincial Spanish authorities. The clouds of war that had gathered so menacingly throughout the fall and early winter suddenly rolled away. But before Pousset arrived at Buffalo Creek, he "met an express" who gave him "the calamitous news": Don Carlos was dead.[42]

On the night of January 30, Percy had taken down his brace of pistols, walked a considerable distance from the house, and stopped at the edge of a nearby bayou, known from then to this day as Percy Creek. Reflecting on the circumstances not long afterward, Robert Dow, Percy's old friend, conjectured that at the last minute he had decided against shooting himself for fear that the report would alarm the household. Perhaps, too, he remembered the example of "poor Sambo" who, a year and a half earlier, had leapt into the water and refused all efforts to save him. Don Carlos tied to his neck a heavy "tin pot" or kettle that perhaps he took from the kitchen. He then waded a distance into the creek, found a spot over his head, and sank into the water. The search party had found his body floating there. Convening the next morning, the coroner's jury reported that only Percy's footprints could be found leading to the site where the guns had been left on the ground. Their conclusion was the only one possible: he had taken his own life in a moment of "insanity of mind." The verdict was no doubt accurate. Hastening up from New Orleans, Robert Dow talked with Susannah and the neighbors and agreed that it had to have been suicide.[43]

As Robert Dow interpreted events, however, difficulties closer to home than phantom armies also had been crowding in upon his friend. The melancholy planter had been deeply affected by the death of Charles, his eldest son in his third marriage, to Susannah. He had doted on his thirteen-year-old. He had done his best for the boy and had left Charles at Opelousas for a year because the climate there was supposedly healthier for a child with severe respiratory problems. "Charly has lost one year in his Education but it is better to loose [sic] that than ruin his constitution," he had written in 1792. But the son apparently had tuberculosis or some other disease of the lungs. The father's demons of grief fed hungrily upon his growing irrationality. The only solace that Charles's friend Robert Dow could muster was the thought that the planter had not for a moment lost his head for business. Rather, as Dow wrote Robert Percy—Charles's son by the first marriage—Charles had left his widow well provided for: a thriving estate, abundant crops, and "some excellent salt meat."[44]

Financial troubles were thus no cause for Percy's unhappy state of mind. To be sure, the local economy was then in poor shape: tobacco prices had fallen disastrously; in 1790, General Wilkinson had broken the local monopoly with Kentucky imports; indigo was also depressed, and large-scale production of cotton had not been widely adopted (the Whitney gin had yet to be introduced). But never in the history of Charles Percy's descendants was the loss of wealth a motivating factor in cases of depression and suicide. The founder of the family had a virtually unencumbered estate with ready cash and notes at his heirs' disposal. He once wrote, "I shall be at my ease for I owe no money." [45]

Instead of financial woes, Percy had become subject to a malady that left him coldly suspicious of all around him—not just invading troops but local people as well. Difficulty with the neighbors was a manifestation of his illness, not its underlying cause. The quarrel with "bad neighbors," as Dr. Dow explained to Lt. Robert Percy, however, illuminated a display of temperament that was to leave a long shadow upon the family's subsequent history. Dow had in mind Percy's quarrel with the Smith family, his indigent neighbors.

Under the leadership of Zachariah Smith, the large clan had come from the "Old Ninety-Six" district of South Carolina shortly after the American Revolution. Like the British under Governor Chester, the Spanish authorities had been liberally distributing land grants to populate the area for purposes of defense and economic stability, the ancient Roman method of populating the frontiers with Goths and Vandals. The Smith boys—James, a ferryboat operator, and his brother Zachariah—belonged to a tough breed of unlettered pioneers. During the American Revolution, their sister Sarah Smith, a woman of considerable beauty, had once refused to reveal the location of family valuables to the commander of a British patrol. The officer had her strung up by the neck, but she refused to break her silence and was cut down from the impromptu gallows. Hard-handed though they were, the Smiths, by all accounts, were uncommonly intelligent and handsome. No one questioned their essential honesty. [46]

As early as 1792, Charles Percy was on poor terms with the Smiths. He had sold Zachariah a chest full of tools but "old Smith," as he contemptuously called him, "could not pay for them," and Don Carlos took them back. [47] Percy had also been squabbling with the Smiths over property boundaries. Such disputes often prompted smoldering hatreds and feuds because surveyors of frontier tracts worked under difficult conditions and boundary-marking rivers and creeks inconveniently changed course.

Not long before his suicide, the planter had convinced himself that young James Smith had burned a hole in the boat which Percy had borrowed from Smith. The magistrate was sure that the ferryman sought to kill him. Actually, some Indians in a nearby swamp, neighbors speculated, were the most likely perpetrators, if any such vandalism had occurred at all. When Smith came to fetch the boat, Percy accused him of attempted murder. Outraged, the young man denied Percy's "malicious and ungrounded" accusation, as Daniel Clark, Jr., Percy's neighbor, later agreed it was. The youth demanded that the magistrate give him back his boat at once. Percy said he had since lost it but would pay for its replacement. Smith, however, felt even more insulted and declared that Percy could "keep" his money "to pay his ferriage over the Styx." Flushed with anger,

Don Carlos, in his role as alcalde, then ordered Smith locked up in the blockhouse overnight. Later, aware that further calamities would soon descend, Zachariah Smith, the father, went to Percy and beseeched him to relent. The magistrate agreed to the plea with smiles and apparent good will. But, he told the old man pleasantly, he and the sons, James and Zachariah, had to sign a statement of apology which he would draw up.

At the second interview, Percy, again genial and almost affectionate, read them the declaration which, in their ignorance, they could barely have read themselves. He placed a document before them to affix their marks and they readily did so. How were they to know that the statement they had signed was different from the one heard from his lips? Percy then asked David Lejeune, his overseer ["preceptor"], to sign as witness, "but Mr. Percy would not let him peruse it, though he showed it so soon as the Smiths were gone," Daniel Clark later reported.

The document to which they affixed their marks and shaky signatures admitted to the sabotaging of the boat and perhaps other crimes conjured up by Percy. Armed with the confession, Percy went immediately to Natchez "to represent the Smiths in a very unfavorable light." Upon his return, he summoned the three to appear at Northumberland House to receive a manor lord's retribution. "The sons," Daniel Clark wrote the governor, "he ordered to proceed to the seat of government and to the father he said, 'Old man, I am determined to destroy you, your seed, being and generations. I have power to send you where you shall not be seen or heard of by anyone in this district again.'" Coldly, he then dismissed him.[48]

Momentarily the deception worked. Governor Gayoso sternly cited Zachariah for "encouraging his children in evil practices," a reprimand that would have stigmatized him as unworthy of credit or trust. The governor ordered the Smith brothers expelled from the district. Zachariah, however, petitioned against a decision that would disperse the family and leave him destitute. He acknowledged that he and his sons "were afraid of the power of Mr. Percy," who was destroying them, just as he had promised. But he entreated the governor to take account of his peaceable nature to which his neighbors could attest.[49]

Most depressives consider their condition their own fault—an alienation from God, a level of performance too contemptible to make living worthwhile, a character or intellect too deficient. These were not the thoughts of Charles Percy—at least as others tried to discern them. But the world he created in his mind conformed very little to the one that his neighbors and family knew. According to Robert Dow, for some time Clark and others had observed that Percy had "talked and acted in the most extravagant and out of way manner." How would Governor Gayoso react when his duplicity of switched documents was unveiled? Charles had always been so proud of his connections with the governor. Once he had swelled that Gayoso "treats me with particular and affec[tiona]te Politeness at all times and places where we meet."[50] Reckless in his loves and hatreds, the founder of the family, it may be said, feared no man. In that respect he was very much like Harry Hotspur in possessing both a testy sense of honor and a churlish melancholy. Yet, what led him to self-destruction was fear, not of others, but of himself and the inner voices that he alone could hear. He had to end his own madness, depression, and intolerable impulses before others—and even himself—discovered who and what he was. Why he chose to be so vindictive toward the Smiths cannot be known, but certainly as humble folk they were vulnerable to someone eager to reassure himself by a bold exercise of lordly power. James Smith had violated his sense of honor in a way Don Carlos clearly found insupportable. Perhaps there was something more, some violent reaction against his own feelings that Percy himself shrank from recognizing but was determined to expel by banishing the whole family from his sight and recollection. At the end, however, he could no longer stand his state of sleeplessness and disorientation.[51]

Undoubtedly the coroner's jury examining Charles Percy's corpse took special care in their detective work. Had there been signs of murder, James Smith would have been the prime suspect. He had the motive, swearing that he would neither leave the country nor go to prison but stay and fight it out with his powerful neighbor. But luckily for him, Percy's condition had already attracted notice. The form of his death confirmed it. As a result, Francis Pousset, Daniel Clark, and other neighbors came forward, just as Zachariah Smith hoped they would. They testified to the father's humble and "quiet" respectability and noted that the only crimes the sons had committed were the rude retorts to the magistrate, issued under provocation.[52] Gayoso rescinded his order, and Zachariah Smith's reputation was restored.

Oddly, the controversy with the Smiths did not end with Percy's death. At least as far as James Smith was concerned, the spirit of Charles Percy remained abroad. Some six years later, the ferryman and the venerable John Ellis, who was to marry Charles Percy's daughter Sarah in 1799, quarrelled hotly. It would not be the last time that the Percy clan would encounter the hostility of the yeomanry. The Ellises, one of the oldest Tory families in the district, was also one of the wealthiest and haughtiest.[53] Judge Ellis had ruled unfavorably on Smith's operation of his ferry across the Homochitto River, which separated the Buffalo Creek residents from Natchez. Moreover, he arranged that a public road being built ran through Smith's property instead of taking a straighter route through his own. Finally, Judge Ellis took the side of his mother-in-law, Charles Percy's heir, on the still unresolved boundary row. The judge rode over to Smith's house to iron out differences, but the encounter ended in shouts and fist-waving. Nursing his grievances, Smith followed up the interview with an intemperate letter. He complained that he had always tried "to obtain The good will of his fellow Citizens and nabours," but Ellis was allied with widow Percy and the Collins relations to carry on "that old grug [grudge]" begun in Charles Percy's time. Smith accused the judge of acting out of his own "exHoste prid [exhausted pride]," dread of losing "honuers," and fear of being discountenanced by his in-laws. Working himself into a passion, he announced that Charles Percy's "devilment with me" had "acasioned him to drownd with the pot about his neck which I expect will be your end if you dont take care." The ferryman closed with an ill-phrased curse almost medieval in style: "if Enny such thing can be that Charles Peerceys gost has Rizen and entered your Mortal Body for I thought I cold perceave His deception in you last Saturday so having that put in moind of him." [54] Smith's malediction was to cost his family a fine of $300, but the incantation served rough justice as a profane antiphony to Charles Percy's actions in January 1794.

As James Smith hoped, his "gost" was indeed to haunt Charles's offspring by Susannah Collins in the coming years.[55] However, thanks in part to early separation from his father and his informal adoption by his commanding officer in the navy, Charles's eldest son by his connection with Margaret in England possessed an entirely different temperament. For reasons not easily explained, none of Robert's descendants would ever follow the example of Don Carlos.

CHAPTER TWO

A Son of Two Fathers

Tho' absent from the hostile shore
Where murdering engines storm and roar,
And stain the field with blood,
Yet here the lonely, rustic plains,
Where fallen melancholy reigns,
Surround my rough abode.

The Rev. Jacob Bailey, Loyalist exile, 1780[1]

In the summer of 1770, H.M.S. *Canceaux* sailed up the Thames and docked at Gallion's Reach after a wearisome voyage from America. The vessel was to undergo extensive repair and refitting in the Royal Dockyards, near the town of Woolwich, just below Greenwich. There on November 8, 1770, Robert Percy was registered as a volunteer, an eighteenth-century term even for one so young. Charles Percy may have accompanied him; he was acquainted with William Hogg, Master, who maintained the list of the complement on *Canceaux.* The designation of "captain's servant" in the entry signified that the lad was no ordinary seaman. From the time of the Restoration, the Royal Navy had permitted captains to nominate neophytes from gentle families for the service.[2] They did not serve as mere cabin boys—polishing the captain's boots and cleaning his quarters. These apprentices were expected to learn the craft of seamanship under their commander's supervision and sit for the stiff examinations to win a commission.

Robert Percy was eight years old when his name appeared on the ship's roster. In the Hanoverian era, that age was not an unusual time to begin a naval career; some recruits were enrolled at age five. William Bligh of the famous Mutiny signed on at seven.[3] Robert Percy's mother and father may have had a prior association with their son's commanding officer, Lieutenant Henry Mowat, a salt originally from the Scottish Orkney Islands. He was to be in effect the boy's surrogate father during his formative years. The small size of the three-masted sloop and the remoteness of its station overseas suggest, however, that Robert's parents were not well placed.

They lacked the wealth and the prominence to secure for their son a prestigious assignment closer to home and on a large, safe, and comfortable ship.

How well would a small boy fare under harsh maritime conditions? Service in the Royal Navy involved long separations from family, unhealthy,
perilous living conditions, and an all-male society with its inevitable aggres-
sions and cruelties. Some historians also claim that sodomy was rife and
the small children aboard often the alleged victims, but evidence is very
slim for so sweeping an indictment.[4] In any event, Robert Percy was never
to show any emotional scars at all—a state of affairs that would contrast
with the fate of the children of his father's later American marriage. Nonetheless, Robert Percy must have experienced a sense of loss when separated from his parents on that rainy, breezy day of his enlistment.[5] Homesick or not, boys like Percy were invaluable. Some as young as ten or
eleven were assigned as topmen, nimbly clambering about the rigging at
work on the topsails, topgallants, and royals. Their small hands and bodies
could handle such tasks better than seasoned mariners. The children
helped to swab decks, mend sails, water the livestock, and perform whatever tasks the adults demanded. Playing about the deck and rigging,
youngsters, making up about 6 percent of a ship's complement, were as
visible—and vexatious—as the tethered goats and cows. They were useful
because they occupied less space and ate less food than their elders. In the
Georgian navy, ships-of-the-line, which assigned four "captain's servants"
per one hundred men, carried schoolmasters. Being on a small ship, Robert
Percy was deprived of that advantage.[6]

Its repairs completed, *Canceaux,* with a crew of forty-five, sailed for Boston early in the summer and arrived on August 24, 1771. To bid his
mother a long farewell, Robert Percy had obtained a short leave at Gallion's Reach. He rejoined the ship in time for the voyage to America.
Attached to the North American squadron, *Canceaux* resumed its regular
surveying duties, making its home base in the Piscataqua River, at Portsmouth, New Hampshire. After his promotion to able-bodied seaman (su-
pernumerary) at age nine, in April 1772, Robert was "discharged" from
service at Portsmouth, as the term went, but it was only a temporary absence. His departure enabled him to attend an American school, probably
run by an Anglican minister. (A staunch churchman, Lieutenant Mowat
would have been reluctant to place his charge in the hands of New England "ranting Dissenters," as his Anglican clerical friends called the Puri-
tans.) The Society for the Propagation of the Gospel in Foreign Parts had
recently permitted the Reverend Samuel Cole to open a missionary academy at Claremont, Cheshire County, New Hampshire. Mowat had a sizable land grant nearby.[7] Possibly Robert Percy was enrolled there. Ship-
masters like Mowat were expected to supervise the education of the small
boys under their authority. The master of *Canceaux* may even have paid
the tuition himself. Robert's mother, Margaret Percy, had little money to
devote to her son's education.[8]

During his American experience, Robert Percy was to serve aboard three vessels—*Canceaux, Albany,* and *La Sophie* under Mowat's command. Ironically, for the formative years of his future vocation as a planter, the lad plied the waters off the coast of New England, not the shorelines of the slave colonies. Robert's whole outlook on life was in large part North European. Most of his associations in America were Scottish friends of his Orcadian master, Henry Mowat. Later in life, he would forsake that heritage and turn to the South.

🎜 🎝

For the length of their common service—some thirteen years of Robert's development—Henry Mowat functioned as guardian. A tall imposing figure in his naval uniform and cocked hat, Mowat proved to be an extraordinary instructor and exemplar for his young charge. According to one superior, the forty-five-year-old salt was "a most vigorous Commander" with an unrivaled knowledge of New England waters. Another praised him as "the most useful person in America" under naval authority, opinions with which Mowat concurred.[9] Robert Percy could learn much about life and seamanship from so skillful a mariner.[10] Mowat's custody flowered into genuine affection for young Percy.

Robert Percy's absence from *Canceaux* extended from 1772 to December 1775.[11] Then, just before Christmas, at age thirteen, he returned with his ship to England, where *Canceaux* underwent repairs at Woolwich on the Thames. During Percy's absence from the ship to attend school in the fall of 1775, *Canceaux* had pounded the port of Falmouth (now called Portland, Maine) as a futile show of military force to overawe the American Patriots. The action had dangerously loosened the ship's timbers. It was Robert Percy's first chance to see his mother since he had left her waving farewell at Gallion's Reach some five years before. No doubt she greeted him with tearful warmth though probably she had trouble recognizing her growing son. Margaret Percy had been living alone in the village of Hammersmith. By then Robert's father Charles had vanished. Mowat took pity on the fatherless boy and assumed even greater responsibility for his development and well being.[12]

When Mowat received command of *Albany,* he took Robert Percy with him, exercising a discretion that the Royal Navy frequently allowed. Patron and client served together on *Albany* from June 3, 1776, to October 25, 1782, their longest service together on the same vessel.[13] Percy's new assignment to *Albany* offered little improvement in physical comfort, though the ship was larger than *Canceaux.* The naval war with the American rebels had deteriorated. Not one town in all New England remained in British hands.[14] In response, General Henry Clinton proposed a combined naval and army campaign at Penobscot at the mouth of the Majabagaduce River (as the Bagaduce was then called). The base would serve as a foothold for the reconquest of the New England provinces, with Mowat assigned to head the flotilla. The expedition was a great success, the only massive naval victory that the British won in the course of the war. Mowat's three ships repulsed the repeated, albeit ill-managed attacks of an American armada of some eighteen ships.[15]

Although the Loyalists looked upon Mowat as their savior, their praise had no effect at Admiralty. He received no promotion in rank and no offer of a better command. Instead, Mowat (and Robert Percy) had to remain aboard the "wretched" *Albany*.[16] In July 1782, a survey commission declared the ship unfit for further service. Frustrated by his lack of advancement in rank and command after twenty-seven years of active service, Mowat asked for permission to return to England. The British naval authorities made poor use of an able commander, and that could possibly affect the standing of his young protégé, Robert Percy. Turning down Mowat's request, Rear-Adm. Robert Digby assured him of eventual promotion to captain and offered him a considerably better command: H.M.S. *La Sophie,* a twenty-eight-gun frigate, captured from the French.[17] Mowat deserved a better posting. His participation in the Falmouth bombardment early in the Revolution had only aroused greater insurgency. Mowat's superiors, who had ordered or acquiesced in the politically inept cannonading, smugly laid the blame for its failure on his shoulders.

ॐ ॐ

Although Robert Percy's naval career began well enough, it later ran a similar course to Mowat's—outstanding performance but little recognition. He joined Mowat on *La Sophie,* their last assignment together. Meanwhile, he had advanced in his career. Having reached the age of seventeen while aboard *Albany*, he was promoted to midshipman in 1779. The designation made Percy eligible for a daily ration of grog and the prestige of being an "oldster." Two years later he reached the grade of master's mate. During this period, he served as master of *Albany*'s tender, the twelve-ton *Prince William Henry.* While in charge, Robert Percy proudly reminded Admiralty many years later, "he cut out of Cape Ann a 20 gun ship letter of Marque, and was thought to have done the enemy much injury in many instances." In addition, he undertook a dangerous reconnaissance mission into Boston harbor to ascertain the strength of the French fleet at anchor there. On the same mission, he "captured three vessels laden with timber, spars &c for the French fleet, also saw a convoy of 14 sail out of Penobscot which had been blocked in by the American State Sloop of 16 guns," as he informed the Admiralty.

Mowat and Percy expected that their accomplishments would soon lead to promotion. The sea war continued after the surrender at Yorktown on October 19, most especially in the Caribbean. While H.M.S. *Albany* had not participated in major engagements, in Admiral Digby, Mowat and

Percy finally had a well-placed patron. In the fall of 1782, Mowat received the rank of captain. As the war was drawing to an end, in May 1783, he commodored the "Spring Fleet," an undertaking famous in eastern Canadian history. It consisted of fifty transports which carried several thousand Tory families and their meager possessions from Sandy Hook, New York, to St. John, on the Bay of Fundy, Nova Scotia. Robert Percy also participated in that operation.[18]

Although Mowat had yet to receive a first-class permanent command, at least his new prestige assisted Robert Percy's advance. In April 1783 on Mowat's recommendation, Admiral Digby convened the board of ship captains to offer the customary examination for Percy's promotion. The young seaman passed handsomely. Mowat thought a show of appreciation on Robert's part would be in order, although presents to superiors were against regulations. Thus when Digby remarried, Mowat advised his informally adopted son "to remind him of your gratitude by some token—I think a couple or three dozen of the very best marten skins fit for the lining of a Cloak would be well received and I can add well bestowed."[19]

Unfortunately for both Mowat and Percy, the ending of the American War for Independence prompted a vast demobilization of the royal forces. They parted as naval colleagues but not as friends in April 1783. Robert Percy took his papers aboard *Delaware,* a captured American ship of twenty-eight guns. He remained with that ship until April 23, 1785.[20] Then, like so many others, Lieutenant Percy was placed on half pay, an eighteenth-century form of unemployment insurance. In return for a small but steady stipend, it bound the recipient to return to service upon receipt of fresh orders from the Admiralty. When not located at Halifax, headquarters for the British North American fleet, Robert Percy considered Castine, Maine, his home. The six hundred Loyalists at Castine were so certain that the Crown would never abandon them that they established themselves in a permanent way. When opportunity permitted, Robert Percy stayed there on the Majabagaduce River so that he could keep in touch with the Mowat kinsmen—David, Henry, and James Ryder Mowat and other Loyalists, including the wealthy Robert Pagan, a shipper; Dr. John Calef, the Reverend Jacob Bailey, Canada's first poet and the Reverend John Wiswall, all of whom were special friends of Henry Mowat. Some residents had begun to invest in local properties. James Ryder Mowat built himself a large home, warehouse, and small shipyard worth, he later claimed, over £900. At the peace table in Paris, fearing the dismemberment of Maine, John Adams had insisted that the home authorities remove the Loyalists and the troops. "Our people will not feel like freemen," he argued, "until this is done."[21]

Whitehall had no desire to prolong the dispute with the former colonies. "New Ireland," as the Penobscot settlement was grandly called, was ceded to the Americans, over the protests of Loyalists like James Ryder Mowat.

When the Union Jack was hauled down from the pole at Fort George overlooking Penobscot Bay, most of the Tory residents, including Robert Percy, the Mowats, Calef, Pagan, and the clergymen sadly left. They first went to Canada, but many of them spent months in London to press Loyalist claims for compensation for confiscated property. Some dismantled their houses, board by board, and reassembled them at St. Andrews, a settlement overlooking Passamaquoddy Bay.[22]

The close of the Revolutionary War did not find Percy unprepared for civilian life. Mowat had not overlooked the assiduous training of his charge in the maritime profession and had taught him the role of purser, a job of great responsibility. Appointment to such a position of trust indicated Percy's favor in Mowat's eyes. No one became a purser based on merit alone. The candidate required a patron because pursers had to be bonded. At some expense to themselves, Henry and David Mowat, a former merchant and shipper of Massachusetts, had furnished their young friend with the necessary guarantee when he had gone aboard H.M.S. *Delaware*. The sum came to £400.[23] Shipboard storekeepers like Robert Percy supervised food provisions, clothing, tobacco, spirits, and fresh water. They were held personally accountable for any missing supplies. Officers like Percy had to keep a running record of the meals consumed by each member of the crew, to work out the credits and debits with vendors—often using their own resources to meet payments—and check on the state of shipboard supplies. To lose one's books, even in shipwreck, was considered a calamitous breach of naval law, and any shortage was charged to the purser personally. Dependent upon the honesty of those who prepared and parceled out the provisions, pursers often had to bribe mess stewards and coopers.

The high risks had their compensations. As a monopoly seller, an officer like Robert Percy could make money through the sale of tobacco and sometimes "slop cloaths" or just "slops" as sailors' canvas apparel was called. He received an eighth of the value of provisions sent him from the Victualling Board. On the other items he was allowed a 5 or 10 percent profit. With ready cash, the purser was the shipboard moneylender—an unpopular but lucrative role. (Sailors claimed that albatrosses bore the spirits of dead pursers.) When prizes were seized, pursers could serve as agents handling the financial side of the cases before Admiralty Court.[24]

By the 1780s, Robert Percy had gained enough business expertise to function in both the naval and the civilian world of shipping, finance, and commerce. Henry Mowat thought the nautical specialty advantageous to his protégé. In 1784 he wrote Percy from London, "Sir Charles Douglas," admiral of the forces at Halifax, "means to continue the Galleys during his Command." He might find a place for Percy if his "books" of accounts were in order, as Mowat fearfully prayed they were. Robert Percy probably heeded the advice; there was no scandal to check his career. To Mowat's gratification, the young lieutenant had prepared himself well as a naval agent, commission merchant, and dealer in small craft whenever the occasion should return him to civilian life. To judge from the scanty documents remaining, Robert Percy achieved modest financial success. He served as ship's purser of *Delaware* but apparently was acting as commander, too. After going on half-pay in April 1785, however, he was more profitably engaged as a prize-ship agent and general dealer in maritime supplies until the outbreak of war with Revolutionary France in 1793.[25]

In a letter from London, the earliest of all American Percy manuscripts, Mowat offered the young naval agent some sound financial and moral advice. In a previous letter, Percy had complained that someone named Turnbull in the village of Castine, Maine, had failed to pay him a very large gambling debt. Mowat admonished Robert in the style of an earnest "friend," probably he noted, "your only one." By "friend," in this context, Mowat meant adviser or interested senior, not companion. The term thus signified that Mowat had long considered Robert virtually fatherless with no one else to counsel him. Mowat urged young Robert to forget the debt. He should remind himself that "had it been your lot to have lost that sum you would not have been able to have paid it any more than the man that lost it." Besides, he cautioned his young protégé, gambling in "your line" of work could lead to disaster.

The senior officer had recently seen Robert's mother, who worried very much about his taking such risks at gaming. Mowat admitted that Robert was owed some $700 at Penobscot, of which he never expected to see "a shilling" and bemoaned ever having gamed himself. Still worse, it could jeopardize Robert's cultivation of Admiral Digby who would show no "patience" with that sort of behavior, given Robert's "situation in life" as a purser and as a ship commander, too. Why jeopardize the admiral's good opinion? As it is, "he asks me how you go on." Mowat did not want Percy to jeopardize his own standing with the only superior ever to have favored him. In his letter to Robert, Mowat stressed that Digby had shown a "Spontaneous Condescension" toward himself, a sign in that hierarchical society then regarded as an uncommon favor.[26]

Mowat and Percy were not just father and son but also business partners, and they naturally associated with mariners from Mowat's homeland, who would prove invaluable in Robert Percy's search for his father Charles when that issue arose. Nearly all of Percy's business associates were Americans and Scots people with close family and business relationships. Among these friends was John Lee, a "man of Honest principles," Henry Mowat maintained. As a Tory merchant of Penobscot, Lee was affiliated with a firm of shippers at Greenock, Scotland. He served for several years as Robert Percy's post office when he was away, particularly after his return to active naval duty in 1793.[27] The wealthy Robert Pagan, a Glasgow emigrant at Castine and then St. Andrews, New Brunswick, was also a member of the company.[28] Robert Percy and these older friends in Maine and

Canada lent money, engaged in shipbuilding and in prize-ship enterprises, and traded in timber and other northern products.[29]

❧ ❧

One reason for Mowat's solicitude about young Robert Percy had been the mystery of Charles Percy's absconding. "We have heard nothing of your Father since I leave him in England," Mowat wrote Robert in 1784. He was referring to the months after Robert's enrollment on H.M.S. *Canceaux* when the ship was still in port under repair before it sailed back to the Piscataqua River in New Hampshire in the summer of 1771. Other members of the Tory cluster from New England, then in London, took an interest in the deserted wife.[30]

Throughout this period, Robert Percy's mother had been living a hand-to-mouth existence. In the late 1770s, if not sooner, she had fallen on especially bad luck since her son could not, as a lowly seaman, remit much money for her support. Her Charles never sent her a farthing, according to one Patrick Morgan, who offered this information in 1804 to Dr. Robert Dow, who had accompanied Charles Percy from St. Eustatius to mainland America in 1776. An old friend of Dow and Charles Percy, Morgan was a London mercer with a shop in Houndsditch. Charles had claimed that he intended to be generous and would use Morgan as his agent, but he never followed through.[31] Increasing poverty had driven Margaret from the respectable location of Hammersmith, a pleasant southwestern London suburb on the Thames. She moved to rooms on Earl Street (now Earlham Street just above Leicester Square). Earl Street was one of the notorious "Seven Dials," where an enterprising builder erected fashionable dwellings in the late seventeenth century. The "Seven Dials" had since become a byword for crime, poverty, and disease. Margaret Percy was not a gin-soaked wretch out of Hogarth's drawings of the St. Giles rookeries. Yet tragedy struck her while she was living surrounded by Hogarthian scenes. She lost her only companion, Sarah, Robert's thirteen-year-old sister, born in happier times. The child was buried at St. Giles Church, off High Street, Holborn, only steps away from Earl Street.[32] Even after winning his lieutenancy, young Percy did little for his mother. His stated pay was four shillings a day at sea, often long in arrears, if he fared no better than most seamen. Yet as an apparently successful gambler, he may have neglected her needs, at least until perhaps Mowat or some other friend admonished him.[33]

Sometime before 1785, however, Margaret Percy moved from the stews of the "Seven Dials" to Westminster. The newer location may have reflected Robert's better financial situation from his sojourn on *Delaware* and a partner in enterprises at Castine and Halifax with the Mowats and Lees. She probably was renting a room from a landlord who paid the rates since her name never appeared in the tax records. How long she lived there is not now known. Her last abode, on St. Ann's Street in the Parish of West-minster, however, indicated a modest improvement over her residence in Soho. The new address placed her within the district that Hugh Lord Percy, heir to the Dukedom of Northumberland, represented in the House of Commons. His Northumberland House was three-quarters of a mile away at Charing Cross, a seat as distant from her world as its humble namesake in America.

Without question Margaret's worries over her son's gambling came from fears of having to return to the slums of St. Giles. At the very least, her situation remained precarious. Captain Mowat urged his young friend to do something about her situation at once. "Her expenses here," the aging mariner reported rather ominously from London in 1784, "is much more than you may judge it to be. I am persuaded that was she settled any where near you she would save you not only the money she spends but otherwise become very useful to you in many ways and much more comfortable for both." He suggested that possession of a "good farm" would be the most suitable arrangement for her.[34]

Percy saw the merit of his informal guardian's suggestion. While serving on *Delaware,* on April 9, 1785, Robert Percy petitioned Governor Thomas Carleton for land in Cambridge Parish, New Brunswick. He received a grant of thirty acres on Lower Musquash Island in the St. Johns River. There on that tiny tract he hoped to settle his mother.[35] Robert acted, however, too late. In October 1785 she died. Although Margaret Percy had moved outside St. Giles Parish, she had continued to worship at the church on High Street, Holborn. In the 1770s and 1780s, the burial grounds at St. Giles-in-the-Fields were notorious, especially with respect to the inmates of the parish workhouse nearby.[36] There, in the churchyard, surrounded by London's worst rookery of prostitutes, costermongers, and unemployed folk largely Irish, Margaret Percy was buried in October 1785, perhaps next to her teenage daughter Sarah, dead for four years.[37]

Dogged persistence finally rewarded Henry Mowat. In 1796, when in his sixties, he took charge of his first ship-of-the-line, the fourth-rate, fifty-gun *Assistance.* Dying in 1798 at sea near Cape Henry, Henry Mowat was buried in the cemetery of the Episcopal church at Hampton, Virginia.[38]

Percy family history would have been vastly different had Robert Percy adopted his friend Mowat's advice and planted himself and his mother in eastern Canada. In such a case, he might never had tried to locate his real father. The American Percys would never have known that their assumption of legitimacy was problematical. In the late spring of 1785, however, Robert Dow had gone to London on business.[39] There the Scottish physician found Margaret Percy in sad circumstances. Perhaps he had met her through mutual Scottish friends and the Loyalist friends of Henry Mowat, then in London.

Not long after Margaret's death in October of that year, Dr. Dow became acquainted with Robert "for the first time," as he recalled. The son had arrived from Maine or Canada, but he was too late to attend his mother's funeral. Exactly how the Scottich physician made the connection between his friend Charles Percy and his new acquaintances, Margaret Percy and then her son Robert Percy, is not known. Yet his wide association with fellow Scots had to have played a major role. Educated at Edinburgh, a leading medical center, Dr. Dow came from the village of Saltcoats, some thirty miles from Greenock, the port of Glasgow. Ann Dow, his sister, had married Alan Ker, the head of Alan Ker and Company of Greenock. The firm traded with the Loyalist merchants of Falmouth, Penobscot, and St. Andrews—the wealthy Robert Pagan (formerly from Greenock), and David and James Ryder Mowat, and John Lee, Robert Percy's Penobscot letter-keeper. The significance of these affiliations lay in the fact that the maritime world was a tightly knit, clan-like arrangement— a community afloat one might say. Although water transportation was slow, it linked together these clusters of mariners and merchants and their families around the Atlantic rim. Dr. Dow's brother, John Dow, a merchant seaman from Saltcoats, plied the waters of the West Indies. He visited such northeastern ports as Baltimore, New York, Boston, and Falmouth, the Scottish ports of the Clyde, and Cork in southern Ireland, a few miles from young Robert's birthplace at Kilkenny. If Charles Percy imagined that he could permanently escape recognition, he underestimated the long reach of Scottish nosiness. He managed the feat for several years, but eventually his whereabouts became well known in the circle to which Robert Percy had attached himself.[40]

Once the connection was made, Dow hastened to advise Robert that he should present himself to his father. Some years later Dow remembered how he had urged Robert to return with him "to the Mississippi." "Obey," he admonished, "the dying request of your Mother who was solicitous you should be reconciled to him [your father], notwithstanding[,] as she said[,] he had ever used you and her cruelly, but that as he was your Father you should look upon [him] as such; that she in a manner pardoned him, &[,] says she, may God forgive him."[41] Perhaps because of pressing business back in Nova Scotia, the son did not pursue the matter at that point.

Even after learning where his father was, probably after his mother's death, Robert delayed the visit for five years. The reason may have been that, before greeting the wayward parent, he wanted to appear financially independent. (Shortly after Robert arrived, he grandly lent his father Charles some $1500.) Meanwhile, long before Robert's arrival, Charles Percy had been boasting proudly of his son's achievements among the neighbors. He even claimed that Robert at eighteen years of age had not won his commission by captains' examination in the usual way but had been recognized for valor during a skirmish at Quebec. No evidence has survived of any such circumstance; Robert Percy never made such a claim when laying before the Admiralty his memorable naval exploits.[42]

Sometime in 1790, probably in late spring, handsome Lieutenant Percy, in his buff blue uniform and sword, at last arrived at Northumberland House on Buffalo Creek. His father greeted him as his son however awkward his appearance might have been for Susannah. The young naval hero, as Don Carlos proudly described him, made a strong impression upon his half-brothers and half-sisters. Little Susan, wrote her proud father Charles, is "forever talking of her brother Bob in London," and Thomas George "often talks of his Brother Bob." Robert's step-mother and neighbors like Daniel Clark, Don Francis Pousset, and Governor Gayoso's circle found him an agreeable acquaintance with his stories of life at sea. Magnanimously Robert waved aside whatever awkwardness there may have been, much to Charles's relief. Afterwards Robert returned to Canada or, perhaps briefly, to London. (He was still attached to *Delaware* but on half-pay.) After his departure, he and his father developed a lively correspondence. The "Dutyful and affectionate Son," as his father exulted, sent him newspapers. When occasion permitted, Robert despatched fellow officers to visit Northumberland House to bring further information. While visiting in Natchez, Robert enjoyed the scientific discussions at William Dunbar's. Some years later, through Thomas Swift, one of Robert's naval agents in London, he helped the ailing Dunbar to obtain a telescope for his astronomical investigations.[43]

Nonetheless, the visit was not entirely free of strain in the elaborate rituals of affection that eighteenth-century etiquette required. Charles Percy was uneasy and displayed it in two ways. First he tried to discourage Robert from settling in the neighborhood, an idea that he had broached several times during the visit and later. "Tho I know you have industry and frugality enough, I cannot approve of such a choice for you as turning planter tho it would be the highest wish of my Heart to have you near me," Charles Percy later advised. To resign from the service would be a mistake because "your half pay . . . is very pretty"—something to be counted on for good times and bad. Second, Charles boasted too intensely about how high he stood in the estimation of Baron de Carondelet and Governor Gayoso. Percy swelled that he was "both respected and esteemed by all ranks of people here, and everywhere Else that I have passed thro, or sojourned in, as an honest Industrious Man. This is a matter that is very needless to tell you as you are already but too well convinced of it." Clearly Don Carlos wanted the esteem of a son whom he acknowledged in an emotional way. Yet he had no intention of embracing him as his legitimate heir. He did promise to allot him some 500 acres at Bayou Sara near Don Francis Pousset's plantation if he ever did leave the navy. Everyone, he wrote Robert, thought the land he had in mind to furnish him was "very fine indeed, and fairly timber'd with black Walnut wild cherry and sassafras and beautifully watered." The offer might sound generous, but it was not. Charles held nearly 5000 acres himself, much of it undeveloped. The amount was less than he had obtained when first arriving in West Florida sixteen years earlier. Robert's father offered no apologies for his past neglect of his son, nor did he mention any regrets for his treatment of Robert's mother. The letter was completely self-aggrandizing.[44]

However unsatisfactory Charles Percy might have been as a father, Robert Percy was eager to luxuriate in the renewed relationship. He seemed to want Charles's approval, perhaps feeling at some level that he had been responsible as a child for his parent's abrupt disappearance. Hence, he had made himself as agreeable as possible with the young Percys, a success to which Charles liked to allude. Happily counting out the loan of $1500, he received assurances of its quick repayment. Two years later, Charles assured him that he would have reimbursed him with interest but circumstances regrettably intervened. Captain McDonough, the carrier, "had every wish to oblige," but found that he "could not take it." The reasons for McDonough's strange incapacity to keep the money safely were not given.[45] Despite the hearty exchanges of good feeling, there was something unreal, overdone in the relationship between the pair. Even so, when Don Carlos took his life, Robert Percy, as the eldest son, could easily have claimed for himself the entire legacy. The fact that he did not spoke well for his character and for the upbringing he had received from Henry Mowat.

※ ※

In settling the estate, Charles Percy's heirs had to deal with the effects of Charles Percy's bigamy. It was a "very delicate" matter, requiring "the greatest reflection," Governor Gayoso mused.[46] Overlooking Daniel Clark, Jr.'s involvement with the aborted French invasion, he ordered the merchant-planter to adjudicate the matter. The bereaved Susannah appealed to Governor Gayoso in her "distressed and perplex'd situation." He reassured her that, as his representative, Clark was to proceed "with the greatest delicacy and equity." [47]

Like her husband, Susannah Collins at first refused to recognize the eldest son's position as the sole legitimate son. Thus, when Clark formally asked her "if she knew of any" children by a previous marriage, she answered, "No." [48] Three neighbors had accompanied the planter during the painful interview. Whispering among themselves, they puzzled over what to do. Finally they threw up their hands and concluded that "the legitimacy of Mr. Robert Percy's nativity is a subject which abounds with uncertainty and legal niceties; therefore they were induced to do but little on that head" out of a regard for "the tender feelings of the widow and the mother." Charles Percy, they decided to agree, "frequently declared that he was not married to Robert's mother." Writing to Governor Gayoso,

Clark observed that "Interest and honor" required Robert to demonstrate that "he was born in Wedlock." If he did prove that he was "not a Bastard," however, the little ones—Sarah, Susannah, Thomas, Catherine, Luke, and William—would "inevitably be [illegitimate]." Spanish law "admits not a plurality of wives," Clark observed. Unfortunately, Daniel Clark added, Charles and Susannah had not remarried after Robert's mother had died in 1785. Clark had been too sensitive to Susannah Collins's feelings to point out the omission.[49] In New Orleans, Robert Dow quickly surmised that the Spanish governor would probably rule in favor of the widow and her children. The physician urged his friend Robert to appear as soon as possible if he expected to gain anything at all. Despite the war then raging against France, the lieutenant, then aboard H.M.S. *Africa,* obtained leave from the navy in late 1794. He hastened to Natchez to look after his interests.[50]

Meanwhile, what was the widow to do? Her husband's first-born was a formidable adversary. Lieutenant Percy was articulate, genial, and self-assured. He could easily turn the heads of such neighbors as the wealthy John Ellis and William Dunbar, who had great influence upon Governor Gayoso. Charles's eldest son had already made a strong impression during his sojourn in 1790. A quick settlement that escaped complications with the Spanish authorities was much to be preferred. Charles's death was itself a family embarrassment the sooner laid to rest the better. Though still denying the outsider's claims, Widow Percy had already fixed on the wisest policy. As early as the interview with Clark in June 1794, she decided to cede Robert Percy "a child's part, whether his legitimacy could or could not be proved."[51] As a result the executors of the estate offered a cash settlement to be paid in installments over the next three years. At the time of Charles Percy's death, the patrimony had an assessed value of $22,400.69. The land was worth $3900; fifty-five slaves, $11,970; cattle and horses, $1340; indigo crop, $1254; notes, $3140; tools, $199; household furnishings, $672.[52] In exchange for relinquishing all further claims, the recipient was to have $2000. After conferring with Dow and Clark, Robert Percy saw the wisdom of keeping the estate out of the hands of a prying Spanish court. The authorities might void the will and appropriate the whole for the state. Much relieved, Susannah Percy took a decided liking to her step-son and after that treated him cordially.[53]

During his step-mother's lifetime, Robert fulfilled his side of the arrangement without complaint. He may have had little choice, not knowing where to find proof of a marriage between Charles and Margaret. Percy was a young bachelor with a promising naval career on rated ships, and a handsome profit from recent prize-ship transactions with Henry Mowat and E. Powell of London. He could afford a degree of magnanimity.[54] Pleased with his arrangements in Louisiana, Percy returned to H.M.S. *Africa.* In 1796, at St. George's Church, Bloomsbury, London, Robert married twenty-four-year-old Jane Middlemist from Edinburgh, daughter of a family of vintners. As early as 1793, the lieutenant had shown a decided interest in her.[55] While her husband was at sea on the *Ville-de-Paris* and *Victory* in Horatio Nelson's fleet, the bride roomed at a friendly boarding-house on Great Russell Street and, later, on Hyde Street, Bloomsbury.[56] Soon the couple was blessed with babies.

With a wife and a family to care for, Percy longed for a life that would not separate him from them. Yet his naval career did not flourish. For some reason he failed to impress the fast-rising Horatio Nelson and others, most particularly a Captain Drury of H.M.S. *Powerful,* upon which battle-ship Robert briefly served.[57] In 1798 Robert wrote a plaintive letter to the Admiralty in the deferential language of military protocol. He argued that he had been in service for "twenty-six years, sixteen of which as an officer during which time I have been three times wounded, three times ship-wrecked, three a prisoner of war. From the above I beg leave to hope their Lordships will have the goodness to appoint me to either a line of battle ships, Frigate, Cutter or any situation from a store ship, as I look upon myself entirely cut off from every prospect of promotion." Yet for some reason, Percy never managed to rise but continued to be an "unhappy . . . old officer," as he put it to the Admiralty.[58]

As early as 1796, Dow was encouraging Robert to leave the navy. He rhapsodized that, with *"Sans Culotism [sic] Principles"* on the wane and peace returning, not a doubt existed "but this will be a flourishing coun-try."[59] Dow was momentarily at Greenock, Scotland, but urged Percy to join him in Louisiana. "On the quiet Banks of the Mississippi," he wrote, "you will find many near and affectionate friends & relatives ready to stretch out their arms & receive you & Mrs. Percy as a valuable acquisition to their society."[60] In late 1801, Percy was once more returned to half-pay and decided to leave the service, being struck off the rolls at last in Sep-tember 1804.[61] Peace with France, though not to last long, made possible his release. In September 1802, he rented and provisioned a schooner, the *Bilboa,* and sailed it to Natchez. The voyage was dangerous in hurricane season, but it was completed without incident.[62] He brought with him his wife Jane and their two baby daughters, and his wife's young nephew. He also carried some slaves whom Patrick Morgan, the New Orleans and Lon-don factor, had procured for him. For a brief period the Percys settled at Fort Adams, near his father's American family. Buying the ship from its master, he kept it in service, much to the convenience of W. C. Claiborne, the new territorial governor, and other dignitaries, to whom the vessel was lent.[63]

In 1804, he bought a large plantation of 2200 acres, Beech Woods. The tract was located on Big Bayou Sara Creek in the Feliciana district of Span-ish Florida, a few miles below the Mississippi Territory, which had been formally turned over to the United States in 1798. The land, sold for 4000 pesos, was owned by William Collins, his father's brother-in-law by marriage to Susannah.[64]

The ex-naval officer was well suited to his new occupation of planter. The authoritarian character of the service lent itself to the martial rule of slaves. In both instances, the first law was unquestioning obedience. Corporal punishment with the whip met any challenge to authority and "flogging through the fleet" was common. The term referred to the practice of transporting prisoners from ship to ship and lashing them aboard each one. The policy served two ostensible purposes: the greater humiliation of the victim and the wider distribution of the painful costs of defying authority.[65] No doubt, as a planter, ex-Lieutenant Percy found occasion to duplicate that style, though no diary or letter survives to inform us of specific instances. The kinds of offenses for which both seamen and slaves were sentenced were very much the same: neglect of work, fighting, insolence, or refusal to obey orders. Handling volatile men under the stresses that both shipboard and plantation work often induced placed a premium upon decisiveness, sense of expectation, and hardiness. Without these attributes in a master, male subordinates could not be controlled—or so contemporary wisdom had it. The navy instilled in Robert Percy the habits requisite for stern command.

Robert Percy's experience as a purser, dispensing "slop cloaths," rum, and provisions also stood him in good stead as a planter. On *Albany* and other smaller vessels, the purser served as apothecary and surgeon, so that treating the medical needs of slaves would have been no novelty. Moreover, Robert Percy already knew something about African Americans. For instance, while he was aboard *Robust,* the master of the log recorded: "Sent the niggers to the Rigging House to fit the Rigging." [66]

Too often slavery is compared to factory work, a relatively new innovation in that early period of industrialization. The analogy that planters would more readily recognize was the world of military service, in which discipline, deference, and hierarchy were all commonplace. In the navy, positive inducements, special favors, and gratuities were also given—additional rations of food or drink or extra liberty ashore, for instance. Likewise, slaveholders doled out prizes or special holidays for exemplary performance. On the darker side, shipboard mutinies and desertions were the forms of resistance to authority most nearly comparable to the insurrection of slaves or their running away. As in slavery, the distinction between mutiny and simple resistance in the Royal Navy was interpreted loosely. On *Albany,* for instance, John Liddy, Doyle and Patrick O'Brian were given 12 lashes each, the first of the offenders for "Mutiny" and the others for "Drunkenness & Quarreling & Insolence." The offenses were indistinguishable; all received the same number of strokes.[67]

Working hands in large groups—gangs or watches—involved the same kinds of leadership, attention to routine and regulation, with periods for specialized work and relaxation, and close surveillance. In both instances, most of the labor took place in the ever present company of others. Sailors had their shanties just as slaves sang or chanted to make the toil less tedious and more communal. Finding chores for hands to perform during slack periods was the same sort of enterprise in both systems. It was thought important never to let idleness become habitual; boredom could lead to petty quarreling which might grow into seething troubles. During one such period on *Albany,* then at anchor at Halifax, Mowat had his "People employed making nippers." (They were the ropes used to direct the anchor chain around the capstans.)[68] Sometimes momentary respites from routine helped morale. "Drunkenness grog to the ships comp[an]y at noon," the master of *Robust* wrote in a moment of candor.[69] Similarly, the occasional distributing of whiskey rations on a plantation was a way to ease tensions and break the monotony of routine labor. Such concessions could not, however, infringe too much on the efficiency of the operation. All adjustments and activities of work and rest require a high degree of social control and the values related to that control. Just as slaves were divided into gangs, sailors were assigned their watches.

Two cultures existed both on ships and plantations: that belonging to the masters and the other to the culture of the underclass. The latter group had to be accommodated through concessions about work and leisure. A powerful ideology cemented the systems. It required ritualized deference and means of command. Like the ship at sea, the plantation was an independent entity unto itself.[70] An experienced naval officer like Robert Percy would be well equipped for running an isolated community. Like his father Charles and his shipboard second father Mowat, Robert was a man of rough but unmistakable cultivation. Most important of all, Robert Percy remained immersed in the special culture of the Royal Navy; it was a solid preparation for his later career as planter and slaveholder.[71]

In 1804, Robert Percy felt the financial pressures of a growing family. Acting only after the death of Susannah, his father's third widow, Robert initiated a lawsuit in the Mississippi Chancery Court against Charles Percy's heirs. By then the estate had almost doubled in value, to $42,000, a considerable fortune in that era. Under John Collins, the executor, the plantation no longer grew indigo. Instead, the Percy heirs raised cotton, which was already inaugurating an era of wealth great enough to make Adams County among the richest in the new American Republic.[72] Robert had received an additional $3075 as the trust grew. Yet his suit charged that John Collins, from whom he had earlier purchased lands, had improperly paid out $1500 to the widow and had deliberately overlooked some tracts of significant value from the inventory upon which the first settlement was based. The omission was probably either a genuine error or an avoidance of Spanish taxes rather than an attempt to deprive Robert of his share. Because of the complicated change of governments in the late 1790s, Collins may have decided that under-reporting would pay off. (At the time of his death Charles Percy's holdings were undoubtedly worth much more than stated anyhow for the same fiscal reason.) Meanwhile, as an investment, Robert bought more land along Bayou Sara.[73]

Robert Dow, who had befriended father and then son, tried to help Robert gain not only his share of the patrimony but also a posthumous validation of his parentage. While still at sea, Robert had asked Dow to locate documents proving his mother's marriage. Dow had no evidence to provide. Yet he assured the litigant that he should not be "anxious when there so many testimonies to be obtained no doubt from Europe." He had in mind Margaret's friends, particularly a Mrs. Davis, at one time her landlady in London, and "Captain Mowat." He probably meant David Mowat of St. Andrews, Nova Scotia, one of Robert's good friends and business associates. (He could not have meant Henry Mowat because he had died off the coast of Virginia some six years earlier.) Dow was no attorney. Hearsay evidence from acquaintances or kin would be no substitute for a marriage certificate or some other legal paper. Yet the physician did his best. He remembered "long conversations" with the errant husband, who, "at different times both in Europe and here," had privately confessed to him facts which Charles Percy then publicly denied. According to Dow, the planter "thanked his God that he was, or soon would be able to provide for his family; that it behooved him however to be frugal & industrious that he had two children by his first wife and now two by his present one who was likely to have many more."[74] Dow enclosed a statement, which had not been notarized, by Patrick Morgan, the London and New Orleans agent. In New Orleans himself in 1804, Morgan declared: "I was well acquainted with the late Mr. Charles Percy from his arrival in the country in the year 1776 to the time of my quitting it in the years 1780 & 1790 that during that period he informed me at different times that he had a wife and family" in England and a son in the navy. Percy promised to send him remittances for his wife and daughter, but he never did so, Morgan affirmed.[75]

Somehow, though, Robert did find a marriage paper of some sort and brought it to America or had it sent. It made no difference at all. Lawyers on both sides of the case urged Judge Thomas Rodney of the Mississippi Territory to ignore the question and not examine the document to ascertain its merits.[76] After lengthy hearings in 1804 and then again in 1807, Judge Rodney concluded that Robert had gone to the well once too often. He ordered, as he phrased it, "that Pl[an]t[i]ff Take nothing by his bill." No doubt, Rodney's friendship with the Collins and Ellis families had some influence on his decision.[77]

Despite the suit over Charles Percy's estate, the two branches of the family managed to keep channels of communication remarkably open. Robert did not hesitate to buy extensive lands from William Collins, the brother of his British mother's marital rival. One might expect a military man to be much cruder in his handling of business matters.[78] No doubt there were financial motivations for the Ellis–Collins–Robert Percy harmony. No one wished to disturb the delicate equipoise reached about the legitimacy of *any* of the heirs. In effect, the American authorities followed Gayoso's precedent when in diplomatic silence they passed over the issue of bigamy. About such issues families often rage for generations; the Percys did not.[79]

Never subjected to the fits of depression that blighted Charles Percy's peace of mind, Robert Percy followed a career that in some respects was similar to that of father Charles (though it lacked a dramatic termination). Robert was well suited to become, long after his death, a legendary hero. Like his father "Don Carlos," Robert served as an alcalde and an attorney in the fourth district of Feliciana. Like his father, too, he held the rank of captain in the Spanish militia. The neighbors, however, appreciated his willingness to serve as the local apothecary and physician to whites and blacks more than his military éclat.[80]

Like other planters at Bayou Sara, Robert Percy raised cotton and prospered. Like his neighbors, he also chaffed under Spanish rule. When revolutionaries elected a legislature and appointed a governor for the "Lone Star" State of West Florida in 1810, he was named an associate justice.[81] The revolt succeeded with little bloodshed. The minuscule republic—the area around Baton Rouge and below Natchez—joined the United States and became part of Louisiana only seventy-nine days after its birth. In December 1810, the annexation took place under the dubious American claim that the district had really been part of the Louisiana Purchase of 1803 anyhow.[82]

In the years remaining to him, Robert resided both on the banks of the Bayou Sara Creek and in Washington, a hamlet on the Pine Ridge, seven miles west of Natchez near St. Catherine's Creek. Among his neighbors were the large and contentious Foster and Smith clans, some of whose members had once quarreled so bitterly with Charles Percy. The village was also home for the widow Susannah and her heirs as well as for others of considerable social prominence. For a short period, Washington served as a meeting place for the Territorial legislature and governor, although the commercial center of the region was Natchez. The gathering of the wealthy landowners in a nearby town defies the popular image of plantation isolation. Instead, those who could afford to maintain two establishments did so, very much as did the English gentry with a house on Belgravia Square and a seat in the country. Robert Percy—and his American relations—were no exceptions in the way they moved from town to plantation as pleasure and business suited them.

However pleasant life in Washington, Mississippi, was, Robert Percy derived his income from the Beech Woods plantation at Bayou Sara, later known as St. Francisville, Louisiana. Though lacking the social life of tiny Washington, Bayou Sara was then a country of "gloomy grandeur," as one oldtimer recalled. The trees—magnolias, poplars, red oak, and black walnut, occasionally a huge sassafras, many covered with tangles of heavy vines and Spanish moss—populated a river-bordered district. Robert's cotton was of the highest quality, and he ably judged when to withhold and when to put it on the market. In July 1810, he received fourteen cents a pound for his prior year's crop and got it safely bound for Europe despite the turmoil of embargoes, Napoleonic decrees, and naval warfare. (As Spanish territory, the Feliciana district, of which Bayou Sara was a part, had earlier escaped the disruptions of embargoes imposed by the administrations of Jefferson and Madison.)[83]

Such success enabled him to play the role an ex-naval officer enjoyed: the lavish dispenser of his good fortune. As open-handed with his hospitality as any Southern gentleman, Robert Percy upheld a tradition that his Anglo-Irish background reinforced. Even the descendants of Susan Collins Percy had come to like him very much. Judge Elijah Smith, who had married Mary Purcell, an orphan whom Jane and Robert had brought with them as a family helper from England, spoke of him respectfully as "our good old Friend Capt. Percy."[84]

During Robert's lifetime, his wife Jane served as his hostess. She was sturdy, well educated, witty, and formidable, and often had a sharp tongue in her head. Like so many other plantation mistresses, she assumed the demanding and unpleasant duties of her post with Scottish conscientiousness. Fortescue Cuming, an English traveler, remarked in 1809 on the high degree of cultivation that her "long residence in London" had afforded the accomplished matron, particularly when compared with the provincial wives in the Bayou Sara neighborhood.[85]

Most slaveholders in the Natchez District would have felt more at home with the Smiths and Fosters than with the Percys. Their tastes and literary interests far exceeded their neighbors'. The "nabobs," as the Natchez elite were called, fell short of an Old World aristocracy. They adopted, however, the manners and style that served, especially on the frontier, as the American equivalent. In that respect, the Natchez circle was little different from other exclusive groups throughout the Old South. Uniformly they held the most strategically located lands and dominated the political and economic life of the community. Unmistakable signs of station and membership in the enclosed group grew out of shared tastes and common political and economic goals. Southern male elites controlled capital and credit through the banking system, promoted Whiggish commercial development with state funds. They financed and organized the election of members of their own faction. The Natchez circle to which the two branches of the Percy family belonged was such an elite.

Under these circumstances, Robert Percy could have achieved more eminence than he did but lacked ambition along those lines. No less than his half-brother, young Thomas George Percy, he could assume his place among the privileged. In keeping with this confident social and political position, Robert Percy and his "lively set of friends" and relations set fine tables and filled their libraries with current literature. By any standard that one could imagine, these highly selective members of the upper class in the Natchez district knew the classics. For the most part well educated, they were acquainted with the formal rhetoric of the day, the literary fashions, and the proper manners of gentility. Such clusters could be found in other parts of the South, but their numbers were always small even among those counted wealthy. Their habit of congregating in small villages rather than rusticating in the countryside made this social intercourse possible. In 1798, on an expedition to Natchez, a young American army officer from Pennsylvania recorded that he had "had no conception there were so many genteel families in that country. I think I saw as many handsome and accomplished women as I ever saw in my life." [86] Twenty or so years later Natchez was beginning to slip into an economic decline as repeated harvests reduced fertility, but its social and cultural life remained impressive. Mingling with the wealthy families on the Pine Ridge and enjoying their music-making and conversation, Adam Hodgson, a well-traveled gentleman, declared, "I could have fancied myself on the banks of the Lune or Mersey." [87]

The parties, balls, family gatherings, and other social events in the planter community which well-recommended visitors found so accommodating were not designed solely for pleasure. They were the means to solidify kin alliances and evaluate the qualities of the scarce number of appropriate mates in the tiny circle. Typically, plantation families supplied each other with wives and husbands. The Percys, Rouths, Prentisses, Surjets, Sargents, Dunbars, and Ellises intermarried not only because they met each other socially but because the close ties of cousinhood provided some predictability about the happiness and economic future of the lines. The men liked their women to be wealthy, very young, and alert.

For the Percys intellectual life was not as barren as in many other parts of the Old South. Neither leisure nor inclination turned large numbers of settlers toward matters of high culture or intellectual endeavor. Washington had the region's first newspaper, Andrew Marschalk's outspoken and partisan *Republican*. Some of the more enlightened members of the Foster clan had founded Jefferson College for men and Elizabeth Academy for women, and the professors there were generally well-qualified. There was also a town reading room and the rudiments of a lending library. Even if outside the tight circle of elite families the general social milieu was anything but sophisticated, few other parts of the Southwest, New Orleans excepted, were culturally better equipped.

Among the leaders of artistic and literary life in that part of the Southwest were William Provan, physician; Benjamin W. C. Wailes, merchant and planter; former Territorial governor Winthrop Sargent, a well-bred New England Federalist; John W. Monette, a physician from Virginia who founded the library; the aged William Dunbar; and Nathaniel A. Ware, a young lawyer of Woodville, just south of Natchez. Some of these gentlemen and their sons were destined to marry women belonging both to the American and the English Percy lines. On more than a superficial level, they were also the lights of amateur science. Some of them, like Governor Winthrop Sargent, Federalist governor of the Mississippi Territory, took an interest in belles-lettres. Benjamin Wailes early began collecting documents and private correspondence that would become the basis for the Mississippi Historical Society's collection. Others, like Provan, Ware, and Monette took up science, especially botany, geology, and archaeology, with the mystery of local Indian mounds an inducement.[88]

In the 1820s Doctor Provan combined both art and zoology in his enthusiastic patronage of the artist John James Audubon. The artist had just embarked on creating *Birds of America,* his monumental portfolio of engravings. Provan was very active with Monette and the other scientific notables whom a memorialist declared "will be remembered . . . as ornaments to their profession."[89] He fed, housed, and even clothed the young artist, and found pupils for him to teach the skill of drawing. Yet he realized that Audubon's interests would best be served if Lucy, his wife, found regular employment. It would bring them both support and free her husband to carry on his work. Learning that Jane Percy was seeking a tutor for her children, Provan made the necessary arrangements. For Provan, a bachelor, it was an opportunity to visit Sarah Catherine, one of Robert and Jane Percy's four daughters. Sarah Percy, named for her father Robert's little sister who had died in London, and William Provan were married in 1828.[90] Lucy Audubon spent several years at Beech Woods, teaching the Percy children and others from neighboring plantations. She earned the handsome sum of $1000 a year and resided in her own cottage.[91]

At the outset the arrangement seemed idyllic. When James Audubon first visited his wife, he and Jane Percy, both intense and hotheaded, proved to be surprisingly compatible. Jane Percy found his conversation delightful. She urged him to remain at Beech Woods long enough to join her brother Charles Middlemist, a painter soon to arrive from London, on a joint sketching expedition in the neighborhood. Her hopes were realized; the pair met and Charles Middlemist was so captivated by Audubon's ambitious project that he planned a series on American wildflowers similar in scope to his friend's *Birds of America.*[92]

Despite these auspicious beginnings, Jane Percy turned out to be less than an ideal employer. She gradually came to dislike Lucy's erratic, disheveled, and excitable husband. Moreover, unlike her husband Robert, she took no pleasure in largess. She had once announced to an unoffending guest whom she had invited to Beech Woods that he remained only at great "sacrifice" of her "Feelings." He left in some bitterness. Peace was maintained largely because Audubon was mostly away on long expeditions in pursuit of his art. When he did turn up, she made no secret of her feelings, and Audubon, whose Gallic temper flared as readily as her Scottish indignation, responded in kind. During one encounter, she ordered him off the place. After fuming for three days, Audubon boldly revisited his wife's tiny cottage in the night. A slave spied him and informed his mistress. With the servant holding the lantern, Jane Percy stormed into the couple's bedroom while they were making love. The angry words awakened the Audubons' boys, adding to the pair's humiliation. She forced him in the dead of night to trudge back to the hamlet of Bayou Sara. Some years later, Audubon had not forgotten the experience. He remarked about a new residence that at least "if I wanted to go to bed to thee there, I would not be sent back 15 miles on foot to Bayou Sara instead!!!" [93]

Angry at her employer though she was, Lucy Audubon could not afford to leave the post. Nonetheless, the relationship between the women was never the same again. In 1827, while Audubon, in England, was beginning to receive recognition, without regret Lucy left Beech Woods after another dispute that Jane Percy had initiated had arisen, and she had delayed payment of Lucy's salary. Exasperated, Lucy found nearby a more congenial plantation household in which to teach while waiting for her husband's return. [94]

By this time, Robert Percy had gone to his grave. In the fall of 1819, he had come down with a mortal disease at his Washington, Mississippi, house. In late November he died of what the obituary vaguely called "a lingering illness." [95] At age fifty-seven, he survived longer than many other nineteenth-century members of this generally short-lived family. Elijah Smith, manager of the Ellis–Percy estates in Mississippi, noted at the time that a "malignant fever" had swept away an alarming number of local worthies. Smith wrote that Captain Percy had stayed up all night with the corpse of his old Irish friend Nathaniel Evans. According to local talk, the wake had brought on Percy's end from the same disease that carried Evans off. If so, the means of his dying seemed appropriate. His sunny temperament and caring nature, learned in part from old Captain Mowat, had been his undoing but could not dim his reputation. [96] Perhaps it was merely coincidence, but Thomas George Percy, Charles's second son, resembled in character his half-brother Robert. Like him, he, too, searched for a father, but not by traversing an ocean. Instead, in friendship with another man he found the affection and sense of order that Charles Percy could not, in his mental illness and death, provide him.

CHAPTER THREE

Brevity of Life

The highest in the council room,
The wittiest in the hall;
The lord of a far distant home,
Adored, revered by all;
Wearing upon a youthful brow,
The power and pride of years.
With yearnings strange, we name him now,
That "child of many tears."

"That Child of Many Tears," Eleanor Percy Lee[1]

Looking back upon the family's history in the 1930s, William Alexander Percy would perceive his great-grandfather as a progenitor dissimilar from the others—unambitious, compliant, and even perhaps a trifle self-satisfied. In the Percys' house in Greenville—the one that Senator LeRoy and his family occupied—Thomas George's elegant portrait hangs over the library fireplace. Gazing at the picture, Will Percy, the Senator's son, readily understood, he observed, why Charles Percy and his wife had adored their Thomas. The artist had captured a charming, affable, young gentleman, fashionably attired "in a black stock and a black waistcoat adorned with five stylish brass buttons." Was "Thomas G.," as his descendants called him, happier, more at ease with himself than all the other Percy men? Will Percy thought so, but he noted there was a hint of something enigmatic in the artist's rendering of his smile. Look closely, Will Percy wrote, and "at the corner of his mouth, very shadowy and knowing," scrutiny will reveal "a little hurt but not at all bitter."[2]

Will Percy did not mention the unusual rate of mortality that this generation and the next had to confront. There were too many occasions to mourn, beginning with Thomas's own childhood. If Thomas George Percy had any inclination toward melancholy, he had ample reason. His father had killed himself when the boy, born in 1786, was eight years old. He had witnessed the deaths of his two younger brothers, William and Luke, in the 1790s from childhood diseases. Thomas Percy's eldest sister Sarah had to be hospitalized with melancholia in her middle years. Another sister, Susan, about whom next to nothing is known, died young—sometime after 1809, when her last appearance was noted—or else she was afflicted in some way that no one ever mentioned her in writing thereafter. At twenty-five, she was a member of the tiny wedding party attending the marriage of her sister Catherine to Dr. Samuel Brown in 1808 before Judge Thomas Rodney, who recorded her presence. In 1809 she left home for further schooling under the Ursuline sisters in New Orleans[3] and after that disappeared from all records.

Perhaps these circumstances had no special impact upon Thomas Percy, but if they did, he hid the effects from those who knew him. Unlike some of, though not all, the sons that he would father, Thomas Percy seldom exerted himself in any cause—religious, philanthropic, or political. Shrewd business transactions proved to be his strong point, but prudence, not risk-taking, was his watchword. He was by no means, wrote Will Percy, a "demanding ancestor." In fact, Thomas himself once confessed that he could boast of "little distinction" but did not mind because planting was a respectable calling.[4] Being happy, in the way that Thomas Percy might have defined it, would always be low on the family's list of priorities.

Though unambitious, Thomas Percy loved the life of the mind and the acquisition of tangible things. With his inherited wealth, from time to time he acquired handsome furnishings and took special pride in an enormous dining-room table supported by carved legs with great brass claws. Yet his most treasured possession was not fine porcelain but his library, which included Wilson's costly and elaborate three-volume *American Ornithology*. From London and elsewhere he imported many scores of leather-bound books, each bearing a modest book-plate and a number for its spot on the shelf. He had no weighty philosophical interests but purchased the best fare of the age—such journals as *Blackwood's* and the *Edinburgh Review*, histories, and editions of Addison, Goldsmith, and Johnson. The obligatory works of Walter Scott and William Shakespeare, without which a Southern gentleman could not lay claim to the title, filled the shelves.[5] Epicurean tastes and habits of acquisition, however, were secondary matters compared with a more singular feature of Thomas Percy's character. Uppermost in his thoughts was a deep longing for friendship, and in that realm he became a devotee in the way other men might pursue more challenging tasks. Thomas was to link his fortunes closely to those of John Williams Walker, an old Princeton companion. Their experience of brotherly affection established a pattern in the family's culture. Some male Percys enjoyed the company of other men more than they liked staying at home. That preference was by no means unusual in the Old South where men loved the sporting life—the hunt, the gaming table, the tavern gossip. A compulsion to create good cheer with neighbors helped to stay the dread of being alone.

Thomas Percy's friend Walker, not the reticent Thomas himself, would be the central figure in the family circle, perhaps because he filled an important psychological need. He had the dynamism that his friend Thomas set aside. Walker's influence prompted the family's shift of location, away from Natchez, away from the patrimonial lands. But the decision to leave could not have been easy. There were sound reasons to remain on the soil that Charles Percy's slaves had cleared and made profitable. Until he chose to resettle in the Alabama sector of the Mississippi Territory in 1813, Thomas devoted himself to the management of his inheritance from his widowed mother. For the career of planter and investor, he was perfectly suited. From earliest manhood, Thomas Percy liked being "head gardener" and "maker of cotton bales." He hired no overseer. Not only did the occupation provide a seasonable income but also neither interrupted his leisure hours nor prevented his elaborate trips to the North and abroad.[6]

Certainly Natchez was one of the grand places to play the gentleman farmer. Even as late as 1860, by which time the region was in relative decline, Adams County still had a higher proportion of estates valued at over $100,000 than Newport, Rhode Island, and the Eighteenth Ward of New York City, places better known for their rich populations. In the early decades of the nineteenth century, the wealth to be gained from slave labor on the riverine soils cleared for cotton was beyond the dreams of the most acquisitive planters. David Ker, a local slaveholder with whose descendants Percys would be later connected, rhapsodized in 1801 that "an industrious planter clears the price of a negro in [one] year from his labour."[7]

Moreover, Natchez had relatively low transportation costs by river, south to New Orleans and the sea, north to St. Louis, Louisville, and Cincinnati. The Percys belonged to the exclusive set that benefited from these advantages. Sarah Percy, Charles's eldest daughter had married the venerable Judge John Ellis in 1799. The Ellises, one of the first English families to settle in the district in the 1760s, were interconnected with most of the leading people. After Charles Percy's suicide, Ellis had served as president of the Orphans' Court at a probating of wills under United States jurisdiction. Later, the elderly judge served as lieutenant colonel in the local militia, president of the territorial legislative council, and Speaker of the House of Representatives. Judge Ellis's brother Abram and brother-in-law John Collins, both magistrates, and Lyman Harding, the Percy family attorney, belonged to a stately legal circle in which Thomas Percy could move when he liked.[8]

With Judge Ellis so highly placed, ceremonial occasions must have been pleasant for Sarah Percy's younger brother Thomas, but he better enjoyed

Robert Percy, Lieutenant, Royal Navy, 1762–1819; son of Charles and Margaret Percy, drawn from a miniature.

Anton Kumanov of Moscow.

Henry Mowat, Captain, Royal Navy, 1734–98, Robert Percy's commanding officer and surrogate father.

Photo by Edward Owen, from a miniature at the Naval Historical Center, Washington, D.C.

Thomas George Percy, 1786–1841, son of Charles Percy and Susannah Collins Percy, planter of Natchez and Huntsville.

Photo by June H. Dorman, miniature in the Charles Brown Percy Family Papers, Tennessee Historical Society, Nashville.

the company of a livelier and younger crowd: George Poindexter, an up-and-coming attorney and Lydia Carter, his wealthy, beautiful bride; Lydia's sister, Mrs. Israel Trask, and James Dunlop and his wife, a daughter of "Sir" William Dunbar, the planter-scientist. In addition, the Percys and Ellises moved in the society of the Minors, Kers, Surgets, Duncans, Sargents, and senior Dunbars, all very substantial planters. Some of them had close ties with Philadelphia and New England families. The Sargents, with whom some Percys (on Robert's side) would later intermarry, were a Gloucester, Massachusetts, tribe. Their paterfamilias, the Federalist Winthrop Sargent, was the first governor of the newly acquired Mississippi Territory after its acquisition from the Spanish in 1798. Such was the social setting for handsome Thomas George Percy. With ease and confidence he associated with the local "nabobs" of Natchez as even they called themselves. A descendant later identified him as "a perfect Sir Charles Grandison—a man without fear, and truly without reproach." [9]

Thomas Percy's first independent appearance in a record was 1803: his entry at Princeton. Thomas's mother, Susannah Collins, died in that year or perhaps in the year following.[10] By either date Charles Percy's original holdings had been doubled in most categories and tripled in others. His widow, her Collins brothers and Judge Ellis, her very wealthy son-in-law, had together built sturdily upon the foundations that "Don Carlos" had left her. The slave force, working on a domain of 5000 acres, had grown from fifty-five to seventy-six. She had a large herd of cattle from which she sold steers to be used by the workmen building a United States fort on the Spanish frontier near Northumberland House.[11] Thomas George continued his schooling at Princeton until graduation in 1806, but immediately afterwards he entered upon a full time career as a planter.[12] The companionship of Thomas Percy and John Walker began at Princeton, where their studies were of much less interest, under a rigid, Presbyterian curriculum, than the students' opportunities to learn from each other.[13]

The reasons for the connection were peculiar to the time and region. Men of comparably high status were often enemies and rivals in the South. Their sense of place in the social order had to be asserted and the position of others challenged, particularly if they took politics seriously, as many did in antebellum times. As a result, male friendships counted for much more than one might expect. First, to trust one's friends was a way to survive in the clashes that the constant flux of hierarchy stimulated. Second, John Walker and Thomas Percy were keenly interested in political topics and belles-lettres, the latter an intellectual avocation that scarcely had a wide following in the hunting and gambling society to which they belonged.

A third factor was much more significant than the other two. Like Percy, John Walker—a native of the wealthy little community of Petersburg, Georgia—had early lost his father, Jeremiah, the son of an immigrant from

Limerick, Ireland.[14] Even if Thomas Percy was free of any psychological effects from the death of his father, he seemed to have turned over his feelings for a friend to embody: Thomas Percy's boon companion was a young man who also in his childhood had lost his father, but Walker had openly expressed his sense of mourning, in contrast to the Percys' reticence. Orphaned at nine years of age in 1792, John Williams Walker looked up to Memorable, his guardian and eldest brother, even after he went off to Moses Waddel's academy, in nearby Vienna, South Carolina, the school that John C. Calhoun had attended. John Walker reported his academic successes to Memorable as if he were father as well as brother, friend, and, said young Walker later, "discriminating genius." Then, in March 1803, Jeremiah, another brother, unexpectedly died. Already ill with tuberculosis, Memorable, John Walker feared, was likely to follow. Despite the grieving brother's nursing, Memorable's hemorrhages and bouts of coughing continued unabated and on April 27, 1803, he died.[15]

The death of his mother, of his father, then of his brothers, had a significant impact upon the young Princetonian. Ambitious though he was for fame and public service, he often felt overwhelmed by gloom. Worse still, John Walker soon discovered that he had contracted tuberculosis. The disease at the time was thought to betoken moral weakness, being attributable to "constitutional peculiarities, perverted humors and various types of inflammations." Such a medical pronouncement would naturally have a depressing effect—what had John Walker done to be so afflicted? Actually, he had contracted the disease from his dying brother whom he had nursed too faithfully. "Solitude & Silence," he once wrote, "are worse than consumption himself." [16] It is ironic that novelist Walker Percy shared the same problems of melancholia and tuberculosis that afflicted the individual from whom his given name was derived. Unlike the case of Walker Percy, though, religion proved to be little solace to John Walker, though Moses Waddel's foreboding sermon from the Book of Job at Memorable's funeral made an impression: " 'Man dieth, and wasteth away; yea man giveth up the ghost, and where is he?' " Walker tried to reassure himself with the thought that "the designs of the Almighty are unsearchable by man's comprehension." Yet he reached the bitter conclusion that if faith in Christ was the only way to salvation then 4/5 of the world will inevitably be damned," including himself. Neither he nor Thomas Percy ever adopted the Christian faith as bulwark against the ravages of melancholy and sense of parental abandonment; that remedy awaited a few in later generations.[17]

Only one other brother, James Walker, remained alive. "I have no father to please, no mother to soothe," Walker wrote him. The notion that a son should pacify his mother, presumably in a state of agitation over something minor, but please his father by his manliness epitomized the patriarchal code by which white Southerners ordered their lives. Equally part of the early nineteenth-century milieu was Walker's lament for toiling under "a sorrow and anguish of mind not to be described." The "blues" or "Blue Devils," as depression was then called, struck him ever more severely shortly after graduation from Princeton. No doubt a young man's uncertainties when facing post-baccalaureate decisions had much to do with his gloominess.

John Walker was a young romantic, rather typical of the day. When J. W. von Goethe had written "The Sorrows of Werther," the sensitive youth who committed suicide because of an unattainable love, he unwittingly unleashed a popular enthusiasm for extravagant mourning among the young for the might-have-been. Indeed, the romantic philosophy of pessimistic idealism that arose in the age of Sterne, Schiller, and Goethe had turned the concept of melancholia away from *acedia,* or alienation from God, to more secular disappointments, most especially an imputed diffidence or hostility of others toward the unappreciated self. John Walker perceived himself in terms that would soon be identified as the Byronic mode.[18]

In hopes of recovering his health and morale, John Walker in the spring of 1808 headed first for Savannah, then Charleston, and finally New Orleans, whose generally prosaic appearance, he thought, provided "little of [the] grand or beautiful to solicit praise."[19] Just before heading home, however, he took a side trip to the Natchez District. There he and Thomas Percy renewed their ties from Princeton days, an affiliation which was to last until Walker's death fourteen years later. Thomas had his intellectual friend stay on to share the family's pleasant life for approximately a year. As John Walker put it, Thomas Percy took the place of "relations, friends, and home and almost of Love."[20]

The alliance was based in part upon their mutual experience of early calamities in their families. Neither one nor the other had to discuss his childhood experiences and fears or write about innermost feelings. Yet to count upon a friend, or set of friends, as if he were a brother—indeed as if he were the advising and consoling father whom both once sorely yearned to have—could have helped to heal some of the psychic wounds inflicted early in their lives. On this point, in the absence of diary entries and intimate correspondence, one can only speculate. One can imagine, however, that John Walker must have felt some relief to live in the company of a genuinely caring friend during his illness.

To deal with the medical issue confronting him, John Walker had another good reason to linger: the presence of Dr. Samuel Brown. The distinguished and well-connected physician had only recently married Catherine Percy, Thomas's younger sister.[21] Despite the seventeen-year difference in their ages, the physician had quickly become a close and lifelong friend of his brother-in-law Thomas Percy. Brown was enormous in size—big enough when he strolled downtown, he said, "to frighten the Dandies off the foot way."[22] With two such solicitous friends to help, the patient rapidly began to recover strength and hope.[23]

🎕 🎕

The close friendship of Thomas Percy and John Walker was the nucleus of a significant brotherhood of in-laws that would ultimately be formed. Relations between brothers and brothers-in-law in the South were sometimes peculiarly tense because a father's patrimony had to be shared among insiders and outsiders—brothers and the husbands the sisters had married. What often resulted were simmering verbal feuds, lawsuits, sometimes slayings—particularly when the manhood of challengers and defendants in these affairs superseded money matters as the chief point of family rivalry.[24] Such was not the case in the Percy clan. In fact, over the generations male Percys and their in-laws rarely quarreled over financial arrangements and inheritances to the point of breaking off relations.

Under the blandishments of Thomas Percy and Samuel Brown, Walker was tempted to stay permanently and surrender his political ambitions. "I am content," Walker noted, but with scarcely disguised frustration, "to walk my little hour upon the stage, to die, to rot, & be forgotten like the common mass of mankind that fall around me every day unheeded and unlamented."[25] Thomas Percy offered to lend him lands until Walker located acres of his own. In a letter to his brother, John, rhapsodized about how much Thomas meant to him: "My heart knows him not as a common man, an every day friend it loves as a brother, & is proud of its love. By heaven, Sir," Walker exclaimed, "we will bring Celibacy into credit; Our bachelor hall shall be the hall of hospitality & content, a caravansary to the weary, the head-quarters of sport and good fellowship."[26]

As Walker's health improved, ambitions began to revive. Even Thomas Percy's energies quickened a little as he detected his friend's growing restlessness. Walker implicitly criticized Thomas for complacency. The convalescent patient wrote home that, after old Judge Ellis died, in November 1808, Thomas had been compelled to assume the duties of the "man of business, though never intended for it by nature & almost disqualified by habit & extreme repugnance." Eager to begin his law and political career back home, in the spring of 1809, Walker and Thomas set out for New Orleans where they would bid each other farewell. Beforehand, however, they spent a week sightseeing and dining in the city. Among their pleasures was a visit with Thomas's "handsome" sister Susan Percy (nicknamed Nancy) at the Ursuline convent where she was studying French. John expressed a mild interest in the young woman about whom no further information is available. Walker then caught a ship to begin the long journey home, never to return to that part of the West.[27]

Rather than resettle in Petersburg, Georgia, however, Walker reestablished himself in northeast Alabama, the easternmost part of the Mississippi Territory. He and other planters from the Broad River district near Petersburg—LeRoy Pope, Thomas Bibb, General John B. Scott, and others—undertook the resettlement together. At about the same time, in 1810, he married Matilda Pope. He had first noticed her when she was merely twelve, then waited until she returned from a Pennsylvania finishing school to propose. A young woman of "tender, engaging and lovely disposition," he said, she was the daughter of the Virginia-born LeRoy Pope, a planter and magistrate of Petersburg, the head of a household so wealthy and powerful that it was known locally as "the Royal family."[28] The newly married couple settled in a log cabin and directly had a working plantation as well as a new addition to the family. Walker christened the plantation Tusculum and his daughter Mary Jane. Not long afterward he opened a second, called Oakland, which later became his principal residence.[29]

The Georgia emigrants soon made Madison County the fastest growing and most prosperous district in that part of the Mississippi Territory. Situated about ten miles from the Tennessee River at the point where rapids prevent navigation, the county seat of Huntsville, eight miles from Oakland, was located in the midst of lands most suitable for the raising of cotton, tobacco, and grains. According to a report that Walker himself later wrote, the average yield of cotton was 1000 pounds for each acre. By 1817 thirty gins, a large number for a newly settled county, prepared some 5000 bales for shipment. "The face of the country is the most beautiful in the world, being in the main a level plain yet affording many mountain prospects and much romantic scenery," Walker wrote.[30]

In urging his friends Percy and Brown to join him in the new country, Walker stressed the economic benefits awaiting them, but he also made clear his own emotional needs. "The heart-sick exile whom you knew in the wane of his thought & brokenness of his spirit, will never cease to cherish next his heart the remembrance of those who so unreservedly noticed & caressed him," he wrote. Walker's blandishments had the effect intended. The pair recognized the need for developing new lands, Adams County having already passed its zenith. But there were fresh territories much closer by—in Warren County up river which was quickly surpassing Adams in new development. Instead, in 1811 Thomas Percy bought land near Walker's plantation.[31] Fighting in the Southwest during the second war with Great Britain, however, delayed all plans for resettlement on the purchased acres. With the Creeks in full war cry, white Mississippians were hard pressed for a time to defend themselves. Governor David Holmes mustered the militia in which Thomas Percy had been a colonel. Thomas Percy did not, however, volunteer his services, another signal that he would not willingly disturb his bland equipoise. Thomas Percy's refusal to rally to arms when his own locale was threatened violated the family's warrior tradition—his half-brother Robert's naval career and his father Charles's military service in the Seven Years' War. He remained a Percy different from the rest.[32]

⚔ 🛡

When military danger receded, the pair of brothers-in-law prepared to leave Natchez, but they did so under additional pressure from unexpected circumstances: a quarrel with a member of their own circle of young friends. The incident further revealed Thomas Percy's determined course of inertia, and the role of male sexual honor in Southern life. George Poindexter was a clever and learned attorney but erratic neighbor, who clearly suffered from chronic mania and depression. A rural Virginian, Poindexter had been early left motherless and, at seventeen, fatherless as well. His tight-fisted and pious eldest brother John, a Baptist preacher, had reared him, but they had constantly quarreled. George Poindexter often transposed his own misery into claims of persecution and hostility against which he would fight as if his life depended on it, and he never relinquished the neurotic pattern.[33] "Here I am," he fumed bitterly not long after arrival in Natchez, "without society, and without the hope of forming any." Actually, Thomas Percy and his group soon welcomed the brilliant and witty stranger into their midst. Yet according to J. F. H. Claiborne, Mississippi's first historian, Poindexter "was all his life subject to fits of despondency" which were punctuated by episodes of compulsive excitement and bouts of heavy gambling and drinking.[34] Later in life, he suffered from hysterical reaction that made it impossible for him to use his limbs and once, suicidally drunk, he fell out of a Natchez hotel window.[35]

Like so many ambitious men of the Old South, Poindexter secured his financial future with a handsome marriage to Lydia Carter, daughter of the wealthy Major Jesse Carter of Natchez. Shrewd land speculations built on the dowry made him a millionaire, and he climbed from one state office to the next. Yet in his periodic cycles of dejection, he thought his manhood and honor threatened, a suspiciousness that led to a number of duels. According to his biographer, it seemed clear from Poindexter's actions "that he had very pronounced manic-depressive tendencies of the paranoid type." The malady was what French alienists (psychologists) then called *folie circulaire.*[36]

Poindexter reacted violently when rumors circulated that he had acted the part of a coward during the Battle of New Orleans. Still worse, Poindexter heard gossip that he had been cuckolded by Thomas Percy, allegedly in love with Poindexter's wife Lydia. Indeed, his marriage to Lydia Carter had been a misery to both. Nicholas Trist, Poindexter's closest friend and a kinsman of Thomas Jefferson, had predicted earlier to Poindexter that he should learn to "dispel gloom when it assails you as your bitterest enemy" because it might ruin his marriage.[37] Picking up the theme of cowardice from his friends in New Orleans, Samuel Brown broadcast his contempt for Poindexter, although Andrew Jackson, the victor at Chalmette, defended the honor and record of his subordinate. Infuriated, Poindexter issued Brown a challenge. When the doctor refused, he then wheeled about in rage against his former friend Percy for his alleged affair with Lydia. "By every law human and divine I should be justified in taking your life," Poindexter wrote Percy, "without affording you an opportunity or the means of resistance." At one time, friendship "gained you admittance to my house," but, Poindexter ranted, he had been betrayed. Percy was no better than "the midnight assassin or the high way Robber" whose appetite had grown insatiable. "Considerations of delicacy towards the feelings of another"—Lydia Carter—prevented his mentioning exactly what Percy had done, but Poindexter felt obliged to "consult more considerately my own vindication and avenge my own wrongs."[38] The letter was a model of dueling invective. Rather than blame himself for any problems in his marriage that his erratic disposition might have engendered, Poindexter stormed against an alleged rival.

Oddly, no contest ensued. Nor did Poindexter carry out his threat to shoot Thomas Percy on sight. If anyone called Thomas Percy a coward, the records do not reveal it. Perhaps everyone knew that Poindexter was temporarily deranged and therefore no longer Percy's moral peer. In any event, Percy simply walked away from the issue altogether—by hastening to Alabama. But Poindexter's young son, the product of the love affair as Poindexter believed, could not so easily move from harm's way. Albert, Poindexter's second son, grew from problem child to alcoholic young man. Poindexter divorced his wife and never acknowledged Albert in any way, despite the boy's pitiable pleas for affection. Albert died in a Louisville, Kentucky, doss-house in 1832.[39] From his father's point of view, Albert's disgrace was Thomas Percy's concern, not his.

Samuel Brown, the third figure in the new cluster of male friends who would settle in Alabama, had as good reasons for deep mourning as his friends Percy and Walker, but in his case the loss was the demise of his wife Catherine, not of parents or brothers. Unlike most Southern men of the time, Brown always treated his wife with an equality quite beyond the conventions. After her death, Samuel Brown mourned, "I found her mind so stored with useful ideas & so capable of forming sound original judgments on every novel occurrence that I in a great degree lost my relish for all other Society. During the happy period of our union *I never once* blushed for what she said or for what she did, on the contrary I felt superior to other men when I recollected that I was the object of the affections of a woman so virtuous & so discerning."[40]

Brown was by no means indifferent to Catherine's fortune in land and slaves, but the exchange was not one-sided. He belonged to an Anglo-Irish lineage—a lineage perhaps more respectable than that of Catherine's father, Don Carlos. His father had been a distinguished Presbyterian dissenter in colonial Virginia. Brown had received the best medical training that the late eighteenth century had to offer. After graduation from Dickinson College in Carlisle, Pennsylvania, he studied medicine at Edinburgh University, Marischal College, University of Aberdeen, and in the Philadelphia surgery of Benjamin Rush, the nation's leading medical practitioner. In 1799 he accepted a professorship at Transylvania University at Lexington, Kentucky, the first medical school beyond the Appalachians, but then moved to New Orleans before his marriage to Catherine Percy.[41]

The amicable household in Natchez had a sadly short history, but before her death Catherine produced two children: Susan, born in 1809, and James Percy, in 1810. During her third pregnancy, however, their mother took to bed, "seized with a fever and vomiting," Brown wrote Margaretta, his brother John's wife. "I had but too much reason to consider her as lost." On January 4, 1813, she gave birth to daughter Catherine Anna, but within two days a high temperature and nausea returned. Brown was in despair because the infant, "my poor *little Nancy* [Catherine Anna]," could draw no nourishment from her mother's breast. He also worried about the older pair, "my poor little Susan and my lovely boy," for whom a father could do so little. On February 16, 1813, Catherine Percy died, and Brown was inconsolable despite all the sympathy offered by Thomas Percy, "my dear friend," as Brown called him.[42]

The major problem for Brown was an issue that would bedevil future members of the gifted clan. He found Southern life barren of ideas and intellectual vitality and therefore begged his relatives to join him in some Eastern city. Brushing aside the suggestion, brother James, a newly elected senator from Louisiana, urged Samuel to settle again in New Orleans as a more practical alternative. Samuel Brown declined: "I scarcely know any earthly consideration that could induce me to attempt to *raise my children* in N. Orleans" because the people were "profligate" and "frivolous." It would be at least half a century "before a man of real worth can be educated at that place," he concluded. "All new countries are objectionable," he complained of Natchez. "This country has now nothing in it which can interest a heart as wounded as mine." Brother John Brown also was not interested, having just left the U.S. Senate to start a flourishing law practice in Frankfort, Kentucky, the state capital. Therefore, the chance to start over in Alabama appealed to Samuel Brown strongly.[43]

Meanwhile in the summer of 1813, Thomas Percy occupied himself in transferring slaves to a site of 1400 acres adjacent to Oakland, John Walker's plantation. Brown soon followed, and the three planters—

Thomas Percy, Samuel Brown, and John Walker—formed a fraternal ring not to be broken so long as they lived.

𝕬 𝕭

The country to which the families moved was a thriving plantation colony in the midst of the wilds. Colonel LeRoy Pope of Petersburg, first judge of the Madison County court, led the fast-growing elite of the district, but was piqued when the inhabitants refused to call the community Twickenham, the name of the country seat of his celebrated literary ancestor Alexander Pope, and preferred Huntsville instead. An old and quite common settler named Hunt had once lived there. Colonel Pope's house, set upon a hill overlooking the growing town, was a model of plantation splendor. Anne Royall, a noted journalist of the day, remarked, "If I admired the exterior, I was amazed at the taste and elegance displayed in every part of the interior: massy plate, cut glass, china ware, vases, sofas and mahogany furniture of the newest fashion decorated the inside." [44]

The area grew rapidly and its institutional arrangements soon rivaled those that Thomas Percy and Samuel Brown left behind in Natchez. As early as 1818, Anne Royall reported that Huntsville, had 260 houses, mostly brick, a bank, twelve stores, a courthouse, and a large square. By 1821, John Walker could boast to his friend Samuel Brown that even depressed cotton prices had not completely halted the kind of progress that Anne Royall had observed. "New houses are going up in sundry places," he said. "The theatre comes on apace, the Presbyterians have bought a beautiful lot, and the Methodists are nearly ready to raise the nasal storm in their own edifice of Brick." Cotton production was responsible for the boom. In 1822, Colonel Pope estimated that over the previous three years "there has been raised about fourteen thousand bales, annually." [45] But more important than Thomas Percy's contribution to that total was his marital success, as he proudly considered it. Even though John Walker's brother James had always hoped to marry Colonel Pope's other daughter, Maria, upon Thomas Percy's meeting her at John Walker's Oakland, he fell in love with John Walker's handsome sister-in-law and the couple married in 1814 or 1815.

The routines which the three friends arranged for themselves came as close to the portrait of plantation life as any sentimental Victorian novelist might have imagined. Thomas Percy had the means to pursue his reading interests. Moreover, the young planter from Natchez organized the Huntsville Library and became its first president, one of the few philanthropies in which he took an active part. Visits to town from the outlying plantations varied the dull regularity of country life. In December 1820, Percy and an assortment of relations went to a play one evening and to a cotillion the next. "The former," Thomas Percy remarked, "was so wretched as to cease to be droll—it was simply disgusting." But the dance was another matter. Mary Jane Walker, John and Matilda Pope's eldest child, age eleven, was the "best dancer" in the room. "We were all very pleased of course & she was as happy as could be," Thomas Percy wrote her proud father.[46] Longer excursions were also frequent, often with young children, but seldom babies, accompanying their parents.

Meanwhile Thomas was managing not only his own estate Belfield but Walker's Oakland as well. In the fall of 1819, the legislature, then dominated by the "Royal party"—Pope, Clement Comer Clay, and other Huntsville leaders—elected John W. Walker to be the first senator from Alabama. Leaving his wife and family at home, the usual practice at that time, Walker entrusted his plantation and finances to his friend Percy, who cheerfully undertook the mission. The extra assignment helped to prevent boredom and kept him in touch with his companion and his affairs.

The inequality in their relationship, however, was bound to find some expression; Thomas Percy could not help feeling a twinge of jealousy. In a letter to Senator Walker in Washington, he reported that Matilda, left at home, was "far gone in the vapours" but, "as for myself—I shall positively move off to Arkansaw or some out of the way place where you will never hear more of Poor Tom unless the folks should be fools enough to send me to congress also."[47] The self-deprecation about his political ineffectiveness hid a certain testiness. He noted more than once that poor mail service explained neither the paucity of letters from his friend nor their brevity, while his were long and filled with local news. John Walker, Percy averred, was perhaps preoccupied with state business—the controversy over Missouri, for instance. "Why do I trouble your excellency, I should say your *honor* or *honorableness* with this law business," Thomas Percy teased on another occasion. "I have not one excuse for it. Tis the only matter of business I have to write about, but stop! No. Witness I have sold Samuel & his wife for 1000 in notes & tomorrow perhaps Polydore may follow them." Such mundane business might bore his friend, but small doings seemed large at home. Indeed, Thomas Percy did sell Polydore, just before Christmas. Indifference to a slave family's fate was all too typical of the times.[48]

The small wedge of conflict between Walker's ambition and Percy's sense of rivalry never grew larger and vanished soon enough. The friendship itself was based upon Percy's accommodation to Walker's strenuous life—and Thomas Percy took guarded pleasure in Walker's success—as if he were a blood brother. By and large all the letters the male members of the family wrote each other—not just Thomas Percy's—testified to a remarkable harmony. Samuel Brown wrote to Walker, for instance, "You must be told how much I love & esteem you Big & little from your Paternal greatness [and] Madams Maternal grace down to the little stranger—I now say & ever will say you are all dear to my heart."[49]

The three friends so much relied on one another that it seemed as if each one drew on the expertise of the other to make up for a deficiency of his own. Thus, Thomas Percy became the home manager and protector of the households when their owners were away. John Walker was the esteemed statesman whose honors reflected well on all the others, and Samuel Brown served as adviser on matters of medicine and education. All three relied on Major Nathaniel Ware, who was married to Thomas's sister Sarah Percy Ellis, for financial capital and counsel. Although they found Ware intellectually alert, he was too detached and formidable to be an intimate with any of them. (Ware and his wife Sarah never lived in Huntsville, but the Major traveled widely, often stopping there for visits.)

With regard to Samuel Brown's contribution, he divided his time between Lexington and Madison County. The doctor was once again teaching at Transylvania Medical School, but he kept fully in touch with Thomas Percy who was overseeing his plantation just as Brown kept an eye on Walker's sons at boarding school in Lexington. At a blacksmith's shop there, a fight broke out involving Alexander and LeRoy Pope, youngest sons of old Colonel Pope, and some Lexington roughnecks. Samuel duly reported the outcome to his friends in Huntsville. He proudly told them how well the Pope boys had acquitted themselves in avenging an earlier attack by the young toughs. Young gentlemen should show spirit, Thomas Percy's circle assured themselves. If reputation demanded, they should use appropriate means—in this case, stones, sticks, and pocket pistols—to defeat inferiors.[50] The kind of solicitous interest that Brown displayed was both personally gratifying; and a perceived necessity. There were few outside the family circle whom one could trust to take an interest, serve *in loco parentis,* or offer a helping hand.

Likewise, Walker's political career benefited from the forms of friendship and patronage that the intensely familial Southern style of life encouraged.[51] All members of the family—the Popes, Walkers, Browns, and Percys—were Republicans since no Federalists were left in the South. Yet wealthy and commercially minded Jeffersonians, like those in the Percy circle, were delighted with the reestablishment of the United States Bank, federally funded internal improvements, relatively expensive rates for federal land sales, and other planks ripped up from the old Federalist decks and nailed down in the Madisonian ship of state. The political interests of the Southwestern slaveholding elite sought predictable interest rates and safe depositories which a federally sponsored bank system helped to provide. Like others involved in the national economy, they saw no end to American economic growth. They reaped high profits as cotton reached twenty-five cents a pound and drove up prices for lands and slaves bought earlier at relatively low costs. England and Europe had need of American crops, particularly cotton, after the Napoleonic wars. That necessity came to an abrupt close, however, when cotton warehouses in Liverpool and elsewhere bulged with unsold bales, and agricultural recovery abroad lessened the demand for American grains.

૪ૡ ૬

The Panic of 1819 was a particular disaster for cotton planters. Rather than squabble over bad advice heeded or mutual investments that failed, the three friends weathered the storm together without a murmur of dissent or any backbiting. For several years the Bank of the United States, reconstituted in 1816, this time under Republican auspices, had been expanding its credit policies through its proliferating branches. The crop of 1819, however, was pegged at no more than fourteen cents on the American and foreign exchanges, a precipitous drop that meant ruin for Southern agrarian borrowers. During the brief era of postwar boom, LeRoy Pope, John Walker, Clement C. Clay, and other major planters in 1816 planned and obtained a legislative charter for the Planters and Mechanics Bank of Huntsville. Percy joined the distinguished group of Huntsvillians on the board of directors, and Walker served as secretary and attorney for the bank. Its doors were first opened for business on the courthouse square in 1817. For the next two years or so, the institution provided the only circulating medium and source of public credit for the planters, farmers, and merchants of north Alabama.[52]

Yet the finances of the group—Percy, Walker, Brown, and Pope—soon became so entangled that they had little choice but to act in concert. Indeed, the kinds of problems these friends faced in the running of the Huntsville bank were to haunt nearly every generation of the Percy clan in the century ahead, as they also threatened the Southern elite generally. The chief problem was serious undercapitalization. Prior to the establishment of the Bank of Mississippi in 1809 in Natchez, settlers in the Mississippi Territory had only Spanish currency and cotton receipts circulating as legal tender. The need for banks in the Alabama portion of the district was imperative; Pope and kinsmen were ready to exploit that need. Serving as speaker of the territorial legislature, Walker introduced a bill that in effect would have given sole privilege of banking throughout the state to the powerful "Royal" faction. Governor William W. Bibb, formerly a member of Pope's Broad River faction, vetoed it as monopolistic—which it was.[53]

In addition, problems of bank fraud arose when bank director John Brahan speculated and lost some $80,000 out of the U.S. Treasury Department account. Walker, Pope, Percy, and friends kept the matter secret while enabling Brahan to slip away quietly. Meanwhile, William Crawford, Secretary of the Treasury, demanded full disclosure and threatened to withdraw federal deposits otherwise. Colonel Pope, the bank president, turned a deaf ear. When the inevitable crash came in 1819, the enemies of the Royal faction exploded in delighted fury in the press, and the state legislature retaliated with new regulations that undid most of John

Walker's recent banking legislation designed to favor the Huntsville faction.[54]

In the midst of the scandal, Thomas Percy was perplexed, not having much experience in the business, so that when Colonel Pope explained that specie payment had to be suspended in June 1820, he accepted the justification of his father-in-law: the insolvency of Tennessee banks was to blame, not local mismanagement. Yet should these speculators, including Thomas Percy, be wholly condemned out of hand? Their liberal lending policies may have been beneficial in the long run, given the underdevelopment of the state. As the Percy annals would later confirm, the family was so often instrumental in the economic evolution of the region in which the members lived, despite the shortage of capital. As usual in such matters, the chief manipulators escaped. Even though the bank closed its doors in 1825, Colonel Pope shrewdly managed to extricate himself and cleared a handsome profit, while the opposition howled in frustration.[55]

During the period when the Huntsville bank was sliding into ruin in 1820 and 1821, Percy and Walker themselves were steering close to the shoals of disaster. Supervising Walker's affairs while he was in Washington, Percy revealed considerable financial ability. From Colonel Pope, he obtained needed credit against his and Walker's cotton, waited patiently for the right moment to sell his friend's 30,000 pounds of raw cotton, and threatened the heirs of a Colonel Newman with a chancery suit in order to regain the principal of a large loan. In managing his own estate, Percy's only error was a speculation in Florence, Alabama, town lots in which the largest proprietor was former President James Madison. Other losses were beyond his powers to have foreseen. Settlers were moving out, leaving unpaid loans behind. According to one recent historian, only 16 percent of those enrolled on the tax list of 1815 were still in residence fifteen years later. Among the missing was a Major Pettus and his brother Freeman of Lawrence County. They had absconded without repaying Thomas Percy a loan of $2000. As a result, in early 1822 Percy himself had to postpone a heavy loan payment to Major Ware, his sister Sarah's husband.[56]

🪶 🜊

The Percy-Walker friendship survived the financial strains. Thomas liked serving as "Physician in ordinary to two ladies and somewhere about 140 negroes & agent & negociator both for the home & foreign departments to a Senator in Congress & a Professor of the university of Transylvania."[57] Knowing Walker's propensity to brood, Thomas Percy tried to cheer him up. Remarking on Matilda's longing for her husband, he reported with reference to Walker's sons, "The blues are gone—to the next generation— for you must know that your good dame in the true spirit of economy has transformed it into holiday suits for Percy and John James." In their mutual affection, Percy and Walker named their children for each other, so there were to be successions of Percy Walkers and Walker Percys well into the twentieth century.

Though not especially outgoing in shows of feeling, Thomas Percy once let down his guard to say, "I begin most vehemently to desire to see your sharp phiz in the neighbourhood of Oakland and Belfield standing as you were wont in the front door ready to receive me drest in your well worn, & well brush'd suit of blue, perfuming the air with your segar; clean shaved in honor of the day & your hair comb'd decently back." Not often in these post-Freudian times do men comment in so openly affectionate a way.[58] A sense of camaraderie of this kind should be seen as part of a larger texture of family interchange involving all its members—fathers, in-laws, and even the children. For instance, in the summer of 1821, Thomas Percy and his family escorted Mary Jane Walker, his friend's eldest daughter, on an overland trip to Philadelphia, where Thomas placed her at Madame Sigoigne's French-speaking academy for young ladies, most of them Southern. Mary Jane, an affectionate child, looked upon her father's friends as if they were kin and called them "Aunt and Uncle Percy." Susan Brown, Samuel's daughter, was already enrolled at the boarding school, along with Mary Jane Ellis, the daughter of Sarah Percy, Thomas's sister, by her first marriage to Judge John Ellis. Samuel Brown, who had joined up with the travelers, reported that Mary Jane Walker "is delighted with Mdm. & Miss Sigoigne & made the acquaintance with all the girls in four hours time."[59]

By shifting their horizons to Philadelphia, Thomas Percy and his colleagues expanded their circle to include a much more sophisticated group. The strategy was to marry their daughters into wealthy Northern families. The Sigoigne establishment was very small and exclusive, with only a dozen or so girls. So impressed was Samuel Brown that he urged his nephew Orlando to visit the place to be introduced to "some young ladies of no ordinary fortunes." Among the well-fixed pupils were Mary Jane Ellis, he observed, and others worth "1, 2 or 300,000$ . . . who might count that sum before they are twenty one." The wealthy Roman Catholic Gaston girls of North Carolina were also enrolled. Madame Sigoigne's fees were high, particularly in light of the Depression: $128 per quarter. The sum covered drawing, music, French, and dancing lessons.[60] Madame Sigoigne's academy would be a gathering spot for parents in the Percy circle throughout the 1820s.

In the fall of 1821 a crisis far more devastating than financial reverses struck without warning. John Walker took his friend Thomas's advice and brought his wife and smallest infant north with him for the next session of Congress. They left the remaining children—four boys—to live at Thomas and Maria's Belfield. After they had been gone for two days, Charles

Henry, one of the little Walkers, came down with a raging fever and influenza. The measures that Thomas Percy took to cure the child were as primitive and futile as most medical practices of the day. Emetics, applications of blisters to the feet, neck, and back had no effect. If anything, they hastened Charles Henry's death, after only six days' illness. Thomas Percy was distraught, as helplessly he watched the child's decline. "I think I never suffer'd as much as from any incident in my life as from this," he confided to Samuel Brown. Other friends have died, but the blows had passed over. "Now I suffer continually from the force of my imagination which, sleeping & waking, busied itself in representing the agonies of these wretched parents when they learn of this dreadful occurrence."[61]

The Huntsville relations sought the gentlest means to convey the news to the parents. Percy composed a long letter to convey his misery. "I writhe with the pain of the soul & in vain flow'd the bitterest tears I have ever shed," he wrote his friend. Percy's equanimity had never cracked before, but now he was overwhelmed by self-recrimination. "You left him in our hands & we cannot return him to you." Still worse, was his realization that nothing would ever again be the same. The loss, he predicted, meant that "our circle is broken & the charm of our lives is gone." If he could pour out his own "heart's blood" he would freely do it, he professed. "Bewilder'd with grief I scarcely know what is real & what is visionary." What he mourned was not only the dead child of his friend but also the death of a friendship. John Walker would never accuse him of incompetence in the sickroom, nor would he remonstrate that a messenger on a swift horse might have reached the parents to turn them back in time to witness their son's last hours. But most of all, Percy recognized that the veil of depression and mourning had come down on their domestic stage, separating the pair and leaving Thomas Percy to face the future by himself. He urged his friend to bear this trial as best he could if only to comfort Charles Henry's mother Matilda. As for himself, he later added in another letter, "How deeply I suffer & sympathize with you, you will perhaps never know until you feel the like for me."[62]

Two months passed in those days of slow mail service before the couple learned of their son's death. At first Matilda was prostrate, but she proved to have greater resilience than her husband, whose control over his moods had never been secure. Walker was barely able to attend to senatorial duties. Almost at once, his tuberculosis flared up again. Pale, emaciated, and bowed in grief, he could not find the strength to fight it, and tuberculosis is particularly subject to psychological factors. Attending the obsequies of a Rhode Island senator, Walker was reported to have bitterly turned to his colleagues under the Capitol rotunda: " 'I know what you are thinking,' their eyes glancing from the living to the dead—*'You are thinking it will be my turn next.' "*[63] The thought was more his than theirs.

Matilda Walker recovered her spirits with a visit to her daughter Mary Jane in Philadelphia, but John Walker continued to decline. On her return to Washington, they quickly set out for Huntsville. By the late fall of 1822, however, John Walker was fatally ill, knew it, and resigned his seat in the Senate. He died at the age of forty in the spring of 1823, a year and a half after little Charles Henry's death. The senator left a widow, six children, and debts equal to the total value of his holdings. Thomas Percy had done his best in managing the estate, but Walker had been more speculative than he. Worried that there might have been something more he could have done for the ailing child that would also have spared the life of his friend, he gained some satisfaction in supervising the estate and retrieving as much property as he could for the widow. Yet at times he became so despondent that he once wrote Samuel Brown how much he tired of a wretched "solitude." Maybe it would be best to start over and escape the scenes where he had and John Walker had lounged and talked while smoking a delicious succession of "segars." "I am often thinking of changing my pursuits & my country," he wrote his remaining friend Brown.[64]

Perhaps Percy did intend to resettle. At the end of the 1820s he purchased extensive lands in Washington County, Mississippi. But the exertion could have proved too great in light of his grief. The remaining years left to him may have been happy or sad, but no papers of note provide a clue. Only one letter, written a few weeks before his death, survives. The recipient was Richard Wilde Walker, a son of his old friend, then attending Princeton. The message suggested no melancholy but rather a happy resignation to the ways of the world. "Candor compels me," Percy advised the young man, "to admit that men do learn by experience sometimes, but not always." Certainly they seldom appreciate "the vexation of being preached at when in trouble." Nonetheless, "*troubles* as well as delights are brief & transitory." Like some later Percys, Thomas George adopted the attitude of the Stoics who proposed the via media as the temperate, prudent course of modest expectation. One may anticipate, Percy declared in his letter, "that the sun shine of tomorrow compensates for the storms of the present day. Youth is very sensitive & debt, love &c are its devils, but when a fellow gets thro' his romance he will find other sources of annoyance in great abundance. He must get thick skinned which in time arrives to all."[65]

Thus, John Walker's death may have had only momentary impact on this gentle Southern planter. His mourning may not have taken on the character of Tennyson's permanent grieving for his friend Hallam. But if he retained his good spirits to the end of his days, Percy stands out from the other members of the clan as an anomaly. Thomas Percy was the last of the line to make his living chiefly by managing a plantation. He was determined that his sons should follow in his footsteps as planters, but he also prepared two of them for law and two for medicine. The two professions were to remain central to family culture thereafter, each generation producing its share of one or both. Perhaps Thomas Percy was "debonair and wistful, expecting nothing," as Will Percy insisted, but he had tried to live as bland a life as possible and once over his grief for John Walker he reverted to old habits of leisurely inactivity. He knew no other course. He was remarkable because even in a life of relative tranquility—at least for a Percy—there was nonetheless much pain.[66]

Not surprisingly, the death of John Walker's son had a much greater impact upon Thomas Percy than had the potentially more disturbing plunge of his sister into mental difficulties, which took place as the economic crisis commenced in 1819. Although the squire of Madison County said little about the melancholia of sister Sarah, that calamity had deep repercussions in family life: it was the catalyst for the first flowering of the Percys' literary imagination.

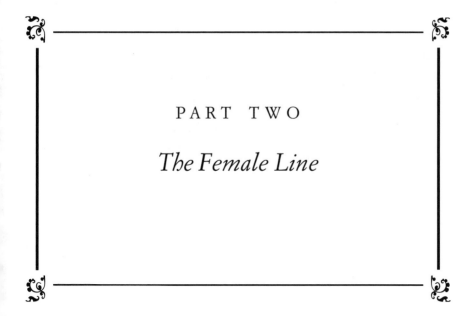

PART TWO

The Female Line

CHAPTER FOUR

The Philadelphia Years

And thou art like that God-struck man,
Forever wandering on;
Thy spirit's doom is weird and wan;
Alone! Alone! Alone!

"They Tell Me There's an Eastern Bird,"
Catherine Ann Warfield and Eleanor Percy Lee[1]

In the 1820s, the Percys and their friends adopted Philadelphia almost as a second home. The circumstances would not have seemed odd to these prosperous planters, although the custom of an urban residence was rarer in Alabama than among the lowland plantation owners in South Carolina with their spacious dwellings along the Battery in Charleston. Philadelphia offered members of the slaveholding class a congenial and conservative atmosphere—as well stocked with stores, sources of financial credit, museums, and sophisticated society as one might desire, without the frantic pace of New York or Eastern snobbery and radicalism of Boston. Also, the city was well equipped with academies for young ladies, and daughters in the Percy circle were enrolled in schools there in preparation for suitable marriages.

A further reason for frequent trips northward was medical. For over a decade, the family thought it best to place Thomas Percy's eldest sister Sarah in the Pennsylvania Hospital. No doubt, at first they hoped that experienced Philadelphia physicians might effect a cure, but was it not also an exile for the daughter of Charles Percy—out of sight, out of mind? If change of scene was supposed to help sister Sarah's condition, however, Philadelphia did not meet expectations. Place had nothing to do with the malady. During the years spent in that city, Sarah Percy, her second husband, Nathaniel Ware, and one of her daughters and her husband were all affected by the ravages of the illness, directly or indirectly. Yet, creativity and remarkable resilience were to grow out of that tragedy, no less than they were to arise in the art of Will and Walker Percy a hundred years later. How deeply Sarah's manifestations of mental instability affected the others can be assessed only by indirection. Family silence was almost total. Oddly, a collective screen memory, as it might be called, offers the most poignant revelation of how much the family wished away what could not be faced without horror. By the term "collective screen" memory is meant the replacement of unpleasant recollection with a set of fantasies that makes remembrance easier to handle.

In the late eighteenth century, Charles Percy and Susannah Collins had raised three daughters—Sarah, born in 1781, Susannah, and Catherine—two of whose life stories were fashioned into legend. Of these, Susannah (called Susan and sometimes referred to as Nancy) remains the most obscure. As the next eldest child after Sarah, she was ten years old when her father killed himself. Susan never married and around her arose a tale of unrequited love. According to the family story, she fell in love with a French count in the cortège of the exiled Louis Philippe of France during his tour of the American West in early 1798. Swayed by his charms, Susan turned down a succession of Mississippi suitors and escaped to Paris, having taken the nobleman's words of undying fealty at face value. Surprised at her appearance, he accepted her, but not on terms of marriage. Years passed, and "the bloom of youth" withered. Then, as if in a Victorian melodrama, the scoundrel discarded her, and she left behind her court costumes and jewels to live as a dependent the rest of her days at Dunleith, a Percy family plantation.[2] According to one account, "Each afternoon she went downstairs to play the harp" which had sat unused until her coming. After her death, the harp could sometimes be heard to play softly with no one plucking the strings. By such means, so the family members said, she could "recapture her lost happiness and unburden her broken heart."[3]

The account is fictional. The storytellers confused her with a sister who never ran off with anyone, let alone a stagey French roué. The future King Louis Philippe and his party had stopped only briefly in Natchez, certainly not long enough for a protracted flirtation with a sheltered fourteen-year-old plantation virgin.[4] With her strange ways, Sarah Percy Ware, not Susan, had been the inmate in the house that the legend-makers specified as Dunleith but was Routhland, its predecessor on the same site. But Sarah spent her days chiefly at White Cliffs, the plantation in the country where she had lived with her first husband, Judge John Ellis, and years later was to live there as ward of her son Thomas George Ellis. The myth about her indicates a point to be raised more than once hereafter: the serviceability of legend as a means of repressing those events and thoughts that few wished to explore very deeply. Through the device of legend-building, Sarah's disconsolate condition was displaced upon a collateral, childless, and long-forgotten aunt. The ghost of "Susan Percy" was melancholia personified.

Daughter Catherine was never enveloped in fantasy, but she served as a sharp contrast to her unmarried and unremembered sister Susan and her unhappy sister Sarah. Judge Thomas Rodney noticed Catherine when she was just seventeen. "Miss Kitty," Rodney beamed, "is a fine sprightly girl and one that may be stiled hansome if not beautiful and gains upon acquaintance." Although "rather short," and "muscular" she was graced with a "delicate Texture and Complexion." Considering himself a connoisseur in such matters, the judge found her reserved at first but on further conversation, Catherine grew "Easy & pleasant in her manner."[5] As a mother to the children of Dr. Samuel Brown, Catherine was no less generous with her attention in the nursery. Kitty "was never absent from them three hours at a time," Brown lamented after her death. When Catherine died, Sarah Ellis did her best to fill the vacancy and virtually ran Samuel Brown's household as well as her own. The physician was very grateful and remarked to a relative that Sarah was looking after his three-year-old daughter Susan Catherine "with unceasing attention" and taking "care of my poor little ones with affectionate care."[6]

Despite Sarah's indispensability by the cradle, something in her temperament and manner aroused mistrust. Because of Samuel Brown's susceptibility in grief, on her deathbed Catherine had urged him not to let Sarah bring up their children. Perhaps Kitty worried that Sarah, a widow, might replace her in Samuel's affections. Kitty warned Brown that Sarah, though "the best of hearts," lacked the requisite intellectual gifts for proper child-keeping. He agreed. "She had married early," the widower wrote his sister-in-law, "& in great affluence has spent her time like the majority of the inhabitants of slave countries, in mental inactivity." Thomas George and Mary Jane Ellis, "her own children," he reported, "are not the examples I should like my children to imitate. But I have no *alternative.*"[7]

Sarah Percy had indeed married early. The elderly Judge Ellis had taken her hand on December 21, 1799, when she was eighteen. Certainly, too, the couple did not lack for money. The Ellises had come from Virginia as early as the 1760s. Settling at Ellis Cliffs, actually a series of low bluffs, twenty miles below Natchez, the family center was Laurel Hill, a plantation house built sometime before 1775. According to a Spanish military intelligence report, Abram Ellis, Sarah Percy's father-in-law, had been known as "the richest and quietest inhabitant" of the district.[8] Like Don Carlos, the Ellises, father and son, had been loyal to the Spanish Crown and provided military information to an agent of Governor Gálvez during the late War for American Independence. Thus, the marriage had united two of the great fortunes in the Southwest whose owners shared compatible social and political views.[9] Without question, Sarah Percy Ellis took her place in

Natchez society with considerable grace and charm. Judge Thomas Rodney, for instance, had found her a "fine easy-behaved woman."[10]

Apparently, in departing for Huntsville, Samuel Brown and Tom Percy deliberately left sister Sarah behind because of her alleged inadequacies as a mother. She would have need of these relatives. In fact, Sarah even suggested that she could join the exodus and give up her comfortable life to help out in the child care, but they refused. Having not yet remarried after Judge Ellis's death in late 1808, she was free to move. Just as she had first married a man who was her senior, she followed the same pattern a second time: her choice was another paterfamilias in his formidability though not in years. She was lonely, perhaps frightened after the others had gone to Madison County. Within months of their departure, Sarah Ellis fell in love with the handsome Nathaniel A. Ware of Woodville, Wilkinson County, near the old Northumberland House plantation, and married him in 1814. He was a well-regarded lawyer in partnership with the Thomas B. Reed, a leading attorney of the region.[11]

Ware's appearance and character made him seem a replication of Sarah's father. Although, unlike Charles Percy, he may never have dreamt of suicide, Ware certainly was neither jocular nor outgoing but instead reclusive and cold. Like one of Edgar Allan Poe's grimly handsome protagonists, Ware had a commanding appearance: ruddy cheeks, dramatically white complexion, as "pure and fair as a young girl's," aquiline nose, glittering eyes, very high, narrow, and prominent forehead, and, in his last years, "thin, white locks falling on his neck." Ambitious, intellectual, and solitary, he was "a man of mark, though not much beloved," a reporter later remarked.[12]

Ware's resemblances to Charles Percy were almost uncanny. Both men married heiresses and made themselves and their descendants very rich. Like Charles Percy, Ware enjoyed titles and the authority that came with political preferment. Unlike him, however, Ware's political career came to an abrupt end through no fault of his own, but rather the changed health of his wife. Ware was on the way to the top until 1819. Secretary of War John C. Calhoun, who had known him in South Carolina, called him "a man of excellent information and correct principles." Josiah Simpson, another admirer, declared that both "in courts of justice and in private circles," Ware proved himself "a gentleman of highly respectable legal acquirements, of a very capacious, vigorous, and enlightened mind, and of the most inflexible integrity."[13] Such characteristics were not in great supply among government officials in the wilderness settlement. Just as "Don Carlos" had cultivated Governor Gayoso of Natchez, so, too, Ware placed his fortunes in the hands of a patron, Governor David Holmes of the Mississippi Territory. A moderate Republican from the Shenandoah Valley, Holmes exhibited strong capacities for administration. Patron-client relations of this kind—that is, between an ambitious newcomer and a senior political figure—were common in antebellum America, particularly in the

South and Southwest. Having no connections in the region, Holmes had need of talented and efficient men like Ware to serve as subordinates and dispatchers of their decisions.

Though otherwise qualified for Holmes's favor, Nathaniel Ware, like Charles Percy, seemed to have come out of the mists, bearing no traces of the past. That was not necessarily a handicap in a region in which adventurers like Percy carved their fortunes. Although accounts differ somewhat, Ware was probably born in 1780 in South Carolina, where he had practiced law before heading west.[14] Like other newcomers, he made up for anonymity with noisy demonstrations of patriotism, fully endorsing war with Great Britain in 1812—but failed to join the armed forces. Even after Governor Holmes called out the militia to meet the assaults of the Choctaws, Ware preferred to serve as a military aide to the governor with the rank of Major.[15] Pleased by his performance, Holmes arranged a promotion. In a close contest with Abner Green, a wealthy and formidable rival, Ware gained appointment to the Governor's Legislative Council, by order of President Madison.[16] The Woodville lawyer's rise to prominence excited growing opposition, one that was also jealous of John Walker's simultaneous success at the eastern end of the enormous Mississippi Territory, as it still was. Factional rivalry, not great issues, were responsible for backland partisanship. In the 1810s, Gabriel Moore and Hugh McVay of fast-growing Madison County, in the future state of Alabama, sought the downfall of Major Ware, Holmes's favorite. These same individuals had opposed Colonel LeRoy Pope's "Royal" party of Georgians. In a legislative election in early 1814, the anti-Ware faction, which was aligned with the "old Republican" or ultra State Rights wing of the Jeffersonian party, favored Beverly R. Grayson, a young and well-connected Virginian of Prince William County.

Indeed, in contrast to young Grayson's credentials, Major Ware appeared to his adversaries as a closet Federalist or at least "not strictly Republican," as it was said against him. Besides, the haughty attorney was nothing but a Johnny-come-lately, complained his rivals. Holmes, however, won approval for the appointment from James Monroe, secretary of state. From April 1815 to May 1816, Ware served as acting governor when Holmes, in wretched health, could not meet the responsibilities.[17] It had not harmed his progress toward these appointments that Ware had married the wealthy widow Sarah Percy Ellis.[18]

More politically minded than his brother-in-law Thomas Percy, Major Ware introduced what later could be called the Whig mode of thinking into a family already inclined toward the nationalistic approach of young politicians like Henry Clay.[19] But, unlike "Harry of the West," Ware had no gift for democratic canvassing, no hearty, even compulsive, earthy manner. When Mississippi was elevated to statehood, he ran for elective office. According to one account, his manners were so stiff and his outlook so aristocratic that he went down to numbing defeat—not the last member of the Percy family to suffer that humiliation. By no means was democracy in full flower, as the frontier historian Frederick Jackson Turner once insisted. The planter class ruled through one party or another, even in Mississippi.[20] Nor was a haughty demeanor invariably a handicap, even in the Southwest. George Poindexter, who wrote the state's penal code as a grisly replication of English law, continued to win office regardless of his reactionary and highhanded ways. What brought Ware's political ambitions to an end was not the 1818 defeat, which could have seasoned him for later tries, so much as the mental collapse of his wife Sarah the following year.

Sarah Percy's second marriage started auspiciously with the birth of Catherine Ann in 1816. Ironically Sarah named her first-born Ware for Catherine Percy Brown, who had cautioned her husband on her deathbed about Sarah's supposed child-rearing deficiencies. Shortly after the birth of a second infant, Eleanor, in 1819, it became clear that Sarah was no longer the "easy-behaved" young woman Judge Rodney had depicted twelve years before. The suicide of her father, Charles Percy, when she was an impressionable twelve must have affected her much more seriously than outward appearance showed. Perhaps she had overly repressed her feelings of anger and grief in assuming the light-headed role of which Samuel Brown had disapproved. Almost immediately after Eleanor's birth, she fell into a deep psychotic state. At the time the cause was attributed to a blood curse from her father as well as to the contraction of puerperal fever during the delivery. Although often fatal, the fever has seldom been associated with mental aberration, but certainly any disease, especially one as life-threatening as childbed fever, would have made her mental state still worse.

There were, however, other somatic factors involved. Sarah Ware was thirty-nine years old when the second Ware child, Eleanor Percy, was born—an age for childbearing that sometimes portends something perilous. In fact, postpartum depression, which involves hormonal changes that affect the mind particularly in older women, may precipitate permanent and severe emotional damage. According to current statistics, "depression psychosis," as a modern clinician might call her condition, occurs in one or two births of every 1000, not an inconsiderable number by any means.[21] It seems likely that an inherited predisposition may well have strengthened the severity of the disorder. Yet, emotional factors had played a major part. One can only speculate, but twice marrying men of patriarchal temperament suggested a dependency that unconsciously she herself found demeaning. Given the status of womankind in Southern culture at that time, such reliance on men was unavoidable. Sarah Percy could well have been lacking much self-esteem, and others sensed and confirmed her self-evaluation. Although she was extraordinarily bright with an artistic and musical temperament, the men whose praise she valued most were dismissive. Some part of her might have inwardly resented their indifference—her father's, husbands', and family males' generally. But she could find no release, save in illness, as with so many other women of her class and place. Such circumstances might have made matters worse for her mental well-being. Admittedly these are speculations in the absence of hard information.[22]

In light of his wife's condition, Major Ware put his political hopes aside. As soon as it was clear that she would not mend on her own, Ware took her to Philadelphia and placed her in the Pennsylvania Hospital. She gave such signs of recovery in the early spring, 1820, that Ware had her discharged; less than three weeks later she was readmitted. She was destined to remain there with a maid-servant as companion for a decade.[23]

No doubt Sam Brown was instrumental in securing Sarah's admission to the prestigious institution. Like other well-supported private hospitals of that time, the Philadelphia center was meant to be distinguishable from an almshouse. Bonds had to be posted. According to historian Charles Rosenberg, it was only by a "written testimonial from a 'respectable' person attesting to the moral worth of an applicant" that one could gain admittance. Access was not easy for another reason. In the entire United States only the New York Hospital also welcomed "lunatics" or the "deranged," as the expressions were. Sam Brown had worked under the renowned Benjamin Rush, a founder and for years an attending physician at the hospital. In addition, Brown knew the medical community of the city, members of which were often old friends and classmates. Thus, as early as the 1820s, the Percy family was to turn to the mid-Atlantic states for medical purposes. That predilection would continue well into the twentieth century. None of the Southern states, then or even a hundred years later, had any sort of facility for the mentally ill to match those that the Percys were to use first in Philadelphia and then in Baltimore.[24]

The Pennsylvania Hospital was primarily devoted at this time to the care of somatic problems. (Its fame as a mental asylum developed after 1841.)[25] But having a son who suffered from melancholia, Rush had successfully introduced wards devoted to patients with mental disorders. Some of the treatments for melancholia at that time were quite reasonable and possibly helpful. In the 1790s Samuel Coates, the hospital director, had arranged for hot and cold baths to be set up in the basement. He reasoned that changes in body temperature would have a soothing effect, and for those suffering from depression, the observation was accurate.

Sarah Ware probably received the same sorts of heroic applications to which patients with physical ailments were then subjected: purging; bleeding; and possibly some dosing with laudanum and other drugs. At the same time, attendants treated patients kindly. The inmates were encouraged to mingle with each other and were neither drugged into insensibility nor kept isolated. The Pennsylvania Hospital was no warehouse of somnambulistic patients.[26]

The premises of the hospital, built in elegant Federalist style, well served the emotionally disturbed. Flanking wide corridors, the rooms—at least those in the upper stories where the wealthier patients lived—were large and airy, with light pouring through broad casements. Attendants took the patients outside to exercise in a kind of dry moat surrounding the building, as can be seen today. Spectators used to pay a small sum to stand above the inmates and watch their behavior as if they were creatures in a zoo. At the Pennsylvania Hospital charges for room and board came to $13.50 a week, a sum quite beyond the reach of the ordinary citizen. Nathaniel Ware considered the sum exorbitant and in 1824 complained in a most peremptory way that the new rates of "$14.25 a weak [*sic*]" were highly "irksome," because he also had to pay the wages of Sarah's servant and for the servant's room and board on the premises. Claiming disingenuously that his fortunes left him no choice, he petitioned for a reduction since "Boarding may be got at fashionable houses in this city for $7 per weak."[27]

A satisfactory adjustment must have been worked out: Sarah stayed on for another seven years. Ware's complaint, however, signified a deeper exasperation. Sarah Percy had become little more than a financial burden, and he grew embittered, unable to live with his wife or with any other woman, except in adultery. The latter option was unavailable to an American gentleman, particularly, as in this case, a man of substance with two small daughters to raise. The watchful eyes of male in-laws and their wives were upon him. Not surprisingly, Ware's initial reactions to his wife's condition were so raw that they underlined his already cold business sense. In the first year of Sarah's madness he found fault with William Collier, plantation overseer on the old Northumberland House property in Wilkinson County, and refused to pay him salary due, a matter that was finally settled by court order against Ware. He was known locally in Natchez for his hard-driving on indebtedness. In his will, one Robert Moore, planter, complained in 1826 that Major Ware had usuriously overcharged his brother on a loan.[28]

Major Ware's unhappy reaction to his wife's unchanging state of mind was to have a profound effect upon his life. He seemed to have slipped his moorings and did not settle anywhere for very long. He refused to buy a house in Philadelphia or its suburbs. Instead, he rented some well-appointed rooms with sufficient shelves for his extensive library. Apparently he changed locations in the city a number of times. Moreover, he took every possible occasion to leave the city and its unhappy associations to pursue his interests in land speculation and exploration. For instance, in 1828 he returned to Natchez to oversee properties still held there. On one such trip away from his deranged wife, Ware, reluctant to return to Philadelphia, was only too happy to oblige the local journalist, Andrew Marschalk, who asked him to escort an old slave on a leisurely trip to the North and freedom. The slave, whom everyone called Prince, was Abdual Rahman Ibrahima, a son and first heir of a West African ruler from Timbo (now in Guinea), though American philanthropists thought he came from Morocco. For forty years, Ibrahima had been a slave, owing to the misfortunes of war and the Atlantic slave trade. By sheer happenstance, his identity became known to the Natchez community and his master, Thomas Foster. (Foster had paid the fine of his brother-in-law, James Smith when old Judge Ellis had cited him for contempt of court.) At last Foster released his aged slave so that he could return to his native land with some members of his American family under the auspices of Henry Clay of the State Department and the American Colonization Society.[29]

On April 8, Ware and Ibrahima, dressed in an outlandish costume that his sponsors thought approximated Moorish fashions in his native land, boarded the squat, uncomfortable little steamboat *Neptune* together. The *Neptune,* clattering "like a hoarse giant," as one historian has remarked, carried the pair to Cincinnati. They then traveled to Wheeling, Virginia, where they boarded a public coach that bumped along the National Road to Baltimore. Everywhere crowds stared at the resplendent old man, with a stage sword dangling at his side, an attention that the fastidious Major probably did not appreciate. There Major Ware left the freedman in the hands of colonizationists for further fund-raising exhibitions. Ware's association with Ibrahima was brief, but he told an inquirer, "I know the worth of Prince" since he had lived so many years quite near Foster Fields, Ibrahima's plantation home.[30]

Travel seemed to force Ware out of himself, a goad, as it were, to his own forms of creativity—the pursuit of natural science, the study of political economy, and the making of money. All three belonged to a single framework in his mind, but he was most successful as an avid land speculator, and invested in textile mills, banks, and other enterprises. When others, including his relations by marriage were skating close to ruin in the 1819 Panic, Ware told Samuel Brown that his business affairs permitted him to boast of being "a fine man for another year."[31]

The second of his priorities was constant movement. Thwarted politically and shackled domestically, Ware became a lonely but determined traveler. He crossed the sea a number of times and, sometime before 1845 explored the desert regions of Morocco and Turkish North Africa. In *Henry Belden,* a novel that he wrote and had printed in 1846, Ware told without much art or originality the story of a white Christian whom Bedouin Moors enslaved.[32] Apart from the adventure story, Ware directed most of his journeys into practical channels. As an expert botanist, soil analyzer, and land surveyor, he used his skills to build his fortune and secure a prosperous development of the wilderness.[33]

Escaping from his wife after her admission to the Pennsylvania Hospital, Ware undertook his most important exploratory mission in the newly acquired territory of Florida. He had met some Philadelphia investors, under the leadership of Peter Stephen Chazotte, an émigré from Saint-Domingue, who had formed the East Florida Coffee Land Association with hopes of creating coffee plantations.[34] Ware assisted the coffee enthusiasts with information he had gathered, but he saw Florida's future in sugar-raising. His associates in that specialty were eventually to establish large slave plantations that thrived until the outbreak of the Second Seminole War.[35] Ware also recognized the possibilities for orange crops. "Fruit culture is very profitable in Florida. A five-acre lot in St Augustine," he observed, "produced 500,000 oranges; which were sold at one dollar per hundred the purchaser gathering them, so that an old widow and her son made 5000 dollars."[36]

Like William Bartram, the famous eighteenth-century botanist and explorer, Ware crossed the wilderness of rivers, forests, and swamps of north central Florida, including the "Alachua plains," which he found extraordinarily fertile, "with beautiful little lakes of clear water and savannas," rich timber stands, and abundant wildlife. But the lands he liked best lay along the Appalachicola River on the upper Gulf coast. There he apparently made large land purchases and raised cotton, but no courthouse records survive to document the extent of his holdings.[37]

Scarcely was the Major back in Philadelphia than he was again planning travel, as if to flee not only from Sarah's pitiable condition but also from his own gloom. "Phil[adelphia] is dull—even science sleeps," he wrote, almost before unpacking his bags. At one point he tried to interest Samuel Brown in joint housekeeping, so that they could rear their children together. Brown refused, knowing that Ware would disappear leaving him with all the duties of minding the daughters at home. Undeterred, Ware returned to Florida again in 1822, where he served as a United States Land Commissioner in Pensacola. Owing to a yellow fever epidemic, he resigned his post sometime during the winter of 1822–23.[38] He reappeared at the side of his long neglected wife and daughters briefly, but soon was trying to wheedle a territorial governorship or some other distant post through Senator John Walker. The family, however, resented his neglect of domestic responsibilities in the search for "exalted" offices, as Thomas Percy sarcastically noted, and he was forced to withdraw his name.[39]

Ware's third interest was the examination of political economy. As something of a Whig philosopher, as it were, he thought the United States would achieve great power through the encouragement of science and industry as well as agriculture. In 1844 he published a tract on the subject, *Notes on Political Economy As Applicable to the United States. By a Southern Planter.* This very Whiggish document stressed the beneficial role that government should play in directing a national economy, basically a call for Henry Clay's "American System" of federal aid to internal improvements, greater emphasis on public education, industrial development, and protective tariffs to aid it.[40]

Ware's own investments followed the lines of his political convictions. In 1831, for instance, he tried to interest Samuel and Henry Austin, the famous Texas land developers, in the construction of a cotton mill with a thousand spindles at Bexar, Texas, then a province of Mexico. Already the major owned a large plantation on the Saltillo River, but he sold it for $40,000 to invest in the textile experiment.[41] Difficulties with the Mexican government over labor arrangements and land sales, however, tried his patience, and he withdrew to invest $200,000 in a sugar plantation. Later he would welcome the Texas Revolution that broke out in 1836, so that his properties might be better protected.[42]

The investments in Texas, as well as others in Arkansas and Mississippi, may have prompted Ware to leave Philadelphia altogether. Samuel Brown, a frequent visitor in Philadelphia, with whom he shared interests in science, had died January 12, 1830.[43] Sarah's condition remained static; it was time for the Major to move on.

As a result of Ware's 1819 decision to move Sarah to Philadelphia, the orientation of the entire Percy clan had shifted geographically. A quick review may help. During the prior years, the family had scattered across the South. Previous to Sarah's illness, Major Ware and family had remained in the vicinity of Natchez, but Tom Percy had meanwhile settled in Huntsville. Then Sam Brown, fitful in his widowerhood, in 1818 returned to the Transylvania Medical School. He left his plantation in Alabama for the always agreeable Tom Percy to supervise. Despite the distances, the family members had kept in touch by correspondence and frequent visits. The decision to place Sarah in Philadelphia, however, provided a common meeting ground.

Unlike Major Ware, Samuel Brown was very willing to experiment with a Philadelphia residence, a decision that undoubtedly encouraged Ware to keep Sarah at the hospital, even though a cure seemed most unlikely. Brown had always been partial to the city, and as early as 1813 had talked of moving there permanently and ridding himself of slave property. (In the abstract he did not approve of bondage, but he was fully appreciative of its personal benefits.)[44] Brown felt an obligation to serve Sarah as best he could in light of her support for him at the time of his wife Catherine's death. Indeed, he sometimes took care of Sarah's two daughters during the major's absences.

In any event, Brown was the first to see the educational advantages of the city, a policy the others soon adopted as well. In 1819 the Kentucky physician placed his Susan in Mrs. Phillips's school, where a number of other Southern families had enrolled their daughters.[45] Later, she married Charles Ingersoll, who was destined to be a distinguished attorney to whom the Percy group usually turned for legal advice. Ware quickly placed his teenage step-daughter, Mary Jane Ellis in the same school, but he did so with such secrecy that Judge Elijah Smith, Ware's business associate and a longstanding family friend, was "kept in the Dark" about where to send the tuition payments. It was a grand choice, Smith acknowledged, for a young lady of great fortune who needed such preparation for "society and happiness in mature life." [46]

Not long afterward, both Mary Jane Ellis and Susan Brown were transferred to Madame Aimée Sigoigne's French-speaking school in nearby Frankford. Ware changed his lodgings on fashionable Spruce Street to rooms on Washington Square, perhaps because it was somewhat closer to the Sigoigne academy. In 1821 John Walker contributed his daughter (another Mary Jane) to the school. In the fall of 1823, the soulful Catherine Ann Ware, age six, entered the female academy. Thus, along with the daughters of Philadelphia blue-bloods, Madame Sigoigne's school was well populated with Percy-related "young ladies," as they were primly called. [47]

Madame Sigoigne was a warmhearted, very Gallic soul and a dedicated professional. Apart from her schoolteaching, she gathered intellectual friends in her salon. Most of them possessed deeply conservative and European convictions. Her daughter Adéle Sigoigne, a beauty whose portrait by Thomas Sully is well known, aided in the children's instruction and also served as a magnet for the social evenings. The Nicholas Biddles of adjacent Andalusia, country estate of the president of the Bank of the United States, were frequent visitors to the Sigoigne household along with the Biddle in-laws, the Craigs, and other wealthy Philadelphia aristocrats whose daughters attended the school. [48]

Also among the Sigoignes' evening guests were the musically talented members of the LaRoche family. Marie Jeanne Condemine, Madame Sigoigne's sister, had married old Dr. René LaRoche. Like Ware's friends, Stephen Chazotte and Peter Vignoles, Florida explorers, both the LaRoche and Condemine families had fled the Saint-Domingue revolution in the early 1790s. The distinguished physician's son, René Marc Marie LaRoche, often joined the soirées at his aunt Aimée Sigoigne's residence. The talented nephew played the violin or piano as a welcome respite from his studies at the University of Pennsylvania Medical School.

Although the sophisticated European colonials at Madame Sigoigne's were bound to dominate the evenings, it was said that Mary Jane Ellis, the melancholy Sarah Percy Ware's daughter and "a leading belle in society," was the "great favorite." [49] Having earned his medical degree in 1818, René LaRoche took special interest in the highly intelligent Southern girl. He visited the Sigoigne academy more often than courtesy to his aunt or dedication to the arts required. Major Ware, however, had to grant his stepdaughter permission to sit in the Sigoigne parlor. The privilege, which had required considerable negotiation, enabled the courtship of the sixteen-year-old Mary Jane to proceed. Though pleased for the sake of her nephew, Madame Sigoigne refused to assume any responsibility for the outcome. The result, gratified LaRoche, however, who was wholly unaware of what the future held. [50]

On July 1, 1824, relatives congregated for the marriage ceremony at

St. Joseph's Catholic Church. Included in the wedding party were Mary Jane's step-father, Nathaniel Ware, and a group of LaRoche's medical classmates, all later prominent in Philadelphia medical circles.[51] Thereafter, LaRoche was very much a part of the Percy circle. Even before the nuptials, LaRoche and Samuel Brown were close friends, despite the twenty-six years separating them. As physicians with a love for scientific discussion, they wrote each other about the latest books in medical science, the course of smallpox epidemics among the almshouse dwellers of Philadelphia, the affairs of the medical journals LaRoche edited or in which he published. When Brown died in 1830, LaRoche penned an affectionate and lengthy memorial in a compilation of American medical biographies.[52]

At the same time, LaRoche adopted the family style of reticence about the medical anomaly in their very midst. Although he published material on depression and puerperal fever in his medical journal, not once in their private communications, did he or Brown allude to Sarah Ware.[53] Disease of the body, not of the mind, was his preoccupation. Science, it would seem, stopped at the threshold of family sensitivity. LaRoche's preference for objective fact, however, would not spare him later tragedy. Walker Percy, himself a physician who explored in his novels the humanistic inadequacies of modern science, would have appreciated that predicament of his distant predecessor.

꩜

Like LaRoche, Thomas George Percy was not at all forthcoming about his sister's condition. At least in writing, he never inquired from family members how Sarah Ware was faring. Nor when he made one of his frequent trips to the North did he give others any gossip of her at all. No news apparently signaled no change. Percy spent June and July 1821 in Philadelphia, having been assigned to enroll Mary Jane Walker, his senator-friend's eldest daughter, in Madame Sigoigne's school. During the sojourn, he visited Princeton, his alma mater, saw old friends, spent two days with Thomas Percy Ellis, Sarah's eldest son, and then met Nathaniel Ware and his daughters at Staten Island on their return from a European tour. Percy said nothing about Sarah's location or condition when reporting on these family encounters.[54]

The reasons for apparent diffidence were several. Inquiries or even references sounded too much like prying and rumor-mongering, but sometimes a short phrase gave some news. In late 1819, a family business associate told Samuel Brown, for instance, that "Mrs[.] Ware if anything improves."[55] Physical illness but not mental was most often a chief topic of conversations and letters. About such matters as the death of little Charles Henry Walker, grief could be expressed in the most open and tender fashion, but mental illness was another matter. Even in the early nineteenth century, when science and secular thought had modified the concept of irrationality as God's punishment for sin, the stigma remained.

Dr. Benjamin Rush, long associated with the Pennsylvania Hospital until his death in 1813, had been the first in America to recognize insanity as an organic disease rather than a curse delivered by the Almighty for human sins. Rush considered it a matter of hypertension of the blood vessels to the brain whereas some neurologists speculated that it was a malfunction of the nervous system. Henry Miller, a Kentucky physician and old corresponding friend of Samuel Brown, faithfully subscribed to Rush's theory at the time Sarah was placed in the Pennsylvania Hospital. "Why in maniacs, does the remembrance of things long past and forgotten revive with all the vividness and directness of reality?" Miller asked Brown. Miller proceeded that the answer was "the increased action of the blood vessels of the brain," which accounted for the "mania" and caused the overstimulated "fibres" to "present themselves to the mind" in a shower of "brilliancy" and an incoherent excitement of thoughts.[56] The description was confused, but Henry Miller, Samuel Brown, and most other contemporary medical men did not see much point in searching for hidden psychological issues.

The notion that some moral flaw was hidden beneath the disease lingered in the popular and even the medical mind of the day. Although claiming to be scientifically objective, physicians, even Benjamin Rush, the most influential theorist in America at the time, could not free themselves entirely from age-old prejudices. At the heart of the matter, Rush asserted, were such excesses as "inordinate sexual desires and gratifications, intense study, frequent and rapid transition of the mind from one subject to another, avarice, joy, terror, grief, and, of course, intemperance." He conjectured that because of the growing signs of "avarice and ambition" in the commercial life of the country, madness would increase, especially among the rich. The lower orders, Rush thought, did not "have the time to worry about the things that make the rich insane."[57] Such a moral diagnosis was all very well in the abstract, but which of these moral lapses had brought Sarah Ware to her state of inanition? The attending physicians would no doubt have been at a loss to say. Whatever they concluded, a moral indictment was unavoidable. In keeping with the notion of individual responsibility for one's actions, whether of will power or reason, the patient, not early environment and upbringing, was deemed culpable. As a result, Sarah's condition gravely embarrassed her kinspeople. In a family that prided itself on its integrity, standing, and honor, madness was a calamity and best guarded by silence.

Another factor in the family attitude was the prejudice about women which assumed that they were more subject to moral weaknesses leading to madness than men were. The mental dissolution of a male member of the clan might have elicited more comment among those of the same sex, but from the evidence so far uncovered the female correspondents were as reticent about their sister-in-law as their husbands were. At the center of the circle was a woman afflicted with, as a mid-nineteenth-century reporter called it, the "family proclivity inherited from her father." [58] They all knew the implications but said as little as possible about them.

Thus was begun the policy of reticence that would continue in the family for years thereafter. Taciturn and forbidding, Major Ware himself set the example. He also made it perfectly clear that Sarah's insanity was not to interfere with his life any more than necessary. Nor was her health to be talked about: Only once did the Major drop a remark. "Mrs[.] Ware," her husband laconically reported to Samuel Brown in 1821, "is very tranquil but her mind in statu quo." Aware of family disapproval about his long absences, Ware increasingly took his children on his travels—to Europe, Florida, and Mississippi. [59] But that was no solution, the others thought. When Ware was planning a trip to Europe in 1822, Thomas Percy, for instance, confided to Sam Brown, "I hope Ware will not take his children, but cannot believe that he will part with them. It fills me with grief to see him continually exposing his dear infants to the unnecessary dangers of voyages by sea & land & the perils of various climates." How much better it would be, if Ware could "settle himself somewhere in a healthy spot if but for their sakes." The major promised his concerned in-laws to buy a plantation near Thomas and Maria Percy's Belfield, Jack and Matilda Walker's Oakland, and Samuel Brown's place. He never did. Like Charles Percy in his younger days, he liked to keep his options open. [60]

Despite Ware's eccentricity, Thomas Percy, Samuel Brown, and John Walker admired him greatly. Perhaps they even respected his silence in suffering. Often they deferred to his judgment about financial matters out of admiration for his wealth, business sense, and knowledge of good opportunities. They borrowed money from him without demur. During the great depression of 1819, Thomas Percy, for instance, had considerable difficulty in repaying money that Ware had lent him, but his creditor was forbearing. Moreover, Percy, Walker, and Brown all consulted Ware about domestic matters: where Brown's son James should go to learn the law or whether Mary, another of Samuel Brown's daughters at Madame Sigoigne's, should be withdrawn from school to enter the marriage arena. [61] Nonetheless, he stood apart.

🙞 🙜

Sarah Ware remained in the hands of physicians in Philadelphia for eleven years. In 1831, however, Ware withdrew her and dispatched his wife to live out her remaining days at Woodlawn, as the Ellises' Cliffs was now called. It was the plantation home of her son Thomas George Ellis, located at White Cliffs, a dozen miles below the city. Ellis's marriage to the very young Mary Routh made possible the transfer. The family disapproved.

Thomas Percy refused to continue as a trustee for an estate of over $100,000 that the major had set up from his wife's properties to benefit their daughter Eleanor. Colonel Percy excused himself on the ground of ignorance about "the particulars," he said, but it was clearly a signal of his displeasure.

Ware may have deserted his wife, but Sarah's first-born son, Thomas George Ellis, and his family were devoted to the troubled lady who meandered about the premises. Years later, Sarah Ellis, Thomas Ellis's eldest daughter, could remember her grandmother in those closing years of her life. Sarah Ware died when her namesake was only seven years old, but she had deeply impressed the child. In one of her semi-autobiographical novels, Sarah recalled that not withstanding her grandmother's beauty and "exquisite hands and moulded form," she was "hopelessly melancholy." Sometimes, Sarah later wrote, there had been "occasional gleams of reason, when she would recognize us, and would busy herself with the plants and music, embroidery, or her pencil," for she was "very gifted." But these moments would pass, leaving "her mind darker than before." In a novel, Sarah [Dorsey] describes how the heroine's great-uncle, a British officer, had deserted his wife, age sixteen, who went insane. (Sarah Dorsey's character is a conflation of Margaret, whom Charles Percy had abandoned in the British Isles, and Sarah Percy Ware.) The novelist observes that the heroine's "great-aunt" (i.e., Sarah Dorsey's grandmother) could rarely be induced to leave her nurse or venture from her room. Yet "sometimes she becomes restless and wanders over the house." Sarah wrote that "her mind is usually in a mazed state," and she had to be retrieved. Living on the upper story of the Ellises' Woodlawn, Sarah chiefly occupied her days tunelessly strumming on a guitar or painting pictures. Once in a while, however, she could be restrained only in a strait-jacket.[62]

Sarah Ware lived in a quiet cocoon, it might be said, dreading the fateful moment when something awful would ravage her desperate calm. Like the Renaissance poet Christopher Hatton's dying swan who, "living had no note," Sarah Percy Ware did not recover her mental faculties. According to a family story, "death approach'd, unlock'd her silent throat" as well as her long imprisoned mind.[63] She was buried in the Routh family's brick-walled cemetery on Homochitto Street, Natchez. A large tombstone identifies her remains without pious reflection: "Sarah Percy Ware, 1835." Actually, the date was wrong. According to the diary of William Johnson, a free black, she died on May 30, 1836—just after large distributions of her property to her two daughters by Nathaniel Ware. Whoever planted the headstone did not even remember the year of her death. Though frequently in Natchez, Major Ware did not set the matter straight, perhaps because he never stopped by. Even court documents, later drawn up in collaboration with family members, recorded her death a year earlier than it was.[64]

Sarah's eldest daughter, Mary Jane Ellis LaRoche, did not escape her mother's fate. In fact her own mental deterioration began not long after Sarah Ware's death in faraway Natchez. Fortunately, for a number of years, the problem did not surface. Her husband René LaRoche, unlike Nathaniel Ware, was most uxorious and giving, but he seized an opportunity to advance his career, having no worries of his wife's health. With Sam Brown he went to Europe in the fall of 1828. There, thanks to James Brown, Samuel's brother and American minister at the Court of Charles X, they gained access to medical centers and scientists in France, Switzerland, and northern Italy. LaRoche reported the latest medical findings in his scientific journals and later won honors for his own advances in medical science.[65]

Although the LaRoches entertained their intellectual friends at musical parties where René could display his virtuosity on his Amati viola, all was not well at their house on the south side of busy Walnut between 9th and 10th streets. At some point in the late 1830s, Mary Jane fell victim to the same melancholia that had afflicted her mother in 1819. Perhaps the reasons were also similar. Mary Jane gave birth to her last child, Charles Percy LaRoche, in 1838 and quite possibly post-partum depression was the consequence. The evidence offers no conclusive answer. As Mary Tardy, a reporter, later remarked, Mary Jane LaRoche, "like her mother, for ten long years suffered like Mary Lamb, under eclipses of reason."[66] (Mary Lamb, the writer Charles Lamb's sister, was a notorious melancholic, being one of the few women in English history to have murdered her mother.)

Unlike most of the Percy women's husbands, LaRoche had no head for business. Absorbed in his scientific pursuits, he was not in a position to afford her a room and servant at the Pennsylvania Hospital. Since the family was Catholic and attended the Rev. William Harold's St. Joseph's Church, she was not an appropriate resident at the well-equipped, handsome Federalist-style Friends Asylum in Frankford, not far from Madame Sigoigne's academy. Probably LaRoche took care of her at home. When she contracted tuberculosis, her husband placed her in the hands of John Bell, who had been a member of his wedding party in 1824. One of LaRoche's closest and most intellectual friends, Bell, formerly of Ireland, was a specialist in pulmonary disorders and the use of mineral waters. Despite his efforts, she died "after great suffering," in 1844, at the age of thirty-five or thirty-six. She had been six or eight years (rather than the reported decade) under the cloud of derangement.[67] The death of their half-sister Mary Jane was a devastating blow to Major Ware's two daughters, most especially Eleanor. Their grief, however, found expression in art—the first family experiments in translating gloom of mind into poetry and fiction.

CHAPTER FIVE

Two Southern Brontës

Their sadness had become their religion and
their art: it provided, as music to a dance, the
tempo and structure of their lives.

Gail Godwin, *A Southern Family*[1]

Major Nathaniel Ware's wanderings and the illness of mother Sarah gave
Catherine Ann and Eleanor reason to feel abandoned, a circumstance that
led them toward literary self-expression.[2] Their poetry concerned the loss
of their mother, and later, their prose fiction explored an ambivalence
about their father. Despite their sense of deprivation, he offered them a
number of compensations. At his Philadelphia apartment the major hired
a Mrs. Mortimer, an English governess. The children loved her dearly,
although one of Eleanor's playmates remembered "old Mrs. Mortimer" as
a querulous tyrant.[3] Winter residence in Florida or Mississippi, where their
father oversaw his plantations, took the girls to new scenes and exposed
them to Southern and rural ways. In Philadelphia the visits of Samuel
Brown, John Walker, and Uncle Thomas Percy, their wives and children
also gave Catherine and Eleanor a further sense of their Percy and Southern heritage.

Despite these advantages, the sisters deeply missed their mother. Catherine was especially upset, at the age of a year and a half having lost her
mother to the affliction of insanity. Forced to find affection and companionship with each other, the sisters were at once both competitive and
mutually dependent. Though their portraits have not been uncovered,
Eleanor was reputed to be the better looking with exceptionally fair complexion and blonde hair. Eleanor's eyes, a reporter wrote, "were as blue as
heaven her features statuesque, her hair black with a purple tinge." In
comparison, Catherine thought herself plain, but according to the same
authority, she "had the Percy eye, dark-gray with black lash" and a forceful
chin. Only five feet three inches tall, Catherine always stood very erect, a
trait then much admired, and her hair was black, like mother Sarah's and
Mary Jane's.[4]

The pair also differed in temperament. When they were first sent to Madame Sigoigne's academy, Catherine rebelled in fright. No doubt she feared that in her absence from home her father would disappear just as her mother had. She ran away to her half-sister Mary Jane LaRoche's house, only a few blocks from the school, and hid in the wood-closet. When Madame Sigoigne found her huddled in a corner, the truant hysterically refused to return. Major Ware had to fetch her home, promising never to send her back to Madame Sigoigne's. Instead the child was tutored in classical English and French literature by her father and by others when he was out of town.

In the meantime, Ellen, as the younger sister Eleanor was often called, flourished at Madame Sigoigne's French-speaking academy. "S.G.M.," one of her closest confidantes, happily recalled the evenings spent in the headmistress's parlor. She pined even for those school days "when a page of Racine was our hardest task and an hour's detention in school our saddest sorrow." (This correspondent, who left no clues about her full name, had had a crush on her beautiful friend that she seemed not yet to have outgrown when she wrote her an impassioned letter years later.)[5] For all her outgoing ways, Eleanor may well have been the more vulnerable of the sisters. She never had a mother to know and thus missed a sense of belonging to someone, but the effects of her deprivation would not emerge until years later. As a child, she was self-assured and outgoing. On Saturdays, Ellen would return to the Philadelphia apartment to show off her social and linguistic skills, chattering in French as fluently as a native. The major had a child-size harp made for her at Erard's, and she was soon proficient. The young women often attended gatherings at half-sister Mary Jane LaRoche's, who became their surrogate mother—a parallel to Henry Mowat's supervision of Robert Percy in this luckless clan. No doubt, René LaRoche took special pleasure in the brief recitals of his wife's baby half-sister, being himself so accomplished a musician. Ellen eagerly accepted the attention of the French-speaking guests. In fact, it was reported, she liked being "a little queen in society, kind and warm-hearted, generous, but *tant soit peu* capricious and rather tyrannical, perhaps, over her more timid sister."[6] Although Ellen's competitive behavior drove Catherine deeper into herself, in their longing for love from parents unable to supply it, the two were almost obliged to be inseparable. From an early age, they began to write poems and stories together. Ellen had the gift of total recall and could recite without error any poem that she fancied.[7] Catherine, however, had greater sensitivity and inventiveness than her sister, but they liked to think that their talents complemented each other's.

The Ware sisters spoke often of their mother and she became almost an icon in their imaginations. In their early teens, the Ware sisters used to spend many weeks at their half-brother Thomas George Percy Ellis's plantation. There they visited their mother Sarah in the upper apartment. Sarah recognized her son, Thomas Ellis and his children Sarah Anne, Stephen

Percy, and Thomas LaRoche. Yet, as Catherine told a journalist, "she would weep sometimes for her baby 'Ellen.'" Yet the old lady would abruptly push away her daughter despite all of Ellen's attempts to have her mother recognize her.[8] After their mother died in 1836, they wrote of her as a saint, not as a woman (through no fault of her own) totally indifferent to their existence. Following a brief controversy over the ownership of a favorite house slave, Ellen in 1843 appealed to her sister by invoking the memory of Sarah Ware: "Catherine when you grow cross, or selfish, or mercenary my beau-ideal will be overthrown here below, and I shall have to await the meeting with our *sainted mother* in Heaven, before I behold a woman above self-interest, a purely noble woman!"[9]

In accordance with the custom of the family, the sisters married early. Their husbands were tolerant, well-born gentlemen of little ambition or talent—good choices for these strong-minded women. At the least, they would not interfere with the constant testing and probing to which the sisters' subjected each other and which they thought was unambiguous love. At age sixteen, on January 3, 1833, Catherine Ann wedded Robert Elisha Warfield in Cincinnati, her father's new residence after leaving Philadelphia.[10] Belonging to a prominent Maryland family, Robert's father, Elisha, had been a business associate in 1829 of Thomas Percy, Samuel Brown, Nathaniel Ware, and Samuel Worthington, another Marylander, in the purchase of lands in the Mississippi Delta. Catherine's father-in-law, Dr. Elisha Warfield of Lexington, taught with Samuel Brown at the Transylvania Medical School. Unlike his father, Elisha (who dropped the Robert) had no professional interests but followed the doctor's avocation of horse-breeding and racing. The Warfield family had founded the Lexington Association Race Course and in the course of the century was to own such famous mounts as Lexington and Darley, progenitor of forty Derby winners.[11]

Although the connection with the Warfields was scarcely objectionable, Major Ware kept a watchful eye on his daughter's welfare. He once thought of buying a large house at Biloxi on the Gulf coast so that the daughters and their families could gather there for summer holidays. As was his custom, though, he changed his mind, not wishing to be tied down himself.[12] Instead, he held on tightly to the financial strings of power. Ware had increased the size of his wife's share of her father Charles's estate. By 1836, the dowry for Catherine consisted of sixty-six slaves, a quantity of land in Arkansas, bank stocks, and half-interest in Utopia plantation on Black Bayou, in Washington County, Mississippi, the total valued at more than $100,000.[13] Ware promised to relinquish control if Elisha Warfield were to "become trustworthy and confidential and show himself worthy" of the responsibilities, but no documents show that a transfer of power ever took place. If the major wanted heirs, he could have asked for little more from Elisha; Catherine bore him six children.[14]

The marital state of her sister Catherine did not lead Ellen at once to follow suit.[15] At twenty, however, she felt an urgency, as Southern women were expected to marry at not much older than that age. Her choice was Henry William Lee, a Norfolk member of the famous Virginia clan and a cousin of Robert E. Lee. "Gay Harry" was a striking figure of a man, over six feet tall and well-proportioned, "a cavalier of 'ye olden times,'" as one contemporary rhapsodized.[16] Harry was too timid, however, to face the major for his daughter's hand. He was worried that she was his mental superior and that the major had typed him as a fortune-hunter.[17] Ellen grew impatient and put her scruples aside to write: "If I followed dear Mrs[.] Willis's rules [of etiquette], I should not write at all." Nonetheless, "I have taken up an idea that you are not entirely happy[,] Mr. Lee" and much too "thoughtful, and anxious." She pointed out that upon her father's return to Louisville, where the Wares were then staying, he better speak up because Ware was himself expecting to hear from him. "And yeild [sic] not to despondency—no, *never,* while life, and life's hopes are before you; and I am yet upon earth," she ordered.[18] Ellen's boldness paid off. Harry Lee promised to act, but, losing heart, he added, "In relation to your Father, what can I say to him? I who am so poor in this world's goods ask him for his daughter, his pride," a woman who could be "the bride of the brightest in the land, would he not scoff at and revile me?" Could she not arrange it all herself without his having to make an appearance? *"You know him,"* he pled.[19]

Eleanor agreed to do her best, confessing, "My Father is wayward and of a peculiar disposition, but *not* cold-hearted, or unfeeling." But if Ware refused to give her away, Eleanor promised to seize "my portion of my mother's heritage" and, "alone on earth, friendless perhaps—half parentless—guided and upheld by strong deep affection alone, I will come to you Harry!"[20] Harry had nothing so rash on his mind, but his fears were unfounded. Ware quickly granted his consent although subjecting Harry Lee to the financial constraints that he had imposed on Elisha Warfield. If Ellen died, her dowry would revert to her elder sister, and if Catherine had died, the estate would fall to Mary Jane LaRoche, her elder half-sister. On May 25, 1840, the couple was married with a sizable property for starting domestic life, thanks to Ware's careful management of his wife's legacy from Don Carlos: a large plantation in Hinds County, Mississippi, with about 85 slaves, assessed in 1838 at the value of $122,000, no small sum for a year in the throes of a severe depression. Some years later the couple also lived at a Deer Creek plantation near Greenville in Washington County, Mississippi. There they were linked by neighborliness and blood with Thomas George Percy's widow and young sons, William Alexander and the others, who had moved in the early 1840s to that newly opened frontier in the Delta.[21]

The two sisters' married lives by no means ended their preoccupation with their elusive and undemonstrative father, who remained for them a patriarch, loved, feared, and resented. He liked them under his control and encouraged their attentiveness to his needs but then withdrew whenever it suited him. Major Ware's Mississippi plantations were located in the Natchez region and he sought to bring newly married Lees into his orbit there. "I positively promised Father that I would return if my health improved," Ellen Lee confessed; "in the fall we go back." [22] Indeed, the major was seldom absent from the young matron's thoughts. "I shall have a room fixed for him and put an arch of greens over the gate and *dress little Catherine and Nat, as cupids with gauze wings to welcome him,* naked if the weather is mild, in highland kilts if the weather is cold. Oh how I long to see Father once more." [23] In daily life Catherine Warfield and Ellen Lee lavished him with affection and demands for lengthy visits. When they pursued their literary inclinations the Ware sisters expressed their displeasure with the major's mercurial habits in their poetry, but otherwise showed no frustration with their difficult parent.

🎐

Catherine and Ellen may have begun their cooperative literary enterprise, years before their marriages, largely to please the major. As precocious children, they both had marveled at the extensive library that Ware had developed. Catherine later remarked how much she enjoyed browsing alone among the books. She read through a "ragged regiment of authors"—Walter Scott, a lavishly illustrated Bible, Amelia Opie's *Ruffian Boy* and "the matchless *Madeline*," Maria Edgeworth's *Castle Rackrent,* Charles Robert Maturin's novel *Melmoth the Wanderer,* with its veiled suggestions of homosexuality, and other gothic tales. But, she confessed, her favorite was *Vathek: An Arabian Tale* (1786), one of the leading gothic stories in the Horace Walpole and Ann Radcliffe tradition. Writing through the medium of a fictional character many years later, Catherine recalled most fondly the eccentric William Beckford's story about a little princess and her feminized brother. They vie for the affection of a mad possessor of hidden knowledge. One of the most grotesque and violent romances in the eighteenth-century genre, Beckford describes scenes in which a Marquis-de-Sade-like character out of a fiendish pleasure hurls children over a precipice. As in Maturin's *Melmoth,* hints of sexual deviance appear in the work. In England, Beckford himself was notorious for his open homosexuality, although American readers were probably ignorant of that facet of his life.[24] The book, Catherine wrote, "saddened her for days, she scarce knew why, and left its imprint of mournful warning on her heart for life." [25] The young Catherine may well have fancied that she was Princess Nouronihar. Her sister Eleanor appeared as Beckford's creation, the boy-girl Gulchenrouz. Naturally, in this female version of the family romance, Vathek was her fearsome but fascinating father in a fiction of blood and incest. Major Ware himself sanctioned the sisters' intellectual pursuits, even though literature of this kind was thought to be gravely harmful for young impressionable minds.

Eleanor Ware may have been less impressed than her sister by the gothic form of fiction as her first surviving experiment at writing was not at all bloodthirsty. At age eleven she penned a five-quatrain ode that dwelt upon lost friendship and broken hearts.[26] Nor did it concern her ambivalent relationship with her father but rather her yearning for her mother. At age seventeen in 1837, not long after Sarah Ware's death, Eleanor wrote a draft of a novella, entitled *Agatha*. In the course of the story, one that concerns a daughter's struggle with the loss of her mother, the writer questions the pleasure of love. Passion was a dangerous "*sea,* upon whose swelling crest/ Floats many a wreck of fond affections lost," preached the teenage author.[27]

This slight production is less interesting for its content than for the circumstances of its creation. Doubtless, *Agatha* was inspired by the presence of other women nearby engaged in developing skills that were prized among the female members of society in Natchez.[28] Trying his hand at the craft, in 1848 Major Ware published *Henry Belden,* an adventure story based on his travels in North Africa, perhaps as his contribution to the local literary circle.[29] Such clusters of poets and writers were not at all uncommon throughout the Old South. Some, like Maria J. McIntosh of Darien, Georgia, specializing in children's literature, went on to establish lucrative careers. This kind of activity by obscure women—and sometimes men like Ware and William Faulkner's romantic and violent great-grandfather, William Clark Falkner—was a source of entertainment and sometimes even modest profit.[30] Despite the literary and social constraints, antebellum Southern female writers, most especially, provided a sturdier foundation in the region for more sophisticated thinkers of later generations than literary historians have acknowledged.[31]

Whether formally organized or not, the *literati* of Natchez were a busy group. The circle included Joseph Holt Ingraham, whose first work, *The South-West, By a Yankee* (1835), a lively social commentary, enjoyed wide circulation.[32] A native of Portland, Maine, he taught for a while at the nearby Jefferson College and over a lifetime he wrote eighty novels. Among them was *The Prince of the House of David* (1855) which sold between four and five million copies as the first of the Biblical sagas.[33] In the late 1830s, the two Percy women were influenced by the examples that Ingraham and others such as Rosa Vertner Jeffrey of Port Gibson offered.[34] Most important as a literary influence was Eliza Ann DuPuy, a well-born Virginian then serving as governess for Sarah Ellis, the Ware sisters' young niece.[35] DuPuy's most popular work (it sold 25,000 copies), *The Conspirator,* inspired by Aaron Burr's famous arrest in Natchez, was written at

Routhland, belonging to Thomas Percy Ellis. Eleanor Ware and the governess held regular symposiums at Routhland, where the women read aloud their productions.[36]

Encouraged by their niece's governess, "The Sisters of the West," as the poets styled themselves, were also gratified that their father thought their work publishable. A Cincinnati printer presented the 268-page volume to the public in 1843 under the title *The Wife of Leon, and Other Poems,* which went into a second edition in 1845. The following year Nathaniel Ware commissioned a New York printer for the pair when they published *The Indian Chamber, and Other Poems.* They dedicated it to William Cullen Bryant in gratitude for his "indulgent opinions" of their first volume.[37]

Their imaginations did not stray far from the conventional, but the poems reveal much about the character of Southern female belle-lettres and even throw light on the authors' inner lives. Not surprisingly they celebrated the code of honor and gentility that undergirded Southern social discourse. But, like Will Percy and Walker Percy many years later, they coupled such precepts with a persistent note of sorrow. Many of their verses sing the praises of noble Indian savages, exemplars of gentleness and stolid bravery—but always sadness knits their brows.[38] A nostalgia for medieval verities and noble gesture was a poetic theme common to the age, but these members of the Percy lineage incorporated that sentiment with their own special mark of melancholia. As Carolyn Heilbrun observes, nostalgia can be a mask for unrecognized anger, a canopy of sentiment to cover resentments one would rather not face head on.[39] In one of their longer examinations of broken love, the poets lament:

> But to the soul
> Where lies a hidden sting of pain, and wrong
> Of vain regret, or darker word—remorse,
> Thou bring'st, O shadowy twilight, brooding gloom,
> And dearth, and restlessness, and agony.[40]

The sisters were more likely to dwell upon "doom," "gloom," and "tomb" than to rime "June" and "moon." Death, especially of mothers and children, not romantic love, was their preoccupation. Yet, occasionally, Catherine Warfield made the topic of untimely death serve larger and rather personal purposes. In "I Walk in Dreams of Poetry," she uses the motif to explore a woman's yearning beyond child-bearing and domestic duty. The poet rejoices in the gift of language that permits communion of the soul with dead loved ones. The poet had long watched "them in their sorrowing hours,/ When, with their spirits tost,/ I heard them wail, with bitter cries,/ Their earthly prospects crossed." Only "in dreams of poetry" can their memory live. Poetic fancies, she concludes, alone can "make a romance of our life;/ They glorify the grave!"[41]

With so many verses connected with their mother's death and sometimes her demented state, only a few were devoted to the sisters' reactions to the major. They expressed their sadness and anger over his long absences and coolness when home. As dutiful daughters, they were never to question his judgment about such matters but used the composing of poetry as a hidden language of quiet protest, much as Bedouin women, in grief hidden from view, do today. The novelist Gail Godwin, quoted at the beginning, captured the mood: "Their sadness had become their religion and their art: it provided, as music to a dance, the tempo and structure of their lives." [42]

For these literary descendants of Charles Percy, writing poetry and fiction gave a sense of control over an undependable world—and over a wayward father. In "The Wanderer," for example, the poet warns the one addressed that "ambition, boundless, uncontroll'd," drives him from the home he should love. Even though he returns bearing great riches, he once again signifies with "the dark eye, the glance of scorn" a "joyless" longing to escape. The poet remonstrates that the years are fleeting by—"Thine eye is dim; thy voice hath lost its tone." But, the poet fears, only the grave will end his roving—as indeed was the case.[43]

Of the two sisters, Catherine was the more accomplished and much more prolific poet. In fact, after her marriage to Harry Lee, Ellen let her sister take command of editing and publishing their books of verses. Ellen even wrote Catherine, "You Kitty, are the leading Star, of us two, in the way of poetry." [44] An episode of depression may have slackened Eleanor's creative energy. At Mississippi Springs in the summer of 1849, she confessed the low state of her morale in one of her few letters to survive. Ellen found the people at the spa "dull," the dresses uninteresting, the ladies vulgar, the men more so. How much she wished to see Harry and her father.[45] A few weeks later, she died of yellow fever in Natchez, knowing how aggrieved her sister Catherine would be to learn of her death. Roman Catholic Bishop John Chanche was summoned to administer extreme unction, and Eleanor Percy Lee met her end "tranquilly." [46]

At the time of Ellen's fatal illness, Catherine was still grieving the deaths of her mother, her half-sister Mary Jane, and her half-brother Thomas George Ellis. Meanwhile, Major Ware had settled far distant from Kentucky, having chosen Galveston, a thriving port that many thought might one day rival New Orleans and in which he acquired blocks of downtown property. For the first time in many years, he bought a house and furnished it completely. In 1853, however, like his daughter Ellen, he came down with yellow fever, which was almost as serious a scourge in that ill-fated city as hurricanes. The major's death deepened Catherine Warfield's melancholy to the point that she refused to trust John L. Darragh, Ware's competent and reliable Galveston lawyer. She dispatched Nathaniel Ware Warfield, her eldest and feckless son, to manage the major's vast "San Jacinto" tract and other properties. Catherine's literary inspiration died with the loss of her sister, and her father's death reinforced her sense of lassitude. To write, she confessed, too much *reminded her of Eleanor.* [47]

Sarah Ellis, her niece, paid a visit to Pee Wee Valley, near Louisville, where the Warfields then lived. She encouraged her Aunt Catherine to honor sister Ellen's memory by resuming her literary career. In a drawer they found a cache of poems, novels written in verse, and "Tales of the Weird and Wonderful," which she and Ellen had written together. Aunt and niece looked over the old manuscripts, and Sarah, herself a brilliant young woman, helped with the editing and preparation of Catherine Warfield's second experiment in belles-lettres, the novel that was to establish her reputation.

With her six children raised, Catherine Warfield, in middle age, did not turn to fiction solely for its own sake, although ambition played a serious part. Her second purpose was to explore the relationship with her father and mother, a pattern to be repeated by the two twentieth-century Percy writers. Major Ware had given her wealth and education but it had been a dreary life. The two daughters had to wander with him, observe his wretchedness, and receive his cold looks and sometimes bitter remarks with the deference due a nineteenth-century father. The result of her renewed labors using themes that her poetry had foretold was a bestseller: *The Household of Bouverie; or, the Elixir of Gold.*[48] Published in the same year as Lincoln's first election, Warfield's most ambitious novel was a two-volume, 783-page gothic romance. Like the Brontës, Charlotte, Emily, and Branwell—Catherine and Eleanor Percy Ware had been lonely children thrown back upon their own devices, who created their own worlds of fantasy. Much of that fairy-tale period in their literary development is present in the Bouverie story. The opening section of *The Household of Bouverie* deals with serious parental conflicts. Yet its romantic settings—castles in England and gloomy plantation mansions in America—endow the circumstances with the sort of unreality that fiction readers then preferred.[49]

Three major aspects of this remarkable novel deserve attention: first, the source of its inspiration, both personal and literary; second, its most salient and interconnected themes—the Oedipal relationship of father and daughter, the moral duty of womanhood, and finally, the Catholic tendencies of Warfield's art. The last was a thread that ran through much of the Percy family history.

The inspiration for *The Household of Bouverie* came largely from Charlotte Brontë's *Jane Eyre*. The heroine Lilian de Courcy (a patronym perhaps copied from Anthony Trollope's Barset series) is a young orphan who arrives from England to live with her long-suffering but strong-willed grandmother, Camilla Bouverie, on a plantation located in a border slave state. Lilian discovers that Erastus Bouverie, her grandfather, long supposed dead, is secretly living on the second floor (site of mother Sarah's habitat on her son Thomas Ellis's plantation outside Natchez). The Brontëan signature should be clear, but in her hands the adoption of the English gothic approach made possible an indirect criticism of the patriarchal world Warfield inhabited. That theme, however muted, was not peculiar to Warfield's writing; it can be found in the work of other Southern female writers as well.[50]

The character of Erastus Bouverie, who dominates the narrative even more than the heroine herself, was created from three sources: the first being Henry Percy, the Ninth Earl of Northumberland, imprisoned for eighteen years in the Tower of London for alleged complicity in the Gunpowder Plot of 1605 (Warfield would know the story from history books and from touring Martin Tower, the "Wizard Earl's" apartment where he experimented with alchemy); second, the progenitor, Charles Percy; and third, her saturnine and distant father, Major Ware. In Bouverie's well-appointed hideout, the mad plantation squire conducts alchemical experiments with an elixir that requires measures of human blood and gold. The potion, the Byronic figure claims, is the source of eternal youth. Too proud to submit himself to God, Bouverie anticipates glory and immortality. Just as Major Ware entertained high ambitions for wealth and fame as an explorer and botanist even at the expense of love and domestic happiness, so too does Bouverie. As reporter Mary Tardy pointed out, the moral lesson of this and other Warfield novels was that "intellect without moral goodness is nothing worth."[51] The idea was already trite by 1860, having been exploited in so many sentimental novels—most notably Augusta Evans's *Beulah*. Yet, the force of Warfield's convictions comes through because of the personal element. It was a hidden critique of her dead father, though, of course, Warfield would not have admitted to implying such an intimate connection.

The sexual overtones of the novel were true to the gothic form. The hero, Jasper Quintilian, who later marries Lilian de Courcy, is virtually a eunuch and described as "feminine" with a "mouth rigidly beautiful, as if from suffering and determined endurance."[52] Borrowing from Charlotte's Brontë's *Jane Eyre,* Warfield places a mad grandfather in an upper story instead of a deranged wife. Yet both characters imbibe incestuous blood. Bertha Antoinette tries to suck dry her brother Richard Mason's life blood, and Erastus Bouverie attempts to revive his youth by drinking his granddaughter Lilian de Courcy's blood.[53] Describing the elixir into which melted sovereigns have been poured, Warfield writes in terms that Freud would understand, "the small gold snake rose, and fell convulsively in the liquid."[54] As in *Vathek* and so many other stories of the type, sexual anarchy and confusion abound. Fathers lust for daughters, husbands prove either ineffectual or perverse. Women must assume roles of manly courage and conform to patriarchal rule only by an indomitable determination not to surrender their femininity. Above all, *The Household of Bouverie* dealt with the very human problem of insanity. The author knew it at first-hand and doubtless feared it might be her own fate.

The female novelist had a further mission in exploiting a subject that already had a long tradition: the dread that women entertained about making marital choices that would ruin their lives with no hope of escape by divorce or separation, owing to their financial dependence and vulnerability to social ostracism. Warfield's Camilla Bouverie had no means of escape from the burden of her marriage to an insane and criminal figure. The same circumstance, of course, applied to men as well. Brontë's Rochester could not initially free himself from his mad wife to marry Jane Eyre. Likewise, in his own life, as his daughter well knew, Major Ware had found that same situation so embittering, so enslaving. Victorians shrank from the peril of marriage to a partner who might be the very opposite of outward appearance—deranged, despicable, weak, or roguish. Brontë dealt with the issue from the perspective of the male victim, Warfield from that of an abused but also resentful wife, no less honorable, no less bound to duty than Brontë's Rochester.[55] Although the lesser artist, Warfield shared with Brontë a tragic personal history that shaped her literary imagination.

In the act of creation, Charlotte Brontë and Catherine Warfield both found a way to deal with the afflictions of familial loss and grief. But Warfield had another incentive that resembled in some respects the one that Abraham Lincoln adopted. In fear of losing his mind, he sought a means to avoid the anonymity that belonged to those who lost their reason. Lincoln's answer was not a pursuit of faith—he was scarcely religious—but fame in the affairs of men.[56] Catherine also felt burdened with a dread of being as wraith-like in madness as her mother, whose existence their father, Major Ware, and his brothers-in-law Samuel Brown and Thomas Percy had barely acknowledged. In response she drove toward the power that came with publishing novels. Luckily for this resourceful woman, her depression no more prevented her from a remarkably productive career than Lincoln's periodic anguish inhibited his political ambitions. That compensatory exercise of will would help to explain the creative energies of so many in the Percy line, but most of all its literary members.

Having thought much about the matter in light of her mother, half-sister, and grandfather's mental history, Warfield provided considerable insight into how madness might arise in a character like Bouverie.[57] The symptoms she ascribes to her anti-hero Bouverie conform with what would now be called manic-depression. Bouverie experiences swift mood shifts in which the "highs" feed his sense of omnipotence, but soon enough he falls back into remorse and lethargy. "As the brilliant vision swayed his mood," Warfield writes, "he would walk the room with steps of pride and power, his form dilating, his eye glittering, and that radiance that I have seen in no other countenance flashing over and illuminating his face like sunshine. Another moment and the dream would vanish before the impotence of reality. His step would slacken, his lifted arm fall heavily by his side, his head droop on his breast, the light die from his face, and he would throw himself depressed and exhausted into a chair to muse and perhaps despair."[58] Possession, not love, dominates Erastus Bouverie's life. The transference of desire to alchemy and electrical experimentation as a way to gain control of the sorely abused women reveals his inner emptiness. As a child, the novelist explained, Bouverie has been terrorized by his father, Ursus (the Bear), a cruel trader in African slaves, so that the son cannot give or receive affection. At the same time he cowers in his hidden sanctuary, dependent upon the reluctant loyalty of a wife whose love for him has long before disappeared.

Catherine Warfield exemplified a theme that was to figure greatly in the Percy family literary history—the role of religion. Catholicism serves as a means to salvation, but also as a way of coping with the family malady of depression. Like Walker Percy a hundred years later, Warfield turned to the most structured and authoritarian forms of Christianity available as a source of redemption. In this regard she was influenced by her half-sister. Ellen Lee, in turn, had converted to Catholicism soon after Mary Jane LaRoche's slip into insanity in 1838. That event, declared a contemporary critic, occasioned "a loss from which Ellen never recovered."[59] Her sister Catherine also mourned in verse, expressing gratitude that Mary Jane had mothered her when her own mother had "waned away,/ Into her dark, unbroken rest," a sentiment that Ellen fully shared.[60]

Ellen, who, according to a close friend, had already been leading "a sorrowful life," was only nineteen when Mary Jane had gone mad.[61] Since the LaRoches were devout Catholics, the young and sensitive poet found the consolations of that faith a source of great strength. Catholicism furnished a bond to link her to her kinswoman, dearer to her than all except her sister Catherine. Frightened by the succession of mental illnesses, she found in her Christian faith a means by which to escape a prison in the mind. In Natchez, Ellen was especially drawn to Roman Catholic Bishop John Chanche of Natchez and must have often written Catherine about her attachment to her spiritual guide. In *The Household of Bouverie,* Warfield presents her sister's father-confessor as Bishop Clare, adviser to Camilla Bouverie.

Throughout that novel and others, Warfield made her own attraction to Catholicism obvious, though she never formally converted to that faith. The appeal of Catholicism, or at least High Anglicanism, as we shall see, was also evident in the fiction of Sarah Dorsey, the Ware sisters' niece.[62] Ritual can be a socially acceptable method of handling the fear of suicide and death. It helps a mourner to reach a reconciliation with the pain of loss. Grief and anger are channeled into a sacred activity that authority and tradition make legitimate. The Catholic faith provided venerated formality in the handling of uncertainties of life and death. By contrast, Protestantism or unbelief leaves such matters in the hands of the individual and may encourage denial and repression of feelings of both anger and guilt. To gain some insight one may best turn to Charlotte Brontë, whose gifts far outshone those of Catherine Warfield. In Brontë's most brilliant novel, *Villette* (1853), Lucy Snow suffers from unremitting depression. Lucy's mother had died. Then Lucy's father abandons her, without offering much explanation for his departure. These were familiar events in the lives of all three Percy women. Similar tragic losses had struck Charlotte Brontë herself. The early death of her mother was later compounded by the desolation and grief that came with the unswerving sequence of deaths of her sisters and brother. At one point Brontë has Lucy Snow seek out confession in hope of some emotional relief. A surprised but understanding Catholic priest declares: "You were made for our faith: depend upon it our faith alone could heal and help you—Protestantism is altogether too dry, cold, prosaic for you."[63] Even though Charlotte Brontë makes clear in the novel her own deep suspicions of the Catholic Church, her words provide an understanding of its appeal to the suffering depressive. Dryness, coldness of death, one recalls, were the conditions associated with black bile, one of the four antique Galenic humors.

For the nineteenth-century Percy writers, the Catholic Church, though patriarchal, personified the feminine in the worship of Mary. In Brontë's *Villette,* Lucy Snow finds the rule of masculine Reason "vindictive as the devil . . . Often has Reason turned me out by night . . . and harshly denied my right to ask better things." But a different voice beckons her away from the despair that austere rationality exacted. She calls that countering force "this daughter of Heaven," with powers "divine, compassionate, succourable." The nurturing spirit, Lucy Snow says, "saw me weep and she came with comfort . . . Sleep, sweetly—I gild thy dreams!"[64] In Catholic terms, that spirit materialized in the form of the mother of mankind—the mother that Catherine had known and loved and yet not known at all. However attracted Warfield was to the faith that had captured her beloved sister Eleanor, she, like Charlotte Brontë, held deep prejudices against it. In her books *Ferne Fleming* and *The Cardinal's Daughter,* she has a Southern planter abruptly leaving his wife to join the Roman priesthood. Ferne Fleming's father eventually is elevated to the cardinalate by Pio Nono (Pius IX) himself. Once again Warfield seems in search of a father. Taciturn, book-minded, Ferne's father, who in Rome calls himself Salvano, never explains his decision to take up holy orders. Salvano does not acknowledge the pain and bitterness he caused his abandoned wife or the vacancy he left in his daughter Ferne's upbringing. In some ways, Salvano is another Bouverie, though only fanatical, not mad. Yet, the portrait is not altogether dark. Through her heroine, Ferne, the novelist admires the intellectuality and even the formality of the Catholic father. At the end Salvano gives his hearty blessing to her marriage, the customary close to romance. Despite her religious misgivings, Warfield, like the other Percys, recognized that order, structure, hierarchy, and a moral imperative could challenge depression. Hope in this life and the next were to be found within the Catholic realm. Such was the faith for some members of the

Percy lineage, a dedication not dissevered from the long record of melancholy.

Warfield's eight other novels, written after the Civil War, show a timidly growing appreciation of a different style for women to follow. In them, feminine integrity is less tied to social and moral constraints. She even allows some modest degree of feminine autonomy. Published in 1867, *The Romance of Beauseincourt* reveals that the heroine, Miriam Monfort, a Jewish woman of independent temperament and intellect, becomes a governess to the children on Colonel Prosper Lavigne's plantation near Savannah.[65] (Apparently Warfield fashioned the story from a tantalizingly undocumented incident that occurred during a childhood visit to her father's Florida estates near Appalachicola.[66]) There Miriam discovers the inadequacies of the patriarchal order. The reactionary colonel's wife is portrayed as "the constant, self-sacrificing wife." She explains that following "a lifetime of submission, first to my father, next to my husband, I could not commence" a domestic "revolution." After witnessing Colonel Lavigne's drunken incompetence, the self-employed Miriam recognizes that his family will face a future filled with "sorrow and poverty." Drawing on the old memory from the Florida tragedy, she has the colonel die in a swamp, his eyes plucked out by vultures. Nor was Warfield uncritical of plantation life. She has her heroine declare, "To vegetate on a Southern plantation, and year by year feel the shackles of prejudice and circumstance more closely confirmed by necessity, did not seem to me the most desirable of conditions, 'noblesse oblige' notwithstanding." Such a life, Miriam continues, was surrounded by "the shadow of mediocrity, self-conceit and dissipation. For me there was no prestige in the mere name of planter." [67]

Although an ardent Confederate and unusually firm supporter of slavery and conservative tradition, Warfield was no Louisa McCord, the South Carolina intellectual who found very little amiss south of the Potomac. In contrast, Warfield had some harsh things to say about plantation management. When Colonel Lavigne gives out Christmas rations of tobacco, whiskey, fireworks, and other favors, he receives the usual "Thankee, Master, thankee" from the hands. But when a chained bear (another Ursus) gets loose and mauls the old reprobate, the field hands stand by and passively watch until at last the white observers rescue him. To be sure, these are exceptional passages in the midst of the customary glorification of Southern mores. She sets, however, the good qualities against what she calls the "petty vanities and social narrowness" of Southern rural life.[68]

In her most popular postwar novels, *Ferne Fleming* and its sequel *The Cardinal's Daughter,* Warfield created one rather memorable character. Warfield seems to have turned her attention to the marginality of the kinless, plain-looking but sturdy woman about whom Charlotte Brontë wrote so effectively. Marian Dormer, the heroine's sometime confidante, eventually marries Ferne Fleming's wealthy uncle, much to the family's distress. She is an aggressive woman who speaks her mind. Mrs. Dormer confesses to Ferne at one point that in her teens, she had married her first husband simply to survive: he was twenty years her senior, an invalid, but wealthy. " 'Mediocre women can never choose their fortunes: they must meekly accept them.' "[69] Yet, unlike Brontë who sympathizes with her struggling, solitary women, Warfield did not altogether countenance Mrs. Dormer's plainspoken determination. After her last, much deplored match to the well-to-do widower, the character disappears from the narrative.

In one of her last composed works, *Hester Howard's Temptation* (1875), Warfield proved more adventurous still—up to a point.[70] For the first time she creates a spirited heroine. Unlike the long-suffering wife of Erastus, Camilla Bouverie, Hester Howard deserts her self-serving husband and goes on the stage. But it was all too daring. Warfield has the heroine give up her promising venture to return to a Southern plantation inheritance, periodically bedeviled, like Camilla Bouverie, by her unreliable mate. After her husband's fortuitous death from drink, and Hester's escape from a feverish, over-repressed lawyer named Mulgrave, she unites with a former physician, Rebel blockade-runner, and all-round hero. Like so many other lucky heroes belonging to the sentimental tradition, he turns out to be heir to an English barony. Despite such predictable plots and characters, throughout these later works, Warfield denounces men who, eager to put matters straight, "think housework a cure-all" for "weary, broken-spirited" women under the yoke of misfortune and bad husbands.[71]

Warfield should be considered one of the transitional women writers of the mid-Victorian period. She was not as genteel and delicate in her themes and portrayals as many of her cohorts—notably Augusta Evans Wilson. As reporter Mary Tardy observed in 1868, "She has lived too much out of the world." Women writers, the critic continued, had to "study men, as well as books." While her "wounded heart" had taught her much, she had not experience in the life of cities and of "men that 'George Sand' and 'George Eliot' have had." As a result she could not be as daring as the late nineteenth-century female novelists Amélie Rives and Kate Ferguson, Warfield's niece and daughter of Eleanor Percy Lee. These two writers of the 1880s belonged to a remarkable cohort of women willing to rejoice in feminine sexual passion in their lives and writing that Warfield would have found un-Southern and most unladylike.[72] Nonetheless, Warfield's writings contributed to feminine letters an attention to the darker aspects of male and female relations. She possessed a psychological seriousness not to be superseded by a Southern female writer until the publication of Kate Chopin's *The Awakening* in 1899, some twenty or so years after Warfield's death.

CHAPTER SIX

Sarah Dorsey

Child of my heart! look on me. Even now
A mournfulness upon my brow is thrown;
Thou hast thy father's lip, the father's brow—
Hast thou thy father's spirit, oh, mine own?

Child of my heart! hold'st thou all deep and
strong
That father's memory in thy spirit's cell,
A charm of life 'gainst injury and wrong,
A sacred dream?—for, oh! *He* loved thee well.

"To "S**** A** E****""
Catherine Ann Warfield and Eleanor Percy Lee[1]

Throughout her life, Sarah Anne Ellis Dorsey sought to combine the routines of a typical plantation lady with a sense of feminine intellectuality which superior learning and wealth made possible. In comparison with Southern white women of similar tastes and high education, Sarah Dorsey, her married name, was much more experimental and extensive in her search for individuality. One reason was her metropolitan links—to Philadelphia and New York, and after the Civil War, to London. By her own choice much of her life would be confined to a rural existence. Yet she would strive to open new avenues of intellectual experience without risk to her marriage or her social and economic position. Romantic by temperament she thought that it would be easy to pursue an intellectual, productive career and give up nothing of her imposing style of living.

※ ※

Sarah's father, Thomas George Percy Ellis, had been named for his mother's only surviving brother when he was born on May 1, 1805.[2] After Ellis's brief career at Princeton in 1820, he had returned to Natchez to oversee his mother's properties. In 1828 the young planter had married Mary Malvina Routh, an heiress barely fifteen years old. Job Routh, her father, had to submit a two-hundred-dollar bond to validate the arrangement.[3] Routh had arrived during the Spanish period as a penniless farmer, probably from Tennessee or possibly Wales. In a short time he had amassed a great fortune and owned vast tracts in upper Concordia Parish, Louisiana, and around Natchez.[4] When in the country, Thomas and Mary Ellis lived at Woodlawn, which had been Judge Ellis's house, not far from Northumberland House. On February 17, 1829, Sarah was born at her parents' town dwelling, Richmond, in Natchez. The rambling place, still standing, combines colonial, provincial Spanish, and brick in its architecture. As the family grew and wealth increased, Ellis sold it, and the family in 1837 moved into Routhland, Job Routh's house until his death some three years earlier.[5] It was a much grander house than Richmond, with a second story and "columns and upper galleries on two sides." Situated on what was originally a 1700-acre tract, just south of the city center, Routhland was surrounded by stone outbuildings in the style of a baronial castle. The grounds were surrounded by walls which, like the garden, had been designed by an English landscape artist.[6]

Thomas Ellis idolized Sarah, and the little girl responded with great affection to her father's interest in her, more so than to her mother Mary. Sarah's preference for her father owed something to the youth of her mother, barely sixteen years her senior. Mary Malvina used to laugh that the child, so grave and intelligent, "was much older than she was."[7] The Rouths were not intellectuals; rather, as Sarah Ellis later reminisced, they were "fond of good living, and of having their friends about them, to aid in the enjoyment of well-stocked cellars; abundant tables, billiard-rooms, libraries, and fast horses." Her beautiful mother was disappointed not to have a child who was equally attractive, and she found Sarah's quickness of mind and constant questions a trial.[8]

Sarah was seven years of age when grandmother Sarah Ware, living in the upper rooms, had died, May 30, 1836. The old lady, for whom the child was named, made a strong impression on her granddaughter. Many years later Sarah Dorsey recalled her as "a beautiful, stately woman, with exquisite hands and moulded form . . . possessing everything that the prestige of birth, and rank, and wealth could give." Nonetheless, the reporter, who recorded her remarks, summarized, "the 'skeleton in the closet' was always there, and for years this dreadful thought pursued her . . . as it had all her family (her gifted aunts [Catherine and Eleanor] as well), making their inner lives deeper and more thoughtful than the life of most people."[9] In more than one novel, Sarah was to create characters based upon her memories of her grandmother.

After Sarah Ellis Ware's death an unexpected and greater blow fell. Early in 1838, Thomas Ellis went to Lake St. Joseph in upper Concordia Parish (later Tensas Parish) to buy a plantation. At the age of thirty-one he died there from causes never specified. Sarah was then almost nine. There had been no preparation for the calamity, no lingering illness during which goodbyes could be said and grief openly expressed. Many years later Sarah confessed that the loss had "made a deep and ineffaceable impression." As so often happened in Southern families like this one, denial was the means for handling death. Sarah created a mythical father who was all goodness and enlightenment. Daughters of Sarah's age are prone to such an idealization, a stage preceding adolescence when they seek a greater distance to achieve a separate identity. Thomas Ellis's early death precluded the latter opportunity. The tendency toward depression was already in her background. Mary Tardy reported from an interview with her in 1869: "Her great-grandfather, grandmother, and aunts suffered in that terribly mysterious dispensation of God," and Sarah Ellis now had this additional wound to endure.[10]

Thomas Ellis was not, however, the perfect representation of manhood and wisdom that Sarah fashioned from her selective memory. Like Thomas Percy of Huntsville, he preferred the unambitious life of leisurely planting. He once refused to stand for public office on the Whig ticket even after he had been nominated by his party. According to Mary Tardy, who interviewed Sarah Dorsey shortly after the Civil War, he was supposed to be hospitable, "very gifted and brilliant." Despite the memorial verses in his memory that Sarah's aunts Catherine and Eleanor composed, he was not a figure to deserve the adoration of a daughter who would prove herself much more brilliant than he had been.

The third formative event in young Sarah's life was the marriage of her mother to Charles Gustavus Dahlgren on October 19, 1840.[11] Mary's second husband inherited a lovely bride from his predecessor but also his staggering accumulation of debts. In the last year or so of his life, Squire Ellis discovered himself $300,000 in debt in the Panic of 1837.[12] Ellis's losses far exceeded those that years before nearly had ruined Thomas George Percy, his uncle in Huntsville for whom he had been named. Mississippians had been particularly hit hard. The Democratic majority of the Mississippi legislature repudiated the state's debts. Although the executors declared the estate insolvent, Dahlgren drew up a marriage contract that protected his fiancée's large paternal inheritance from seizure by her deceased husband's creditors.[13] Moreover, the enterprising financier rescued Ellis's slaves already on the auction block. With creditors happily raising the bids, he had to pay over $90,000 to retain them. All of her property had to be placed under a mortgage requiring repayment within six months. At risk were household goods, including ten chairs, silverware, and other amenities. In the fields, barns, and storehouses, 75 head of swine, 55 mules and field horses, a thoroughbred, two carriage horses, 95 barrels of "Prime Pork," and 70 head of cattle were slated for sale. Mary also had to borrow nearly $5000 from her portion of Job Routh's considerable estate.[14]

Without question, the Ellis family would have been reduced to near penury had it not been for Charles Dahlgren's timely financial intervention. Sarah's education would have been minimal and her marital prospects reduced—not to mention the humiliation that so drastic a loss of power and wealth entailed. As it was, Dahlgren managed to provide Sarah, Stephen Percy, Thomas LaRoche, and Inez, Sarah's younger brothers and sister, with an elaborate education and style of living. Young Sarah's mother, Mary Dahlgren, was very much obliged to her husband. Years later, she would declare that he alone and not her Ellis children should be considered sole owner of everything, "except those [properties] he settled on me from the Estate of my father." [15]

Like Henry Mowat's care-taking of midshipman Robert Percy, Dahlgren, when assuming the role of paterfamilias, came on the scene as an outsider. Unlike her cousin Robert Percy, however, young Sarah never acknowledged an indebtedness for what the step-father did for her and the other family members. In many ways, Dahlgren was like Captain Mowat—outspoken, quick in temper, energetic, and honest. Yet he was insensitive to a child's feelings. To a nine-year-old girl, accustomed to her father's special interest and affection, he seemed a hard-hearted taskmaster.[16]

The Dahlgrens were Swedish aristocrats with claims to a direct descent from King Gustavus Adolphus, famed for his military triumphs in the Thirty Years' War. Charles Dahlgren's father Bernhard had had enough influence at the Swedish court to outweigh an indiscreet attraction to French Revolutionary thought. Instead of prison he won appointment as consul in Philadelphia. It was a form of political exile for a once promising member of the Swedish diplomatic corps. Bernhard Dahlgren died suddenly in 1824, and Charles Gustavus and his eldest brother John had to receive their education at sea. As Charles Dahlgren recalled years later, obligations to support his widowed mother, however, required him to leave the U. S. Navy. His brother John Adolphus Dahlgren remained in the service and rose to the rank of rear-admiral on the strength of his invention of the famous Dahlgren gun.[17]

In 1826 Nicholas Biddle, a family friend, appointed fifteen-year-old Charles an employee of the branch office of the Bank of the United States at New Orleans. Charles Dahlgren later entered the plantation supply business and cotton-growing itself in Natchez. With large plantations in Concordia Parish and Tensas Parish, Louisiana, across the river from Natchez, and real estate holdings at Beersheba Springs, Tennessee, Dahlgren was reputed to be worth three-quarters of a million dollars, and just before the Civil War his income was said to reach $100,000 a year.[18] Yet, like so many other transplanted Yankees, over the years Charles Dahlgren became more Southern than the native-borns, adopting the behavior of a man of honor and associating with adventurers like Rezin Bowie, inventor of the famous knife, and David Crockett.[19] William Johnson, a black barber and diarist of Natchez, reported that Dahlgren had insulted one Charles Stewart, who called him "a Damned Lyar and a Dd Scoundrel & a Dmd Coward." After exchanging insults and fists in the face, the pair resorted to pistols and knives and stalked each other about the town. In a store Dahlgren shot his adversary so that it seemed for a while that Stewart was "so Dead that he Barely Breathed." Dahlgren carried evidence of his valorous conduct in the form of a knife-blade chip in his skull and two balls in his rib cage to his natural death.[20] These indications of character, however, did not appeal to his little step-daughter.

Adding to the child's sense of distance from her family was the steady succession of little Dahlgrens. Years later the rivalries burst out in disputes over Mary Routh's bequests in the late 1850s. On her deathbed, Mary Malvina prayed that no "bitter or evil feeling or words between my children and Mr. Dahlgren" should arise but only "peace and kindness—and kind intercourse" should prevail so that "no differences of name" should separate them all. In particular, she urged "those who are strong to help the poor & weak—to cling to each thro the trials of life." With regard to the "poor and weak," she had in mind Inez, her favorite and youngest child, who should make "her home with the rest of my Dahlgren Children."[21] In early March 1858, Mary Routh died after much suffering from heart trouble.[22]

Continuing family quarrels prompted Dahlgren to place Routhland on the market less than three weeks after his wife's death for distribution to the Ellis heirs. Meanwhile, to Sarah's disgust, he remarried all too quickly, his second bride being nineteen-year-old Mary Vannoy of Nashville, who was no doubt pleased not to live in her predecessor's mansion. In July 1855, the original Routhland, struck by lightning, had burned to the ground while the Dahlgrens were vacationing in Saratoga, New York. Dahlgren had a new structure, with its ring of two-story white columns, built on the same site. For his new bride, he erected yet another great house, which he called Llangollen. From his two marriages, Charles Dahlgren had a total of thirteen offspring.[23]

Years later, Charles Dahlgren claimed that he had always hoped that Sarah Dorsey would demonstrate his belief in women's innate abilities. "When I took charge of the family," he reminisced, "I discovered she had a wonderful intellect, which I determined to develop. I spent a fortune doing it, but I never regretted the result."[24] First, despite the straitened finances of the family, Dahlgren continued the employment of Eliza Ann DuPuy at Routhland as the child's governess. This young and prolific novelist, whose literary advice and company Catherine Warfield and Eleanor Percy Lee had enjoyed, heightened her young pupil's already intense love of literature and writing. When the governess and Aunt Ellen gathered friends to read each other's work, little Sarah could be seen "hiding in a corner to listen" intently, as DuPuy recalled.[25]

At some point, but most likely between 1838 and 1841, Dahlgren sent Sarah to Madame Deborah Grelaud's French School in Philadelphia. Associated with the wealthy Stephen Girard family, the strict headmistress catered to Maryland and Virginia planters, though a handful came from as far away as Mississippi. A native of France, Madame Grelaud, like the LaRoche and Sigoigne families, had fled the Revolution and founded her small academy in the 1790s and kept it open until 1849. The pupils were chiefly Episcopalian but the discipline and theology were along Presbyterian lines, as Deborah Grelaud was a Huguenot.[26]

Dahlgren also recognized Sarah's musical talents. Aunt Ellen Lee perhaps had encouraged him to advance her training on the harp, which she, too, had mastered. Residing in Philadelphia, Sarah took lessons from "Boscha, the great harp player," Dahlgren later boasted. "I purchased the instrument that he played on for her." Under Dahlgren's choice of art instructor, she became adept with pencil, water-color, and oils. As one who enjoyed the full social life that Natchez and Philadelphia afforded, she also quickly exhausted the repertoire of her dancing-master.[27]

Gifted as she was in art, dance, and music, Sarah showed even greater precocity with languages. Like most girls of the American upper classes, she began with French but soon outdistanced her schoolmates in her fluency with Italian, Spanish, and German. Some years later she knew the last language well enough to publish in *DeBow's Review* a serialized translation of *Uriel Acosta* (1849) by Karl Gutzkow. Finally, Sarah's step-father had her trained in law and bookkeeping, and she kept up her interest in legal studies years later, though as an intellectual rather than practical specialty. These were scarcely typical subjects for a belle in mid-nineteenth-century America, particularly a Southern one.[28]

During Sarah Ellis's years of education in Philadelphia, the teacher she found most exciting was Anne Charlotte Lynch, who became her lifelong friend. As beautiful as Sarah was plain, Anne Lynch had also lost her father, a banished Irish rebel and intellectual, when she was only four years old. In addition to this shared misfortune, both tutor and student had lively minds, high literary ambitions, and Whiggish sentiments. Like Sarah's earlier governess, Eliza Ann DuPuy, Anne Lynch, a follower of the principles of Dr. Thomas Arnold of Rugby, was already well known for her educational as well as her literary gifts.[29] Sarah, it might be said, continued to be the Northern schoolteacher's pupil for nearly the rest of her life. Although they kept up with each other until the mid-1870s, for some forty years, only one letter survives from their extensive correspondence. The friendship could be characterized as the feminine equivalent of the companionship of Thomas George Percy and John Walker, some years before.[30] Anne Lynch opened the first and most famous salon in the history of nineteenth-century Manhattan. Without much money when she began, she nevertheless gathered about her the leading intellectuals of her day. Among the guests at her "Saturday afternoons," were Horace Greeley, William Cullen Bryant, Ralph Waldo Emerson (who called her place "the house of the expanding doors"), Julia Ward Howe, Margaret Fuller, Mabel Mapes Dodge, novelist Catharine Sedgwick, the actress Fanny Kemble, G. P. Morris (known for "Woodman Spare That Tree"), and many others. Visiting celebrities also were her guests: Anthony Trollope, Charles Dickens, and Charles Kingsley among them. Charles Butler, a wealthy investment broker in New York and Rhode Island, created a trust for her, the income from which provided her with ever more elegant town houses in which to hold her Saturday gatherings. Poe gave the first reading of "The Raven" at her house on 9th Street, and he also helped her with her poetic efforts. Herman Melville, "with his cigar and his Spanish eyes," regaled her guests with stories of his adventures in the South Seas. But she was best known for her *Handbook of Universal Literature* (1860), which remained in print for over fifty years. Her contacts with the intellectual world were expanded when in 1855 she married Vincenzo Botta, an aristocrat from Savoy, whom Sarah Dorsey always referred to as "the Professor" because he taught Italian literature at New York University.[31]

Sarah Ellis's aesthetic and literary tastes almost exactly paralleled those of her friend in New York City. Sarah tried to bring some Northern sophistication to Natchez by introducing a salon similar to Anne Botta's. Although conventional in her social ambitions, Sarah was too competitive, talented, and impatient to be popular with the local belles and matrons. As early as 1849, Eliza Quitman, wife of John A. Quitman, a wealthy Natchez planter, militia general, and sometime governor of the state, gossiped that "Sarah Ellis is practicing so I am told for a great Soiree, she tries hard poor girl to be thought fashionable."[32] Sarah would have been better advised to entertain after a horse-race rather than invite guests to discuss the latest work of John Stuart Mill or Thomas Carlyle.

Sarah Ellis was not handsome; she had long black hair, parted in the middle—the same color as her grandmother Sarah's. Yet she had determination and vivacity—and a sizable fortune—making her quite eligible for a match to be universally applauded. In late 1852, Sarah became affianced to Samuel Worthington Dorsey, originally from Ellicott Mills, Maryland, eighteen years her senior. Dorsey's family tree had roots traceable to the mid-seventeenth century in Baltimore and Howard counties, Maryland. Dorsey's father, Thomas B. Dorsey, had served as Chief Justice of the Maryland Supreme Court. In 1838, his son, a graduate of the Yale School of Law, seeking a place where he could establish his independence from the large Dorsey clan, left Maryland to build a law practice in Vicksburg. The competition proved very stiff, however, and he turned to managing large plantations in Tensas Parish in the possession of his own family as well as those in the Dahlgren-Routh-Ellis connection: Elkridge (belonging to Thomas himself); Last Retreat (which had been one of the Rouths' properties); Limerick; Point Pleasant; and Buck Ridge, (the latter three Ellis and Dahlgren lands). With 155 slaves producing 515 bales of cotton, Elkridge alone grew in value to $122,840. The other, smaller plantations were also successful under his overseeing.[33]

Samuel Dorsey had not inherited his father's intellectuality or force of personality. According to one source, in all their married life of twenty-two years, "he made no material contribution to the superior abilities of Mrs. Dorsey." Sarah Dorsey had chosen the same kind of husband that her aunts Catherine Warfield and Ellen Percy Lee had picked. Dorsey was practical-minded, vigorous in the planting profession, respected by his neighbors, and at ease with hunting friends and associates in the International Order of Odd Fellows.[34] Marriages of intellectual women to men of lesser mental exertion were not uncommon in the greater world beyond Natchez. Lydia Sigourney, the Connecticut poet, Lydia Maria Child, the abolitionist and novelist, Elizabeth Cady Stanton, the suffragist, all married men of lesser gifts than their own. In the South, however, the kind of match that Sarah Dorsey made could scarcely be helped. A woman with unusual talents had few options since so few Southern planters of Sarah's social rank took an interest in matters of the mind.

At Routhland in Natchez, before three hundred guests, the couple was married by Dr. Joseph B. Stratton, the local Presbyterian clergyman, on the evening of January 19, 1853. The groom was forty-two, his bride twenty-four. Step-father Dahlgren lavished upon his step-daughter silver goblets, a full set of silver flatware, a gold thimble, and other items of considerable worth.[35] Yet, the gifts did not overcome a persistent coolness between them. Sarah Dorsey had long sensed Dahlgren's tacit disapproval of the match. Shortly before the wedding Sarah had asked him for his opinion of her choice. Dahlgren replied that Dorsey's respectability was beyond question but, as he recalled years later, he explained that her fiancé was mentally "inactive, and it was like wedding the living to the dead to marry such an animated creature to a man of phlegmatic temperament who was so many years her senior." After the ceremony, Sarah made sure that their paths crossed as seldom as possible.[36]

Having moved to Elkridge, one of the Dorseys' Tensas Parish plantations, the couple depended on their neighbors near Lake St. Joseph for their social life. There were a number of Rouths in the parish—Matilda, Stephen, Andrew, John Knox, and Calvin. Each had a fortune as large as that represented by the Dorseys' Elkridge, if not larger. Aunt Matilda Routh had married Dr. Allen T. Bowie of Maryland, who was the brother of Senator Reverdy Johnson's wife. John Routh was married to Margaret Williams, the granddaughter of former Royal Navy Lieutenant Robert Percy of the "legitimate" Percy line and sister of Mississippi Senator Seargent A. Prentiss's wife, Mary Williams. John Routh alone grew nearly 9000 bales of cotton in one year. In total, the fifteen Routh plantations around Lake St. Joseph utilized the labor of 5000 slaves on land comprising 20,000 acres.[37]

In 1803 old Job Routh of Natchez, founder of the family, had built a spacious house called Winter Quarters in the future Tensas Parish to serve as a hunting lodge on lands he had acquired from the Spanish authorities. Dr. Haller Nutt, a Routh descendant, was its owner when the Dorseys arrived. A graduate in medicine from the University of Kentucky, he was a planter of considerable learning and scientific interests, a figure much like Dr. Samuel Brown. Also close by the Dorseys' Elkridge plantation was the estate of Sarah Dorsey's first cousin, John Knox Routh, and her Uncle John was not far away. The latter owned Holly Wood consisting of 10,000 acres. According to the census of 1860, he was worth over $500,000 in real estate and $300,000 in personal property. He and his son, John Knox Routh, possessed more than 500 slaves.[38] At Christmas, Sarah's Uncle John used to gather the family from far and wide for a banquet over which he, "the Patriarchal Head of the family," as she put it, presided in splendor.[39]

Although surrounded by kinspeople and living at a distance from Natchez, the Dorseys could not easily separate themselves from Sarah's step-father. From time to time, Dahlgren and the newlyweds both had need of each other's capital, and, though few documents survive, transactions beneficial to all parties were doubtless arranged often.[40] By the customs—and laws—of the day Samuel Dorsey, not his wife, would have directed matters involving her properties.[41] Although Dahlgren had tried to prepare her for the exactitudes of business, Sarah's refusal to participate in the financial side of family affairs had much to do with her resentment of her step-father.

One suspects that aunts Catherine Warfield and Ellen Lee encouraged her to worship the memory of Thomas George Ellis. On their long summer visits the aunts told and retold stories illustrating their half-brother's qualities. The poem, lines of which appear at the beginning of the chapter, reminded her never to forget her indebtedness to him. Thomas Ellis had been the Ware sisters' only brother, a circumstance that could well have encouraged their hero-worship. At the same time, death claimed so many in Catherine Warfield's life, until by 1853, none of her family was left. Along with her mother and father, she had lost this favored half-brother, Tom Ellis, and then her half-sister, the deranged Mary Jane Ellis LaRoche—both dead by their early thirties—and finally, her sister Ellen Lee, who was not yet thirty. Catherine's attention was bound to focus upon this gifted niece, the precocious, interesting child of the dead brother whose life should always remain a model for other family members to emulate. Sarah reciprocated her aunt's regard for her.

Indeed, after Ellen Lee's death in 1849, Sarah and her aunt Catherine shared intimacies in a way that she and her mother Mary Malvina Routh

Dahlgren, one suspects, could not because of their temperamental differences. During the mid-1850s Sarah had helped Aunt Catherine through her depression and grief over the loss of sister and father so that she resumed writing fiction once more. (Sarah would not herself adopt that career until some years later.) As time passed, aunt and niece became ever more like mother and daughter in their relationship, particularly after Mary Dahlgren's death from heart disease in 1858.[42] The connection of niece and aunt kept the flame of her father's memory aglow. Sarah's search for an ideal father—something Dahlgren could never have personified—was to have substantial consequences many years after her marriage to the elderly—and fatherly—Samuel Dorsey.

In those relatively tranquil prewar years, Sarah Dorsey had secured her self-esteem in marriage. But what was the cultivated woman supposed to do at home? A Memphis journalist in 1924 caught something of her spirit when noting that Sarah Dorsey "had felt an infinite longing all her life for something higher and better than the ordinary routine."[43] A lonely plantation existence could not suffice, and so she organized a heavy calendar of events, setting a magnificent table and inviting guests from far and wide for lengthy stays. With all her talents and vigor, Sarah Dorsey threw herself into organizing these occasions—the staging of small dinners of learned friends and large parties for the local squires, ladies' teas and fêtes, poetry and fiction readings, and musical recitals, during which she played her harp. Moreover, she guided the discourse in parlor and dining room.

Like so many Southerners of her day, she preferred the romantic literary tradition. In her biography of Henry Watkins Allen, the second Confederate governor of Louisiana and a close friend, she provided a glimpse of the social life that she had arranged, very much in imitation of Anne Botta's "conversazioni" in New York, but with a distinctly Southern style.[44] She recalled that on one occasion, her gamekeeper had shot one of seven swans that had made their winter quarters at Lake St. Joseph, and his mistress added the bird to the evening's menu. After the cygnet was brought to the table, stuffed, at her direction, with mashed apples and celery sauce, only one guest ventured to name the creature they were consuming, calling it "the tenderest goose" and largest he had ever tasted. The hostess laughed and replied, " 'Yes, it was the *Moeonian* goose." Beating the other guests to the mark, Allen at once saw her meaning and said: "It was a swan! Et quæ Moeonias celebrârant carmine rapas/ Fluminæ volucres medio caluere Caystro."[45] "And those winged creatures [swans] which crowded the Moeonian banks in song were singed with fires in the channel of Cayster." The reference, from Ovid's *Metamorphoses* (II, 1.252), deals with Phaeton, who drives the chariot of his father, Sol, the sun god, too close to earth and dries up such rivers as the Caystro and destroys the water fowl. Such were the classical exchanges of the gentry class—at least as Sarah Dorsey liked to recall in grimmer times after the Civil War.[46]

Also in keeping with the Old South's reputation for refinement and romance, the hostess at Elkridge arranged elaborate "tournaments," as they were called. Gentlemen of the surrounding countryside were invited to ride in exhibition or play a form of polo. The Clyde Ratcliffs, neighbors who many years later bought Elkridge from her estate, recalled those happy days. The contests, they remembered, reached their climax when a young lady was crowned queen of the tournament and given the task of dispensing prizes. An elaborate ball usually followed.[47] No doubt such activities, especially when the guests were gifted conversationalists, were the talk—and envy—of the community. But these fêtes and balls for the rich among the nine hundred whites in the county were unlikely to satisfy Sarah Dorsey's fitful spirit.[48]

Unable to bear children, Sarah Dorsey threw herself into the task of treating her slaves as if they were her youngsters. An early step was to have the Rev. J. W. Philson of St. Joseph's Episcopal Church marry slave couples. Although such unions were not recognized in law, four couples wed at the Episcopal church between 1855 and 1857. In July 1855, as their sponsor, she had the rector baptize forty-seven of the Dorsey family's slave children. A year and a half later Bishop Leonidas Polk confirmed Sarah and Samuel Dorsey at St. Joseph's, along with four of their slaves.[49] Braving the laws of Louisiana, she founded a school where sixty to seventy slaves, young and old, learned to read and write. Her first objective was Bible study, but the plantation academy gradually became more secular and utilitarian, and religious instruction was confined to Sundays. As late as 1940, Dave Dodson, who remembered that era as a pupil, warmly spoke of the July 4 "Exhibition" that closed the school year with class exercises and picnics. Icy Jenkins, another graduate of "Miss Sarah's," recalled her teaching the Bible and playing the harp in a log house used for Sunday school. She added that after emancipation Thomas Wright, a young Englishman hired by Sarah, ran the school for the freed people of Elkridge, most of whom did not leave the premises. She also sold to some former slaves small tracts of land at the price of a bale of cotton (400 pounds). Icy Jenkins told a visitor in 1940, "Everybody looked up to Miss Sarah." [50]

In perhaps her first literary venture Sarah Dorsey wrote an Episcopal Service Manual that was designed specifically, as she saw it, for the slave mind and temperament. Before the religious guide appeared in print, however, the war came, and publication was postponed, never to be revived.[51] How the subjects of her benevolence reacted to Episcopalian High Churchmanship cannot be known. Yet, as a plantation mistress, she was by far the most personally involved in the improvement of black life of all the Percy connections, male or female, until the planter-poet Will Percy's day. She also was solicitous about the plight of handicapped children. In her later novel *Athalie* she describes an efficient and solicitous staff of a hospital devoted to their care. Since much of her fiction consists of barely disguised autobiography, perhaps she was herself engaged in a similar charity, though helping handicapped children in an organized fashion was a rarity in the United States of that time.

ૹ ૹ

Like most Southerners, Sarah Dorsey found her life profoundly altered as a result of disunion and war. The exciting events of secession and military preparation were bound to arouse new feelings. Like most of her neighbors and relations, that is, her Percy, Ellis, and Dahlgren kinfolk, she and her husband were nationally minded Whigs—followers of Henry Clay, whom her step-grandfather Nathaniel Ware had most particularly admired. That conservative position, with a Burkean cast, would remain a persistent theme in Percy family history—an opposition to a mobocracy that threatened social order. In part it was based upon traditional American values. As the historian Daniel Howe observes, Whiggery in America was not merely a party. It was a way of living, most particularly for those belonging to the upper classes, North and South.[52] There was, however, almost an English quality to the political beliefs of the Percy contingent—as if Charles Percy's Tory sympathies and Robert Percy's naval loyalties reached from beyond the grave. Sarah Dorsey's politics were affected by her strong affiliations with upper-class Northern families, by friendship with such dedicated Unionists as Anne Lynch Botta, and by her own broadly transatlantic outlook in tastes and literary preferences. As a result, she as well as her husband and others in their Whiggish Louisiana circle looked upon such fire-eaters as Robert Barnwell Rhett of South Carolina or Albert Gallatin Brown of Mississippi as reckless, rabble-rousing zealots.

After Lincoln's election and the popular outcry in the Lower South against "Black Republicanism," the Dorseys and their friends still hoped for some compromise to save the Union. Like so many other Conditional Unionists, as they were called, Samuel Dorsey thought the Lower South should await a general consensus among all Southerners before undertaking so dangerous a step as disunion. As a delegate from Tensas Parish to the state secession convention meeting in January 1861, Samuel Dorsey had opposed immediate withdrawal, a stipulation that hotheads quickly overrode.[53]

Armed with the zeal with which she had organized her parties and her plantation Sunday school, Sarah Dorsey turned to the war effort. The hostilities broke out just as she had passed the age of thirty. Wars create heroes by the score, and, as Sarah Dorsey saw it, heroes needed their priestesses. P. G. T. Beauregard of Louisiana, hero at First Manassas, was one of her deities. She thought his military instincts were derived in part from "the ducal family of the Reggios of Genoa" on his maternal side. "*Lineage tells,* the Southern people think!"[54] She also considered General Albert Sidney Johnston, who died at Shiloh, a worthy addition to her collection of icons. "Truly, his was a noble heart." In showering praise upon

Confederates, Sarah Dorsey "was actuated," declared a reporter, "not only by friendship and zeal, but a sort of hero-worship, which our late disastrous struggle was well calculated to arouse in the Southern breast." [55]

Above all others, however, she most admired manly divines. The Rev. Joseph Buck Stratton, the handsome minister of the First Presbyterian Church in Natchez, had once caught Sarah Ellis's eye before she married Samuel Dorsey in 1853.[56] Sarah Dorsey found her Confederate ideal manifested in the Right Rev. Leonidas L. Polk. The imposing West Pointer had left the army in 1827, two years before she was born, converted to the Episcopal faith, and risen to the rank of bishop of Louisiana. Polk may have been flattered by Sarah Dorsey's animated regard because his own wife, Frances Devereux, was a rather timorous, unadventurous soul. Before the outbreak of sectional hostilities, Sarah Dorsey had hoped to establish an order of deaconesses with his help. Polk had encouraged her plans, stating on their last visit in 1860 "that she should do everything in her power, as long as she lived, toward the establishment of a Sisterhood of Mercy in New Orleans." [57]

When the war came, Bishop Polk put aside his pastoral staff, cope, and miter to wear the sword and uniform of a brigadier-general, although a civilian since resigning his army commission after graduation from West Point thirty-four years earlier. Sarah Dorsey could scarcely have been more mesmerized: a clergyman in Confederate regalia. She organized the family to prepare a proper battalion standard. "The staff was made for me by my Cousin John Bowie," she wrote the warrior-clergyman-slaveholder. "The lance head [was] fashioned & polished by the hand of my Uncle John Routh," the wealthiest planter in her neighborhood. She devised the banner herself, based on the Labarum of Constantine the Great. "Recognizing the holiness of our Cause I have not feared to use the Sacred Christian symbol, especially as I designed to put it in the hands of a Christian Apostle." In her opinion, the Confederate cause was as sacred and moral as any that Constantine or medieval crusader ever fought. Earlier Christians had battled against savage heathens and infidels, but "we are fighting the Battle of the Cross against the Modern Barbarians who would rob a Christian people of Country, Liberty, and Life." The outcome could not be doubted, but if God willed Confederate defeat, she continued, "there will live defiance and resistance to those who would tread us beneath their feet." The donor of the colors concluded, "When the land is conquered it will be time for us to die." [58]

From her perspective, the war increased her sense of slaveholding responsibility. Sometime in 1863, probably at the time the Dorsey plantation Elkridge was burned to the ground by a contingent of Ulysses S. Grant's troops, she and her husband accompanied well over a hundred slaves and two overseers to new lands in East Texas. As the Dorseys hastened westward, they learned of the plundering and burning of the houses in their neighborhood—the destruction of rosewood dining tables, desks, chairs, and of pianos and harps from Erard's and Pleyel. "From one house alone, that of Mr. J[ohn] R[outh], Ellett's Marine Brigade stole over thirty thousand dollars worth of table silver," she later wrote.[59] The "Patriarch" would not be entertaining his kinspeople at Christmas banquets in the grand style any more.

The journey was harsh, particularly since measles broke out, and many died. Sarah Dorsey shared the hardships with her field hands. She supervised the nursing and preparation of meals. Her tent, which had been made from carpet material, leaked in the rain. For some ten days during their flight, she ran the encampment herself in the absence of her husband. Although she had only a small supply of quinine in her medical stock, she gave it all to the mother of two slave children, stricken with malaria, and did not withhold it for possible future use by whites in the camp.[60]

Once they arrived somewhere in East Texas, Sarah Dorsey sought to help the cause as best she could. Unlike Virginia Clay, Mary Chesnut, and other well-known Rebel matrons who did little more than roll bandages or attend patriotic fairs, Sarah Dorsey worked as a regular nurse in a Texas Confederate hospital.[61] The proprieties mattered to her not at all. By no means were these charitable activities simply a way to kill time or promote self-congratulation, but with a sense of romantic heroism often to be repeated by the male members of the family, she found in war that purposefulness and glorious risk-taking that not only galvanized her energies but also provided a welcome relief from the perils of boredom and vacuity. Always working within the framework of Southern convention, she was a firm believer in the code of honor in all its noblest manifestations, as she deemed them. By such means she and other Southerners—rich and poor alike—justified their rejection of Northern, especially abolitionist, indignities and asserted their claims to independence. In her extensive library, Sarah Dorsey owned and knew thoroughly *Meditations of Marcus Aurelius,* in which the Stoic philosopher and Roman emperor stressed the steadiness of purpose that could face down inevitable adversity. In light of defeat and the horrors of war, the principles of Marcus Aurelius inspired Sarah Dorsey just as they did Anne Botta and others belonging to the Whig circles in which these women moved.[62] Later, other members of the family would also seek to live by the precepts of Aurelian honor.

Somehow, in the midst of the troubles that war, dislocation, and mere survival entailed, Sarah Dorsey found the time—and the need—to write. For her, the creative act helped to alleviate anxieties and the sense of helplessness that war engendered. From June 1863 to January 1864 the *Southern Literary Messenger* published her novel *Agnes Graham* in serial form. Scenes shift abruptly, characters materialize in one place or another without explanation. Its defects revealed a novice with much to learn about the craft. The novel was a fantasy about life in the now fast disappearing Old South—a society of well-traveled grandees, parties, and philosophical discussion around the tea table. But the theme that generates the plot consisted of the Percy family's misfortune with mental illness and its persistence through the generations.

The heroine, whose name the title bears, was based upon Sarah Dorsey herself. In the fashion of the sentimental genre of the day, Agnes, a young virgin of Natchez society with great talents in music and linguistics, falls in love with her first cousin Robert Selman, a well-educated young physician. The pair plan to marry until an aunt informs Agnes that their common grandmother's insanity, which she reveals to Agnes for the first time, suggests a problem of blood inheritance. Madness, the aunt recounts, has run through the family's history. The great-grandfather, an English army officer of ancient lineage, who had begun a life in Louisiana with an heiress, had drowned himself in a lake, Agnes Graham's aunt relates. The news staggers the susceptible heroine, and, following recovery from the obligatory attack of brain fever, she promises God never to marry cousin Robert and thus prevent the family curse from arising in future generations.

The novelist reflected how the women in the Percy line of that generation were concerned with the fate of the family. Disappointed in love, Robert disappears, while Agnes fends off a fortune-hunting villain during a European tour—until she marries a Samuel Dorsey-like character, an elderly family friend to whom she feels kindly but is not emotionally attached. After the husband's death, Agnes converts to High Anglicanism, and, just as Sarah herself had dreamed of applying her great wealth to a religious purpose, so Agnes endows a hospital for the poor of New Orleans and heads an Episcopalian order of nuns to run it. Thus, in fiction at least, Agnes Graham fulfills the pledge that the author had made to Bishop Polk years before. Quite abruptly, Robert Selman reappears, and Agnes, suffering from a weak heart, cannot master her surprise and expires. Her life ends in a state of grace—chaste and true to her pledge to put genetic duty over love. Although the novel had little artistic merit, it revealed, as had her aunts' poems and novels, the self-consciousness of these women regarding the family's history. The serialized work enjoyed much popularity and was reprinted in book form by Catherine Warfield's Philadelphia publisher, Claxton, Remsen, and Haffelfinger, after the war.

Sarah Dorsey's second major venture into print offered the contemporary reader a much deeper and highly evocative experience. Her topic might seem most unpromising: the life of an old-fashioned, guileless, and gravely charming wartime governor of Louisiana: Henry Watkins Allen. The work appeared before the end of 1866. Having traversed the Rhine River Valley and toured the sights of Paris with Henry Allen in 1859, the Dorseys were very fond of the bluff planter and lawyer who shared their Whig convictions. After serving two terms in the state legislature as a Whig and Know Nothing, in 1860 he had joined the Democrats. Like Leonidas Polk, Allen, as Sarah Dorsey put it, *"worshipped intellect"* in women.[63] Also like Polk, Allen belonged on her roster of heroes and father figures, being twenty years her senior. As a leader of wartime relief for the poor, an advocate of emancipation for slaves as reward for Confederate service, and other bold if not always welcomed innovations, Allen much deserved her praise.[64]

Sarah Dorsey's study of Governor Allen was surprising in its perceptiveness of the subject, its easy command of military events, and the energy of the prose—much superior to the pedestrian nature of *Agnes Graham*. But it also showed her dedication to the code to which the Percys then and later adhered. Commenting on an incident in which Allen challenged a Union officer to a duel, duly ignored, she remarked, "The federal did not understand *Sir Lancelot, redivivus!* " Sarah Dorsey defended Allen as "a Representative Man—his virtues and his faults were entirely Southern." Such conduct, she rhapsodized, set the South apart as a civilization superior to the money-grubbing North. In pagan times, the duel, she argued, was thought to represent "the direct interposition of the Gods in behalf of the just sword," which superstition "was grafted by popular custom upon Christianity, and gave the laws to knight-errantry." Expanding on the theme of honor, the biographer quoted a long letter in which a friend had defended Allen's conduct and the duel in general. Its author argued that civil law could not properly handle calumnies upon a lady's or a gentleman's reputation. Couldn't a monetary settlement take the duel's place? the correspondent asked. The answer was: never. "Men of honor and the brothers of women of honor" never deviated from that reply. All must be risked on the gamble of life itself because "true honor is an inestimable jewel; the desire to preserve it overcomes the love of life."[65] In the Percy branch of Sarah's family adherence to that code would outlast the erosion of honor in the post-Civil War South.

In writing the biography of her neighbor and friend, Sarah Dorsey's literary purpose, however, went beyond the biographical—and filial. She used her study of Allen to work out her understanding of a Southern woman's role in a male world and even the status of women as writers and thinkers in general, conceding, however, that biographical writing was a most unfeminine occupation. She proposed that the "feminine mind," for all its subtlety and occasional acuteness, was "entirely too *subjective,* to attempt in any way the writing of *history*." She was apparently unaware that such women as Emma Willard, whose American history text was to appear in twenty-four editions, had long since overcome the barrier that Dorsey approached so demurely.[66] Despite her misgivings, Sarah Dorsey wrote a most engaging life history, as contemporary critics recognized.[67] In her evaluation of the women's contribution to the war effort, Sarah Dorsey showed much less modesty, arguing that the men may have stumbled into an unnecessary war and managed it miserably, but white women of the Confederacy, almost without exception, had done much more than their part. They had undertaken all those hard chores once in the province of their slaves. "We were proud to be the mothers, wives, and sisters of our heroes, *and to suffer with them*," she exulted, and "we were right, *very* right, to aid *'our own,'* even, like our Pelican, with our very heart's blood. We are not to be blamed for the instinct of nature and true woman-hood." [68] Although truculently expressed, such sentiments were anything but feminist. Women in war, particularly in the honor-conscious South, were always expected to rise to the occasion, offering themselves as examples of self-sacrifice, resoluteness, and physical courage.

Her life of Henry Allen was also a contribution to the development of the Lost Cause legend that would continue to dominate Southern memory over the next fifty years or more. She might even be called the mother of the Lost Cause, that curious postwar movement that mixed legend, mourning, and anger. There existed, she remarked, three forms of virtue: "With the Christian martyr it is faith; with the savage it is honor; with the republican it is liberty." In forming the Confederacy, the whites of the South "conscientiously believed all these to be attacked." No answer, she claimed, except war for Southern independence could erase the stigma of insult and degradation that the Yankees had thrust upon them. [69]

Perhaps, she admitted, the Southern people had been wrong, but even at the end of the conflict, she continued, "The 'Confederate Cross,' we were persuaded, was raised in honor," and in defeat, "we felt it went down behind the purple sea of war without *dishonor*." Nonetheless, hope is gone, "Be silent, then, and let us weep!" The only recourse was to live by the Stoic principles of Marcus Aurelius who exemplified the virtues of patience, endurance, coolness, and strength to rise up from pain to glory. Determination and pride, she believed, provided reasons for "some glimmering trust, some faint hopes, in the resurrection of my native land. Allah, Akbar!" These sentiments were hardly signals of much optimism. In the preface she spoke feelingly, for instance, of her hope to freshen "the epitaphs, which are already yielding to the corroding tooth of Time, on the grave stones of Southern heroes." Only in her mid-thirties, she was rather young to concern herself with "Old Mortality," as she put it. [70] Undoubtedly Sarah Dorsey had found the historical genre aroused her passionate nature in a way that fiction never did. Her reading in the field was impressive in its range and depth. She wrote a friend in 1872, "I think I read more history than most people." Her list included all the modern German, Spanish, French, and English scholarly works from Henry Hart Milman on early Christianity (eight volumes) and Bartold Georg Niebuhr on Rome before the Punic Wars (two volumes) to Blackstone's legal *Commentaries* as well as texts in Greek, Latin, and German, along with assorted works on Louisiana's *Code Napoléon* and American civil laws. [71]

Dorsey's strength lay in applications of history and events that she had personally witnessed and could depict with her painterly skill. In *Lucia Dare*, for instance, her basically non-fictional account of the flight from Louisiana to Texas has an authentic and compelling intensity. With an

artist's eye, she describes a pastoral scene during the hegira. The long cara-
van, as she calls it, passes a great meadow and stream. "Beautiful cattle,
white, speckled, and mixed with red, were quietly feeding on the rich
grasses. Some of the negroes, mounted on horses of varied color, white,
black, sorrel, were splashing across the sparkling shallow stream; the heavy
wagons, slowly descending or ascending the precipitous roads cut through
the high banks on either side; the negroes swarming about these wagons,
clinging around them, like so many bees about their comb; the variety or
color in costume; the heavier grays and purples relieved by garments more
fanciful of bright crimsons or yellows; the laughing, shouting, heaving,
pulling, holding back by the huge wagons, and the brilliant, radiant canopy
of blue fire we call 'sky,' over it all,—made one of the most striking land-
scapes I have ever seen." [72]

Although this passage would not have offended, Sarah Dorsey gained a
reputation for a harsh realism only barely detectable by the modern reader.
So stark was *Lucia Dare* thought to be that a critic as late as 1907 argued
that if Northern readers "could not appreciate" the suffering of the story's
white and black Civil War refugees, Southern readers had always found
"the scenes . . . too harrowing." [73] In *Panola,* a much more popular work,
Sarah Dorsey rather anticipates Kate Chopin by careful dissection of Louisiana upper-class society. Although no challenge to Chopin's eminence,
Dorsey offers some spirited portraits of Southern vulgarity.

Despite Sarah Dorsey's relative success as a writer of romances, a chain
of events began that might have led her along a different path, one that
would have removed her from Louisiana society. *Athalie* appeared in 1872,
but *Panola,* which was begun in 1871, was not completed and published
until 1877, by which time Sarah Dorsey knew her end was near. During
this interlude, other matters slowed her fictional creativity. One might call
it a mid-life moratorium. For her it was a time of unplanned reassessment
and also exciting intellectual ferment, as if for a time defeat and emancipation had liberated her mind along with the lives of her slaves.

CHAPTER SEVEN

Collision of Minds

> I wish I would write magnificently or do some
> little good in this world, but my work is to wait
> & learn patience.
>
> Sarah Dorsey, 1872 [1]

With the ending of war and the installation of Radical Republican government in Louisiana, Sarah Dorsey and her husband had every reason to
escape the unhappy conditions at home. They hastened from Louisiana to
renew friendships in England and the North that they had acquired in the
1850s. Despite their wartime losses, they somehow retained a large fortune,
which permitted their expensive sojourn abroad in 1871, a luxury few
other Southern plantation owners could manage even six years after the
conflict. Their itinerary included London, Paris—and, oddly, the Arabian
desert, where Samuel Dorsey decided to hunt game.

In any event, the whole experience abroad was nearly disastrous for
Sarah if not for him. In the first incident she came close to losing her life.
During the Arabian trip, Samuel Dorsey ordered the whipping of a Bedouin for theft, the common penalty of the desert. Bent on revenge, the
offender crept into Sarah Dorsey's tent one night when her husband and
party were hunting in the mountains. Armed with a long knife, the in-
truder would have slashed her, but the Dorsey's watchdog Traveler, a Russian bulldog, caught him and held him in its jaws until help arrived. At
another time during their travels, Traveler, which the couple had bought
in the Bernese Alps, prevented the theft of her jewels in a Paris hotel. She
had worn a glittering array of diamonds to a ball at the Tuilieries, which
caught the notice of a professional thief who broke in while Sarah Dorsey
was asleep and Samuel was smoking nearby with friends. The Parisian
culprit was even less lucky, however, than the malevolent Bedouin. Traveler leapt upon him and tore out his throat and, after his capture, the
burglar expired.[2] The final episode took place not long after their return
from Europe. On a trip north, the Dorseys again were lucky to survive
unharmed when their ship collided with another vessel. "It was very terrible," she wrote. "One could hear from the water around us the hoarse

cries for help from the drowning men." Boats from their ship set out but found no survivors.[3] The Dorseys' ship was not even damaged.

These adventures were sidelights as far as Sarah Dorsey was concerned. Armed with letters of introduction from Anne Botta, she was eager to strike up new friendships in the literary circles of London and reestablish connections from previous excursions. By that means, after her return to isolated Tensas Parish, she could correspond with those who shared her intellectual interests. Later reports indicate that she corresponded with some of England's leading intellectual figures. Yet her only major surviving letters were written to Edward Lyulph Stanley. Judging from the length of her responses, however, he was probably the most significant of her English contacts and one of the best placed in society. Lyulph Stanley's bitingly witty father, Edward John, the second Lord Stanley of Alderley, took a seat in all the Whig cabinets over which Lord Palmerston, his close friend, presided.[4]

The most likely first occasion for the Dorseys' association with the Stanleys was during the European tour of 1859. They were probably introduced by way of Blanche, the handsome, outspoken, and haughty Countess of Airlie and Lyulph Stanley's sister. She once averred that "no gentleman ever goes into business," a sentiment that few in the Victorian aristocracy could any longer afford to uphold as fortunes dwindled. With investments to oversee, the Earl of Airlie and his countess were frequent visitors to the United States and had become acquainted with Anne Botta. The relationship of Lady Blanche and her fox-hunting husband very much paralleled that of Sarah Dorsey and hers. By his own admission, Lord Airlie was not as "clever" as she. Lady Henrietta Maria Stanley, his mother-in-law, worried about his gaming proclivities, the losses from which had almost threatened the engagement. "His ignorance is surprising," she once complained. On the other hand, Blanche shared the Stanley women's trait of brusque manners, wicked tongue, and lively literary curiosity. Like Sarah Dorsey she was a romantic with an interest in German poetry.[5]

The relationship of the English couple casts some light on Sarah's marriage to Samuel Dorsey. In dullish husbands these intellectual women found an anchor that tethered them in the social waters of their kinspeople. As unmarried women, they had not enjoyed the mindless distractions of courtship, yet when Lord Airlie turned serious, Blanche Stanley had welcomed his professions of love. He would provide her with wealth, secure social position, and contact with the ordinary world that she thought missing from her own life. At the same time, he would seldom interfere with her own interests. Yet, her mother, Lady Stanley, gossiped, "She rather talks to him as if he were to be civilized."[6] The same may have been the case with Sarah Ellis when she met and married Samuel. Unfortunately the necessary evidence from correspondence has not survived. The arrangements were by no means perfect in the case of either couple. Yet the alternative was spinsterhood and still greater frustration. These women with intellectual ambitions had almost no professional outlet. With such similarities in their situations, Sarah Dorsey no doubt enjoyed associating with Blanche Airlie. She hoped to assist the Airlies with introductions on their next American visit.[7] The twentieth-century writer Nancy Mitford, however, remembered her grandmother Blanche as a tartar. So Sarah Dorsey must have found Maude Stanley, Lyulph's "quiet, ladylike," unmarried sister much more companionable. Maude shared her interests in painting and sketching, and they spent hours together at the National Gallery in London.[8]

Lyulph Stanley visited the Southern states in 1870. Most probably he stayed with the Dorseys at Elkridge plantation and resided in Louisiana long enough to become familiar with its tumultuous politics under Radical Republican leadership. When the Dorseys toured England in 1871, they reconfirmed their friendship with the young aristocrat's family. Lyulph Stanley himself was on the Continent at the time, but Sarah visited with his mother, Henrietta Maria, and his sister Maude, the "saint" of the family. Maude held a literary salon in Smith Square, very like Anne Botta's in New York, and did much work with the London poor. In contrast to Maude's open-heartedness, Henrietta Maria Stanley, the mother of twelve children, was almost overwhelming to the childless Sarah Dorsey. The Stanleys' Alderley Park in Cheshire, with its sixty-bedroom mansion and extensive Italianate grounds, famous among Victorian landscape enthusiasts, put the plantations of Tensas Parish in the shadows. Lyulph's mother took Sarah Dorsey to the Kensington Museum, held a dinner party in her honor, and wrote her son, "I found her very pleasant & we got on very well together."[9]

The reasons for Sarah Dorsey's attraction to young Stanley were evident from the start. First, he was an intellectual with broad interests in the same sorts of subjects—literature, history, psychology, contemporary politics, and religious controversy—that she so much enjoyed. Most particularly Stanley believed in universal manhood suffrage and republican government—an admiration of American politics that swelled Sarah's pride in her homeland.[10] Second, his bachelor state, athletic physique, and blond whiskers made him an attractive correspondent to write to and think about. The intimacy between the American plantation mistress and the English aristocrat also rested upon similarities of temperament and moral values. As the epitome of Victorian rectitude, Lyulph Stanley detested human sin and failure and made few allowances for them. It was a characteristic of Anne Botta as well. Stanley regarded Sarah Dorsey, who was ten years his senior, more as a friendly aunt than as an intellectual companion. Upon first meeting Sarah Dorsey, Henrietta Maria Stanley wrote her son, "She is much younger than you represented her."[11]

Evangelical convictions about moral obligations survived among transatlantic intellectuals even as they were losing faith in the doctrine of the Trinity. Sarah Dorsey shared the Stanley family's common perspective that the world was the arena in which Good and Evil battled for supremacy. In fact, she argued that "every pain & *sin* have their place in the lifting up of man into a higher plane." [12] Being the Victorians they were, both the American and Englishman believed that tenacity of purpose and consolidated focus would win the day, a belief that the nineteenth-century members of the Percy clan fervently espoused. Stanley also had opinions sure to attract a woman of Mrs. Dorsey's nationalistic feelings. His ideas about the march of progress, universal suffrage, at least for men, and the need for other earnest reforms of the Empire along "American" lines appealed to her. [13] Although a brother had become a Roman Catholic bishop with the tastes of a Renaissance Pope, Lyulph prided himself on his own free-thinking principles. (Years later he passed on his iconoclasm to his daughter Venetia, a free spirit who was Lord Asquith's mistress during World War I.) [14] For Sarah Dorsey, association with such an interesting and exotic English family must have been exciting.

Another factor was subtler—the moral tenor of the Stanley family. Sarah was deeply impressed by the strong-mindedness of the Stanley women, particularly Henrietta Maria. She was a member of the ancient house of Dillon, and had become "a personage" noted for her advanced feminism, including the founding of Girton College, Cambridge. The philosopher and mathematician Bertrand Russell considered his grandmother one of the most "intimidating" people he had ever known. In one of her pronouncements, famous in family annals, she included Russell when she once sniffed, "I have no intelligent grandchildren." Sarah Dorsey admired Lady Stanley's ardent liberalism as much as her "rare social qualities." On one occasion, Sarah Dorsey gushed to Lyulph, if only "all mothers" could be "like your Mother! I don't think I ever told you how much I admired Lady Stanley." [15] With Lyulph abroad, Sarah Dorsey did not meet his most intimate intellectual friends, for one, Benjamin Jowett, the Platonist scholar at Oxford. She was later to say that she wished she knew Jowett because she expected great insights from his forthcoming book on religion. The redoubtable Lady Stanley, however, had decided that a visit at the house of splenetic Thomas Carlyle would be more entertaining than tea with the timid Oxford don. In July 1871 the mistress of Alderley Hall took Sarah to meet the renowned critic of modern middle-class vulgarity. According to Lady Stanley's report to Lyulph, Carlyle "discoursed" to her American guest "for one hour & a half & she was most delighted." [16]

Sarah Dorsey was most impressed with Lyulph Stanley's dedication to humanitarian causes. At the time their correspondence was drawing to a close in 1872, he became an assistant commissioner under the Friendly Societies. Although differing from his American friend in his strident agnosticism, he was Evangelical in his enthusiasm for moral and educational reform. As a Southerner suspicious of voluntary organizations like the Northern abolitionist chapters before the war, she teased him for undue trust in the efficacy of his beloved "friendly societies." Stanley was little different from many Victorians of his day. Intellectuals such as he—as well as the Southern plantation lady—tried to unite the contradictions of modernism and science on the one hand and tradition and moral, if not spiritual, faith on the other. They sought a balance between Belief and Unbelief in the natural order of things even as the foundations of Christian morality were eroding.[17]

Sarah Dorsey was not immune to such unsettling trends in Victorian culture. Having experienced war, emancipation, and disruptions of every sort, she might well have questioned the existence of a God. After all, her deity had not favored the cause in whose name she had given Bishop Polk the regimental banner. In one of his letters, Stanley had argued that he could not "accept the revelations of the religions of the world," whereas, she replied, she could. But having reached the conclusion that all religions were valid or at least valuable, she came close to questioning whether Christianity had a transcendent claim of authenticity. This position was one that Matthew Arnold had articulated in his poem "Dover Beach" in 1854—the receding tide in the "Sea of Faith." [18] Arnold, a favorite poet among the Percy connections, then and later, was well appreciated in the Stanley household. He was a particular friend of Sarah's sometime correspondent, Arthur Penryhn Stanley, Dean of Westminster Abbey and Lyulph's cousin.

All that Sarah Dorsey could offer on this point was the sentiment that had I "been Socrates I should also have sacrificed the cock to Aesculapius." She admitted that she responded to the culture in which she was brought up. "I should be a Theist anywhere and *here* I am a Xtian because it is the best for our civilization & I require such a faith." Such a position would have precluded missionizing the world. She criticized Lyulph Stanley for making "apologies for those *'unconscious'* scoundrels"—the Mrs. Jellybys of the age—who ran the mission agencies. "Ah! it is well, perhaps, that the heart of my friend is softer, than his *head,"* Sarah Dorsey chided the young philanthropist. A culturally based Christianity was sufficient for her. Augusta Jane Evans Wilson, another but religiously more conventional contemporary Southern novelist, however, would have found Sarah Dorsey's faith heretical in its acceptance of relative rather than absolute superiority.[19]

Yet, Sarah Dorsey was cautious in expressing all her religious ideas to her skeptical friend. Perhaps she sensed that a full revelation might open a breach between them. If so, she was right. Henry Stanley, Lyulph's eldest brother, and heir to the titles and estates, had joined the Muhammedan faith and dressed like an Arab, much to the Stanleys' dismay. (When his funeral at Alderley Park was conducted according to its unfamiliar rites, one of his brothers remarked that he had "lived like a dog" and deserved to be "buried like a dog.") Thus, Sarah Dorsey's reports about the allurements of Eastern religions would have had no welcome at Alderley Hall. Nor did Lady Stanley favor speculations about reincarnation and other forms of spiritualism which Sarah Dorsey and other Victorians found intriguing. Lady Stanley wrote him that she had received from "Mrs. Dorsey" a novel by her aunt, Catherine Warfield, and "a book on the Other World which is not in my way."[20]

No matter what the Stanleys thought of her religious pursuits, while in England in 1871, Sarah Dorsey ventured into the realms of Emanuel Swedenborg and Eastern mysticism. Her interest was probably first aroused by Anne Botta and Anna Leonowens. Sarah Dorsey had come to admire not only their inquiries into religion but also their reformist principles about women and slavery. Anna Leonowens's books, *The English Governess at the Siamese Court* and *The Romance of the Harem,* were very much the rage in the early 1870s. Both friends—Anne Botta and Anna Leonowens—had taken up the study of religions in the Far East. Eagerly they read the "old Vedic teachings" of India as well as works on Buddhism. Anna Leonowens romantically believed that the latter religion better recognized the rights of women than did Western cultures.[21]

The case for Anna Leonowens, however, was not so self-evident as Dorsey and Botta fancied. She is known today through the Rogers and Hammerstein musical comedy based on Margaret Landon's *Anna and the King of Siam* (1944), but in her own time she was a very controversial figure. Travelers in Siam disputed her accounts of courtly life and her claims regarding feminist influences in the Buddhist monasteries. Nor was she reliable about her own background, claiming to be a Welsh-born daughter of an army officer when her father was a poor sergeant and her birthplace India. In her adolescence she apparently linked herself to various men in the Middle East, south Asia, and Australia about whom little was known and much suspected. Whatever her background was, her stories about King Mongkut's harem of eighty-two concubines stirred strong feminist reactions. Leonowens explained in her work *The English Governess:* "how I have pitied those ill-fated sisters of mine, imprisoned without a crime!"[22] As critics at the time pointed out, Mrs. Leonowens had no sense of cultural context. She portrayed King Mongkut as an unconscionable villain, who ruled over victimized innocents. In actuality, the harem served as an institutional means to hold the country together, its inmates being privileged hostages from the ranks of the inland nobility.

Sarah Dorsey and her liberal friend Anne Botta saw matters through the eyes of the English governess. They detected no irony in a former slaveholder denouncing the king of Siam. Yet Mongkut was more an authentic reformer in his culture than almost anyone in the old Confederacy had been in an American context. No doubt Sarah Dorsey could easily applaud such ennobling examples of womanhood as the exotic harem inmates offered. To have found parallels in the lives of women closer to home— Sojourner Truth, Harriet Tubman, and the ordinary female slave—would not, however, have occurred to her. Putting aside all the questions about their heroine's arguable past, she and Anne Botta urged Anna Leonowens to undertake a tour. She was to publicize her ideas about freedom for all people—but especially women. "In truth A. B. & I have [been] instrumental in persuading Mrs. Leonowens to give these Lectures," Sarah proudly wrote Lyulph, "hence the interest we both take in her success, which has been so far quite remarkable." When Stanley expressed his doubts about the motives of Sarah Dorsey's client, she replied, "I would like you to know at any rate she is making money & that's something for a poor [woman] without any."[23] Women, after all, had as much right to profit from their experiences as any man, she reasoned.

Stanley remained unconvinced about Anna Leonowens. To counter his influence Sarah Dorsey sought to win over the male intellectuals whom she knew. She wrote Thomas Carlyle, enclosing a copy of her friend's book, and told Stanley that one of Anne Botta's kindred had once known Anna Leonowens in Siam and thought "most highly of her." She also distributed copies of Anna Leonowens's feminist works to Dean Stanley of Westminster Abbey, Gabriel Rossetti, and others whom she thought would benefit from the exposure. Sarah Dorsey's defense of the romantic Leonowens represented the high water-mark of her interest in radical ideas: feminism, antislavery, and religious exploration. All three were very much in the atmosphere of the early post-Civil War period, although such concerns would have been thought insufferable in her native Deep South. Often at this juncture of her life she spoke of hoping to learn new things, meet new people, and reflect on fresh ideas. "I envy you your Oxford Dinners!" your "constant communion with such intellects as you have about every where," she wrote Lyulph Stanley. "Collision with such minds would be to me *ecstatic.* I should learn all the time, so delightfully."[24]

With regard to religion, she was no less experimental than she was about women's issues and the plight of female slaves at the Siamese court. While abroad, she became acquainted with "a Hindu gentleman of high caste" and his wife. The latter was one of the first women, Sarah Dorsey marveled, to break through "the superstitious fetters of caste to cross the seas."[25] Outside of Oxford, Cambridge, and London, few in the Anglo-American world at large considered India, then under the imperial banner, worthy of intellectual respect. Challenging such prejudice, Sarah Dorsey later lectured a New Orleans audience that Indians were a "Noble Race of men." To them, she continued, "we owe not only our [Aryan] blood but the characteristics of our intelligence, of our Philosophies, and much of our Theology."[26] After the crowning of Queen Victoria as Empress of India, however, the English intelligentsia grew curious about the intellectual and spiritual life of the teeming domain.

Sarah Dorsey's interest should be seen, then, to be not quite as exotic as it might first appear. (After all, Henry David Thoreau, one of her favorite authors, carried a copy of the *Bhagavad-Gita* to his hut on Walden Pond.) To take up Hinduism was really a part of her Anglophilia. After all, Anna Leonowens, whom she greatly esteemed, was herself a conventional

Anglican. Furthermore, the study of Vedic moral prescriptions was a partial escape from the provinciality and monotony of Louisiana life. So serious was her interest, however, that she learned Sanskrit in order to read the sacred texts. She called the Indians' faith "the Aryan philosophy." Not until 1877 was the English term "Hinduism" applied to it.[27]

ॐ ॐ

In the midst of her spiritual searchings an unexpected event made her speculations seem even more significant. It also drove her back to traditional theological and moral premises. After her return from Europe, the Dorseys had settled once more at Lake St. Joseph. On Christmas morning, 1871, a young neighbor committed suicide. As soon as she had the opportunity, she wrote Lyulph Stanley about the affair. Word reached her from a nearby plantation that Henry Johnson, about eighteen years old, had shot himself in the head in the woods. She and Mortimer Dahlgren, her young half-brother, set out at once and discovered him fatally wounded and lying under a tree. She took scissors and "clipped off all the poor boy's antique brown hair & then saw the ugly wounds from which the blood was pouring." Mortimer hurried to get a surgeon and she administered camphor and cold compresses. Then, she watched as "the brain began to ooze slowly out of the wound." She knew that the boy was beyond medical help. The tragedy had a powerful effect upon her. "What a *cowardly* thing suicide is, Mr. Stanley! Such a lack of true courage & manly fortitude, so weak! so pitiful. My heart bled for the poor fellow who was too weak to face his daily life, who fled from it, in the very beginning of life's struggle. He was a *deserter* from the banner of humanity! It is so much *greater* to endure patiently." If pity and even contempt were her first reactions, anger soon followed. The boy's decision had touched a raw nerve. She later claimed that nothing had ever given her "more intense pain."[28]

Sarah Dorsey tried to sort the matter out in intellectual terms as best she could. Two months later the incident was still preying on her mind. Henry Johnson's death violated her sense of heroic manhood. "The brave, true man is like Medea. He knows he is valuable in himself & to the Universe, if all else fails him," she insisted. But the allusion to classical mythology reminded her that her convictions differed from those of the ancient philosophers. "I know the reasoning of the Stoics," she told Stanley, "—if death could *possibly* be annihilation there might be some reason in their reasoning but life is eternal. We *cannot* escape from it. Somewhere, we *must* be," and "what we shall be depends much upon what we make of ourselves here."[29] She needed reassurance, as if such an act threatened her own life in some way.

Sarah Dorsey took solace in her pantheistic readings, having become intrigued with James Hinton, author of *Man and His Dwelling Place;* he was a philosopher of whose mysticism Stanley did not approve. From this sage she learned that to die was not to end life but to enter a different phase, and to exterminate oneself was therefore no escape at all. Pain "& what we call Evil, exercises most wondrous power in the elevation & spiritualizing of Man," she claimed. "In a very ingenious manner he reconciles the old battle of the Nominalists & Realists—the modern strife of the Positivists & Idealists," she had recently informed Stanley. Hinton "shows how every pain & *sin* have their place in the lifting up of man into a higher plane of Existence. How this human life is not educational as a *probation* but as a *resurrection* from the *present* death," the pain of which Hinton wrote, she contended, was the very force from which so many good things arise. In contrast to the cynicism of the suicide, she asserted, "I *like* to *be a human being!* and to suffer like my fellows." [30]

Sarah Dorsey was further incensed that a motive for young Henry Johnson's death was rejection by a young girl. No woman was ever worth a man's life, which was given and sustained by God. It was a serious sin to elevate "the *glamour* of Passion" to such heights. How base the young man was to be prompted by mere sexual indulgence when any woman was only to be appreciated in the goodness that she shared with all other women. "Mr. Stanley I stood by that dying boy & wrung my hands in grief over his mad folly, and I feel *angry* at him, that he did not comprehend better the value of human life." She did admit that the suicide did not act "in a state of entire sanity." Although intellectually she could survey the suicide with some detachment, emotionally she could not and kept returning to the subject. In reaction she reflected the conventional view of the matter: suicide was not a desperate act over which the victim had little control but rather an unmanly, deliberate violation of criminal, moral, and divine law, by which suicide was still considered a felony, punishable by imprisonment in most Western countries. Yet, the issue for Johnson, we can assume, was either his terror of an approaching madness or the absolute emotional emptiness in him that made rational thought impossible. [31]

Living in that day, Sarah Dorsey had no means to understand the nature of the problem. Her times, her religion, her regional culture had no access into the way her neighbor's mind might be struggling against helplessness, dread, and pain. As her understanding of Hinton demonstrated, "pain" was affliction from the outside, not from within. Besides, the act threw into question the existence of God. So long as God was the ultimate will, then individuals had no autonomy to do with their lives as they pleased. Thus, in Sarah Dorsey's opinion, suicide was more than a pitiable deed, it was a blasphemy far more dangerous than any conjectures about metaphysics, pantheism, and Hindu "philosophy." As the philosopher Ludwig Wittgenstein later pointed out, "If suicide is allowed then everything is allowed. If anything is not allowed then suicide is not allowed." [32] Reticent even with her English confidant, Sarah Dorsey did not inform Stanley that her great-grandfather had killed himself, when quite insane, as her novel *Agnes Graham* explained. Yet, she must have reflected on the issue of insanity and suicide in her own bloodline even as she mourned, in wrath and pity, the wasted life of her young neighbor and wondered how God would judge his crime.

As Sarah Dorsey had earlier declared, throughout this period she was suffering not only because of Henry Johnson's death but for other, more personal reasons. She lost some Natchez relatives to a vicious assault of yellow fever upon the city, but financial calamity was sometimes a more persistent adversary than disease. Only a few weeks before Johnson's suicide, Sarah had explained to Lyulph that she was depressed to "see on every side of you those near & dear to you by ties of blood & kinship struggling so hard & so ineffectually in this hard hard Battle of Life." For instance, her first cousin, John Knox Routh, once a planter worth half a million dollars, was barely managing to survive. A credit reporter came to the blunt conclusion that he was worth not "a cent" of credit, having lost all his slaves and gained only an enormous load of debts. Besides, he said, Routh was "too indolent & stupid ever to work out."[33]

Even Sarah Dorsey had close friends who were often driven to despair. Her neighbor Caleb Forshey, a gentle soul with scientific interests, sometimes felt as if the world were crashing about his head. Writing to a former classmate at West Point, Forshey declared, "There seemed to be little to live for after the death & burial of our country, the slaughter of the flower of our land" that "neither you [n]or I would have given much for life. Certainly I had a thousand wishes that we could have all *sunk* together." Such sentiments were common in the bleak years after the war. Only the duty and love that one owed to "family ties," as Forshey explained, kept him going.[34]

Sarah Dorsey's sense of loyalty was as strong as Forshey's. It sustained her through the troubles of Reconstruction—that "Mountain of Wickedness" as she viewed it. She determined to help her kinfolk as much as possible. Her sister Inez had lost her husband and, with a son and daughter to raise, Inez's Lake St. Joseph plantation provided only a modest return. Still living in the overseer's lately expanded cottage after the burning of the Big House, Sarah Dorsey promised to add a wing to accommodate the newcomers.[35] Inez, still a great beauty even in middle age, soon afterwards married Edward Peckham, an Englishman, and went back to her own plantation. Sarah Dorsey may have been relieved at her sister's departure, having always been a little jealous of the beautiful Inez.

※ ※

Though faithful to the old precepts of family life during the early 1870s, Sarah Dorsey's bold religious explorations were matched by a shift to the left in her political leanings. In her letters to Stanley she sought to please both him and herself by taking a more democratic position in Reconstruction politics than most of her neighbors would care to follow. Despite his

father's skepticism about the rights of the lower orders, Stanley was a devoted democrat—by English standards—and ran unsuccessfully for the
Oldham seat against a Tory incumbent in 1872.

In the early 1870s, the Republicans were firmly in control of Louisiana,
but two factions split the party, as Stanley had learned during his visit to
Louisiana in 1870. One was the "Custom-House" ring, under James F.
Casey, President Grant's brother-in-law. He saw his chief duty to be his
patron's reelection in 1872. Allied with this group was George W. Carter,
speaker of the lower house, a completely unscrupulous former Methodist
preacher. Sarah Dorsey mistrusted Carter: "He promises every thing, but
I doubt whether he has the power to prevail." The rival faction was headed
by carpetbagger governor Henry Clay Warmoth. Though only thirty, Warmoth was the shrewdest politician in the state and the handsomest and
most marriageable. A number of women of Sarah Dorsey's social class
were intrigued with Warmoth because of his "genius." More important,
for some at least, was what a plantation lady wrote the Republican governor: "his grand physical beauty." Nor could a man named for the great
Whig leader be totally evil, some may have reasoned.[36]

Certainly these were all assets that drew Sarah Dorsey's attention. "Warmoth must be a man of extraordinary abilities & I have nearly a curiosity
to know him, carpetbagger as he is," she wrote her English correspondent.
At the request of the editor of the New Orleans *Times,* she began writing
letters urging fellow conservatives, the Democrats, to support Warmoth's
battle against Lieutenant-Governor Oscar Dunn, a former slave, House
Speaker Carter, and the corrupt custom-house faction. The Democrats of
the city gleefully united with the Grant forces, hoping to oust Warmoth
from power. But in the countryside, Warmoth himself recalled, conservative Democrats like Sarah Dorsey stood by the beleaguered governor.
"There is no use of our people sitting down any longer in dust & ashes &
wringing their hands. The good men of all Parties will have to unite for
the common weal," she insisted in a letter to Stanley. Indeed, she was
following at that time a policy that some Democrats in the legislature had
already initiated at Warmoth's own suggestion. It was only, of course, a
marriage of convenience and would not last.[37]

Like other Louisiana Democrats—straight-outs and moderates alike—
Sarah Dorsey could not forgive Warmoth for championing the black underclass, but that was better than a continuation of federal Reconstruction.
She most admired him for his stand against Grant and his dramatic con-
frontations with the "Custom-House" gang. Amid the political chaos of
post-Civil-War Louisiana, she repeated to Stanley the hopes that she expressed to her friends and newspaper readers: "A new party must come
now & that soon. A Party of all good men *of all sorts* of opinions in the
Past." Sarah Dorsey anticipated "a new Liberal Reform Party" along English lines that could unite the broadcloth class. Yet, she did find politics
a curious game. "Warmoth who was detested last year is now the most

popular man in the State. He is turned *liberal*. It is a queer world! I am glad I have not the responsibility of managing it." [38] Sarah Dorsey's sympathy for Warmoth and liberal reform aroused resentment among her most conservative peers because of her outspoken moderation and because of her sex, which was thought incapable of rational political judgment. She confessed to Lyulph Stanley, "I have stirred up a good many of my friends with what I have said lately. One told me recently that I had become 'a rabid Republican.' I replied 'that I was only a philosopher.' " [39]

Looking for political survival and not philosophical truth, Warmoth on the national level linked his fortunes to the anti-Grant Liberal Republican cause that was developing across the nation under the leadership of Charles Francis Adams, Gratz Brown, and Charles Sumner, politicians who united with the Democrats in choosing Horace Greeley, a former Whig and antislavery editor of the New York *Tribune,* as their common standard-bearer. Thanks to her friendship with Colonel J. M. Sandidge, one of the Louisiana delegates, Sarah Dorsey was seated in the gallery during the Democratic convention in Baltimore. In her view, the Democrats, whom she had formerly criticized for not supporting Warmoth, had at last vindicated themselves "in the noblest manner when they sacrificed their party to the country's pacification. Some of the chief men are friends of mine & I know how they suffered . . . I am glad I have known heroes." When Grant was reelected in the fall of 1872, Sarah Dorsey sympathized with "poor old Greeley," who ran an abysmal campaign, as she observed, and died three weeks afterwards. All along, she told Stanley, she would have preferred the candidacy of the Boston patrician Charles Francis Adams. He was the very model of Whiggery that her lineage and class generally favored. [40]

Yet, even though she was a woman outside the inner corridors of power, Sarah Dorsey's defense of Warmoth and her activities to unite Southern Whig and Northern Republican forces represented a less severe break with Southern political orthodoxy than one might expect. Whig women had long been active in party affairs, though Sarah herself did not seem to awaken until the dark days of Reconstruction, as she perceived them. But long before the Civil War other well-born women had served as partisan cheerleaders and fund- raisers for campaigns. So long as their opinions coincided with those of their husbands, such activity, at least among Whigs, was not thought to be indelicate. Sarah Dorsey, however, was realistic enough to know that politics was a sooty business. "It seems impossible for an honest man to touch this political pitch without defilement. It makes me despair." But determined to preserve her Southern ideals of honor, she could not let such cynicism weigh her down for long: "That is if one ever does despair which I do not. In reading History I find things work out for man eventually for good somehow & some way." She denied the terror of hopelessness, just as she denied understanding why Henry Johnson had ended his life. [41]

Not religion, ethics, or politics but rather a yearning for career and intellectual fulfillment kept Sarah Dorsey mentally alive. As she wrote Lyulph Stanley, she was even "half ashamed" of her boldness in letting her signed work on current events and other matters appear in the public prints.[42] What she sought was a sense of competency in *one* field of endeavor instead of being amateurishly adept, in ladylike fashion, in quite a number.

Throughout this period she was developing something of a literary following with *Agnes Graham,* and she was pleased that *Athalie,* published in 1872, won praise from local Acadians on which people the fiction was centered. She wrote Stanley at length about how a Creole gentleman from Opelousas had stopped her on the street to praise her accuracy in depicting his countrymen. Moreover, she thought herself a better novelist than some of her female literary acquaintances, one of whose works she thought "commonplace & stupid" and the other's "not pure." Yet she knew that her literary talent was limited and her self-confidence inadequate. She told Lyulph Stanley that the close of *Athalie* "was made to please the Publishers who said that there was complaint made against my *endings* as being always too *sad.*" Sarah Dorsey justified her submission on the grounds that "it is my earnest desire to improve and progress as a writer . . . & to use such influence as I possess worthily."[43] Yet, there was still something missing from her life.

In November 1871 an opportunity arose that might have been the answer to her half-realized dissatisfaction. She received an invitation to apply for the headship of the Patapsco Institute, a female academy at Ellicott Mills, near Baltimore. The wealthy Ellicott family as well as a number of Dorseys in the Worthington Valley had founded and long supported the school. The job would literally have been Sarah Dorsey's simply for the asking.[44] In the antebellum period, the clientele had expanded beyond local Maryland families to include young girls from the Southwest. Winnie, daughter of Jefferson and Varina Davis, for instance, may have briefly attended Patapsco after the war. In more settled, antebellum times, under Almira Hart Lincoln Phelps, an impressive and experienced school principal from Baltimore, Patapsco had almost achieved collegiate standards rather than being merely a finishing school. Before her departure in 1849, the headmistress insisted, "Accomplishments should be valued chiefly" because they enhanced domestic life and strengthened a woman's confidence rather than merely entertained "parents, brothers or sisters," not to mention the young ladies' suitors. After the Civil War, however, Deep South planters could no longer afford to give their daughters so expensive an education. Headmaster Robert H. Archer, beset by financial woes and presumably personal problems, had entered a local mental asylum, and his wife had temporarily but ineffectually taken control. The board of trustees concluded that Sarah

Dorsey with her reputation for ingenuity and drive could "restore it to more than its pristine glory."[45]

At once she wrote to Lyulph Stanley for advice because of his educational interests. Her lengthy letter revealed a woman torn between the safety of continuity and the liberation of change. On the one hand, her husband Samuel already had been urging that they should move to Baltimore. He wished to end his days in the bosom of his kinspeople. Sarah Dorsey had successfully delayed agreement, finding the prospect gave her "a feeling of blankness to the monotony of life." To begin housekeeping in Baltimore would compel her to deal with her husband's enormous flock of relatives. She hated the dreariness of "formal society, & balls &c &c &c, and restless flitting from place to place & person to person. I can't do it long."[46]

In contrast to a life of party-going and arranging teas, running a school would be exciting but also exhausting. Sarah Dorsey wanted to control her own time. Moreover, she yearned to develop her literary skills. She had both the leisure and solitude to explore her interests in many fields, so long as she remained on her Louisiana plantation. "I sometimes feel as if it would be pleasant to be brought into collision with other & superior intellects," she later repeated, "but I live here among my books in great peacefulness and the calmness & repose of my life become dearer to me every day."[47] On the other hand, the advantages of a headship were appealing. Baltimore was close to her friend Anne Botta and other intellectuals, and, with ten or fifteen thousand dollars of her own money invested in the school to give it stability from the start, she could experiment with fresh *"ideas of female education."* She pledged to keep her "domestic life carefully separate from the school" for the sake of her husband, and, once resettled in his native Maryland, he would be happy. *"I can make him so,"* Sarah asserted with aplomb.[48]

Finally, in undertaking this mission, would she not exemplify the courage and sense of moral duty that her friend Stanley strenuously enjoined? "I have all my life *preached loudly,* the dignity of & the value of labour," she contended. Not for a moment did she doubt her capacity to run the academy: "I never do any thing except with my *utmost.*" With good reason she expected a hearty endorsement of such a scheme. Lyulph Stanley's chief occupation was the reforming of education in England, attempts to improve teaching methods and to reach the masses. And yet, Sarah Dorsey closed, "I pause—*Is it all* self indulgence that I should hesitate? *Is it?* What do you think? Answer me as soon as you can."[49]

CHAPTER EIGHT

Enshrining the Lost Cause

There is no time, there is no spot,
There is no thought, nor dream,
Wherein that aspect cometh not—
I cannot banish him.

"Unholy Love" Catherine Ann Warfield[1]

Sarah Dorsey answered her own question about running the Patapsco Institute before Lyulph Stanley could give his reply. She declined the offer. In doing so she set the stage for playing out the closing years of her life. The reasons, which she explained to her English correspondent, were plausible, but on closer scrutiny lame. Old Samuel Dorsey's health suddenly— and, for his sake, conveniently—deteriorated. Complaining of chronic "gout" and "neuralgia," he might need her for a nurse. "I don't believe I should be satisfied if you took the school because when I suffer so I require your constant attention & I am afraid the climate of Maryland will be *too cold* for me," he had told her querulously. At least, Sarah Dorsey disclosed, she heard nothing more about keeping house in Baltimore. She agreed with her husband that the weather in Maryland was much too cold for them.[2] She had always done what she had liked before in their marriage, but this time she preferred to heed his wishes.

As if unwilling to admit any loss of former prerogatives, she found a more elevated motive. Mrs. Archer, acting headmistress, had to rely upon the salary. Sarah Dorsey thought it was "only *right* & *just*" that she, a mistress of plantations, should defer to the hapless Mrs. Archer. She did not explain why the former principal's wife could not simply become a teacher on the staff. After all, Sarah had planned to put ten to fifteen thousand dollars of her own into the school.

The truth, though, was different. Sarah Dorsey did not wish to relinquish her position as a lady of grace and leisure, an honored and enviable role in the Southern scheme of things. To accept the appointment would mean a rejection of her father's values and a surrender to the temptations of independence. Besides, as she noted later, she felt it a matter of loyalty to remain in the South to endure the toils of Reconstruction with her friends and kin. "I am bound by so many ties of relationships & interest here that I . . . think it is best to stay & suffer with those who *can't* get away. I know how Demosthenes felt when he had to live & witness the decay of Athens! I wish I did not care. I wish I could bury myself in my books & ignore every thing in my daily life, but I cannot," she later wrote Stanley.[3]

The English reformer had led Sarah Dorsey to question her own decision after it was made, but that consequence was ironic for two reasons. First, it contradicted his own relationship to women of intellect. Stanley replied to her first letter before learning of her refusal. He challenged the wisdom of her directing the school. Her first and only duty, he admonished her, was to make her husband's life as smooth as possible. When Sarah Dorsey received this response, she was taken aback, expecting Stanley to call her to the colors of feminist "duty," the Victorian intellectuals' favorite word. Previously he had made some remarks in that vein.

A second irony also appeared. Beginning in the early 1870s, Stanley was developing his own ideas regarding education. He might have looked upon Sarah Dorsey as a potential ally in the field of education. She had looked forward to experimenting with the ideas of Thomas Arnold. As the headmaster of Rugby, Arnold had been a noted educator and mentor of Lyulph's cousin Arthur Penrhyn Stanley, Dean of Wesminster Abbey. Later, Lyulph Stanley (by then known as Lord Sheffield) would become famous in England for his work on the London School Board. He failed, however, to achieve his plans for higher education to serve the English masses.[4] Nonetheless, the outspoken adversary of British monarchy, champion of manhood suffrage and universal secular education had not extended his egalitarianism to include the rights of women. Instead, he undermined his counsel by criticizing Sarah Dorsey's plans that would mean neglect of her marital obligations. "Didn't you give me a neat little reprimand," Sarah Dorsey answered sarcastically. "Of course Mr[.] Dorsey 'would not mind' and don't I know 'that one does not belong to oneself when one is *married.*' Perhaps it was a little selfish in me to want to take the school. But I thought it was a good work & that I might manage to make my husband comfortable too." [5]

Sarah Dorsey's reaction guided her to other, more rebellious thoughts about woman's place in the social order. She showered upon her correspondent all her customary compliments on the brilliance of his mind and the prolixity of his activities. She noted particularly his recent lecture at Leeds. Yet she also felt helpless and vaguely indignant. "Here you go about and occupy your life so usefully & with diverse interests, while most women have such stupid times," she chided the younger man. "If I was not really opposed to publicity in a woman's life, I should like to lecture a little myself. Suppose I were to make my Début as a Lecturer solely to *women,* would you acknowledge me as a friend?" She had a great deal to tell her fellow women. These were intimate matters that "I can't put into books or even into '*articles* for the newspaper.' " Sarah Dorsey complained that her onetime flame, the handsome Dr. Joseph Buck Stratton of the Presbyterian Church in Natchez, had told her, "You can do the book but I should not like *my wife to undertake*" the management of a school. Had Sarah Dorsey not half-believed them right in the first place, the condescension of Stratton and Stanley would have seemed more of an affront to her. Yet, she wondered, "Were women created solely to exist for one man's gratification?" Mothers had their duties clearly laid out, she observed. Yet what was to become of her, she asked, a childless wife with hardly "*much housekeeping* to look after." [6]

Still worse, Sarah Dorsey continued, philosophy, literature, and psychology, one of her favorite subjects, did not seem to equip her for practical utility in any field. "*What* must *I* read, what training must I individually go through, in order to escape from this fault? If you tell me I will go through that study & that training. I read the books that Men read but they do not educate me as a man is educated by them. Is it that I do not apply them? & how am I to apply them?" [7] She meant that Stanley and his friends had the advantage of college and specialized training in one field or another. For instance, Stanley himself had earned a first-class degree in *litterae humaniores* at Balliol College. Through the endorsement of the Platonist Benjamin Jowett, he had won a fellowship at the Oxford college (1862–69). He was called to the bar by the Inner Temple in 1865, then took up philanthropy and educational administration. [8] By contrast, she had received private tutoring, attended a boarding school briefly, and had taught herself as well. Yet, she was given no aim beyond the pleasing of herself, her family, and the husband of her choice. Unlike the rigors of collegiate training and the general recognition that competition for honor creates, she had been immersed in the deliberately non-competitive world of female letters. Like most other educated women of her day, she felt herself to be merely a dabbler in many things, a master of none. Despite her brilliance of mind, which her step-father Dahlgren had quickly discerned, she was not equipped with much intellectual confidence. The special tutoring in law and accounting that Dahlgren had provided her might have helped its development, but the kind of unstructured academic work she had undertaken had no coherence, no ultimate objective.

Nor could literary work engross her attention. By her own lights, Sarah Dorsey thought of fiction as a means to an end—the ennoblement of humanity rather than as a way to explore the subtleties and dilemmas of existence. "I resolved when I began to write that I would never use my pen deceitfully for the public," she had confessed to her English friend. The notion of realism in novel-writing was quite antithetical to her literary sensibility: "I am not fiendish but I hate impure books & morbid conceptions." With elevated thoughts and spotless language the criteria by which to judge a woman's fiction, she left herself little room for dealing with problems that life presented.[9] Also, there was the problem of background material. A woman's experience with so many facets of male activities was limited; the Southern female writer was largely dependent on incidents, people, and scenes known to her. To publish, even in fictional disguise, stories of corruption, abuse, or sense of hopelessness that one could see on every hand, would mean hurt feelings, ostracism, outrage. Could a woman writer endure the kind of reaction that would ensue from disclosure of private matters? Sarah Dorsey did use characters and incidents close to home in *Agnes Graham* and *Panola* in particular, but literary formulations were so standardized that no one was likely to take offense.

Many years later the English novelist Virginia Woolf pointed out that writing had appealed to Victorian women because it was "a reputable and harmless occupation. The family peace was not broken by the scratching of a pen." Paper and ink for the aspiring female romancer were cheap enough to make no rude depletions of coins in the sugar bowl. The female novelist of previous generations, Woolf remarked, was expected to be like all other women—self-effacing and sympathetic to the greater burdens of active men. "Above all—I need not say it—" Woolf concluded, this "Angel in the House" was supposed to be "pure." These requirements were bound to inhibit free writing as much as corset stays restrained free breathing. Woolf's appraisal of her female predecessors, most of them "unknown and forgotten," would have horrified Sarah Dorsey.[10]

Woolf's idea that the "Angel in the House" was a formidable adversary to any woman of intellect would have quite astonished Stanley as well. He had eagerly strengthened Sarah Dorsey's ladylike approach to literary effort. To judge from Sarah Dorsey's responses to him, Stanley constantly encouraged her creative impulses, and she considered him a literary critic worthy of the utmost respect. "Your friendship is a refreshment & an inspiration to me," she wrote him. "I know you like to do good & therefore I tell you frankly that you have done me *great good.*"[11] As a result, in some ways she was less willing to confront human evil than was her aunt Catherine Warfield in the novels she was currently writing. In some of her work, Sarah Dorsey did contribute to the "local color" school that was beginning to flourish in Louisiana as elsewhere in the Reconstruction South. After Dorsey's death, the local colorists would include the New Orleanian writers Mary McEnery Stuart, Grace King, and George Washington Cable, all of whose early fiction combined sentimental conventions with local dialects and scenes that readers found charming and unthreatening.[12] Dorsey's experiments with Cajun and Creole society were not, however, very memorable even within this restricted genre.

Neither Stanley nor Sarah Dorsey herself recognized that her real talent lay in history-writing, not telling stories. But, who had ever heard of a female historian? Sappho was a poet, but there was no female equivalent to Thucydides, she reflected. Sarah Dorsey could only name as historians Anna Commena and Doria D'Istria, author of the "History of Roumania." "It was a mistake," Sarah Dorsey declared, "in the wise Greeks to make the Deity presiding over History, a woman. It needs the broad, objective grasp of the masculine soul to do justice to general History." Women, who are good story-tellers anyhow, can attempt biographies, she conceded, "just as they paint best, flowers, animals, subjects of still life, that require close, refined, loving scrutiny" and "dainty touches of the pencil and minute, careful elaboration." [13] Although it was true that women were barred from direct participation in the subjects of history as it was then understood—wars, diplomacy, politics—these were public matters and written about within very strict rules of propriety. As a result, the topic was quite accessible to a woman confined to the experiences of home, church, and library.

According to intellectuals like Sarah Dorsey, fiction-writing belonged in the feminine domain. Yet, after the publication of Gustave Flaubert's *Madame Bovary* (1857), the range of experiences and perceptions which the genre provided was far too great for a woman with her sense of propriety to cultivate. Flaubert had revealed the frustration that could afflict middle-class womanhood, but many years would pass before Kate Chopin, another resident of Louisiana, would treat women in the way that Flaubert handled his female figures. For the most part, nineteenth-century women writers like Sarah Dorsey had to function in a very narrow frame of reference. They could not make full use of the crises in their own lives, much less those of others. Fanny Kemble, the actress and friend of Anne Botta, once declared bitterly that heroic women like Cleopatra had "lived their tragedies instead of writing them." Ever since, women had not been expected to do otherwise. [14]

Besides, fiction-writing was a mixed blessing. In the public mind the literary imagination, with little awareness of contradiction, was associated with effeminacy in the spinning out of untruths on the one hand and "impurities" too coarse and barbaric to be sanctioned on the other. It was therefore treated with ambivalence and sometimes downright moral hostility. Lyulph Stanley was himself guilty of these reactions. He claimed to be impressed with the delicacy and high-mindedness to be found in Sarah Dorsey's works—an antidote to the dangers of irrationality, deceit, and crudity. These were common judgments of fiction in that period. For instance, Dean Arthur Penryhn Stanley of Westminster Abbey, with whom Sarah Dorsey corresponded, delivered a funeral sermon on June 19, 1870, for Charles Dickens in the Abbey. The Dean dwelt upon the moral limitations of the novel and the dangers of inflaming readers' passions—the kinds of moral perils that Sarah Dorsey also piously deplored. Dean Stanley praised Dickens chiefly for finding "even in the humblest and worst of mankind, a soul of goodness and nobleness, a soul worth redeeming." [15]

The Dean's cousin, Lyulph Stanley, though not a devout worshiper at the Abbey, shared such generally conventional views that were especially popular among contemporary male spokesmen.

Thus, the pair—the American lady and the English aristocrat—heartily agreed on the nature of fiction and the enclosed sphere in which women, most particularly, should create fiction. Their harmony on this point helps to explain why, in her correspondence with Stanley, Sarah Dorsey was so tentative in expressing her feelings regarding a literary or educational career. In a speech to young women professionals, Virginia Woolf in 1931 observed that Woolf herself and other women might seem free to pursue any calling. Yet "phantoms and obstacles," she argued, constantly loomed in the way.[16] In Sarah Dorsey's time, the impediments were not vague apparitions but actual men like Stanley and women like Dorsey herself. It was made clear how Duty and Morality commanded restrictions upon female experimentation. The supposed feared outcome of alternative behavior was the precipitous fall of civilization into ruins.

Sarah Dorsey, herself an "Angel in the House," dared not risk her friendship with the young reformer. Yet, clearly her friend's presumption in questioning her loyalty to conventional values made her *almost* aware that something was deeply wrong. In her view the issue of being both a lady of leisure and a woman of intellect and ambition had to be squared. Anne Botta, she believed, had met the challenge. Sarah Dorsey wrote the Englishman that her friend in New York "is immersed in all sorts of causes & amusements. Her 'Sunday evenings' are quite brilliant, I learn from friends who attend them. Her last enthusiasm was a French clergyman whom she says 'it was an epoch in her life to know.' "[17] Andrew Carnegie would soon be Anne Botta's most prominent conquest at her salon on Murray Hill. As she had for Sarah Dorsey, she introduced the industrialist millionaire to English friends—Anthony Froude, Charles Kingsley, Matthew Arnold, and probably the Airlies and Stanleys. (Carnegie was not as famous in the 1870s as the Pittsburgh steel-maker was later to become.) Literary figures like Poe and Washington Irving had been replaced with inflated celebrities such as Henry Ward Beecher. But that was more the fault of the Gilded Age than of the beautiful Anne Botta's aging.[18] In any event, whatever the state of her "evenings," Sarah Dorsey was sure that women like her friend in New York could achieve new heights in literature and art without losing a fraction of inherent daintiness. Sarah Dorsey believed that at salons like Anne Botta's and her own at Elkridge and her New Orleans townhouse, men and women could exchange ideas with no loss of delicacy or propriety. "The minds of women should be widened, without lessening their womanly qualities," she argued.[19]

Such reflections as these were all very well in theory, but choices had to be made if the imagination was to be served and not society. She had decided against any sort of professional advancement. By the kind of self-effacement that Woolf later was to denounce, Sarah Dorsey had sacrificed her own plans and let Mrs. Archer run the school, while knowing the record of the woman's incompetence.[20]

Despite her decision, for the next few months Sarah Dorsey looked further into the question of who she was and what she wanted to be. She met too many people in too many Northern circles not to be affected politically and intellectually. Even some of her favorite kinspeople held what seemed to her fanatical ideas. Among them was her uncle, Dr. René LaRoche, in Philadelphia, whom she tried to see whenever taking a trip up the east coast. "He is a violent Republican," she acknowledged, but his differentness was part of his attraction. "I am very fond of him. He is so *French* & so peculiar & so charming." She was proud of his eminence as a scholarly physician, writer of an influential treatise on malaria. She also boasted to her noble English correspondent that LaRoche's lineage entitled him to be called the Marquis of "Faubourg St. Germain," had he so wished.[21]

Likewise, in July 1872, she was thrown into contact with people whom Southern whites would ordinarily have avoided at all costs. Sarah and Samuel Dorsey visited Bedford Springs, in southwestern Pennsylvania, so that he, in failing health, could have the benefit of the mineral baths. Simon Cameron, Lincoln's first Secretary of War, and other leading Grant Republicans were staying at the elegant hotel that still stands, and Sarah Dorsey joined in their gatherings and greeted them on the promenades. Although she was not won over to their political position, she found among them women intensely involved in political affairs—much like Henry Adams's Madeleine Lee in his contemporaneous novel *Democracy*. She told Stanley of her long conversations with a Mrs. Cunningham of the Women's Labor Association which sought to supply scholarships for young women seeking medical degrees in a virtually all-male profession. Mrs. Cunningham, she confessed, "interests me greatly," but, Dorsey added rebelliously, "My husband complains 'that everybody speaks to me,' " and " 'nobody seems to be afraid' which he considers rather too democratic in his wife but I am glad of it." [22]

Alarmed by her interest in such people as the earnest Mrs. Cunningham, Samuel Dorsey planned for his wife to have as little further association as possible with Anne Botta, Lyulph Stanley, and other notables with dangerously advanced opinions. Sarah Dorsey was looking forward to a visit with her party-giving friend who would be vacationing in Newport, Rhode Island, in the summer of 1871. Samuel Dorsey remembered, however, the unpleasantness of a previous sojourn. When the Dorseys first had returned from Europe some months before, Sarah Dorsey had already spent some days with Anne Botta and her circle. On that earlier occasion Charles Butler, Anne Botta's financial adviser and friend, and "the Professor," her husband, who taught Italian literature at New York University, had accompanied Sarah Dorsey by train to Long Branch, Long Island. "What a night we had! & how we talked!" Sarah Dorsey had reported. Meanwhile her "disconsolate" husband Samuel endured the heat and dust of the city at the St. Nicholas Hotel. He and other relatives had grown more than a little impatient with her extended absence.[23] A year later, upon their reaching Dorsey's Howard County relatives after leaving Bedford Springs, Sarah Dorsey came down with a serious bronchial infection and high fever. Her husband, much relieved by the circumstances, arranged for her further recuperation at Point Comfort, a beach resort just below Norfolk, Virginia. Undoubtedly Samuel Dorsey encouraged the attending physician strictly to forbid her to go anywhere except home to Louisiana. It was "a bitter disappointment" to Anne Botta and to Sarah Dorsey that she could not once again enjoy the intellectual stimulation of the previous summer's visit.[24]

Just as Sarah Dorsey lost contact with Anne Botta, her rather tentative effort to introduce a new era in her life faltered as well. Even her friendship with Stanley would soon atrophy. As the Englishman grew ever more democratic in politics, Sarah Dorsey was becoming more conservative. "How does your own class (& your own friends) receive your Radical utterances?" she asked him very pointedly. "I should think somewhat as *we* used to take Cassius Clay & others whom we used to regard as leading Abolitionists."[25] She warned him that democracy had its limits, particularly in Louisiana where ignorant blacks, she maintained, had nearly bankrupted the state. The former slaveholder could not see why Stanley, who questioned Anna Leonowens's rendition of facts about slave women in Oriental harems, found Leonowens's championing of black intellectuality in her work so compelling. "I don't see what more you want for those 'Wards of the Nation' than they have already got. They are not interfered with in any way that I see." Southerners, she insisted, objected solely to the whites who irresponsibly encouraged black unrest. "We could get along very well with the negroes if they were let alone."[26] She played the usual chords of prejudice so favored by white Southerners. The relationship between Dorsey and Stanley was bound, however, to come to a close soon anyhow. In the fall of 1872, Lyulph Stanley wrote her about his impending marriage. Sarah Dorsey was gracious about "the fair Queen" of his "affections," the beautiful aristocrat Mary Bell, but clearly Stanley could not treat Sarah in a special way ever again.[27] To fill the vacancy in her spirit, something or someone else would have to take its place.

Samuel Dorsey's health deteriorated rapidly over the following years. He died in October 1875. After months of mourning her loss, Sarah Dorsey at last found a new purpose in life, one that she considered much more significant than the running of a girls' school or even the re-establishment of a united Northern and Southern Whiggery. Having returned from Europe in late 1876, Jefferson Davis was searching for a place to write his memoirs. Davis had failed in various business ventures but hoped to sell his memoirs at a good profit. In December 1876, Sarah Dorsey invited the former President of the Confederacy to visit in January her plantation home on the Gulf Coast. She promised him accommodations at a quiet site ideally suited for his literary purposes.[28]

The circumstances, some would soon say, were indeed the fruits of an "Unholy Love," as her Aunt Catherine's poem at the opening of this chapter is entitled. Davis was married to Varina Howell, a woman of great spirit and beauty, who was three years older than Sarah Dorsey, a fact of which the jealous wife was well aware. Despite being married and the nearly twenty years' difference in their ages, Sarah Dorsey allowed her attachment to go far beyond simple admiration for a former leader of a dead cause.

In 1873 the Dorseys had moved to Beauvoir, as she called the place, from Elkridge, their Lake St. Joseph plantation with all its memories of better times. Their new location consisted of a fine house and outbuildings on a 680-acre densely timbered property, six miles from the village of Mississippi City and near the hamlet of Biloxi, overlooking the Gulf of Mexico. The main house, constructed in 1849, was built in the Louisiana Plantation architectural style—tall ceilings, crushed-shell floors, cool passageways, and the whole edifice raised on pillars so that the Gulf breezes could circulate underneath. No doubt the decision to move from Elkridge was a response to Samuel Dorsey's ill-health, though it failed to improve his condition.

When Jefferson Davis arrived on a permanent basis, she arranged for him to occupy a modest but generously proportioned cottage only yards east of the main house. The dwelling became Davis's quarters and office.[29] Allegedly he paid rent—probably a nominal sum—fixed up his own bookshelves, and agreed to board at her table. The arrangement seemed ideal for both parties, but Sarah soon discovered that her distinguished boarder required more attention than she had imagined. On May 1, 1877, Sarah Dorsey wrote to Major W. T. Walthall, a nearby resident who served as an aide-de-camp in the preparation of Davis's memoir, that he was "in a very troubled condition of mind," being too depressed to settle into the work. Obligingly, she stepped in and soon organized his day so that he began to function more productively.[30]

The widow reveled in the opportunities opened to her by his presence. Not surprisingly in her withdrawal from reform and expanded interests, Sarah Dorsey had reverted to old patterns, one of devotion to father-like men generally many years older than she. Sometimes they were clergymen, like Dr. Joseph Stratton and Bishop Leonidas Polk. Others were generals and colonels of the Confederacy. After her flirtation with advanced thinking in politics and social order ended, she was at last to find the individual who embodied all the virtues and winning ways that she imagined Thomas George Ellis, her father, to have possessed. Fitting this pattern, Jefferson Davis was ideal for her psychological needs. She oversaw the improvement of his health, warded off unwanted visitors, cautioned him against public appearances, and kept his friends informed about his physical condition. Moreover, she lavished hospitality upon his comrades from the war years. As one historian has put it, she entertained "delegations from Lee memorial societies, Jackson bands, gallant Forresters, and Davis clubs, eager to pay their respects to their old chief." These impositions must have taxed her resources, which were much diminished from their prewar condition. Yet according to Maud Walthall, whose husband was Davis's chief secretary, Sarah Dorsey spared no expense: "She even sent to Cuba for the special brand of cigars which she knew Mr. Davis liked."[31]

Finally, Sarah Dorsey corresponded with sundry politicians and generals to enlist their memory of specific events to be treated in what became Davis's *The Rise and Fall of the Confederate Government*.[32] She transcribed notes, took dictation, corrected prose, and offered advice about style and organization—most of it, unfortunately, not taken. In contrast to her vigorous biographical rendering of Governor Allen, Davis's approach to his subject was legalistic, dull, and unconvincing. Defeat and imprisonment had taught him nothing. Davis assumed that despite the outcome of the war and the Reconstruction amendments, the states retained their sovereignty. He seemed to believe that the Constitution had simply duplicated the Articles of the Confederation with but a few modifications. However opinionated Davis remained on such matters, Sarah Dorsey saw him as a generous-hearted, much abused leader, who deserved the gratitude and acclaim of Southerners and the respect of gentlemen everywhere.[33] Always drawn to vulnerable elderly men, she could both worship him as the father whom she had lost so early in her life and nurse him as the child she had never had.

Curiously enough, Davis and Sarah Dorsey shared in common a psychological predisposition: both were troubled by the early deaths of their fathers and both sought out elderly heroes to admire and love. Earlier in his life, Davis had not been very secure despite his outward claims of self-reliance. He hero-worshiped John C. Calhoun, elder statesman of the South, Andrew Jackson, and Zachary Taylor, father of his first wife. Those were perhaps understandable preferences for a young Mississippi Congressman. Reverence for the austere, antislavery John Quincy Adams, however, was certainly a strange choice. Davis's father had been so reserved, unaffectionate, and demanding that when he died his teenage son had difficulty resolving his feelings. "What could be more revealing," Davis's most recent biographer concludes, "than the subsequent succession of father figures whom Davis adopted almost worshipfully?"[34] He developed a rigid self-defensiveness and a vulnerability to flattery that would severely diminish his abilities to lead a people at war many years later.

Though unable to tolerate the criticism or independent spirit of peers, Davis was nevertheless the soul of charm and generosity toward those subordinates who understood their station—self-effacing generals and politicians, women, and children. Among the military favorites was Leonidas Polk, whom Sarah Dorsey had so greatly admired herself. Despite Polk's inexperience and, later, demonstrated incompetence, Davis held him in overblown regard and promoted him over highly skilled seniors to major general. (General Polk's blunders were many, but the most serious had been his occupation of Columbia in 1862 which violated Kentucky's neutrality at a time when leaving matters as they were would have greatly benefited the Confederacy.) No doubt, Sarah was delighted that her new hero so grandly revered the memory of her old one.[35]

Sarah Dorsey found in Davis the perfect master, and his needs filled her day. For his part, Davis found in her the ideal disciple. Curiously, though, Davis sought something more than just adoration from his female votary. He needed someone to reassure him that he was everything he claimed to be, and Sarah Dorsey's unfulfilled motherly instincts provided him a source of constant nurture. Every day she took dictation. She had to keep in touch with Major Walthall regarding the editorial work, which always seemed to be in arrears. When a chapter was completed, she packaged it and had it sent to him. Walthall eventually settled nearby and undertook some of the dictation, but other chores on Davis's behalf crowded her hours. Above all, she had to keep prodding the autobiographer not to relive the old controversies in hand-ringing ruminations but to keep the pen busy on the page. Even as a writer, Davis found it hard to make up his mind what to say. He did so eventually, however, even Sarah Dorsey admitted, "only with a forced interest."[36]

Keeping up the former president's spirits was perhaps her most serious contribution as a sometime nurse and mother. Aside from his delicate health, particularly after his two-year incarceration in Fortress Monroe, Virginia, Davis suffered even more profoundly from depression than when undergoing the severe pressures of wartime administration. In her reminiscences, Varina Davis later called him "a nervous dyspeptic by habit," a condition that added to his general irritability. Other bodily problems included: periodic insomnia; neuralgia; facial dysfunction; and even blindness in one eye. In the language of the late 1870s and 1880s, he was afflicted with "neurasthenia," a condition both physical and mental. Even before the war he had been compelled to take long vacations to recover his spirits and strength.[37] Women like Sarah Dorsey were certain that the basic trouble with such an ailing hero as Davis was purely overwork and physical ailment. Varina Davis, however, took a more realistic view, calling attention to his hypersensitivity about criticism, so much so that "even a child's disapproval discomposed him."[38]

For the first year or so of this arrangement, even Sarah's kinspeople saw no calamity looming. Inez Ellis Peckham did not object to her sister's relationship with Davis. Periodically she came for long stays at Beauvoir. Inez and Edward Peckham, her English-born husband, ran a somewhat down at the heels post-Civil War plantation near Elkridge, which Sarah Dorsey still owned and operated. Moreover, Sarah had appointed her penniless half-brother, twenty-year-old Mortimer Dahlgren of Brooklyn, New York, to manage Beauvoir while she and Jefferson Davis worked on the memoirs. Only weeks after Jefferson Davis settled in, Mortimer Dahlgren arrived, in early March 1877.

The young half-brother found himself in the midst of unaccustomed luxury. The house, he wrote his step-mother in Brooklyn, was "built in true old Southern style upon columns twelve feet high," had a gallery that banded the house, and encompassed living space of 100 by 120 feet. "[G]rand old live oaks," decorated with a "picturesque garb of iron-gray moss," pushed "their proud heads high." His hostess was no less lavish in these grim postwar years than she had been in more prosperous times. Mortimer reported that the Lee Association, numbering some seven hundred guests, were treated as if their honoring of the former President at Beauvoir were a royal fête at Windsor, with lengthy processions and exchanges of dignities. Wearing a "flashing medal," a rosette in the lapel of a new black frock coat, and white vest, the twenty-year-old took special pride in standing near the onetime Confederate Commander in Chief on a platform built for the occasion. Sarah Dorsey liked to surround herself with high-toned, intellectual young men. She wrote a friend, Dahlgren learned, that she thought him "as good as *ten girls,* besides being a *boy.*"[39] She told the servants that Mortimer was after that the "head of her household" whose orders should be promptly obeyed.[40] Soon enough, the young man was studying law under the supervision of Jefferson Davis and General Joseph R. Davis, Davis's nephew. So well did the group get along in those early days that Joseph Davis and Mortimer Dahlgren formed a partnership to run a newspaper, the *Seashore Gazette,* at nearby Pass Christian, Mississippi. Moreover, the ex-President and the young man together built "a Clipper race boat."[41] Mary Routh Ellis, Sarah Dorsey's niece and a pleasant companion for Mortimer, was also in residence for a long and friendly stay, adding to the general harmony.

Stephen Percy Ellis, one of Sarah Dorsey's two full brothers, might have entertained suspicions, but the early reports from his young half-brother Mortimer were reassuring. Stephen Ellis resided in Brooklyn, where he kept in touch with his step-father, Charles Dahlgren. Neither had much money. Dahlgren's property, including his Marydale plantation in Tensas Parish, had been confiscated by the federal authorities.[42] Ellis was an ill-paid newspaperman. The old gentleman, who practiced law at 117 Broadway, was faring only modestly, not having been invited to join General Burton Harrison's flourishing circle of ex-Confederate lawyers in uptown Manhattan. Harrison, the former President's private secretary, still considered Jefferson Davis "our great chieftain," but General Dahlgren disagreed.[43]

Another relative who might have registered concern over Sarah's household arrangement was Mrs. Appoline Ingraham Ellis. She was the widow of Thomas LaRoche Ellis, Sarah's Rebel brother who saw action but had died of tuberculosis at home in 1862. Widow Ellis owed her position at a Philadelphia post office to her uncle General George G. Meade, victor at Gettysburg. She and her daughter, Mary Routh Ellis (the niece staying at Beauvoir), lived in genteel poverty. But apart from the permanent estrangement between the blunt Confederate brigadier and his impulsive step-daughter, none in the family was aware of any deep-seated antagonisms between themselves and the owner of Beauvoir.

Varina Davis's situation, however, was quite different. Bad health kept her in Europe. Then she learned through a newspaper column that Sarah Dorsey, her former schoolmate in Philadelphia, had become her husband's amanuensis and landlady, roles that might easily lead to more intimate relations.[44] Foolishly Sarah Dorsey had herself initiated the newspaper account to help Davis receive publicity for his forthcoming book and to remind readers of how the Rebel ex-President was suffering a financial and political "martyrdom." The article ardently described Sarah Dorsey's contributions to Davis's comfort and literary progress. Varina Davis was dismayed and her daughter Margaret in Memphis disgusted. "I never liked Mrs. Dorsey," she wrote Varina. "I think she is manish & her conduct to you extremely ill-bred to say the very least of it. You will not go there if any thing I can say will prevent it. I told Father what I thought of her when he was here, & said I did not think you would [have] enjoyed being her guest." Sarah Dorsey's brilliance of mind and the way that she collected male intellectuals seldom earned her esteem among other Southern ladies. "She assumes a superiority over all other women which is very disgusting to me & makes men her friends." Actually, Margaret later changed her mind about her mother's enemy. She lost a baby and, needing someone to comfort her while her mother was still in Europe, accepted Sarah's invitation to visit Beauvoir. During a month-long summer vacation, her hostess made Margaret and Addison Hayes, her husband, feel so much at home in the west *garçonnière* that Varina's daughter was quite won over. Generous by nature, Sarah Dorsey knew how to please.[45]

When at last Varina Davis returned to America in the fall of 1877, she went immediately to Memphis to help Margaret Hayes through her continuing grief. She expected her husband to come to her and refused any form of reconciliation with his hostess at Beauvoir, explaining, "Nothing on earth would pain me like living in that kind of community in her house." Varina had long been certain that the newspaper reports of Sarah Dorsey's aid to her husband were part of her rival's strategy to claim co-authorship of the memoirs.[46]

At Christmastide, 1877, Sarah Dorsey entertained in a style that few in the South could have afforded, even in prewar days. For the holiday dinner, the guests consumed oysters, raw, in soup, and fried, the customary turkey, followed by mutton, beef, salmon, crabs, both sweet and Irish potatoes, vegetables, cranberry sauce and jellies. All this was washed down with quantities of sherry and excellent claret. The main dish had yet to appear. It took two servants to carry a silver salver three feet by four feet, upon which was placed a "magnificent peacock," roasted, with the feathers, some five feet long, in full display "(arranged as if alive)," Mortimer Dahlgren marveled. The bird was stuffed with yet more oysters. Present were Sarah Dorsey's young relatives, Generals Jubul Early and Joseph Davis and their wives, Jefferson Davis—but no Varina.[47] Even the year-end holidays did not bring the couple together. Sarah's elaborate dinner was simply another example of her compulsion to entertain—with her dramas of delectable swans and peacocks, hundreds of wax candles blazing, music on harp and violin, and elegant conversations. However well intentioned, such activities were ill-suited to assure domestic peace in the Davis household.

In April 1878, Varina, then in Memphis, made her views unmistakably clear: "Do not—please do not let Mrs. Dorsey come to see me" or she would have to be "uncivil." In light of his stubborn absence, she questioned his historical project, one doomed, she protested, to be a "bitter, *bitter work*." Some even said Sarah Dorsey was the real author anyhow, an opinion that Varina said made her feel "aggravated to death." Sarah Dorsey's editorial help galled her because that once had been Varina's privilege.[48]

Finally, curiosity and impatience overcame Varina Davis's pride and she arrived in May 1878, on the day of a large garden party that Sarah Dorsey had arranged to honor her, not knowing if she would appear or not. Barely had Varina Davis unpacked her valise when she flared up in a temper, denounced the widow for alienating her husband, and flew off to the woods. Somehow Sarah Dorsey coaxed her back, still fuming. But rising to the occasion as the guests arrived, Varina Davis was graciousness and dignity personified before the unsuspecting throng.[49]

With Sarah Dorsey at all times discreet, hospitable, and accommodating, Varina Davis gradually was appeased, and Sarah Dorsey shrewdly slipped into the background. "She has a charming temper and makes us very comfortable," Varina Davis finally acknowledged. Nonetheless she could not endure the place, finding the heat—and the company—unbearable, whereas, Dorsey and the ex-President thought the climate and surroundings "an absolute necessity" for their "well being." Varina Davis preferred city life and was happy to leave "the beauties of nature" to farmers, romantic poets, and "man-haters" as she could neither grow things, versify, nor do without admiring male attendants.[50]

To nurse—and soon to bury—son Jefferson Davis, Jr., fatally ill from

Thomas George Percy Ellis, 1805–38, planter of Natchez, son of Sarah Percy Ellis Ware and Jude John Ellis, and father of Sarah Anne Ellis Dorsey. *Telfair Academy of Arts and Sciences, Inc., Savannah, Georgia.*

Mary Routh Ellis, 1813–58, wife of Thomas George Percy Ellis and of Charles Gustavus Dahlgren, and mother of Sarah Anne Ellis Dorsey. *Telfair Academy of Arts and Sciences, Inc., Savannah, Georgia.*

Charles Gustavus Dahlgren, 1811–88, General, C.S.A., planter, financier, attorney, who saved the Ellis-Routh property in 1840 and educated Sarah Dorsey, his step-daughter. Portrait by Washington B. Cooper.
Photo by June H. Dorman, courtesy, Tennessee State Museum, Tennessee Historical Society Collection.

Sarah Anne Ellis Dorsey, 1829–79, novelist and biographer, and owner of Beauvoir plantation, bequeathed to Jefferson Davis.
Courtesy, Beauvoir, the Jefferson Davis Shrine, Biloxi, Mississippi.

Anne Charlotte Lynch Botta, 1815–
1891, Sarah Anne Ellis's governess and
lifelong friend. She sustained a salon of
intellectuals in New York City from
the 1840s to her death.
*Courtesy, Metropolitan Museum of Art,
Bequest of Vincenzio Botta, 1895.*

Edward Lyulph Stanley, 1839–1925,
2nd Lord Stanley of Alderley, leading
Liberal reformer, and friend of Sarah
Dorsey.
Nancy Mitford, ed., The Stanleys of
Alderley: Their Letters Between the Years
1851–1865 *(London: Chapman & Hall,
1939), opp. p. 286.*

Routhland, site of the Ellis family's residence. The original house having burned in 1855, Charles Dahlgren erected this house (later called Dunleith) in Natchez, Mississippi; the Ellis-Ware graveyard is across the street.

Courtesy, Mississippi Department of Archives and History, Jackson, Mississippi.

Beauvoir, plantation home of Sarah
Dorsey, who bequeathed it to Jefferson
Davis before her death in 1879.
*Courtesy, Beauvoir, the Jefferson Davis
Shrine, Biloxi, Mississippi.*

Jefferson Davis, ex-President of the
Confederacy, and Varina Howell
Davis, recipients of Sarah Dorsey's
bequest.
*Courtesy, Beauvoir, the Jefferson Davis
Shrine, Biloxi, Mississippi.*

yellow fever, Varina Davis left Beauvoir for Memphis in October 1878. Despite her insistence that he accompany her, Davis, feebly excused himself on grounds of illness. To be sure, he grieved for the loss of his twenty-one-year-old son and wondered how long it would be before he joined his four sons—all now dead.[51] His wife had good reason to fret over his absence from the funeral party.

Throughout these months of Davis's presence at Beauvoir, the connection between Sarah Dorsey and her boarder became a matter of almost open scandal. Yet both were impervious to the gossip. Convinced, as always, of his own pure motives, the onetime President of the Confederacy was as intractable, obstinate, proud in domestic affairs as he had been as a war leader. One historian has noted that a basic trait in Davis's character "was the strict observance of internalized standards of honor." As a result he was often self-righteous in a way that "gave him a repellent manner," as Varina Davis later styled it. His inelasticity had much to do with his inclination to despondency. That problem partly grew out of the early loss of his father and, in 1835, the premature death of his first wife, "Knoxie" Taylor, for which he might have held himself accountable, were he capable of self-understanding. (Against his own better judgment he had moved his bride to Hurricane plantation at the height of a summer pestilence.) Unable ever to say "I was wrong," Davis did not feel that he could afford to let down his guard without forfeiting his manliness.[52]

As early as November or December 1877, Sarah Dorsey had realized that she had not long to live. Although only forty-eight years old, she had breast cancer. Despite promises made to various family members about the help she intended to give them by gift or bequest, she resolved to make her sole commitment to Jefferson Davis's ease in retirement. During the Christmas season, 1877, she had her suspicions of Davis's financial state confirmed. Through her friend General Jubal Early, then a lawyer in New Orleans, she learned that he had just about exhausted what little capital he had.[53]

On January 4, 1878, Sarah Dorsey signed a new will at the home of Major W. T. Walthall in nearby Mississippi City, making her "most honored and esteemed friend Jefferson Davis" the only heir of her fortune. "I do not intend to share the ingratitude of my country toward the man who is in my eyes the highest and noblest in existence," she explained. Should Davis die before her, his sole surviving child Winnie was named the next heir. As it turned out, Davis's daughter lived a solitary existence under her parents' roof because they had refused her permission to marry into a prominent Yankee and abolitionist family. Winnie died in 1898, not outliving her mother who inherited Sarah Dorsey's property from her daughter, although Sarah Dorsey, her rival, had never so intended.[54] As for the Dahlgren and Ellis relations, Sarah Dorsey declared in her will, "I owe no obligation of any sort whatever to any relative of my own. I have done all I could for them during my life."[55] Her words revealed considerable bitterness.

In the months before her death, Sarah Dorsey broke her connections with her Dahlgren relatives one by one without much regret. First Mortimer Dahlgren left Beauvoir when he discovered that he was no longer the manager of the estate; Davis had taken full control. Then, Sarah and her sister Inez had a row which they never settled. Beginning with childhood, their relationship had never been close, Sarah, having been a favorite of her father, whereas Inez was doted on by her mother because Inez's beauty, tastes, and intellect more resembled her own. Considering her sister light-headed, Sarah confided to Lyulph Stanley, "She was very pretty & a spoiled belle in society." The two sisters had both been interested at one time in Arthur Haliburton of Halifax, Nova Scotia, whose father had been a prominent jurist and Canada's first comic novelist ("Sam Slick"). At this time an adjutant-general of India, who later would be knighted for his work on British army reforms, Arthur Haliburton had once courted Inez Ellis but took no interest in Sarah. Thirty years later Sarah still harbored her jealousy. The break came when, at the instigation of half-brother Adolphe Dahlgren of Nashville, Tennessee, Inez Peckham confronted Davis and Sarah Dorsey with the public rumors about their relationship. At the height of the squabble she pulled out Adolphe's letter objecting to their arrangement. Recriminations and angry words flew even thicker and faster; Sarah Dorsey resolved never to associate with Inez Peckham again.[56]

In June 1879, Sarah Dorsey left Beauvoir to undergo surgery in New Orleans which proved unsuccessful. She spent the post-operative days in the St. Charles Hotel and the only relative she would see was young Mortimer, to whom she renewed promises made earlier to leave him her lands in Arkansas. She refused a deathbed reconciliation with Inez Peckham and told a friend at the bedside: "I do not blame her for anything she has said or done to me; but I can never forgive her for her attack on Mr. Davis."[57] Sarah Dorsey died on July 4, a day of double irony. It was the anniversary date of the fall of Vicksburg and also the birthday of the Union from which she became as alienated as her elderly hero had been.

A further sign of a hidden anger about the past was Sarah Dorsey's decision not to lie in death next to her husband Samuel but rather to be buried beside her father in the Routh family plot on Homochitto Street, Natchez, opposite the great mansion Dunleith. In her novel *Lucia Dare,* she had all but prefigured her choice. In 1867 she wrote, "City of my heart—city of my love—city of my childish joy. Oh, city of my dead!"[58] One is reminded of Ellen Lee's poem, "The Lighthouse of Natchez," verses that commemorated mother Sarah Percy's grave site. Ellen Lee's grave is located next to her mother's. For Sarah Dorsey, father, not mother, was the object of mourning. Long after burial, both of these parents, separated from their children so early, had exercised profound influence upon their sensibilities.

⚜ ⚜

Within a week of Sarah Dorsey's death, Jefferson Davis applied to the court for the probating of the will, the contents of which soon appeared in the newspapers.[59] To their complete chagrin, the Dahlgrens and Ellises discovered the extent of Sarah Dorsey's munificence toward the former President of the Confederacy. With bitter memories of the war and Reconstruction still very much alive in the swirl of partisan politics, Davis's windfall became the center of a minor storm. The former President's friends and admirers rushed to his defense, publicly insisting that the Dahlgrens and Ellises were living in "easy circumstances," especially when compared with the penniless Davis family.[60] In addition, they insisted that Sarah Dorsey had been not only a close girlhood friend and classmate of Varina but also an admirer of Jefferson Davis even as a little child in Natchez, an affection that had never diminished over the years.[61]

Sarah Dorsey's Ellis and Dahlgren sisters and brothers found themselves portrayed as slanderers of Davis's glorious name, with no legal, much less moral ground for challenging the will. Their complaints, declared the always aggrieved ex-President, were "born of greed and hate—the filthy progeny of the *auri sacra fames.*" The charges were "unqualifiedly false, malicious and contemptible" and, thundered Davis, the slanderers were inviting the dead widow's "lustrous eyes" to "wake from the lethargy of the grave and pierce with their scornful glances the foul ghouls, who, under the guise of relationship," were resorting to a malicious lawsuit.[62] Such, however, was not the case. Old General Dahlgren had lost everything in the war, but only a little desperation, not greed, was uppermost in his thoughts. The Philadelphia reporter who interviewed the old soldier—"tall and gray," with "a steady step and clear eye"—had no doubt that Dahlgren was telling the truth—as Dahlgren saw it. Though not a party in the upcoming lawsuit, Dahlgren wished his own children and the Ellis heirs to gain some financial security.[63]

What chiefly hurt Dahlgren to the quick, he claimed, was Sarah Dorsey's complete rejection of him and all the others in the family, despite everything he had done to take her father's place in her heart. Discreetly, he said nothing about his financial rescue of the family fortune after Thomas Ellis had lost it in speculations. Others in the family were also dismayed. Particularly hard for postmistress Appoline Ellis of Philadelphia and Stephen Percy Ellis to accept was Sarah Dorsey's apparent disinheritance of their respective daughters, Mary and Lilian. Both were young, unmarried dependents of financially vulnerable parents. They would have no dowry to bring to a marriage.

In working up challenges to the probating of the will, the Dahlgrens insisted that Davis had violated the law by insinuating himself into the widow's affections when she was mentally vulnerable. But actually there was no evidence to support their charges. Davis was most likely monogamous, despite Varina's suspicions, and Sarah looked for emotional and intellectual gratification but not sexual fulfillment. Besides both were so often ill—he with an accumulation of depressive disorders and she with breast cancer. Moreover, Sarah was a thorough Victorian about such matters. In *Panola* (1877), her last novel, she had reflected on sexual passion: "the reason why there are so many wretched marriages is because men and women mistake this common and universal magnetism, for *real preference,* for true sympathy, for holiest love; and it fails them, as all mere physical impulses do." The important element, she continued, was not the act of love but "being *perfectly* appreciated and *understood.*" That, for her, was what she had found in her relationship with Jefferson Davis. This lonely "high-strung" pair had genuinely achieved the inner repose with each other that she had long sought.[64]

After a long search for a lawyer to take their case, the Dahlgrens hired attorney William Reed Mills of New Orleans, who entered a bill in equity in December 1879 against Davis. The plaintiffs professed that Sarah Dorsey had been temporarily irrational and subject to "undue influence" in her disposition of the estate, a claim effectively refuted by Davis's attorney, Clement Walker.[65] Charles Dahlgren tried to introduce the long record of mental illness from the Percy line, but Attorney Mills probably saw that such a tactic would be counterproductive since Stephen Ellis and other litigants were themselves genetically tainted, as it were. But Charles Dahlgren let the word reach the press. "There is something unbalanced about the family, and there have been seven cases of mental derangement in their history in this country," he told a reporter. First, there was the suicide of "Capt. Percy," he enumerated, along with Sarah Dorsey's grandmother "who died insane in my house," something of a misrepresentation since he did not live at Routhland until five years after her death.[66] There were other misstatements in his account as well.

Yet why did Sarah Dorsey give Jefferson Davis all her property? Her antagonism toward her step-father as well as her own people was a factor. One might even call Sarah Dorsey's repudiation of her family a singular mark of vindictiveness. Legally she had every right to bestow her property in any way she liked. But she had been a woman determined to adopt Davis as the embodiment of the lost cause. Her hostility was directed less toward her younger brothers and sisters than it was toward Charles Dahlgren who had refused to recognize her virtuosity of mind without also charging that she "had," as he put it, "the family characteristic, which was impulsiveness."[67] Dahlgren represented something she could not tolerate, a passionate skepticism about her judgment and her Confederate hero. As Sarah Dorsey well knew, General Dahlgren had long resented Davis as his Commander in Chief. In 1863, he had offered a scheme to save the Confederacy that was forwarded to the President in Richmond, but his design would have left Virginia virtually undefended, hardly a wise risk from any perspective. Davis had rejected it, and Dahlgren never forgave him. It galled the old general with his law office on Broadway, a "monotonous" thoroughfare of "huddled buildings," to think that his nemesis should enjoy the fruits of Dahlgren's own labors as savior of the bankrupt Ellis estate. Tears welled up in his eyes when he talked with a Philadelphia reporter. The principle involved was not money alone, the estate being worth about $50,000, but a question of family integrity. Aristee Tissot, the presiding judge, rejected the plea without comment. The case was not appealed to the United States Supreme Court probably because the Dahlgrens saw little chance of success.[68]

Sarah Dorsey should not be judged too harshly. Like most others of her time and section, she suffered from unusual pressures that were bound to weigh down the spirit. Demoralization of Southern white families was a serious consequence of the war—the mourning for lost kindred and neighbors, the wrenching adjustments to be made in race relations, the woes of lost investments and treasure, ruined homesteads. Above all, a devastation of spirit far outlasted the destructive boom of cannons, the wreckage of a once proud and prosperous country. The Southern whites had brought the misery on themselves, but that circumstance hardly made the situation more endurable. Indeed, the conflict led so many Southerners toward a degree of insensitivity. Lost self-esteem, alcoholism, "neurasthenia," and mindless violence were sometimes the consequences. Veterans of a more recent conflict, it may be said, would recognize the tragic emotional effect of defeat and rejection. The distortions of character that the widow's decision brought to the surface should be seen as a partial result of a postwar Southern malaise.

In addition, there was a sense of feminine self-sacrifice for the good of a worthy knight, as Sarah Dorsey saw the matter. She had already relinquished her ambitions in order to retain her standing as a Southern lady of culture. Her family history, so rooted in Southern conservatism, had constrained and ultimately defeated her efforts as author and educator. So determined was she to reject fame and intellectual recognition—so unsuitable for a Southern matron—that she had Jefferson Davis burn all her papers upon her death, except those needed for legal and financial purposes. That was a greater loss to posterity than the way in which she disinherited kinfolk and bestowed wealth on an ill-tempered and distracted old man.[69] Her decision to leave everything in the hands of her idol revealed a heart deadened against her kindred but alive to a legend that would animate the South for years to come. She would not be the last of Charles Percy's descendants to live in the realms of the imagination.

PART THREE

The Greenville Percys

CHAPTER NINE

A Knight-errant's Defeat

"Nothing is so sad as defeat, except victory."
William Alexander Percy[1]

Sarah Dorsey would not be the last Percy to taste the bitter dregs of defeat for yet another "lost cause" lay ahead for the family. Just as Sarah Dorsey and other members of the extended Percy clan had rejoiced patriotically in the early days of the Confederacy, so, too, did the next generation as though they were riding the tides of power. In 1910, LeRoy Percy was elected to the United States Senate from Mississippi, the highest office that any family member had achieved in America.

Percy's friends fully expected his selection to be the first step toward a national career, but the Greenville attorney fell far short of any political goal after that initial triumph. Several contingencies conspired against his advancement. First, no Percy had ever enjoyed or sought public popularity. Although his father, Colonel William Alexander Percy, had returned from the Civil War a hero and had ruled a small kingdom of local power in the Delta from his law office in Greenville, he retired from politics after 1878 in spite of having helped as Speaker of the Mississippi House of Representatives to overthrow "Black Republicanism." The "Gray Eagle," as the Rebel veteran was known, devoted himself to serving his corporate clients, to building levees and railroads in the Delta, and to other civic and financial enterprises. LeRoy Percy, like his father and senior partner at law, ordinarily preferred to be behind the scenes, directing political affairs with Captain John S. McNeily of the Greenville *Times* (and later Vicksburg *Herald*), and other conservative cronies. He enjoyed his reputation among his father's circle of conservatives for getting things done, especially in the Delta, but he did not push himself forward to gain statewide notice.[2]

Old rivalries that Colonel Percy had first aroused in the 1870s also bedeviled him. Confederate General Alexander G. Paxton, a neighbor at Deer Creek who had supported the various independent tickets that ineffectually challenged the Percys' power, in 1885 denounced the cotton assessment that funded the Percy-controlled Levee Board. It was "a tax upon labor, a tax on the poor, while the rich go free," Paxton protested.[3] In the next generation, John Hebron, a wealthy Paxton kinsman, and Ray Toombs, who had married the general's granddaughter Nellie Paxton, carried the family grievances well into the twentieth century. Hebron ran for county sheriff against the Percy nominee, Nathan Goldstein. "Goldstein beaten, and the Jews very bitter over it. I can't say I think much of Hebron, the successful candidate," Harry Ball, a faithful Percy enthusiast of Greenville, recorded in his diary. Still worse, Governor James Vardaman later put John Hebron on the Levee Board rather than a Percy placeman. Hebron and Percy Bell, a young lawyer, would be Vardaman's key supporters in the Delta.[4]

Percy's chief political weakness was unabashed corporate conservatism. The close-knit oligarchy to which the Percys belonged had not lessened Mississippians' dependence on cotton, a crop too often overproduced and undervalued. A mediocre system of education for both races ill prepared workers for skilled jobs. Mississippi's forty-six banks had no more than ten million dollars in deposits. Nearly everyone, even the richest planters, was constantly in debt to someone else. LeRoy Percy lamented, "Easy credit has been the curse of this section," but keeping out of debt was scarcely easy.[5] Unlike industrializing Alabama, where Walker Percy, LeRoy's brother had settled in the early 1880s, Mississippi had no iron or coal deposits to exploit, and general manufacturing did not take their place. As LeRoy Percy pointed out himself, cotton profits in Mississippi, no matter how great, would probably never "find investment in factories."[6] Meanwhile, Delta plantations were growing larger and small freeholders were being driven from the land.[7]

A further obstacle to Percy's long-term political hopes was a declining base of regional power. The Delta no longer exercised the kind of muscle it once had within the state political system. From 1896 to 1908, a succession of administrations—those of McLaurin, Longino, and Vardaman—had undermined the Percy faction's control of offices in the region. Instead, men with loyalties to the governors dominated the state agencies.[8] Moreover, Vardaman's reform projects as governor shook the corporate establishment which LeRoy Percy so often represented in litigation.[9] When prohibition became a major factor in the state at the beginning of the twentieth century, prohibitionist resentment of the high-flying, dance-crazy aristocrats of the Delta was bound to doom the statewide candidacy of any Delta politician. The highly popular Senator John Sharp Williams was the only statewide leader with a boozy reputation.[10] In 1902 a further shock to conservative and Delta interests was the passage of a new primary law that withdrew power from the state convention, a body dominated by planters and corporation leaders. As a major figure at the once powerful state conventions, Percy had to face a new order of the day.

Percy did have a few political advantages. Among the most important was the rootedness of the family in the Delta. A few retrospective remarks are necessary to indicate the Percys' role in the district, but the continuity of troubles faced by the family members helps to explain why the achievement of power came with a degree of desperation. Squire Thomas George Percy of Huntsville, Alabama, had first bought land on Deer Creek in 1829. To develop a vast plantation operation on lands recently seized from the Choctaws, he joined financial forces with other family members. Those involved were: Major Nathaniel Ware (who sold out early); Samuel Brown; Elisha Warfield, husband of the novelist Catherine; and a Warfield kinsman, Samuel Worthington of Baltimore County, Maryland. The last was also related to the Dorseys (although Sarah's marriage took place many years later). From Belfield, Squire Percy dispatched some ninety slaves to clear the wilderness and expose the rich alluvial soil along Deer Creek for cotton-planting. An absentee landlord, he did not, however, live long enough to leave Huntsville himself and move to the raw frontier. After his death in 1841, widow Maria Pope Percy carried out her husband's plan and resettled on Deer Creek, some twelve miles east of the future village of Greenville. Charles Brown Percy, the squire's eldest son, brought the remaining slaves, the household goods, and tools on barges by way of the Tennessee and Mississippi rivers. Death, however, traveled with them. Maria and Squire Thomas had already lost several youngsters in Huntsville; after 1841, more died in the 1840s. From a brood of eight only three sons survived to middle age: William Alexander, a lawyer trained at the University of Virginia; John Walker and LeRoy Pope. The latter pair devoted themselves to medicine though neither practiced.

When secession fever struck Mississippi in 1860, the Percys, still loyal to Whiggery, were no less Unionist than Sarah Dorsey or Catherine Warfield. William Alexander, though, eagerly seized the chance to prove Percy valor. He organized a cavalry outfit which he dubbed the Mississippi Swamp Rangers. Eventually reaching the rank of colonel, he survived the siege of Vicksburg. He then joined the Army of Northern Virginia, serving in the Second Corps, under General Armistead L. Long, chief of artillery. Long, a highly experienced West Pointer, was one of Lee's most competent and reliable subordinates. Colonel Percy remained with that unit until the surrender at Appomattox.[11] For his heroic exploits in the Shenandoah of Virginia, he earned the soubriquet "the Gray Eagle of the Valley."[12]

By 1865 the war had ravaged the Deer Creek neighborhood. Percy Place, as the Deer Creek plantation was called, however, survived intact. Nannie Armstrong Percy, the "Gray Eagle's" wife with a Presbyterian heritage, proved herself a worthy daughter of a general and friend of Andrew Jackson. During the war, Nannie Percy managed the property alone and kept her brood of five growing children alive and well throughout the conflict: Fannie; LeRoy; William Armstrong; Walker; and Lady, named for Nannie Armstrong's mother. Walker Percy, the novelist, had Nannie Armstrong in mind when, in *The Last Gentleman,* he characterized the Confederate women as those "lovely little bitty steel-hearted women" who guarded the cotton rows with a gun across their knees or quietly rocked on the front porch and "made everybody do right."[13] Nannie had saved not only the Percy cotton for peacetime sale but also "Bill Jack," the last horse in the Percy stable. She hid the nag in the woods. Mounted on the unhandsome creature, the "Gray Eagle," on his return, went down the long, muddy road to Greenville to open the doors of his fledgling law practice.[14]

Colonel Percy thrived in business and politics. During Reconstruction, to oust Governor Adelbert Ames and the rest of the "Black Republicans," he advocated a "fusion" policy. Rich planters, mostly of Whiggish persuasion, joined with those Delta blacks who could be enticed, bribed, or coerced to vote Democratic. A few offices were set aside for blacks to fill. The policy was shoddy and at times plainly dishonorable, but it was at least a less violent approach than that of the "straight-outs" or anti-black zealots in Democratic ranks. Elected to the state legislature when the Redeemers seized the reins of government in 1876, Percy was elected speaker of the lower chamber in Jackson. With the Republicans virtually eliminated from the political scene, Percy retired from office-holding in 1878 to devote his energies to building his law practice and his power on the Levee Board. That agency—on which served Percy's kinsman by marriage, General Ferguson—was the best source of patronage in the Delta. The colonel's advocacy in Washington and throughout the Mississippi Valley for sturdier levees and his persistent efforts for bringing in railroads were his outstanding contributions to the local economy. Though mentioned several times as a worthy, conservative nominee for a Senate seat, governor's chair, or cabinet post in Washington, invariably he declined.[15] The colonel's son LeRoy would have been wise to follow his father's example.

Yet for the Percys, peace, restored white rule, and an increasingly comfortable living did not satisfy the claims of death. Colonel Percy's brother John Walker Percy (for whom the colonel had named his son Walker) had already died very young before the end of the war. The non-practicing physician left a widow, Fannie, and a daughter, May, for his brother William Alexander and Nannie Percy to care for. Then in 1882 came a double tragedy. LeRoy Pope Percy, the family's intellectual and last of the Colonel's brothers, suffered greatly from hypertension.[16] All his life, the sad-eyed bachelor, "Uncle Lee," as he was called, lived under the same roof with William Alexander, Nannie, four of their children, Fannie, brother John Walker's widow, and her daughter, May. In 1873, LeRoy Pope expressed his gratitude by bequeathing to his energetic brother all his property. "I do this," LeRoy Pope Percy advised, "out of the great love and affection I have for him, having never received any thing but kindness and brotherly love from him." These are his only written words to have been preserved. "Uncle Lee" took special interest in Fannie, his brother William Alexander's eldest child. In 1882 she fell desperately ill at Eureka Springs, Arkansas, a summer resort and health-cure location. As her condition worsened, LeRoy Pope blamed himself for having put her in the hands of a quack. In despair for reasons that family reticence and his own silence obliterated long ago, LeRoy Pope Percy deliberately ended his life with an overdose of laudanum on June 27, 1882. It was a day before his niece Fannie expired. He was fifty-eight; she, a young married woman, just twenty-three. Colonel Percy and Fannie came by train to Eureka Springs to escort two coffins to Greenville.[17]

Under these trying circumstances Colonel Percy felt a special weight of responsibility on his shoulders. If he did not reestablish the fortunes of the Percy tribe, no one else would. He moved the family from Deer Creek to a new house in Greenville, seat of Washington County, to be nearer the courts and his law office. Yet with so many kinfolk to lodge, he had had to build a large, rambling dwelling at considerable cost. He also had to pay for the educations of his sons LeRoy, William (Willie) Armstrong, and Walker. The colonel decided that he could not afford the tuition at Princeton, his alma mater, so, they attended the University of the South, in Sewanee, Tennessee. Then all three went on to law school, a further imposition on his resources. With a household of dependents, and his daughter Lady still at home, the grocery and doctors' bills made heavy demands on his income. While these obligations might have broken someone less driven, the cost Percy paid in health was much higher than he knew at the time. Six years after burying "Uncle Lee," the colonel's health was shattered. Alarmed, Nannie Percy wrote her sister in Nashville, in early 1888, "My dear husband is never very well now—suffers with colds & a cough that comes on in the early fall & keeps up all winter—& quite wears him out at times."[18] She tried to slow him down, Nannie wrote, but it was impossible. "I regret so much with all the money he has had made & given away & spent—that he is. not able to leave off working so hard but his labours are greater every year." Within three weeks of conveying her fears, her husband, the last heir of Squire Thomas George Percy, was dead at the age of fifty-three.[19] Eleanor Percy Lee's daughter Kate, who lived with her husband ex-Rebel General Samuel Wragg Ferguson next door, dedicated one of her mother's frequently reprinted poems to William Alexander Percy's memory.[20] Like an eagle, the colonel's admirers believed, he had striven too hard and plunged to a defeat in death. Yet he had bequeathed a legacy of substantial accomplishment. The last lines reflected the poet's own cast of mind. She wrote:

> Then comes the hour of sudden dread
> Then is the blasting sun-light shed;
> And *the gifted* fall in their agony,
> Sun-struck eagle! to die like thee!

The theme of glorious defeat that Ellen Lee first evoked would reappear in the Percy family annals.

❦

With little difficulty LeRoy Percy, already a partner in his father's law firm, filled his father's place in the law firm and community. For that purpose he was physically well suited. As a child, the novelist Walker Percy remembered his standing in the L & N station in Birmingham in 1928. The train on which he was booked stopped only momentarily but it afforded a quick visit with his nephew LeRoy Pratt Percy, who was the novelist's father. Dressed in a light tropical suit, he had an air of vitality, but, said the novelist, his great-uncle "was small, smaller than I expected. He was a very handsome and trim figure of a man with a white moustache, very erect and rather imperial looking." [21]

LeRoy Percy's early career demonstrated that he was a gambler by instinct. He knew his cards well, but sometimes overplayed his hand, leading to losses at both poker and politics. He had a vitality that few men possess, but also an inclination, at times, to serious dejection. His son Will Percy sometimes overstated his father's virtues, but he perceived the two sides that his father exhibited: LeRoy could carouse like an Elizabethan, but also descend in gloom while perspiration dropped from his face and "you could feel him bleed inside." He could laugh and enjoy the good things of life but never, Will Percy insisted, did he forget that human existence was "unbearably tragic." [22]

Joe Rice Dockery, a rich planter's son remembered fondly how his father and he used to hunt ducks with Percy. Before taking their guns to Lake Charles, Louisiana, the trio would spend a few days in New Orleans. The seniors would play poker or bridge all day at the Boston Club, after which dinner at Antoine's was often the capstone of the evening. With the dash and good looks of "a Hollywood movie star" and the steady composure of an old-school gentleman, "he was my idol," Dockery concluded. [23] Such bonhomie assured him an informal network of fellow lawyers, bankers, and other men of means around the state. Camaraderie and the Percys' record of noblesse oblige and honor-conscious behavior, however, would be insufficient to meet the challenge of a populist insurgency. Reality and the Percys' almost mythical sense of indomitablity would struggle, and reality would be the victor.

Building on the tide of racism flooding the South during the 1890s and the years following, James Vardaman aroused the voters to near frenzy with his flamboyant appeals to white supremacy—and to reform. Historian Neil McMillen points out, "As a social ideal," the Percys' kind of genteel paternalism "was no match for the more savage impulses of racism." [24] Politicians, including such patricians as John Sharp Williams and LeRoy

Percy, could not escape the dictates of the Savage Ideal, as journalist W. J. Cash called it. Later, as senator, for instance, Percy joined Williams to protest in high places the retention of a Mississippi black postmaster with twenty years' tenure. Obligingly President Taft moved him to another federal job. Such efforts were well within the boundaries of contemporary prejudice. Yet neither Delta leader would match Vardaman who declared in 1907, "If it is necessary every Negro in the state will be lynched, it will be done to maintain white supremacy." [25]

The Percys typed James Vardaman, with his white suits and flowing hair, as a race-baiting rabble-rouser or at best as Will Percy sneered, "a top-notch medicine man." [26] Though enemy to the black race, as governor he initiated significant reforms: higher taxes to help the wards of the state—the orphaned, the deaf, blind, and insane; increased school funds; and regulatory laws to control the utilities, timber interests, whiskey trust, and railroads. Although hostile to black education, Vardaman battled the convict lease system to which more blacks than whites were subject. [27] The Percys' hostility was not just a revulsion against Vardaman's racial tirades but a deep-seated antagonism against his populist, anti-corporate state program.

Governor Edmund F. Noel, Vardaman's conservative successor, appointed James Gordon, an old Confederate hero, to fill the seat of Senator Anselm J. McLaurin, who had died suddenly just before Christmas in 1909. The move was a temporary expedient until the Democratic legislative caucus could meet to elect a permanent replacement. In the Delta the politicians expected that LeRoy Percy and James Vardaman would be the chief contenders. Elsewhere in the state, however, Vardaman's immense popularity was thought to have virtually assured him the appointment. To head off a stampede for Vardaman, Governor Noel skillfully arranged for an array of minor candidates to come forward. A New York reporter cynically wrote, "Every 'favorite son' from up the forks of the creek and elsewhere was brought to Jackson, patted on the back," and pledged undying support. [28]

In early January 1910, the Jackson hotel managers, boardinghouse matrons, cafe owners—the Busy Bee was a favorite spot—and liquor dispensers must have greeted the New Year with special joy. Jackson was filled to the brim with legislators, candidates, their friends and retainers, and seedy professional camp-followers—the gamblers and prostitutes who always turned up when the politicians and lobbyists gathered. Among the "Freebooters of Fortune," as a reporter labeled them, were Mrs. Carrol Johnson Neil, a tall, thin, middle-aged Southern-born woman, who called herself a traveling real-estate representative, and her friend Ruby Hall, who was married to the manager of the Lemon Hotel, headquarters for the Vardaman faction. Both were prepared to help any candidate who had the money to buy their services. Meanwhile, LeRoy Percy's faction had engaged ten rooms at the Edwards House. Brothers William Armstrong Percy and Walker Percy established themselves there. William Armstrong Percy was then a thriving attorney in Memphis who participated in local political affairs and was considered a rising politician on the state scene. LeRoy was sure that brother Willie's expertise would help his campaign. Walker Percy also added strength to the Percy cause. As counsel for the Tennessee Coal and Iron Company in Birmingham, he had wide experience in the business world and in Jackson could mingle with the visiting corporation leaders on a basis of equality. Walker had recently become politically active in his hometown, and in 1911 would successfully run for state representative from Jefferson County. He had come to help LeRoy win office but also to learn about campaigning for his own canvass. LeRoy Percy's son, young Will, came along "to be with Father and to help as best I could," he later remembered.[29]

A handicap that the conservatives did not mention was the reputation of their candidate as an aristocrat. Though an obscure figure outside the Delta, those from other parts of the state who did know LeRoy Percy could easily understand why he might raise suspicions among common Protestant folk. He had graduated from the University of the South in Tennessee and the University of Virginia Law School rather than attending local institutions. True he was a family man, rearing two sons, one of whom, sad to say, had died very young. His wife, Camille Bourges, however, was a Roman Catholic of French descent. That connection seemed in the public mind characteristic of a high-living Delta planter who liked to drink and gamble. These attributes would acquire in state politics even more sinister implications in the post-World War I era of the Ku Klux Klan, but such factors did not strengthen his position even at this time. The Delta aristocrats were already disliked in the rest of the increasingly prohibitionist uplands.

A further detriment to his political hopes was his association with powerful planters and businessmen, whom his father, the "Gray Eagle," had first collected. When LeRoy inherited the law firm, he continued to lead the Levee Board cronies in managing Delta affairs. The Percy clique had been embarrassed in 1894 by General Ferguson's abrupt flight to Ecuador when Levee Board funds, for which he was accountable, were discovered to be missing. That incident was particularly hard on his wife, Kate, who had published a racy novel in an effort to keep alive the female literary tradition in the family. His defalcation left her penniless and depressed. To be sure, the scandal was ancient history by the time LeRoy Percy was running for high office, but Ferguson had briefly reappeared only two years before the 1910 election, seemingly intent to revive a scandal so painful to the Percy family.[30]

At the first meeting of the caucus on January 7, Governor Noel's conservatives displayed their control by passing a rule assuring the secrecy of caucus balloting in order to encourage Vardaman backers to break ranks without jeopardy to their reelection. Vardaman was outraged.[31] Some 58
ballots would be cast by 171 delegates before the issue was decided. Over
the six weeks of frantic politicking, Vardaman had the highest plurality
with no more than 78 and seldom less than 65 on all but the last ballot.
Vardaman himself was surprised at his failure to gain a quick majority.
John Hebron and Percy Bell, his Delta backers, warned him that LeRoy
Percy was a tenacious infighter. They knew his mettle from local contests.

January faded into February, with neither side gaining advantage, and
both getting weary. Finally on the evening of February 22, Governor Noel,
Percy, and other conservatives forced the last of the also-rans to retire and
rally behind LeRoy Percy. Shortly before the count began, Percy was alleged to have leaned over to Will Crump, his campaign manager, and said,
"Crump, let's just put it to the touch." A motion to begin the final count
passed. Percy won narrowly, 87 to 82.[32] An uproar followed as the guards
opened the doors to admit the crowd of reporters and spectators, and
when the clamor subsided, Percy pledged that "all the manhood, all the
courage, all the ability and all the industry" with which God had endowed
him would be devoted to the people's interests. Vardaman rose to congratulate the winner but also to announce his candidacy for the full term. The
following day, the legislature, by a vote of 157 to 1, ratified the previous
evening's result.[33]

When the word spread of Percy's selection, hundreds of people in Jackson ran into the streets to celebrate. "It was plainly manifest that the nomination of Percy was popular," concluded a Memphis reporter.[34] Conservatives all over the state rejoiced, but in the Delta the jubilation for the
district's favorite son was truly widespread. While the Percy contingent
traveled back to Greenville on February 25, the town fathers arranged for
a massive demonstration of local pride. Some 30,000 paraded through the
streets with torches to greet the victor as the train from Jackson pulled in
at 7:05. The celebrants had even brought a small cannon up from
Vicksburg.[35]

Throughout those happy days, close observers remarked that LeRoy
Percy presented a "masterful mien which sits naturally with him." Yet he
also exhibited a coolness and detachment almost unnerving. Herman Solo-
man, a Greenville high-school principal, recalled that LeRoy Percy usually
spoke as if he were "a little tired." Even during the victory procession he
seemed drawn, worn out, even grim. A few observers worried that he
might collapse while standing up in the automobile during the parade.
Even if his fatigue had been less a function of melancholy than physical

weariness, the senator-elect had good reasons for pessimism. As he well knew, the conservatives had made no permanent inroads on Vardaman's political strength. Already Percy was on the defensive when he addressed the cheering Greenvillians on that first evening home. His opponents, he pointed out, were slandering his name by calling him "a politician" who had won only "by trickery" and by pushing all the others out of the running until "I pushed Jim Vardaman out." [36]

Over the coming days, LeRoy grew more hopeful. Newspapers across the urban South exulted over the defeat of Vardaman radicalism. Frederick Sullens, editor of the Jackson *Daily News,* hailed the "far-seeing, sagacious, conservative and cool-headed" senator-elect "so resolute as to 'Dare do all that may become a man.' " In the North, the New York *Times* applauded Percy's selection over a diehard demagogue. The incoming senator, the paper declared, was a descendant of "the Northumberland family of which Harry Hotspur was a member." He was more noteworthy, though, as "a level-headed lawyer and business man, who has given much thought to public matters." [37] Flattered by the compliments, Percy may have felt vindicated for having run. His instincts had earlier warned him not to pursue the goal.[38]

※ ※

As soon as he had settled his local affairs, Percy packed his bags and headed for Washington. He was the underdog in the race for the full Senate term, with the primary set for August 1911. A good plan would have been to stay at home to shore up his supporters. Percy, however, was oddly passive. On March 1, 1910, he wrote a friend in Yazoo, "I don't know anything that can be done towards perfecting any special organization" for "months" to come. A full year later—February 1911—Percy had yet to organize a campaign finance committee. There was not a moment to lose. W. A. Speakes, a planter, wrote a friend that he and other Percy friends ought to urge him to build a strong state organization of conservatives. They, too, worried about the rumors of corruption in the legislative caucus.[39]

The political work ahead was daunting, particularly in light of Percy's reputation for being aloof and imperious. According to a New York *Times* reporter, Percy claimed descent from "Hotspur, and all that outfit," but such a background hurt more than it helped. Percy was "suave and dignifiedly courteous" toward his peers, "condescending but still affable" with those he held beneath "his estimate of himself on birth or money." But, the reporter noted, his manner was lofty, "not to say overbearing, toward the hoi-polloi beneath his altitudinous orbit." The journalist wondered how Percy could hope to win.[40]

Then a greater calamity descended. Rumors of bribery and low tactics abruptly became outright charges. Six weeks after the caucus ended, Vardaman, then editing *The Issue* in Jackson, charged that special interests under Percy's direction had offered lobbyists and lawyers special enticements as local counsel, passing out railroad passes, and other inducements. Vardaman thundered that while he had been bravely battling for "white supremacy" and the good of the yeomanry, "every railroad attorney" and the representatives of every trust "that does business in Mississippi" had been scheming his defeat.[41] After a Hinds County grand jury met on March 22 to investigate the stories of corruption, Mississippi newspapers exposed a pattern of conduct that left few caucus participants unscathed. District Attorney M. S. McNeill and the jurors showed much interest in the distribution of liquor, largely because prohibition had become a major issue of the day. According to S. H. Johnson, head clerk at Edwards House, Walker Percy was apparently in charge of his brother's campaign logistics. He "generally had whiskey in his room, I wouldn't say how much," one witness declared, "but you could always get a drink in his room." According to gossip, the Percy faction had liquored up State Representative A. J. Jones, a preacher of Union County. Jones had supposedly chased a chambermaid around the Edwards House corridors, and the campaign managers then allegedly tried to blackmail him into switching his vote to Percy.[42]

A more substantive matter concerned State Senator Walter Robinson of Copiah County, whose zest for whiskey outmatched his zeal for Vardaman. The newsman B. T. Hobbs found his friend from Brookhaven in the room of Frank Cannon, a Percy manager, too drunk even to move. According to Hobbs, later that same evening, Frank Cannon shoved Robinson into a cab and heaved him into the caucus room at the state capitol. After Robinson voted for Percy, he was returned to the Edwards House to swill more alcohol. Hobbs worried that his friend might die of alcoholic poisoning and late that night aroused LeRoy Percy to warn him of the danger. Despite promises to investigate, the candidate did nothing then or later. All of the Percys knew about Robinson's condition, Hobbs insisted, and they wandered in and out of Cannon's room unconcerned. Having covered the story in his paper, Hobbs felt obliged to pack a .32 caliber Smith & Wesson because Frank Cannon had threatened his life. Shortly after that, Hobbs related, delirium tremens overtook the inebriate. The Percy managers hustled him to a hospital. After his recovery, he disowned the card announcing his support for Percy.[43]

Hobbs's testimony was convincing but difficult to prove in a court of law. Less impressive was another witness, State Senator Joseph Oliver Cowart, a down-at-the-heels attorney from Jefferson Davis County. Cowart claimed that to weaken Vardaman's support, two managers of another candidate, Charlton Alexander, tried to bribe him to switch to their man in exchange for an offer of a circuit judgeship. "I told them as for selling my vote," Cowart piously declared, "I wouldn't sell it for no sort of appointment, or anything else."[44] "Will Percy"—that is, William Armstrong Percy of Memphis—invited him to his room at the Edwards House in order to change his mind. Percy, he testified, boasted that he and his brothers "represented practically all of the most important corporations in this country." If Cowart "wanted a position, why, that he was in a position to give me anything I wanted." Cowart could go to Greenville to serve as counsel for the Yazoo and Mississippi Valley Railroad. Cowart said he replied that he no use for the "delta" and was "sorter scared of it." Even more surprising was his claim that Willie Percy of Memphis had promised to get him a job as consul to Japan or China, the Percys having strong connections in Washington. Cowart reported, "I told them I didn't care about leaving the country, and I says, I am not qualified to fill a position like that anyway." Those words were indisputable, but little else in his testimony was.[45]

Despite all the talk, there had not been sufficient evidence of outright bribery to justify indictments. The Edwards Hotel clerk offered meager help and had an uncommonly bad memory about who paid for what rooms reserved for the Percy campaign organizers. Cowart had no presentable witnesses to endorse his reliability.[46] Brother Willie Percy, the only Percy to be subpoenaed, contended that Cowart offered his services for a price that Percy claimed he had at once refused, saying, "Well . . . you can't do business with me." Willie Percy's testimony sounded as plausible as anyone else's.[47]

Embarrassed but undaunted, Percy supporters assured the grand jury that their candidate's campaign had been principled and honest. Van Buren Boddie, Percy's floor manager in the caucus, declared unequivocally that the men who had brought the charges "were liars." On the other hand, Percy, he testified, was "a brilliant high class man of the highest integrity" who would never stoop to "any means that wasn't highly honorable and didn't comport with honor." As for pro-Vardaman Robinson and his binge, Boddie said that the Percy people had rescued him from drink, not plied him with it. They only doled out small amounts to keep him from trembling. Congressman Thomas Spight came to Percy's side to remind voters that the senator-elect was the son of the "Gray Eagle," about whom it had to be said "no nobler gentleman" had ever served the state. "I believe that blood will tell in men as in horses," the congressman continued, and that an "illustrious lineage" was almost proof sufficient in itself to assure Percy's integrity.[48] Under the circumstances, the grand jury made no indictments regarding these matters. A charge more difficult to refute than any raised before, however, lay ahead.

———

In early March, Theodore G. Bilbo, a Vardaman stalwart, announced that a Percy supporter had given him money to change his vote during the caucus balloting. The Percys in Greenville were mystified and dazed, as

LeRoy's son Will Percy recalled in *Lanterns on the Levee.* All they knew was that Bilbo was untrustworthy. The same had to be said of Lorraine Catchings Dulaney, the alleged bribe-giver, who was fanatically anti-Vardaman but not necessarily pro-Percy. He was a flush-faced, middle-aged planter and levee contractor from Issaquena County, "with cold fishy-gray eyes and a stubby, sandy moustache." In 1894, Dulaney's accounts with the state penitentiary revealed a misappropriation of some eighty bales of cotton belonging to the state. Political influence kept him out of prison—and well supplied with its inmates under convict lease arrangements.[49]

The Percys wondered whether Dulaney had been "fool enough to endanger the whole cause of conservatism in Mississippi" by spending money—presumably his own—in a move so fraught with peril. Senator John Sharp Williams and Percy were both perplexed. They knew Dulaney's long affiliation with the late Senator Anse McLaurin, a friendship that scarcely endeared him to the Percys. Some years later a friend wrote John Sharp Williams, Mississippi's senior senator, that "from what I saw and knew . . . improper influences *were* used to defeat" Vardaman. That did not mean, however, that LeRoy Percy was familiar with Dulaney's activities in his behalf.[50] On March 25, 1910, Bilbo told his story to the grand jury. He swore that Ruby Hall and Carrol Neil, the two Percy campaign hostesses, as they might be called, had approached him about switching sides. Bilbo explained that Carrol Neil told him how LeRoy Percy could do much more for him than Vardaman could. The Delta attorney had better connections—corporations in need of county attorneys to represent them. She confessed that Bilbo seemed to her "a bright prospect, and so reported to Dulaney," but claimed not to have discussed a sum. Carrol Neil testified that she thought she was "playing a game" and claimed that she had quit before knowing the results of the negotiations. Disgusted with the low pay for politicking, she took a job with a patent medicine company selling a nostrum for women's complaints.[51]

According to Bilbo's testimony, he and friends planned to have Dulaney bring the bribe money to a whorehouse. It was run by an "octoroon" named Mary ("Mamie") Stamps, then very busy in the legislative season. Bilbo lined up a Jackson policeman to be a hidden witness. The schemers feared a Percy double-cross, so the meeting took place in Dulaney's room at the Edwards House instead. Suspicious, Dulaney demanded to know if Bilbo would "tote fair with us or not," but soon enough he handed over $150 for Bilbo to throw his vote away that night on a write-in nomination. By that means his ballot could be spotted.[52] Dulaney promised to hand over an equivalent amount the following day if Bilbo then voted for Percy. Bilbo, gleeful that his plot was succeeding, showed his roommate, S. B. Culpeper, his stack of small bills and boasted that he had caught a bribe-giver red-handed. Culpeper was president of Clarke Memorial Baptist College and a relative of Bilbo's wife. The next morning and over the next

several days Dulaney paid him the additional money promised, Bilbo testified. The total came to $645, on the understanding that he had voted for
Percy—although he did not do so, the ballots being secret.[53] In essentials,
Bilbo's account did not deviate from testimony of the Vardaman partisans
with whom he had consulted. Corroboration meant little because, declared
one supposedly neutral legislator, most fellow lawmakers "didn't put no
faith in all such rumors, because it is a very easy matter in a contest like
this to get all kinds of rumors up."[54]

On this matter, the grand jury seems well justified in returning an indictment for bribery against Dulaney. Nevertheless, conservatives in the two
state houses did their best to throw the weight of blame upon Theodore
Bilbo and to exonerate the Percy managers if not Dulaney himself. Bilbo,
however, stuck to his story. The senators eagerly collected some 510 pages
of testimony from Ruby Hall, Carrol Neil, Bilbo, Cowart, Dulaney, William Armstrong Percy, and a score of others. Dulaney testified that Bilbo
had solicited the bribe and he had refused to give it. The planter had come
to Jackson simply to defeat Vardaman because his racist diatribes were
driving blacks from his county "by the hundreds into Arkansas." (The only
motion of blacks in the county, according to a newspaper quip, was the
departure of some convicts from Dulaney's plantation, from whom he had
extracted "a liberal profit.")[55]

Bilbo's friends rallied to his side, but they made little impression. S. B.
Culpeper feared losing the conservative patrons of his Baptist college and
told the senators that when Bilbo spoke of "corrupt money" he thought
his roommate was being "jocular." For the benefit of the legislators,
Walker Percy produced a set of affidavits from Chattanooga, Tennessee.
The local police had characterized Carrol Neil's reputation as that of "a
blackmailer, procuress and prostitute."[56] The anti-Vardamanites almost
managed to have Bilbo expelled from the Senate. Though unsuccessful,
the senators congratulated themselves for the "dignified, honorable and
upright" way the hearings had been conducted. The politicians proudly
concluded, "we record with pleasure our confidence" in the newly elected
senator's "chivalrous honor and personal and political integrity."[57]

By a change of venue, Dulaney's trial for corruption took place in Yazoo
City. The town was not far from his native Issaquena County, and very
distant from Hinds, where public sentiment would have surely aided the
prosecution. As expected, the result was acquittal; jury deliberations took
eighteen minutes. The prosecution never had a chance.[58] Most significant
in Dulaney's defense was the credibility of Bilbo's account that Dulaney
had given him a set of small bills. He had carefully placed them in the vault
of the Capital National Bank in Poplarville. Dulaney's attorneys brought in
a Treasury Department official to point out that among the notes turned
over to the grand jury were several bills so new that they had not been
officially issued until after the date of the alleged bribe. Bilbo could not
account for the discrepancy. The novelist Shelby Foote, who obtained

hints of the story from an uncle who participated in the Percy campaign, has suggested that Dulaney supporters may have reached the Poplarville bank president. A switch of currency in the vault could well have been effected, but who did it remains a mystery. Equally possible, Bilbo could have made up the whole story.[59]

LeRoy Percy's friends rejoiced in their moment of triumph, but few senatorial incumbents ever faced more daunting prospects for reelection than LeRoy Percy. Unknown throughout most of the state before his selection, afterwards he was notorious—and disliked—everywhere. Ordinarily he did not have a rhetorical flair to strike back in the language of common folk as Vardaman and Bilbo did. Brodie Crump, whose father, William Crump, served as Percy's campaign manager in 1910 and 1911, thought his most obvious failing lay in his inability to remember voters' names. He left them with the impression of indifference and haughtiness.[60] In this respect he rather resembled Major Nathaniel Ware, when acting governor of Mississippi, whose high-toned manners had alienated the Jeffersonian voters of his day.

In contrast, Bilbo, a little gamecock, was admired for his boastful humor. Bilbo once depicted J. J. Henry, a former penitentiary warden, as "a cross between a hyena and a mongrel," who had been "suckled by a sow and educated by a fool." That episode and others like it sometimes landed Bilbo in the hospital with broken bones, but by playing the amoral trickster role, Bilbo ordinarily won the cheers of the crowd. To the Mississippi farmers, he was, as Will Percy in *Lanterns on the Levee* described the relationship, "a slick little bastard" who could dish it out and take his punishment like a man.[61]

Confident of his popularity, Vardaman centered his senatorial campaign on the issues of corruption and class rather than race. The heart of his strategy was to remind voters of the "secret caucus" question. Constantly he threw in references to the social status of his opponents. In the fall of 1910, Vardaman's *Issue* called Percy "the dead-game plumed-knight of the Poker-table, the Crowned Victor of the Rotten Secret Caucus."[62] His political operatives did likewise. "Prince Percy" and his "Secret Caucus henchmen," a Vardaman manager thundered, sought to "defeat the wish and will of the people of Mississippi."[63]

LeRoy Percy played directly into Vardaman's hands. In 1910, at a county fair at Godbold's Wells, the attorney encountered hecklers who kept him from being heard from the platform. Over the growing tumult the crowd detected the word "cattle" coming from the speaker's mouth and assumed it referred to themselves. Vardaman translated the incident into a popular campaign gimmick. At the Mississippi State Fair in Jackson on October 29, 1910, Percy was greeted with signs proudly bearing the labels, "Low Brows," "Red Necks," "Simple Minded Folks," and "Cattle." At another rally, John Hebron, the Percy family's longtime enemy, was said to "have pitched" the feed for the so-called redneck "cattle" every which way "by the bundle." As the summer wore on, Bilbo retold his story of bribery and corruption with increasing expertise and humor. His audience howled with delight. Even someone as loyal as Will Percy, LeRoy's son, grew worried and wrote his father, then in Washington: "Bilbo has been canvassing this part of the country, very closely, and I believe he is doing harm." Although our kind, he continued, "see nothing in him, except cheap arrogance, and mendacity," his patent medicine pitches "certainly catch the ignorant country vote." [64]

Percy answered the statewide uproar as best he could. F. O. Ingram, a Percy supporter, recalled hearing him argue, "They say I'm a big Greenville aristocrat, and don't care anything about the common man. There are people on my place, white and dark, who have lived there all their lives. I've taken care of them, and I'll continue to care for them." Unwittingly he spoke like a grandee. Percy invariably found himself on the defensive but tried to stain his opponent by charging him with churning the racial waters simply to gain votes. Never in Mississippi's history had race relations been better than at present: "The negro does not fill any offices. They do not vote." [65] Percy did not point with pride to his ancestry, but conservative editors boasted of his descent "from a noble race of men." Among his ancestors, chimed the Memphis *Commercial Appeal,* was a knight who had ridden with William the Conqueror. An eighteenth-century member of the family had been "an intimate friend and companion of Oliver Goldsmith [Bishop Thomas Percy]." Why voters in Jefferson Davis County or Kosciusko should care about his lineage did not occur to the Memphis editor. Moreover, the support of Charles Scott of Rosedale, Governor Noel, Stevenson Archer, a Presbyterian clergyman, and even Senator Williams merely confirmed the impression of establishment support for the incumbent. (Ironically, Vardaman belonged to the same high-toned society in which Percy and these friends moved. He was not, as conservatives characterized him, a "mountebank astride a hobby-horse." [66])

Old issues reappeared to haunt Percy's candidacy as well. Federal authorities, led by a skillful attorney named Mary Grace Quackenbos from New York City, had investigated his management of the huge Sunnyside Plantation across the river from Greenville in Chicot County, Arkansas. From 1896 to 1907, Percy and his partners had imported North Italian immigrants to rent the land and raise cotton. The arrangement, however, violated federal contract labor laws. In addition, with the backing of the Italian consulate officials, the renters complained that they had been reduced to a state of peonage. Percy's guards and employees, they protested, forced them to work until debts to the Sunnyside Plantation were paid—at high rates of interest. Percy's reputation had been stained by the revelations released in the national press, but no federal charge was ever issued. His friend Teddy Roosevelt took his side in the dispute with the Justice Department. Yet the President did not, as some expected, appoint Percy to a federal district bench. John Hebron and other Vardamanite leaders raised the peonage charges once again to embarrass the Delta leader. Indeed, Mary Grace Quackenbos wrote an article in a national magazine which helped to rekindle the Sunnyside controversy. Will Percy, LeRoy's son, moaned in his diary, "How long, O Lord!"[67]

The climax of the campaign occurred at Lauderdale Springs. Bilbo had invited the senator to join him in a debate there and, after first refusing, Percy agreed but called upon brother Walker to meet him there. Will Percy, along with his first cousin, young LeRoy Pratt Percy (son of John Walker Percy and father of the novelist), joined the campaign party, and in *Lanterns on the Levee* Will Percy recorded the scene. After midnight, the memorialist recalled, Uncle Walker came to his room and proposed that Bilbo had to be shot. Before the mirror, Will confessed that he spent half the night pulling out his weapon, trying to remember to release the safety. At six o'clock the next morning, the Percys assembled in the bare little hotel dining room. A few yards away sat Bilbo, by himself. Walker Percy strode into the room, took a seat, and boomed, according to Brodie Crump, "I think I'm going to kill that little son-of-a-bitch sitting over there." Will Percy related that Bilbo pretended not to hear and instead plunged even more intently into his cereal. The point of the incident, as the Percys perceived it, was its illustration of Bilbo's utter cowardice and ungentlemanly behavior. What it also revealed was the desperation of the senator's camp and the almost insane behavior of Walker Percy himself. Seated with two inexperienced young men, he was apparently willing to start a gun battle in which he risked not only his own life but their lives, too. Will Percy observed that "Uncle Walker" was the poorest marksman among the family males, who took pride in being crack shots.[68]

At the rally that followed, Bilbo effectively denounced the "kangaroo court" of the Senate hearing. He claimed to hold Dulaney in higher respect than "old Granny" Noel whose patronage offers were attempts to sell "something that didn't belong to him." At least Dulaney went about getting what he wanted "in a business-like manner" in the exchange of cash for Percy votes. If Percy knew nothing about corruption in his selection, he must have been sound asleep. The crowds cheered upon hearing each charge.[69] In the afternoon, when Percy rose to speak the throng was primed to jeer and hoot. Seated on the hotel gallery, the senator was in the blackest of moods. A constituent named Thompson came up and asked him why he had used the franking privilege to send out his campaign material. Retorting that the question was "contemptible," the senator tried to slug his accuser. Walker Percy, however, intervened. Then the senator rose and, facing Bilbo, exclaimed that his opponent was nothing more than "a low-flung scullion, who disgraces the form of man, a vile degenerate, and a moral leper." He predicted that Vardaman would rue the day that he had enlisted "this bribe-taker, this liar, this consorter with lewd women and frequenter of assignation houses." Alluding to Carrol Neil, the senator declared that Bilbo had only one ally who would collaborate with him, "a poor, broken-down shameless woman of the streets." The audience was so stunned that a gentleman would stoop to Bilbo's oratorical level that they remained silent. Will Percy, however, loyally claimed that his father had "cowed them" with his exciting barrage of "invective."[70]

The campaign turned violent and corrosive, for which result Percy was himself largely to blame. To make matters worse, the conservatives themselves had divided. Charlton Alexander, who had involuntarily retired from the caucus nomination in January 1910, had entered the race in June 1911. The conservatives' joint appearances, designed to show unity, merely led voters to suspect that the old "secret caucus" conspiracy was still functioning.[71] On the hot and sultry election day, August 1, Mississippians turned out in historic numbers, over 60 percent of the eligible voters (nearly all white). Vardaman carried all but five of Mississippi's seventy-nine counties, sixty-one of them by a majority over both candidates. His 79,369 votes overwhelmed Alexander's 31,490 and Percy's pitiable 21,521. Percy had garnered the majority in three counties and a plurality in two more. Vardaman's vote topped the combined conservative vote by a higher count than Percy garnered by himself.[72]

To heap further humiliation upon the Percy forces, Bilbo's 76,240 votes for lieutenant governor almost matched Vardaman's total. Vardamanites were swept into all the other state offices, too. Of the eighty-seven "secret caucus" legislators who had nominated Percy only five survived the Vardaman landslide. Dispensing $20,000 on the campaign, Percy achieved little more than one vote for each dollar spent. Vardaman had seized nearly 80,000 ballots with only $2,000 expended, about three cents apiece.[73]

Standing on his lawn in Greenville, LeRoy Percy promised to resign the seat so that Vardaman could take his place as soon as possible. Friends like Governor Noel, however, demurred. In a typical statement Percy replied to Fred Sullens, editor of the Jackson *News,* "If the result had been a close one[,] the opinions of friends like you" could have changed his mind. Yet "unpalatable and bitter as the truth may be," the people had unmistakably "repudiated" his leadership. He represented no one apart from "an insignificant minority." Nor was he mistaken. Self-interested friends of the senator suddenly discovered new virtues in Vardaman without a moment's thought about the fact that "Right is Right," as cousin Prentiss Knut complained to Percy. In November 1912, Knut hoped that President-elect Woodrow Wilson might select Percy to be his attorney general; he did not. A minority President could hardly afford to alienate the Vardaman people in Mississippi.[74] Disheartened, Percy left with his wife Camille and son Will for a vacation in Greece.

While Percy was absent, the muckraking reporter George Creel of *Cosmopolitan* blasted him as the darling of "the Southern Railroad, the Illinois Central," and several other corporations and banks. He invariably voted their interests, Creel charged: "against the direct election of United States Senators, the Commerce Court, and the Tariff Board."[75] Creel's assault, however, was a gross misreading of Percy's senatorial years. He served conscientiously. Harris Dickson, another conservative like Percy, declared that "no State in the Union was more ably represented than Mississippi" during his incumbency. Whether Dickson's praise was fully justified or not, he had not been corrupt, as Creel had implied.[76] When the Vardaman-dominated state legislature demanded Percy's resignation, Percy refused to quit early after all. He thought Vardaman responsible for Creel's libel in the national press.

The election result left deep psychological scars among the members of the family. LeRoy Percy took his humiliation to heart and felt demeaned and diminished. In a letter to a friend he plotted out for himself a much reduced terrain of activity. "If I can keep this small corner of the United States in which I reside, comparatively clean and decent in politics and fit for a man to live in, and in such condition that he may not be ashamed to pass it on to his children, I will have accomplished all that I hope to do." The sentiment reflected the gentility of its author and suggested a conciliatory mildness. Will Percy observed that his father hated to lose at cards, golf, or politics and showed it. So profound was this loss, though, that he adopted a reticent tranquility. Yet Will Percy detected "an inner sadness" that could not be touched; his father had the "look I suppose Lazarus never outgrew after he had once died."[77] From that response grew Will Percy's own dedication to a Stoic posture—the noble sense of resignation to the indifference of fate, the waywardness of human affairs, and the inevitable ruination of honor in the modern world.

LeRoy Percy was not the only member of the family to suffer over the critical defeat in 1911. All three brothers took it as a deeply personal judgment, and it may have played a hidden role in their declining health. None of them, however, took the loss as hard as LeRoy's son, William Alexander Percy.

CHAPTER TEN

Will Percy: The Years of Testing

> What can I say now that autumn is upon me
> and the frost has pierced to the bone?
>
> William Alexander Percy[1]

With the exception of Walker Percy, the novelist, no other member of the family in the United States ever matched the subtlety and individuality of William Alexander Percy. Unpretentious and self-effacing, he exercised an extraordinary influence upon those around him. In his adult later years, men and women of wit and intellect filled the guest rooms of his house in Greenville. Socially he flourished in the company of young people and genial Southern women, married, widowed, or single. His interests in women, however, were solely gratified in parlor intimacies and never, so far as is known, developed further than that. Nonetheless, he was widely known for his facility for companionship. He was carrying on the tradition which Thomas George Percy had begun and which he in turn was to pass on to his adoptive son Walker Percy.

Equally important in the family annals was his articulation of the Percys' sense of honor. From his father, LeRoy, and from his own studies and personal needs, he was to develop a Stoic outlook, a determination to confront the battles of life with courage and to accept defeat as an inevitable result of great action. Yet idealizing honor in this form had its drawbacks. To win acclaim within the household and in the public arena as well required an agonizing struggle for perfection. But Will Percy strove against the frailties of human nature itself not only to develop in himself virtues that Percys and the Southern public could respect but also to set an example of noblesse oblige for others to follow.

In this highly conscious effort, Will Percy became the most gifted myth-maker in the family, raising the aim toward honor ever higher. Yet because of his aid to struggling artists and his magnetic power over those who came under his spell, he was also the subject of myths. Even his appearance suggested romance, enigma. He was small and frail but his blue-gray eyes could smolder darkly, turn inward to sorrow, or light up with abandon in laughter. In later years, his face looked youthful and his hair, though prematurely silver-gray, still grew thick. Hodding Carter, the Greenville journalist, once noted that he had a "sensitive mouth above a fighter's jaw," a description that captured the twin aspects of his character. He had a musical, sophisticated voice and a soft Southern accent that Northern visitors to Greenville found especially captivating. The writer Lucas Myers, introduced to him at age ten at Sewanee in 1940, remembers him as one of the most arresting figures he was ever to meet, along with the dapper and equally animated Allen Tate, the poet and another resident of the Sewanee mountains.[2]

How effortless it was to idolize Will Percy. He was a good man, but friends and relations refused to recognize him as the vulnerable, troubled human being he was. Some of his literary friends were acutely aware that behind the laughter and graciousness a deep sadness enveloped him. Jonathan Daniels, the North Carolina writer, remarked, "I had a feeling that [his] weariness was deeper than the physical." David Cohn, Will's friend and fellow writer in Greenville, declared, "Loneliness sat with him when he played the piano . . . sometimes hovered as an aura about his head as he presided at his own table bright with laughter." Recalling Will Percy's quick temper, Walker Percy would remark that his first cousin once removed could shift so quickly from telling a funny story "to a level gray gaze cold with reproof. They were terrible and beautiful eyes, eyes to be careful around." Above all, he added in recollection, "I cannot see them otherwise than as shadowed by sadness."[3] The factors that induced the mourning and anger they described and the life of isolation and single state that he adopted can be traced back to his infancy, his upbringing, and his very young manhood.

※ ※

Will Percy was born on May 15, 1885, a little over seven months after his parents' marriage on December 9, 1884. The young couple was then living in the house of Colonel William Alexander Percy and his wife, Nannie Armstrong, an arrangement that was bound to cause tension under the best of circumstances.[4] In that Victorian era, little Will's appearance had to have been a matter of considerable embarrassment and one that provoked gossip. No doubt Mur and Fafar (Colonel William Alexander Percy and Nannie Armstrong), as Will Percy later called them, had moved up the young couple's wedding date as much as possible. Will himself reflected on the ambivalence that reigned at the time. In *Lanterns on the Levee,* he observes, his birth "overjoyed no one" and added that his parents were just starting life with the advantages of good looks and good lineage but no money. The memorialist guessed that "the blessed event" would have been much "more blessed" had it come a "year or two" later—he might have admitted, two months later.[5]

Another handicap was his fragile health and small size. He seemed to take after his "Uncle Lee," dead by suicide in 1882, three years before Will's birth. Like the physician, who had been stricken by paralysis sometime during or just after the Civil War, Will Percy was to suffer from hypertension and other ailments all his life. And also like his uncle, he was never to marry and always to feel extraneous to family life.[6] The Percys' tiny, delicately beautiful child sensed quite early his parents' distance from him. As he grew, he proved himself to be unusually quick and very, very good, as if compliance in all things would bring him greater acceptance.

Quite understandably, the youngster loved nurse Nain, a sixteen-year-old, "divinely café-au-lait." According to psychiatrists, Will Percy scoffs in *Lanterns on the Levee,* he had undoubtedly found in Nain "the comfort of the womb, from which I had so recently been ejected and for which I was still homesick." Nain's undemanding nature and her freely given love drew from little "Peeps," as she called him, some of his most wistful recollections. Sometimes he sobbed disconsolately when cuddled in Nain's arms while she sang to him: " 'Whut's de madder, Peeps?' she would say. 'What you cryin' fur?' But I was learning not so much how lonely I could be as how lonely everybody could be, and I could not explain," he recalls. In contrast, the author is relatively silent about his own mother. He mentions only that they attended Mass together, and he attributes his early and precocious interest in church ritual and sacred music to her influence.[7]

Other women in the family helped to make life a joy for the child—perhaps more than his mother did. Aunt Nana, Camille Bourges's genial sister, was a great favorite. Mur, the Gray Eagle's widow, must have been keenly aware that her grandchild was a living reminder of the parents' youthful indiscretion. She compensated by offering a special attentiveness toward the little boy that her daughter-in-law could not as freely provide. Young Will slept in Mur's bed-chamber. Nightly he watched her fascinating but rather unnerving bedtime habits. The old lady was accustomed to changing from widow's weeds to shining white nightgown and removing "her switch," a "scrawny" knot of artificial hair. Then she would take from her mouth a single tooth "attached to an amazing red thing" that she dropped into a glass of water. The ritual ended as she swallowed some sort of liquid in a brown bottle that she called "Crab Orchard Water."[8]

These mysteries aside, Mur taught him to love flowers, music, and such stories as Mark Twain's *Huckleberry Finn,* Lewis Carroll's *Alice in Wonderland,* and Charles Dickens's "A Christmas Carol." With a little acerbity, he remarks in *Lanterns on the Levee* that some might think that Mur should have read him books on aviation and electricity or equipped him with a "diluted" course in Lenin and Marx. These would have been better preparations for a boy than what she selected. Instead, Will points out, she supplied him lessons "in the human heart," that spirit which never changes. After all the contemporary ideologies of communism, fascism, and capitalism have disappeared, even from memory, "as completely as slavery and the old South, that same headstrong human heart," he writes, "will be clamoring for the old things it wept for in Eden—love and a chance to be noble, laughter and a chance to adore something, someone, somewhere." Will's retrospective thoughts suggest how sorely he missed the 1880s, the time when kind people in Fafar's house responded to his young grief and held him close. So powerful is this theme that one suspects that it underlies his conservative, Stoic philosophy in *Lanterns on the Levee*—the return to the innocence of childhood when a boy could yearn for greatness and parental love—what the historian Richard King has called Will Percy's "longing toward a past heroic age." [9]

While finding warmth among these older women, as youngster and adult, too, Will Percy never could reconcile himself to his father's ambivalence toward him. Regarding that issue, neither he nor LeRoy Percy was fully conscious of just how different they were in temperament and habit. LeRoy used to call him "a queer chicken" but the father meant the term as half endearment for someone whom he could not understand. [10] To acknowledge any genuine antipathy, however momentary, would have been much too dangerous while both of them lived. Instead, the son worshiped him as a god—who was not always a loving one—and demeaned himself as unworthy of the respect and love which, at some level, he knew that LeRoy Percy half-withheld. Almost from his first experiments with toys, Will Percy had bewildered his father. The child took little interest in the kind of aggressive play with bats, balls, and guns that LeRoy Percy would have found reassuring.

As if in defiance of that expectation, Will Percy early showed an artistic and literary aptitude quite mistrusted in that agrarian, conservative part of the South. Once when Will was seven, his father exploded in fury because Aunt Nana, Will's beloved companion, was reading him yet another sentimental romance. Snatching the offending book, LeRoy Percy replaced it with *Ivanhoe,* which he himself read at least once a year. He reacted by identifying with Walter Scott's portrayals of monastic celibacy, not with those of knightly heroism. "It was hard having such a dazzling father," he reminisced; "no wonder I wanted to be a hermit." In *Lanterns on the Levee,* Will Percy declares, "Because of or in spite of Don Carlos he [LeRoy Percy] was kin to Hotspur and blood-brother to Richard Coeur de Lion, and he looked the part," a veritable "cross between Phoebus Apollo and the Archangel Michael . . . He loved life, and never forgot it was unbearably tragic." [11]

Yet despite these romantic attributes that in his adult years Will Percy assigned his father, the young Will could not love him very much. Although they later learned how to accept each other, their moods in these early days, Will Percy reminisced, never seemed to coincide. "He was stern," Will Percy says, "though he never corrected me, and shy, and high-spirited at all the points where I was flat." [12] Will Percy always blamed himself for any deficiency, a common reaction in anyone who had been forced to deal with the disaffection of parents. It signified a wish to avoid any sort of conflict with an older male rival who had all the advantages and commanded the son's veneration. But Will Percy also felt resentment and sense of loss beneath the adulation. The modern reader's sympathy lies with Will Percy who, after all, had the last word on the subject to posterity. His father, of course, had no idea that he might be treated as both sainted hero and half-devil in his son's memoirs, although Will Percy would have denied any such intention. But it must have been very hard for a man of the world to have his first-born and only surviving son seem so prone to cry and run to a woman, and to have so small a frame that he might be mistaken for a girl. It just wasn't what a Southern father of that era expected or wanted. He was mystified.

Camille Percy, who shared all her husband's worries as if they were her own, made no exception with regard to her son. She sought to furnish Will with an education in the "manly" sciences rather than the "feminine" humanities that he loved. When he once announced that, upon growing up, he intended to take holy orders, she immediately pulled him out of the parochial school he was attending. Loyal Catholic though she was, Camille had no intention of producing a celibate priest. Despite her response, Will Percy always associated his mother with the Roman faith. From age ten to sixteen, he was a religious fanatic, much to the exasperation of his parents. His father was proud of his own indifference to religion in any denominational form, and in oedipal fashion, young Will "resented his unchurchliness," or so he recalled in *Lanterns on the Levee*. Characteristically, the son took the blame upon himself for being uncharitable toward a father whom he "boundlessly" admired: "I must have been a hard child to get close to." [13]

Will Percy prayed, fasted, attended Mass, and made his confession "at the slightest provocation," as he recalled. His behavior seemed designed as a statement of fidelity to his mother—even though he knew his zealotry displeased her. He had sought, Will reminisced, an impossible, saintly "perfection." Yet at the same time, "the Satan of my disbelief was at my elbow scoffing, insinuating, arguing, day and night." What was the internal argument about? One can guess that it may have been not just theological matters but in all likelihood the issue of sexuality—so often uppermost in teenage boys' thoughts. One is reminded of the pious terrors that linked sex and religion in James Joyce's Stephen Dedalus in *A Portrait of the Artist as a Young Man*. In Will Percy's case—so innocent compared with the sexually experienced hero in Joyce's novel—the adolescent's showy self-abnegation aroused strong feelings of guilt and rebellion against parents. They, in turn, found young Will both deeply worrying and irresistibly winsome. Later, he shed some light on the matter in a poem called "On Sunday Morning," in which he fondly remembers attending church with his mother, but then he abruptly concludes, "There's something lost, there's something lost,/ Some wisdom has beguiled!" He feels "a thousand miles" away at heart, though he kneels next to his mother who is absorbed in vain prayer for his spiritual return.[14]

In part, Percy's reaction to his mother was a reflection of deep-seated cultural traits in the South. Men counted much more than women. The male Percys of these earlier generations were particularly jealous of their power and pre-eminence. Sometimes it took the form of pride in lineage, although vainglory could be masked in genuine humor. By and large, according to their lights, their wives came from less distinguished stock—even the well-connected Armstrongs, whose genealogical roots in Scotland were much more verifiable than those of the Percy strain. For instance, Will Percy remembered an oil painting of Queen Elizabeth's death that Mur had hung in the gloomy parlor, where it presided over horsehair sofas and heavy, stiff-back chairs. After years of gazing at the monstrosity, he wrote, "I understand why one of those fool early Percys was beheaded for attempting to rescue Mary Queen of Scots." The reader was thus treated to a double message: the Mississippi Percys belonged to the nobility, even in their folly; the Armstrongs fell short. Likewise, Will Percy, perhaps learning the lesson from his father, considered his mother's people a rung or so below the station of the Percy line. The characterization was unfair. The nineteenth-century Bourges had indeed fallen on hard times. The decline of cotton prices during the Panic of 1873 had swept away the wealth of Ernest Bourges, Camille Percy's father. Yet the family was more than "bon bourgeois," as Will Percy condescendingly labels them in *Lanterns on the Levee*. Even he finally conceded that the Bourges's French realism helped to modify "that moony strain of Don Carlos." [15]

To be sure, Will Percy was by no means ill-disposed toward his mother. He worshiped her, too, though saying little about his feelings toward her in *Lanterns on the Levee*. "Southern women were expected to show courage and to remind men of their martial, protective duties," an historian has written. To rear brave sons, the mothers had to be brave themselves.[16] Camille Percy belonged to the admirable and formidable species. Will Percy appreciated his mother's sturdy character as well as her delightfully Gallic humor and endearing qualities. In a letter to his distant cousin and confidante, Janet Dana Longcope of New York, Percy was later to write, "She's one lovely & lovesome person. It's an awful pity I have such a wide queer streak in me—she would have enjoyed so a lot of normal children." [17] The tone of irony is unmistakable. It very much resembles the pervasive air of self-mockery that Will permitted himself in *Lanterns on the Levee*—undercutting his own achievements in the realm of honor and duty that he advocated as life's purpose. His mother was very much a product of conventional culture. Instinctively Will always knew that in some ways he was isolated from her and her expectations.

Compounding his difficulties with his parents was the appearance of a rival in the household when Will Percy was six years old. LeRoy, as he was christened, grew to be superbly virile in his liveliness and interests. Will Percy registered understandable jealousy against the new arrival, who threatened his status as the only child. Writing to Aunt Lelia, another of Camille Percy's sisters, Will, then eight years old, remarked, "I miss you so much I want you to come home" and then the afterthought: "LeRoy is all-right and Mama." [18]

Little LeRoy immediately became the favorite of his father. When he was older, he proved to be a natural athlete and loved to hunt, fish, and play baseball. On one occasion, LeRoy, Sr., took his wife with him to Arkansas so that they could see their son's abilities at the plate. The proud father treated the teams to ice cream afterwards. LeRoy loved to wrestle and romp with the black boys in the neighborhood. He used to ride his pony, bareback, to their section of town to talk with them and their families as they sat on their porches. LeRoy Percy, Sr., understood this boy, "a chip off the old block," as Southerners of that generation never tired of saying. The relationship of the young and the old LeRoy matured into mutual affection and respect. Meanwhile, his older brother was taking piano lessons from Aunt Nana at home, reading, or day-dreaming about knights and castles.[19]

In its singularity, Will Percy's education contributed to his sense of being apart. Indeed, most of his mentors in his youth, as Richard King notes, were, like him, solitary and eccentric. Among them were Sister Evangelist, "a midget of a nun," and Father Koestenbrock, a Dutch-born, alcoholic Roman Catholic priest who, says Percy, was lonely and would be or could be nothing else. Later, Will Percy found a soulmate in the solitary Carrie Stern, his English teacher, whose longstanding friendship rested on a mutual love of poetry. Camille Percy always disliked their association. Carrie Stern encouraged Percy's experimentation with versifying. He used to visit the house of the little Jewish poet, whose modest lyrics appeared in a slim volume that no one reviewed, much to her distress. After she died of cancer, Percy wrote that he had many Jewish friends, but Miss Carrie "was not my favorite Jew. She was my favorite friend." [20] None of the family was anti-Semitic, though conscious of ethnic differences. Rather, the Percys, allied themselves with the Jews in the community, admiring their business acumen, European ways, and sophistication. Will Percy was attracted to them for the additional reason that they knew what apartness from the majority meant.

Sister Evangelist, Father Koestenbrock, Carrie Stern, and other souls whom young Percy admired had a singular courage, observes Richard King, like Percy's own. Oddly enough, LeRoy and Camille Percy were themselves responsible for bringing their boy into contact with these eccentric figures. For instance, rather than send him to Greenville's excellent public school, they dispatched their son across the street to the home of a totally untrained teacher named Judge Griffin. In his cluttered library, the old judge, a former Confederate general, whispered that he was writing an epic called *Ruin Robed* but never read a line to his pupil. Together they pored over Shakespeare, the *Divine Comedy,* and *Paradise Lost.* They also began reading *Othello,* but Will Percy grew increasingly uncomfortable. The play's explicit, even graphic references to sex made him feel deeply ashamed—mortified by thoughts he could not seem to repress. The ten-year-old prudishly persuaded himself that Iago's insinuations were "un-adulterated smut," which, Percy later realized, he nonetheless had enjoyed "exquisitely." Terrified of raising the issue and being denounced and also terrified of saying nothing and dooming his soul, he finally blurted out, "I don't think we ought to read any more *Othello.* It's—it's immoral." The old gentlemen, Will Percy recalls, was rendered "speechless" but "mourn-fully" substituted *The Merchant of Venice.*[21] *Othello* had aroused not just his sexual interests but also a bothersome resentment against Camille, a powerful maternal presence who frightened him and, he imagined, did not provide him the full-hearted love he required.

Perhaps the incident was reported to the parents. In any event, Will Percy's mother decided that the tutorial across the street was not working out. Will Percy interpreted her decision for a change along these lines: "What with learning the eternal verities from my old friend and talking poetry instead of doing sums, Mother judged I was growing a trifle remote from ordinary doings." Perhaps so, but her concerns were greater than that. She feared that he was not going to be the sort of rough and tumble boy that she and LeRoy wanted. Yet she was protective and did not subject him to the schoolyard razzing that he would have had to endure if sent to the public school. Instead, the parents hired E. E. Bass, the Greenville schools' superintendent, to tutor the boy at home in the afternoons.[22]

In June 1900, Will's parents packed him off to attend a military academy associated with the University of the South at Sewanee. No doubt their object was to stimulate the boy's sense of manliness. But, "the small chap," as his father confided to Vice-Chancellor Wiggins, had his permission to apply for the University, if he so wished. Wisely, the brilliant young student did so, sailed through the qualifying examinations, and was admitted at the age of only fifteen.[23] There he passed the happiest days of his life. Sewanee was a celibate young man's paradise. Though secluded in the Tennessee forests, there were scores of lively young men with whom to make friends, hike in the mountains, debate such weighty questions as the existence of God or the Meaning of Life, and compete for honors. Like most colleges of that era, Sewanee provided a world without young women. They came up only for dance weekends or made a fleeting appear-ance when released from a finishing school at nearby Monteagle.

At fifteen, Will Percy found the Tennessee "Arcadia" perfect, and his opinion never changed. There in winter, under a powder of snow, the "pines sag like ladies in ermine" and in spring, he writes in *Lanterns on the Levee,* the dogwood looks like "puffs of ghost caught under the higher trees." He recalled the teachers as kindly "Centaurs." For him, the most important of them was Huger Jervey, who taught romance languages. (The name was pronounced "Hugger" in Sewanee and Mississippi where the pretensions of South Carolinians, saying Hew-gee, were sometimes mocked.) Will Percy especially enjoyed the literature classes of John Bell Henneman, who introduced him to Chaucer. He also studied ethics under the dreamy William DuBose, a renowned theologian of his day. He called DuBose "a tiny silver saint" who sometimes would "suspend, rapt, in some mid air beyond our ken, murmuring: 'The starry heavens—' followed by indefinite silence." The students would quietly remove themselves, "feeling luminous, and never knowing when he returned to time and space." [24]

Will Percy studied hard and performed brilliantly, especially in the classics and literature. Rather than face the quizzical looks of his father, he could rely upon some older students as uncritical mentors: "Percy Huger, noble and beautiful like a sleepy St. Bernard; Elliott Cage, full of dance-steps and song-snatches, tender and protective, and sad beneath; Paul Ellerbe, who first read me *Dover Beach,*" by Matthew Arnold, Will's favorite poet. Arnold, who also had lost his Christian faith, laments that a world which once seemed radiant with fresh promise "Hath really neither joy, nor love, nor light/ Nor certitude, nor peace, nor help for pain"—sentiments that Will Percy carried with him all his life. [25]

Then came a blow so stunning that he wrote not a word about it in his chapter celebrating the Sewanee interlude. During Will Percy's sophomore year in 1902, his brother LeRoy came to a violent death. Delighted with his son's skill at games and school, LeRoy Percy, Sr. had presented him with a .22 caliber rifle. The father carefully instructed him in how to shoot it and keep it in good condition. Together, while Will Percy was away at college, the pair hunted the Delta wilderness. On a vacation at Hot Springs, Arkansas, young LeRoy and a playmate were romping about, when, in the hands of his inexperienced friend, the gun went off and shot LeRoy through the stomach. Initially it did not seem mortal. When he first returned to the hotel, the boy greeted his father, "Hello pop, I am all right." [26] Camille called in four doctors, but they could not find the bullet in his stomach, and the pain he suffered could not be relieved. Fever ensued, and the boy was sure, Camille wrote her son at Sewanee, that he "was going to die." Within a week, little LeRoy was dead. Before the end had come, LeRoy Percy, Sr., mourned with an eloquence that arose so naturally in that family: he wrote his remaining son at Sewanee that soon "the blue would be gone from the sky and the music from the laughter of children forever." Years later the father was still grieving the loss. In 1919 he at last relinquished little Roy's favorite gun to his nephew, William Armstrong Percy, young son of his dead brother Willie. It was not the firearm that killed him, he told his nephew, but another which the boy only lived long enough to use once. [27]

Will Percy felt keenly in his own right the loss of his brother but he also recognized the sadness and heavy disappointment of his parents. He would later write that his father's "heart must often have called piteously for the little brother I had lost, all boy, all sturdy, obstreperous charm." No matter how hard he tried, he knew that somehow the death had lengthened, not closed the distance between himself and his parents. They might say little about their feelings, but he sensed that they knew why he never could fulfil their parental desires. For the most part, Will Percy dutifully repressed his resentment of a disapproving paterfamilias. Yet at the time of young Le-Roy's death, brother Will allowed himself some harsher thoughts. In his pastoral poem, "A Legend of Lacedaemon," which tells of a young classical Greek hunter's death, he wrote: "I am your son, and you have slain my brother." [28]

Percy often chose to write within the Victorian tradition regarding classical Greece and medieval Europe as a means of burying still deeper the anger and resentment involved in his struggle against a dominating father. In the case of the dead brother, the undeserving survivor may have conquered a rival for fatherly affection, but he had also lost a sibling who could have shouldered the major responsibilities for carrying on the Percy family line. In only one of two direct references to the child, Will Percy in the cemetery chapter of *Lanterns on the Levee* calls him "the small brother who should be representing and perpetuating the name." [29]

Years later a friend remarked, "Often Will withdrew himself from life, not to an ivory tower where the living and dying world could not touch him, but rather to an Olympus of his own where he could observe with truer perspective and sharper clarity the realities below." [30] No doubt young LeRoy's death heightened his appreciation of many realities, most especially his temperamental differentness from the other Percys and from most of his school chums.

In addition, he found his religious convictions flickering out on the mountain where they were supposed to burn as fiercely as the desire for humanistic knowledge. The nearest Catholic church was down in the valley, at Winchester. It was about fourteen miles away, but the trip down the winding road from the mountain was unpleasant and solitary. There was more, however, to his disillusionment than that. His brother's death may have played a part. Whereas others might have had their faith rekindled under that tragedy, his was snuffed out. He found that he could "no longer pretend to myself or cry: Mea culpa. Help thou mine unbelief." [31]

Will Percy's religion may have no longer seemed capable of damming up his sexual feelings. Belief fell away as he awakened to a sense of his autonomy—away from parents, away from the Mother Church. In *A Portrait of the Artist as a Young Man,* Stephen Dedalus undergoes a similar inner struggle over faith and sin, but Joyce has his alienated hero in search of career and honor emerge with at least a momentarily lighter heart: "Welcome, O Life! I go to encounter for the millionth time the reality of experience and to forge in the smithy of my soul the uncreated conscience

of my race," sings the hero. Will Percy did not rejoice in his newly discovered freedom but instead resigned himself to "breathe a starker and colder
air, with no place to go when I was tired." Thereafter, he declared, "I
would be living with my own self" with none to help.[32] Many young men
of his generation lost the religion of their childhood, but Percy was so
sensitive a soul that his was not a common case. Nor did he really ever
lose a sense of spirituality even as he turned away from the theology of
Catholicism. His poetry and his life revealed just how important the religion of St. Francis and others would be for him. Their faith permitted
them a robust endurance against defeat, and that inspiration remained a
part of his life thereafter.

After graduation from Sewanee at nineteen in 1904, Will Percy had little
idea what he wanted to do in life. Family pressure implacably pointed
toward law school, but he could not face it without a respite. With the
reluctant approval of his parents, he decided to spend a year abroad. He
went to Paris, with Camille and LeRoy Percy in escort to help him settle
in. They located, for a mere eight dollars a month rent, a small, centrally
located flat, notable for the "clammy sleaziness" that seeped from the
cracks "like mold or gangrene." "To please Father," he even went to fenc-
ing school three times a week. The exercise did little for his self-esteem
or his coordination, since his instructor turned out to be disappointingly
"ordinary"—untemperamental, sane, and "married!" as Will Percy put it.[33]
   Primarily, the young American haunted the galleries, museums, opera
houses, theaters, and gardens, especially the Luxembourg, and practiced
on the "tinkly" piano that he had installed in his dismal-looking flat. He
spent at least an hour every day at the Louvre. His letters home differed
considerably in tone from the melancholy reflections on the European experience in *Lanterns on the Levee.* He told his parents only the names of
people met, pictures seen, music heard, small adventures enjoyed or lamented, and never his deepest thoughts. "I have been exceptionally gay &
giddy, going to the theatre every night," he wrote his mother in late 1904.
He had been escorting a "Miss Hargis," and he assured Camille Percy that
the "damsel" had enjoyed herself. In deep mid-winter he headed for Florence, Pisa, Rome, Naples, and even Egypt. The Italian leg of the trip
brought him together with Huger Jervey and Elliott Cage, Sewanee friends,
and a whole party of Americans they knew. One American family hoped
that he would take an interest in one of their daughters, but he did not. A
Miss Bradford, a young lady of high birth and wealth from New York City,
he complained, "gasps, wrings her hands & rhapsodizes over everything
indiscriminately." But he liked her and took her on excursions around the
city. Mrs. Bradford observed the relationship and encouraged Will Percy
to pursue her daughter. Finally, however, as Will wrote his mother, Mrs.

Bradford gave him up "as hopeless." After returning from Egypt, he and Elliott Cage became good companions on a further tour of Italy. During an excursion to Germany that followed, Will Percy was unimpressed with the "flaxen-haired . . . Mädchens" of "receptive mood" because they seemed "to lack that something—temperament—Chaucer would say—which rouses one to make sacrifices, do great deeds."[34]

It was probably at some point during the Grand Tour that Will Percy first admitted to himself his sexual identity, though he made no confession in surviving letters. The art work at the Louvre set his thoughts ablaze—particularly Greek statuary. In his chapter, "Year Abroad," in *Lanterns on the Levee,* Percy mused on what he had learned about the Greeks from examining a representation of a hermaphrodite, a "sleazy mock-modest little monster." It haunted his thoughts; he felt, he recalled, guilty and unclean. Later, he said, he understood better that "the Greeks practiced bisexuality" without considering it indecent or repellent rather than acknowledge only one form of love. However much Will Percy yearned for male sexual companionship, he apparently did not find it in Paris. Instead, he mostly remembered how forsaken he felt: "I was sick for a home I had never seen and lonely for a hand I had never touched." Throughout that year he could venture nowhere without his companion of "loneliness until she was so familiar I came not to hate her but to know whatever happened in however many after years she alone would be faithful to me."[35]

Will Percy then satisfied his father by agreeing to attend law school. He took up a legal career only because it was the expectation for most male Percys. LeRoy Percy wanted him to join the Greenville firm just as LeRoy himself had gratified his father, the Colonel, by doing likewise, years before. LeRoy Percy was relieved that his son would not become an idle poet or Roman priest. As reward, he later took Will abroad again, for one of several trips there before the World War I. Yet LeRoy Percy did wonder if "this European business is going to fit, or unfit, him for the prosaic work of digging a living out of law."[36]

Will Percy chose Harvard rather than the University of Virginia Law School, the family alma mater, not for any alleged academic superiority. It was a question of location. He loved Cambridge and Boston and the social and aesthetic opportunities they offered. But he did not like the law. He made many friends among his classmates at Winthrop Hall and graduated without difficulty but also without distinction. He belonged to the Southern Club at Harvard where young gentlemen like Percy could reassure each other that the home region had attractions that the North could not match. His Southern attitudes showed up when his father was preoccupied in the Sunnyside episode in 1907. Will Percy sympathized with him for having to engage in "swapping oratory with a female lawyer" as unladylike as Mary Grace Quackenbos. Homesickness flared up now and again. After reading a biography of the Southern poet Sidney Lanier, "a wonderful man," Will Percy expressed a yearning "to go dashing off to Mine Own

People." Such moods were as fleeting, however, as his interest in "enter-taining" Miss Singmaster, a short story writer whom he briefly squired around Boston.[37] The Cambridge idyll came to a close all too soon in 1908.

After passing the Mississippi bar exam, Will Percy had a reprieve from taking up law practice at once. He joined the faculty at Sewanee as a temporary replacement for John Bell Henneman, who had died unexpect-edly. Clearly the academic life would have suited Will Percy, had he stuck to it. Phinizy Percy, his youngest ward of later years, recalled, "I think he enjoyed his teaching at Sewanee as much as anything he ever did." Cer-tainly the students thought so. At the end of the semester, they wrote him a letter of appreciation for his "enthusiastic efforts and well proven competency." His letters of the period reflected intellectual self-confidence—his frantic preparations for five courses notwithstanding. He shared with Huger Jervey quarters that they called "the Bachelors." The workload at Sewanee, particularly for someone without graduate training, was so great, however, that he resented the lack of time for writing. As a result, he urged his father not to fret about his return to the law firm. "Your being in the law *naturally* suggested it to me, but if I had strong predilections for any other 'pursuit of happiness' I should certainly not have allowed the *law* to turn me from it. I have no such predilection, least of all for teaching." He reassured him that "Uncle Willie" in Memphis was wrong to encourage him to continue as a teacher. "The life is too narrow, dry, & cold-blooded," he concluded. If his talent and interest proved suf-ficient, Will Percy claimed that he could aspire to a literary career as ad-junct to the law more easily than to teaching.[38]

Yet after the semester at Sewanee, Will Percy found the return to Greenville by no means easy. The provinciality of the Delta weighed down his spirits, whereas up North he had flourished. His Yankee friends had liked his appreciation of the absurd. No doubt he regaled them with his description of a formal dinner in the "bolt-upright atmosphere" of a Cam-bridge academic crowd. According to his recounting, as he was talking with customary animation and gesture, he had casually flipped open a snowy-white napkin. Cleverly folded almost to resemble a battleship, inside it contained a roll, "shaped like a torpedo." The projectile flew into the air and crashed noisily into a corner where a wire-cage of canaries stood. The startled birds began to sing hysterically as if they were a chorus from Stra-vinsky. That was a scene to be recalled more than once.[39]

His Northern friends also shared his intellectual and artistic interests. All his experiences since college graduation in 1904 had sharpened his differences with the society into which he was immersed some five years later. As he observed in *Lanterns on the Levee,* he had "no endearing vices." Gambling provided no pleasure, and getting drunk was not his idea of fun. "Rutting," he reiterated many times, was for him "overrated and degrading." Some might wish to call him "an idealist," but most others would have typed him as "a sissy."[40] The ambitions that stirred his father, grandfather, and two Percy uncles and toward which his now dead brother had been progressing did not touch him in the slightest. He wanted no legal, civic, political, or financial fame and power. But to be an intellectual in the South—particularly one so sexually sequestered and vulnerable—was no career at all. Catherine Warfield, Eleanor Percy Lee, and Sarah Dorsey could pursue their literary interests. Writing romances and poetry were women's prerogatives; men should find more virile things to do—so white Southerners, both male and female, believed.

Male writers in the South long had chafed under the layers of conservatism, bigotry, and narrow preoccupations of their neighborhoods. Walter Hines Page, a North Carolinian, in 1881 had complained that the intellectual could not live long under the burden of the "mental stagnation of his surroundings." He had to flee or "be caught by the spell of inertness, and live out his life and die before he decides whether to go away or not." In reference to Southern contempt for humanistic pursuits, social critic W. J. Cash, Will Percy's contemporary, pointed out that early in Southern history the ideal was to be "a captain in the struggle against the Yankee," preferably a fire-eater "ramping through the land with a demand for the sword." On the other hand, aspirations for intellectual matters, "the writing of books, the painting of pictures, the life of the mind, seemed an anemic and despicable business, fit only for eunuchs." That popular Southern sentiment persisted into the years of Will Percy's development. In a sense his father no doubt wondered, as had a friend of an antebellum Virginia aristocrat, "Why do you waste your time on a damned thing like poetry? A man of your position could be a useful man." A cultivated gentleman himself, LeRoy Percy would never have openly said something so wounding, but in unmistakable ways he let his son know his disquiet.[41]

Could Will Percy have escaped? He might have joined in New York his college friend Huger Jervey of Charleston who was later to become dean of the Parker School of International Studies at Columbia University. But he felt too burdened to desert his parents. He feared their censure, their confirmation of how inadequate he felt himself to be. LeRoy and Camille Percy were still grieving for the lost boy of their hopes. Yet by staying home, he ran the risk of the kind of stultification that Page had criticized. In retrospect Will Percy declared, with a witty play on words, "I didn't exactly plunge into life, rather I tipped in, trepidly."[42]

In this disheartening period of his life, Will Percy tried to be as agreeable and conscientious as possible about those things that mattered to his father. On political and social topics, they shared exactly the same opinions. Upon reading LeRoy Percy's address on educating the Southern blacks, his son Will noted that it spoke truths "which few men who had the brains to conceive would have had the courage to express." Gradually he learned to tolerate if not very much enjoy the life of the law. He took over the cases of the ailing Judge C. C. Moody, his father's partner, and ran the family plantations. These activities kept him occupied. "I am learning some law and a considerable amount of human nature," he told Judge Moody.[43] He was equally loyal to the senior's clique of friends. In 1910, for instance, Will Percy urged a publisher to reach old Captain McNeily because his reminiscence about being an intrepid "fighter for white supremacy" under the Redeemers was "well worth while publishing."[44]

Although his father certainly had no intention of compelling his son to share his grief over the 1911 election defeat, Will Percy took the loss excessively hard. He expressed his bitterness in *Lanterns on the Levee,* complaining that he had learned a bruising lesson about the blindness and inhumanity of the world. "Thus at twenty-seven I became inured to defeat; I have never since expected victory."[45] Father and son had fought side by side in that campaign, but the aftermath proved even worse—the steady flow of bad publicity even after the contest had been lost. On the Senate floor, December 1911, LeRoy Percy sought to answer George Creel's muckraking article in *Cosmopolitan,* a national magazine, that had grossly distorted Percy's role in the legislative election scandal of 1910. Despite his hopes that rebuttal would be unnecessary, Percy's reply covered four pages in the *Congressional Record.* Will Percy felt quite helpless in trying to remedy his father's periodic bouts of depression. The best he could do was to throw such matters into poetry. "We were so close!" Will Percy has a son declare in his narrative poem, "Enzio's Kingdom," written some years later, "yet I could not reach out/ And soothe the grief of his profound despair." Yet curiously, "To the Mocking Bird," composed on the very night of the 1911 defeat took up a second theme: a yearning for a return to Europe—an escape from the necessity to praise his parent, to do his bidding, to live in the glass house of Greenville's prying society. Thus, when "the courage and the joy are gone," the poet could forget "this western flaunt of living" and "the battles and ceaseless clash." Instead, he could savor such pleasures as catching the notes of "the anguished nightingale that Sappho heard," seeing the "Sicilian shepherd boys /Piping across their shining pastures," and feeling "an alien sweetness that /Long vision hath made sad."[46]

Will Percy would not assume the role of husband and father that his parents wished for him to adopt. Like Dr. LeRoy Pope Percy, his great-uncle "Lee," he remained in the house of his birth all his life, unmarried and tied to Percy kindred. From the start his rebellion was internal, like Binx Bolling's when the character in Walker Percy's *The Moviegoer* resolves that "he will put on the outward forms which are trivial. The inner content will be his own." But it was a much more self-defeating, unhappy resistance than that of Walker Percy's hero. Greenville was most unlike Gentilly, the faceless, anonymous New Orleans suburb, in which Binx resides.[47] As Hodding Carter put it, Will Percy was "Orpheus in a small town, perplexing to his father and suspect to his fellow river folk." After his return from the Paris sojourn and his years at Harvard, Will Percy alluded to his situation in a letter to a Percy cousin, Janet Dana, who learned that he thought himself to be "unmothered of Aphrodite."[48]

An unpublished sketch, titled "The Fifth Autumn" spoke more directly to the anguish he felt, but he kept the document to himself. The undated piece was written some time after his return to Greenville from Harvard Law School. In it he does not resort to verse and classical invention which had served so many Victorian poets and writers as a means of expressing similar feelings.[49] "It was the fifth autumn," he begins. "For the first time there was a definite chill in the air." Some five years earlier, he continues, "I knew nothing of what was taking place. My father and mother looked at me strangely. My mother gave thanks to God that I was untouched by sin, but she would stop in the midst of her words and weep bitterly. My father said, 'It is in the spring that the seed is eager, is it not?' But my mother would cover his lips with her hands. 'Do not speak,' she would say, 'We do not know what we may be saying.'" He used to walk for hours, Will Percy explains, a solitary figure under the autumnal trees, whose "brown leaves had fallen in slow spirals." He watched "the dark movement of the water" before returning late at night to "hear my mother crying out in her sleep and my father in his room pacing the floor." He would go to his own room, move his chair to the window, pull a bathrobe about his shoulders, "and smoke cigarettes." He confessed, "Sometimes I would sit that way all night. 'The fifth autumn is upon me,' I said, 'And I have not forgotten.'" Spring, he mused, "is to me a release from pain. But always in autumn I shall be stricken and confused with memory."[50]

That sense of incompleteness and loneliness, of not meeting the high demands of family expectation, would haunt him the rest of his life. Yet self-dissatisfaction led him to write poetry, to seek glory in war, to adopt causes and family burdens that would have major effects upon his community and his lineage.

CHAPTER ELEVEN

At War

Though friendless, childless, honorless I come,
They will know I am theirs; they will make room.
William Alexander Percy, "In France"[1]

In the summer of 1914, Will Percy was again abroad—in Sicily. He was mounting the slope of Etna with a group of aged "donkey-boys," most of them drunk out of fear of the climb. It turned out that Percy was the first to ascend Etna from the village of Taormina since the most recent eruption. That disaster had occurred, they told him, shortly after they had escorted an Austrian Grand Duke to the top of the crater some months before. According to the newspaper, they told the tourist, that same Archduke had been assassinated only the day before at Sarajevo. Oblivious to the impending "doom," Percy did not care how many archdukes had been killed; he simply rejoiced: "Taormina and Assisi and Paris. What a fascinating World!"[2] But actually, throughout this period when his artistic life was developing so well and should have cheered him, he was desperately unhappy. He expressed his bitterness in "Girgenti," a poem composed at Taormina. The subject was the fall of a great medieval city, but the poet wishes to stand with other brave souls "in stubborn rank against the wall of doom."[3] He would soon have his wish.

The Great War in Europe had begun, and, upon returning to Greenville, Will Percy remembered that he was "miserable." He longed to help preserve the old civilization in France. Even his usual "opiates" of travel and versifying held no charm. Then, inspiration came from Janet Dana, his distant New York cousin (on the Robert Percy side), a romantic, enthusiastic young woman who shared Will Percy's conservative tastes in art and literature. In this friendship so "peculiarly" tender, as she declared, he drew from her equal measures of Platonic love and sympathy. Through correspondence with her he could express his feelings of anguish and self-doubt, whereas letters to Camille Percy were invariably buoyant. In late April 1915, Janet did what Will Percy had only talked about doing: she left the Dana mansion at One Fifth Avenue, Manhattan, to serve as a nurse in hospitals at Dunkirk and Dieppe.[4] Receiving complaints about his worthlessness, even before her departure, she did her best to cheer Will Percy, but admitted, "We are both going through the despondent slough, so let's talk busily to keep our courage up."[5] At Dieppe, she confided to Will that the charm of the French countryside was such a contrast to the war, the anguished wounded for whom she was responsible, and the reports of "unspeakable crimes & sorrows which seem to be engulfing all mankind."[6]

Not long afterward Will Percy, daily trudging to the Greenville law office in the Weinburg building, hinted rather strongly that his "usefulness down here is ended." He felt utterly alone and distinctly unwanted. First uncertain of his meaning, Janet Dana soon realized that what he had revealed in his last letter was a yearning for being "needed utterly"—a test of mettle that made possible the capacity to separate reality from illusion. She urged him to "speak the truth" about himself. "We live so veiled perhaps you will be repelled by what I am saying. Will, I seem to feel that the ultimate test is courage." Sometimes, she continued, we must violate "our own ideals even, for the sake of seeing the truth" and by that means "truly live." She admitted that it was "a strange letter," but she saw that he ought to join the war effort as soon as possible as a way of meeting his craving for "self-sacrifice" and fulfillment of duty. He did so by volunteering for Herbert Hoover's Belgian Relief agency. Yet the prospect of leaving Greenville met the resistance of his parents who made him feel both solitary and desperately needed, as if they had not yet overcome the death of their first son. He wrote Janet that if he got the place in Belgium, he would depart with "no great feeling of gusto. Isn't it fearful how one attains freedom only at the expense of the blood and tears of others?"[7]

Without fully explaining her reasons to Will Percy, Janet Dana had abruptly returned from France to New York City in the summer of 1915. He guessed that she was about to marry because "nothing else," he wrote, "has so often & so constantly sapped the carefully built fortifications of my friendship." He complained how unfair it was, since she knew of his preference for bachelorhood, that he had to erect his "last line of defenses" on the terrain of "philosophy." For all our caring for each other, in the last analysis, he wrote, "all our fights are lonely fights."[8] At thirty, Will Percy had given up entirely on the idea of marriage without indicating exactly why and she, by the same unspoken code, never asked for frank explanation. Upon that basis their friendship could continue.

In reply, Janet Dana admitted that a wedding would soon change her life but not of course her feelings about her cousin. She had fallen in love with Warfield Theobald Longcope, a professor at Columbia University and head of medicine at the Presbyterian Hospital. They were married on December 2. (Her husband was later a long revered head of medicine at Johns Hopkins University Hospital in Baltimore, where they lived the rest of their lives.)[9] Although Janet Dana Longcope remained a loyal correspondent and friend, Will Percy felt more isolated than ever. He was reconciled to his cousin's marriage when at last the Hoover agency accepted his application.

The new recruit was stationed in German-occupied Brussels and, like some forty-two other American co-workers, became, as he later reminisced, one of the "spoiled darlings of Belgian society." Yet he felt superfluous because the relief work had become a bureaucratic routine. More acutely than ever he wished to flee a tame life without nobility or purpose.[10] Moreover, he felt helpless and disgusted as he watched hundreds of Belgian civilians marched off in bondage to labor in Germany. When the United States broke off relations with Germany, Will Percy and six other relief workers at once applied for safe conduct out of Belgium in order to join the armed forces. Fearful that at any moment they might be thrown into a concentration camp, Percy and his friends traveled through German-occupied territory and then through Germany itself until they reached Switzerland and safety. The following day, the United States declared war on Germany. Their escape had been timely indeed.[11]

As soon as he could, Will Percy enlisted in the army with the object of earning a commission. It was the only way he could serve because he was a year over the draft age. By drinking quarts of water and eating more than his tiny frame could handle, he barely met the minimum weight requirement for admission to officers' training school at Fort Logan H. Root in Arkansas. During his training, along with various generals and other notables, he was asked to speak at a Liberty Loan rally at the camp. He addressed some three or four thousand soldiers with great aplomb and high passion. The troops gave him "a fifteen minute standing ovation," as Groom Leftwich, a fellow trainee, wrote his father, a Mississippi politician. Janet Longcope was delighted that Will had made the grade because, as she wrote him, it furnished him "the blessedness of action," a "boon to be prayed for," especially in his case, because, she believed, her cousin dwelt too much on his uselessness.[12]

Will Percy's experiences in 1917 and 1918 were intense enough to provide him a grim seasoning in war's terror and boredom. Yet they did not permanently or radically alter his opinions about the sanctities of honor, race, class, and the purpose of literature, which he thought should be morally uplifting and beautiful in the Victorian sense. As a soldier, Will Percy began to develop some new ideas, but as in the case of Sarah Dorsey with her flirtation with feminism and radical politics, he would later subside into old personal patterns and return to the culture of his father and forefathers. Even so, in recalling his life in the army some twenty-odd years later in *Lanterns on the Levee*, he coupled his conservatism with self-deprecation, humor, and insight.

His description of life in the infantry at Camp Stanley, Leon Springs, Texas, captures the anxiety, absurdity, and poignancy of young civilians thrust into the mindless exigencies of officers' training camp.[13] He found himself in the midst of similarly miniature physiques—what he called the "Pee Wee Squad." Resenting the ridicule of the six-footers, they stuck together, helped each other through. With amused contempt, the Pee Wees watched as great hulks—models of military manhood—fell like timber when faced with that weapon of war on disease, the hypodermic needle. Meanwhile Percy and friends withstood much greater ordeals such as hiking under the Texas sun at double-time with a seventy-pound pack.[14]

After reading Will's reports home, his father wrote a cousin that Will "thinks he has detected a symptom of a little muscle in his right arm." As father of the delicate recruit, he was pricking his own pride as he made fun of his son: "I think there is an even chance of his getting through."[15] Will, who had uncommon grit when it counted, performed far better in military life than his father's near contempt would have brought to mind. At Fort Logan H. Root he had been something of a camp hero for totally denouncing a stupid training officer in the Liberty Loan speech. He got away with that challenge to authority and was also equally blessed in his assignments. Later, at Camp Pike in Arkansas, he disputed the fairness of prohibiting the ordinary trooper's access to alcohol, when officers could drink all they liked. In his outrage, Will took the teetotal pledge, so to speak. (He never did like hard liquor.) LeRoy Percy was, as usual, dumbfounded by his son's idiosyncrasies. He considered abstinence a violation of divine order and urged his son to "think carefully" before giving up on drink altogether. He might find it useful, after all, for mingling with fellow officers, and by all means Will should join a local country club to entertain himself and friends. On this occasion, the son felt liberated enough to plunge into H. Rider Haggard's *She* (1887), a novel that his father had forbidden him as a youngster to read at home.[16] The protagonist was an angelic and chaste but monstrously powerful demi-goddess who had to be obeyed—the late Victorian male's nightmare of what women might be like.[17] Disembarking at Le Havre on January 29, 1918, with his friend Gerstle Mack, he hastened on to Tours and later to Paris, where he served in various office jobs because of his French-speaking skills. Soon enough, however, he wangled a transfer to the front. Ironically the heir to LeRoy Percy's cotton lands discovered that his assignment brought him to the 92nd, the first African-American division ever created and largely officered by blacks.

Will Percy's racial ideas did not change very much as a result of his experience. He was not selected to lead a platoon, as he wished, and therefore was not thrust into the company of foot soldiers by circumstance. Nor did he choose to get thoroughly acquainted with them on his own. His task, the training of the troops in communications and other specialties, made it possible to return to headquarters without free and easy contact with the officers and men. He kept both the black officers he liked and those he disliked at arm's length by a "meticulous politeness" and turned down an invitation to mess with them.[18] Oblivious to his own contribution to the problem, Percy recalled that morale in the 92nd was generally low. A group of black junior officers approached the young instructor to express their concern that in a heavy engagement the black troops might break ranks because they had too little trust in their own black leaders. "A Negro won't follow a Negro," one of them confessed, as if to confirm regular army wisdom—and prejudice—of that day.

Like most of his fellow white officers, whether Northern or Southern, he was blind to how racial discrimination could undermine black troop morale from officer to private and failed to open his eyes to examples of leadership and bravery. Will Percy learned nothing lasting from his army experience to alter his Southern views of the race, in part because it came to an end before battle was begun in earnest. His transfer to another unit led to the opportunity for re-examining some of the old Southern ways upon which he had been raised, but he did not seize the chance to grow.

Will Percy's regimental commander in the 92nd Division was William P. Jackson, an affable and keen gentleman who carried himself like Lewis Carroll's White Knight, reported the memorialist in *Lanterns on the Levee*. Promoted to brigadier-general, Jackson chose Will Percy as his aide in the all-white 74th Brigade.[19] Percy was pleased to have fewer ambivalent feelings about the 74th than about the black division. He eagerly—and innocently—awaited a chance to prove himself as valorous as his grandfather, the "Gray Eagle," but the summer of 1918 went by without his seeing much action. Percy carried his gas mask everywhere but thought it mostly useful for giving himself "a serious air." As for combat, he ruefully remarked to his mother, "I've resigned myself to losing all chances of glory, and what's more, of the deep human satisfaction of suffering and fighting with the men."[20]

His duties required escorting General Jackson on inspection tours of the trenches at night, the daytime sniper-fire being too hazardous. Only three times did the pair come under fire. On one moonless night, however, danger crept up unexpectedly. With no lights allowed, Lieutenant Percy and his driver crashed into another vehicle. The "blithe, blue-eyed youngster" broke his collar-bone, Will Percy reported home, but he himself stepped out of the wreckage without a scratch. On a more menacing occasion during an offensive, he found himself alone in an open field when the shells began to drop all around him. "To be shelled when you are in the open is one of the most terrible of human experiences," he wrote his father. "You hear this rushing, tearing sound as the thing comes toward you and then the huge explosion as it strikes, and, infinitely worse, you see its hideous work as men stagger, fall, struggle, or lie quiet and unrecognisable." Yet the explosions and shrapnel missed him altogether. "I'm alive and awfully glad to be alive," he rejoiced. He retained that kind of luck throughout the war, having, as he recounted, gone "thro hell and returned without a scar."[21]

Many of his trench-mates were less lucky than he, especially during the Ypres-Lys offensive. Situated in the center of the advancing line of over a million Americans, the V Corps, to which Percy's 37th Division was attached, had to capture the great German fortress of Montfauçon. The fort fell in only two days—a quicker result than the French planners had anticipated. But as the troops moved forward, matters grew worse. Seeing no purpose or plan in the operation, the soldiers morosely struggled through mud, smoke, gas, and shell bursts. When the Germans launched a counter offensive, Percy helped to rally the men, particularly on one occasion when a heavy enemy artillery barrage sent a company into head-long retreat. He rallied the foot-soldiers to return to order and hold the ground.[22]

After the fall of the great German redoubt at Montfauçon, the 37th Division was ordered out of the battle-line for a respite. Yet almost at once the troops were sent to the Belgian front, where fresh units were expected to tip the balance for the Allies. Fortunately, the war ended before that plan was tested, and Will Percy could exult that "the wrecked world is once more at peace." The Americans, he reported, were quiet on first hearing the news just as the offensive was about to begin. The French, however, began singing and "childishly burned flares and rockets."[23]

When Pershing reviewed the 74th just before its return to the United States, Percy was full of pride for the men. Their uniforms were "ill-fitting" and "shoddy," he conceded. "But when our boys get their shoes shined, clean their wrapped leggings, cock their overseas caps," he boasted, "they are the most capable looking and endearing bunch in the world." In a letter to his mother, later reprinted in the Greenville *Delta Democrat,* he wrote, "In all the horror and pity of the thing it's certainly well to remember this—it's the shining and the splendor of it all." Such a judgment was very much in vogue among the American "doughboys."[24]

Percy pride and love of action inspired the young officer throughout the conflict. The young lieutenant had reason to rejoice not merely in his surviving but also in proving himself as a man among other brave men. Next to the battle of the Somme, the offensive in the Argonne Forest—the site that the historian, John Keegan, has called "that awful wilderness of shredded woods and choked-up streams"—was among the grimmest of the war. In Percy's words: "What they suffer in hunger and cold and exhaustion would earn them eternal reverence"; he was happy in the knowledge that he had been with them through such privations.[25] He wrote Camille Percy that it would be hard for a woman to understand what he had endured: "There is so much to say that of course I can't write about. Experiences that I wouldn't take a million for having been allowed to go thru, and that I wouldn't give ten cents to go thru again."[26] Moreover, he had won a conquering hero's rewards: the *Croix de Guerre,* with a gold and silver star, and *L'Ordre du Corps d'Armee* from the French authorities; and *Le Médaille du Roi Albert* from the Belgians. More gratifying were the praises of his commanding officer. After the Armistice, Jackson wrote Camille Percy that her son had shown "the utmost coolness and bravery" under fire. The general mentioned for special commendation how during the Argonne offensive Percy had delayed his return to headquarters in order "voluntarily" to assist in regrouping troops from a line that had all but collapsed. With so strong a record, Will Percy was promoted to captain in the Army Reserve after being mustered out.[27]

Will Percy was determined to retain his wartime enthusiasms into the postwar period as best he could and not reject the values that Woodrow Wilson had proclaimed and the ideals that had animated the Percys of past times. Yet his sense of the tragic and the inevitability of defeat was much deepened rather than lightened by the Allied victory. As early as January 1919 he thought that the participants at Versailles were most likely to be "avaricious" and "provincial," and the settlement would be even more dangerous to world peace than the balance of power system of prewar times. Then, in their antipathy toward Woodrow Wilson's "essential undemocracy" and "self satisfaction," the Americans would undermine the President's authority. As a result of these factors, predicted Will Percy, the Treaty would become "the most tragic failure in history."[28] He was not far from right.

Once the United States entered the conflict, LeRoy Percy had taken a pessimistic view of the war. At first he hoped that America would fight long enough to have control of the peace process. He was to be disappointed: the war ended within months of American entry on the battlefields of Flanders, and American influence declined as the United States swiftly demobilized. A skeptic by nature, and a Southerner who had seen causes in which he believed defeated, LeRoy Percy mistrusted the overoptimism that military victory often engenders.[29] In contrast, LeRoy Percy's son remained a steadfast believer in war from start to finish. For him, war was not disillusioning but ennobling, a sentiment that so many Americans, even intellectuals, shared in 1918. British and French thinkers and writers took a darker view. But Will Percy's reaction did not arise from simple naïveté alone. He had personal reasons for extolling the warrior's code. Like other soldiers at the front, he longed for peace, but fighting was the only proud male activity of his own making that his father never had the chance to hazard. The old senator had been much too young for the Civil War, far too old for the Great War. To be sure, he and LeRoy Pratt Percy, his nephew and companion, loved camping out in the wilderness to shoot duck and geese in Louisiana or Canada. The older Percy had found in this nephew (the novelist Walker Percy's father) a replication of his own LeRoy, dead since 1902. Will Percy was not jealous that his first cousin had assumed first place in the senator's heart. The unappreciated son could see how happy his father was in the association. It actually helped to relieve a strain in their father-son relationship. Yet Will Percy could reflect that shooting birds and elk and enjoying the sociability of hunting trips were tame indeed. They were nothing compared with the harrowing ordeals and the bonding of soldiers under fire that he, the self-deprecating "sissy," experienced in the trenches of France.

Although spared the full range of horrors that the European Allies underwent, Will Percy saw in the fighting a seemingly petty advantage but one that had much meaning for him: a degree of political vindication for the campaign loss in 1911. Senator Vardaman, his father's vanquisher, had denounced American entry in 1917; Mississippi soldiers were quick to tell Will Percy how sorry they were that the "White Chief" and not his father represented the state in the Senate.

There had been more, however, than just Percy gloom with which to contend—the very reality of battle itself. One letter, out of the many sent home, captured its horror without resort to sentimentality or overwriting. During the Meuse-Argonne campaign in late October 1918, he had written his father to describe "the old No Man's land which for four years first our side and then the other would dash in waves of blood vainly attempting to break through." Percy broke his own rules of elegant convention to adopt what he called "the natural speech of raw emotion." In that "nightmare" landscape, he wrote his father, the combatant stumbles "in the mad welter of shell holes and filth and mud," where, "like prehistoric animals from the slime of creation, the wrecks of battles lost and won—shelters of elephant iron" loomed up. The witness passes "concrete pillboxes torn apart till the iron ribs shattered in gigantic explosions, tanks fantastic and terrible, that had crawled to the roadside or into a shell hole to die (you could not believe they belonged to men til you looked inside and saw the skeletons still by the wheel and the guns)." Continuing his ghastly catalogue, he described the "barbed-wire, a crown of thorns on the mangled landscape" and the tall, branchless stumps of trees "rising white and distorted and twisted out of the mud, like the skeleton fingers of creatures drawn into the slough, raking and tearing at the dismal sky."[30]

These and other lines of stunning authority were written to LeRoy Percy, not, of course, to Camille. As Will Percy remarked in his introduction to the letters, such communications seemed to describe events written at the very moment of their occurrence despite "a forced cheerfulness for eyes that must not fill when reading them." Other letters may have a "gagging eloquence," and he had in mind the letter of October 25. Indeed, it was not meant for someone of delicate sensibilities. Rather his letter to LeRoy was really a kind of internal monologue, a recording of Will talking essentially to himself. In 1940 Harold Straus, his editor at Knopf, urged Percy to remove these powerful words about the horrors of war for political reasons. America had not yet entered the conflict, but Straus, indeed Percy himself, sought to offer no excuses for continued American isolationism. While the removal of such material made contemporary sense, it would have added further depth to Percy's memoir.[31]

Lewis Baker, the family biographer, observes that this kind of stream of consciousness was more typical of contemporary British poets and writers at the front than of the American writers trying to convey the madness and perversity of modern warfare. In fact, Percy's effort was an early example of the surrealistic mode that arose among some disillusioned members of the French intelligentsia after the war. Yet Percy's approach may also have had ancient roots as well.[32] The style was what linguists call parataxis, in which the discourse gives all phrases, often simply linked by a series of "ands," an equal significance. The result can convey a sense of how awesome a whole scene may appear, an overloading of the senses, as it were. This rhetorical device was common in the archaic Greek literature that Will Percy knew so well.[33] He employed it to describe No Man's Land, not to strike a Homeric pose, but to make the words match his reactions to what he saw and smelled. It was a kind of anti-epiphany, that is, a plunge into hell rather than a climb to heaven.

Parataxis involves the language of participation. For once in his life, Will Percy was not the alienated observer or the chronicler of his father's court. Rather he was an actor in his own right, voicing real agonies and letting a degree of incoherence, commensurate with the irrationality of war itself, be heard. As Baker notes, words that Will Percy generally threw about with abandon—*honor, gallantry,* and the like—were thus replaced with the primeval imagery of tanks as monsters, slime, and "elephant iron." All those grand ideals of nobility and right action dissolved in the enormity of endless casualty lists and the stench of rotting corpses. Thereafter Will Percy spoke the language of honor in Victorian innocence no more. When he invoked the old precepts it was to complain that while he would remain faithful to the ethic, his was a dying cause. In *Lanterns on the Levee,* he mourned, "The North destroyed my South; the Germans destroyed my world." Like Sarah Dorsey after the Civil War, his reaction to the great, shattering conflict of his life was to claim for the prewar years a legendary grandeur, of moral principle and uprightness to contrast against the tawdry present. Thus participation in the war did not shake his faith in old verities but made him aware of their obsolescence or unacceptability in the face of harsh reality.[34]

Although he glorified the risks of death in battle, in subsequent years Will Percy came to realize that he had not found battle action a certain remedy for the persistent melancholy to which he and others in the family were subject. During the turbulent battle in the Meuse valley, he had felt particularly low and powerless as he bedded down alone one night in a bombed-out and abandoned cottage. Even there memories of failures to please his kindred and find his own independent way haunted him. On the wall was a torn print of an Italian Madonna. He could not remember who had painted it and where he had seen the original. What did it matter? "Art?" he had cried out in anguish, as he reported in *Lanterns on the Levee.* What was it all but "child's play, the pastime of weaklings, pointless, useless, unmanly, weak, weak, weak." These self-flagellating words Will Percy remembered thinking on that cold night in the empty, unheated room, sentiments that he believed deserved a public airing even as he omitted the bitter words of meaninglessness and negation in the letter of October 25.[35]

Once the war ended and the noise of victory parades and cheers died away, Will Percy's sense of isolation quickly reappeared.[36] Meeting the troopship when it docked in New York, Janet Longcope realized that her cousin was perhaps even more melancholy than he had been before joining Hoover's Relief Commission in 1916. "Keep whistling, Will," she wrote him kindly. "It helps so to know there's someone not far off in the dark." She urged him to expand his intellectual horizons, too. Janet and Warfield Longcope had spent the war in Washington, where Warfield was engaged in government medical work. Having spent some time in the company of the dying Henry Adams, Janet Longcope sent Will Percy a copy of *Mont-St. Michel and Chartres.* Her neighbor Adams, "an old, old man," she remarked, "could have written Ecclesiastes there was such a taste of ashes in his philosophy, but I am sure that you would have been interested by him." Also, she recommended the "Bloomsbury Set"—"Dorothea [*sic,* Virginia] Woolf," whose *Voyage Out,* she admired; Clive Bell; and Vanessa Bell. "They're worth finding out about."[37] Although Will Percy never showed interest in the Bloomsbury writers, he certainly was influenced by Henry Adams, not only in rediscovering Chartres Cathedral after reading Adams's account but also in shaping his *Lanterns on the Levee,* a work as pessimistic as Adams's memoir, *The Education of Henry Adams.*

Life in Greenville resumed its familiar and unsatisfactory routines. Yet Will Percy returned with a greater degree of self-confidence than he had when he left. As a decorated veteran, he did not by any means allow his moods of depression to interfere with his business, social, or civic life. He gave a number of public speeches for which he earned much praise. Colonel Catchings, his father's old crony of bygone days, wrote that Will's address at a Vicksburg college commencement had been "perfect." Will liked associating with fellow lawyers and businessmen.[38] He briefly taught English at Sewanee again, but he wrote a letter to Jervey of a "disheartening" character about the "charmlessness" of the place. Huger tried to encourage him by remarking that "if you have your boys to teach, & if you can thrill them with the teaching, you can forget the rest."[39] The trustees of the Episcopal college, however, took the decision out of Percy's hands. They disapproved the hiring of a Roman Catholic (apostate though he was) on a permanent basis. For that reason, when elected to the Board of Trustees, he felt bound to resign. Twice the board resolved not to have any but Episcopalians serve. Hurt though he was by these insults at a time when anti-Catholicism, fed in part by the Ku Klux Klan, was rampant in the South, he lost none of his affection for Sewanee. His dignity on this point demonstrated his moral superiority even as the Episcopalian trustees fell short. But the early months after the war were a grim period in his life.[40]

What saved Will Percy from still greater desperation was the sense that he could periodically escape whenever he felt the need. It was hard for an adult to live under the parental roof and not feel somewhat trapped. But rather than take quarters elsewhere in town, he used his wealth in flights from home. For all practical purposes, his bags were permanently packed. As often as possible—in the summers of 1922, 1923, and 1924—he went back to the Mediterranean countries, including Greece. His friends Gerstle Mack and "Hugger" Jervey made the experience less lonely. He heard, too, from a New York City friend and fellow intellectual named Lindley Hubbell, whom Will Percy met through Jervey. On one occasion, Lindley Hubbell reported that "Hugger" had been ill, "And hasn't heard from you for months. A depressing note, poor darling." Effeminate talk of this kind was probably not something Camille and LeRoy Percy liked to know about. Nonetheless, their friendship was significant. According to Shelby Foote, Hubbell, who worked at the New York Public Library, was instrumental in keeping his friend Will abreast of trends in modern poetry, even though Percy much preferred the ancients and the Victorians.[41]

Every Southern town had its eccentric, somewhat alienated bachelor for whom there was a condescending tolerance along with a degree of misgiving. With his vivid personality, irrepressible unselfishness, high social standing, and recognized military bravery, Will Percy weathered the rumors that materialized in the little hothouse community on the banks of the Mississippi. His war record partially subdued many tongues, no doubt. Frederick W. Galbraith, Jr., an infantry colonel, wrote Will Percy's father to say that "I have seen your son go calmly into the front lines under the most violent fire—never hesitating—always cheerful—doing his duty without even a thought of self or safety. If he were my son I should be most proud—as he is yours—I know you are."[42] Yet military honors and mentions in dispatches had limited value at home, Will recognized, especially for the aesthete that he was. Gervys Lusk, a Greenville friend, joked that Will should have made "the supreme sacrifice" at the front, since the townspeople thought him useless. Who needed poets? as Lusk posed the issue. Percy admitted that he felt similarly, "now that the opportunity was safely out of hand."[43]

The sexual feelings that Will Percy entertained gave him little apparent pleasure, but when abroad both before and after the Great War, he drifted into the orbit of a group of poetic Englishmen, who had first formed a circle in the 1880s. They called themselves "Uranians."[44] Often living on the Continent, they celebrated in verse the merits of young male beauty in the nude. The ideal had been first expressed in an essay by Walter Pater (1867) which explored J. J. Winckelmann's *History of Ancient Art* (1764) and dwelt on classical concepts of how mind and body could be naturally and wholly integrated, in contrast to the Christian tradition of soul-body separation of an almost Gnostic character. For the Uranians, chaste aestheticism was the ideal. Romantic Edwardian agony, particularly the death of boys—as in A. E. Housman's "A Shropshire Lad"—lent a lofty sentimentality to the Uranian movement. It found further expression in the war poetry of Wilfred Owen with its references to blond foot-soldiers, who caught Owen's admiration: "His head was golden like the oranges/ That catch their brightness from Las Palmas sun." Unlike the chaste Owen, some Uranians let aesthetic appreciation degenerate into "ordinary pederastic sodomy," as literary historian Paul Fussell remarks.[45]

Will Percy moved in this circle when he was abroad in the 1920s. Even as early as 1909, he and Gerstle Mack paid the first of many visits to Taormina below Mount Etna. With a Mediterranean atmosphere that sanctioned an unpuritanical perspective on life, Taormina had become a popular summer resort, particularly for the Uranians. Will Percy judged Taormina one of several ideal locations for pursuing his poetic interests. To a friend, he remarked, "The writing of longer pieces is generally done during my summer vacations and always out-of-doors in the loveliest spot I can find, Sewanee, Jackson's Hole, Wyoming, Taormina, and Capri."[46]

On one of his holidays in Italy after the war, probably in 1922, Will struck up a friendship with Norman Douglas of Capri. Douglas was outwardly a conventional English gentleman. Many who knew him well were, however, aware of his Uranian proclivities, as the gays of that time used the term. He was the author of small, limited-edition travel books and of *South Wind* (1917), a novel about the pagan character of southern Italian and British expatriate life. In America it sold over 200,000 copies in the 1920s. An admirer summed up Douglas's hedonistic ways by noting that Douglas loved "life, women, boys, food, drink, and knowledge."[47] Boys, however, figured somewhat more prominently among his interests than the comment suggests. Despite his egotistical claims of freedom from the instincts of the "common herd" of men, Douglas despised himself and those like him. "The uranians of both sexes," he deplored in his autobiography, "are more close-fisted than heterosexuals; self-centred, like oysters in their shell . . . A bankrupt uranian is as rare as a bankrupt spinster." As an Englishman in self-imposed exile, he established himself at Capri, an island resort which, like Taormina, attracted a wide assortment of wealthy, eccentric, and homosexual Europeans. Douglas sometimes brought his street pick-ups along on excursions with friends simply to be outrageous. At the same time he was a man of great dignity, wit, and sensitivity when he wished, and many who knew him never saw at first-hand his seamier side. With his puritanical views about public display of vice, Will Percy undoubtedly belonged to the latter group of his admirers. Percy and Douglas remained in touch by correspondence through the 1930s.[48]

Percy first met the English novelist in a Neapolitan restaurant in Florence, where Douglas, always a showman, made a scene in the kitchen (probably for Percy's benefit). A day or so later, Will Percy reported, their paths crossed again as the American was heading for Santa Maria Novella to see the Giotto murals. Though he refused an invitation to join Percy's expedition, Douglas sighed "tenderly," as Percy reported, that "it's the most famous and convenient place in Florence for lovers' meetings." Douglas advised his new friend to see the Etruscan statuary at Volterra— "charming boys" who "are all lightly powdered with alabaster dust, even their eyelashes." Percy did not follow the suggestion. Later on the tour, Percy stayed at a hotel on Capri. In writing his mother, however, he did not mention by name his acquaintance with Douglas and his friends on the island where "everybody knows everybody else." Percy did, however, speak of meeting most of the English expatriates of Capri, thanks to "an elderly & homely Englishman."[49] He might have meant Douglas, who was sixteen years his senior.

Despite differences in age and cultural background, Douglas and Percy shared a number of important intellectual and even political tastes. Each in a separate way was highly conservative on political matters in general. More abstractly, both Douglas and Percy thought pernicious ideologies offered the modern world a dismal road to chaos. Neither could tolerate the notion of socialism or any other means of yoking individuals under the will of the state. In his *Birds and Beasts of the Greek Anthology,* Douglas went out of his way to condemn ants and bees as despicable sports of nature because of what he considered their robot-like totalitarianism. Percy and Douglas were both skeptical of democracy and often identified it with vulgarity and stupidity. Nor did they celebrate the technological innovations of the modern era—from railroads to radios. Like his father, who was also very unmechanical, Will Percy never learned to drive a car. Douglas railed against the telephone.[50]

Their intellectual compatibility was not, however, purely negative. Percy and Douglas felt a special affinity for Mediterranean culture, for Hellenism, and for what has been called the "elegiac cadences" of a sadness that crept into their prose as well as their lives. Will Percy believed it was human nature to be alone with no likelihood of redemption, least of all the kind of renewal that the austere Catholicism of his childhood had promised. Rather than turn to Marx in reaction against Christian dogma, he adopted the Stoic philosophy of Marcus Aurelius Antoninus, and read and re-read his *Meditations* as others might thumb their Bibles.

Like Thomas Jefferson and other early Southern skeptics, Will Percy admitted the goodness of Jesus Christ but not his divinity or the Christians' monopoly upon ethical truth. In *Lanterns on the Levee* he argued that, seated in the ruins of the Greek amphitheater above Taormina, an observer would look down at the "wine-dark sea below and Ætna against the sunset," would think of Christ and Aurelius and be "assured a god had made earth and man. And this is all we need to know." Though pagan, the Stoics recognized the brotherhood of man. The greatest virtue was helping others for one's own sake and peace of mind as well as theirs. Justice, goodness of heart, duty, courage, and fidelity to fellow creatures, great and lowly, were abstractions requiring no divine authority to sustain them; they were worth pursuing on their own.[51]

Like the Roman emperor's, Will Percy's Stoicism was neither a doctrine of despair nor one of purely sensual indulgence because of the brevity of life. Yet it did not offer hope of eternal reward, only fortitude. Adopting it was one way to overcome the dolor that he recognized in himself. Human beings are too prone to fret themselves with unwise misgivings about "the fear of death, the hope of survival, forgiveness, heaven, hell." Christians demand of their God "bribes" for a "perfunctory righteousness!" Will Percy maintained. His credo was not as gloomy or misanthropic as Douglas's. Nonetheless it was based on the impossibility of some kind of transcending victory. The true dread of life was "its apartness, its eternal isolation," Percy insisted. The only rapture of joy and peace on earth came in such flashes of ecstasy as when we lie "on the bosom we love" or are "lost in a sunset." Then "we dissolve and become part of the strength and radiance and pathos of creation," he concluded. These moments of enchantment were brief. Loneliness was the chief experience.[52]

Like Will Percy, Douglas fell into periods of gloom. He was a "sad and lonely man," as a friend observed, who sometimes tried to hide behind "a last smile of lurking mockery." Douglas liked to argue that the ancient Greeks were peculiarly subject to what Walter Pater had called a "pagan melancholy" or gravitas about the inevitability of death and change. He too rejected the Christian concept of an afterlife and adopted instead a bleak, pagan perspective on life—even more desolate than Percy's and also more pleasure-seeking.[53]

Drawn perhaps by these common prejudices and ideas, Percy wrote the foreword to Douglas's *Beasts and Birds of the Greek Anthology,* only published in 1929 but completed much earlier. *The Greek Anthology* is a large collection of ancient poetry, some of which, in the famous Book Twelve, solemnizes male love of boys. Percy's introductory comments captured Douglas's literary and personal traits, especially his wide knowledge in botany and zoology, his dedication to meticulous accuracy in his writings, and his snobbery. But underneath a light, open style, Percy was no uncritical admirer of Capri's most celebrated resident. He shared Douglas's love of repartee, but, unlike the English cynic, he did not consider "Goodness" a "fell disease." Not for a moment did the Mississippian accept Douglas's aesthetic amorality that justified pleasure for its own sake. Douglas always scorned what he called the Anglo-Saxons' "Gothic mistrust of clean thinking," by which the classicist had in mind the ancient Greeks' *joi de vivre* and supposed preference for Uranian love.[54]

Douglas outlived his American acquaintance of the 1920s by ten years. Broken in health, alone, and depressed—as he was most of his life—Norman Douglas killed himself in 1952.[55] With a strenuous rigidity, Will Percy fought against the impulse to which Douglas fell victim. A Southern gentleman of the old school, he could not have enjoyed for very long the vulgarity of which Douglas was capable. Appearances, not principle alone, mattered greatly to Will Percy. In fact, as model host himself, he equated courtesy and hospitality with uprightness. To be sure, "good morals" had their appropriate place in life, but what also mattered was "good manners," he wrote. The remark might be taken lightly, but that would be a mistake. Percy genuinely thought that the rituals of politeness to all and sundry were inducements toward appreciation of another's feelings, a notion that was fast losing any following in America, he thought, under the quickening pace of modern life. The Percys' sense of class was very much involved, but he had no apology to make for cleaving to such ideas.[56]

და

A bachelor with severe inhibitions, Will Percy used poetry as the medium by which to gain some control and direction over his emotions of fear, sensuality, and self-despising. Most notable among his themes was his complicated attitude toward his father. Many years before, Eleanor Percy Lee, his great-aunt, had adopted versifying to articulate her resentment against her unmindful father Nathaniel Ware and distracted mother Sarah Percy. Likewise, Will Percy used the medium to express mixed emotions toward his parent and his own sexual nature. The result was ambiguity. How could it have been otherwise? With reference to the sexual issue, he was most circumspect. In "A Page's Song," a lyric which was anthologized in the 1920s, the medieval persona of the poem sings to Jesus a request— "And fringe my boyhood's path, both sides,/ With lads-love fine and free."[57] The poem was meant to be ethereal and delicate—much yearning, no touching. Percy expected other poets to do likewise. In a letter to Witter Bynner, a poet with whom he had begun a correspondence, he lambasted Webster Ford, a fellow poet. His verses "about a soldier in the Philippines," Percy gossiped, were "surely inexcusably indecent."[58]

Will Percy's most serious lines were written as laments over love unfulfilled. The variations on this romantic and classical theme were probably based on a schoolboy's surreptitious reading of Virgil's *Second Eclogue,* in which Corydon never succeeds in winning over the disdainful Alexis. At Harvard, Percy had written a poem, "To Lucrezia," which reflected his awareness of an inability to love a woman. The poet tells Lucrezia that he had been swayed by her beauty, but his infatuation had died. Even Christ, who "could not claim my soul as friend," had deserted him. Meanwhile, "some young god,/ With blown, bright hair and fillet golden" had come with "the blossoming rod of beauty" and cast upon Lucrezia "a pagan spell." The poem suggests that Will's loss of faith in Christianity, and particularly in Catholicism, had much to do with his shame at his own sexual feelings for which the Church had no more sympathy than had his parents or Greenville society. According to *Lanterns on the Levee,* during his European trips he enjoyed moments of joy that yet had the same unrequited outcome. Once in Turkey, he writes, he and a companion heard a boy singing a rude Turkish song. They followed the sound to the edge of a hidden pool where "a young man, white and naked, with a mop of gold hair, was swimming beneath us." Will Percy translated the incident into his distinctive idiom: "Oblivious of us, enraptured and alone," the young swimmer "clove the flashing water and sang into the sun." [59]

Some of Percy's lyric poems are written with an indeterminate persona—male or female—but always with sexual passion unfulfilled. Among such verses is one that includes the lines: "And so we part! . . . You to your vague sweet ways,/ I where the failures start." But among his lengthier and more ambitious poems are those which identify the narrator as a woman vainly in love with a youth who finds the advances repugnant. The most significant of these was "Sappho at Levkas," which he had composed in its totality at Sewanee in the summer of 1913. In the poem Sappho explains to Zeus her love for Phaon of her native Lesbos. Her first sight of the "slim, brown shepherd boy with windy eyes" made her breathlessly aware of "the poison of his loveliness," she tells her father-God.[60] Sappho is filled with alternating moments of gratitude for "the life Thou hast given me," passion, yearning for understanding on the one hand and on the other, grief and anger—for "shame's rebellion in my blood" cannot be quelled. Zeus, however, remains studiously silent throughout the monologue, but clearly the father's silence means cold, humiliating rejection of the wayward offspring. "Father," Sappho confesses, "it seemed not evil then—so sweet/ He was," whereas Sappho who hated "lust" and cherished "purity" came to loathe herself. Caught in the grasp of guilt, craven desire, and a raging jealousy that Phaon will soon "flaunt" his "manhood's proof" before some earthly "wench," Sappho leaves her immobile father to fling herself over a precipice. A chorus mourns that mankind is doomed to becoming "wise only in our own futility." [61]

By including "Sappho in Levkas" in an anthology, editor and friend William Stanley Braithwaite hailed it as a poem exhibiting "a magnificence that is rare, a flawlessness of expression in the old manner that is unusual" because it dealt inspiringly with "the struggle between pride and chastity and love and sensual instinct." In the New York *Sun* an admirer likened his poems to the "well wrought verse" of Rupert Brooke but observed that Percy avoided the English poet's "grossness." Yet the praise was not universal. Another critic was almost insulting, finding the title poem "so de-

void of feeling, that when he seeks to paint voluptuousness sympathetically
. . . and when he strives for tenderness, he can compass nothing but coldness and sparkle." [62] Young William Faulkner of Oxford, Mississippi, with
whom Will Percy was acquainted, declared in a review that *In April Once,*
another slim volume, revealed the poet to be a Miniver Cheevy. Faulkner
speculated that he was "a little boy closing his eyes against the dark of
modernity" with his fancies about chivalry and the Middle Ages. Likewise,
"H. M." in *Poetry* (Chicago) protested his "words and phrases imitative of
a bygone diction or manner, like *guerdon, methinks, of yore, the empurpled
air,*" particularly in "Sappho in Levkas." The shorter poems, "H. M." concluded, were less "flagrantly mediocre," but on the whole Percy smothered
what little inspiration he had to produce "an absolutely artificial
product." [63]

Southern newspaper critics generally gushed about the Keatsian qualities
that the Northern reviewers found dull, constrained, and derivative. Nonetheless, Caroline Gordon, the novelist and poet, guessed that Will Percy's
mediocrity, evident in the often trite closing lines, grew out of an awareness of his limited talent that inhibited the hard work necessary to reach
excellence. Like his family predecessors in the literary line—Warfield, Lee,
and Dorsey—Will Percy wrote about his emotional life, using, in his case,
the Edwardian convention of classicism, as his vehicle. His three major
themes—father-son relations, unrequited love, and natural beauty—left
him with a limited range since he knew that the Greco-Roman and medieval settings for his long poems were unfashionable.

Critics complained—he thought unfairly—of his indifference to historical authenticity. "Another thing that irritates me," he protested to Professor Donald Davidson, a leader of the conservative Agrarian movement at
Vanderbilt University, "is the expectation that all artists in prose or verse
should write about the poor and the illiterate and the ill-bred. I know
nothing about the psychology of the negro nor of the poor white. But I do
know something of the feelings and problems of that class which was once
the slave owner class in the South." His literary interests, like Walker
Percy's, were inescapably elitist. Unfortunately, Will Percy could not reflect with any conscious objectivity about the Southern elite. Years later
his adopted son Walker achieved that salutary detachment. "I never could
see any point when you are born a gentleman in trying to act as if you
were not one," Will Percy testily concluded.[64]

Will Percy's prewar verse did display a bloodless quality. In *In April
Once,* published in 1919, one finds, however, a greater maturity. The domi-
nant tone of his war poems was a melancholy poignancy, as "In France,"
the poem in the epigraph of this chapter. Some poems expressed the view
that the war was worth the fighting and dying, but other verses were angry.
In "After Any Battle" the poet denounces the initiators of the struggle for
blasphemously calling "this holocaust" a crusade and "Turning the sham-
bles to an altar stone/ And butchery to sacrifice!" [65] But by and large

Percy's verse lacked concreteness and fresh imagery even when the sentiments were themselves authentic.

Much of the pessimism of the poetry he wrote in the postwar period
stemmed from his complex reaction to war and unfulfilling peace and to
the internal conflicts that kept him a dependent upon his parents at home
and only a temporary wayfarer abroad. Despite the gloom of his writing,
however, Will Percy actually had reached a plateau of relative contentment
in the first postwar decade. Despite his frequent flights away from Greenville, he and his father—Will Percy's Zeus as it were—reached a rather
close relationship in the last years of the Senator's life. Their friendship
and collaboration helped them both to weather not only two dramatic crises—the destructive torrents that washed over the Mississippi Delta—the
metaphorical deluge of Ku Klux Klanism in 1922 and the real Mississippi
River flood in 1927—but a series of family calamities as well.

CHAPTER TWELVE

The Terrors of Klan and Flood

What we were slow to forgive was hardness of
heart and all unkindness.

William Alexander Percy[1]

LeRoy Percy considered the rebirth of the Ku Klux Klan as a powerful movement in the twentieth century a folly that would die of its own absurdity. To those not affected by antagonisms toward ethnic minorities, such a description might have seemed very apt, but some eighteen million Americans were sufficiently disturbed by the wrenching changes in post-World War I America to join the ranks of the KKK. The organization was built upon a long history of nativist sentiment, stretching back to the old anti-Irish Know-Nothings and anti-abolitionist, anti-black mobs in the North before the Civil War and the fear of black insurgency and advance in the South, anxieties that persisted and even grew worse after emancipation and Confederate defeat in 1865.

The modern Klan, however, had no direct connection—except in terms of continued bigotry—to the earlier Klan which had sought to reinstall Democratic regimes throughout the South and destroy the Republican experiment in Reconstruction. William J. Simmons, a small-time insurance salesman, Edward Young Clarke, Elizabeth Tyler, and, later, Hiram Evans built the organization from small beginnings in 1915, when Simmons was inspired by D. W. Griffith's film *The Birth of a Nation*. The Klan flourished in the postwar atmosphere of economic uncertainty, the hasty and unsettling demobilization of American troops, the return of black veterans willing to assert themselves, the recent exodus of black labor to Northern war industries, and upheaval and revolution in Europe—especially in Bolshevik Russia. Latent anti-Semitism, anti-Catholicism, racism, and suspicion of radicals and suffragettes churned into rage throughout small-town America. Seizing the moment, Simmons and company recruited members and formed chapters everywhere, but with particular success in the Deep South. Violence, lynchings, beatings, and other atrocities—all performed in the name of justice and 100 Per Cent Americanism—followed in their path. Politicians bowed under the tide of hatred. They said nothing or, like Hugo Black of Alabama, joined the populist fraternal order, as Walker Percy's law partner Augustus Benners later disgustedly reported to Will Percy.[2]

The Mississippi Klan, like other state chapters in the South, claimed to be defending society from hordes of Italians, Jews, Catholics, and "sullen" blacks. Few stood in the way, but LeRoy Percy was one who did—and he did so to great effect. He saw the Klan's presence in Greenville as an invasion by "an alien breed of Anglo-Saxon" from the hill country similar to the mobocratic Vardamanism that had driven Percy and his class from elected office a decade before. They had met the poor whites, as they perceived the Klan to be, when on the hustings in 1911. In former times, Greenville might have been "overstocked with sinners and pariahs and publicans," Will Percy conceded, "but they kept the churches in their places and preserved the tradition of sprightliness."[3]

LeRoy Percy applauded his son's opinions and expressed similar sentiments to his friends. He wrote one of them, for instance, that, though the town had grown, "there were more men and women possessing individuality, personality and charm in the dear dead days when you knew it, then there are today." He had always taken a rather benign view of human failings. Once, when a sitting senator, he wrote a cousin about a Natchez postmaster who had allegedly run off with another man's wife. "That crime, as you know, is neither unheard of nor uncommon." Live and let live had been his credo.[4] The Percys, however, saw the recent arrivals as a serious threat to community stability. They represented a new moral and religious fundamentalism, enforced by lawless means—back to the old charivari of a barbaric, witch-hunting culture. The South, Will Percy wrote in *Lanterns on the Levee*, had "two major deficiencies—character and education—" and both deficiencies contributed to the ascendancy of the Klan.[5]

Much more was involved than a simple righteous stand against intolerance. The ascendancy of the Percys in the Delta was at risk. By no means were all anti-Klan stalwarts under Percy influence, but without the efforts of the Percys the Klan would have assumed complete control of the county offices with ugly results not only for the blacks but also the substantial number of Catholics, Jews, and members of other ethnic minorities in Greenville. The Percys were well aware that a victory for the Klan would have meant the end of their dynastic leverage in local affairs. Moreover, the anti-Catholic character of the Klan affected the family personally, since Camille Percy and her kin belonged to that much suspected faith. In addition, the anti-Negro aspect of the hooded order threatened the stability of the Delta labor supply in general and the Percys' economic interests in particular. Indeed, during both the Klan and the Flood crises, LeRoy Percy was as determined to hold cheap labor in the Delta as he had been in the Sunnyside affair years before. Finally, the Klan episode stirred LeRoy

Percy's blood in a way that was almost intoxicating. This was his World War—waged at a time when his son Will was feeling downcast. The battle also made him gauge other things with greater confidence. His relationship with LeRoy Pratt Percy—commonly called Roy—was especially strong during the period of the Klan's rise because he saw in his nephew such great promise as a lawyer, and possible statesman too. The future of the family name would be Roy Percy's responsibility.

At the start of the anti-Klan contest, the former senator was ready for any ordeal. His health was good and Camille, his wife, was still vigorous and a great support. Cotton prices were high, and the boll weevil did not affect his plantations. The law business flourished, so much so that LeRoy Percy did not hesitate to help send William Armstrong Percy II to Stanford University, to aid his nephew's mother Caroline Percy in coping with her widowhood in Los Angeles, and to take care of Aunt Nana (Mrs. George Pearce), Camille's sister. His work for the Mississippi Y.M.C.A. was going well.[6]

Recent scholarship about the Klan insurgency elsewhere in the country has played down religious and racial bigotries and stressed the quarrel with big-business capitalism, concern for community morality, and resentment of local and business elites.[7] Actually these elements were practically inseparable. The Klansmen's first agenda was not to bring down Wall Street but to restore a Protestant moral order, but their resentment of high-toned traditional leaders like the Percys and their alien friends—Catholics, Jews, and dependent blacks—had its origins in economic discontent and the widespread suspicion that people like the Percys had no respect for the lower orders. Indeed, the organization displayed characteristics likely to disgust sophisticated folk. The Klan combined a narrow righteousness with the American love of ritual, especially initiation rites, and fraternal bonding, a style that most suited small-town America, North and South.[8]

Like their Klan enemies, Will Percy and his father ventured a return to an earlier and simpler day, but they envisioned a past different from the one the Klan hoped to restore. Both parties—the Percys and the Klan leaders—used the language of honor to enfold their convictions. The Percys, however, assumed the mantle of noblesse oblige and the rule of dignity and law to which they were professionally devoted, whereas Klan leaders upheld the honor of rigid community conformity and tradition. The Percys did not believe that men should snoop into other men's private affairs—how they treated their wives, how much they drank, how often they gambled. In Greenville before the arrival of the Klan, "drunkenness and lechery, Sabbath-breaking and gambling," Will Percy contended, had been regarded not as atrocities on the scale of rape and armed robbery but rather as lapses into "poor judgment or poor taste."[9]

The Percys' anti-Klan activities were to have significant repercussions in later times as well. During the Civil Rights movement of the 1950s and

60s, when Southern politicians and their supporters were howling against the march of integration, the Percys would defend the blacks against the same class of people their forebears had opposed long before. Thus, David L. Cohn, long a member of the Percy circle in Greenville, declared bitterly, "This is the Age of the Lout. The gentleman in our times is here on sufferance and he may be permitted to live and die obscurely if he keeps his mouth shut." With its elitist overtones and dislike of white racist rabble-rousing, the campaign that Senator LeRoy Percy launched in Greenville so many years before made it easier for the next generation of Percys to support the blacks: to do so was part of family tradition. Hodding Carter of the *Delta Democrat-Times,* Walker Percy the novelist and his younger brother LeRoy Percy opposed the White Citizens Councils of the 1950s and 1960s. The courageous struggle in the early twenties would bear rich fruit in later years.[10]

The Klan arrived in Greenville in the person of one Colonel Joseph G. Camp, a former Chatauqua lecturer. County and town officials secretly recruited before his appearance secured for Camp the use of the courthouse to open his campaign. LeRoy Percy was outraged when he learned of it. At first he tried to countermand the authorization but soon saw advantages in direct confrontation. Ray Toombs, son of an old deceased friend of the Percy family, warned him in Percy's own office not to interfere at the Ku Klux rally, but Percy retorted, "I told him if Colonel Camp made a speech at the Court House I would make a speech, and he says, 'I would not do that; I would wait. . . .' I says, 'Well, I am going to do it and I hope you will be there.' He says, 'I will' and he left." Astonished that Toombs, the county prosecuting attorney, had already joined the order, Percy saw at once that the epidemic of irrationality was much more serious than he had imagined. Moreover, in his mind the incident with Toombs reflected the enormous changes in the social order that separated the world of old Dr. Toombs, Ray's father, and the present age. The young attorney's behavior, Percy concluded, was not "the kind of conduct gentlemen who are not Klansmen indulge in." Toombs's father would have been ashamed of his son's fall from good taste and sound principle, LeRoy Percy asserted.[11]

On the evening of March 1, 1922, the courthouse was as packed as if the murder case of the century were being tried. When the audience settled down, Percy shrewdly proposed that Sheriff L. M. Nicholson take the chair. Some in the crowd had arrived armed and tension was running high. Colonel Camp's speech covered the expected ground. He introduced his topic by declaring that "the Catholics are organized, the Jews are organized, and the negro is organized," and all of them were conspiring against the liberties of the country. Only true-blue Americans were "unorganized." He finished his lengthy remarks with a boast of the Klan's clandestine moral surveillance of individuals and neighborhoods.[12]

As the shouts of "Percy, Percy, Percy" rang through the hall, the former senator rose to give the speech of his life. He began by comparing the alleged virtues of the original Klan to the hypocrisies of the Klan national leaders, Doc Simmons and Hiram Evans, then squabbling scandalously for control of the headquarters in Atlanta. (Like the Lost Cause of the Confederacy, the First Klan of the Reconstruction period had to be paid homage or the Southern spokesman of the 1920s would lose his following.) Percy argued that the two were nothing more than swindlers whose chief interest was in the ten-dollar initiation fee and the selling of Klan apparel and trinkets—all in the name of a spurious Americanism. Besides, on what battlefield did Camp get his commission? In patriotic reference to American participation in the recent war, Percy observed that General Ferdinand Foch, Allied commander and one of the world's greatest soldiers, was a Catholic Knight of Columbus, who never had found it necessary to hide behind a mask.

LeRoy Percy's main point was the damage that the Klan could cause. Already "thousands and thousands of acres lie idle today in the most fertile part of the State of Louisiana," Percy noted. "Why? For lack of labor." The lure of industry in the North that offers "better opportunity" was already having an appalling economic effect. With only three parades, no matter how peaceful, the Klan could sweep all the remaining blacks out of the region, and grass would soon be "growing in the streets of Greenville." The senator warned that although the Klan claimed not to injure Negroes unless they misbehaved, the black people in the Delta "don't know whether they are going to behave so as to suit those 1,000,000 Klansmen or not." Turning to sarcasm, he observed, "Can't you see Sheriff Nicholson, if he wanted to arrest a negro for robbing a henroost, writing to Nashville for a posse of klansmen and going down the road with a gang of white-robed men behind him to arrest the negro? You would have to advertise to find the negro after that parade."

No less important was the ruinous effect the Klan had on community life. Reaching the most eloquent part of the address, Percy showed that he, too, had rare gifts. With a rising voice, he declared, these strangers have come among us, knowing nothing about the people of the Delta. "They don't know how united we have faced the floods of the mighty river; faced the scourge of epidemic, faced bankruptcy and trouble and poverty; they don't know how we have feasted together at the weddings of our young people; they don't know how with bowed heads we have stood together around the graves of our loved ones; they don't know how the love and pride the people of this county and community have felt in the fact that we stand together and undivided." The repetitions, rhythmic cadences, and juxtaposition of weddings and burials as community rituals provided a telling contrast with the tawdriness of Camp's diatribe. Percy continued by arguing that mob violence, personal acts of lawless revenge, gained a degree of social acceptance in the Klan-controlled community, even when the Klan was not directly responsible. Wherever the Klan ap-

peared, neighbor could not trust neighbor, and even families fell to quarreling, Percy contended.

Giving almost as much time to religious as to racial bigotry, LeRoy Percy
pointed out that the very courthouse where they gathered had been built
by Protestant, Catholic, and Jewish taxpayers. Perhaps the Klan would go
after Percy's business partner (Morris Rosenstock) who was then lending
over $150,000 to Washington Countians at the reasonable rate of 6 per-
cent—scarcely Shylockian usury. With equal derision, he pointed out that
even the town police force had its dangerous Papists. "They have got
Boots, as constable. He is tainted, his wife is a Catholic. They are creeping
up on us." Finally, he argued that the Klan interfered with regular law
enforcement, although its oaths of allegiance pledged members to assist
police officers in their duties. Klansmen claimed to protect Southern womanhood, Percy scoffed: "Since when has Southern womanhood needed to
be defended by men in masks?" As the crowd laughed and clapped its
approval, Camp was becoming increasingly apprehensive. He asked for
police protection to get him safely back to his hotel. Nicholson's deputy,
an Irish Catholic, with elaborate civility, honored his request while Percy
and his supporters passed resolutions denouncing the divisiveness and ugly
principles of the Klan.[13]

The speech earned LeRoy Percy headlines and praise not just at home
but across the country, largely because outspoken opposition to the Klan
by prominent Southerners was so rare. Marcellus Foster, owner of the
Houston *Chronicle,* a virulently anti-Klan paper in a state that was riddled
with Ku Kluxism, informed Percy that he intended to carry his stirring
address in full, in hopes of awakening the thinking public to the danger.
"The Chronicle has been fighting the Klan in this state for many months,"
Foster wrote, but how discouraging was the response. "It is the most difficult fight we have ever attempted owing to the intolerance and the racial
and religious prejudices that have been engendered through Klan activities." After the Greenville address appeared in the *Chronicle,* LeRoy Percy
received word from wellwishers in Texas that it was helping to turn public
opinion in the state against the Klan.[14] In the Northeast, news of his eloquent attack also spread quickly. Ellery Sedgwick, editor of the *Atlantic
Monthly,* urged Percy to write up the speech in the form of a journalistic
essay. Busy with law cases, LeRoy Percy asked his son to ghost it for him,
but the article itself seems less in Will Percy's style than in LeRoy's.[15]

Over the next two years, with growing intensity, requests poured into
Greenville from across the nation for copies of Percy's courthouse speech
and others to follow.[16] Meanwhile, Percy was himself sending out reprints
to influential national associates, whose friends reproduced the tract for
distribution to larger constituencies. Most important in the anti-Klan crusade were leaders of the Knights of Columbus, who found in Percy's words
the perfect retort. They had learned that the Percy family had Catholic
members and that Percy was himself most concerned with the anti-

Catholic aspect of the Klan's activities. From the Midwest, the North, and Far West, K. of C. chapters invited Percy to special anti-Klan gatherings. He always responded with advice or help. For instance, he offered his opinion that much anti-Catholic sentiment sprang from Scottish Rite Masons, who seemed to reflect Ulster hostility toward Catholic Ireland. With some bitterness, he claimed that the Southern clergy had proved slender reeds in the storm. He turned down most invitations, however; he did not wish to make anti-Klan work a new profession. That would have put him on the same level as the itinerant Colonel Camp. Percy had more than enough to do already: his work as a corporate attorney, a director of the regional Federal Reserve Board in St. Louis, member of the American Law Institute, trustee of the Carnegie Foundation for International Peace, and other duties.[17]

In his national anti-Klan activity, Percy benefited from the Louisiana Klan's political blunder in Morehouse Parish, just west of Greenville and Vicksburg. It was a brutal atrocity against two locally prominent white men. Since the 1880s, Morehouse had been one of the most lynch-prone districts in the country. In the Morehouse Klan's estimation, bootleggers and other open (as opposed to surreptitious) violators of local mores should be the first targets. The blacks were already cowed, and Catholics were rare in that part of Louisiana. Not long after Percy's speech at the Greenville courthouse, J. K. Skipworth, a superannuated Confederate veteran, gathered some fifty of his hooded friends on a highway between Bastrop and Mer Rouge, where they stopped all cars until they found the men they were hunting: J. L. and Watt Daniel and Thomas F. Richards—all planters of Mer Rouge—and three others. Watt Daniel, a graduate of Louisiana State University, and Richards had served in the same tank unit in the recent war and they belonged in the upper echelons of the community and treated the Klansmen as loutish buffoons. Although class antagonisms had been aroused on both sides, the Klansmen denied that they were retaliating for the mockery but insisted that they were trying to clean up Mer Rouge by punishing some bootlegging sinners. After subjecting them all to a severe beating, the Klansmen let J. L. Daniel and the other, older men go home, but held Daniel's son Watt and Richards. Watt Daniel and Thomas Richards were unmercifully tortured to death. When their bodies surfaced in nearby Lake Lafourche some three months later, the autopsies revealed bones broken, genitals cut off, and the bodies crushed under the iron wheels of a road-grading tractor.[18]

Meanwhile, "Old Skip," as the Exalted Cyclops of Morehouse Parish was affectionately called, publicly defied the state authorities. Governor John M. Parker of Louisiana, a fiscal conservative with socially progressive tendencies, was outraged by the murders and other vigilante incidents in the parish. Parker and Percy had grown up together at Deer Creek many years before and had remained friends, as both were almost fanatical huntsmen. They had only recently collaborated in the founding of a cooperative organization to limit cotton production to hold up prices.[19] Like his friend in Mississippi, Parker was a fighter. "Daily," he wrote LeRoy Percy with some heat, "I receive my full share of abuse from these people, and this only adds to my determination to do everything that lies in my power to put them out of business."[20] By this time, the kidnaping had become a case of murder upon the discovery of the mud-encrusted bodies, but Klan-dominated grand juries refused to indict Skipworth and company.

Seizing the advantage of so blatant and nationally damaging a coverup, LeRoy Percy made the most of the Morehouse Parish affair. He and Governor Parker traveled together to Chicago to attend an anti-Klan rally. Heaping scorn on the low-class ignorance of the opposition, Percy explained that the hooded order wanted Americans to believe that the army and navy were in the hands of the Pope to reduce the credulous to "a condition of nervous apprehension bordering upon imbecility, seeing the air crowded with Catholic hobgoblins, popish dragons and the terrors of the inquisition." Chicago Klansmen were quick to rejoin. With sarcasm to match Percy's contempt, a Chicago Klan paper headlined an attack on his speech with: "PERCY'S PUNY PROPAGANDA PLAY POLITICAL PRANKS PERVERTLY" and claimed that Percy and Parker, whose aristocratic wife Cecille Airey was Catholic, were mere automatons manipulated by the Pope. They insisted that Percy and Parker had a fiscal interest in destroying the Klan, the Pope having supposedly contributed six million dollars to the undertaking. Such claims suggested that behind the nativist rhetoric was a deep class bias against the pair and others of their class. In turn, Percy and Parker revealed a similar antipathy in their considerably more accurate charges that Klan leaders were petty confidence men.[21]

Exciting and important as Percy's anti-Klan ventures upon the national scene were, he enjoyed the local struggle much more, taking special pleasure in trying to shame the Klansmen who stood on the lower rungs of the town hierarchy. At a meeting held on April 23, 1923, in the old Peoples Theatre in Greenville, a huge crowd heard him deliver a scathing assault upon Skipworth, the instigators of the Mer Rouge incident, and the Washington County Klan. "P.P.P."—for "Percy, Parker and Pope"— he said, seemed to be the watchword of the local K.K.K.. He was proud that he could associate with Parker, "a gallant, Christian gentleman," a designation not fitting the men to be discovered underneath the white sheets of the opposition. Anyone who believed the Klan's nonsense that the bodies found in Lake Lafourche had been planted by Irishmen working for the Pope and that Governor Parker had received a war chest from the Vatican to campaign against the order had to be a "blathering idiot." In respect to the events in nearby Louisiana, "We ought to build a monument to Skip; it ought to be of white marble painted with blood." Then he attacked the issue of class with no subtlety whatsoever. At nearby Leland on Deer

Creek, the Grand Cyclops of the Klan had called Percy " 'the Big Cheese.' " Percy remarked that some were crowing "that the day of Kings had passed." Perhaps so, Percy acknowledged, "but the day when Wizards will rule Washington County will never come." He named all the Klan leaders individually—including Ray Toombs, prosecuting attorney, and one of the kinsmen of old General Paxton, a Percy adversary of the 1870s, Torrey Woods, candidate for sheriff, and Ben Hatch, Supervisor of Education, who was no scholar everybody agreed, but was thought to be merely "simple and straight and true." With bold condescension, Percy beseeched the politicians to take off their hoods and help to heal a disunited community, and he denounced the immigration restrictions that the Klan, One Hundred Per Centers, and the labor unions sought to impose on the country. Far from being a danger to law and order, he later argued in the Memphis *Commercial Appeal,* the immigrants were hardworking and law-abiding, a characteristic contrasting with those of their sheet-clad adversaries. The kind of democracy he had in mind was of the old Tory variety—the union of the upper stratum with the dependent poor who, if white, smart, and eventually wealthy enough, ought to be welcomed as equals. (After all, Percy's Jewish friends, the Rosenstocks and Goldsteins, were founding members of the Greenville Country Club, one of the few anywhere in the nation, North or South, that brought Jews and Gentiles together.)[22]

Class and history lay behind Percy's thundering against the Klan. What he sought was vengeance, a vindication of his stand against Vardaman and the allegedly unthinking masses who had so humiliated him eleven years before. The enemy was scum. They were nothing, he asserted, but "a cowardly, skulky bunch and no thorough-bred ought to have anything but a feeling of contempt for them."[23] The trouble was that "thorough-breds" made up so small a part of the populace in Mississippi where Theodore Bilbo and his piney woods friends reigned in places once held by Percy's well-born, high-living friends of old—Catchings, McNeily, Ferguson, Alfred H. Stone, Charles Scott, and the rest. LeRoy Percy was determined to defy the teetotalling know-nothings even in his social habits. As if to mock the pretentiousness of a Klan, lately burdened at the Atlanta headquarters with scandals about sex and corruption, he gambled and drank as he always had. In February 1923, for instance, he wrote a New Orleans friend to make sure the bearer of his introductory letter, who was on his way to New Orleans, was put in the hands of a safe bootlegger for "some good old red liquor." After shooting ducks and snipes in Louisiana in late January with his nephew Roy Percy, he had won $220 playing cards at the Boston Club in New Orleans. For all its boasts of having spies in every corner of the South, the Klan apparently knew nothing of these adventures.[24]

The class warfare between Percy and his skulking opponents reached a climax when Skipworth, then on a Mississippi speaking tour, demanded that Percy explain his words at the recent Peoples Theatre anti-Klan rally in Greenville. Failure to do so, he implied, would result in unpleasantness. In his speech, Percy had characterized "Old Skip" as no less murderous in intent than "Lenine or Trotsky"—as Skipworth reported it, with little regard for spelling. The senator at once gleefully replied that it was his "conviction that the Bastrop Ku Klux Klan was responsible for the deaths of Watt Daniel and Richards and you, as the head of the Klan, were morally responsible therefor." An evening or so later, during a heavy downpour, a stranger banged on the door of the Percys' home. Calling himself a Mr. Keith from Arcola, he asked LeRoy Percy to help him with his car which had broken down with his two sisters stranded some distance away. As a man of honor, LeRoy Percy felt obliged to help a stranger, who, it was later learned, had stationed two other men nearby to wait in ambush. As Percy went off to fetch his coat, Sheriff Nicholson fortuitously appeared on some errand. Priding himself on knowing everybody in Washington County, Nicholson said he had never heard of a Keith from Arcola. But before the Sheriff, LeRoy or Will Percy could question him further, "Keith" mumbled that he had to take a leak and disappeared into the rainstorm.[25]

With a tight election coming soon, LeRoy Percy described the whole incident in an open letter to Exalted Cyclops Ray Toombs published in the Greenville *Delta Democrat-Times* and the Memphis *Commercial Appeal.* Obviously the stranger meant him harm and therefore the Washington County Klan should be held responsible. Although Toombs denied any involvement, Percy pointed out that a cardinal boast of the organization was its omniscience about local affairs. Furious, Will Percy went over to Toombs's office and told him that if anything happened to his father, he and his friends would run Toombs to ground and kill him. The actual murderer need not be caught because Percy would know who gave the orders. Toombs undoubtedly had heard that one of the Percy brothers had been ready to kill Theodore Bilbo in a shoot-out during the election of 1911. As for Skipworth, Will Percy told his friend Charlotte Gailor of Sewanee that he could never permit the Morehouse Parish Cyclops to attack his father in a public way should the old Klansman ever dare to show up in Washington County. Skipworth prudently stayed away. Indeed, there was no violence, no lynching, no midnight demonstrations in Washington County thereafter. As for the stranded motorist, Will Percy had had a good look at him that evening. Two years later, he spotted "Keith" when he was brought up on charges of robbery. At the Greenville jail, the deadbeat realized that Will Percy knew who he was, and with a wry grin remarked: "Old Skip nearly put that one over."[26]

The episode dampened ardor for lawlessness and prepared the way for the Klan's political decline in the county as well. On election day, the townspeople were in a state of near hysteria from excitement, and men went armed in the streets as they had, according to Will Percy, since the spring. The race for sheriff—the office most useful for protecting future Klan activities—was between Torrey Woods and George B. Alexander, one of LeRoy Percy's hunting companions and anti-Klan supporters. He and others on the same ticket were supported by the Protestant Committee of Fifty Opposed to the Ku Klux Klan which the Percys, Judge Percy Bell, and the Hamm family had organized. The outcome was expected to be close. Such old-timers as former Governor Edmund Noel had signed up with the Klan, lending it a little respectability. But in Washington County the Klan had virtually gone underground, and no one knew what their true strength was. Will Percy hovered around downtown where the votes were being counted, while LeRoy Percy played bridge at the house. At nine o'clock, the results were ready. An anti-Klan supporter burst outside to announce, "We've won! We've won! Alexander's elected! God damn the Klan!" Will Percy rushed back to the house to bring the news, but almost immediately afterward a huge crowd arrived to begin a long night of celebration. According to *Lanterns on the Levee,* his father was "nonplussed." He pointed out to Adah Williams and his son that the crowd seemed intent to party but not a drop of whiskey—at least not the kind suitable for entertaining so large a throng—was in the house. On his instructions, Adah Williams, Camille's friend, went off to get four kegs as the Senator threw the house open to the happy company. Weighing some "twenty stone," Lucille, a local musician, pulled the Steinway into her lap and she and her band got the dancing started. Social distinctions, Will Percy recalled, soon fell by the wayside. "A banker's wife hobnobbed with the hot-tamale man, a lawyer's careened with a bootlegger." Folks, long at odds, made up their differences and swore to be friends forever. Greenville had won a small victory and, for once in this bleak world, "righteousness had prevailed." [27]

How greatly this political episode differed from that of 1911. For the Percy family, the victory was almost enough to restore faith in human nature and the benevolence of the deities. Nevertheless, LeRoy Percy still longed for an earlier time. To a friend in Natchez he had once written that the Klan insurgency "is a demonstration of the fading away of the old aristocracy of the South, which with its many faults and weaknesses is yet far in a way of the best thing the South has yet produced. In the olden days as gentlemen we were something of a success." But those times were gone, he lamented. As money-makers, Southerners could not compete "with the more highly trained products of the West. When you destroy the traditions which furnish a background for a people you leave them like a rudderless ship on a[n] unchartered sea." He despaired; only the most light-headed optimist could "name the day or point the way" for a return to civilization.

Will Percy was no more sanguine than his father. Even serving as editor for the Young Poets' Series for Yale University Press, then the most prestigious in the poetic world, did not raise his spirits. Worse still, his longest and most ambitious poem, "Enzio's Kingdom," excited almost no critical interest. In it, the author reflected not only his antipathy toward unchecked democracy, Vardamanism, and Ku Kluxism but also his half-conscious ambivalence about his father. LeRoy Percy served as the model in the poem for his portrayal of Frederick II of the Holy Roman Empire, whose dreams for a well-ordered world are shattered in pettiness and popular greed. " 'Enzio' was as flat a failure as I've ever known." For the romantic Will Percy it was yet another sign that the old values—in poetry as in politics—had washed away in the democratic tide.[28]

As if to prove Will Percy's animadversions against mobocracy the victory over the Klan in Greenville did not spell the end of the fraternal order statewide. At the State Democratic Convention in Jackson, June 1924, the party hacks, including ex-Governor Edmund Noel, a Klansman, refused to let the Washington County anti-Klan leaders take their seats. The setback came at a time when LeRoy Percy was beginning to feel his age. He was only sixty-three, but in the Percy clan that was already living on borrowed time. Under a doctor's strict orders to slow down, he cut back on the alcohol, cigars, and traveling. In addition, Camille came down with appendicitis and underwent a lengthy operation. All these troubles, he wrote his nephew LeRoy Pratt Percy in Birmingham, had left him feeling "very low in spirits." Fearful that the Democrats might be overwhelmed by Ku Kluxism at their Presidential convention in 1924, LeRoy Percy had to follow events helplessly from a sickbed. By 1928 he recovered and courageously fought locally for Al Smith's selection. LeRoy Percy approved the New York governor's opposition to Prohibition, but he was certain that Smith had no chance of election whatsoever. Reflecting perhaps the influence of H. L. Mencken's political punditry, Percy told his friend Senator Pat Harrison of Mississippi, "Hypocrisy is the pet vice of Americans and bunk is their faborite [sic] diet." [29]

Will Percy had not been very active in the Klan battle. For part of that period, he had influenza, a disease that had carried off hundreds of thousands during the Great War. Much of his lengthy vacation time was spent abroad or at Brinkwood in Sewanee, Tennessee, which he and Huger Jervey eventually bought in 1925. In fact, his father thought that his son's health had been undermined by a "weakened heart condition left by the flu." In the midst of the anti-Klan struggle, all three—Will, LeRoy, and Camille—went to fashionable Palm Beach, Florida, where they were appalled—and fascinated by—"the manifold diversions of the idle rich," frivolities that helped to explain "the unrest of the masses," as LeRoy Percy mused. Will Percy proceeded to Panama by steamer for the benefit of the sea air.[30] After his return, he was busy speaking against the Klan at various men's clubs in the small towns around the Delta and apparently was very effective. An irate writer anonymously complained to LeRoy Percy, "Your son, William A. is making a very shabby appearance by playing a jumping Johnnie or Jack in the box, at Rotary Clubs and Legion meetings." What made things worse, the writer continued, was that he had voted for Percy in 1911, not knowing then, he claimed, that the Percys were on the Vatican payroll. Will Percy had filled in at the law office or as speaker when his father's heavy schedule required such help, and he also had undertaken his own writing campaign against the Klan to friends.[31] But in these efforts he kept well under the shadow of his father. Will Percy's chance for glory came with the floodwater sweeping downriver in the late spring of 1927.

The populist thrust of Mississippi politics could not be checked as the Percys had once dreamed. The same sense of embittered helplessness would be experienced when the family confronted the devastation of the Flood of 1927. In *Life on the Mississippi,* Mark Twain said that "ten thousand River Commissions, with the mines of the world at their back, cannot tame that lawless stream, cannot curb it or confine it, cannot say to it, Go here, or Go there, and make it obey."[32] For two generations, the Percy family had gamely tried to channel the river into safe directions, as they had the people of the Delta—efforts in which they gained only indifferent success. William Alexander Percy, "the Gray Eagle," had been the first to reform the levee system with the primitive and local means available during the thirty years after the Civil War. His son LeRoy Percy had been highly active in the same enterprise, attending meetings on flood control and drawing up reports, starting as early as 1879.[33] Sometimes these calamities inspired a momentarily deepened sense of community. Harry Ball, a local diarist, reported that when a "hastily erected" levee four blocks from his house threatened to collapse, "the whole town turned out to work, a strange scene was presented. Here a little squad of Irishmen, working like clockwork; gangs of negroes, shouting and singing over their labor; bunches of Jew clerks, coats off and doing perhaps the first honest labor of their lives, and elegant young dudes, white handed and dressed in flannel shirts and boots like comic opera choruses, with solid business men wielding spade and shovel and puffing and perspiring with the unwonted toil."[34] The townspeople generally came together on such occasion in an impressive way, but economic necessity would have compelled some level of discipline.

To be sure, the Percys had vital interests at stake. Trail Lake, a plantation of 3200 acres and Panther Burn, with 14,000 acres, in which the Percy family had an interest, were important sources of income. In 1926, the year before the great flood, Trail Lake alone had produced almost 2700 bales of cotton valued at $275,000.[35] Both properties were to be devastated when the river overflowed its banks. But in the face of natural disaster, the tendency in the Delta was to take a sanguine view. LeRoy Percy did so when he reassured his sister, Lady McKinney in Knoxville, that the Mississippi "is just at that stage that when any big rain over the upper valleys will give us a dangerous river. But we may get by without that and at any rate, our levees are in very much better condition than ever before and should be able to stand a big water." River engineers had been most reassuring to the inhabitants.[36]

After the spring thaw, the river poured some 60 cubic miles of water into the million square-mile basin. At one point, the volume was enough to force the tributary Ohio River to reverse course. The waters destroyed crops, farm tools and machinery, houses, and businesses worth almost a half billion dollars. Before a Congressional Committee in November 1927, LeRoy Percy described it as a great "yellow sea, stretching a thousand miles from Missouri to the Gulf of Mexico, from 50 to 120 miles in width, rendering more than 700,000 people homeless, putting 600,000 of them on the charity of the American people."[37]

These circumstances underlined a fatalistic and melancholy sense of human transiency that Southerners entertained as soon as a calamity descended. At the same hearings, LeRoy Percy told the congressmen that the people of the Delta had been once more reminded "how puny and futile their efforts to secure protection have been." As if reflecting on his own political misfortunes, he observed that against the "mighty river" they had "made the fight and lost" and now believed themselves "powerless to continue the struggle." But it was the overwhelming force of the river, not the losses alone, that robbed them of "courage and hope" and left them with a foreboding that the river had mocked them and devastated their once proud levees, so long in construction.[38] Of course, his purpose before the House Flood Control Committee was not to adumbrate upon the mysteries of God's order, yet this practical-minded, unreligious attorney did reveal that special Percy gift of reflection and existential wonder and identified it with the plight of his fellow Mississippians.

Just before the flood struck, Will Percy was oblivious of coming disaster, just as he had been about the origins of the Great War. He later admitted that he was working on the final proofs of some poems while 5000 blacks, National Guardsmen, planters, merchants, levee engineers "and old-time high-water fighters" were patching a weakened part of the levee fifteen miles north of town. Frantically they carried sandbags to the levee, but the crest was coming fast upon them, and the levee dissolved practically under the workmen's feet. "The terrible wall of water like an imbecile blind Titan strode triumphantly into our country," Will Percy recalled. Dry land would not be seen again in many parts of the Delta for another four months.[39]

Refugees poured into Greenville—mostly black tenant farmers and their families. Meanwhile white residents prepared to leave as quickly as possible. The Greenville levee, some forty feet high, "with its crowded refugees and all the bustle of getting people" into the waiting steamers, looked like "a war scene," reported Percy Bell.[40] At first pandemonium spread throughout the town, but gradually people who intended to stay settled down as the flood waters silently crept up the streets. The Percys moved their furniture to the second floor, filled bathtubs—and waited. Then, reminisced Will Percy, they saw the water making its insidious way, like "a wavering brown snake," up Percy Street toward the garden, the house. Seeing the crisis as an opportunity for Will Percy to try his hand as a community leader, LeRoy Percy did not leap to the rescue of the drowning city as he had five years earlier in the anti-Klan struggle. Instead, he turned to his son and said, as Will remembered, "Guess you'd better go while you can. I'll be along." Newly appointed by the mayor because of his experience in Belgium, Will Percy waded to the headquarters to take charge of the Greenville Relief Committee under the auspices of the American Red Cross. As he shortly wrote Gerstle Mack, his Army comrade and European traveling companion, he was entering a time that reminded him of "the Argonne in its strain and confusion and distress." [41] How long his father would remain in the background remained to be seen.

At the start, Will Percy proved a capable organizer. He and his committee quickly arranged with Mississippi Governor Dennis Murphree for the National Guard to patrol the streets, commandeered transportation—boats, trucks, and wagons—fed 5000 blacks on a levee seven miles long, another 5000 people, black and white, in town, and 12,000 head of cattle, and telegraphed friends and Red Cross officials for assistance. The response was overwhelming. Northern friends sent Will Percy $10,000, local residents matched the sum, and, thanks to his old boss in Belgium, Herbert Hoover, Secretary of Commerce and head of the Red Cross effort, millions rolled in through that agency.

The problems facing the Delta were on a scale that justified every dollar applied to them. The dangers to health from untreated water and the carcasses of dead animals floating about, as well as from the difficulty of distributing food, mounted. Those who lived in one-story houses had to seek refuge on roofs and in the trees until rescued, sometimes by bootleggers with power boats. Fresh meat, vegetables, and milk disappeared quickly. Boil water for twenty minutes, Will Percy's committee advised, but fuel and pots were as scarce as fresh bread. Percy Bell reported that as the water receded, an inch at a time, the "Buffalo gnats" and mosquitoes increased proportionately. "Every store in town," Bell wrote his relatives, exiled to the state capital by the overflow, "smells horribly and the entrance to the Weinberg building is like walking into a sewer." The anomalies that arose from flood conditions struck residents with peculiar force—to see roses blooming in gardens, just peeping above the water line, and at the same time to look inside the "pretty houses" where living-room furniture was floating silently in deathly dance with a putrefying mule. Unless they were pets under careful supervision, dogs were shot, and sent drifting off in the scummy waters, to save food and prevent rabies. The sooner white residents left the district the better was the general opinion. Will Percy and his colleagues enlisted the help of the Standard Oil Company, whose barges and boats carried off as many as possible to Vicksburg. Before long nearly all the women and children had been safely evacuated.

(Camille and Aunt Adah Williams refused to obey Will's orders and stayed to care for the menfolks at the house on Percy Street.) [42]

If the women and children were considered an impediment, Will Percy himself must have felt at times as if he were as well. On one level, he turned to his father, who, he wrote Gerstle Mack, "has been wonderful." What Will most admired was the senator's appreciation of the "tragedy in its entirety." His father's moral support, his son rhapsodized, had been the only thing to prevent him from having a serious "breakdown," but there was another plane of emotion which the son did not wish to recognize. An issue arose that tested his mettle and put him at odds with his father. It concerned what to do about the black tenants who were shivering in the upper stories of town buildings and in the gins, compresses, barn lofts, and other outbuildings in the country. To get food, blankets, and clothing to these tiny islands was complicated, particularly because undertows, especially at street intersections, and objects hidden in the water could unexpectedly capsize a supply boat. Will Percy and his committee tried to gather up as many of the blacks as possible and locate them on the levee. There the cooking and eating could be centralized, but no tents were available to house them in the continuing cold weather, and blanket supplies were running out. As a result, he and his co-workers decided to ship the 7500 blacks to Vicksburg, and two large vessels arrived to carry them downriver.

At first LeRoy Percy tried to take a lesser role in events that his son was overseeing. But after a lifetime of activity and customary command, he could not sit quietly on the sidelines. His son had won battle decorations which were a source of paternal pride, but perhaps, too, he experienced some feelings of jealousy. Will Percy had never directly confronted his own feelings when his father exhibited an aggressiveness that was bound to dishearten him. For instance, after the 1911 defeat, LeRoy, Camille, and Will Percy had fled to Greece for a much needed vacation. One morning in Athens, Will Percy arose at dawn to explore the Acropolis and report his impressions to his breakfasting parents. But before he reached the steps leading toward the Parthenon, he heard "a great hubbub." Then, climbing upward, he saw his father in the midst of some workmen protesting his entry upon the site of their repairs: "Father had beaten me to it. . . . The curative morning was flooding over him, and he laughed when he saw me." [43] LeRoy Percy hated to lose not just to men like Vardaman, Skipworth, or Ray Toombs, but to his own son as well. It was unfortunately a competitiveness that could be destructive.

Despite his stated desire to leave the management of relief work to his son Will, LeRoy Percy almost immediately was working as hard as if he were just starting a law practice from scratch. The local paper hailed him as the "guiding genius" who brought order out of chaos in the first twenty-four hours of the overflow. [44] Although he recognized the dangers of subverting Will Percy's authority, he intervened when the decision was made to remove the black tenants to Vicksburg. Fearful that the old system of labor was about to collapse, LeRoy Percy and his fellow planters were concerned that if the tenants dispersed, they would use the occasion to move permanently up north. Legally they could do so, without having to work off old debts, because by state law natural disaster provided that sort of debtor relief. LeRoy Percy advised his son to poll his volunteers again, and, though determined to carry out the original plan, Will complied. He was dumbfounded when the group unanimously voted to reverse policy. Chagrined, Will Percy gave in and ordered the infuriated ship captains to leave empty. In 1929, after his father's death, Will Percy discovered that LeRoy had spent the day convincing volunteers such as Percy Bell to change their vote, swearing them all to secrecy. As it happened, a supply boat materialized the next morning with all the necessary equipment for supporting the blacks on the levees. Always the gambler, LeRoy Percy once more had the advantage of good luck.[45]

Historian Richard King holds that LeRoy Percy's intervention represents a "betrayal" that exposed the true state of the relationship—the domineering father and the humiliated son. That construction is persuasive. Yet LeRoy Percy was quite incapable of acting otherwise. By temperament and cultural background, he was unable to see that his manipulations would have any harmful effects, either on his son or on the community, white and black. From one perspective, it might be argued that given the hard-boiled attitude of the planter class, Will Percy, heir to his father's principality, as it were, would have been the loser if his own orders had been carried out. Will Percy's idea of noblesse oblige simply was not compatible with his father's more autocratic spirit, one that Colonel John Sartoris or Thomas Sutpen in William Faulkner's fiction would have understood entirely. But if Will Percy's original policy led to a loss of labor for which he was then held responsible, he might have been forced to leave the community altogether. In the long run, exile might have been a surer way to independence than Will would ever find by staying at home. LeRoy, however, was just as determined that his son would stay in Greenville as that the black toilers would. Both Will Percy and the blacks on the levee were necessary to LeRoy Percy's well being, not just for economic reasons but also for psychological ones that depended on his ability to continue personal control of his lands and family. In a psychological sense, Will Percy, it might be said, was serving a term of peonage on his father's estate, however willingly. A more favorable reading might stress that LeRoy had saved his son from the future repudiation of the community. A less subtle or caring father might simply have run roughshod over a son similarly placed whereas LeRoy had the delicacy not to exert his authority blatantly, for he loved Will dearly in spite of their differences in temperament. Nonetheless, LeRoy Percy had to prevail.[46]

Will Percy's reactions were equally complex. He always had strong convictions about everything, except with respect to matters that might challenge his father and the ethical patterns, the form of rule, that he thought his father almost divinely embodied. Throughout these years of their association, they walked to the courthouse or the law office together, conferred frequently during the day, returned home arm-in-arm after work, and often spent the evenings in each other's company. No wonder Will Percy flew off on lengthy vacations so often; the intensity of the oedipal relationship was too much to bear for long.

During the crisis of the flood, however, Will showed modest signs of rebellion against the approach that his father and others took toward the blacks. He recognized that his fellow whites considered coercion, under most circumstances, the preferred way of dealing with the race. In *Lanterns on the Levee,* the memorialist defended that culture of white supremacy without qualification. In the spring of 1927, however, he had been momentarily much more critical, knowing very well that in the Delta, even in Washington County, planters were using their monopoly of Red Cross supplies to coerce tenants to stay put. Writing to Oscar T. Johnston of Memphis, president of the largest plantation company in the South, Will Percy denounced those landowners who "were guilty of acts which profoundly and justly made the negroes fear them."[47]

Will Percy's attempts to remove the blacks to safer ground violated the harsh principles of Delta rule. Like Sarah Dorsey at a similar juncture of her life during Radical Reconstruction, he had been a little too long under Northern influence—at least as his neighbors perceived his actions. (Percy Bell was especially critical.) Yet he was a member of the established order. Therefore he would never have agreed with the equally just comment of historian Pete Daniel, who noted that the flood waters flushed out "living things" and exposed "stagnant customs," that is, "the authoritarianism" and "the antediluvian labor system" of the Delta.[48]

Well intentioned though he was, Will Percy betrayed the black community just as his father had betrayed him. He could not fully skirt responsibility for the increased tension between blacks and whites, and he was drawn into a larger context that involved his old chief in Belgium. Herbert Hoover was staking his chances for the Republican nomination on his reputation for efficiency and humanitarian solicitude—in Belgium earlier and at this point in the Mississippi Flood crisis. Once Hoover learned the facts from investigatory commissions of black leaders whom he had appointed, however, he realized that mistreatment of black refugees was rampant. He admitted his blindness and tried as best he could to correct mistakes and right wrongs.

In contrast, Will Percy did not have the reputation, national spotlight, and immunity from heavy-handed local pressures available to Herbert Hoover for redressing racial injustice even in the constrained way that Hoover undertook. Instead, he found himself the subject of attacks that further alienated him from the blacks in Greenville. The Chicago *Defender,* an African-American journal, ran a series of articles on the plight of black flood victims and the efforts to reimpose conditions of peonage upon them in the Delta. The paper reprinted from the *Delta Democrat-Times* a statement that seemed to suggest that Will Percy was withholding Red Cross supplies from those black families without a male as head of household. The rumor fed suspicion and discontent among the Greenville blacks. The story, however, was completely fallacious. The misrepresentation arose because of some garbled lines in the Greenville newspaper, as Will Percy quickly rejoined. Then further unsubstantiated charges appeared in the Chicago paper: that whites were playing golf at the country club in the midst of ruin; dead Negroes were opened up like dug-out canoes, filled with sand, and dumped in the river; and finally, that raw sewage was being deposited into the black residential section of town. Actually, the fairways were under four feet of water; corpses, whether black or white, were weighted down with ropes and stones but not scooped out, because burial by other means was impossible; and the city's waste disposal system never faltered.[49]

False though the charges were, they aroused great resentment in the black community. Their acceptance as gospel truth revealed a deeper problem: the chronic mistrust and antipathy between the Delta blacks and the planter class. That longstanding division was bound to surface during a crisis when a sense of desperation gripped the community. Another factor to make matters even more tense was the continuation of the flood long after it should have passed. Ordinarily in the periodic flood seasons in the Delta, the waters receded in May or early June. In 1927, for a while the water line did drop with exasperating slowness. In late May, Will Percy, his Relief Committee, the remaining whites, and the 7500 or so blacks housed in tents on the levee were preparing to go back to their muck-covered houses when the water began to rise again. With that frustrating change there arose a spirit of selfishness that common danger had formerly tempered. As a result, Will could not find sufficient black workers to unload the supplies from the relief vessels that docked at Greenville.[50] Sometimes the boats slipped away to more cooperative river ports.

To inspire some public spirit, Percy organized an all-black committee that consisted of a physician's widow and a few others who were thought in the white community to be leaders in the black. Their task was to guarantee the appearance of work crews to empty the boats. According to Will Percy's later claim, the committee members were helpless in the face of the indifference and even hostility of their neighbors. Desperate, the relief committee whites won Will Percy's consent to send a police expedition to round up conscripts. When a black man refused, however, a young patrolman shot him dead. The black community was up in arms. Percy then called a meeting and thoroughly lambasted the outraged audience for being as murderous as the inexperienced policeman, then in jail for the crime. "Because of your sinful laziness," he chided arrogantly, "one of your race has been killed." According to his recollection, they fell on their knees, but Percy did not realize that from the assembly's point of view, it seemed necessary to appear contrite when the white boss so commanded. Yet their true feelings were expressed soon enough. When Percy asked for more volunteers, only four stood up. Two of them were old retainers from slavery days on the Percys' Deer Creek plantation. His attitude, so typical of his time and place, was bound to elicit from his captive audience the kind of response that the spiritual "We Shall Not Be Moved" exemplified.

Gradually the waters receded, and life assumed a more familiar pattern. Yet the closing episode over the hauling of river freight had revealed as much about Will Percy's attitudes as about the so-characterized lazy blacks. It did not occur to him or apparently to anyone else that whites might have joined in the unloading of the boats. At a later point in race relations, a cooperative venture would have been a reasonable solution, but not in the 1920s. At that time, any white so engaged would have been stigmatized for doing the kind of labor that blacks alone were supposed to do. The crisis of the flood brought out some of the disagreeable prejudices of the white community.

Aid to the blacks was sometimes grudgingly given. Percy Bell, for instance, explained to his family that his friend Maurice Finkelstein had given him two huge boxes of clothing to distribute at the levee. As soon as the weather warmed up, Bell complained, the recipients "stretched out in the sun and went to sleep as though nothing had ever happened. Their dependence on the white man is pitiful."[51] Such were the almost universal judgments of black behavior at the time, and Will Percy, despite his sweetness of temper and frequent sensitivity, shared them all.

Attitudes in the black community were equally frozen. Generations of suspicion of whites, discrimination, and violence had demoralized the blacks in the Delta. Percy's appointment of a committee had done nothing to help: the chosen group would inevitably be seen as simply black servants of the white overlords, not leaders. He might have asked the blacks whom they would like to see take charge, but that would have raised an alarm among the whites, none of whom wanted the formation of an autonomous corps of black leaders to challenge white hegemony: That was a nightmare as perilous as the existing problem—the gradual flight of laborers to Chicago. Will Percy was caught between the exigencies of white supremacy and the stubborn resistance of the blacks, who were then denounced as ungrateful wretches ill-deserving the kind attentions of their superiors. Such a situation was scarcely designed to create much sense of self-regard in black quarters or much trust between the races.

Yet in all fairness, Will Percy's situation was not an enviable one. He cannot be wholly blamed for acting within the rules of his regional culture. Most people do so, and few, including critics from a different time and place, are brave enough to disregard the conventions of their group. Furthermore, if they do, they cannot get anything done, pragmatically speaking. Though far from what a subsequent generation would consider appropriate in race relations, at least he showed that he cared about the blacks' welfare when most of his fellow townsmen did not. Although mistrust would continue into the thirties, Percy's form of noblesse oblige would eventually earn him more respect in the black districts of town than it did at this time of desperate trouble. Yet the crisis of 1927 illuminated his limitations as a benevolent despot—a kind of Richard II, faltering in the footprints left by a dynamic father, an Edward III.

Exhausted from the experience, Will Percy resigned his relief chairmanship in favor of Hazlewood Farish. He had done his best, but the regional Red Cross authorities judged him not up to the mark. Percy's "rich experience in human understanding" led him to be inadequately "practical in his planning," a report to national headquarters concluded. Too often the Greenville chairman found himself "at the mercy of the cross currents of local opinion." Nevertheless, the regional officers tepidly observed that "he was deep rooted in his desire to render genuine service." Hazlewood Farish, however, was to receive unstinting commendation, but by then the crisis had passed. Although he never actually saw this evaluation, Will felt disheartened and unappreciated.[52] He took a vacation to Japan in the fall of 1927 and found the Japanese delightfully pagan—like the people of the Mediterranean. On longer observation, though, he concluded that they were not really pleasant—too "remote, impersonal." As a result, he felt exceedingly lonely. He wrote Charlotte Gailor, his close Sewanee friend, that he suffered from "an inner weariness like that following a long illness."[53] To make matters worse, he soon learned that in his absence the health of both his father and Camille had deteriorated, and he hastened home.

CHAPTER THIRTEEN

An Acquaintance with Grief

> Something or other lay in wait for him, amid
> the twists and turns of the months and the
> years, like a crouching beast in the jungle.
>
> Henry James, "The Beast in the Jungle" [1]

Along with the fight with the Klan and the Mississippi River Flood, burdens of a personal nature lay heavy on the shoulders of LeRoy Percy and his son Will beginning in 1917. The first of a series of family calamities occurred when tragedy struck LeRoy's brother Walker, the Birmingham attorney. Born at Deer Creek in 1864, Walker Percy had graduated from the University of the South in 1883. He earned his law degree at the University of Virginia two years later. Rather than enter the firm of his father, Colonel William Alexander Percy, and his elder brother in Greenville, he had quickly established a growing practice in the industrial boom town of Birmingham, Alabama. [2]

In the spring of 1888, Walker married Mary Pratt DeBardeleben, daughter of Henry Fairchild DeBardeleben and Ellen Pratt. [3] At the time DeBardeleben was among the richest industrialists in Alabama. He had acquired his wealth through his connection with Daniel Pratt, his father-in-law and one of the founders of the coal and iron industry in the state. After DeBardeleben bought himself a vice-presidency of the Tennessee Coal and Iron Company, the largest iron producer in the South, Walker Percy became chief counsel. He held that lucrative position throughout his career, and he managed DeBardeleben's legal affairs during and after DeBardeleben's departure from T.C.I. in 1895.

An attorney with a quickness of mind and a thoroughness of preparation for trial, Percy appeared to be favored by the gods in every way. In addition he and his wife had two handsome and intelligent children, LeRoy Pratt (the father of the novelist), born in 1889, and Ellen, born in 1893. With these circumstances possibly in mind, novelist Walker Percy, his namesake and grandson, would later remark, "Men can be well off, judging by their own criteria, with all their needs satisfied," but "as time goes on, life is almost unbearable. Amazing!" [4]

From all that anyone could tell at the time, Walker Percy had completely recovered from a nervous breakdown in 1911 that had sent him to a clinic, probably Shepherd-Pratt Institute in Towson, outside Baltimore. According to a newspaper report, he had come back from Maryland after a month "as fit as a fiddle."[5] Walker Percy had never displayed outward signs of melancholia. Certain that his condition was simply a temporary aberration, the lively group, who surrounded Walker and his wife Mary, rejoiced in his apparent return to conviviality. The DeBardelebens and Percys moved in a circle of substantial and respected leaders of local society—the Fulenwiders, Badhams, Tutwilers, Crawfords. The heads of these interrelated families were the chief officers of the Tennessee Coal and Iron Company, local banks, and other substantial firms in Birmingham. According to Sallie Lathrop's memoir of Jefferson County society, they entertained lavishly and organized themselves as the "Harveys." "All my friends admired Walker Percy," she recalled. On one occasion, Sallie Lathrop recorded, he was supposed to have told a friend just before launching a speech against an enemy, "I can take care of my front—you protect my back."[6] A bantering assertiveness was much admired in hard-minded Birmingham society.

Always ready with a joke or open-handed welcome, Walker Percy belonged to a number of clubs—the Roebuck, the Southern, and the Country Club, which he helped to found in 1898. Southern businessmen took to golf the way their ancestors had hunted with hounds or shot deer and quail on the frontier. A fanatically dedicated player, Percy was among those who initiated the business golf round, whereby gentlemen set the stage for deals while knocking a little ball in and out of roughs and over unreliable greens. (The early courses were not the carpets of clipped grass of later years.)[7] Fearless, determined, and brilliant as a lawyer, he seemed to have full command of himself and of any situation into which he entered. Such, however, was not the case.

As so often happens in a case of suicide, the day it took place was quite ordinary. On a dull, Saturday afternoon, February 7, 1917, LeRoy Pratt Percy—Roy as he was usually called—came over to see his father about a hunting trip to the Delta. Walker Percy's Victorian house on Arlington Avenue, a fashionable and busy part of town, had a gloomy appearance, with heavy furniture, thick draperies, somber carpets, and dark panelling. Yet it was comfortable and spacious. Roy Percy's father appeared to be in good spirits, though he had complained of overwork, fatigue. He was thinking about taking a vacation. Walker and young Roy talked over the plan to meet the senator on the following Thursday in Greenville, from whence they would head for the duck blinds. He left his father cleaning his guns in the trunk room where they were stored. A little after three o'clock, while reading in the library, Roy heard a muffled report from upstairs and hastened to the trunk room to discover his father's body with a massive wound in the chest. He had used a .12 bore shotgun. There was no sign of life. It was the first suicide in the family since the reclusive LeRoy Pope Percy, the "Gray Eagle's" brother, had taken his life in 1882.

What had gone so wrong? Certainly the way Walker Percy had lived suggested that he had been running from something internal. He was driven to activity of any kind, from golf and hunting to speech-making and the practice of law. Constantly on the move, Walker Percy had accomplished significant things. The press justifiably stressed his achievements instead of the manner of his dying. An editorial in the Birmingham *News* praised his work for the Y.M.C.A., Red Cross, and the Mercy Home, his instrumentality in the purchase of Tennessee Coal and Iron by the United States Steel Corporation, his board memberships of banks, country clubs, and newspapers. One editorial observed, "He had the truest of pride, and was the embodiment of honor in all his relations." In 1911 he had won his election to the lower house of the Alabama legislature on a reform ticket and steered some measures important to Jefferson County through to passage before his first mental collapse.[8] But Walker Percy's determination to keep busy may have been a way of warding off what eventually stirred him to the fatal decision. The newspaper headline provided about as much information as anyone could venture: "Melancholia Is Given as Cause of Shooting."[9]

Like all the Percys, Walker had been reared under the code of honor, a regional ethic that all the sophistication of city living could not erase. As Jay Tolson points out, Walker Percy was a "scion of one of those great planter families on whom the old order so heavily depended," but who "finally failed to hold together the old system and so were now working to replace it" with a replication of Northern capitalism. The very transformation of the South from agrarian values to industrial complexity may have contributed to a yearning for primordial roots, in him and in others who had grown up in the country but made their living thereafter in the city. To be sure, the social milieu of Birmingham was not nearly so refined as that of Nashville or Richmond, but rather retained the rawness that Henry DeBardeleben, Walker Percy's father-in-law, had brought with him from frontier Autauga County years before. Perhaps he felt that his life fell far short of the ideal which his father, the "Gray Eagle of the Valley," had established long ago.

Yet, in contrast to DeBardeleben's erstwhile conquests, what had Walker Percy accomplished by 1917? DeBardeleben had once watched the shattering of his dream of a Southern-controlled coal and iron industry. Southern raw materials and enterprise gradually had slipped into the hands of outsiders from Wall Street. Perhaps Henry DeBardeleben had not won his struggle, but at least he had not betrayed it. If Walker chose to adopt the perspective, he had grounds to call himself a Judas of sorts in that he had helped to surrender the T.C.I. Company to the United States Steel

Corporation in Pittsburgh and New York. Moreover, as general counsel for a captive company, his own work had diminished in importance. He had made money but tarnished his honor in the process—or so he may have reasoned. While his father had earned luster for his bravery against the Union forces in the Civil War, Percy had no military achievement to boast of, no saber-rattling defiance of Yankees to recall for the moral instruction of his son. Instead, he had become a mouthpiece for Northern interests. In a few weeks' time the United States would enter the Great War. Walker could have discovered in that crisis some means to meet the old warrior tradition of the Percys. At his mature age the opportunity to match the martial successes of his father was perhaps out of the question, but he might have found a way to make a difference in military affairs or in the process of reconstruction, as his father, the Gray Eagle, had done. For a man of Walker Percy's pride, pondering comparisons with his father may have been most distressing. Admittedly in the near absence of any surviving letter or records from Walker Percy's life these are speculations based on the logic of the circumstances.

Honor could also have played another role in Walker Percy's depression. The new order did not have the certainty of convictions that had marked the Old South when slaveholders were quite confident that their slaves were happy and contented, and the hands were scarcely in a position to challenge such complacent self-justification. Such was not the case in the postwar years when a sense of inferiority set the South apart in a way that engendered an increased defensiveness in meeting Northern snobbery and indifference. Constant commemorations of the Lost Cause in parades and Confederate gatherings in the industrialized as well as the agrarian South were searing reminders that the military defeat continued to place the region in an inferior role in national economic, social, and political life.

Following his father's suicide, Roy and his growing family moved into the Arlington Avenue mausoleum. Given the sad event that had taken place in that ugly, almost Charles Addams-like house, it was by no means a healthy choice. Unfortunately, along with the mansion LeRoy Pratt Percy inherited his father's misery as well.

⧨ ⧩

Walker Percy's death reawakened old fears in the family circle as if a banished demon had returned to ravage the members once again. Senator Percy was especially stunned by his brother's sudden end. It was a reminder, too, of his own son's death by gunshot. "Walker's death has left me with a feeling of loneliness which I will carry to the end," he wrote a cousin.[10] LeRoy was now the only surviving son of the "Gray Eagle." His Memphis brother, William Armstrong, had died in 1912. Yet as if this sign of suicidal tendency in the family were not sad enough, Lady McKinney, sister of the senator and his two deceased brothers, began to show signs of mental instability within a few months of her brother's death. She was admitted to the newly opened Phipps Psychiatric Clinic at the Johns Hopkins Hospital. While she was there, C. J. McKinney, her husband, unexpectedly took seriously ill. LeRoy Percy arranged for the McKinneys' son to leave naval air training to assist his mother's return from Baltimore to be with her husband in Knoxville. Lady's brother LeRoy told young Percy McKinney's wartime commanding officer that she was "a singularly helpless woman." [11] Although her mental condition improved in the 1930s, Lady McKinney was often ill during the 1920s. In 1922, for instance, LeRoy wrote Caroline Percy, widow of his brother William Armstrong Percy of Memphis, "Lady has had one of her breakdowns and been in quite bad shape for the past few months, but is better." He and Camille tried several times to induce Lady to stay with them in Greenville. Customarily she refused, but perhaps through the urging of her son Percy McKinney, who had by then become an engineer in Knoxville, she finally agreed. LeRoy was much relieved. "Lady is with us and is well and in good spirits," he wrote his nephew, Roy Pratt Percy, in Birmingham. Yet her chronic depression could return at any time. [12]

The most devastating blow for the senator was not the state of his sister's health so much as that of nephew LeRoy Pratt Percy, his frequent correspondent and companion. The senator esteemed him without reservation or ambiguity. He had highly approved of Roy's marriage to Martha Susan Phinizy of Athens, Georgia, and took an interest in their succession of healthy, good-looking sons—Walker (1916), LeRoy (1917), and Phinizy (1922). When the brilliant young graduate of Harvard Law School completed naval air training in 1917, Senator Percy was as proud of Roy as he was of his own son Will, then in the infantry. Roy Percy loved flying, and, according to first-cousin Will Percy, wrote about it with enviable literary skill. It was a sore disappointment for young Roy that the war ended before he had the chance to engage the enemy. He was so skillful an aviator that he had been assigned to remain in the United States as an instructor. The ex-senator was delighted that his nephew had overcome the family's laughable incompetence when it came to "machinery of any kind." [13]

Like his cousin Will, Roy Percy, the Birmingham attorney named for Will's father, was a reader and a thinker of uncommon gifts. Yet he was almost addicted to the outdoor life, a joy in which his uncle also partook. "What are the chances of your taking a whirl at mountain sheep this Fall?" Roy Percy asked his Greenville uncle in a typical invitation for yet another trip in pursuit of game. Their expeditions to Wyoming, Alabama, Louisiana, Arkansas, and Canada were occasions not just to try skills and breathe the outdoor life but to enjoy each other's company. [14]

After the death of Walker Percy, the pair grew ever closer. One reason for the intensity of their bonding was that Senator LeRoy Percy had lost his two brothers so early in their lives. At an earlier time, the trio of brilliant lawyers had stood by one another. After George Creel had published his almost libelous article in *Cosmopolitan* in 1911, for instance, Walker Percy had written Willie in Memphis, that all three brothers should meet soon in New York. They should confer, he argued, not to coordinate a response to Creel but rather to set a precedent for gathering "whenever any one of us is attacked." Combining forces would ensure that the family honor would never be stained with impunity. The second object Walker Percy had in mind was to cheer up their beleaguered brother and "see that he is not unduly worried or depressed."[15] From whom could the senator, in his sixties, expect similar acts of thoughtfulness and camaraderie now that brothers Willie and Walker were dead? The young Birmingham nephew would do his best to fill the gap. He would also try to embody the ten-year-old son whom the Senator still idolized. The burden was perhaps heavy, but Roy Percy welcomed it.

Further cementing the ties of the two LeRoy Percys was the fact that they agreed about almost everything. Uncle and nephew shared the Percy contempt for mendacity, vulgarity, and mindless populism. During the anti-Klan struggle, for instance, Roy Percy complimented his uncle for his courthouse speech against Colonel Camp and compared the ex-Senator's boldness with the pusillanimity of Birmingham's leaders. The summer before, Roy Percy reported, "a jack-legged Methodist preacher" had murdered a Catholic priest in cold blood. Hugo Black, a labor-union lawyer with whom Walker Percy, Roy's father, had often crossed verbal swords in the courtroom, had defended his client with such hideous "True-American" diatribes that the jury had acquitted his client after only perfunctory deliberations. Black was a populist member of the Ku Klux Klan (and later one of the great liberal jurists on the Supreme Court). Roy Percy complained that he was typical of most Birmingham politicians: they all belonged to one or more of the nativistic fraternal orders. "I believe that I am the only man in Jefferson County who does not belong to anything." It was a point of pride—not to run with the common herd.[16]

Roy Percy did not say so, but he and his uncle both knew how much difference it would have made if Walker Percy had still been alive. He would have led the fight against the Klan. Others in town would have agreed: "Alabama had no more fearless leader, as private citizen and otherwise, than your lamented brother, Mr. Walker Percy," a Birmingham attorney told Senator Percy, when contrasting the latter's valor in Greenville with the dismal situation in Birmingham. A young man with a growing family, LeRoy Pratt Percy shrank from the anti-Klan crusade. He did so not out of fear but because he felt inadequate to match the zeal and skill that his father and uncle would have displayed. Underneath the role of expert huntsman, golfer, and gambler, Roy Percy was not the extrovert his seniors were. Even these manly activities that brought nephew and uncle together were a means to escape problems for which Roy Percy knew no cure. Possibly his extravagant interest in hunting was the analogue to Will Percy's poetry-writing: a means to deal with mental depression. Roy's hunting, though, offered the possibility of a lethal outcome, as it did with the other LeRoy who died when accidentally shot with his own rifle. Even his interest in flying the fragile and mechanically untrustworthy planes of that era could have been a deliberate courting of death. If so, Roy's fascination with such risk-taking resembled Will Percy's defiance of fate on the battlefields of the Argonne. Roy and cousin Will Percy may have had more in common than it seemed.[17]

The two LeRoys—uncle and nephew—also shared a number of characteristics, notably a belligerent regard for reputation. In 1923, Roy Percy and Will Denson, a rival lawyer, exchanged heated words over a Birmingham law case. Feeling insulted but getting no reply from his opponent, Roy dispatched a friend named Henley to gain an apology. Denson refused to admit wrongdoing and asked whether Percy was issuing a challenge. Henley replied, "Mr. Percy desires me to inform you that he is at your service now, and will be at all times in the future, to give you any satisfaction you now or hereafter desire in any manner, shape or form." No fight ensued. On this occasion, the state Supreme Court heard arguments from the two warring attorneys and then rendered a decision so quickly and decisively in Roy's favor that the young lawyer was sure the judges "meant to give emphasis to their disapproval of Denson's course."[18] A bully who had already killed one man in so-called "self-defense," Denson was known to be a first-rate marksman, but so was Roy Percy. Throughout the affair, Roy asked for and received the advice of his friend and uncle in Greenville. A story among the city's attorneys has it that over a similar fracas later on, they went to the woods and practiced hitting targets for a while until both realized that neither might survive an exchange of fire and agreed to cancel the shoot-out.[19]

Roy Percy's situation was very much like that of his father, Walker. He, too, was a man of great charm, good looks, and legal brilliance. Just how aware the ex-Senator was about his kinsman's darker moods is not easy to ascertain. The young attorney's career was so promising—"head of his profession in Alabama"—LeRoy Percy boasted to a distant cousin in Pennsylvania, as if he had reared him himself.[20] Yet in the fall of 1925, when ordinarily Roy Percy went on his hunting trips, he committed himself to the Phipps Psychiatric Clinic at the Johns Hopkins Hospital in Baltimore. The medical papers, of course, are sealed, but at that time Emil Kraepelin's ideas of somatic factors in depression were still in vogue. As a result, the physicians probably recorded the observable symptoms—and waited, having no drugs to counteract depression at that time.[21] After a few weeks under observation, Roy seemed no less well than his father had been after his breakdown in 1911. The senator learned about the crisis and worried until his nephew returned from Baltimore. "LeRoy was dangerously sick but is back home and all right again and threatens to make me a visit," his uncle LeRoy rejoiced in a letter to his sister Lady McKinney's mother-in-law in Knoxville. He may never have heard about Roy's subsequent failed attempt to end his life in 1928. As reported to Jay Tolson, novelist Walker Percy's biographer, Robert Smith, a Birmingham neighbor, remembered that during a drive with his father he saw Roy Percy working in his garden with white bandages on his wrists. The boy asked his father what had happened to Mr. Percy, and the reply was that he "had had an accident in his bathroom."[22]

🎴 🏮

By 1928, when Roy Percy's mental health was clearly in jeopardy, Senator Percy had troubles of his own. He had to face the immediate problem of Camille's alarming decline, the tensions and exertions brought about by the Flood of 1927 having damaged her health more than either she or her husband realized. (She was sixty-four when her husband spent the fall and winter of 1927-28 in Washington to make his last major effort for the Delta community.) LeRoy Percy's mission was highly successful, but before the final votes were taken, he had to hurry back to Greenville: Camille had suffered a nearly fatal heart attack. She, her friend Adah Williams, LeRoy, and a trained nurse spent most of the fall, winter, and spring, 1928-29, at Pass Christian on the Mississippi coast or in southern Florida while she struggled toward recovery.[23]

Camille Percy's frailty, however, was merely the first of several blows that soon struck the family. Roy Percy was suffering once again from depression, aggravated by a degree of overdrinking, a problem with a genetic relationship to affective disorders.[24] Walker Percy recalled that in 1926, at the age of ten, he had watched his father prepare for the aging of his Bourbon in a charcoal keg in the basement of the house and sometimes lie, face on the cement floor, to extract the liquor with a siphon. Not much is known about the circumstances surrounding Roy Percy's troubled state of mind, but certainly he felt, as his son often recorded in his novels, the triviality or "everydayness" of life in the suburbs. So severe did the problem become that Roy's wife Martha Susan—Mattie.Sue—beseeched her husband's uncle to visit Birmingham to raise Roy's menacingly low spirits. It was a great sacrifice on the senator's part because of Camille Percy's frail condition, and Mattie Sue Percy appreciated his prompt response. After he returned to Greenville sometime after June 20, she reported in a brief thank-you note that the visit "helped us all *so much*. Today is the best day Roy has had. He has had no tenseness at all, in spite of 'the Crouching Beast.' I do feel so much better about him in every way. I will try hard to get him to do what we agreed was best." She signed herself, "Yours with a lighter heart, Mattie Sue."[25]

According to Walker Percy, the novelist, the "Crouching Beast" was his family's name for Roy Percy's condition, a phrase adopted from Henry James's short story, "The Beast in the Jungle" (1903). James was distraught over the death of a female friend, and "The Beast in the Jungle" was his way of preserving forever his insights into his own reaction of evasive diffidence during her life and his misery after her death.[26]

As in previous cases of severe depression in the family, beginning with Don Carlos in 1794, Roy Percy was not burdened with financial worries, though one might have expected such a problem. Although the Great Crash of 1929 did not arrive until the fall, ominous signs began to appear during that fatal summer. Five Birmingham banks shut their doors on their depositors. Two high ranking bank officials in Birmingham shot themselves to death in the summer of 1929. Yet Roy Percy's situation was different; his personal finances were in such excellent shape that the couple had recently built a splendid Tudor-style house at Fairway Drive on Country Club Road, out of town beyond Red Mountain.

With a strong financial situation, a healthy family, a loving wife, Roy had everything to live for, and his periodic swings of mood might be worrisome but not ominous. Even the message that Mattie Sue sent to Senator Percy suggests a misunderstanding based on outward appearances. All too often a depressive's behavior becomes very composed, even serene, once the final decision has been made, but the observer sees only the absence of former agitation and inanition and assumes that the composure means a return to normal living. As a result, the caretaker becomes less watchful. Assuming that her husband was much improved, Mattie Sue left him at home to do some shopping downtown. When she heard the newsboys hawking the afternoon paper's headlines about a prominent lawyer's suicide, she knew at once that they were announcing Roy's death.[27]

Roy Percy had just returned from French Lick, an Indiana resort hotel where various members of the Percy clan often vacationed, and it seemed to have done him good. At eleven a.m. the maid heard a report ring out; she ran to the attic where the sporting equipment was stored and there she found Roy Percy dead, the shot having destroyed the jaw and exited through the top of his head. He had removed his outer garments, perhaps to leave them unsoiled for his burial. Roy Percy had killed himself with the same gauge and type of gun that his father had used a dozen years before, and he had committed the act in the same sort of surroundings. He was only forty years old, youngest of all the Percys who had taken their own lives. At this time, Walker Percy, his eldest son, was at Camp Winnipee in Wisconsin with his younger brother LeRoy. Phinizy, eight years old, was at home.[28]

For Roy's uncle, the senator in Greenville, the suicide was particularly hard to bear. He had lavished so much affection upon the nephew whom he hoped would one day exceed his own achievements in law and politics. As always in times of crisis, the family pulled together in a most remarkable way. LeRoy Percy tried to comfort Mattie Sue, writing her that she had been "brave beyond words" and urging her to stay in Birmingham rather than return to Athens, where she had grown up. The boys should not be uprooted and, besides, Birmingham would "offer them more in the future than Athens."[29] Mattie Sue, however, thought she needed the support of the Phinizys and Spaldings, and so the house was sold and they moved into her mother's house in Athens.

One can only guess how deeply the survivors were affected, how they might have wondered what could have been done to prevent the tragedy. Self-recriminations, though undeserved, usually accompany loss, natural or otherwise. Little was put on paper and saved. Yet undoubtedly Roy's death hastened the ends of Camille and her husband and undermined the already fragile health of their son Will. He had never fully recovered from an influenza attack in the early twenties when he and his father were defying the Ku Klux Klan.

Devastated, Will Percy took off for the Grand Canyon on vacation; he felt it necessary to get far away. During his absence, Camille Percy's health rapidly deteriorated. She died on October 15, shortly after his return. Three days later, the anguished father and his son went to French Lick, but Will Percy would find the senator with a club in hand standing on the golf course, staring vacantly into the middle distance. On the return trip by train to Greenville, Will Percy had to take him to a Memphis hospital. LeRoy's appendix had ruptured. The operation was medically successful, but he had lost the will to live. The senator managed to write a final report on flood control, and by all accounts it was a brilliant exposition. The effort, however, overstrained his heart. Knowing his tendency toward despondency, his old colleague in the Senate, John Sharp Williams, urged him not to give up but to stay with him in this world even if only on the "outskirts" in retirement.[30] Williams's sound advice went unheeded. Refusing to take much nourishment, Percy grew ever weaker and had to be placed in the Baptist Hospital in Memphis. Harris Dickson, an old friend, paid him a final visit there and found him in very low spirits. "I never expected to find you among the Baptists," Dickson quipped; he later recalled, "I think that was the last time he ever smiled."[31]

Oddly Will Percy seemed to have predicted a sad, unfulfilled ending for his father. In his longest poem, "Enzio's Kingdom," Enzio tells a story to a priest about how King Frederick II of the Holy Roman Empire dies with his plans for a world of peace and order shattered. He feels his life to have been a series of base betrayals; his kingdoms has become "a boundary, bounding nothing./He died because he had no heart to live. . . ."[32] Senator Percy had stopped eating altogether some days before Christmas. Then a heart attack on December 24, 1929, and he failed to rally. He was sixty-eight and the sole male descendant of Charles Percy ever to live to that age over the previous 150 years. Eulogies praised him for his civic labors, which had been quite remarkable in the 1920s, ironically, long after his period of greatest sway in Mississippi politics.

Will Percy's reaction to the death of his cousin Roy, his mother, and his father—all within six months—was uncomplaining but deeply melancholy. In mid-December of that deadly year Janet Longcope had tried to comfort

Charles Brown Percy, 1820–1850, son of Thomas George Percy of Huntsville. In the early 1840s, he organized the family's resettlement to Deer Creek, near the future town of Greenville. Died in Nashville, Tennessee, age thirty.

Henry William (Harry) Lee, widowered husband of Eleanor Percy Lee (1819–1849), planter of Hinds County and Deer Creek, Washington County, Mississippi. His dates of birth and death are not known.

In the Eleanor Percy Lee and Catherine Warfield Papers, reproduced courtesy of the Special Collections, Hill Memorial Library, Louisiana State University Library, Baton Rouge, Louisiana.

William Alexander Percy, 1834–88,
Colonel, C.S.A., planter of Deer Creek,
and attorney of Greenville, Mississippi,
father of LeRoy, Walker, and William
Armstrong Percy, and grandfather of
William Alexander (Will) Percy.
From Lewis Baker, The Percys of
Mississippi: Politics and Literature in the
New South *(Baton Rouge: Louisiana State
University Press, 1983), p. 2.*

Nanny I. Armstrong (1835–1897), wife
of William Alexander Percy ("the Gray
Eagle") and grandmother of Will Percy
who called her "Mur" in *Lanterns on
the Levee.*
*Courtesy of John Seymour Erwin, Sun City,
Florida.*

William Armstrong Percy, 1863–1912, Class of 1882 at Sewanee, attorney of Memphis.
Courtesy, Archives, Jessie Ball Dupont Library, University of the South, Sewanee, Tennessee.

John Walker Percy, 1864–1917, Class of 1883 at Sewanee, attorney of Birmingham, Alabama, married to Mary Pratt DeBardeleben, 1888.
Courtesy, Archives, Jessie Ball Dupont Library, University of the South, Sewanee, Tennessee.

LeRoy Percy, 1860–1929, Class
of 1879 at Sewanee, attorney of
Greenville, Mississippi.
*Courtesy, Archives, Jessie Ball Dupont
Library, University of the South, Sewanee,
Tennessee.*

William Armstrong Percy, Memphis
lawyer, shortly before his death from
Bright's disease at age 49.
Courtesy of William Armstrong Percy III.

him by letter, but then came his father's death on Christmas Eve. Upon hearing the news, she wrote him at once, commiserating afterwards that "one's own emotions are so weary & so confused" when faced with an overwhelming sense of loss. She worried that his "fatigue & anxiety" might distort a necessary sense of " 'courage ' & 'beauty' " which were "gallant words" to revive "a weary body & a spirit that's sad." Will Percy shared her Stoic principles, and perhaps her thoughts did him some good. A few years later, he was reconciled to the losses. He remarked to a friend that gradually one learns "to endure the dark and the solitude with an incredible sort of dignity." It helped his morale to assume the role of studied acceptance. It was a performance for which the "gods" responsible for setting the drama of life "should feel very proud." [33]

Despite his willingness to live by his own and Janet Longcope's code of duty and composed resignation, at some level Will felt that both he and his poetic spirit had figuratively died with them all. Later Will Percy wrote a friend, "Whether the loss of my father and mother is the direct cause of writing no more poetry I do not know." [34] Perhaps, he added, he had nothing left to say. In a sense he repeated the pattern of Catherine Warfield, whose poetic inspiration withered during her depression following the deaths of her sister Eleanor Percy Lee and Nathaniel Ware, their father. Also like Catherine Warfield, he was to find in prose, not verse, his strongest voice, an ironic turn for one who always considered himself chiefly a poet.

There was a further irony. Some years before, LeRoy and Camille had suffered the emptiness that Will Percy's absence during the Great War created in their home. They had brought William Armstrong Percy, Jr., the eldest, teenage son of the Memphis brother to live with them. The adjustment must have been hard on them all, including the boy's widowed mother, Caroline, who had moved her family to Los Angeles. (Later in his life, like so many others in the lineage, William Armstrong Percy, Jr., would know the trials of melancholia.) "The older I get the more I appreciate that year with you and Aunt Camille," the Stanford graduate had written Uncle LeRoy in 1924. "I feel that it helped me a great deal." The family always cared for its own. In likewise filling a void in a lonely house and solitary heart, Will Percy would soon take on a similar burden. [35]

CHAPTER FOURTEEN

Stoic Honor

> Love the art, poor as it may be, which thou hast
> learned, and be content with it; and pass
> through the rest of life like one who has in-
> trusted to the gods with his whole soul all that
> he has, making thyself neither the tyrant nor the
> slave of any man.
>
> Marcus Aurelius[1]

After his father's funeral at the end of 1929, Will Percy went to New York
to visit his bachelor friends Huger Jervey, Lindley Hubbell, and Gerstle
Mack to ease his pain and loneliness. Periodically he had needed to leave
the Delta on trips to the North or even farther away. In Greenville, Percy
had no sympathetic male friends of high intellect in whom to confide and
with whom to share his delight in art and music. Aunts Adah and Nana
were kind ladies who loved him like a son, but they could not meet these
needs. It was doubtless one of his companions in New York, perhaps Gerstle Mack, a well-known art historian, who suggested Malvina Hoffman
as sculptor and designer of the memorial to Senator Percy. Will felt a
discriminating and substantial monument was required, although his
practical-minded father would have been dismayed at the expense. It cost
over $25,000, a sum which could have been invested in some local enter-
prise. Commissioned in 1930 and cast in bronze in Italy, the statue was
mounted a few years later by the exotic, chain-smoking Malvina Hoffman
herself with the help of black masons.[2]

Having settled upon the tribute to his father that he wanted, Percy decided during his New York trip to assume the mantle of leadership that
his father had worn so long: he continued his legal practice as a family
commitment; he joined forces with a highly capable partner, Hazlewood
Farish, who had been his successor as chair of the Red Cross Relief effort.[3]
Will took even longer vacations than he had when under his father's quizzical gaze, feeling it necessary to get away from the provinciality of a Mississippi town. Despite his war record, proven courage, and steely will
power, he was regarded as "rather effeminate, but not extremely so," re-

called Leon Koury, the Greenville sculptor who, thanks to Percy's introduction and sponsorship, later studied with Malvina Hoffman. "Some people were very unkind," Koury remembered, but "those who knew him well
loved him dearly for all his great qualities of mind and soul." Devotion to
art was permissible as a temporary affectation in youth, but virile men were
supposed to use deeds, not mere words on a page, to express themselves.
Percy went his own way and, according to Koury "always remained
himself."[4]

The ambivalence that surrounded an intellectual's local reputation affected other sectors of Will Percy's life. No doubt his vigorous civic activities were in part a fulfillment of his father's wishes that the family continue
to exert a salutary influence in the Delta. The municipal ventures into
which Will Percy entered represented the highly masculine side of the
Percy code. Yet that kind of public labor was also a demonstration of his
own pleasure in exercising power, an understated determination not to
become merely a reclusive dabbler in poetry but to contribute to its improvement, come what might. A commanding voice about parochial concerns was part of the family's self-definition, which, Percy was tacitly saying, would remain unaffected by the narrow minds of neighbors. Given
the complications of his life, Cousin Will's legacy for the next generation
of Percys had a double edge. He embodied moral strength, love of stability
and tradition, and reverence for Stoic principle but also vulnerability as
one who loved the arts, about which Greenvillians had their suspicions.
That contradictory mixture, of which he was himself only partially aware,
would appear in his memoir *Lanterns on the Levee,* giving its texture a
tension and depth that otherwise it would have lacked. Equally important,
Will Percy's intellectual concerns would ironically become in time a source
of inspiration for Walker Percy's art. Such an outcome was a tribute to
Will Percy himself. His exemplary compassion and paternal nurturing and
advice were crucial to the development of Walker Percy as a writer and
thinker.

🙞 🙜

As Will Percy strode into the Weinburg Building upon his return from
New York in early 1930, Holt Collier, LeRoy Percy's tall black guide and
companion, greeted him at the door to his law office. Aged but still alert,
Collier pointed at LeRoy Percy's desk and boldly commanded, "Set there
where he sot. That's where you b'long." The old hunter who had once
stalked bear with Teddy Roosevelt and Will's father, took a seat opposite
and then, with his massive hands resting on his cane, shuddered in grief,
"I am out in the dark and the cold alone. I want to go where he is." Percy
felt the same way. Without LeRoy and Camille, he recalled, "my life
seemed superfluous." Yet that reaction scarcely meant any withdrawal

from the kinds of affairs that his father and he himself considered the duty of the family.[5]

Thus, despite an enduring grief, the bachelor-attorney followed Collier's orders for the next ten years. Useful as he was to the railroad interests and the corporate community, he intensely disliked legal practice. Brodie Crump, a friend of the family, conjectured that "he stayed on with it" after his father's death to make up for "the great loss" of his young dead brother.[6] Will Percy could barely rise before noon on work days, a signal of insomnia and depression. Often he felt "a spasm of nerves before and after" a courtroom appearance.[7] Driven by a sense of duty that at times he wished he could ignore, he took full part in Greenville's political and social life, just as if he were the reincarnation of his father. The Percy code of noblesse oblige, recalled the Greenville journalist Hodding Carter, meant "doing things for your fellows that you don't always want to do, and don't really have to; doing them because you consider it not only your inherited but your moral obligation."[8] Many of his civic efforts fell under that rubric. The Delta Cotton Council, which served as a political lobby, was planned in his spacious living-room on Percy Street. At the weekly meetings, Percy managed to convince the Rotary Club to do less group singing and more serious thinking about current problems, at home and abroad. After the New Deal was under way, he organized the Greenville Art Center as a federal art project.[9]

In politics, Will Percy was instrumental in combining the family's traditional liberalism—in the old Whiggish sense of that term—with New Deal experimentation. Percy admired Franklin Delano Roosevelt, a patrician who seemed determined to pull the South out of the economic doldrums. Yet in Will Percy's eyes the kind of democracy that Roosevelt promoted had its limits. He could not forget what the masses had done to his father years before. In his poem "Enzio's Kingdom," Will Percy had warned, through the figure of Frederick II, that rulers had to protect the poor "in their breeding moil" but never should "build for them" since they were ignorant, unworthy, and "doomed to everyday contents and grievances." He returned to that position in the late thirties. For instance, he learned to his horror that Roosevelt's denunciation of sharecropping was based in part upon his reading of reports about Percy's own Trail Lake. Uncle Will stormed that, thanks to Roosevelt and his bluestocking wife Eleanor, from the lecture halls in Moscow to the parlors of California leftists, do-gooders could now censure something fresh in Southern affairs. From his point of view, no other arrangement in the capitalist order extended to a pauper several hundred dollars credit for a year with no security on the simple promise of producing a crop at the end of twelve months. Of course, faced with starvation and homelessness, the indigent in question had little choice, particularly during the Depression.[10]

A sensible approach required that the people be properly led, Will Percy believed. To that end, he thought Greenville and Washington County in great need of civic enlightenment. As it turned out one of his most important local achievements was his enlistment of William Hodding Carter to revive Greenville journalism. Along with David Cohn who had first spotted Carter when the editor was struggling in Hammond, Louisiana, against the Long machine, Percy helped to gather funds from their Greenville friends to bring Carter to town. The young newspaperman, eager to reform county and state politics, needed a means to overcome Greenville's sense of clannish honor. He was a stranger. "We don't need outsiders to tell us how to behave," the natives might have grumbled. Will Percy furnished the necessary endorsement: he made sure the journalist gained immediate membership into the local establishment.[11]

On the first visit to Greenville, with his lively wife, Betty Werlein, in December 1935, Carter was most impressed with his patron's warm hospitality. The young couple had skidded into a ditch in heavy weather and arrived, bedraggled, wet, and three hours overdue for dinner. As they struggled out of their coats, Percy smiled and said, "You've got Delta mud on you. Now we'll never get rid of you."[12] Carter would indeed stick to the Delta. By 1937, his newspaper, the Greenville *Star* merged into the *Delta Democrat-Times*, which Carter quickly transformed into one of the South's most courageous papers. The crusading editor began laying the foundations for his greatest contribution: the 1960s crusade against segregation and racial discrimination in the state, a policy even more controversial than the Percys' anti-Klan struggle of the twenties. In 1946 Hodding Carter won a Pulitzer Prize for his editorials against racial and religious bigotry. Although Will Percy did not live to see the erosion of segregation, a policy to which he was ever faithful, he had contributed, ironically, to that result by wholeheartedly supporting Carter's early labors.[13]

Will Percy's sense of public duty included giving speeches for public causes. In that pre-television era, oratory was more appreciated than it is today. He was a toastmaster without peer, and whenever a charitable organization or Democratic party event called upon him, he was ready to oblige. For instance, in late August 1931, in Greenville, Will Percy gave a rousing introduction to Martin (Mike) Conner of Hattiesburg, a business-minded reformer running for governor. Conner's landslide primary victory a few days later was a happy vindication for the candidate. He had resoundingly lost the gubernatorial election four years earlier to Theodore Bilbo, the Percys' nemesis. With success to crown Conner's second try, there was much rejoicing on Percy Street.[14]

Will Percy also continued the family's efforts for flood control. For Greenville, the disaster of 1927 and his father's final lobbying efforts in Washington in 1929 had important political effects. Throughout the Depression, federal money poured into the reconstruction of the levee system under the direction of the Army Corps of Engineers. The multi-million dollar program made Greenville an oasis of steady employment in the midst of a population that, as Percy's friend David Cohn recalled, was living "on whippoorwill peas and cornbread." Simultaneously, federal dollars were also used to link Greenville by a new bridge to the rich Delta lands of Arkansas and Louisiana on the west bank of the Mississippi.[15]

In living up to the code of noblesse oblige, Percy extended his philanthropy from public activity to private assistance. The town would remember him more for the latter benefactions than his speeches or endorsements. Years later, Adah Williams declared, "He was the most tender, sympathetic person, I don't care what you had done with your life or fortune Will was absolutely sympathetic. He knew that all people were weak."[16] Helping friends of his parents was high on his list of obligations. Among the early recipients of his benevolence was Harry Ball, the Greenville diarist. He was among the 60 percent of Delta landowners whose property was mortgaged to the hilt—a higher ratio than anywhere else in the state. Thousands of tenants were destined to be thrown off the land in the coming years.[17] Will Percy heard about Ball's difficulties with the local bank and assumed the mortgage at reduced rates just before foreclosure. "This act of Will Percy's is the strongest evidence of disinterested friendship that has ever been shown us," Ball rhapsodized. Will Percy kept up a family tradition of generosity toward Harry Ball, who had once been Camille Percy's favorite walking companion.[18]

Likewise, Percy befriended a sweet-tempered but incorrigible alcoholic named Tommy Shields, who had what Will Percy thought of as the misfortune to fail the draft board physical exam in 1917. In April 1941, when his old, penurious friend Shields took ill with a brain tumor that proved fatal, Percy was himself suffering the effects of high blood pressure. As he wrote Charlotte Gailor, he had very little "pep" from worry over Shields's condition and the tragic news from Europe. Nevertheless, he spent fifteen hours a day at his bedside, even though the patient had lapsed into a deep coma. Asked why he stayed so long, Percy replied simply, "Tommy needs me." After Shields died, he had him buried next to the rows of Percys.[19]

Percy's open-heartedness was repeated scores of times. It led Cynthia Ware of New Orleans, one of his many admirers, to declare, "I have known two saints in my life, and Will Percy was one." According to Hodding Carter, he "sent penniless youngsters to college, helped jobless men find work, set up ambitious people in small businesses." The problem of any friend became his problem. He hated to see suffering and did his best to make things go well for others—even when he was himself in deep mourning or ill from fatigue, as he often was.[20] This approach to life was an essential part of his sense of Aurelian honor. Yet it was also his link to that unadmired antebellum Percy—Thomas George—whose passivity mingled with kindness was the obverse side of the Percys' competitiveness.

Will Percy's interest in others extended beyond the white community. With much greater solicitude than his father had ever showed, he took an active role in the civic affairs of the black section, sometimes in ways that whites did not appreciate. Once he challenged the police authorities when he was convinced that they had jailed "Jim," a young black, on false charges. The sheriff was infuriated and became a bitter foe, Percy recalled. Nonetheless he secured bail for his indigent client. He then extracted a few hundred dollars for injuries sustained in jail and whisked him off to the remoteness of Trail Lake plantation until the sheriff cooled down. Recognizing that Jim had intelligence and ambition, Percy installed him at the mansion on Percy Street as a house servant. Not long afterward, however, Jim stole several items from the house, boasted of his cleverness in the black community, and fled to Memphis. He was soon apprehended and returned to Greenville, but Percy and Cohn, some of whose property was also found in Jim's possession, decided not to press charges.[21]

At some level he could see how a young man might become so resentful toward whites, even toward benefactors, that he might steal out of sheer malice. He also understood the wounded pride and misery that Jim Crow attitudes might engender. For instance, Cynthia Ware, who knew him when she was growing up in Sewanee, has said that he never would wear a hat. To do so would have required him to tip it to white but never to black women. By going hatless, he was not compelled to make that discrimination on his strolls along the Greenville sidewalks. On such matters, though, he was generally much more conventional than these anecdotes suggest. Defiance of Southern racial rules could only go so far.[22]

Will Percy's interest in Greenville's poor could not have come at a more appropriate moment. Harry Ball, Greenville's most dedicated diarist, reported in the winter of 1931, "The negroes are starving." Alberta, the cook whom Nell Ball, Harry's wife in his late years had hired, supported a large family on very meager wages. One day she failed to appear. "Going into the kitchen Nell found the cupboard bare—all our groceries gone—the place fairly looted." The incident made Ball sad rather than angry. The blacks, he wrote, "throng about us daily, begging for work and food."[23] Throughout the Delta, tenants were being forced off the land. To raise crop prices, the New Deal's Agricultural Adjustment Administration (AAA) was paying landowners to reduce acreage. The result was that fewer hands were needed year round. The labor pool grew so large that day workers could easily be hired for low wages at cotton-picking time.[24] Planters damned the government for offering the alternative of WPA work because, they whined, it demoralized the workers, who would expect handouts while doing no labor. Yet when convenient, the same employers fired these workers or forced them off the land, salving their consciences by advising a trip to the WPA office to enroll. Other forms of injustice were common, too. Ever since the Civil War, black education, particularly in mathematics, was so meager that tenants could not work out credits and debits with the all-powerful landlord.[25]

In the face of these conditions, to have a white man with special solicitude for the black separated Washington County from the rest of the region. First and foremost, Percy strove to make Trail Lake a model estate that other planters might emulate. In 1932 he had recast it as a company, the Trail Lake Planting Company, with family-held shares of stock. In 1936, during the height of the Depression, Percy obtained an income of $35,314.96 from the plantation, then a considerable sum. Populated by 600 members of sharecropping and tenant families, the property consisted of over 3000 acres. About half the land was planted in cotton and much of the remainder in hay and corn. Fifty acres were provided for garden plots.[26]

When Percy first took over the family property, he assembled the managers and announced that the "Golden Rule" would be followed thereafter. Under that strict rubric, no policy of mechanization would drive off unneeded tenants.[27] All 124 families were thus assured of employment throughout the hard times. Moreover, in 1936, their income was modest but ample—well over $400 net—with free water, pasturage, housing, and fuel. All but a handful stayed on the land. "We've got to think of the human side," he told his friend Hodding Carter. "The tenants have their homes and their roots here, and I'm not going to pull them up." Indeed, the historian Jack Kirby demonstrates that Will Percy's concern for the welfare of his people, paternalistic thought it was, compares most favorably with the brutality and indifference of Delta plantation owners whose only concern was machine-like efficiency and profit.[28]

Unlike most other plantation owners, Will Percy arranged for the tenants to buy their own land, and he had the commissary run at cost. His father would have been dismayed by such unbusinesslike management. Will Percy's neighbors were also uneasy about the example his benevolence produced in the black tenantry. He took little interest in the day-to-day management of the place. As Hodding Carter admitted, "When a manager or tenant pointed out a rich stand of cotton, Will would stray off to the cabin yard to look at the flowers he encouraged the tenant wives to plant."[29] Yet the journalist faithfully insisted that despite his good works for the tenants, "Trail Lake thrived." Actually it did not, but its ill-success had much to do with inefficient and under-supervised managers. Some years later when young LeRoy Percy, Will's successor at Trail Lake, assumed control he discovered grave problems.[30]

Yet for all the worthy projects he undertook, two Will Percys materialized. One Will Percy was the sympathetic listener who gave advice or something more substantial to all and sundry supplicants. After Mattie Sue and the boys arrived in time for school in the fall of 1930, they were all impressed with how public their new home was. Phinizy remembered how he used to return "from playing softball or football at say 5:30, and there'd be like a line of people in the hall waiting to see him [Will Percy]—people ranging from doctors to drunks. One at a time they would go in and talk to him."[31] In good Aurelian fashion, Will Percy once called up Hodding Carter in 1937 to complain hotly that no editorial had appeared about a gruesome lynching in another part of Mississippi. "Isn't a lynching worth commenting upon?" Will Percy huffed. "Look at the front page," Carter rejoined. "That's where I put my editorials when I'm really mad." In his outrage over the murder, Percy had simply overlooked the first page.[32]

Moreover, Will Percy could be an exceedingly forbearing employer. To make the newcomers feel at home, he hired Lige, their black man-servant in Birmingham. Lige, however, proved to be a mixed blessing to the household. Will Percy had to adjust to Lige's sometimes trying alcoholic episodes. On one memorable occasion when Betty Carter's mother, Mrs. Werlein, was the featured visitor at the house, Percy poked at the roast mallard too hard with the carving knife and it flew off to settle in the lap of the guest of honor. Gamely rescuing the wayward bird, Lige with tipsy hilarity exclaimed to her, "Please, ma'am, us needs the duck, 'cause us ain't got no more out in the kitchen." After he reinstalled the duck on the silver platter, Lige returned it to the host for another try. The following morning, Percy and Lige went through their antiphonal rite of warning and penitence. Soon, however, they dropped the unpleasant subject and began discussing how to tend the rose bushes near the back gate.[33]

Percy's patience, however, was not inexhaustible. The Percy family had long boasted of employing the best cook in town. Louisa's fried chicken, beaten biscuits, and other delicacies were locally renowned. Will Percy christened her "the Queenly Woman" because of her memorable proportions of three hundred pounds, regal dignity, and fierce temper. Yet for reasons of some unknown "malady of the spirit," as David Cohn recalled the matter, Louisa became so thoroughly demoralized and probably alcoholic that her food became inedible, her kitchen management slovenly. With heavy heart, Percy finally called her in to give her notice. "And so it was that this once majestic figure, a canker at her heart, left the household," Cohn recounted. She was replaced by "the gentle Theresa who remained as long as Will lived."[34]

Yet in Percy's handling of black employees there was a second and darker side, one that followed the contemporary segregationist line without deviation or second thought. Will Percy was more successful than most of his class and period in recognizing the cultivation and humanity of the Jewish people. He used to tease David Cohn that the Jews of the South were becoming so acculturated that they had "fallen to the level of Gentiles." In his last days when ill-health confined his movements, Will used to say, "Now that I can't talk to the Jews I sit here a lonely man."[35]

Yet despite his empathy for those habitually misunderstood or alienated, Percy invariably failed to understand blacks. Like Thomas Jefferson and many other intellectuals throughout Southern history, he could not examine the subject without first complaining how Southern whites suffered both morally and emotionally from the heavy yoke of superiority that God in His wisdom had thrust upon their reluctant shoulders. Living with a benighted race in his midst, Percy insisted, the white Southerner merited some compassion from outsiders. To be sure, he conceded, the ordinary white could not resist the temptation to cheat, rob, and penalize the black—to the ruin of their own white souls. Lackluster as the record was, white Southerners had handled their racial troubles better than anyone could realistically expect, he liked to think. As far as he was concerned, recalled Hortense Powdermaker, "Negroes were happy Pan-like beings living only in the present." After talking with him for many hours, she was convinced that black people were simply not people in his eyes. The sociologist noted that even his nurse-maid Nain, who had lovingly called him "Peeps," was not very real to him. In *Lanterns on the Levee* he wrote, Nain appeared to him "more an emanation or aura than" as an individual. His black playmates had not imprinted themselves on his consciousness; he could imagine his best black friend in boyhood, Skillet, only as a Pullman car porter or a family man with "many little crawfishers." The black preachers, physicians, teachers, barbers, and small proprietors have no names or even much presence in the work. The same disregard, of course, applied to his treatment of the lower- and even middle-class whites of the town. Such was the nature of Percy's view; black or white, the people outside the family circle—unless enemies like Bilbo or dependents like Lige—were simply invisible.[36]

He admitted that white people could not fathom the black mind but considered that incomprehension the fault of a race whose affinity for violence, in Percy's opinion, confounded any outside observer. A black nurse-maid, Percy argued, might slice her lover's throat from ear to ear and not long afterward be changing the diapers of the white baby and crooning a quaint lullaby. It never occurred to him that whites in the South hardly set a better example when it came to murder and atrocity.[37] Will Percy took an almost anthropological interest in black folklore and habit. He did so, however, only to demonstrate how apart the race was from white society. Differences in black and white social values, Percy thought, amply justified Jim Crow segregation in custom and law.

Priding himself on his insights, Percy relied on Ford Atkins as his chief source of sociological data. Son of Percy's cook Louisa, Atkins as an adolescent became his house servant, factotum, and chauffeur. "Fode," as "Mr. Will" liked to call him, told his employer what was happening in the black community and why. For instance, Atkins explained to him the custom of the "dozens"—that is, the verbal escalations of ritual insult among young men that sometimes ended up in a fight and murder. What sort of insults? asked Percy. Delicately, the servant answered: when somebody called out "Well, your mommer hists her tail like a alley cat. Then the shootin' begins."[38] Such examples, Percy believed, suggested the happy life of a race incapable of self-control and dignity. What he missed was its parallel with Southern white notions of honor. Deriving his ideas from Will Percy's code of ethics, the novelist Walker Percy has the hero Lance Lamar in *Lancelot* boast that an ancestor in Spanish times had coolly dispatched a gambler with a bowie knife. The offense that prompted the fight was an affront to the reputation of the victor's mother. Will Percy could not have imagined that blacks might have a similar sense of honor. Accordingly, a Mississippi black man considered his women, mother or lover, as his dependents, the devaluing of whom affected his own esteem.[39] Such views still had pertinence in both the white and the black Delta as late as the 1930s.

Percy and his fellow conservatives knew only what the superficialities showed them. To list all the offenses which had occurred on his plantation during the decade of the thirties would take considerable labor, Will Percy professed; there was so much petty thievery, bootlegging, mayhem, and homicide.[40] Will Percy was unaware that his philosophy of helping the downtrodden could possibly contribute to this behavior. He felt that he followed as best he knew how the precepts of Marcus Aurelius, cited in the epigram at the opening of this chapter. Well meaning as Will's philanthropy was, it could not replace genuine independence and a lessening of the self-hatred that economic and political dependency engenders in all people, whatever the color of their skin. Percy devoutly believed that such aspirations were inherently beyond the capacities of the race. His generosity, though much beyond that of other Delta planters, was always on the donor's, not the recipient's, terms. Given the blacks' poverty and set of habits arising from inequalities of every kind, what else might one expect but a certain compulsiveness, crudeness, and anger?[41] The Will who stood up to sheriffs to help blacks in trouble never challenged or doubted the social rules of the day.[42]

Despite or really because of his doubts of black potentiality, Percy took an uncommon interest in black community life, only to discover that things were not always as they appeared to be. Even a white Southern sociologist saw the difference of perspectives between landlord and tenant. After taking his field notes in the mid-thirties, he reported that Trail Lake's landlord "has a high sense of honesty" and treats the tenants fairly. Yet they "probably do not trust him any more than they trust the other landlords under whom they may have worked in the past."[43] Although Percy had the forthrightness to tell Ford Atkins's stories against himself, they revealed more than he realized. For instance, in a dispute with another planter's chauffeur, Atkins had boasted that his employer had traveled all over the world, even to Africa. Yet rejoined the other servant, Percy went there solely to plan for the return of American blacks to slavery. On hearing this account, Percy exploded, Ford, do you believe such nonsense? Ford replied that he had heard the story many times—even from his mother Louisa. Though clearly an embroidery to get Percy's goat, the message was that even Mr. Will's goodness could not be wholly accepted. Other blacks, however, recognized that he did more to help the African-American community than his white contemporaries. In the black quarters he was known for a time as the "little Jesus." In a case of fraudulent medical practice, his passionate oratory gained an acquittal for a black healer, who claimed to cure in the name of Christ. His white detractors honored him, as it might be said, with a pejorative that the novelist Walker Percy later proudly and bluntly put into print: "nigger-lover." [44]

Percy did not permit community prejudice to govern his relations with the blacks—or with anyone else. Yet on occasion his stubbornness could result in an insensitivity toward the blacks in Greenville. David Cohn reported that the leaders of the black sector of town came to Will Percy's door requesting a donation to build a Y.M.C.A. building. After several days' reflection, he agreed to sponsor their plans, but the petitioners would have to accept a stipulation. If they all united in one huge Baptist Church, Percy and other whites would construct the church building to which a well-equipped and spacious recreational complex would be attached. The existing fifty or so churches, which Percy claimed were dissipating black resources, would have to be closed down. The proposition met "stony silence," Cohn commented. That was the end of the project. One suspects that Percy had grown frustrated with numerous requests from the various preachers seeking help for their struggling missions during the hard times. A less heavy-handed approach, however, might have been worked out. Percy could have tried to enlist the various preachers in a coordinated effort, using black volunteer labor, with whites providing financial assistance. Instead, Percy presented the black community fathers with a Hobson's choice that affronted their self-respect and their interests. Cohn and Percy thought they failed to appreciate the white philanthropist's logic. The outcome reflected badly, the white philanthropists were convinced, on black leadership rather than on the way Percy handled the matter.[45]

The same attitude was evident in Percy's relations with his Trail Lake tenants. As a thoroughly sympathetic Southern journalist reported, he had "the feudal lord's love for his serfs." He "loved Negroes as another gentleman might love dogs," the reporter gushed, "and that somehow the fiercer the beast the more he might prefer it." Yet contrary to the favorable press and the praise of casual visitors, the plantation was poorly run. Trail Lake managers did as they pleased out of his sight. Upon taking over the property at age twenty-one in 1939, LeRoy Percy (Walker's brother) found that some of the bosses were using a two-by-four to strike tenants who crossed them. At once he put a stop to the practice.[46]

In Lanterns on the Levee, Percy himself described a telling incident. Atkins drove "Mr. Will" out to Trail Lake. In his own estimation and that of most whites, Percy had done a great many things for that community. He ordered that the cabins be neatly painted, garden plots cultivated, venereal disease controlled, managers kept from tyrannizing, and, at the plantation store, fair prices set for goods and crops.[47] Nonetheless, all was not as utopian as Percy thought. Since his last visit, Percy had traded in his old Ford for a new shiny limousine. As Ford Atkins and his employer drove up to the supply store, one tenant asked whose car it was. Someone in the gathering replied, as Will Percy heard it: "Dat's us car." Percy mused how pleasant that the relation of employer and tenant had become so tender that to them his car was also theirs. On the way home, basking in the sunlight of his philanthropy, he asked Ford Atkins for his opinion of the "funny" sentiment. "Funnier than you think," he muttered. How so, asked Percy. "He meant that's the car *you* has bought with *us* money." The Trail Lake tenants had understood perfectly but knew that Will Percy had missed the point. "They wuz laughing to theyselves," Ford chuckled.[48]

In telling the story on himself, Percy stressed that Ford Atkins's candor—which his employer permitted and enjoyed—not the reaction of the tenants was the significant point. His relations with Atkins illustrated something of the bonding that could occur between white employer and black servant. Such a link had long been celebrated in the white South from slavery days to the more recent past. Yet the pair's undoubted devotion to each other could not overcome all the antipathies between them. Will Percy never acknowledged his servant's prescience without a reference to foibles that were supposedly typical of Ford Atkins's race. Being part of the culture that also produced Percy's stock responses as patrician, Ford accepted the position in life that his patron assigned him. He knew exactly how to play the trickster to his own advantage. As biographer Jay Tolson points out, he was "fool, jester, and licensed truth-teller." Percy proudly admitted that he was himself one of the white men who was the property of a black whom he had thought he almost owned. The weaker party called upon the more powerful to a degree that weighed down the master, a state of affairs, Percy thought, that was the white man's burden in Mississippi.[49]

Thus, over the years, employer and servant danced their dance together. Each leaned on the other's dependency. That inclination did not make the bond any less strong. Yet such a relationship could only last as long as power was so unequally distributed between white and black in the society at large. As he grew older, Ford Atkins increasingly resented his situation; perhaps unpleasant remarks made in the black quarters rankled. From his own point of view, Will Percy told the sad story of what happened in *Lanterns on the Levee*. Ford Atkins enters the bathroom where Will Percy is showering. Atkins, he reports, remarked, "You ain't nothing but a little old fat man." Percy, whose temper could erupt suddenly, spluttered an epithet; he was as proud of his good looks as any bachelor ever was; reminders of his aging were most unwelcome. Ford Atkins had overstepped the boundary and paid dearly for his off-hand remark. Not a week passed before Percy decided it was time for servant "Fode" to make his own way in the world.[50]

Percy sent him to a mechanics' school in Chicago, but Atkins was soon back in Greenville. Percy went off to Samoa for a while but, upon return, continued to help out, always with a sigh and condescending thought about poor Ford. He had to support his former chauffeur, Percy wrote in *Lanterns on the Levee*. Ford Atkins was his sole link to "Pan and the Satyrs and all earth creatures" who beamed "sunshine" and mutely understood him.[51]

One disaster after another marked Atkins's downward plunge, with each fall prompting a frantic plea for help. Percy rendered assistance as need appeared. Each act of benevolence confirmed him in his conviction that blacks were incapable of self-reliance. In this age his attitude might seem uniquely callous and unthinking, but for someone of Percy's class whether Southern, Northern, or British, servants were almost invisible, to be petted or disciplined because of their unreliability. He was reared in that tradition; there was very little to prepare him for any other approach. It would never have occurred to him that he was in any way irresponsible and would have indignantly denied that he mistreated or neglected his chauffeur. Yet an unexpressed tension and moral confusion lay deep in Percy's concept of Stoic honor whereby patron and servant performed their roles as master alone prescribed. Thus Ford put on the costume, as it were, and said the ritual lines that Will Percy handed him. Yet as a black man in the Mississippi Delta and not a Pan or Satyr or some other metaphorical creature, he must have wondered exactly who he was. Paternalism could make its clients feel like children, instead of men or women of independent spirit.

A complete termination in their affiliation came when Atkins was fired from a job for being drunk. Will Percy had procured him the rare chance of employment in the Depression, and Atkins, sobbing in distress, came to see him after his dismissal. He mourned that Mr. Will could not rescue him because no matter how hard he tried, "I ain't never gonner be nuthin' but jest Fode." Percy had the sensitivity to wish that his former companion had not said that. Yet in Percy's mind it corroborated long-settled views—Ford's personal dilemma but also that of his race in a world with which blacks could not cope.[52] Ford Atkins disappeared from his former employer's life. Will Percy was no less embedded in the culture of inequality than Ford Atkins was. To expect him to violate customs that entangled both himself and servant would have been unrealistic. The Southern white code with which he had no serious quarrel was never meant to apply even as broadly as Will Percy extended it. Instead, Southern racial customs were designed to maintain the historic, hierarchical distinctions of race. Rare it was in the 1930s to find any white who disputed the tradition.

Will Percy's charity was soon to settle closer to home and would require more of him than serving as a visiting Sir Roger de Coverley at Trail Lake or in helping Ford Atkins find work up north. Assuming responsibility for an entire family would be one of his greatest legacies as well as the inspiration for the writing of his memoirs.

CHAPTER FIFTEEN

New Duties and Old Memories

When I look on the youth of the world I
weep. . . .

William Alexander Percy, "Youth"[1]

After having lived with his parents for the greater part of his life, Will
Percy wanted to fill the rambling place with young voices, perhaps to help
him banish some of the ghosts and memories of earlier times. As Walker
Percy was later to remark, so serious a decision must have caused his
guardian much worry. Did it make sense for a lonely, world-traveling bachelor to assist the rearing of his cousin's children? Knowing Will's large-
heartedness, his New York friends Mack and Jervey probably supported
him in his idea when he visited them shortly after Senator Percy's funeral
in late 1929. Undoubtedly Adah Williams and Aunt Nana, whose tour
abroad he had recently financed in another gesture of generosity, encouraged his plan.[2]

In the meantime, Mattie Sue Percy was trying to pull her life together.
Will Percy's father LeRoy had advised her not to disrupt her life any more
than necessary. She should not leave Birmingham, he counseled, but con-
centrate on giving the boys as much emotional stability as possible. Mattie
Sue, however, wanted a chance for a new start. Her desire was understandable but may have masked a dark apprehension—denial of the tragedy and
the episodes of affliction preceding it. According to one of her husband's
DeBardeleben cousins, Mrs. Charles Allison, the guests caught their breath
in amazement when Mattie Sue appeared in a red dress at a reception
following her husband's funeral. Perhaps she meant unconsciously to express her anger at fate and at the husband who had deserted her and their
three sons—uncontrollable though his misery had been.[3]

If the Percys were reticent to acknowledge their inmost feelings, the
same was true of Mattie Sue's family, the Phinizys. They, too, were people
with a strong sense of identity, privacy, and pride. Huguenot in background and Calvinist in the form of Presbyterianism by religion, Mattie
Sue's forebears and parents saw life as a serious struggle requiring rectitude and intelligence. Her widowed mother, Nellie Stovall Phinizy, had

come from foreign missionary stock, and Mattie Sue, one of five daughters, shared her inner determination. Like so many of the women the Percys married, she had great beauty and graceful manners. Outgoing and likeable in every respect, she had the social advantage of playing a skillful game of tennis and an expert hand of bridge. After returning from a stay in Bora Bora, Tahiti, Percy put his proposal before Mattie Sue Percy, his first cousin's wife. She and the boys were living at her mother Nellie Phinizy's large and comfortable mansion on Milledge Avenue in Athens, Georgia. Mattie Sue accepted the invitation, and the family moved to Greenville in the late summer of 1930.[4]

The newcomers were soon made very welcome in the commodious, rambling house. Standing on the corner of Percy and Broadway, its location was too low-lying to be fashionable, and the frequent downpours typical of the Delta country surrounded the place at times with almost enough water to form a shallow lake. The house had once been handsomer, in a "bastard Greek Revival" style, as Walker Percy later remarked. Nevertheless it was neither as large nor as elegant as Mary Routh and General Dahlgren's Routhland. An overzealous local contractor had modernized the place in the 1920s. He tore down the columns and portico, covered the wooden frame with stucco, installed an elevator because of Camille's poor health, and put a porte-cochère on one side and a sun parlor on the other. Camille, then convalescing, and LeRoy Percy had taken a long vacation to avoid the strain of watching the contractor's amputations and additions.[5] As if to make up for its unprepossessing look, Will Percy had surrounded it with an elaborate and luxuriant garden in which he and his frequent guest, Charlotte Gailor from Sewanee, spent hours puttering about. Azaleas, roses, and forsythia bloomed in a riot of color.

The boys were much attracted to their gentle, animated, story-telling cousin and had hailed the move to his house, if only to escape the dreary Presbyterian Sundays in Athens. "I immediately took to him. There was no way not to like him," Phinizy Percy reminisced.[6] Soon enough they made the old place, with its odd-angled rooms, a permanent treasure-hunt. Mixed in with plantation furnishings that Will's grandparents had bequeathed was a veritable museum of strange acquisitions by way of the family's, but especially Will's, excursions to foreign places. "Moroccan rugs, Persian vases, Mexican wood screens, Japanese paintings, Victorian bric-a-brac, old-fashioned mahogany furniture, and brass beds, all somehow achieved a harmony that defied the rules and evaded analysis," declared David Cohn.[7] The attic was filled with things boys would enjoy much more than the assortment downstairs: war souvenirs—German helmets, canteens, belts, uniforms, puttees, rifles and bayonets—from Will Percy's World War I experience.[8] All in all, the arrangement "seemed," as Walker Percy later recalled, "like a good idea."[9]

Yet Mattie Sue was running unanticipated risks. One Percy, her husband, had committed the ultimate rejection by killing himself. If she had entertained any thoughts of remarrying, the second Percy was implacably committed to the bachelor life. Some people in town expected the couple to marry. Why else was she living under his roof, the gossips clucked. Will Percy's biographer Carol Malone reported that people whom she interviewed in the 1960s "have stated that Will Percy was in love with his first cousin's wife, Mattie Sue." Harry Ball also expected a similar outcome. "We all like young Mrs[.] LeRoy Percy very much," Ball reported in his diary. Later, he lamented, "We had hoped that she and Will might marry." The Percy family today, however, denies any such thing. She may have found him too mercurial. As Adah Williams later remarked, "He had two natures; he was sad as could be and as gay as could be. He had that lively, gay spirit, but he was always worried about somebody or some thing." In a chilling way, the often melancholy bachelor might well have reminded Mattie Sue, in this respect, of her depressive husband, especially when Will Percy made such mordant remarks as "[D]eath is the best cure for many diseases," a comment likely to raise unhappy memories.[10] In any event, after a year and a half in the house, she must have realized that no romance—either on her part or his—could ever flower.

More important, her role as mother to three boys must have been compromised in her dependency upon a provider who was neither husband nor lover nor step-father to her children nor blood kin to her. With his tales of past family glories, classical training, and mannered Old South gentility, Will was fitting the boys into the Percy heritage—all with the best of intentions. In a sense she had already become superfluous. Will's servants did all the work; she was a permanent guest, not an easy thing to be. Mattie Sue might have eventually found compensation for living in the glass house of Greenville society under Will Percy's protection by taking pride in rearing three strapping, highly intelligent sons. Yet another tragedy, a car accident, prevented further testing.

Walker Percy recalled that his mother "was not well" at that time, although neither he nor the younger boys would have noticed much about what their mother was doing. They accepted things as they were. As Walker Percy later mused, "What with youth's incapacity for astonishment or gratitude," it never occurred to him that it might appear odd to be left a teenage orphan and "adopted by a bachelor-poet-lawyer-planter and living in an all-male household."[11] As the eldest, he needed his mother less than the others and was undoubtedly trying to break away from maternal ties in natural, adolescent fashion. Though polite and interested in people, Walker Percy was always remote, even with boys his own age. He proved too shy and diffident to begin a relationship with a girl, but instead pined after several school beauties from a distance. One was Camille Sarasson, a very bright girl whose family belonged to the wealthy Jewish circle. Another was Margaret Kirk, who fulfilled the model of the perfect Southern belle of the thirties.[12] Embarrassed by a social awkwardness that prevented him from any effective pursuit of these popular girls, he could well have given his mother an impression of rejecting her as he mooned about the house. An air of teenage detachment may have been a minor matter to her feelings, but Mattie Sue had no experience with rearing a boy at Walker's stage of development. She could have taken the slightest rebuff as a further sign of the Percy curse that had separated her from her husband—and not without some reason. Walker Percy kept his feelings to himself.

Besides, the boys were a handful, running and jumping about, competing and quarreling as youngsters are accustomed to doing. Such behavior could have been a source of satisfaction in ordinary circumstances, but with her nerves taut and with Will Percy's health worsening from hypertension, the situation might seem chaotic. "Looking back on it now, it must have been extremely traumatic for my mother," Walker Percy later suggested.[13] Nellie Phinizy, the boys' grandmother, came for a visit. Perhaps the women consulted about the situation in which Mattie Sue was placed, with no prospect of any alteration in her relationship to Will Percy.[14] Shortly after Nellie Phinizy's departure, tragedy struck.

On April 2, 1932, a fateful Easter Saturday, Mattie Sue Percy and her youngest son Phinizy, age ten, plunged in her Buick coupe some twenty feet into the swollen waters of Deer Creek from an unrailed bridge outside Greenville. As the water rose inside, Phinizy Percy realized that the only way to safety was through the right rear window, still above the water line. His mother, holding his hand in paralyzing terror, would not let go, and even held tighter as her fright mounted. Vainly he tried to pull her along with him. Then she suddenly released him. He escaped, scrambled up the bank, and shouted for help. Mattie Sue remained seated in the sinking car.[15]

Mattie Sue and Phinizy had been traveling down the road to the property of the Metcalfs, who belonged to the Percy circle of friends. Apparently she was not heading there but simply driving as a diversion. The unpaved road toward the bridge was quite steep, sharply curved at the bottom, and very muddy. Harry Ball's diary, written in Greenville, indicated that it had been raining for several days previously. The car's steering mechanism probably made it hard to turn, especially if the driver had misjudged the slope and the sudden twist that the road took before reaching the slippery wood-plank bridge. The question arises, why did Mattie Sue not try to save herself? "When taken from the car she was dead, but unwounded," reported Harry Ball in his diary. "It is conjectured she may have died of heart failure." In other words, she had not lost consciousness from a blow nor was she otherwise physically impeded or hurt in an effort to get out. Panic, complicated by her continued grieving for Roy and anomalous place in Will's household, would seem the best explanation. It was most unlikely that she deliberately sought the death of her son as well as herself.[16]

Although few would have expected it, Will Percy ably responded to loss and became thereafter both mother and father to the boys—Phinizy age ten, LeRoy fourteen, and Walker sixteen. It was a double role that might have provided recompense for not having quite filled his younger brother's place in their father LeRoy's heart. Although Percy related his loss of poetic inspiration to the series of family deaths, he may really have turned from versifying because of the new parietal duties. His first responsibility was to deal with Phinizy's reaction. The boy was having night terrors. "Frequently," recalled Phinizy, "I would wake up . . . screaming from a nightmare, and he would come in and we would go in his sitting room and he would try to talk to me about what the nightmare was about, and then he would read to me, Greek mythology or something. You know it might have been a night when he had been throwing up for the fear of a trial. He was totally selfless. His only thought was comforting me and getting me to go to sleep. Needless to say, I'll never forget it." [17] Percy took the child to the Phipps Clinic, at the Johns Hopkins Hospital, in Baltimore, where Phinizy talked with a woman psychiatrist. The attention and love that Will Percy gave him proved much more helpful than the session or two in Baltimore. Percy's willingness to try a professional psychological approach showed a level of sophistication and liberal thought that ran counter to his Victorian attitudes and Southern ultra-conservatism. Undoubtedly he was reassured in reaching such decisions by his New York bachelor friends, Huger Jervey, Lindley Hubbell, and Gerstle Mack. [18]

Among Will Percy's many remarkable qualities, as Walker Percy recalls, was his "extraordinary capacity for communicating enthusiasm for beauty." [19] He was a born teacher, with an unusual talent for imparting to others his personal enthusiasm for literature, art, and music. Walker Percy remembers that once his guardian had given him Romain Rolland's *Jean-Christophe,* "a big, thick book," no longer much admired, "but it made a great impression on me." He learned that it was possible "to enter the world of a book, you know, to get lost in a book." In 1935, when *Gone with the Wind* appeared, "Uncle Will" handed Walker a copy, and the young reader could not put it down. [20] No doubt the senior Percy was very gratified that his charges listened to his suggestions about aesthetic matters. Most boys their ages would have found his opinions and reading suggestions boring.

Will Percy's house was well equipped for the informal tutoring that often took place there. In the living room stood an enormous Capehart, a machine that could automatically flip records over and play the other side. The record library consisted chiefly of the classics—the romantics and Bach. As Walker Percy reminisced, the player sometimes "would have a fit, take a dislike to Tchaikovsky and sling records every which way." The apparatus was the talk of the community, and visitors would often ask for a demonstration. Once, when the Capehart felt out of sorts, Will Percy, who loved a joke, obliged a group's request and put a record on the turntable. When the music stopped, nothing happened. Having prepared the scenario beforehand, he rang a bell. A black boy soon ambled in and turned the record over. That method was probably more reliable than the quirky mechanical device.[21] Withdrawing into himself, Walker often played the classics on the Capehart while curled up immersed in a book.

Will Percy's library was another source of wonder for the boys, especially for Walker. The books that Thomas George Percy, the intellectual ancestor, had collected in the early part of the nineteenth century were still there, leather-bound and dusty. Will Percy added his editions of Matthew Arnold and other Victorians whom he read and reread. Walker recalled that Will Percy did not like the " 'moderns,' " as he called them. Not even his distinguished contemporaries and fellow Southerners, the Nashville poets, Allen Tate, John Crowe Ransom and company, met his Edwardian tastes. Yet he had a variety of nineteenth-century stories of adventure and romance upon which his young cousin voraciously fed.[22]

Moreover, Will Percy provided a rich intellectual atmosphere for them to enjoy. Any celebrity who passed through his corner of the world was likely to spend some days or longer under his hospitable roof. According to Walker Percy, David Cohn, the novelist and a conversationalist reputedly as skillful as Samuel Johnson, came for a weekend and ended up staying over a year. Probably the energetic Aunt Nana, who ran Will's establishment, never objected: Cohn was a model guest.[23] Son of a Polish-born merchant in Greenville, Cohn, like Will Percy, had been a great favorite of Carrie Stern, who predicted his later literary success. After attending the University of Virginia and Yale, Cohn had made a fortune in retailing in New Orleans. At the beginning of the 1930s he returned home to start a career as a writer. *God Shakes Creation,* a memoir of Mississippi life, was written in his room on Percy Street. Although a dozen years younger than Will, Cohn had an influence on his host, modifying, however slightly, his aesthetic conservatism. Through him, for instance, Percy was introduced to the sculpture of Jacob Epstein, whose first exhibition in the United States Cohn had financed in 1927. In the late 1920s and 1930s, Epstein's work was extremely controversial partly because of his scandalous succession of mistresses and his "primitive" and not at all classically Grecian representations of the human body—aspects that ordinarily affronted Will Percy's conventionally Victorian views.[24] After buying a house for himself and later marrying, Cohn continued to attend nearly every function that took place at the Percy house.

The Delta attracted a number of Northern investigators on Southern race relations. Each one, it seemed, trooped into town armed with a letter of introduction or a personal invitation from Will Percy himself. In either case, he was eager to disarm critics and make new friends. Planning a newspaper series on sharecropping, Raymond Gram Swing and Dorothy Thompson brought with them Gordon Selfridge, Jr., of the famous London store on Regent Street. He was dressed in Savile Row's finest and sported the customary bowler. Both his apparel and incomprehensible accent were a sensation among the tenants at Trail Lake. A more academic guest than Swing and Thompson was Hortense Powdermaker, a young sociologist, who came to study racial conditions in Indianola some forty miles away. The townspeople there were suspicious and uncooperative. Desperate for help, she remembered having read Will Percy's poetry with pleasure and telephoned him for assistance. Percy opened doors for her in Indianola, finding her a comfortable lodging with private bath (then a rarity). He also provided his hospitality as a sanctuary when the difficulties of her project weighed her down.[25] "You never knew who was going to be at dinner," Phinizy Percy has recalled. "It was almost like living in a hotel." The younger boys no doubt only partially appreciated the guests' dinner conversation. Already mature enough to grasp *Brothers Karamazov,* Walker Percy, as the eldest, found that listening to brainy visitors was no trial at all.

In 1939, Harry Stack Sullivan, the famous psychiatrist, who had been a guest some years before, returned to see his friend Will Percy and investigate race relations for a national foundation. As Walker remembered this occasion, the guest spent most of the time in the kitchen and pantry drinking vodka martinis. The concoction was unknown to most Mississippians of the 1930s. Sullivan would talk to "any and all comers," Walker Percy reported, but how he could learn much about the Delta in so confined a spot was a mystery. On further reflection, however, Walker Percy realized that "between the white folks in the front and the cook [Theresa] and her friends and friends of the cook's friends in the back," the shrewd psychiatrist had found an excellent observation post where "the traffic was heaviest and race relations liveliest."[26]

The theater critic of the *New Republic,* Stark Young, journalists Jonathan Daniels and Dorothy Parker, poets Vachel Lindsay, Langston Hughes, and Stephen Vincent Benét, and many others also visited. Hughes, the great poet of the Harlem Renaissance, stayed overnight in the house, no doubt to the consternation of race-conscious neighbors. At a meeting of the local literati, Percy introduced him by saying, as Walker Percy later recalled, "Now here's a man who's black and a poet and who has risen above the issues of race." To Will Percy's unpleasant surprise, however, Hughes then read "the most ideologically aggressive poetry you can imagine." Hughes's host did not flinch or remonstrate; he was a gentleman, and a fearless one to boot.[27]

The North Carolina journalist Jonathan Daniels was particularly impressed with Percy's bearing and old world charm. He titled a chapter of a book on the contemporary South, "Hotspur's House," to celebrate an unforgettable experience. Daniels's choice signified a respect for his host's genealogical credentials and an appreciation for his nobility of character. The journalist spent more than one evening in the company of David Cohn, Will Percy, and Roark Bradford, another Mississippi intellectual who enjoyed Will's hospitality. Hard on their neighbors' foibles, they were a witty band, Daniels reminisced, and lit "with anger and humor a darkness like despair" and shared "an unloving knowledge of the people on the land which they loved."[28] More to the liking of the boys was the entertainment that Carl Sandburg supplied when he unpacked his guitar. He sang "none too well," Walker remembered with amusement. On another occasion during the Depression a black transient with a harmonica appeared "from God knows where" and "played the blues" with greater effect than had the Chicago poet.[29]

The guests' skill in conversation was sure to win Will Percy's favor, especially if they could draw in the boys. Some fell short. William Faulkner, for instance, proved most unsatisfactory. Although polite to his visitor from Oxford, Mississippi, Will Percy could not forget the novelist's mocking critique of *In April Once*. In the University of Mississippi student paper, the arrogant young writer in 1920 had remarked that Percy "should have . . . gone to Italy with Swinburne, for like Swinburne, he is a mixture of passionate adoration of beauty and as passionate a despair and disgust with its manifestation and accessories in the human race." Will Percy never forgot old slights, but he was always gracious. Running into Faulkner in New York City in 1921, he introduced him to his friend Lindley Hubbell at the New York Public Library. Some years later, Faulkner found himself drawn into a tennis match, Will Percy's favorite form of exercise. Having arrived half-drunk, he "never managed once to bring racket into contact with ball," Walker Percy recalled. As Faulkner reeled about the court, Will urged Ben Wasson to rescue his friend by taking him away for a drive. The pair left post haste.

On the whole Will Percy's guests were more affable than the brooding Faulkner. With "their unfailing French gayety and 'soft hilarity,' " as Harry Ball, the Greenville diarist, remarked, Adah Williams and Aunt Nana could always be counted on to draw out the shy members of a party. Having installed them in a house across the street, Percy had the pair over every Sunday afternoon for dinner and a cocktail or two. The drinks invariably went to the old ladies' heads and quickened their departure. In addition, they were in and out of his house more or less every day.[30]

Will Percy's exercise of Southern largesse was very much like the intellectual "conversaziones" that Sarah Dorsey had initiated years before. Will Percy's rich sense of humor, however, gave his social functions a much lighter air than the heavy earnestness that seemed to hover over the lavish festivities of his predecessor in Louisiana. Unlike the childless Sarah Dorsey, however, Percy designed his entertainments at the house neither simply to gratify his own pleasure or curiosity nor to raise the cultural tone of the neighborhood. Instead, the surrogate father saw the welcoming of guests from distant places as part of the boys' upbringing. Exposing them to the world of letters was a much richer experience than to let them listen to the radio or laze about the house.

༜ ༜

After his parents' deaths, Will Percy had given up his poetry-writing but not his principles. Perhaps he undertook to serve as father for his cousin's boys to transmit to them something of his Stoic credo of endurance, respect for classical learning, and love for an irretrievable Southern past—as he idealized it. In the late 1930s, he realized that his time was limited, given his health and the family record for longevity. To be sure, the boys had heard all the stories that found their way into *Lanterns on the Levee.* The memoir was largely a compilation of legends passed down to Will that he then further embellished. Yet the oral tradition could be easily lost. The remedy was to write a memoir explaining what he had learned and thought valuable as a legacy for Walker, LeRoy, and Phinizy.

A visit by Alfred Knopf to Greenville set the wheels in motion. Knopf had published Will Percy's *Selected Poems* in 1930 and wanted him to compose a memoir of a small-town attorney. "Damned if I'll write about the law!" was Percy's reaction. In the summer of 1936, however, Percy sailed to Tahiti from Los Angeles. On the way back, according to Ben Wasson, he began a study of the island people, an effort in prose that inspired further experimentation. David Cohn urged him to try his hand at reminiscence, and Percy began in earnest. Considering Percy too poetically inclined to write prose, Janet Dana and others expressed doubts of his success, however, and he put the manuscript aside. On a hot summer day while seated in the Percy library, Cohn found some loose pages stuffed behind the cushions on a sofa. Scooping them up, he went out to the gallery, read and liked them. He beseeched Will at once to resume work on a very promising autobiography.[31]

Thus encouraged and with a feeling that the winds of death were blowing his way, Percy made rapid progress for a while. Sometime in the late thirties, he vacationed at Fort Walton, Florida, but it was bitter cold. He complained to Charlotte Gailor that icicles dangled from his nose and roaches were nestling in his ears at night. Nevertheless, he doggedly worked on the chapters about his Harvard years and his old friend Carrie Stern. He was grateful to Charlotte Gailor for typing his almost illegible scrawl and correcting his spelling.[32] Perhaps more conscious than those around him of physical decline, Percy grew depressed as the work drew to a close. On August 28, 1939, he warned Harold Straus at Knopf headquarters in New York that the book would never sell and might even have to be canceled because of the impending war in Europe (in fact, to begin within a few days.)[33] Moreover, he was concerned about four chapters he had written on race relations. Two female readers—Charlotte Gailor and Adah Williams, no doubt—thought them the best in the book, he reported. Yet David Cohn feared that his reflections on race would "mean nothing to northern readers" and made dull reading anyhow. Huger Jervey who read all the chapters before their submission to Knopf, agreed that the ones on race were inappropriate. Percy withheld them for the moment. Knopf, however, was delighted with what he had so far received, including the controversial ones. "As publishers we feel that it is so strong and honest and genuine as well as beautifully written, that it cannot fail to attract wide attention," he reassured the nervous author.[34] Nonetheless, Percy should have heeded the advice of Jervey and Cohn rather than his publisher's.

Though almost completed, the work was still not ready for a final submission a year later, Percy insisted. He complained to Jervey, "I'm at the end of my rope." Everything was more or less in order except the "Sharecropper" chapter. Yet he wrote Charlotte Gailor, "I am completely bogged down on it." For that reason he booked a room at the Hotel El Tovar on the edge of the Grand Canyon, probably his first visit since the tragic year of 1929.[35] Thoughtfully, he wanted to be out of the way anyhow. His adopted son LeRoy and Sarah Farish, newlyweds, should be allowed to "learn the cost of housekeeping and the responsibilities of running a menage" without the intervention of his superintending eye. In that bleakly romantic Western setting, Percy put the final touches on the work and then carried it to New York, where he saw his old friend Huger and his ward Walker, then in the midst of his medical training at Columbia. He dedicated the work to "Walker, Roy, & Phin" and to Adah Williams, Charlotte Gailor, and Tommy Shields, an old Greenville friend who was then slowly dying of cancer. The first set represented the future of the family; the latter were his dearest friends. Receiving an advance copy, Roark Bradford wrote him that it was "the 'goddamndest' book he ever read," Will Percy commenting, "whatever that means."[36]

A conservative and highly romantic Southern memoir might not be expected to win either sympathy or audience among the Northern intelligentsia even if David O. Selznick's *Gone with the Wind* was currently exciting the movie-going masses. In designing the cover for *Lanterns on the Levee,* the illustrator must have been inspired by Selznick's glamorized plantation sets. Percy pronounced the dust-jacket "horrible" in "the most ghastly magnolia tradition" that "a Yankee" could imagine.[37] Despite the tasteless packaging, *Lanterns on the Levee* had a remarkably favorable reception in both the popular and academic press. In Pulitzer Prize speculations, it ranked third among newspaper critics on a list of fifteen book selections.[38] Carl Sandburg praised the memoir and said that his friend was to Mississippi what William Allen White was to Kansas. Lawrence Olson in the New York *Herald Tribune* considered the chapters on race "an eloquent and valid defense of the Southern farm system." The compliment seemed to vindicate Percy's inclusion of the race material. Herschel Brickell in the Sunday New York *Times* hailed it as "a work of exceptional merit and importance," written in a style that entitled it to "a permanent place in our literature." [39]

One critic—from the Deep South—trumpeted a contrary but refreshing blast. Lilian Smith in the *North Georgia Review* told some plain truths when she acidly observed that, "those who wear the aura of racial superiority will acknowledge with satisfaction the halo which the author has woven so delicately around his own head." She found *Lanterns on the Levee* much more disturbing than "a Georgia demagogue's cheap tricks." Intelligent people were too easily seduced by "well-bred softness" while smugly despising the vulgar rantings of "race chauvinism." Moreover, she found Percy's gentility callow and pretentious. We in the South, she argued, "feverishly continue to blow ourselves up from miniature dimensions to the magnificent proportions of a super race and a super class." Percy's work encouraged that self-satisfied response, she insisted.[40]

Lilian Smith's criticisms hit the mark, but two other Southern liberals applauded the memoir. Both W. J. Cash of Charlotte, North Carolina, and James Agee, originally from East Tennessee, had both written major works in 1941 that were highly critical of the South that Percy glorified. Cash, author of *The Mind of the South,* and Agee, who wrote *Let Us Now Praise Famous Men,* treated *Lanterns on the Levee* with surprising respect. Agee, who had gone to St. Andrew's, an Episcopal school near the University of the South, loved to read aloud the Sewanee passages to his co-workers at *Time* magazine. The reasons for these writers' enthusiasm had little to do with Percy's politics and much to do with his elegant note of melancholy and winsome self-deprecation. Like Percy himself, Agee and Cash were depressives whose brilliance as writers did not release them from its toils. Their favorable readings reflected a recognition of Will Percy as a kindred spirit. Only a few weeks after writing his review, Cash committed suicide during a psychotic attack. Agee died at age forty-five in 1954 after long abuse of his body with alcohol and cigarettes.[41]

Lanterns on the Levee remains in print after fifty years, and many consider it a classic Southern text. Recently, literary critic Fred Hobson pronounced both Cash's sole book, *The Mind of the South,* and Percy's only prose writing to be "brilliantly conceived and controlled works of art, triumphs of tone and style, and as deserving of a place in American literature as the works of Faulkner and Wolfe, Warren and Welty." [42] A case can plausibly be made for such high praise, despite the racial blindness and self-deluding romanticism of Percy's book. Yet a closer reading finds it more intriguing than beguiling. Besides being a work of art, *Lanterns on the Levee* illuminates a Southern intellectual's anguish. At all events, the historian finds the memoir a complex document. It is sumptuous and subversive, clever and saddening both for what the author says and what he seemed not to grasp. Its duality of theme and counter-theme and its internal contradictions, both recognized and unacknowledged, rescue it from banality. As a literary historian has observed, *Lanterns on the Levee* is never "morbid or whining." [43] Instead it changes tonality and mood with astonishing arpeggios and modulations from major to minor modes. Yet confusion is evident everywhere. Percy worships his father but only half-consciously reveals his father's insensitivities. He mingles cosmopolitan tastes with a safe insularity, insight with an outworn idealism, in such intricate ways that the modern reader, knowing something of his character and unfulfilled life, can decode it. At the same time Percy's contemporaries saw the work as a straightforward and uncomplicated threnody on the old order. No critical reading today would fail to notice its homoerotic passages, but not a single reviewer fifty years ago mentioned that aspect of the work. Will Percy was by no means coy or deliberately obscure; his critics simply ignored what they found dismaying, puzzling, or too confounding to bear close scrutiny.

Even more curious was the contemporary failure to recognize the fanciful aspects, as if Percy wrote factually and as if the characters he described were as charming or noble as he asserted. Gone were the days of true nobility, Will mourned throughout the pages. Men with little conscience and no dignity now ruled the land. "The moral anemics" of the current era, he thundered, could not match in stature his father's political friends of the 1890s. They were worthy of installation next to the solemn knights over a portal at Chartres Cathedral, he argued. In reality, LeRoy's cronies—General Thomas Catchings, a retired, undistinguished congressman and others—fell considerably short of Will's appraisal. The reader is not meant to laugh, but Percy's characterization inadvertently parodies the sometimes pretentious romanticism of the white South. Only Will Percy could have identified General Catchings, with his cold manner and questionable veracity, as a divinely inspired medieval crusader. The analogy was even too exaggerated to suit the author himself. Within a paragraph he slips into a different guise, stripping off the cloak of a modern Jeremiah. In its place he dons the short pants of the little boy raptly listening to his elders—as if they, he says, were "the patriarchs of Chartres . . . sipping the dregs of a julep." [44]

Yet *Lanterns on the Levee* is a remarkable document, not in its insights into Southern realities but in its exposition of Southern mythology in a delightful and psychologically intriguing way. Percy opened the work with a romantic view of the "Delta Folks," describing the land itself, those who first settled it, and their descendants, particularly his own ancestors. He recalled his own childhood, his playmates, both white and black, but most mournfully the motherly figures, again of both races, who had made him feel welcome in the world but who had long since passed away. Recounting his schooling, particularly his chapter on Sewanee, offers him reflections on the merits of an old-fashioned education in the classics, an approach that helps to explain his reluctance to venture into modern literary practice as a poet.

Also memorable is his description of a Southerner at Harvard. His comments bring to mind the contrasting experiences of Faulkner's Quentin Compson and that of the less fictionalized Henry Adams in his *Education,* to which *Lanterns on the Levee* seems a Southern counterpart. Like Quentin and like Adams's classmate Rooney Lee, a son of Robert E. Lee, whom Adams had characterized as a typically hearty but "ignorant," "childlike," and belligerent Virginian, Percy found Northern aristocrats a snobbish breed—as Rooney had earlier. One of Percy's acquaintances in law school was Freddie, who would speak to him in class but refused to return his greeting in the Yard. Will Percy remarked that Freddie, a typical specimen, felt privileged above other law students because he was a true "Hah-vahd" man before his misfortune to mingle with lesser beings at the professional school.

Too charming and too well connected to be wholly ignored, Will Percy was once invited to a dinner given by a law professor with long roots into the Bostonian past. Telling an anecdote in his customary voluble way, Percy flipped out his napkin for emphasis. To his surprise, the napkin cleverly hid a hard dinner roll which shot out, like a projectile, sailed into the air and crashed against a nearby bird cage with a noise resembling "a Stravinsky chord on an untuned harp." The canaries, stricken in their agitation, replied in a great cacophony, but the host and guests pretended as if nothing untoward had occurred at all. Percy commented that in the South, at least somebody "would surely have been silly and merciful" enough to have cracked such a remark as "the last time Senator Omygosh did that he hit two canaries and killed the auk." [45] The advantage of being melancholy was that in his case it gave him liberty to be funny and to see the inanity of human reactions.

Percy was likewise critical of such exiled Southerners as a Mrs. Lovell, who asked him whether he had actually met any Northerner who qualified as a gentleman. He replied that he had. The unreconstructed lady, a daughter of Mississippi General John A. Quitman, testily observed, "I'm certain that you will find you are mistaken." Although hating to admit his fascination with Northern urban life, Percy admitted that despite their reputation for high manners, his fellow Southern whites "are easier to meet and never so intimate after the meeting." [46]

The strongest chapters, however, concern his defense of his father in the 1911 campaign, his experience in World War I, and the Percys' fight against Klan and Flood. The last section of the book, which deals with Will's thoughts about race, particularly "Fode" Atkins, is strident and dull. Yet as he figuratively walks through the cemetery and sees the Percys' graves, his ruminations vividly restore the mood of nostalgia and bitter loneliness that contrasts with his sense of paradox and humor. Although in a vague way his recollections conform with a reality, the memoir is essentially a justification for the Percys' sense of specialness, not an objective history. "Autobiography," declares Georges Gusdorf, "appeases the more or less anguished uneasiness of an aging man who wonders if his life has not been lived in vain." The comment applies to *Lanterns on the Levee*.[47] Given that purpose, Will Percy had written an *apologia*, a subtle and memorable rendition of a world that never existed except as the Percys fashioned it in their minds.

In both his writing and his self-understanding, Will Percy closed his eyes to the cultural maze in which he lived. He could not face head-on the symbolic import of "Small Boy's Heroes" who sometimes descended to a shabbiness that honor, no matter how defined, could wash clean. To have conceded the point, however, would have been an indictment of his all-knowing father, whose power rested on a group of traditional politicians—some of them kinfolk and few of them with hands not altogether clean.[48] Thus, the honor Percy celebrated actually consisted of the honor of blood loyalty. He described it as some noble abstraction worthy of Tennyson's Arthurian band. Among such motives, however, was also that of family self-protectiveness in a chronically mistrustful world. Yet Percy had no wish to reduce his imposing ethical construction to a vulgar self-aggrandizement, the kind of familial honor identified with Sicilian peasants. It should not be attached to plantation lords of the Delta. As Walker Percy put it many years later, "The whole of the Delta, indeed of white Mississippi, is one big kinship lodge." [49]

In the richness of its texture and in the way Will Percy conducted his life and projected his convictions of love and hate, joy and grief, he was to exercise a profound influence upon Walker Percy, the eldest son of his first cousin. Yet for the younger Percy, his surrogate father would always be an enigma. As late as 1975, he was still bemused. In "The Delta Factor," first published in Lewis Simpson's *Southern Review,* the novelist asked why his cousin rejoiced when news came on the afternoon of December 7, that the Japanese had attacked Pearl Harbor. Why had he been happiest in the Argonne Forest, shooting Germans? "Why was he sad from 1918 to 1941, even though he lived in as good an environment as man can devise, indeed had the best of all possible worlds in literature, music, and art?" The question was rhetorical. In *Lanterns on the Levee,* Will Percy had written in the late 1930s about how he felt when he was mustered out of the army in 1918. "It's over," he had said to himself at the time, "the only great thing you were ever part of." How hard it was to return to "the old petty things without purpose, direction, or unity"—humdrum lawsuits, "defending a railroad for killing a cow." Briefly, he had known how to forget the melancholy that burdened him, a time when "it, somehow, had meaning, and daily life hasn't; it was part of a common endeavor, and daily life is isolated and lonely." As a Percy, Walker Percy knew precisely what he meant and found ways of saying it in his fiction.[50]

During a visit to Sewanee in 1941, Walker Percy, then a young physician, accompanied Will to the home of two old friends: Charlotte Elliott, a former member of the Metropolitan Opera chorus; and her lifelong companion, Marie Truslow, a sculptor. Will Percy had long owned a stone cottage, Brinkwood, near Sewanee, and vacationed there almost every summer. As a boy growing up on the mountain myself, I found them a most startling pair. Charlotte Elliott was tall, dignified, and benevolent, Marie Truslow, stumpy, bucktoothed, and vivacious. They wore long dresses, black or dazzling white, and heavy, chinking amber beads and pearls, pendant over very ample bosoms. The dowagers were serving tea and cakes to some Sewanee undergraduates. Will Percy had been regaling the guests with his customary wit when suddenly he faltered, unable to pronounce certain words. He had Walker drive him back to Brinkwood at once. The work attending the publication of *Lanterns on the Levee* had taxed his strength considerably. Another attack—what Will Percy called momentary "aphasia"—took place at the Sewanee home of Charlotte Gailor. Tests at Johns Hopkins Hospital in Baltimore revealed severe hypertension. Relentlessly a series of small strokes began to weaken his frail body.[51] At the relatively young age of fifty-seven, Will Percy died on January 21, 1942, at Kings' Daughters Hospital in Greenville.

For all his old-fashioned ways and opinions, Will Percy was clearly a man who engendered love from those who knew him. In his dignity he extracted deference "normally shown to a patriarch," as one scholar concludes.[52] In character and strength Will Percy was by far the most impressive member of the family. Despite his diminutive size, he had great moral stature. Throughout his life he showed a profundity of spirit that his young adoptive sons glimpsed and could not help but admire. His capacity for affection was almost boundless. No wonder that Roy and Mattie Sue's sons found in Will Percy's death cause for intense mourning. Will's influence would linger on in the memories of all those who knew him but most especially in the mind of Walker Percy. The pair did not live very long under the same roof. Will Percy was often away on vacation; Walker began his college career in fall 1933, only a year and a half after his mother's death. Despite the brevity of their association, the senior Percy made a deep impression on the future novelist during the months of every year in the 1930s that they spent together at Greenville or Sewanee.

PART FOUR

Fiction, Legend, and Lineage

CHAPTER SIXTEEN

Walker and the Legacy of "Uncle Will"

> A young man am I, twenty nine, but I am as
> full of dreams as an ancient. At night the years
> come back and perch around my bed like
> ghosts.
>
> Walker Percy, *The Moviegoer*[1]

Walker Percy's relationship with his adoptive father Will was one of deep love, gratitude, and dependency. How could it have been otherwise? After Roy Percy's death, Will Percy sacrificed his comfort and freedom of movement for the sake of the fatherless family. Reflecting upon their ties, Walker some thirty or so years later remarked that his guardian had been willing to shoulder "the burden of parenthood without the consolations of marriage." The elder Percy may have obtained great satisfaction from rearing the boys for he enjoyed his new role, and they reciprocated the love he showed them. Yet whatever "Uncle Will" obtained from the experience, Walker Percy confessed, "I know what I gained: a vocation, and in a real sense a second self, that is, the work and the self which, for better or worse, would not otherwise have been open to me." Will Percy had placed him under an obligation that could not be repaid.[2]

In an introduction to a reprinted *Lanterns on the Levee,* Walker Percy wrote those words from the heart. The situation, however, had been more complicated than he sketched in recollection. For the teenager, the bond of affection between himself and his adoptive father furnished a source of certainty in a problematic world. The rawness of the wound that Roy Percy's death had inflicted made Walker's emotional reliance upon his Greenville cousin deeper still. For Walker Percy, the problem became the effort to break away effectively. He had to find his own voice and ideals and yet remain loyal to the Southern values that his guardian represented. The search for self-mastery affected the novelist's life in two respects: the effort to reach maturity and the struggle toward religious conviction. In both ventures, Percy toiled hard. Although outwardly he seemed casual, his inner feelings were very intense. Always the courteous and soft-spoken gentleman, he hid a layer of bitterness, doubt, and anger that later found an outlet in the practice of art. Oddly enough, as it turned out, he was to be the greater artist when he was angriest and demonic, the least convincing when he was benign and conventional. Throughout his life, but most especially before he reached middle age in the 1960s, the spirit of his guardian remained very much alive in Walker's thoughts. After that, his sense of dependence lessened to a degree, but never his gratitude.

Athletic and sociable, Walker Percy as a teenager in Greenville quickly made friends. Given his sometimes distant manner, though, he limited his closest companions to those who shared his intellectual interests. His best friend in Greenville was Shelby Foote, to whom he entrusted his inmost thoughts throughout his life. Their comradeship had characteristics very similar to those of Thomas George Percy and John Williams Walker, whose name the novelist carried. Foote was the author of several novels, including *Tournament, Jordan Country,* and *Love in a Dry Season.* Later, he won lasting recognition for his stirring three-volume narrative of the Civil War and earned more widespread fame with appearances in Ken Burns's television documentary series on the Civil War.[3] In an interview not a few years ago, Foote remembered the day at the country club that Will Percy invited him to visit his young cousins any time he liked. "Soon afterwards they arrived and I began to go over to their house," Foote recalled, "and they began to come over to my house, and we became good and close friends, which we have been ever since."[4]

Like Walker, young Foote had lost his father when he was very young. Common deprivation may have helped to strengthen the tie between the two boys, but they also held in common a love for—and fear of—Will Percy. Forever getting into scrapes of one kind or another, Foote, helped by young LeRoy, once placed some tennis balls in "Uncle Will's" dining-room chandelier. Phinizy tried to extract them, and the contraption came crashing down. Dutifully the trio marched to the law office. On hearing their confession, "Mr. Will" exploded: "Godammit, people who don't know how to take care of good property shouldn't be allowed around it!" Foote explained that they all "were scared to death of him." At the same time, Will Percy intervened with Foote's mother and his uncle, Morris Rosenstock, to let the boy use his library and famous Capehart phonograph for a week. The school principal had expelled him temporarily for some prank or display of insubordination.[5]

Another schoolmate, Charles Bell, who had a most inquisitive mind, was also drawn into a friendship with Foote and Walker Percy. He was the son of Judge Percy Bell, who had supported Vardaman against Senator's Percy's reelection. Young Bell took special delight in a brass telescope that the boys sometimes hauled out of the house. Walker had inherited it from his father, who had built a terrace off the master bedroom of his house in Birmingham to study the heavens while battling insomnia. (For Walker Percy the instrument was endowed with special meanings of alienation and detachment. In *The Last Gentleman,* the narrator has Will Barrett purchase one in New York to watch, from a great distance, peregrines and passers-by in Central Park.[6]) Charles Bell himself borrowed heavily from the Percy family history in one of his novels, *The Half Gods.* In this semi-autobiography, he created a moody character named Hazlewood, based on Will Percy. As Bell recalled from those early days, Walker's adoptive father had "the outward manner that the mythopoeic type of old gentry displayed."[7]

If melancholy enters Charles Bell's depiction of his friend's guardian, mental disability of a very serious kind was no stranger to the Bell family. Bell's father, a Washington County judge, held strict notions of schoolwork and decorum that contrasted grimly with the free atmosphere of Will Percy's home. Charles Bell continues to blame his father for the soul-killing manner of discipline to which he subjected his children. He used to quiz them on their studies, punishing them when they did not measure up. In 1937, as a Sewanee freshman, Charles's younger brother Percy, a fat but brilliant sixteen-year-old, pushed aside his manuscript poems. He lay on his bed and swallowed a fatal dose of cyanide he had taken from the chemistry laboratory. Lonely and feeling out of place, he chose to die on a dance weekend with girls imported from Ward Belmont in Nashville and other fashionable schools for the annual "Germans." Some years later, desperately ill with cancer, Judge Bell killed himself with a gun that he insisted his son Charles bring to his hospital bed. Thus, depression had more than one victim in the town of Greenville and included individuals whom Walker Percy knew.[8] It might have seemed to him that depression was not solely a family problem but one with wider social implications; as a novelist he was to use the ailment as a metaphor for the barrenness and vacuity of the modern age.

The years in Greenville were hardly unrelieved gloom. Young Percy took part in debating society events and wrote for the school paper, *The Pica.* Walker was at a forensic contest in a neighboring town the day his mother died in the car crash. Camille Sarasson, an attractive and very intelligent editor of *The Pica,* picked Walker to write a gossip column called "The Man in the Moon." The assignment provided a shy boy with a means to reach out to schoolmates. Although he tried to exhibit an outward indifference toward grades and study, Percy possessed an unusual gift of concentration and quick comprehension. He did extremely well at his precollegiate studies.[9]

When as a high school senior Walker Percy began the process of choosing a college, Will Percy passed over his own alma mater, Sewanee. He steered him toward the University of North Carolina. The reason for Will Percy's preference was that Frank Graham, president at Chapel Hill, had gained his respect as an admirable fighter for Southern higher education. By fall 1933 Walker Percy was involved in the typical pursuits of undergraduates. He joined the Sigma Alpha Epsilon fraternity and made many friends but always felt out of place among football fans and undergraduate jokesters. Walker professed to have "sat on the porch for four years, drinking and observing the scene." In truth, he did spend hours in the dark and comfort of the local moviehouse, watching films. He resembled the alienated hero, Binx Bolling, in *The Moviegoer*. Yet he was scarcely as idle in his activities or studies as he claimed. Periodically he wrote for the undergraduate literary journal, the *Carolina Magazine*.[10] According to a recent scholar, he spent considerable time in college pondering "not only the question of vocation but the melancholier one still of what life was really all about."[11] He decided, however, not to pursue literature as Shelby Foote and Charles Bell, later a professor of humanities at St. John's College, were destined to do.[12]

Since Walker Percy was away from home for the first time, a change in outlook might have been expected. Instead he remained faithful to the ideals and tastes of Will Percy. He shared Will's racial views and thought the very idea of integration a betrayal of Southern civilization. Yet young Walker was more politically conservative than his adoptive father. Will Percy supported Franklin Roosevelt with as much ardor as his father LeRoy had championed the President's cousin Theodore many years before. Walker's cynicism reflected his experience in the family; it had taught him to fear abrupt change and rely on tradition.

Yet in choosing a career toward which to direct his studies, Walker Percy distanced himself from the gentlemanly role that Will Percy represented. Unlike "Uncle Will," he hoped not to practice a profession out of a sense of duty to meet family expectations. Nor did he expect to become a writer or poet. Instead, Walker Percy wished to be a man of decision, simplicity, and self-reliance. He sought absolute authority, absolute certainty in coping with a world of unpredictability and tragedy. The pursuit of cold rationality in his array of science courses thus represented something of a break from Will Percy's authority. It defied his adoptive father's distaste for things mathematical, practical, and unromantic. To excel in an area in which his guardian had no expertise at all established a realm apart from Will Percy and his old-fashioned ideals. Walker Percy majored in chemistry and mathematics with the intention of becoming a physician. "I spent four years in the laboratories," he later recalled. "I loved the idea of looking at a microscope slide and seeing all those beautifully stained cells."[13] Another aspect of his scientific interests was their masculine character, contrasting sharply as they did, with the allegedly feminine humanities to which Will Percy was devoted.

Determined that his charges should be allowed to choose their own destiny in a way denied him, Will Percy nevertheless sought to point them toward a good career—so long as it was not the law, in which he had taken so little pleasure. Will helped LeRoy take up farming on a large scale by handing him Trail Lake to manage. He did so, however, only because LeRoy already saw that as his own special interest. With Phinizy, whom he sent off to military school in Chattanooga and then Annapolis, "Uncle Will" was more prescriptive because of the early trauma over the fatal car accident and because Phinizy was the youngest and longest under his direction. Though perhaps more devoted to "Uncle Will" than the others, Phinizy defied his guardian's advice against a legal career. Following World War II, Phinizy left the navy for which career his graduation from Annapolis had prepared him and took up the traditional family profession. Specializing in admiralty law, he practiced for several years in New Orleans and then devoted himself to teaching in the Tulane University Law School. Doubtless, Will Percy, who had died while Phinizy was still at the Naval Academy, would have been immensely proud of his youngest ward's legal career, had he lived to see the outcome.[14]

Will Percy's relationship with Walker was more complex than with the two younger brothers. Sensitive and bookish even when an adolescent in Athens, Georgia, Walker too much resembled his guardian and found it hard to fashion his own sense of specialness. Will Percy understood his needs and recognized that his influence on his adopted son Walker lay less in the kind of vocation that he would adopt than in the sort of moral attitudes he would espouse in his life. He claimed that he would not equip the boys with obsolete instructions for following the code of medieval knights. Yet he came very close to doing exactly that—in the Victorian interpretation of that code—under the rubrics of rectitude, honor, justice, and truth. They could easily identify and follow these unambiguous ideals, Will Percy assured them. Vulgarity often might triumph in the rush of aggrandizers who mocked American honor and sought profit and popularity with the vulgar masses, Percy contended. At the start of World War II, he told a convention of Mississippi editors that the democracies needed "a Peter the Hermit, or a St. Francis" to ignite "a great religious revival" to save Western civilization. Once when Walker Percy was momentarily unhappy about his academic progress, Will Percy wrote him, "My whole theory about life is that glory and accomplishment are of far less importance than the creation of character and the individual good life." Will's stress upon the "broad-sword virtues" of Stoicism belied the more modest sentiment of a "good life" in a contradiction that had been long a part of family sensibility. Yet his advice only made matters worse in a sense. How could anyone live up to the credo—the "unassailable wintry kingdom of Marcus Aurelius" with all its demands for perfection in the face of worldly corruption?[15]

Walker Percy in college was not satisfied with making a small mark in his world. Rather, as Jay Tolson argues, he "was fascinated with heroism and greatness, and wanted both for himself." Like so many perfectionists—Percys and otherwise—Walker feared the humiliation of failure and developed a pose of seeming indifference to the outcome of ambition. Besides, nonchalance was the expected behavior of gentlemen. Fellow collegians and medical-school students wondered how Walker could master topics so easily, since he appeared to spend most of his time prone on a couch reading a novel. One is reminded of Castiglione's *The Book of the Courtier,* in which the writer advises the sixteenth-century gentleman to practice "a certain *sprezzatura* [nonchalance], so as to conceal all art and make whatever is done or said appear to be without effort and almost without any thought about it." Coolness lent an individual grace and caused wonder in others; Walker Percy had that facility. The underside of this manner of appearing was a medieval haughtiness that found expression in Percy's gothic protagonist, Lancelot Lamar, in *Lancelot.*[16]

Summer vacations during both college and medical school prolonged Walker Percy's dependence upon his guardian. With a black chauffeur at the wheel, Will Percy, sometimes aunts Nana and Adah, the boys, and assorted young friends escaped the Delta heat and humidity by fleeing to "the mountain," Sewanee, Tennessee. In 1925 Will Percy and his good friend Huger Jervey had purchased the summer cottage within the University domain that was called Brinkwood. In February 1934, Jervey sold his share to his partner, no doubt because Will Percy would need more room for his adopted sons and their young guests.[17] The sandstone house had six bedrooms and a large living room. It perched over a beautiful ravine (a cove as it is called in the region) on the road to Sherwood, a tiny settlement of mountain people. On one occasion in the late 1930s, Shelby Foote and Walker Percy built a stone pavilion—they called it a "tea house"—on the promontory over the cove. It was a present for "Uncle Will."[18]

For both Will and his adopted sons, Sewanee had many intellectual and recreational attractions. Will Percy could visit with George Boggan Myers, a professor at St. Luke's Seminary and a resident expert on Hegel, William DuBose, and other nineteenth-century philosophers and theologians. He also favored the unmarried women and widows of the mountain with his lively company: Charlotte Gailor, his gardening friend, Mrs. Mary More Sanborn, Mrs. Telfair Hodgson, and others whose company he enjoyed. Sons and daughters of professors and Episcopal bishops and clergymen were in small but lively supply—Robert Daniel, whose great-uncle had been Bishop Frank Gailor of Tennessee; Currin Gass, son of a classics professor; Ted and Buddy Bratton; Mary Shepherd and Jervey Quintard, Huger Jervey's cousins; Rosamond Myers, stunning black-haired daughter of Will's friends George and Margaret Myers.

In the daytime there was golfing, tennis, and woodland swimming at the cascading Fiery Gizzard in neighboring Grundy County. Also, the young people could organize picnics at exquisite mountain views. The group managed to visit all the caves on the plateau before summer ended in 1938. A favorite place for exploring was Lost Cove Cave, just below Brink-wood.[19] The site figures in Percy's *The Second Coming,* although the novel-ist situates it in North Carolina. Near Sewanee was the Monteagle Assem-bly, a Southern Methodist Chatauqua-like enclave. It was the summer home for the Tennessee family of Peter Taylor, another Southern fiction writer, and his wife Eleanor Ross, a poet studying under Caroline Gordon. Father James Flye, mentor and friend of James Agee, the novelist and film critic, was situated at St. Andrew's School for mountain boys, halfway be-tween the two little literary communities. In the mid-1940s, Robert Penn Warren, Andrew Lytle, Robert Lowell and Jean Stafford, Allen Tate, as editor of the *Sewanee Review,* and his wife Caroline Gordon occupied houses in the Monteagle Assembly grounds. Some of them developed life-long ties to Will Percy's charges, Walker, LeRoy, and Phinizy.[20]

As handsome as any Southern young woman could dream of, Walker Percy garnered his share of teenage crushes among the young women on Sewanee mountain. Nearby was Barbara Kirkland, who often brought up young friends from Houston. The young people, including Roz Myers and Alice Hodgson, learned to love the classics from hearing them played on Will's record-player at Brinkwood. Walker, then twenty-four, became in-fatuated with the vivacious seventeen-year-old, Mary Shepherd (Shep) Quintard. She was a freshman at St. Mary's College in Raleigh, North Carolina, at the time. When she lost in the grass the SAE fraternity pin that Walker had given her, the school paper teased her for being suspi-ciously eager to rake leaves on the school's front lawn. As Peter Taylor records in his short stories, in the interwar South summer romances of this variety were likely to be pretty tame by today's standards. As far as Will Percy was concerned, that was as it should be.[21]

Will Percy's influence did not erode even after Walker established him-self in New York. There, in 1937, he began his medical training at the Columbia University's College of Physicians and Surgeons. Huger Jervey periodically fed the busy medical student at his well-appointed West Side apartment. "Hugger" used to go with him to concerts and the theater—whenever Walker Percy's training permitted. "Uncle Will" would arrive in New York, and all three would attend the opera—for instance, Wagner's *Tristan,* which Walker did not much enjoy. The medical student was very impressed, however, with Lotte Lehman's singing in the role of the Marschallin in Strauss's *Der Rosenkavalier.*[22]

Yet on another level Walker Percy recognized that all was not well in his feelings about himself and his family. In need of psychiatric help in sorting things out, he turned to one of Will Percy's friends. From 1930 to 1939, Harry Stack Sullivan maintained a private practice in New York City. Having experienced mental difficulties himself and sometimes in de-spair over his homosexual leanings, Sullivan was particularly effective with depressives and potential suicides. He found it more practical to probe the

earliest rather than the more recent self-destructive temptations and un-
cover the buried language of his patient's fears. Some analysts thought his
approach bordered on the brutal, but patients were more intrigued than
disheartened by his sometimes humorous dismissal of immediate crises.
Walker Percy remembered Sullivan's three-week stay in Will Percy's
house. When he had watched the analyst conducting his field research on
race relations, the young physician had thought him very wrongheaded.
Percy was absorbing matter-of-fact medicine, in which the speculative had
no place. The attraction of science for him had always been its disembodied, detached character. In contrast to the romanticism and subjective sensibilities of "Uncle Will," Walker could adopt the role of the disengaged
investigator. Yet conversations with Sullivan at this time had a marked
effect on Walker, although he perhaps was not aware of it. He later reflected that he had misunderstood Sullivan during the analyst's Greenville
sojourn. His "silence and his peculiar way of doing field work I can only
interpret now as signifying not that there was not a 'problem,' but rather
that the human condition is a very complex business," scarcely to be
grasped through "instant psychoanalysis." [23]

At the end of the 1930s, while he was still in medical school, Percy
did not wish to appreciate Sullivan's subjective, open-minded approach to
medicine, particularly the analyst's insistence upon a physician's engagement with the minds and hearts of patients. Later, in the 1940s and 1950s,
he came to see that the psychiatrist's practice was both humane and humanistic. "Here's the peculiar thing, and I'll never understand why this is
so," Percy quoted Sullivan as saying, "each patient this side of psychosis,
and even some psychotics, has the means of obtaining what he needs, she
needs with a little help from you." [24] Yet whether repelled or attracted by
Sullivan's methods, Percy knew that he had to work things out or suffer
consequences about which he dared not think.

Recognizing the complications of professional and personal exigencies,
the analyst did not take Walker as a patient, although his influence on
the young medical student was nonetheless significant. Sullivan considered
himself too close to the family, having at Will's request, visited Phinizy in
Greenville not long after the car tragedy. Instead, he recommended Janet
Rioch, a New York psychoanalyst from Canada and a most promising pro-
tégée. She was developing a large practice and would in the future treat
some of the leading intellectuals of Manhattan. Long associated with Sullivan, Karen Horney, Erich Fromm, and Clara Thompson, Rioch was less
concerned with theory than with the urgent requirements of the patient.
Like her own analyst, Harry Sullivan, she believed that regional or ethnic
culture played a role in determining the forms in which serious mental
problems appeared. She had been reared by a Canadian father and English
mother in India, where they had been Christian missionaries. Her experience abroad gave her a sophisticated understanding of cultural variation.

The Southern code of honor established very high criteria by which men were expected to prove their manliness and superiority over others. That heritage of high expectation had affected the annals of the Percys. It also marked the Southern elite as a whole, even after the growth of an industrial New South. The penalty for defeat in the arena of honor could sometimes be harsh—as a succession of Percys well recognized. The need to present a brave front in the face of disaster imposed further burdens. How aware Rioch was of such circumstances would be hard to gauge. Undoubtedly she heard enough from Walker about the family's travails to respond with some grasp of the regional context.

Rioch's office at 17 East Fifty-fourth Street was then the typically under-decorated and neutral looking apartment of an analyst.[25] For three years Percy underwent the rigors of prolonged therapy, five days a week. A female analyst might not have seemed the wisest choice for a proud young Southerner, steeped in conservative traditions about the sexual divide. Yet Rioch's distance from the ways of the South could have been itself a great help in their mutual work.[26]

Percy's representation of the experience in Will Barrett's sessions with Dr. Gamov, a fashionable analyst in *The Last Gentleman,* may have come from this experience. If so, the expected transference and degree of openness it is supposed to engender were never completed. Will Barrett parries the doctor's inquiries with Southern courtesy which, for the first year of treatment, "royally *entertained*" the analyst. During the second year of association, however, Gamov grows weary of his dance with a "Southern belle" of a partner, "light on his feet and giving nothing away." Although he likes, even admires the analyst, Will Barrett fashions his "amiability" into a weapon of defense. He secretly feels superior to the lisping doctor and silently mocks the fresh-faced, middle-class Ohioans whom he meets in the group therapy sessions that Gamov has him join. The only clue to his inner life that the patient discloses is a confession of having a "hollowness" at the core of his being. Yet the cause of it never emerges in the years of treatment under Gamov's supervision. The patient still has not learned who he really is when he terminates their relationship early in the story.

Percy's astute rendering of an analytic experience that ends in failure does not, however, necessarily mirror exactly what occurred in his own life. Although experiencing the common difficulties of such an association, most probably he gained more insight into his own life than Will Barrett did. Although he never said so, Walker learned that some uncontrollable force would not inevitably carry him toward the same end that his father had met. At times, though, he may have worried that it might. As analyst Felix Brown has pointed out, the loss of a father is highly calamitous for a child, and the result is very often a strongly depressive reaction. Yet Brown speculates, the mourning process may lead the orphan, if gifted, to develop his or her own resources and imagination. As "a virtue" arising from "necessity," deprivation could have remarkable results. So it was, anyhow, in

Walker Percy's case.[27] Yet Percy himself only reluctantly admitted that the psychoanalytic experience had been worthwhile. He revealed to biographer Linda Hobson that he had been fond of Janet Rioch. Nevertheless, he felt that "he was somehow on the stage in that darkened room talking to her, that he was supposed to talk even when there was nothing to say."[28] There should have been much to say. The problem was Percy's reluctance to speak freely without a disabling fear of shame. For obvious reasons, Rioch's impression of Walker Percy cannot be ascertained. She wrote, however, one article on obstacles in transference in which the case of her brilliant, albeit disguised, Southern patient almost surely emerges.[29]

Transference, Rioch asserted, was itself no easy matter. One of her patients developed "intense feelings of attachment to a father surrogate in his every day life." In working through the essence of that relationship, he grew ever more aware of his resentment of his "real father." When attachment to the surrogate diminished as self-confidence emerged, however, Rioch's patient became increasingly distant from Rioch herself, "believing," as she recounted, "that she was untrustworthy and hostile." What had occurred was a "reëxperiencing" of "an ancient triangle in which he was driven to submissive attachment to a dominating father, due to the utter untrustworthiness of his weak mother." The danger lay in regressing to a submissiveness toward "the surrogate father" rather than maturing toward independence. Yet she reported, her patient worked through the problem to achieve "a new insight."[30] In reporting their findings, analysts often condense their case histories to the point where complexities and nuances of the situation are omitted: such was Rioch's account. No mention was made of the violence of the parents' deaths—circumstances that made transference and trust hard to achieve. Nor did she comment on the bachelorhood of the surrogate father.[31]

No one will ever know with indisputable certainty how Walker Percy's psychoanalytic experience ought to be assessed. He gave out different readings, all of which made sense but showed an ambivalence toward the field of medicine he once might have entered himself. "Sullivan," the novelist recalled, "wasn't sure what ailed me, and I wasn't either. I must say that, after three years, five days a week, Dr. Rioch and I still weren't sure."[32] He confessed that he had once thought "Freud was the answer, and he is indeed a great man." Nevertheless, he continued, "I elevated him far beyond the point that even he would place himself."[33] Later, to an interviewer he offered his chief objection to Freud. Unlike the more optimistic Sullivan, whose attitudes Percy placed in the words and activities of psychiatrist Tom More of *The Thanatos Syndrome,* Freud had erred in his predetermined pessimism. Percy criticized Freud's conclusion "that we are no longer sovereigns of our own consciousness."[34] In one of his most thoughtful articles on life in contemporary America, he was more generous-minded about the profession. In a show of medical snobbery, he remarked that in contrast to the amateur—"the social worker in Des

Moines or the sophomore psychology student"—the expert analyst "is more apt to be eclectic," a description, perhaps, of Sullivan and Rioch.[35] Yet Percy had learned much about himself even if much yet remained to be nailed down.

To judge by the literary results, the experience was not wasted because he showed an unusual awareness of the human dilemma. As Donald Winnicott, the English analyst, declared, psychoanalysis offers the patient "the possibility of self-knowledge" and "the opportunity for a second chance."[36] Perhaps that was the case in Walker Percy's experience, one that he later translated into the "second coming" of the religious conversion. The question naturally arises: what was the character of Will Percy's role in Walker Percy's psychological development? Their relationship was complicated. Courageous, witty, sophisticated, and generous, Will expected great things from the boys, a degree of perfection that had been the family criterion for generations. The goals he set could be inspirational but also paralyzing.

Even more perplexing is the question of Will Percy's sexuality and what Walker Percy made of it. Anne Jones, a recent reviewer of Jay Tolson's biography of Walker Percy, remarks that he failed to mention this matter. She proposes that at the least the novelist "lived in a world of great epistemological pain because he could not have missed the clues."[37] No evidence exists that Walker Percy knew anything much about his adoptive father's private life, whether by willful denial or not. He had such serious concerns about his biological parents that he did not give the matter much thought. Yet Will Percy's habit of populating the house largely with men helped to reinforce a general Southern pattern of privileging men over women. Yet too much could be made of that issue. After all, Charlotte Gailor, Adah Williams and Aunt Nana, and other single women were residents or neighbors, and Will Percy welcomed having young people of both sexes in his house in Greenville or at Brinkwood. Yet a rigid Victorian code about the proprieties was very much observed on the premises—as indeed they were in many upper-class houses of that day in the South and elsewhere. Yet outward conformities could not hide the ambivalences of Southern sexual mores, particularly in regard to Will Percy's bachelorhood.

Walker Percy no doubt thought much more about his adoptive father's unmarried state than he cared to express. His position on this point was very traditional in the South. In the 1930s, collegians like Walker Percy, even the athletes, happily tolerated and even made close friends with teachers or older bachelor mentors. Today, fairly or not, anyone would at once suspect the advisers of being closet homosexuals. At an earlier day, however, such figures would have been stigmatized as effeminate or, more delicately, "funny" fellows, and the matter would end there. Curiously, the South of the mid-twentieth century countenanced eccentrics of all kinds because they were rare enough to be harmless so long as public scandal did not erupt about them. When he was growing up, Walker felt at ease with his guardian's friends whose sexual orientation differed greatly from Walker's inclinations. As a medical student he often seemed to place himself in the kind of company that Will favored because it was familiar and unthreatening. His teacher of pathology, a subject to which he was intellectually drawn, was well known for both his erudition and his favoritism toward handsome male students.

Bachelor counselors, usually learned and witty, served as significant father figures but restrained themselves from criticizing their young friends in a way that real fathers seldom did. Many Southern colleges had their avuncular, unmarried professors—the Centaurs, teachers of the gods, as Will Percy dubbed them. As far as the community was concerned their lives were unblemished and for the most part probably were. Sewanee had its examples of the chaste breed to whom Walker Percy, Shelby Foote, and many others were genuinely devoted. They were the male counterparts of the genteel widows and unmarried women of meager resources who served as fraternity house and dormitory mothers. No one gave a thought about the sexual interests of these nurturing figures, male or female. Yet these same young collegians fully endorsed the Southern cultural taboo against homosexuality and condemned it along with effeminacy of manner whenever it appeared among their giddier classmates. Appearances, as always, mattered. What no one saw or heard about directly had no greater repercussions in the mid-twentieth-century South than in the military services.

This approach, so much a part of upper-class Southern culture itself, was complementary to a young adult male's ambivalence about women. The opposite sex was supposed to be gentle, lovable, and chaste, but another sort of woman was alleged to be "bad," carnal, and corrupting of a young man's morals. The either/or aspect of womanhood bred confusion and even hostility in the well-brought-up, young, Southern white man. For instance, in the mid-1930s Katherine Grantham Rogers, a friend of the North Carolina writer W. J. Cash, mocked his prissy and Victorian views of women. "You are subconsciously just another sentimental Victorian male, strictly dividing females into just two classes—the all good and all bad," she reported later to have scolded him. Walker Percy has Will Barrett echo these familiar Southern sentiments. The hero laments that he is "neither Christian nor pagan nor proper lusty gentleman, for I've never really got the straight of this lady-and-whore business." Kitty Vaught, Will Barrett's girl friend, agrees: "You've been brought up to think it an ugly thing whereas it should be the most beautiful thing in the world." [38]

Walker Percy's ambivalence about sex was almost Victorian. Though much was said about lechery in his novels, he was seldom graphic in descriptions of bedroom scenes (*The Second Coming* excepted). Instead, he followed the older practice of fadeouts or satirical remarks, "all her charms in his arms." From his perspective, the erotic, as he told Foote, diverted the writer and the reader from greater concerns about genuine love and other motions of the soul.[39] At the same time, the fiction-writer recognized that a degree of lustiness, according to the Southern code of honor, was to be prized. Homoerotic behavior was a sin of deepest shame. Such were the fixed rules of sexuality in which Walker Percy grew to maturity. Yet in *The Last Gentleman,* Dr. Sutter Vaught, perhaps speaking for the author, argues for a more generous perspective. "The major discovery of my practice: that there are probably no such entities as 'schizophrenia' and 'homosexuality,' conceived as Platonic categories, but only peevishness, revenge, spitefulness, dishonesty, fear, loneliness, lust and despair." Thus what makes up a person is not psychosis or sexual orientation but the sins of the flesh and of the world. Sutter Vaught finds no mental or spiritual release in his heterosexuality although he keeps trying through heedless promiscuity to discover himself. Percy's heroic figure of the grandly melancholic physician becomes almost Faustian in his concupiscence. Vaught sells his soul, so to speak, by fornicating with women to divert his thoughts from both depression and the compulsion to kill himself. He cannot really love a woman but only bed with her in movements that the sterile relationship renders meaningless. Will Percy stigmatized such behavior as "rutting," and Walker Percy agreed with that condemnation even as he found something distinctly heroic and manly in it, too.[40]

Behind the matter of fornication as opposed to love was the issue of father-son relations in Walker's life. The subject ran like a recurring theme in a symphony throughout the Percys' history. It began, in a sense when the genial Lieutenant Robert Percy set out literally to reestablish his link with his absconding parent, the founder of the American family. It took a new turn when Thomas George, in a life of placid gentility and brotherly affection for John Walker, found a way to overcome paternal abandonment. Will Percy's yearning for Senator LeRoy Percy's respect remained central in their troubled relationship. Similarly, Walker Percy's love for and gratitude toward Will Percy extended as far as to make his life, in a sense, a fulfillment of his surrogate father's. He would love and marry a woman, an achievement that Will Percy's nature precluded. Walker would have the children that Will could never have sired. In addition, he would complete the religious journey that Will Percy had deserted in his cheerless adoption of Stoic integrity. Walker would fulfill the literary promise that had steadily eluded his surrogate father. Perhaps Will Percy had the finer sensibilities, but as a writer he could never have achieved as much as Walker. Will Percy could not bear to venture beyond the Victorian conventions and the memories of his childhood years. Walker was fortunate to mature in a less burdened, less mannered age. In following or even completing his surrogate father's course and improving on it, Walker Percy would also perpetuate the extraordinary vitality and glory of the family. Above all he would show his gratitude for a guardian who loved him in a way that the real father had been too dejected to offer.

Not long after the decision to stop the analysis with Janet Rioch, Percy faced two major misfortunes—the death of his guardian and his own loss of good health. He graduated with honors from medical school in 1941 and looked forward to specializing in pathology or psychiatry. The cold exactitude of pathology much attracted him. Yet he was also captivated by Janet Rioch's field. "I think I would've ended up in psychiatry," he later was reported to have said. "Pathology is the most elegant of the medical fields, and psychiatry the most interesting. I felt more at home on the psychiatric ward than anywhere else. . . . Maybe it takes one to know one." [41] Yet before he could reach a decision, Walker discovered that "Uncle Will's" health was declining rapidly. When he died, in January 1942, the blow fell heavily on all three of his adopted sons. An Annapolis midshipman at the time, Phinizy Percy was the least prepared. His brothers had not informed him about "Uncle Will's" decline during the previous months. He mourned him most deeply. "Nothing like that had ever happened to me before or since," Phinizy later recalled. "I felt cut adrift. The anchor was gone." Knowing the inevitability of his death, Walker's reaction was less passionate, but he mourned perhaps longer than anyone else. [42]

A second misfortune was equally serious for the medical student. Working with destitute patients at Bellevue Hospital during his internship, in the year preceding his guardian's death, Walker Percy grew overtired. Perhaps, too, he was disstracted by Will Percy's failing health. Like three others in his group of twelve interns, Walker neglected the precautions necessary when close to the diseases that a city hospital must treat. The interns had to work with little time for sleep; in their haste they sometimes forgot to wear masks or surgical gloves, when examining the cadavers of transients and "floaters"—bodies hauled out of the Hudson and East rivers. Chest pains and a persistent cough alerted him. He had developed pulmonary tuberculosis.

Spiritually and also physically the disease laid him low for the next few years—throughout World War II. Perhaps he wondered if he were not destined for an early death like so many of the male Percys. (Later, in his seventies, he loved to rejoice that he had outlived all the men in the American clan.) Literary critic Lewis Lawson suggests that he may have felt a sense of providential betrayal: the scientist, bent on a detached approach to humanity, finds himself instead the victim of a predictable natural order in which he had invested his hopes. Immediately he hastened to the Adirondack Cottage Sanitarium at Saranac Lake. The tuberculosis center, founded by Edward L. Trudeau in 1885, had by this time achieved world fame. Once installed there, Walker had a chance to ruminate on his misfortune and the vagaries of fate. "I was in bed so much, alone so much,"

Walker Percy recalled, "I had nothing to do but read and think. I began to question everything I had once believed. . . . I knew so very much *about* man, but had little idea what man is." He might have also added that he wished to know what it meant to be a Percy in a war-torn world that seemed headed for the apocalyptic ruin that his guardian had predicted.[43]

With his career checked, his intellectual confidence shattered, Walker Percy grew despondent. On a visit to Saranac, his friend Shelby Foote found him "gaunt and pale," and resigned to the "life of a hermit." He would have preferred to see his invalid friend "out in the world, near people." To Phinizy on leave from naval training, his brother "looked shattered and uncertain." Adding to his other worries, Walker was grieving still for the loss of "Uncle Will." Writing a very short note to a former Chapel Hill classmate in 1943, he mentioned a miniature of his guardian that he had left in New York; clearly "Uncle Will" was much on his mind. In the same letter, Walker tried to sound as cheerful as possible. He declared himself almost cured, he wrote his friend, a naval officer stationed in Alaska, as though he were trying to convince himself. Nevertheless, he admitted that he felt a tremendous weight of self-loathing. Dejection never aids medical healing, and with tuberculosis it may lead to decline and death. A Swiss sanitarium for consumptives once displayed the inscription, "Hilares mox sani." It meant the cheerful are soon cured. Under the circumstances, however, good spirits were not easy to sustain.[44]

Years later, Walker Percy remembered the period of his illness with more fondness than he felt at the time, claiming: "I was the happiest man ever to contract tuberculosis, because it enabled me to get out of Bellevue and quit medicine."[45] Such a resolve may have been the outcome. Reaching it was another matter. At the time he was still undecided about whether to enter pathology or psychiatry. The first choice engages the doctor in a confrontation with tissues and bone instead of a living and demanding patient. The second career would mean a rejection of scientific precision. Moreover, the results would be as uncertain as those he had reached in Janet Rioch's office. No doubt he must have wondered if his own analysis had left too many issues still unresolved. Enforced rest, with naps every afternoon, and structured routines were then considered the best remedies for the disease.

Life at Trudeau was comfortable, perhaps too much so because it was like being incarcerated in a well-maintained nursery for grown-ups. The regimen sent Walker Percy back to those earlier days when he had listened to "Uncle Will's" Capehart and read novels while lounging on the veranda. The invalid was ridden with guilt and became restless. He avidly followed the news bulletins and cursed a fate that denied him the experience of military combat. "Uncle Will" had proclaimed warfare a source of his own empowerment, and through the generations, Percys had always carried a martial spirit. His brothers were engaged in a war that made much greater sense than the one in which Will Percy had fought. Like his father in World War I, Walker's brother LeRoy had become an Army Air Force pilot. An Annapolis graduate, brother Phinizy served in the Pacific and, repeating Will Percy's success, won high military honors, including the Navy Cross. (One of Phinizy's shipmates in the squadron of patrol boats, was John F. Kennedy.)[46] Under these circumstances, for a proud man like Walker Percy a bedroom instead of a wardroom or cockpit seemed infantile.

"To be homeless and in exile," declares the theologian and philosopher Ralph Harper, "is as old and sad as the hills; to be metaphysically homeless and to care is new."[47] The recovering consumptive at the end of World War II must have felt this way. As Robert Coles observes, Walker Percy's brothers returned from the war and quickly settled themselves. They got on with the business of life, in contrast to his own loneliness and irresolution in the face of his future. LeRoy Percy returned to the management of Trail Lake plantation turned over to him by "Uncle Will" in 1939. LeRoy had married Sarah Farish, exquisite daughter of Hazelwood Farish, Will Percy's gentle, shrewd law partner. Forsaking a continued career in the navy, Phinizy took some courses at Sewanee in the summer and fall of 1946, while enjoying the company of the local young people. In 1952 he entered the law school at the University of Virginia. Like Walker, the two brothers were also fulfilling aspects of Will's life that had not been so successful. Finding a wretched state of affairs at Trail Lake, LeRoy learned how to make it both a model plantation and a profitable one. He filled his surrogate father's shoes in local civic affairs. After graduating high in his class at law school, Phinizy became the fully dedicated legal professional that Will Percy never was. Thus all three built upon and, in their separate spheres of action, surpassed the record bequeathed them by their guardian.[48]

Yet for all the negative aspects of Walker Percy's illness, he had not wasted his time at Saranac. Instead, he later perceived it in the light of what Erik Erikson describes as a sensitive young man's "moratorium." At this time of reflection, the youthful male finally settles on his choice of career. Percy called the period at Saranac "turning the corner." By the phrase he meant his discovery that while science could explain mechanisms, its practitioners could not explore the experience of pain, the reality of beauty, or the puzzle of human existence. The process of knowing himself and the strength of his aims had begun, but progress was slow. More than most writers, his apprenticeship in the craft was so prolonged that his first novel was not published until he was forty-five years old.

Gradually, the illness abated, and he was discharged from the Trudeau Sanitarium. In the spring of 1945 Percy took up residence with Huger Jervey and began teaching in the Columbia medical school. In May, however, an X-ray revealed a resurgence of the bacillus. Rather than return to Saranac, Percy went to a similar institution, Gaylord Farm, in Wallingford,

Connecticut. It was most disheartening to start all over again. According to Jay Tolson, at this time Walker came up with the idea of leaving medicine to start a literary career despite his scientific training. He arrived at Gaylord fully armed with boxes of books. In a sense, a return to the pen instead of the scalpel was a coming home—to the life of the mind to which Will Percy would have loved to have pledged his days. Walker Percy found that he could best free himself from "Uncle Will" by making good on the dreams of literary achievement that his guardian had entertained but could not wholly realize. Several agonizing years would pass, however, before the resolve became firm. Although the eldest brother, he was still unmarried. He hoped to remedy the situation promptly but still lacked a clear idea about what kind of woman would suit him best.[49]

Although he quickly regained his health and was discharged, Walker Percy had to recognize that the illness inhibited his chances for marriage. Uncertain of his next move, he took up residence at Brinkwood, at age twenty-nine. Events that took place there were to provide the mood and themes of both *The Moviegoer* and *The Last Gentleman*. By spring 1945, when he arrived in Sewanee, Rosamond Myers, whom he had dated before the war, had returned to the mountain. After graduating from "Ole Miss" in Oxford, where she was "Cotton Queen" in 1942, she joined the American Red Cross and served in the North African and Italian theaters campaigns.[50] While overseas, she had received Walker's letters from his sickbed at Saranac. Her formidable, Long Island-bred mother had discovered that a relationship with Walker was budding and was most concerned. "I have written her a very strong letter, which I hated to do," Margaret Myers recorded in her diary. "He has tuberculosis, and more than that, he is fundamentally poles apart from [Rosamond]." By that she meant his Catholic background, a matter of deep religious and cultural concern to the Myers, all of them Episcopalians. In a reply from North Africa to her mother, Rosamond stoutly retorted that she was no "Miss Romantic" and much too busy to get tied down to anyone. Soon afterwards, she fell in love with a British Army officer, Peter Thornton, and returned home all but formally affianced. Despite her commitment to Thornton, who was unable to come at once to Sewanee to claim her, Walker Percy pursued Rosamond as if she were still unattached—or at least that was the appearance of things. Walker was traveling back and forth between Sewanee and Greenville throughout the winter, spring, and early summer of 1946.[51]

To her unnecessarily worried parents' relief, Rosamond decided to marry Peter Thornton and relinquish whatever suit Walker had in mind. "In such desperate straits because of his TB," Margaret Myers recorded, Walker "had decided to fill up his life" chasing Mary Shepherd Quintard, "as a life saver" after Rosamond had turned him down. The facts were somewhat different. All along Percy's chief love interest had been "Sheppie" Quintard. To her alone he had confided his having seen an analyst in New York. By this time Mary Shepherd had married an Episcopal clergyman, then struggling in the Baptist ocean of southeastern Georgia, and she escaped for a time by visiting her mother in Sewanee. Members of the Episcopalian community clucked noisily about the scandal of Walker's pursuit of Rosamond, who was pledged to an English war hero, and then of Mary Shepherd, married to a man of the Anglican cloth. Anthony Trollope could not have fancied a more cloistered romance at Barchester.[52] Sundry faculty, matrons, and widows, the reigning vice chancellor, and various church canons scuttled back and forth among the principals. Then the storm clouds passed in a matter of weeks. Percy retreated from romantic adventures and spent the mid-summer of 1946 reading and visiting with Robert Daniel, Charlotte Gailor's nephew. Charlotte Gailor served as the parentless Robert's legal guardian, a position parallel to that of her friend Will Percy.[53]

"After stirring up the dove cotes" at Sewanee, as novelist Caroline Gordon gossiped, Walker Percy returned to Greenville unattached.[54] Yet he continued to act for a short time in ways that the Sewanee elders considered ill-judged. He acted during this time as if confused about who he was and what he wanted to become. Unable to resolve key issues, he sought to nerve himself by proposing marriage to one or another woman, only this time in Greenville, just as he had in Sewanee. When things looked most promising, he would then slip out of sight. Did he try to emulate Roy Pratt Percy's marriage to the elegant Mattie Sue but then fear he could not measure up? He was very much like his character Binx Bolling in *The Moviegoer,* whose self-characterization opens this chapter. For Walker Percy the mid-1940s were years of particular anguish as he sought to free himself from a past that hovered so menacingly.

The episodes of thwarted love signified a desire for positive relationships with women but also a contrary fear of some kind of inadequacy. Walker seemed especially conflicted about the kind of women whom most of his contemporaries would have prized above all others. These were the beauty queens, the lively talkers, the ones to be found at the college stadium on fall afternoons cheering the football heroes. He dreamed of being a success with women of that sort but usually found some convenient impediment in the situation which he thought excused him from further engagement. The women he chose were not college flirts but very appropriate choices for a man of intellect, had they been free of entanglement. Undoubtedly the experience at Sewanee had helped him mature so that he was prepared for marriage in earnest within a few months.[55]

For several years in Greenville he had been periodically dating Bernice (Bunt) Townsend. They had met at a Greenville dispensary where both were working, she as a medical technician, and a mutual interest developed. In the late summer of 1946 Percy postponed any final decision about marriage and career, however, by suggesting to Shelby Foote a motor excursion to Santa Fe, New Mexico. Walker Percy recalled, "I went to Indian corn dances out at the pueblos, met some of the writers and artists who had settled there in the wake of D. H. Lawrence and Georgia O'Keeffe, and saw plenty of their hangers-on, like wealthy divorcees from Westchester." With thoughts of finding a job nearby, he stayed for several weeks on a dude ranch owned by a befriending bachelor named Jim Whittaker.[56] After four months in New Mexico, when Percy and Shelby Foote returned east, Walker had decided to marry. Walker came to realize that Bunt was the only woman with whom he wished to spend the rest of his life. With Foote on hand as best man, the couple were wed in a New Orleans Baptist church on November 6, 1946.

The match could hardly have been more beneficial to the future author. From the start Bunt understood her husband's need for stability. Just as Will Percy had provided him with independent means, making steady work unnecessary, she protected him from an intruding world. Never robust after the sieges of consumption, Walker required the continuation of a steadying, commonsensical influence. Fulfilling that need, Bunt also had an intuitive sense about what was best for her brilliant husband who required time and peace for reading and writing.

Walker Percy had already begun preparing himself for the literary life that he would pursue with Bunt's assistance. During the years of recovery from tuberculosis, at Saranac, Gaylord, and Sewanee, the future novelist spent his days reading, almost obsessively. Shelby Foote recalled a visit with Walker Percy not long after his friend had entered Saranac. He was serenely lying "flat on his back and holding on to those books for dear life."[57] Where Will Percy and other members of the family found warfare a means to forget themselves and meet a family duty, Walker Percy sought the same sense of fulfillment by taking the exacting path of philosophical and religious self-instruction. "Suffering," he later exclaimed, "is an evil, yet at the same time through the ordeal of suffering one gets these strange benefits of lucidity, of seeing things afresh."[58]

Most of the writers who attracted him had themselves undertaken a quest for release from an inner agony. As a youngster he had voraciously consumed the nineteenth-century romantic classics, Dickens, Scott, and the poetry of Arnold, Tennyson, and Browning. These were authors who had fit the tastes of Will Percy. In his mature years Walker Percy did not forget them—Dickens's *Bleak House* was a favorite. However, he expanded his horizons by immersing himself in those who wrote of a world drained of honor, chivalry, and sentiment. Knowing his inclinations, Shelby Foote urged Walker Percy to read the work of Marcel Proust. The French novelist had declared that a writer was forced to compose because he had to find his own mislaid history. Such a position had relevance to both these Southern writers. Although he was himself, like Proust, a victim of depression, Percy did not at first heed Foote's advice. He could not finish

Swann's Way and thought the author too pretentious and snobbish. Proust's works, however, later became part of his library.[59]

Walker Percy found the fiction of Feodor Dostoevsky preferable, and the Russian novelist remained his steadfast companion on the way toward self-knowledge: *The Brothers Karamazov; Notes from the Underground; The Idiot; Crime and Punishment.* Walker Percy named *Brothers Karamazov,* first read when he was still a teenager, as one of the greatest influences on his intellectual development. The work explains the theme of suffering as an agent of redemption. Years later Walker Percy claimed that Dostoevsky's fiction introduced him to the intimate connection that may exist between novelist and reader. "How can I not connect *The Brothers Karamazov* with the big fat Random House edition, fat as a Bible, its pages slightly pulpy, crumbling at the corners and smelling like bread? . . . And how can I disconnect Ivan and Mitya from reading about them sitting in a swing on my grandmother's porch in Athens, Georgia, in the 1930s?"[60]

In the search for something in which modern men could believe, Percy judged Dostoevsky's work particularly relevant. The Russian romantic, pessimistic and conservative, understood both the emptiness of dejection and its antidote, faith in God by which self-alienation could be overcome. In the wayfarer's search for salvation, Dostoevsky claimed, all the negative elements of the human psyche, even a wooing of despair had to be honored as prelude to the rapture of the mystical experience. "Dostoevsky," Percy once said, "knew how hungry we all are for faith, but how hard it is to find—and to keep."[61] All his reading, Percy later remarked, brought him to an inspired realization of literary intent. "I discovered that my feeling of outsidedness, of abstraction, of distance, of alienation, or whatever, was nothing more nor less than what the modern writers had been writing about for a hundred years."[62]

Thomas Mann's autobiographical novel *The Magic Mountain,* about a young sanitarium inmate in search of meaning in life, when, as Goethe had put it, "viewed from the heights of reason, all life looks like a disease and the world like a madhouse."[63] So powerful was this influence that Percy's unpublished, apprentice-novel, *The Gramercy Winner* is based upon *The Magic Mountain* and his own experience at Saranac. Franz Kafka, yet another alienated writer, and Count Tolstoy were the melancholy Southerner's other natural companions.[64]

Percy's reading was directed toward a better understanding of depression and also a search for religious truth which involved a return to the church that his guardian had quit a half-century before. Will, however, would never have admitted just how spiritually inclined he always had been. Will's poems spoke of inmost feelings and often dealt with problems of belief, spiritual life, and wonder at the mystery of God. He had a thirst that had not been quenched when he abandoned the religion of his mother Camille.

Some of Will Percy's most impressive and simplest verses, written in

1924, were called "His Peace." In them, Will had dwelt upon a consequence of divine grace that Walker would many years later make a theme
in his novels: the solitariness and affliction that the Christian pilgrim experiences even when equipped with the favor of grace. In "His Peace," the
poet recalls the simple, contented "fisher-folk" whose hearts had been
filled by the peace of God, a blessing that also "broke them." John died
alone at Patmos; Peter was crucified "head-down." They had followed
their Savior but discovered, as all mortals would, that "The peace of God,
it is no peace,/ But strife closed in the sod." Yet despite the accompanying
anguish, the poet urges his Christian brothers to "pray for but one thing,/
The marvelous peace of God." With music set by David M. Williams, the
verses were incorporated into the 1940 hymnbook for the Episcopal
Church. Percy gave permission for some changes in the poem to make it
more suitable for worship but refused to let the last verse be omitted. To
do so would render the poem meaningless, he insisted.[65]

As Walker Percy contemplated his religious yearnings, he recognized
that "Uncle Will" was right in insisting that the human condition did not
allow easy answers. In Will's opinion there was no rest in life, no freedom
from pain, only temporary moments of companionship and rapture. Such
had been his own experience, and indeed, the experience of a family, always striving for perfection, for honor, for justice. That was what mattered—the heroic struggle for a noble cause. In Will's judgment, redemption ends in a bleak prospect, in the "sod," not in heaven. In another of
Will's work called "An Epistle from Corinth," the poet as Greek warrior
argues with the Apostle Paul, whose asceticism distorts human realities. "I
know the loveliness/ Of flesh and its sweet snare," the Greek soldier
boasts, but Paul considers his statement nearly blasphemous and the Greek
is "hurt" and retreats into solitude. Will Percy felt that one of his solitary
temperament could not find even an anguished peace in God, but Walker
Percy, more hopeful than his guardian, would do so.[66] Part of Walker
Percy's understanding of the Christian message remained tied to Will
Percy's vision of agonized moral struggle. Moreover, he found in his guardian's severe and morally demanding code an authoritarian undertone which
could be translated into the hierarchy and rule of Catholicism. By becoming a Catholic, Walker Percy in a sense was fulfilling a mission that Will
Percy as his surrogate father had begun but cast aside. In mid-December
1947, he was baptized at Holy Name Church in New Orleans. Walker
used the name John as his baptismal name.[67] It was first derived from his
grandfather, John Walker Percy (the TCI attorney), then his great-great-
uncle, the non-practicing physician who had died in 1864, and finally
his great-great-grandfather Thomas George's best friend, John Williams
Walker. The onomastic choice symbolized the continuity of his religious
decision itself, for within the family annals there were precedents for Catholic allegiance: Cousin Will, Camille Percy, Eleanor Percy Lee, Jane
Percy LaRoche.

Percy's conversion to Rome was very closely tied to his psychoanalytic experience, which was, in a sense, a secular version of the confessional sacrament. During his consumptive years, he came to realize that the scientific and medical approach was insufficient because it led toward diagnosis, categorization, and typology, not particularity. One of his closest friends at Saranac had been Arthur Fortugno, a devout Catholic from whom he learned much about the church he eventually joined.[68] As Walker and Bunt settled into their life in New Orleans, the future novelist became ever more certain that he had made the right decision.

Shelby Foote was among the first to learn of his friend's sincerity and was appalled. He found his conversion a grave disappointment and a timid withdrawal from the demands of the artist. In a writer especially, Foote insisted, doubt was a source of inspiration, whereas religious conviction forced one to draw back. Writers served as a vanguard for God's holy men and women, Foote argued, and delved into corners where they dared not enter. If that be sin, then he would proudly bear the consequences. Percy, however, did not think of himself as an artist in the way Foote did, and so informed him. Was the choice really between suicide and sin? Foote asked. In *The Last Gentleman,* the character Sutter Vaught draws exactly that conclusion about his life of loveless love-making—lewdness and self-destruction—one or the other, perhaps both.[69]

Despite Foote's predictions, once Walker Percy became a convert to Rome, he felt free to experiment with writing. His first published efforts, however, were not fiction.[70] From 1953 to 1958, he published articles in philosophical journals. They proved his mastery of the professional language. The ideas, though, might strike generalists as disembodied, as if he were trying to evade those human emotions which he could not yet face. Percy was most attracted to those philosophers of language in that confident postwar era who were much influenced by behavioral psychology. To the man of medicine in him, their work at first had seemed to provide answers to all manner of human difficulties. Gradually, however, he found that uncritical faith in empiricism created what he was to call "the disastrous mind-matter split."[71] Scientific rationalism was a source of spiritual malaise in the modern world. It also failed to fill a sense of emptiness which he found in himself. In the 1950s, dissatisfied, he began to challenge the behavioral approach in the field of linguistics. He anticipated a position that Noam Chomsky was to adopt in his 1959 review of B. F. Skinner's *Verbal Behavior* and in subsequent, revolutionary studies.[72]

Meanwhile Percy was also reading Jean-Paul Sartre, Gabriel Marcel, and Martin Heidegger. He rejected, however, the nihilism and, of course, the communism of Sartre, and Heidegger's disclosure of "being-for-death" in the human psyche.[73] Throughout his life as an artist Walker Percy frequently returned to Dante, Pascal, and Cervantes, all of whom had much to say of loneliness and despair. Yet sometime during the early fifties, he undertook the more arduous business of coming to grips with Søren Kierkegaard, another "melancholy Dane." The French existentialists honored Kierkegaard as their intellectual progenitor. Existentialist thought was then a major concern among American philosophers. Percy steeped himself in that tradition. He called attention to the vacuity of "everydayness," the monotonous routines that dulled the senses and the minds of ordinary people, but most especially the upper-class professional heroes of his novels. In "The Man on the Train (1958)" he pointed out that writing, even reading, about alienation, was "affirmatory and glad," whereas to feel estranged was an "unspeakable" hell.[74]

Walker Percy was preparing himself to become a novelist. He and his wife moved to Covington, Louisiana, in 1948. The small community across Lake Ponchartrain from New Orleans was conveniently close to city life, yet quiet enough for a writer to do his work without distractions. On Wednesdays he customarily met with brother Phinizy who taught law at Tulane, and other friends, some of them also writers and artists, for an extended lunch hour. They ate and drank in the back room at Bechac's, a hundred-year-old restaurant on the lake shore. The camaraderie broke the monotony, and sometimes the company raised issues for which Percy found literary uses. He once remarked that the weekly gathering helped to disperse "the special demons that haunt writers."[75]

CHAPTER SEVENTEEN

Walker Percy: The Making of a Southern Novelist

> Your friend, William Faulkner said many fool-
> ish things but he said one true thing: if a writer
> doesn't write, he is sure to commit moral out-
> rages.
>
> Walker Percy to Caroline Gordon, 1972[1]

Walker Percy's venture into novel-writing was unusually slow for a major author. The translation of disturbing recollections into fiction can be a formidable task. Despite the difficulties, the process makes possible a sense of distance from the immediacy of personal pain. Very few, however, have the talent, self-possession, or persistence to achieve a successful degree of objectivity. Percy possessed the attributes, and they account for his impact on readers. His novels especially move those who recognize their own situations and moments of despair in his presentation of characters and plot. As the literary critic Lewis Lawson puts it, a close reading of Percy's work taught him "what to think about, the uncertainties," and to understand that "not thinking about them is a wasted life."[2]

In reaching the plateau of highly engaging self-expression, the novelist exceeded his guardian's attempts in both poetry and memoir. Walker had advantages, though, that his guardian lacked, most particularly the companionship of a wife. Being married and rearing children furnished him with social permission to be a writer, an occupation too often regarded in the South as emasculating. Beyond that, his wife Bunt gave him the encouragement, freedom from distracting routines, and above all, the stability that Walker, often depressed, needed to carry on. Will Percy, as a bachelor whose mannerisms aroused suspicions, had neither social license nor a wife to help him over the hard places. The family had forced him to be a small-town lawyer with demanding civic responsibilities instead of urging him to become the full-time writer he might have been. Besides, needing the income, Will Percy had little choice. In contrast, Walker Percy benefited from his guardian's earlier sacrifice; his share of Will Percy's estate sustained him during years of apprenticeship and rejection slips.

Also, Walker inherited the legacy of the Southern Renaissance in letters that had produced Faulkner, Eudora Welty, Robert Penn Warren, Allen Tate, and Tennessee Williams. The regional literary profession had become almost a cottage industry, partly a result of the South's economic revival and diversification after World War II. The old mistrust of reclusives who spent their days huddled over a typewriter was gradually eroding. Walker, in need of a more metropolitan location, abandoned Greenville for the environs of New Orleans. Nonetheless the hometown fathers were proud that its remarkable string of twentieth-century authors, including Hodding Carter, David Cohn, and Will Percy—and later Shelby Foote and Ellen Douglas—brought national or at least regional fame to the Delta community.[3]

In short, Walker Percy could be exactly who he wanted to be, and no one could gainsay his choice. Moreover, the postwar climate of intellectual expansiveness washed away the repressive atmosphere in which Will Percy had functioned. Instead, Walker Percy felt no social impediments about what he wrote—whether it concerned race, sex, psychiatry, religion, or any other topic. (Walker, however, was no hack writing bodice-rippers, and only in later works did gentlemanly inhibitions drop away.) For that liberty of expression he could in part thank William Faulkner. Even had he so wished, Will Percy could not have dealt frankly with matters about which most men and women in Greenville of his social class spoke only in whispers—and do even today.

෫ ඊ

Free from the obstacles that had restricted Will Percy's literary ventures, Walker Percy entered the profession at a moment well suited to his intellectual needs. Recollections differ, but he may have begun his first effort, *The Charterhouse,* in Sewanee, when he and Bunt lived at Brinkwood shortly after their marriage in 1946. The site was not congenial for writing. Brinkwood, the summer cottage on the edge of the mountain, was distractingly cold. More important, at that juncture he was devoting himself to religious study—from Thomas Aquinas and St. Augustine to Kierkegaard and Karl Barth. Nonetheless he persisted, interrupted by a move to New Orleans, where husband and wife both officially entered the Catholic faith.[4]

In 1948 the pair, along with their adopted baby, Mary Pratt, moved to Covington, Louisiana. (Bunt gave birth to Ann Boyd, their second child, on July 11, 1954.) Situated on the north side of Lake Ponchartrain, the community of about six thousand was close to New Orleans where his brother Phinizy and family and other old friends lived in the handsome Garden District. In a house overlooking a tributary of the Bogue Falaya and set among the old water oaks and pines of Feliciana, Percy found a location ideal for reading, thinking, and continuing work on his first novel.[5] All of his early writing took place in the master bedroom with yellow pad and pencil while he reclined on the bed, just as he had done in college. Later he did his writing in a small room above the Kumquat, a thriving bookstore that his daughter Ann Boyd and Bunt operated in downtown Covington. The office was quiet and fitted with only the bare essentials—workbench, lamp, typewriter, bookrest, coffee, Jack Daniels, mobile, small stove, refrigerator, equipment for filing drafts and other papers, and one extra chair sufficiently uncomfortable to discourage the rare visitor.[6]

The manuscript of *The Charterhouse* has disappeared, but Jay Tolson has reconstructed its themes from Walker Percy's privately held notes.[7] The novel was short on plot and long on grand abstractions about life and divinity. Yet the writer created a hero who was to appear under different guises in the rest of his work. Ben Cleburne of *The Charterhouse* resembles William Grey *(The Gramercy Winner)*, John (Binx) Bolling *(The Moviegoer,* 1961), Williston Barrett (Will) *(The Last Gentleman,* 1966, and *The Second Coming,* 1980), Thomas More *(Love in the Ruins,* 1971, and *The Thanatos Syndrome,* 1987), and Lancelot Andrewes (Lance) Lamar *(Lancelot,* 1977). All of them are well-born, well-educated men, very young at heart if not always in age. They have lost their fathers under tragic circumstances, and rediscovery of that disaster often moves the story to its denouement. Though viewing the world with passive detachment and inner anguish, Percy's heroes possess charm and unique character that other figures in the stories find winning. In other words, they were in many ways like Percy himself. That singleness of approach lent coherence to his plots but limited the range of his concerns to those of solitude and recovery in spiritual and emotional terms.

Like his father Roy, Percy's central figures suffer from what he called elsewhere an "alienation, which is unspeakable."[8] In depicting this temperament, the novelist was much influenced by the existentialist Jean-Paul Sartre's portrayal of the suicidal Roquentin in *La Nausée.* (Walker's characters, however, are much less intense and more attractive than Sartre's unpleasant egotist.) From first to last, Percy made his Roquentin-like heroes search for an antidote to thoughts of self-elimination and for advancement toward self-understanding. In the tradition of the romantic self-absorbed hero, Roquentin—and Percy's fictional alter egos—cannot be satisfied with ordinary living in a middle-class world. Instead they must search for something singular, even divine, as a remedy for feelings of isolation, self-disgust, and lack of authenticity. In the Percy family the life span was short; thus the novelist emphasizes the young adulthood that many of these characters share. That focus conformed with literary traditions of the Western world. Yet as an author ages, other and equally complicated circumstances can replace a search for a father, a fulfillment of romantic love, or an acquirement of personal mission—all of which are largely paramount in youth. Despite living to be seventy-three, Percy did not venture very far into the later stages of life.[9]

The Charterhouse set the pattern of his lifelong preoccupations: the theme of a son's disillusionment and gradual discovery of a father's moral weakness; an attraction to a woman that is neither romantic nor wholly convincing but off-handed; a religious climax that marks a tentative ending of the hero's pilgrimage toward, but still uncompleted, maturity. In *The Charterhouse*, Ben Cleburne's fury is so palpable that he prevents himself from murdering his father only by submitting his life to the Lord. By finding an anchor in religious faith, Ben can continue his quarrel while still treating his parent with honor. In addition, *The Charterhouse* foreshadowed Percy's persistent use of close personal attachments as a source for the hero's regeneration. A character named Ignatz plays a key role in Ben Cleburne's development toward spiritual grace. The favoring of male affection over the love story was to appear in most of his other novels, too. That ranking of emotional priorities had long been a Southern cultural feature. In his family heritage women were greatly cherished but often accorded a secondary role. Nevertheless, Percy wives found it easy to accept their husbands' intense male links (Thomas Percy and John Walker, Senator Percy and his nephew Roy, Walker himself and Shelby Foote, for instance).[10]

Although Walker Percy had identified his subject of alienation and partial restoration, he still needed literary instruction to employ his ideas successfully. He turned to the capable and almost motherly Caroline Gordon, novelist and wife of the poet Allen Tate. The Tates had been Will Percy's friends. Although not himself actively involved, Will had much admired the Nashville Agrarian movement of which Allen Tate and Donald Davidson, Will's particular friend, were leaders in the 1920s and 1930s. Walker Percy had known the Tates in Sewanee, where Allen edited the *Sewanee Review* in the mid-1940s. Sometime late in 1951 Percy sent Caroline Gordon a draft of his novel. "I have a new pupil; Walker Percy, Will Percy's nephew," Caroline Gordon rejoiced in a letter to poet Robert Lowell. (Like many others, she was misled by the family members' habit of calling their first cousin once removed "Uncle Will.") *The Charterhouse*, she exclaimed, is "really terrific, or will be when he gets it licked into shape. It's wonderful, having a pupil who is smarter than you are. Really, he's extraordinary, that boy!" Caroline Gordon was most gratified that he and Flannery O'Connor, her two protégés, both with excellent, semi-religious first novels, were members of the Roman Church.[11]

In a characteristically heartfelt response that blended their mutual interests with literary matters, Walker explained his hopes for the conversion of the Protestant South. He concurred with Caroline Gordon's high opinion of Thomas More who, he wrote, "is the spiritual ancestor of Lee. He is the man to pray to for the conversion of the South." (The region had prayed long enough to Lee himself, Will Percy being among the devotees.) Percy would name one of his later fictional heroes for the English saint. Yet leading the Protestant South to Rome, he admitted, would not be easy, especially the recruitment of the upper classes. The wealthy sophisticate could not easily embrace Catholicism because such a convert "must go in with his face averted and his nose held against this odor of Italian-Irish pietism and all the bad statues and architecture." These were prejudices that Percy himself, abashedly, confessed to entertaining.[12]

Despite such social misgivings, Percy found in Catholicism a way to deal with some deep-seated feelings about his two fathers: Will Percy, whose apostasy he rectified by joining the church; and his biological father, whose Protestantism repelled him but whose piety was a source of wonderment and even emulation. Introduced to Presbyterianism by his wife Martha Susan and her kinfolk, Roy Percy had striven for spiritual truth. Such a longing for God had not been seen in this otherwise secular-minded, nominally Episcopalian family since the days of Sarah Dorsey. Like her, Roy Percy had faithfully taught Sunday school; he also collected a number of theological works and Biblical reference guides, Bibles, and devotional literature and made meticulous preparations for the weekly lessons. Walker Percy confided to Caroline Gordon that it gave him "the creeps" whenever he gazed at his father's religious library. It consisted largely of volumes by coldly rational, nineteenth-century German and English Protestant divines. Yet Walker may have engaged himself in the lifelong spiritual search partly because of his father. An attorney of intellect and integrity, Roy had sought a meaning to life greater than that to be found on the No. 5 fairway, the hunting blind, or cockpit of a flimsy training plane—important though these activities were for him.[13]

In keeping with his emphasis upon a young man's wayfaring toward redemption, two institutions in *The Charterhouse,* symbolize the "prisons" that hold him back: an asylum and a country club, named "the Charterhouse," to which Ben Cleburne and his set belonged. Walker Percy's father had been a founder and president of the Birmingham Country Club, but Charterhouse, of course, refers to the monastic order of Carthusians.[14] The country club in the unpublished novel and in such later works as *The Last Gentleman* symbolizes the character of modern secular religion—the golf game on Sunday morning—which in this hedonistic age is seen as the unworthy replacement for the institutions of the medieval age of faith.[15] *The Charterhouse* included satirical portraits of New South businessmen— the kind to be found in bright shirts on the golf links while their wives play bridge at the clubhouse. As in *The Second Coming,* written many years later, in *The Charterhouse* Percy satirized the undemanding complacency of the Anglican approach to divinity that often consorted with the values of the country club.

The second institution in *The Charterhouse* carries darker connotations—"the Retreat," which was the Episcopalians' "caste-ridden mental nursing home!" as Caroline Gordon called it.[16] The confused Ben Cleburne undergoes therapy with "Dr. Betty Jane," who tries to help him resolve his conflicts about his father. At Sewanee there lived a Dr. Betty

Kirby-Smith, a down-to-earth general practitioner who was always known as "Dr. Betty" and was a most unlikely model for the figure of a psychiatrist. Walker probably had in mind an analyst resembling Janet Rioch. The nature of Ben Cleburne's illness is not clear from the surviving notes for the novel, for Caroline Gordon queried why Percy claimed that his hero was "hurtling towards an event: the Beast." She complained that a beast could not represent an action. Thus, she asked, isn't he "hurtling towards the Beast who will annihilate him?"[17] Percy was referring to the "beast" by which his father had identified his struggles with depression and dissolution of feeling. Henry James had proposed that name in "The Beast in the Jungle." Aware of his father's use of the Jamesian phrase, the "crouching beast," to describe his own dejection, Walker Percy had to have read the story himself before writing *The Charterhouse*. John Marcher, James's protagonist, describes "the beast" as an "event" that will overtake and destroy him at an unpredictable moment. Gordon had failed to recognize the source for Walker's metaphor. The mysterious adversary, Marcher discovers, was not, after all, an external catastrophe of some kind. Instead he finds himself stung to the quick by a sense of frightening incompleteness. At the end of the story Marcher is left alone to mourn not only the death of May Bartram who had discovered his incapacity for love and felt betrayed, but also his own ungiving deadened nature.[18] Walker Percy borrowed something from the numbed temperament of James's John Marcher in his portrayal of Ben Cleburne. Yet if Caroline Gordon failed to grasp his point, then Percy may have treated it in too understated and opaque a fashion. In Percy's later fiction, he did not try to imitate Henry James whose sexual repression involved what Eva Sedgwick calls "homosexual panic."[19] Not having that theme in mind, Percy adopted a more straightforward approach—the sense of unending darkness and paralyzing dread of melancholia.

In more than one of Percy's novels, psychiatric therapy fails to relieve the hero of his problems. Percy defines the illness as a spiritual rather than an emotional malady. As the novelist argued, a mortal sickness of the soul, not unlike that which James had depicted, cannot respond to superficial nostrums. In his short story James proposed no remedy at all, but Percy offered in his fiction a salvation that could only be glimpsed yet never fully realized. On one level, Percy knew how hard and imperfect the work of psychotherapy is. Two flawed people—analyst and patient—must somehow come to grips with tough emotional issues, and the patient must learn to accept personal limitations and carry on with them. On the other hand, Percy drew characters who are attracted to an immediate and more idealistic solution: the overcoming of a deep disquietude by means of magical— or spiritual—thinking. Yet from his own psychiatric experience, Percy recognized that whatever release religion had to offer his heroes, Ben Cleburne and the rest, it could only yield up, in the words of his adoptive father Will Percy's hymn, the "marvelous peace of God." That peace, as

Will Percy had pointed out, held no promise of serenity but granted only a recognition of human fallibility and permanent sense of loss and isolation. Later, in the portrayal of the austere Val Vaught in *The Last Gentleman,* the novelist tried to demonstrate that an uncalled-for bitchiness rather than warmth and sweet reasonableness can dominate those touched with spirituality.[20] Percy's first venture into fiction-writing indicated that he was developing a profound and richly ambivalent approach to fiction, religion, and self-understanding. As his first work hinted, most of the chief voices who speak in his fiction were fragments of Walker himself. The personalities of Will Percy and of Roy, Walker's father, appear among the major figures, but more than in the case of many major writers, Percy drew upon parts of his own psyche for the creation of figures.

Both Shelby Foote and Caroline Gordon recognized the originality of the apprentice's approach to fiction but insisted that their friend had much to learn. Philosophical elaborations could not take precedence in works of the imagination, they warned him. In long letters Caroline Gordon urged the novice to develop his characters and move the plot along, using the example of James Joyce in *A Portrait of the Artist as a Young Man,* a work similar in character to Percy's experiment. As Walker returned emended chapters, Gordon became increasingly certain that his work would soon deserve a reading at a publishing house. While fleshing out his heroines would be a continuing problem in his fiction, Gordon's protégé had even managed to enliven the character Abby, Ben Cleburne's love. Satisfied with his progress, she wrote, "You are in a position to receive help from the Holy Ghost, which none of my other students has been in. I really feel that in this novel He is using you as His agent."[21] Publishers, however, were seemingly unacquainted with divine intentions. At Scribner's, where Caroline and Allen Tate had sent it, John Hall Wheelock rejected *The Charterhouse.* The editor recognized "flashes of great talent" but also "serious weaknesses" and thought that the ending had been ill-prepared for—a judgment that Gordon thought displayed Wheelock's missing the point of the work.[22]

While awaiting word on the fate of *The Charterhouse,* Percy began at once writing another narrative. Titled *The Gramercy Winner,* it was consciously fashioned along the lines of Thomas Mann's *The Magic Mountain.* Mann, like Walker Percy, during his adolescence had lost his stern and exacting father and suffered from nearly suicidal depressions—a family tendency. Yet these complications had stimulated his grand literary preoccupations with the themes of conflicted sexual identity and death.[23] Percy's story is set in a sylvan hospital complex that at once resembles Percy's Saranac Lake and Mann's Sanitarium Berghof. William Grey—the only Northerner in Percy's stable of heroes—is a very nebulous figure. Yet *The Gramercy Winner* indicated that the source of Walker's own melancholy in the early loss of his parents remained hidden from view, as if the author were still unable to deal with the problem, even in fictional form. William

Grey all but fails to show up for his own life. He drifts through the story as an intellectually gifted but passive spectator. The young hero's inability to mourn the death of a charismatic older friend and fellow inmate, Major Laverne Sutter, is the fundamental issue of the story. Grey whistles tunelessly as he watches his physician friends dissect Sutter's body at the coroner's office. That scene is one of the most thoroughly realized moments in an otherwise pallid novel. Percy's masterful descriptive powers were evident when he provided rich details of the cold marble slab, upon which the cadaver rests, the expert incisions and generous flushings of organs as they are removed, with the civilized cane-back chairs scattered about the room. Percy was making good use of his own experience as a resident at Bellevue Hospital.

In *The Charterhouse,* Ben Cleburne's friendship with Ignatz is a central feature of the story; likewise, in *The Gramercy Winner* young Grey finds a male friend who can replace Major Sutter, the defective and surrogate father, as a source of affection and guidance. The novelist found philosophical backing for this point in the work of Gabriel Marcel, with his celebration of "intersubjectivity" or "I-thou" connection, but a pattern of male friendship had long been a part of Percy tradition as well.[24] E. M. Forster spelled out its nature when he wrote, "But two people pulling each other into salvation is the only theme I find worthwhile. Not rescuer and rescued, not the alternating performance of good turns, but It takes two to make a Hero."[25] Colonel Thomas Percy, with his friend John Williams Walker in mind, would have agreed.

The novel has its moments of genuine persuasiveness, but Percy offered no reasons for the hero's world-weariness. William Grey's parents, not fully realized characters, are depicted as distant, wealthy New Yorkers. He had not yet developed the confidence to exploit the Percy saga to create family figures of verisimilitude like the Chandler Vaughts of the Birmingham country-club crowd in *The Last Gentleman.* (The Vaughts are the same kind of people that his DeBardeleben cousins in Birmingham society were, though he probably had no specific individuals in mind.) Other defects appear as well. William Grey's self-absorption denies him a full relationship with Sutter's widow, although they sleep together once. Given his devotion to the Major, Grey seems almost engaged in an oedipal relationship. The author, however, never makes clear the hero's ambivalence or recognizes his character's subtle sexual treachery against a friend and father-like figure who deserted him by dying. Alone among all his narratives, the novel ends with the death of the main character. Beforehand, William Grey makes a new friend, a heavy-drinking, iconoclastic physician named Scanlon. In a penultimate scene, Scanlon asks Grey what makes him sad. "I don't know, Scanlon, I'm homesick." For how long, Scanlon rejoins. "All my life." One is tempted to guess that the sentiment had personal meaning for a writer who had been uprooted from Birmingham and Athens before reaching Greenville, scene of the second family tragedy, the death of Mattie Sue. Unfortunately, the reason for William Grey's grieving is unexplored. The actual closure of the narrative includes an account of Scanlon's baptizing Grey with tap-water from a bathroom glass, but the scene of the ritual, which could have been very moving, is clumsily handled. Percy would improve on this kind of sacramental event in the rendering of young Jamie Vaught's death and baptismal absolution in *The Last Gentleman*.[26] Walker Percy learned much from the experiments of *The Charterhouse* and *The Gramercy Winner*. He was then prepared to reach into his own and his family's past more directly and assuredly for fictional materials.

His third novel and the first published, *The Moviegoer,* showed a bolder but still cautious approach into personal and family history. In this work the disengaged but yearning young hero is given more individuality and vitality than was accorded the wraith-like William Grey. Set in New Orleans, the narrative describes the angst and confusion of Binx Bolling, a twenty-nine-year-old stockbroker in Gentilly, an unfashionable suburb. Unlike the almost sexless Grey, Binx is promiscuous with a succession of secretaries. But his indulgence springs from a nagging sense of malaise, an "everydayness" as Percy has Binx call it. Watching films also serves to distract the hero from a sense of emptiness. The cause of his uneasiness, never clearly articulated, is universalized as an outgrowth of Southern—indeed American—materialism and moral shallowness after World War II. For the first time, however, Percy introduced the thoughts and character of Will Percy as a way of symbolizing the obsolescence of the Old South's code of honor. He has Binx reared by a rigidly moralistic Emily Cutrer who voices her chivalric convictions with a vigor that mirrored Will Percy's own style.

In his quest for selfhood, Binx struggles against his forceful great-aunt. Emily Cutrer says that the old way of life "has come crashing down around my ears," a sentiment Will Percy had often registered.[27] Like so many others in *The Moviegoer,* she seeks the means to escape authentic feeling. The novelist suggests the inadequacy of his adoptive father's philosophy, its disembodied barren intellectuality, by which Emily Cutrer maintains a constricted equipoise.[28] Binx's method of dealing with her stern admonitions is to tune out, so to speak. Almost as if addressing "Uncle Will" himself, the novelist provided a telling exchange. Aunt Emily appeals to memories of evenings shared years before: "Don't you remember discovering Euripides and Jean-Christophe?" But the nephew replies that actually she had found them for him to read. " 'It was always through you that'—All at once I am sleepy." The symptoms suggest the depth of unspoken loss, incompleteness, and childish resentment. Aunt Emily's offense was to intrude too much, robbing him of spontaneity. As a result, Binx has trouble knowing his own feelings. Moreover, the malaise—"cold and fishy"—which his cousin and lover, the suicidal Kate Cutrer, shares with him—prevents at one point the consummation of their love.[29]

Although Percy made use of his adoptive father, he had yet to deal with his real father's suicide. Binx's melancholy, therefore, only mirrors the general tendencies of solitude and loneliness that Percy attributed to the moral decay of the postwar era. Of course, Percy was scarcely obliged to convert the family saga into fiction, but the interior reasons for Binx's unhappiness were not much explored. The hero's father, Major John Bolling, has died while flying over Crete in World War II. Aunt Emily assumed the responsibility of his upbringing when Binx was fourteen. The situation roughly paralleled Walker's own experience, but without the trauma of suicide that led to a sense of uncompleted grieving.[30]

If Percy in *The Moviegoer* had delved more assiduously into the family past, he would not have gratified his publisher, Alfred Knopf, who disliked the novel as it was. The aging giant of the New York literary establishment may have disliked the existential mode that Percy exhibited and could have objected to Walker's portrayal of William Alexander Percy as an out-of-date Southern lady. *The Moviegoer* had only won approval for publication out of courtesy to the memory of the author's guardian. Knopf had produced *Lanterns on the Levee,* a commercial success, and Will's last two collections of his poetry. The first printing of *The Moviegoer* had been small (1500 copies). Despite favorable notice in *Time* and the *New York Times Book Review,* no plans developed at Knopf for a sales campaign. Stanley Kauffmann (later film critic for the *New Republic*) was its sole supporter in the publishing house, and soon enough he quit the firm for reasons having nothing to do with the in-house reception of the novel. Percy was apprised of Knopf's antipathy. "My former editor at Knopf was down here recently (he got fired by Alfred)—Stanley (Kauffmann) was talking about what a bastard Alfred was, is," Percy wrote to his friend Robert Daniel, Charlotte Gailor's nephew, then editor of the *Kenyon Review.*[31]

A. J. Liebling of the *New Yorker* had read *The Moviegoer* with much enthusiasm while in New Orleans. Liebling was there preparing a work on Earl Long, the "Kingfish's" brother and perennial Louisiana politician. He recommended it to his wife Jean Stafford, herself a well-known writer, who was serving on the National Book Award committee. Equally impressed, she tried to obtain copies from Knopf. Her request refused, Stafford then turned to the National Book Foundation, and someone there found the books and forwarded them to Herbert Gold and Lewis Gannett, her fellow judges. They, too, were captivated. Its selection over Joseph Heller's *Catch-22* was a great surprise in New York literary circles.

Jean Stafford's response to *The Moviegoer* helps to explain Percy's appeal to readers for the next thirty years. As a professional writer, she liked the lean and forceful prose, the taciturnity of Binx and other characters, the easy command the novelist displayed over his material. These attributes

made his fiction memorable, particularly to someone with Stafford's literary sensibilities. But more than that, the book seemed to her well suited to
the mood of the day, a vague uneasiness in the midst of American domina-
tion of world events during the Cold War. Readers like Stafford also found
his evocation of life in the 1950s easy to grasp and very moving but with
hints of meaning that did not intimidate. Percy knew how to make the
middle-class suburbanite look foolish without being unduly malicious. His
dissection of his times was coolly anthropological. Walker examined
WASP culture as if it were a Polynesian tribe with peculiarities worthy of
special notice rather than a normative standard by which other ethnic cultures in America should be judged.

In adopting this detached approach, Percy offered a fitting analogy in
his acceptance speech at the National Book Award ceremony at the Astor
Hotel in New York City on March 13, 1962. Calling attention to his former career at the Bellevue morgue, he remarked that the nation's moral
health required the diagnosis of a pathologist who suspected "that something is wrong." In fact, he continued, "the pathology in this case had to
do with the loss of individuality and the loss of identity at the very time
when words like the 'dignity of the individual' and 'self-realization' are
being heard more frequently than ever." In a nation increasingly fascinated with medical science and its triumphs, Percy was on a popular
course when treating fiction as an instrument for probing illnesses of the
soul. Moreover, his combining of idealism about man as "a wayfarer and
a pilgrim" with a physician's eye for bothersome symptoms fit the
quiet and anxious mood of the country before the turbulent mid-sixties
arrived.[32]

Above all other factors, Percy's fictional depiction of the depressive state
of mind, sympathy for the afflicted characters, and wit struck notes of
recognition, particularly for those who had confronted such emotional difficulties themselves. Jean Stafford was a case in point. As a Catholic, depressive, and an alcoholic once under psychiatric treatment, she appreciated the dilemmas with which Percy had endowed his central characters.
The author had no idea about the close affinity that Jean Stafford had
discovered in her own life and his art. As men at that time were likely to
do, Percy thought that she had been simply swayed by the opinion of her
pugnacious husband. As far as Walker Percy was concerned, however, the
irony of his prize-winning lay elsewhere. Through Liebling's journalistic
labors in New Orleans, Percy's literary arrival owed something to a member of the Long dynasty. Huey Long's brother was just the sort of demagogue the Percys had fought for over fifty years.[33]

Percy's second novel to be published was begun even before *The Moviegoer* had appeared. Feeling new confidence in his literary powers, Percy

now in his mid-forties tackled the family story more directly. *The Last Gentleman,* as the novel would be called, was another study of a young hero's search for career, love, and meaning. Will Barrett is younger (twenty-five), gentler, more dependent upon family ties than Binx Bolling (twenty-nine), and considerably less certain of himself sexually. He lives a reclusive life in New York, refusing to engage himself fully in anything. Yet Will Barrett longs for a return of those times when "bad was bad and good good and a man was himself and knew straight up which was which." [34] His leisure is devoted to watching peregrines and people in Central Park through an elaborate telescope, symbolizing his distance from his own feelings. Barrett's periodic bouts of amnesia—one of them on a Civil War battlefield—sense of déjà vu, nervous tics, and mildly epileptic seizures warn him that something is very much amiss. Confessing nothing significant, however, he ends several years of psychiatric therapy with Dr. Gamov. Snobbishly he inwardly mocks the analyst's comic imperfections and silently ridicules at group therapy sessions fellow patients with their shallow Ohio niceness. He will seek his own cure.

The novel not only drew upon Walker's own observations about psychiatry when he worked with Janet Rioch but also resembled his state of mind during those months in 1946 when pursuing the young women of Sewanee and Greenville. The reader expects that Barrett will later marry the pretty, vivacious Kitty Vaught. When the hero, however, speaks repeatedly in banalities about love as "marry a wife and live a life," Kitty's loss of significance in Will Barrett's life becomes evident long before the novel ends. [35] No marriage takes place, but the reader barely notices the omission. Almost overshadowing the hero and his mental episodes is the brilliantly created character, Sutter Vaught, Kitty's older brother. A former psychiatrist turned renegade pathologist, Sutter, like Binx Bolling, pursues salvation in sexual excesses (all off stage) and worries about his attraction to suicide. Interpreting Sutter's diary which he discovers, Will Barrett muses that his friend saw only extreme alternatives: "God and not-God, getting under women's dresses and blowing your brains out." Barrett reflects that his own difficulty is much more pedestrian—merely "how to live from one ordinary minute to the next on a Wednesday afternoon." [36] In a significant way Sutter Vaught resembles Major Laverne Sutter of *The Gramercy Winner* in that Will Barrett looks to him as he would to a father. The embittered Sutter, however, refuses to play the part.

Barrett's highway toward renewal is a literal journey southward. The trip has its mock-heroic moments, illustrating the manners and mores of the well brought up Southern gentleman who receives mixed signals about what is expected of him. He feels he is "neither Christian nor proper lusty gentleman" and cannot get "straight of this lady-and-whore business." [37] In a confrontation with some racists at Levittown, "strive" as Will Barrett might, "to keep his anger pure and honorable, it was no use." An irate woman, certain he is a blockbusting real estate agent from New Jersey, strikes him hard on the nose, already swollen from an undignified attack of hay fever.[38] Only occasionally does Will Barrett win a small victory for the old code of his ancestors—as when he knocks out an obnoxious Southern policeman.[39]

Behind these feints and evasions that constantly trip the hero into ludicrous or misapprehended situations looms the young hero's inarticulate grieving for a father. That yearning was a poignant and oddly enduring problem in the Percy family annals. What happens to trust when a father kills himself? Will Barrett is too ill to do more than drift but (somewhat unbelievably) he guides himself toward the site of his father's suicide. Arriving at last in Ithaca (Greenville), Mississippi, he recalls how Ed Barrett had rejected his company although Ed had just won a victory of honor against a mob. A family celebration was in order. As his father moves away to walk among the trees, young Barrett feels the chill of a night that was supposed to be filled with happy noises. Instead: "(Victory is the saddest of all, said the father)"—an echo of Will's favorite theme. And then with reference to Will Percy's renowned Capehart phonograph, Will Barrett refers to the Brahms he had heard in his father Ed Barrett's house. Yet "the victorious sonority of the Great Horn Theme was false, fake, fake. Underneath all was unwell."[40] Undoubtedly, Percy had in mind, too, the lines from Baudelaire's "Le Cygne": "And in the forest where my mind wanders in exile/ An old Memory loudly blows its horn!" The father goes up to the attic. There he shoots himself without saying farewell to his son or making his action understandable, except as some kind of empty Stoic gesture. Trust of father and son is broken. In the portrayal of Ed Barrett, Walker conflated aspects of his own father Roy and his guardian. Ed voices Will Percy's prejudices and opinions, but the senior Barrett's actions mirror those of Walker's father Roy. The elder Barrett finds that he could no longer live every day as if it were "a perfect dance of honor."[41] Much still remained in the family saga for Percy to treat in fiction, but *The Last Gentleman* has an urgency and a complexity that his previous fiction lacked.

In 1965 Percy gave the work to Robert Giroux of Farrar, Straus & Giroux. Giroux shrewdly saw literary qualities and good profits in Percy's fiction that his rival Alfred Knopf never did. *The Last Gentleman* drew widespread acclaim from such critics as Joyce Carol Oates in *The Nation*, Granville Hicks in the *Saturday Review*, and Benjamin DeMott, in the *Washington Post Book World*. Frederick Crews in *Commentary*, however, wondered why the author seemed so reluctant to "inspect Will Barrett's conflicts at close range or to understand them much more clearly than Barrett does himself."[42] That reticence, that fear of self-disclosure, was very much a part of the family culture. Critics like Crews could only see the results, not the cause.

In a sense, *Love in the Ruins*, which appeared in 1971, represented a retreat from further exploration of family themes. Much less introspective than *The Last Gentleman,* the narrative belongs to the genre of science-fiction in satirical form. The subtitle explains: *The Adventures of a Bad Catholic at a Time Near the End of the World.* Thomas More, a forty-five-year-old psychiatrist, with a strong taste for bourbon and women, lives in an unidentified future America, a Southern dystopia—the opposite of the imagined Eden which the character's sainted namesake had created. Tom More, inventor of an electronic device that could diagnose mental conflicts, faces the challenge of a behavioral psychology run amok—Percy's most severe critique of the psychoanalytic enterprise. The machine was supposed to heal the mind-body split that Descartes, in the name of Reason, had inaugurated. More finds himself despairing and humorously bemused by the rising ideologies of Right and Left, in and out of the Roman Church. The zealots provide solutions to human ills no more efficacious than More's own mind-altering "lapsometer."

More than his other novels, *Love in the Ruins* revealed the concerns of a Southern writer facing the dilemmas of a region in rapid, disturbing transition. In the 1950s as a self-acknowledged "Southern moderate," he had mourned "the growing depersonalization of Southern life" but wondered if a "secure anonymity" might not help to lessen racial tensions in the long run.[43] He could not approve the racially conservative tradition of Will Percy. Nor did he have much faith in Northern white or Black Nationalist prescriptions for the world's ills. At least, the South, in his opinion, was no longer the pariah it once had been. Shortly before *Love in the Ruins* reached the public, he told a New York audience, "It's not that the South has got rid of its ancient stigma and is out of trouble. It is rather that the rest of the country is now also stigmatized and is in even deeper trouble."[44]

Like William Faulkner, Percy made no pretense at social and political advocacy. *Love in the Ruins* betokened a spirit skeptical about any plans for social uplift. Yet he did provide testimony at a federal court trial over the presence of the Confederate flag in the St. Tammany high school principal's office. Black students objected through the judiciary, and Walker Percy lent support to their cause on the grounds that culturally the flag had lately come to symbolize perpetual segregation. When the court ruled for the black plaintiffs, some of Percy's fellow Louisianans thought his part in the victory almost treacherous enough to require an old-fashioned lynching or assassination. As if living the incidents of *Love in the Ruins* himself, he and his family had to sleep in the attic for a while.[45]

Walker's deep sense of Percyan noblesse oblige toward those in need was a factor, but more important was the religious imperative. In 1965, for instance, Walker called attention to the "calamitous" but "unremarkable" negligence of the white churches in a helpful approach toward the "Negro revolution." In 1970, Percy turned on his fellow Catholics who defied Archbishop Joseph Rummel's efforts to desegregate the Louisiana parochial schools.[46] For a time it seemed that he was engaged in the kind of opposition to white mobocracy that Senator LeRoy and Will Percy had undertaken against the Klan of 1922. In an article in *Commonweal* he pointed out, however, that the old Southern Stoic tradition, to which he was no stranger himself, no longer sufficed. The decent, gentle Stoic tradition belonged to an agrarian and authoritarian era, very much at odds with the values of a modern democracy. Yet wealthy Southern whites still trotted out the old precepts to congratulate themselves for deploring lower-class racism while damning the Supreme Court and the NAACP. Percy was unconsciously repeating what Lilian Smith had criticized in her review of *Lanterns on the Levee*. She had scourged the dangerous racial complacency of "decent" whites that Will Percy's work had represented. Walker Percy was less harsh but reached the same conclusion. "How immediately," Walker Percy wrote, "we recognize the best of the South in the words of the Emperor: 'Every moment think steadily, as a Roman and a man, to do what thou hast in hand with perfect and simple dignity, and a feeling of affection, and freedom, and justice.' " The fight that Stoics like Will Percy waged against the Klan had been noble, Percy admitted, but the motives behind their opposition would no longer serve the South's genuine needs.[47]

Love in the Ruins, which has a happy, almost Edenic ending, reflected Walker Percy's mood after a decade of literary success. The 1970s, however, presented him with deep anxieties, some of them longstanding but others quite new. One factor was the changing political and social climate in the late years of the Vietnam War. His distress was partly a matter of growing older. With dismay he witnessed the upsurge of a new and seemingly callow generation. American young people appeared to be devoted only to self-gratification, an attitude so different from his own disciplined and gentlemanly upbringing. He admitted to his daughter Ann, a student at Louisiana State University, that for some time he had been feeling low and unable to write much. "There doesn't seem to be a great deal of point," he told her. "Middle-age depression no doubt, plus a Percyean disposition toward melancholia."[48]

Another source of gloom may have been a realization that his mourning for his father and for Will Percy had not yet been wholly resolved. With reference to his guardian, Louisiana State University Press came out with a new edition of *Lanterns on the Levee*. Obligingly Percy provided an eloquent testimonial and critique of its author. The short piece revealed his profound love for the man and yet strong opposition to the agnostic and racial views he had espoused. In the introduction Walker reported, "What he was to me was a fixed point in a confusing world." Yet immediately he qualified the remark by adding "This is not to say I always took him for my true north and set my course accordingly. I did not." He distanced himself from Will Percy's antiquated notions about race, a rejection of a long family tradition. Jay Tolson argues that Will Percy's noble ethic could "never work" for Walker "—and wouldn't for the simple yet decisive reason that he lacked the strength of character, the *virtu*" that the ethic required. Too often a sense of "self-disgust" and unworthiness enveloped him.

Walker Percy did not, however, renounce Will Percy altogether. The novelist recoiled whenever "a lady, not necessarily Southern," gushed that the memorialist "was right! The Old South was right!" Walker also bristled when complacent and present-minded liberals dismissed *Lanterns* as "racist, white supremacist, reactionary, paternalist, Bourbon, etc etc."[49] He even came close to endorsing what he had previously rejected, declaring that *"paternalism, noblesse oblige"* were "dirty words these days." But why was it so wrong for someone to acknowledge that wealth and position carried social obligations in behalf of the less fortunate? In a sense he was begging the question. The problem was not the appropriateness of an abiding sense of responsibility. Instead, it was the often blind, dictatorial, father-knows-best aspect of the patrician's role to which a democratic society could no longer defer. Walker felt trapped between two flawed societies—an Old South that had shaped his character yet was irretrievable and fundamentally wrong-headed and a New South that was both liberating and perilous to the old stabilities of his personal life.

Percy's health was a problem as well. He had developed a case of hepatitis. The disease made him feel miserable but proved a blessing. He was forced into abstinence from liquor, and for a time, alcohol, a depressant, would not contribute to his wretchedness. Added to physical discomfort was his momentary alienation from the Catholic faith which had been his anchor for so long. Maybe it was "male menopause or the devil," he wrote Caroline Gordon. "Anyhow it takes the form in my case of disinterest [*sic,* lack of interest is meant], accidie [acedia], little or no use for the things of God and the old virtues. I'd rather chase women (not that I do)."[50] Like other conservative Catholics of his generation he had watched the reforming effects of the Second Vatican Council with growing dismay. His lights had been Jacques Maritain, Romano Guardini, and other leading Catholic thinkers, most of whom would turn against the kinds of reform that the Church experienced in the 1960s.[51] He had the feeling that changes were accelerating with dangerous momentum, the Church hierarchy allowed guitar twanging in the sanctuary, raised the hems on nuns' robes, tossed out ecclesiastical Latin, permitted questioning of the hierarchical system itself, and worst of all, was infected with the moral relativism that an unreconstructed Catholic convert of the 1940s like Percy could not countenance.[52] In political affairs, matters were no better than in the Church. Campaign skulduggery and corruption—Watergate and Vice President Spiro Agnew's disgrace—sullied the conservative cause. The liberal tradition of Franklin Roosevelt, Percy could reason, had degenerated into the same moral anarchy that swept through contemporary theology. Percy thought it gave license to any kind of perversity or form of taste-lessness.

On the positive side, however, Percy sought to jostle himself out of his misery. In the fall of 1974 he began teaching a course in creative writing at Louisiana State University. The change of scene stimulated his literary ambition enough to overcome acedia, the medieval and priestly term for depression. Moreover, rubbing elbows with young people drew him out, even at the oddest of moments. Once, an undergraduate paused at the door of Percy's English Department office. Much to the young man's sur-prise, the novelist beckoned to him and said in a casual tone, "I guess the central mystery of my life will always be why my father killed himself. Come here, have a seat." [53] Uncannily, the first lines of his next novel, *Lancelot,* would follow the same formulation: "Come into my cell. Make yourself at home." Clearly, the author of these lines still had not left be-hind resentment of a paternal betrayal that no contact with the next gener-ation could eliminate. [54]

After a second semester at LSU, Percy was almost at his wit's end. In early August he suddenly boarded a plane for Las Vegas, rented a car and some camping equipment, crossed the desert, and went up into the Sierra Nevada for a few days. Apparently the experience did him some good. Will Percy had chosen that sort of location, the Grand Canyon, first, for mourning the death of his cousin Roy and later, for completing *Lanterns on the Levee,* and Walker had lived for a time near Santa Fe, before decid-ing to marry Bunt. [55] When Percy wrote *Lancelot,* he had the hero remark, "We will begin in the Wilderness where Lee lost. Deserts are clean places. Corpses turn quickly into simple pure chemicals." [56] The paradox of re-newal in the deadness of the wild caught the Catholic novelist's imagi-nation.

After his return from the Sierra Nevada, Percy settled down to complete the novel that all along had been the source of much anguish. Even when the composing began to flow more smoothly, Percy could be savage with himself and against others. Irritably he chided Shelby Foote for his claim to be reading Shelley for five hours day. Percy thought it a signal of a most inappropriate tranquility of mind when Percy himself, in contrast, was so wretched. "Don't you ever want to (1) shoot your wife (2) burn your house (3) run off with" a buxom University of North Carolina coed? Bitterly Percy added, "Please forward the secret of your maturity to a demoralized Catholic." [57] Was Percy worried that as a member of a short-lived family he was breathing on borrowed time? No certain answer is possible.

रो ज़

Because of the agony that accompanied its writing, *Lancelot* was his most sophisticated and accomplished work of fiction. Not coincidentally the work also dealt most directly with his ambivalent feelings regarding Will Percy and also the family as a whole. In it, the novelist divided his own and the Percys' history into two parts: Lance Lamar, the murderer and would-be suicide, and Percival or Father John, his old friend and confessor. Lance's father is portrayed as an amalgam of Walker himself, Will, and Roy Percy: a versifier good enough to win the title "Poet Laureate of Feliciana Parish" from the Kiwanis Club (Will Percy); a tubercular "semi-invalid" (Walker); and a suicidally depressed attorney with a law degree from Harvard (Roy). Percy has Lance speak in these biting terms of his father's state of mind: "Secretly I believe he was afraid that of all the people on earth he alone would fail and the world would come to an end out of shame for him." [58]

While writing *Lancelot,* he was forming a friendship with Robert Coles, the psychiatrist and popular author on the Harvard University faculty. They became very close, but, Percy complained, Coles earnestly sought to perceive him as the generous and liberal soul that Coles was himself. "He didn't want to recognize my nasty, conservative, mean side." [59] In the anti-hero of *Lancelot,* Percy concentrated all the unhappy traits that he sought to fight in himself. Through his character Lance Lamar, he could be the unrepentant snob, caustic husband, benumbed angry child of suicidal parents that the writer tried—mostly with success—*not* to be in real life.

Since Percy was wrestling in *Lancelot* with a range of family and personal issues, it was his most Southern novel. He used legends about frontier violence over traded insults, Civil War gallantry, male proprietary rights over wives, and other patriarchal attitudes—and even a decaying plantation mansion being restored to serve as a Tara for a Hollywood film. As in *The Moviegoer,* he treated Will Percy's "broad-sword virtues" as a foil against which to pose the emptiness and relativism of a modern world. [60] Lance's inner rage and his disillusionment with the family's code of honor explain his bitterness when he says, "Dishonor is sweeter and more mysterious than honor. It holds a secret. There is no secret in honor." [61] Honor, it seems, is handmaid to power—arrogant and self-serving—a view that Walker's guardian Will did not acknowledge. [62] As if to symbolize the end of the Old South and all its pretensions, Lance destroys the family's antebellum mansion and kills his wife and her lover for their violations of the sacred code. Yet Walker Percy would have felt bereft in a world that failed to grant the preeminence of honor and family loyalty.

Will Percy resides as well in the character of the priest, identified as Father John, who hears Lance's confession of these offenses. He is the voice of Will Percy rendered silent. (Both Father John and Will Percy share a love of walking among graves.) The articulate Will must passively listen for once to the extremes to which his concepts of honor might lead—the righteous vengeance of a cuckolded husband. Lance points out that their families were close and equally "honorable." The Lamars were convivial, hell-for-leather, and "politically active," whereas the Percivals "tended toward depression and early suicide." [63] Walker has distributed Percy characteristics to clothe the families of the two characters. As Lance Lamar's childhood friend, Father John was originally named Harry Percival, who grew up at Northumberland plantation (home of "Don Carlos") and whose name recalls Harry Hotspur. As Lance recollects, in their childhood games, Harry also took the name "Parsifal, who found the grail and brought life to a dead land." Quite ingeniously the author turns the myth upside down. Lance chides Father John for his metaphorical search for a Holy Grail. As for himself, Lance pursues an "unholy grail": the source of evil instead of salvation. Walker Percy is playing skillfully with the family name and the legends of nobility surrounding it even as he places the claims in the mouth of a mad, garrulous, but satanically engaging anti-hero. [64]

In reaching back to legends of Percy nobility, the novelist fashioned the plot of *Lancelot* along lines almost identical with that of his nineteenth-century cousin's *Household of Bouverie*. Both novels concern men who dread the passage of time and the withering of their capabilities. Catherine Warfield's protagonist, Erastus Bouverie, showing no sign of self-understanding from start to finish, is a figure from gothic fantasy. He seeks to regain lost youth by drinking a special elixir made of molten gold sovereigns and the extracted blood of his grand-daughter, Lilian de Courcy. No less melancholic and narcissistic than Bouverie, Lance Lamar seeks to catch his wife fornicating with a man more virile than he. With the same cool detachment with which Bouverie applies shocks from a galvanic battery to his wife's brain, Lance arranges the video camera that will detect his wife Margot's fornications. These wild events convey their authors' similar moods of rebelliousness and iconoclasm, their obsession with scientific power, their resentment of paternal gloom and abandonment, and their search for spiritual renewal. Just as Erastus Bouverie was based on the melancholic Nathaniel Ware, Warfield's father, and the suicidal Charles Percy, so was Lance an amalgam of more recent Percy depressives—Roy, Will, and Walker himself. Both Bouverie and Lance Lamar are frightened of independent-spirited women, despite their chest-thumping and conservative rants about honor. Both seek young and vulnerable women, with strong hints of a father and daughter form of incest, instead of meeting the demands of their wives. (Wide disparity in age between hero and heroine reappears in Percy's *The Second Coming*.) Occupying the cell adjacent to Lamar's, young Anna in *Lancelot* is virtually mute; Lilian in Warfield's story is too young to know what the lecherous grandfather is after. The two protagonists, Bouverie and Lamar, are unable to experience love but only anger, jealousy, and impotent frustration. When I told Walker Percy that one of his collateral ancestors had written a story about a mad, Faustian hero with scientific interests, who murdered his wife's lover, and spent most of his life self-imprisoned for the crime, he replied with a laugh, "I'd never use a hokey plot like that." [65]

His wry humor could not hide the high seriousness of a novel that transcended its plot. On a very visible level Walker Percy's creation of Lance Lamar involved a reaction to those terrible losses that the Percy family endured—the snatching away of parents and of normal expectations by the violence of sudden death and, more subtly, by their replacement with an exotic tradition that stimulated the mind but taught too little of joy and certainty. The world is unjust, Walker Percy's heroes would like to cry out. But instead, the shout dies in the throat, memory fails, passion shrivels to a twitch of the knee, a tic in the face. Or, as in Lance Lamar's case, the repressed outrage might find release in vengeance as if the act could restore a sense of belonging.

Yet even as Walker adopted the Percyan legacy he also condemned it. The family legend of glory and honorable defeat that *Lanterns on the Levee* celebrates has in *Lancelot* a sarcastic, disbelieving tone. How different Lance is from Will Percy's persona who gazes on Malvina Hoffman's creation in the cemetery and memorializes a father whom he claims bold enough to find a place among the stone knights on the west portal of Chartres Cathedral. The author of *Lanterns on the Levee* ponders the fate of a world long since departed from the code his father espoused to the end of his life. "On the tower of the rampart stand the glorious high gods, Death and the rest, insolent and watching," he writes in the last paragraph of the work. Beneath them comes the parade of a wearied, wretched, and humbled humanity. Then, from the looming spire, "the High God descends" to confront the foot-sore traveler, and utters "three slow words: 'Who are you?' " The wayfarer, Will Percy knows, should be able to come forward, with head erect and shoulders squared, to reply manfully: " 'I am your son.' " [66] In this moment of self-assertion, however, Will had couched it in the subjunctive. Had he been worthy?

Walker rejected the inhibiting principles of a "flawed and dissonant" honor that had so restricted Will Percy's creativity. Yet the attention he gave the matter in *Lancelot* suggested his continued fascination with the Stoic ethic. In fact, he recognized its dangerous seductiveness. Honor remains in his novels and essays a tempting way toward certitude and self-acclaim, but its mandates must be resisted and Christian affirmation asserted. Out of the tension that a rich but troubled legacy created in Walker Percy's mind, he found the strength to slay the crouching beast—through the medium of art. *Lancelot* was his masterpiece. Not coincidentally it was the only novel that denied the reader a glimpse of an artificially imposed salvation. As a result it achieved an authenticity that had been compromised in the others. Instead, when Lance indicates his desire to start over, the series of questions elicits from Father John an equal number of "yeses." [67] The colloquy means that the search for Will Percy's "marvelous peace of God" had only begun. And the road ahead would not be easy. Percy's use of a question to close the story was his way of stating the defiant challenge arising from the void of modern life, "Why am I here?" Perhaps in posing it, Walker Percy finally ended his literary quarrel with the ever-formidable Will Percy. He had not, however, resolved his internal controversy with his father Roy.

❦ ❦

Percy's penultimate novel, *The Second Coming* (1980), was apparently meant to end at last his mourning for the suicidal father. The hero is once again Will Barrett of *The Last Gentleman,* who, of all Percy's heroes, was the most involved with the troubling issue of self-inflicted death. Now, however, Barrett is about forty-eight, on the edge of late middle age but seems even older in body if not in spirit and in a recurrent fear of death. (Walker Percy was sixty-four when the work appeared.) Unlike Lance Lamar, Barrett in *The Second Coming* resorts neither to myth-making about grails nor to expressions of nostalgia for Lee-like gentility. Instead, he seeks to dispel his melancholy by repression and unconscious escape from painful thoughts. While playing golf, Barrett, a wealthy widower and prematurely retired New York attorney, is bedeviled by curious snatches of memory of a traumatic but still hidden moment early in his life. Walker Percy had once spoken of an unpleasant trip with his father Roy to hunting grounds near Thomasville, Georgia.[68] In his fictional re-creation of it, the incident takes an ominous turn. The novelist has the father nearly kill his son Will, ostensibly to spare him the internal torture that he himself is undergoing before he dies. Although the scene suggests an encounter like that of Abraham and Isaac in the wilderness, Percy seems to offer a more personal note: was he like his father? In a moment of awkward affection from which the son shrinks, Ed Barrett says: *"I saw the way you lay in bed last night and slept or didn't sleep. You're one of us, I'm afraid."* [69]

In Walker's imagination, Percy blood appeared to have condemned a son to misery if not to early death. With this issue finally given full expression in *The Second Coming,* Percy may have thought that he had freed himself from the old spell. He had confronted Hamlet's ghost, as it were. The story's narrator calls Will Barrett's father "the old mole," which phrase is Hamlet's retort to his father's persistent, vengeful ghost early in the tragedy: "Well said old mole! Canst work i' th' earth so fast!" But the Shakespearean allusion only reinforces Walker's theme of an abiding rancor against "a death-dealing father." [70]

Despite its tragic theme of melancholy and renewal, the novel has the most unpersuasive conclusion of any of his works. Expertly Percy weaves his themes of religious quest, semiotics, and psychiatry—all frequent topics of his prose and fiction—into the narrative. Yet toward the end he leads away from the central theme of personal anguish about the relationship with the depressive father to conclude on a note of contrived redemption. The agent for the change from Will Barrett's Stoical skepticism to Christian faith is a curiously opaque androgynous figure, Allison Huger. At the beginning of the novel, the beguiling young heroine, described as boyish in appearance, is recovering from a nervous breakdown, having escaped from a mental institution. Will Barrett's chief claim to salvation seems to be a sense of victorious affirmation over his father and his passion for death. But in the closing pages the theme of love for a young woman (young enough to be Will's daughter) serves as the vehicle for his epiphany. Barrett metaphorically rejects the beckoning of his father's ghost and forswears ever to contemplate suicide. But he then asks, "Could it be that the Lord is here, masquerading behind this simple silly holy face? Am I crazy to want both, her and Him? No, not want, must have. And will have." [71]

Love of man for woman, it seems, can conquer all, even unbelief. The cliché does not ring true. Allison is more like an adolescent Walker Percy himself than a fully adult woman. Putting aside the romance of spiritual awakening—and an accompanying sexual one—the novelist made a much more convincing point earlier: the banishing of fear about self-inflicted death, a defiant answer to the lure of the unreliable father. That decision seemed also to have at last erased the author's own perplexity over his father Roy Percy's suicide. As if the distance between author and fictional hero were not very great, the novelist gives Will Barrett the body of a man sixty or more years old, like that of Walker Percy himself. Moreover, Barrett has difficulties with a prostate that his physicians think might be cancerous and to have metastasized in the brain. Dr. Vance reports, however, that he had been mistaken: instead, the hero has always been afflicted with "Hausmann's Syndrome," a form of petit-mal epilepsy that causes "depression, fugues, certain delusions, sexual dysfunctions alternating between impotence and satyriasis" and a condition called *"wahnsinnige Sehnucht,* meaning "inappropriate longing." Nonetheless, the problem with the prostate gland presumably remains although the narrator says nothing further about it. As it happened, Walker Percy's fatal cancer originated in that gland only a few years later. Perhaps the author had some premonition of his fate. If so it may help to explain the preoccupation with life, death, and immortality that the novel reveals, and it does so with a finality that the reader easily ascertains. [72] As a result, *The Second Coming,* one of his most popular novels, strikes one as his final statement. What more was there to say? As it turned out, however, he had not disposed of all the ghosts in the Percy household.

CHAPTER EIGHTEEN

Thanatos and Lineage

What's lyfe to me, Northumberland's proud pere?
Lyfe without love is erth without a sunn;
Why did the fates then ever place me here,
Why was I domed life's cheerless course to run?

F. R. Surtees, "Lamente of Henry Percye"[1]

The legacy of Charles Percy has led his descendants, over the years, to make efforts—fictional, genealogical, and legend-making—to sustain a special sense of belonging. Those engaged in such efforts gave meaning to themselves; the fruits of their work gave courage to their descendants. The fiction writers among the Percys, epitomized by Walker Percy himself, drew repeatedly on the family history for their characters as well as their themes. And dominating them all was the melancholy that besieged them over the generations. Yet just as Don Carlos founded two familial lines, his heirs followed separate courses to achieve familial self-projection by searching for their origins and kinship with the House of Northumberland. Descendants of Robert Percy, Charles's eldest son, undertook genealogical study to trace the noble line. Members of both branches, however, in an ironical musical resolution, came to recognize a temperamental if not blood relationship with the noble house. The complicated account of these themes may help to explain how families, consciously and sometimes unconsciously, recapitulate old issues in new settings, displaying both resilience and occasionally a sense of the absurd in the process.

※ ※

Walker Percy's art had one major objective: the transformation of personal pain into a more universal and philosophical observation about human destiny and the imperfections of the world. He took considerable pride in adopting this perspective because it set himself and his clan apart from and even above ordinary mankind. The creation of usable abstraction was one of the more obvious means for raising up sensitive issues without exposing the hidden life of the Percys. Yet he never shrank from naming the familial sources of his inspiration, even if he did not offer details: "I come from a long line of manic depressives," Walker Percy told Phil McCombs, an interviewer, who had come to see him after the publication in 1987 of *The Thanatos Syndrome*. Bunt, Percy added, "kids me. She says, 'Why, you're not manic depressive. A manic depressive has his highs and you're depressed all the time." Percy then shrugged off the comment and claimed that her remarks were a way of saying "that I'm not really depressed" at all.[2] Percy admitted that "some guy had claimed to have discovered the gene for manic depressive psychosis," but, even if he had, "a good deal of the anxiety, the alienation, and the depression in the modern world" had nothing to do with genes. Rather, Percy contended, such difficulties were "due to something wrong with the modern world and something wrong with the way we live."[3]

Percy's attempt to objectify the ravages of personal inanition, blaming the state of the world and human desertion of God, was scarcely new with him, as he well understood. For generations, critics have named the destruction of the patriarchal family, the anomie of bored aristocrats and idle, overstuffed burghers, the rise of the city with its crime and impersonality, the decline of honor and loss of rural virtue, and the very progress of a sophisticated and highly literate "civilization" of science and art as the sources of social malaise in Western society. The most often cited symptom of this low state of morale was a perceived increase in the number of suicides. Since the seventeenth century, authorities, many of them clergy, have argued that debauchery and wickedness among the rich inevitably led to crushed vanity and then to self-immolation. John Brown, an eighteenth-century English satirist, for example, observed, "The Roman killed himself, because he had been unfortunate in *War;* the *Englishman,* because he hath been unfortunate at Whist."[4]

Without much sense of irony or paradox, poets, philosophers, and imaginative writers have simultaneously adopted a contrary view, insisting that melancholia, though conducive to suicide, was a state of mind that betokened seriousness of purpose, whereas feelings of happiness signified shallowness. Percy also embraced that point of view. A fatalistic expectation of suffering and disaster, he argued, had always challenged the notion that human mastery over events was possible. Percy proposed that a writer of fiction, in spiritual kinship to Thomas More and Saint Francis, "is most cheerful with Brother Death in the neighborhood." As a novelist, he continued, he found it easier to write about "catastrophe" than "flower people."[5] Referring to Mickey La Faye, a mental patient in *The Thanatos Syndrome,* Percy remarked to McCombs that "at the end she's better off with her anxiety and depression than being without them. This is the proposition of the book." Happiness, Percy contended, is a state of unawareness such as a "chimp" might enjoy; by its very nature being human is an exercise in low spirits. Likewise, John Milton, Robert Burton, and other thinkers of their era had long before hailed melancholy as a means to achieve a heightened self-awareness and self-criticism. Milton called melancholia "a goddess, sage and holy."[6]

Yet rooted as Percy was in the traditions of Western thought, he must have realized that these concepts of melancholy—its lamentable connection with suicide as well as its chastening philosophical uses—had little to do with the effects of the malady in his own family. Some Percys had killed themselves in the country, far from the alleged dangers of high-living city life. Others had died by their own hand amidst active, urban careers, but, as if to defy Émile Durkheim's propositions about modern, industrial anomie, their place in the social order had always been secure. If they had ever thought the social order responsible for their inner malaise, they never whispered it to a soul or wrote about it—at least as far as the rest of the world knows.

With regard to the genetic puzzle, Percy was most curious about his family's tendency to chronic depression. Ten years before the appearance of *The Thanatos Syndrome,* the novelist had written Shelby Foote that he was either prepared to match the achievements of Kant, Spinoza, or Verdi or to leap into the stream running behind his house in Covington with a sooty pot tied to his neck. Recently, the novelist added, he had felt more like trying old Charles Percy's method rather than strive for literary greatness.[7] The remark revealed the wry way that he handled his perplexity. In his Pascalean collection of essays titled *Lost in the Cosmos,* he often repeated his concerns, but drollery frequently accompanied the questioning: "The only cure for depression is suicide," he states. The age is unbalanced and that is reason enough; besides "chuckleheads, California surfers, and fundamental Christians" are the only "adults" not in a state of despair. That mood, Percy implies, is a function of superior education, class upbringing, and insight into the way the world really is. If you take "the Roman option," as Cato did, one might benefit the attorneys, but "your psychiatrist will be displeased." Neighbors will feign shock, while your family will feel "the disgrace" but miss you only briefly, Percy concludes. The tone is meant to be bantering, but a certain degree of self-pity detracts from the humor.[8] Indeed, the light approach served the same purpose that moral objectification had in all his novels, as a distraction from the deadening reality itself.

The two approaches—what we might call embattled whimsy and the use of abstraction—were combined in *The Thanatos Syndrome* with a third element: the employment of legend—all of them ways for Percy to grasp a familial enigma. The confluence of these themes owed something to his recognition that this might well be his final novel. Having spent his life *not* committing suicide, it was perhaps natural that his last work should allude in its title to Freud's concept of the human attraction to death—Thanatos, the counter-impulse to Eros. He had begun the novel during a busy period of his life in the early 1980s—trips to Europe and California, where he accepted an award from the Los Angeles *Times* for *Lost in the Cosmos.* By 1987, when the novel appeared, Percy was himself aware that he was besieged by a cancer that might well prove fatal.[9]

As a recent critic observed, *The Thanatos Syndrome* is designed, as late-life novels often are, as a "legacy for the next generation," a message in the bottle, to borrow Percy's title for a collection of essays.[10] His decision to write it could have arisen from his sense of aging, a time when the ancestral voices might speak louder than ever before. Feliciana had been populated, he writes in the opening pages, by *"all manner of malcontents,"* ranging from *"disgruntled Huguenots"* to outright criminals. They were amusingly splendid in what Percy saw as their virile unconventionality.[11] As if to join the world of Charles Percy with his own environment, there is much geographical confusion about places in Feliciana. For instance, Percy conflates his own neighborhood with that of Charles Percy's Bayou Sara some sixty or more miles to the west.[12]

Within the framework of the novel, two themes emerge: the first and more obvious repeats some of Percy's social and moral concerns, in which his personal experience in Germany before World War II plays a part; and the second deals with equally dark aspects of the Percyan past. In regard to the first, the "Syndrome" of the title concerns the evil work of some scientists who seek to "reform" human behavior by reducing the restraints of personal guilt and promoting the euthanasia of "useless" old people and unwanted fetuses, a sanitized version of the Nazi Holocaust. By administering doses of heavy sodium to an unsuspecting population, Bob Comeaux, one of the villains, dreams of creating a utopia, in which the lower orders know their place and depend upon the kind of direction that planters like Charles Percy had once seized in order to fashion their slaveholding world. Bob Comeaux calls his scheme a retrieval of "the best of the Southern Way of Life." [13] Just as Faulkner saw almost a divine curse upon the South for its racial sins, Percy suggests a similar retribution. An old family plantation house, Belle Ame, becomes the site for hideous sexual abuses of children, as if such crimes were not only consequences of modern permissiveness but also outgrowths of the rigidly hierarchical system that produced the antebellum mansion. Tom More, aided by a very competent and rational young cousin and doctor, Lucy Lipscombe, eventually uncovers the plot and saves the world from the band of eugenicists, euthanasianists, and abortionists.

Beneath the sometimes shrill call for conservative values, Percy offers two other themes, one personal and the second familial, both of which take on the character of romantic myth. Percy has Tom More locate the origin of the thanatos syndrome in the merciless and overpowering destructiveness of World War I, about which Will Percy had so often spoken to Walker as he grew up in the 1930s. Through Father Smith's confession (which almost overwhelms the story), Percy shows the unchecked evolution of modern fiendishness during the era of World War II. The Nazis learned to hide their schemes of mass death in antiseptic, "tender" applications. These notions stemmed in part from Walker Percy's visit to Germany in 1934, not long after Adolf Hitler came to power. The collegian was enthralled by the military regime, the flag-waving, and the cult of manliness. A literary critic suggests that the young Percy's "emotional conflicts with his two weak fathers—the biological one suicidal, the adopted one of questionable masculinity"—induced this attraction. In *The Thanatos Syndrome,* Percy has Father Smith recall how, in the early 1930s, Helmut, his handsome Nazi comrade solemnly presented him with a bayonet engraved with the words, *"Blut und Ehre,"* that is, Blood and Honor. Percy was very aware that the Nazi cause was a horrible delusion.[14]

The second and more sexual confrontation with death emerges from the relationship of Tom More and his medical associate Lucy Lipscombe. Early in their alliance, Percy prepares for their eventual breakup by explaining their odd lineage from the loins of their rascally progenitor (Charles Percy). Glad to find that Tom More is her only surviving relative aside from an old, half-crazy uncle, Lucy shows her distant cousin "the grave of our common ancestor, an English army officer on the wrong side of the Revolution. It is a blackened granite block surmounted by an angel holding an urn." Reflecting on their forebear, Lucy says, "We come from a melancholy family. . . . He married a beautiful American girl half his age, only to have his first, English wife show up." Tom More reminds her, "He suffered spells of terrible melancholy" and persuaded himself that enemies were coming upon him in the night. The hero adds, "No wonder he jumped in the river."[15]

Despite the casual tone of Tom More's reflections on his ancestor, the author of *The Thanatos Syndrome* recognized that genetic implications arose from the union of Lucy Lipscombe and Tom More. In Lucy, he created one of his more believable women, but More's love affair with her founders because she is too much like him—being an equal in occupation, self-confidence, and lineage. Equality between the man and woman makes her threatening to him in a sexual way as well. But, in addition, she bears the same blood heritage as More. Because he recognizes his own near suicides earlier in his life, Tom More cannot marry Lucy. It would simply bring down on the family a continuation of the hereditary legacy.[16] After their collaboration in unmasking the villains, More returns to his more submissive and more typically Southern wife Ellen, by then cured of her animal-like sexual habits that Comeaux's sodium doses induced.

Perhaps coincidence alone explains the correlation, but the familial configuration of *The Thanatos Syndrome* very much resembles that of Sarah Dorsey's *Agnes Graham.* The heroine of that story rejects a suitor because of their mutual descent from depressive parent and grandparent (characters based on Dorsey's great-grandfather Charles and her grandmother Sarah Percy Ware). Both Dorsey's and Percy's characters like the effortlessness of their association with a female cousin: "It is a pleasure telling her," Tom says, "talking easily, she listening."[17] But in both cases the prospective romantic interests disappear from the respective plots. The figures are unsuitable as mates for each other. To be sure, the analogy between the two novels cannot be pressed too far because Sarah Dorsey did not surmount the liabilities of the sentimental novel, in which genre she and her mentor Catherine Ann Warfield had been steeped. Nevertheless, the legend of a burdensome but also appealing cousinship had its roots in the Percys' Southern culture and in their own history.[18]

⁂

The second approach to family identity, genealogical research, contrasted with and took the place of the more imaginative approach of myth-making. The members of the lineage stemming from Margaret and her son Robert Percy sought to clear up the mystery of Charles Percy's origins. Assiduous work in archives and courthouses provided a means to establish that branch's legitimacy and sense of distinction. In the last years of the nineteenth century, the Louisiana line, which had descended from Margaret, felt a need to make claims of high birth, perhaps because the great-grandchildren of Susannah Collins and her husband Charles—LeRoy, Walker, and William Armstrong—were then becoming so prominent in regional affairs. The difficulty for the investigators was the obscurity of Charles Percy's origins in the British Isles. Certainly the forefather was no historical figure of any importance and scarcely appeared prominently in official records. Only what others made of Don Carlos lent him significance at all. But that turned out to be vastly more important than anything Charles Percy did on his own account. The bigamy, the record of depression and suicide, the boast of patrician birth, and the fortune over which descendants occasionally disputed were Charles Percy's contributions to a complicated process of myth-making upon which Walker Percy had built some of his fiction and upon which Don Carlos's legitimate successors placed their hopes for proving a claim of noble blood.

For the first fifty years or so after Charles's death, both in the first and second family lines, silence had been the sole response.* Squire Thomas George Percy, his sisters, and their sons and daughters had studiously turned away from embarrassing questions about who Charles was and why he acted as he had. When the estate was being settled in the mid-1790s, the modest demands of his first son, the English lieutenant Robert Percy, for a child's share enabled the Mississippi widow to hold the rich properties that Charles Percy had bequeathed her. Being in his youth a gambling man, the only surviving offspring of his father's family, he could have risked a sequestration by the Spanish authorities, taking all the property, or, if the government intervened, gaining nothing. Illegitimacy, after all, was no casual matter in the South or anywhere else in the Western world. With nothing to be gained by keeping Charles Percy's records, someone, perhaps Colonel Thomas Percy, had them destroyed.

Lieutenant Robert Percy's children had little desire to open the matter

---

* For genealogical guides of the family wings discussed herein, see the genealogical charts, pp. 356-58.

to public scrutiny. Margaret's death in London in straitened circumstances was not a cause for boasting. Besides, only their father had known her personally. She had died long before Robert had established his family in America and had slipped out of family consciousness. Finally, even for the legitimate descendants of Charles Percy, his suicide involved a moral stigma.[19] Documents were handled carelessly, and, with a Civil War impending, no one had the time or desire to hunt down ancestral links to the tangled web of Northumbrian aristocracy.

In the post-Civil War period, the Percys who moved to the Delta were much too busy to devote much thought to the issue. Gradually, however, it became family custom to state bluntly that a connection with the Northumberland household existed. The Gray Eagle and his sons, Walker, LeRoy, and William Armstrong, took it as a matter of course. In 1907, LeRoy Percy, Will's father, for instance, boasted to a cousin, "We claim back to the Northumberland Percys." Will Percy also harbored such notions. In the 1920s he visited the Percys' famous Alnwick Castle in Northumberland and struck up a friendship with the Rt. Hon. Eustace Sutherland Percy, a younger brother of the Seventh duke. According to Will's cousin John Seymour Erwin, who toured the battlements himself in 1972, a guard on the castle staff still remembered Will's visits. Friends of the Percy family sometimes supported the noble claims as well. As late as 1938 Jonathan Daniels, a well-known Southern columnist, called his friend Will Percy "the true last of the great family of Hotspurs."[20] Yet as members of the ostensibly "illegitimate" line, they had no wish to pursue the genealogical trail. Legend-making would suffice, and that tradition eventually found its spokesman in Will Percy. He codified it in *Lanterns on the Levee* and passed it on in the form of semi-historical memoir to his ward Walker, who then wove it into his fiction.

Though less complicated than Walker's use of Charles Percy as one component of Lance Lamar, Will Percy's description of the founder was based on the family's oral reminiscences and guesses. Yet he made the story serve his evasive design by the use of somewhat adolescent humor with only an intimation of darker themes. From the familial storehouse of half-knowledge, Will Percy had extracted the notion that Don Carlos had been a bigamist. Abandoning history in the account presented in *Lanterns on the Levee,* he has Charles Percy's first wife Margaret and her adult son Robert arrive together on the doorstep of the Spanish alcalde's plantation home, Northumberland House. The English matron, he writes, promptly announced, " 'I am the long lost wife of your bosom.' " As if her own appearance was insufficient testimony to Charles's absconding, she pointed to a "full-grown Captain in the English Navy, also ycelpt Charles [*sic*]." To Will Percy, the affair seemed "a discouraging business all round." Left unchronicled was whether Don Carlos struck her, but, Percy adds, one can imagine the planter's sense of provocation. The parties soon began vigorously to sue each other.[21]

In the midst of the pandemonium, Will Percy relates, the unhappy En-glishman strolled down to a nearby creek, secured an iron pot to his neck, and "hopped in." He is suggesting that the appearance of the first wife and son triggered Don Carlos's calamitous reaction. Will Percy, who knew that such a motive was hardly plausible, relished the fact that it bordered on the comical.[22] The Chekhovian delight he takes in creating a comic scene helped him to handle the melancholy that frequently enveloped him.

Stung by the wild inaccuracies that colored or discolored nearly every sentence in Percy's tale, John Hereford Percy, the family's most dedicated genealogist on the Robert Percy side, could not resist making a few critical remarks about Will's best-selling book even though the gentle-hearted dis-senter admired the family's famous memorialist. "Other readers will be amused," admitted the Baton Rouge banker, but "I would not have recog-nized your description of our Percy ancestry."[23] In offering an apology, Will Percy addressed his distant Louisiana cousin, "Dear Head-of-the-House-of-Percy." Yet the cavalier tone disclosed his barely hidden dis-missal of the historical dimension. In fact, Will excused himself with the remark, "The account I gave followed pretty closely the facts as I had gotten them vaguely, but as I always considered it rather cockeyed and ludicrous that is the way I wrote it down." To judge from Henry James's equally casual mis-statements in recounting the history of his Irish ances-tors, Will Percy was in good company. Better to tell a good tale than to keep the record straight. Certainly such an approach conformed with the Southern habit of withholding more intimate revelations by providing a di-version.[24]

Will Percy's purpose, however, was far more serious than the light re-marks suggest. He wrote in the foreword to *Lanterns on the Levee* that the destruction of the world he had loved was imminent, and he was therefore determined to "indulge a heart beginning to be fretful by repeating to it the stories it knows and loves of my own country and my own people."[25] For him, as for Walker Percy, memory of the past was a source of ambiva-lence, presenting itself both as a duty and a menace. On the one hand, as a traditionalist who mourned the passing of the old order, Will lamented in his last work what he considered the corruption and madness of modern times and the contemporary naïveté about the prospects of Science, Ratio-nality, and Progress—a theme that Walker Percy reiterated, most especially in his swan-song novel *The Thanatos Syndrome*. Story-telling was a sort of counterargument against abstract analysis, linear progression, and "his-tory." Will Percy mocked the precision that professional historians are ac-customed to demand. As a figure of Will Percy's imagination, ancestor Charles also represented the transitory nature of life, rank, and pretension, the rise and fall of families and nations—ideas thoroughly typical of the Southern conservative mentality. Yet Will Percy did not really wish to know too much about his forebear or any other figure on the family tree.

In a sense, denial and fancy were one and the same. To have undertaken extensive research might have revealed corruption, weakness, even madness. Will Percy was no Jack Burden (in Robert Penn Warren's *All the King's Men*), a figure who found his identity by uncovering the truth of his wayward father. Nor did Will Percy resemble Walker's Lance Lamar, who discovers his suicidal father's money-making fraud. Exposures of a father's iniquities could have shattered Will's faith in the antique values whose passing he mourned. Legend and story-telling, then, were not mere diversions. They were an escape from a truth about Charles Percy and others in his train. Above all, Will Percy sought to deflect notice of the family's mental burden in his delight with the romantic qualities of the founder's adventures. "Don Carlos came from nowhere, he issued suddenly from the sea," the memorialist observes. Cousin Mary Dana, he notes, "once darkly confided" that Charles Percy's record in the Caribbean islands could only be described as "lamentable, lamentable." Perhaps he was a Caribbean buccaneer or a "lost heir of the earls of Northumberland." To these queries, the speculator meets only, Will says, "Silence. Mystery."[26]

The author of *Lanterns on the Levee* recounts that he once motored down to sleepy Woodville, near "the old Percy place." He was looking for the ancestral grave and was directed to an agreeable country idler with a plug in his cheek who upon inquiry replied that no one had ever located "where the old bird was buried." Probably the creek had washed his bones away long before, Will's distant cousin guessed. "Playing Tarzan in the family tree is hazardous business; there are too many rotten branches," Will Percy concludes.[27] Wit took much of the pain out of the family history.

When a member of the Susannah Collins line took up the genealogical cause, his effort rather resembled the garbled account that Will Percy later formulated for *Lanterns on the Levee*. William Armstrong Percy, the Memphis lawyer and brother of Senator LeRoy and Walker Percy, Sr., created parody, but he sought no ironic artfulness. William Armstrong contented himself with fabricating a family tree for the progenitor Charles from only one source. On vacation in Leipzig, Germany, in 1904, he had bought for twenty-five dollars a copy of Edward Barrington de Fonblanque's monumental *Annals of the House of Percy* (1885) from a book dealer. Fonblanque's *Annals* was the family Bible to the more diligent genealogists of the Louisiana branch. After reading it, Willie Percy came to the unwarranted conclusion that the family descended from Thomas Percy, the leader of the Gunpowder Plot of 1605. He wrote a relative from the Robert Percy branch regarding his speculations about Thomas, the conspirator. "This cheerfully disposed old gentleman," the Memphis attorney declared, "was descended from the 4th Earl of Northumberland." The rebel's descendants had included two naval captains, father and son, from Cambridgeshire. Robert, the second of these seafarers, the Memphis lawyer observed, had gone to Ireland in 1763 as a "Gentleman" in the company of Hugh Percy, Lord Lieutenant and heir to the dukedom. Robert Percy was often seen at Northumberland House in the Strand, the noble family's London residence. "I fancy," William Armstrong Percy surmised, "this man must have been the father of Charles." [28]

William Armstrong Percy's desire to find aristocratic origins for Don Carlos may well have been a compensatory act to lift his own sense of inferiority to his younger brothers, the senator and the attorney for TCI. For some reason, they always treated him with affectionate condescension, owing in part to his second marriage below the social stratum from which Percys usually drew their spouses. Essentially, however, his genealogical conjectures reflected the sense of class of the Percy clan as a whole. Like Will and Walker Percy later in their celebration of Charles Percy, William enjoyed the prospect of decorating the family tree with colorful scoundrels. After all, what Southern family lacked its "black sheep?" None could be blacker—or more significant—than the thwarted assassin of James I. Unfortunately for his case, Robert of the Cambridgeshire Percys died without legitimate issue, as William Armstrong Percy himself admitted, thereby insinuating that the Cambridgeshire Robert's son Charles of West Florida had been a bastard.[29] The more earnest family genealogists did not take their Memphis cousin's fancy seriously.

While legend-making sufficed for the American-born line of Percys, genealogical investigation best suited the descendants of Charles and Margaret of St. Giles, London, the mother of Robert. The latter group was convinced that they were descended from the progenitor's first and only legitimate marriage contract—wherever it had been certified in the British Isles. From the 1890s to the recent past, their efforts to nail down the facts were more quest than hobby.[30] The changed circumstances of the post-Civil War South encouraged such inquiries. After defeat at war and the imposition of slave emancipation, some members of former slaveholding families sought new means to affirm respectability. For many of them, glorification of the "Lost Cause" sufficed. Others, like the Percys, found the search for ancient roots inspiring. After the Civil War wealthy descendants from both sides of the family had regathered in Natchez. Sargent Prentiss Knut, a member of the Louisiana tribe, recalled, "It used to be sport for Mother to get Mrs. Veazie, Mrs. Percy and cousin Margaret Routh, who was a sister of Mrs. S[eargent] S. Prentiss and daughter of Mrs. Jane Williams into a discussion as to which of these ladies belonged to the legitimate branch and a royal battle always resulted." Later on, he continued, they decided that *all* the Percys were legitimate (as their grandparents had conveniently agreed long before).[31]

At the close of the nineteenth century, Americans like the Percys and their collateral families had achieved material success. Yet they wanted something more, an enlarged sense of family roots and social standing. Daughters of the American Revolution, Colonial Dames, the United Daughters of the Confederacy, state and local historical societies, published genealogical aids and registries, and other institutional means were

created for members of the middle and upper classes in search of aristocratic forebears. By 1895, some forty-seven patriotic societies had been
established. Many of these activities had an unabashedly conservative purpose. At this time enormous waves of immigrants from eastern and southern Europe and Scandinavia seemed to threaten the sway of the Anglo-
Americans, among whom the Percys and their kinspeople counted themselves.[32]

While all the Margaret Percy line's genealogists eagerly participated in
the Anglo-Saxon revival, they were divided into two distinct circles. The
first consisted of male enthusiasts in Louisiana.[33] The group was large, led
by Clarence Percy, a Confederate veteran, and John Hereford Percy, his
son who carried the avocation into the 1940s. The second group was entirely female and Northern. With occasional help from female cousins in
Philadelphia and elsewhere, Jane Percy Sargent Duncan, Clarence Percy's
first cousin, took up the mission with special zeal. Later, Mary Butler Duncan Dana, her daughter, continued the enterprise after her mother's death
in 1905.

The circle of female genealogists reflected a change in circumstances of
the Robert Percy line that had begun in the antebellum years: the marriage
of Southern daughters to extremely wealthy and well-placed Northern men
of business. One of Robert's daughters had married the son of Winthrop
Sargent, a prominent Massachusetts Federalist, who served as the first ter-
ritorial governor of Mississippi.[34] Mrs. Charles Dana Gibson (the "Gibson
Girl"), Lady Astor, and Mrs. Wilton Phipps of London, wife of a knighted
English general, were also connected with this branch of the family. John
Singer Sargent, the famous nineteenth-century painter of Philadelphia and
London, was a cousin in this branch of the family and his portraits of the
extraordinarily handsome women in the line—Mary Dana, Rachel Heale
Phipps, and Jessie Percy Duncan Phipps—are among his best work. Mary
Dana's daughter Janet, Will Percy's friend and the wife of Warfield Long-
cope, was perhaps the most beautiful of them all, as her photograph in old
age suggests.[35]

These associations with substantial families at home and abroad bring
to mind Henry James's social comedy *The American*. It tells the story of
Christopher Newman, a rich, middle-aged American bachelor, who goes
to Paris to acquire an aristocratic wife. Continental duplicity—based upon
principles of an ancient, unfathomable honor—frustrate his pursuit.[36] Madame de Cintré, the object of his desire, eludes him. In much the same
fashion, the Northern wing of the Robert Percy line sought to obtain a
suitable ancestor—with little more success than James's humbled protagonist enjoyed. Jane Percy Sargent Duncan knew exactly the sort of ancestor
she would like to find. She lived in New York at No. 1 Fifth Avenue and
in Glen Cove, Long Island, on a large property later sold, according to
family story, to J. P. Morgan. Her historical acquisition could reasonably
be expected to match such well-appointed surroundings.[37] William Butler

Duncan, Jane's husband, whom she married in 1853, was the son of Alexander Duncan of Providence, Rhode Island. Duncan's father, a Scotsman in the eighteenth-century East India trade, had made a fortune speculating in western New York lands, and Alexander himself amassed even greater wealth in American banking and railroads before removing himself to a large estate near London in 1863.[38] He was reputed to be one of the richest men of his time, though much was lost in the Panic of 1873. His son William and his wife Jane inherited a comfortable estate. In 1884, their daughter, Mary Butler Duncan, married Paul Dana, Harvard-educated editor of the New York *Sun,* a post that he assumed when his father, the brilliant Charles Anderson Dana, retired.[39]

Together, mother Jane and daughter Mary Dana, undertook to locate Charles Percy's pedigree, hoping to find evidence of his gentility if not his link to the Northumbrian nobility at Alnwick Castle. The results of their labors, however, were disappointing for two reasons. The first was beyond their control.[40] By the late nineteenth century the trail had grown cold. Private records were scattered about, and much was destroyed when Windsor, one of widow Jane Middlemist Percy's plantation homes, burned to the ground in 1859 at Pine Ridge, near Natchez.[41] Those Percys holding key documents seemed to the genealogists exasperatingly inept at times. Even Clarence Percy himself forwarded some papers that Jane Percy Duncan found of "little use." Ones which could help—particularly a letter from Margaret Percy to her son Robert, dated 1781 and concerning the death of Robert's sister Sarah in London—had been lost by a careless kinsman. From New York, Jane Duncan wrote cousin Clarence Percy that their relative " 'Job' (I do not know how else to describe him)" had not returned crucial items for the investigators' use. At one point, Jane Duncan learned that her uncle, a son of Lieutenant Robert Percy, had found a paper of some kind that provided evidence of Margaret and Charles's marriage. Such a document would have provided major leads for their inquiry; the old gentleman had discovered it when removing the backing of the retired naval officer's portrait that had once hung in the parlor at Beech Woods, Robert's plantation at Big Bayou Lake.[42] Jane Duncan's Louisiana cousin then managed to lose it before anyone had a chance to find out what evidence it might offer. Worse still, knowledgeable kinspeople had long since died. In the fall of 1895, on a visit to London, Jane Duncan interviewed descendants of Jane Percy, Robert's Scottish wife, for whom Jane Duncan had been named. They were "members of the Middlemist family," Jane Duncan reported, "but they could tell me nothing." [43] Some of Robert and Jane Middlemist Percy's friends in London were still known by name in the family. However, their parents and grandparents had carried whatever secrets they knew to the grave years before.[44]

The second difficulty was the problem of investigation at so great a distance, the Louisiana Percys not being rich enough to venture across the ocean. Jane Duncan, however, had the funds and determination; she specialized in the British inquiries. Yet as she delved deeper into the matter, she realized that her quarry was not only elusive but also unsavory. For reasons no longer known, she thought that Charles Percy had perhaps been a "surgeon in the Army" after training in Scotland. Since Robert Dow, Charles Percy's early friend in America, and many of Robert Percy's associates in Canada were Scottish, her intuition was not unjustified. She planned to pursue that possibility by visiting the region herself and hiring experts. But, she concluded, "I fear we know all we will ever know & maybe all we would really care to know!—as I do not believe that Charles Percy was a very reputable character." In fact, in a later communication with cousin Clarence in Louisiana, she declared that Charles's children by "Miss Collins" were "not legitimate but they got most of the property after Mr C. Percy's death even though he owed money to our grandfather [Robert] from whom he had borrowed it."[45] Like historians, genealogists sometimes take up issues long since laid to rest.

A Scottish background for the family story would have been welcome. Yet as early as 1893, Jane Percy Prentiss, Jane Duncan's unmarried cousin, had pointed out that their ancestor had come from a less respectable part of the British Isles. In 1870, Jane Prentiss recalled that a Louisiana kinsman had told her of a letter (since lost), written by Charles himself, which had referred to Ireland as *"his home."*[46] Clarence Percy, who generally concerned himself with searches in Louisiana graveyards and church registries, confirmed that unpleasant news. As a youth, he had seen "an old legal document" among the papers of his father, Thomas Butler Percy. It began, he wrote, with the words: "Be it remembered that I, Charles Percy formerly of Ireland but more recently from the islands of Bermuda. . . ."[47]

Perhaps in the hope that Charles Percy was an Anglo-Irish gentlemen and not simply a peasant, Jane Duncan abandoned the Scottish trail that she had been pursuing. In 1896 she and her husband William Butler Duncan hired a law firm at the Inns of Court to establish his identity by way of the Public Record Office in both London and Dublin. Hardy and Page of Lincoln's Inn reported back surprising news. The firm and its agents could not find a Charles Percy on any officer muster roll or half-pay list. They did, however, discover a Charles Percy, private, in the 83rd Regiment of Foot. It had been first formed in Ireland in 1758 and permanently disbanded in 1763. Beside his name in Captain Holliol's company, the London lawyers reported, was written the letter "I." It stood for Irish, since other foot soldiers were designated "B" for English, Welsh, and Scottish, but nearly all the soldiers were Irish. As the regiment was stationed in Kilkenny, where Charles and Margaret's son, Robert, was born in 1762, there could be little doubt.[48]

Although Jane Percy Sargent Duncan told her daughter Mary Dana about her suspicions regarding Charles Percy's marital roguery, she did not circulate Hardy and Page's report. Her worst misgivings had been realized. The ancestor was neither an officer nor a gentleman—and he was a lowly Irishman besides. Nor had he belonged to a venerable regiment of Grenadiers, Horse Guards, or Fusiliers but rather to one without history and prestige. Moreover, the 83rd had seen little action. The unit served only briefly in a minor campaign of the Seven Years' War—the Portuguese campaign led by "Gentleman Johnny" Burgoyne, who was later to lose the Battle of Saratoga in the Revolution. Indeed, well-situated officers would never have selected a regiment so newly formed as the 83rd for fear of disbandment after paying for the commission. A regiment that existed only five years had scarcely time to develop an esprit de corps, instill self-confidence, and stimulate "family" loyalty, as eighteenth-century military experts liked to phrase it.[49] No wonder Charles Percy never boasted about his regimental affiliation. Jane Duncan must have been sorely disappointed on receipt of Hardy and Page's report.

After her mother Jane's death in 1905, Mary Dana took up the genealogical enterprise. She called on Clarence Percy for assistance but still withheld the information that Hardy and Page had provided.[50] In their ignorance, the Louisiana relatives pursued the cause with unremitting zeal but inevitable futility. Clarence Percy continued his correspondence with Irish Percys, members of the landed gentry. They lived in County Leitrim but knew most of the Kilkenny and Wicklow members of the small and scattered clan. They could not, however, identify a single Charles among their dead, antique or recent.[51] Although there were, in truth, some tantalizing possibilities in the Irish records, Clarence Percy could not gather the sum needed to visit the island.[52] By the time of his death in 1909, he could offer the family nothing so solid—or so deflating—as the Duncans' lengthy report from Hardy and Page, still unmentioned and uncirculated.

Some thirty or so years later, building on his father Clarence's labors, John Hereford Percy published his incomplete but indispensable genealogical history of the family. By correspondence he began to reconstruct the naval career of Robert Percy from the Admiralty files at the London Public Record Office on Chancery Lane. Moreover, he reconfirmed the burial listings of Margaret and daughter Sarah Percy in London that Jane Duncan had unearthed after combing the ancient records of the city's parishes. (Although no existing contemporary document gives the information, the idea that Robert's mother was named Margaret rested on family tradition and the fact that Robert had had his second daughter christened with that name.)[53] Knowing nothing of Jane and William Butler Duncan's discovery of Charles's military career with the 83rd, he could only designate Charles as either "English or Irish." His endeavors followed the destruction in 1922 of the Public Record Office in Dublin, which had eliminated all traces of Charles's existence in its enormous archives. The Baton Rouge banker still believed his ancestor to have been a former army officer, regiment and career unknown.[54]

Despite her misgivings, Jane Duncan need not have been as embarrassed about her ancestor as she apparently was. Also in her possession and also not shared with others was a letter from Charles to his son Robert, written in 1792. The document indicates not only that Charles was literate but that he had the graces associated with the gentlemanly class. In all likelihood, Mrs. Duncan's chagrin about the gentle birth of her ancestor was possibly misplaced. Charles Percy could well have been a cadet in the 83rd. Following its dissolution in 1763, young Percy may have transferred to another unit in which he did gain a commission.[55] Such possibilities apparently escaped her notice, but that was scarcely the only irony in the history of the Percy tribe.

Yet one must suspect that Jane Duncan kept her own counsel about Hardy and Page's unexpected findings not simply because his social standing did not measure up to her standards. The report from the lawyers at Lincoln's Inn was altogether negative. Their investigators had found no baptismal record in Kilkenny for Robert Percy, no marriage entry for Margaret and Charles, no will for Margaret at Somerset House, although the Lincoln's Inn law firm had been given the precise date of her death, October 21, 1785, as recorded in the Duncan family Bible. Worst of all from Jane Duncan's point of view was that Hardy and Page's agents had vainly combed the records "of the military chapel at Kilmainham, of Chapelizod, and the parish in Dublin (St. Paul's) in which the old barracks were situated." Charles's regiment had been located in that district for the months prior to departure for Kilkenny, where Robert Percy was born. Jane Duncan perhaps surmised that the only marriage ceremony to which the absconding Charles had subjected himself had been the one attaching him to the young heiress Susannah in Louisiana. That, she might have thought, explained why Lieutenant Robert Percy had let his step-mother Susannah receive the bulk of her husband's estate without demur. To be sure, though never identifying her by her Christian name, Dr. Robert Dow and mercer Patrick Morgan, Charles's friends in New Orleans and London, had referred to Margaret as his "wife," but perhaps out of delicacy. After all, Jane Duncan could have reasoned that when the lonely dying woman had told Dow how Robert's father had "used" her and her son "most cruelly," she might have meant that he had not only deserted her but also had never in their years together legalized their union. Understandably, Jane Duncan had no desire to challenge a tradition of equal legitimacy that both families had come to accept.[56]

For the later descendants of Susannah Collins Percy—Will and Walker Percy most particularly—a touch of roguery invested their past with romance, daring, and even aristocratic unconventionality. For Will Percy, himself a soul apart, the idea of a bar sinister on the family escutcheon was a source of delight, not shame, and he nearly boasted of that heritage in *Lanterns on the Levee*. The doubtfulness of everything related to the American Percys' progenitor raises the story to the level of inspired drama, like Tom Stoppard's brilliant play, *Arcadia,* or of historical mystery, like Natalie Zemon Davis's *The Return of Martin Guerre.*

Indeed, irony lies at the heart of the intermixture of genealogical actuality and fancy, not only because of the information received about Don Carlos's problematic origins and adventurous early life but for another reason: the history of the Northumberland Percys, a story that suggests the possibility that myth and reality were more closely joined than one might have guessed. Both the legitimate and the illegitimate wings of the family—whichever was which—had reason to feel a psychological connection with the Northumbrian lineage. Substance to their claim for noble blood rested in genetic resemblances of a darker nature than genealogists usually expect to unearth.[57]

The American Percys of both houses sensed in themselves a blood relationship to the distant Border lords that was based in part upon that combination of intellect, honor, and melancholy that figured in the chain of Percys on both sides of the Atlantic. Surprisingly, Charles Percy's Irish birth makes blood kinship to the noble house on the Scottish border more likely than if he had come from a district closer to the Northumbrian seat at Alnwick Castle (just north of Newcastle-on-Tyne). All the Irish Percys, a relatively small band, were either close kinspeople or direct descendants of James Percy (1619–90?), known as "the Trunkmaker," and his wife, Sarah Sayer of Norwich in East Anglia.[58] (He had engaged in that craft as a youth but went on to make a fortune in general trade.) Late in the seventeenth century, this Percy had achieved a peculiar notoriety. Before the four courts at Westminster he was forced to wear a paper sign on his breast, reading "The False and Impudent Pretender to the Earldom of Northumberland." The tradesman had had the temerity to claim the princely domain and title when Josceline, the eleventh Earl, died in 1670. The nobleman's daughter, later the Duchess of Somerset, had had no son.[59] By the law of primogeniture, the Northumberland honors could only devolve upon a male relation. James Percy wrecked his health and his capital in hiring lawyers to forward his claim which he could never prove beyond doubt.[60] Nevertheless, one genealogist claims that he was probably a direct descendant of Edward Percy, the fourth son of the fourth Earl. Perhaps that connection explains why Josceline, the eleventh Earl, on his deathbed had acknowledged James Percy as his cousin and heir.[61]

Even though conventional genealogical work led nowhere, temperamental factors seem to link the American Percys with the Northumbrian house: similar patterns of intelligence; material shrewdness; early death; and problems with chronic depression.[62] The American Percys read and told each other stories gleaned from the family chronicles, most particularly Fon-blanque's *Annals* and, later, Gerald Brenan's two thick volumes. Percy Ferguson, a daughter of Confederate General Samuel Wragg Ferguson and his novel-writing wife Kate, declared that in her reading she saw "in living members of our brilliant and self-willed tribe" many of the traits that the Northumbrian earls had once exhibited. The whole breed, she summed up, consisted of a "peculiar people!" Like many others in the extended clan she felt most intrigued by her "Percy blood, because perhaps they were people of artistic talents, literary ability and most pronounced character and personalities." [63]

With regard to the English Percys, such a characterization was not inaccurate. Setting aside Shakespeare's depressive and truculent Hotspur of the fourteenth century, the gloomy record began with the assassination of Henry Percy, the fourth Earl, probably at the behest of Henry VII. The king was suspicious of the nobleman who had placed him on the throne. Henry Percy had switched sides at Bosworth Field, assuring the defeat of Richard III. Playing king-maker had its disadvantage. [64] By the time Percy's son and heir reached maturity, his father had fallen into a melancholy that seldom lifted. The fifth Earl revised the armigerous motto from "Esperaunce ma comforte"—"In hope is my comfort"—to "Esperaunce en dieu." One could not trust man, only God. [65] The mood persisted in his son, the sixth Earl, known as "Henry, the Unhappy." From an early age this Henry Percy was separated from his mother and compelled to live at the court of Henry VIII. [66] While a page of Cardinal Wolsey, the youth fell in love with the exquisite Anne Boleyn, one of Queen Catherine's ladies-in-waiting. Their young love, however, was quickly suppressed by order of the king. [67] Still in his adolescence, Henry Percy was married off to Lady Mary Talbot, daughter of the Earl of Shrewsbury. The couple quickly came to despise each other heartily and produced no heirs.

Sonless and unloved, Henry Percy took little interest in life, assumed a haughty and dissipated manner, and used the crises of combat as a means to overcome his severe depressions. In a manner so characteristic of the family, Henry met his personal mood and the needs of the hour with consummate skill and bravery against England's Scottish enemies. As part of his reaction to the political crisis, the sixth Earl raised his household to new heights of military effectiveness on the Border and conducted vigorous campaigns against the Scots, particularly a major raid in 1532. [68] Nonetheless the king was not pleased and through Wolsey demanded that the Border lord should prove himself "comformable to his Hyghness's pleesor" by repudiating his tendency toward "sulleness, mistrust, disdayne" and drunkenness. [69]

When Henry VIII turned against Queen Anne, his sonless wife, he seized upon Henry Percy as the author of his troubles. Percy had allegedly made a prenuptial arrangement years before. On grounds that her honor had been sullied, Henry accused Anne of treason and other offenses. By

LeRoy Percy, father of William Alexander Percy, at mid-career in the early 1900s.
From the Percy Family Papers, courtesy, Mississippi Department of Archives and History, Jackson, Mississippi.

Camille Bourges Percy, 1862–1929, wife of LeRoy Percy and mother of William Alexander Percy.
From the Percy Family Papers, courtesy, Mississippi Department of Archives and History, Jackson, Mississippi.

LeRoy Percy (1891–1902), second son of LeRoy and Camille Percy and brother of Will Percy; killed in a gun accident.
From the Percy Family Papers, Courtesy of the Mississippi Department of Archives and History.

LeRoy Percy in his declining years.
From the Percy Family Papers, courtesy, Mississippi Department of Archives and History, Jackson, Mississippi.

The Greenville, Mississippi, home of
LeRoy and Camille Percy prior to its
renovation in the 1920s.
From the Percy Family Papers, courtesy,
Mississippi Department of Archives and
History, Jackson, Mississippi.

The Percy family automobile, parked
above the 1927 Flood Line, in front of
the Percys' house, Greenville.
From the Percy Family Papers, courtesy of
the Mississippi Department of Archives and
History, Jackson, Mississippi.

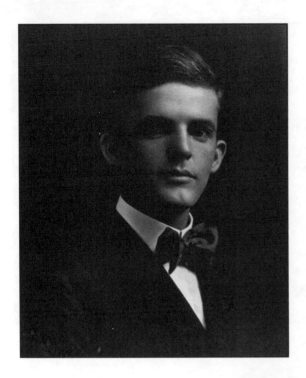

William Alexander (Will) Percy, 1885–1942, as a young man at Sewanee and Harvard in the early 1900s.
From the Percy Family Papers, courtesy, Mississippi Department of Archives and History, Jackson, Mississippi.

William Alexander Percy, Paris, 1918, portrait photograph by the famous Alice Boughton.
Courtesy of John Seymour Erwin, Sun City, Florida.

Will Percy, Herbert Hoover, and LeRoy Percy inspecting the flood damage in downtown Greenville, 1927.
From the Percy Family Papers, courtesy of the Mississippi Department of Archives and History, Jackson, Mississippi.

Huger Wilkinson Jervey, 1878–1949, friend of Will Percy and co-owner with Will Percy of Brinkwood, Sewanee, later Dean of the Parker School of International Studies and Professor of Law, Columbia University.
Courtesy of the Archives, Jessie Ball DuPont Library, University of the South, Sewanee, Tennessee.

(above, left) LeRoy Pratt Percy, 1889–
1929, as a rising Birmingham,
Alabama, attorney in the 1920s.
*Courtesy, Photographic Collections of the
Birmingham Public Library, Birmingham,
Alabama.*

(above, right) Martha Susan Phinizy
Percy, 1890–1932, wife of LeRoy Pratt
Percy and mother of Walker, LeRoy,
and Phinizy Percy.
*From the Percy Family Papers, courtesy,
Mississippi Department of Archives and
History, Jackson, Mississippi.*

John Walker Percy, in 1911, as a mem-
ber of the Alabama legislature. He suf-
fered a nervous collapse later that year.
*Courtesy, Photographic Collections of the
Birmingham Public Library, Birmingham,
Alabama.*

William Alexander Percy, c. 1935.
From the Percy Family Papers, courtesy of the Mississippi Department of Archives and History, Jackson, Mississippi.

Will Percy with his lifelong friend, Janet Longcope, August, 1941, at Cornhill Farm, Lee, Massachusetts.
Courtesy, Mary Lee Johansen and Duncan Longcope, Lee, Massachusetts.

Will Percy, author of *Lanterns on the Levee,* some months before his death on January 21, 1942.
From the Percy Family Papers, courtesy, Mississippi Department of Archives and History, Jackson, Mississippi.

Janet Percy Dana Longcope on her 80th birthday. Her radiance suggests why Will Percy found her so endearing.
Photo by Lisa Gamble Bartle, Stockbridge, Massachusetts, courtesy, Mary Lee Johansen and Duncan Longcope, Lee, Massachusetts.

(above, left) Mary Shepherd Quintard, Sewanee friend of Walker Percy, c. 1940.
Mrs. Charles Wyatt-Brown, Beaufort, South Carolina.

(above, right) Rosamond Myers, Sewanee friend of Walker Percy, c. 1941.
From the Margaret Jeffery Myers Papers, courtesy, Archives, Jessie Ball Dupont Library, University of the South, Sewanee, Tennessee.

Walker Percy and Mary Bernice Townsend, newlyweds, late 1940s in New Orleans.
Courtesy of Jay Tolson and Mrs. Walker Percy.

Mary Butler Duncan Dana, initiator of
the Percy genealogical enterprise.
*Photo by Lisa Gamble Bartle, Stockbridge,
Massachusetts, courtesy of Mary Lee
Johansen and Duncan Longcope, Lee,
Massachusetts.*

Henry Percy, Ninth Earl of Northumberland, known as the "Wizard Earl," imprisoned in the Tower of London for eighteen years after the exposure of the Gunpowder Plot. Engraving from a portrait by Sir Anthony Van Dyck.
Courtesy, Photographic Division, Library of Congress, Washington, D.C.

Algernon Percy, Tenth Earl of Northumberland, was as melancholy as his father, the Ninth Earl. Engraving from a portrait by Sir Anthony Van Dyck.
Courtesy, Photographic Division, Library of Congress, Washington, D.C.

Walker Percy, 1916–1990, at Bechac's Restaurant, Mandeville, Louisiana, 1984, at the weekly gathering of his friends.
Photo by Rhoda Faust, New Orleans, Louisiana.

Walker Percy and Mary Bernice Townsend Percy, New Orleans, c. 1984.
Photo by Linda Hobson, New Orleans, Louisiana.

Walker Percy, novelist and essayist.
Photo by Mark Morrow, Alexandria,
Virginia.

Shelby Foote, 1993.
*Photo by Crissie Wilson, courtesy of the
Department of Archives and History,
Jackson, Mississippi.*

cruel and deliberate irony, he named the sixth Earl as one of the twenty-five lords to sit in special judgment on her case in 1536. When the Lord Steward of the trial announced the unanimous verdict of guilty of treason with execution to be a burning at the stake while she was still alive, Henry Percy swooned and had to be removed from the chamber.[70] Percy's dejection—*"languens in extremis,"* pronounced a courtier—grew increasingly more serious. In a suicidal moment, he begged his retainers to kill him so as to *"rid him of much pain."* On June 29, 1537, at age thirty-five, Henry Percy died in a state of delirium and anguish.[71] F. R. Surtees, a nineteenth-century novelist known chiefly for his sporting tales, adopted the language and style of Tudor poetry to capture something of Henry Percy's disheartened spirit in the lines at the opening of this chapter. The earl even renounced all his property and willed it to his monarch on the grounds that he feared "the debylytery and unnaturalness of those of my name" and deplored his childlessness.[72]

Although the family recovered power under the reigns of Edward VI and Mary, Thomas Percy, the sixth Earl's nephew was heedlessly brave in warfare but dim-witted. He rebelled against the Crown and was decapitated at York in 1572 for seeking the restoration of Catholicism. For all to see, the Earl's head was affixed on a pole above Micklegate Bar, portal to the city of York. Some of the literary Percys in America were Catholic, most notably Ellen Lee and Walker Percy. For them the Northumbrian earl's last words were appropriate: "Remember that I die in the Communion of the Catholic Church, and that I am a Percy in life and death."[73] Though later beatified, Thomas Percy was no figure like Sir Thomas More, whose image Walker Percy would signify as a recognition of his connection with the period in which the Catholic Northumberland household flourished. The career of Thomas Percy's younger brother and heir was equally violent. He shot himself in the chest in 1584 while imprisoned in the Tower of London for suspected acts of treason in the Catholic cause.[74] Suicide was a relatively rare occurrence in the Elizabethan age. Men of honor ordinarily projected their feelings of despair in violent assaults against others rather than in taking their own lives. Nonetheless, historians largely agree that melancholia, not fears of legal proceedings, led him to that extremity.[75]

Though not suicidal, young Henry Percy, the ninth Earl, was deeply embittered by his father's death. "For weeks," Gerald Brenan writes, the new earl's "door remained closed to the world."[76] Henry Percy was no less afflicted with depression than his father. "For years," the Percys' historian reports, "he was accustomed to give way to fits of melancholy." He styled himself "a wretched parricide for serving under those whose hands were red with the blood of so loving a sire." Never did Henry Percy believe his father capable of killing himself. In consequence, fairly or not, he was suspected of a secret and treasonous faith in Catholicism. As a courtier observed, Romanism was an antidote to his open "discontent" with himself and the unjustified loss of his father. That response would have its American analogies. In the earl's case, however, his attraction to the faith was also based on his relationship to the North country. The many families of Percys as well as other well-born kinspeople and their tenants remained loyal to the old traditions.[77]

The ninth Earl found much solace in study and in the principles of Aurelian Stoicism, a philosophy which attracted him because of its rationale for melancholy, fatalism, self-deprecation, attributes that, centuries later, Sarah Dorsey and Will Percy also found in the emperor's work. The earl preferred association with intellectuals—especially astronomers and mathematicians—to affairs at court. For his interest in learning, he was known as the "Mæcænas of learned men." [78] Henry Percy found women's intellect weak, being "as wyse at fifteen as at fifty," and their sense of morality too swayed by base ambitions and lust. Their utility was confined, he asserted, to making love, bearing heirs, and being the means for the formation of family alliances and the transference of dowries. The melancholy earl's disparagement of womankind was directly related to his resentment of his mother's decision to send him away from her when he was five, a common practice among the nobility. Moreover, he knew how much his mother detested his father, the eighth Earl, whom her eldest son so greatly admired.

Northumberland had special reason for gloom, however, when cousin Thomas Percy, a client under the earl's patronage, organized the infamous "Gunpowder Plot" in 1605.[79] The zealot, *"hote as any Hotspur himself,"* Guido Fawkes, and a few other co-conspirators dug a tunnel to the House of Commons from the basement of a house that Percy had leased and prepared to blow up Commons with barrels of gunpowder when the king arrived to open Parliament. The plot was uncovered, the fanatics run down and killed, and the earl, ignorant of his cousin's conspiracy, thrown into the Tower of London, where his father had killed himself. Anticipating a long stay, he filled his apartments in Martin Tower with scientific instruments and books in many languages. Other well-born and highly intellectual inmates included Sir Francis Bacon and Sir Walter Raleigh. The earl was especially close to Raleigh and did much to make his sojourn in the Tower more bearable before his execution.[80] Although handsomely rewarded for their favors, the Tower guards took a dim view of Henry Percy's coterie. They whispered about the mysterious scientific experiments with telescopes and alchemical powders, the clouds of noxious smoke (Virginia pipe tobacco) issuing from the library and laboratory, the preparation and consumption of a *"Greate Cordiall,"* which Northumberland and his learned friends called the *"Elixir Vitae."* In the guards' opinion, he was the "Wizard Earl," engaged in *"black magick."* [81] The earl's temperament found expression in Catherine Warfield's representation of Erastus Bouverie and in Walker Percy's Lancelot Lamar. In a sense, Henry Percy was as self-imprisoned as these fictional heroes. James I offered Northumberland a pardon, but he refused it because the king had granted the earl's daughter permission to marry a Scottish commoner, one of the king's wealthy favorites. On matters of class, Henry Percy could be unforgiving, but clearly depression as well as pride kept him entombed, as it were. Even when released from prison after eighteen years, the earl, in his melancholy, took residence in apartments in view of the Tower walls, as if he could not relinquish sight of where his father had ended his life and where he had nearly ended his own.

Raised in the gloomy battlements of the Tower, Algernon, the tenth Earl, born in 1602, also suffered from a despondency that "nothing," declares Brenan, "could efface." [82] Through his second marriage to Lady Elizabeth Howard, he acquired her father's great London palace on the Strand.[83] Until its demolition in 1870, it was known as "Northumberland House," the name Charles Percy gave to his comparatively modest dwelling on Buffalo Creek in the 1780s. After the death of the tenth Earl's sickly and only son, Josceline, in 1670, and the failures of the trunk-making James Percy's petitions, the male line died out. In 1740 Elizabeth Percy, Earl Josceline's descendant, married Sir Hugh Smithson, a member of the gentry but, by the prevailing standards of nobility, virtually a commoner. In 1750, George II conferred the Northumberland arms and properties upon Sir Hugh, a political ally of Horace Walpole, prime minister. (The Smithsonian Institution in Washington owes its existence to the first Duke's illegitimate son.) Sir Hugh successfully petitioned the House of Lords to change his name to Percy. For his continued political support, George III elevated him in 1766 to the titles of Earl Percy and Duke of Northumberland.[84]

From the most cursory reading of Fonblanque and Brenan, the American Percys discerned these facets of the earls' lives—their early deaths and their problems with depression. They could also claim that they, unlike the latter-day household of Northumberland, were genuine Percys, not parvenus like the Smithsons. In the 1920s, Percy Ferguson of Mississippi City, granddaughter of poet Ellen Lee, had by correspondence become acquainted with the reigning duke. To cousin John Hereford Percy she recounted how she had confronted the nobleman with the observation that he was not a "real" Percy but only a Smithson who had changed his family patronym to his wife's maiden name. The duke had been rather "testy" in response. As far as Percy Ferguson was concerned, the duke, along with his son, Lord Henry Algernon George Percy, "was no more to be compared with cousin Will—cousin Le Roy Percy's magnificent and brilliant father [the Gray Eagle], or cousin Le Roy himself [—] than a potato to a bright star in the heavens!" Berating a duke might have comforted Percy Ferguson, whose father, the heroic General Ferguson, had scandalized LeRoy Percy's Levee Board by absconding to Latin America years before. Were not the Smithsons, after all, frauds on a scale unimaginable in the impoverished South of her father's time? Ironically the unmarried elderly woman depended upon occasional donations from nearby kinfolk in Bi-loxi, a monthly check of ten dollars from Will Percy until his death, and charity from the United Daughters of the Confederacy to keep her out of the county home.[85] In contrast to Percy Ferguson's pluckiness, most of the clan in America, thought the alleged connection with the House of Northumberland too insubstantial for such familiar remonstrances. In fact, the mystery of a blood relationship was as baffling as the doctrine of "Apostolic Succession," as John Hereford Percy once lamented.[86]

With little to show for years of genealogical labor, John Hereford Percy nonetheless hated to think that his ancestor Charles Percy had no monument, and that perhaps, as Will Percy said, the creek into which he had flung himself had changed course and washed away his bones. So, on the grounds of Grace Episcopal Church in St. Francisville, you can find the slab that the Louisiana banker placed there to honor Charles Percy—a more unassuming memorial than the one Will Percy commissioned for the Greenville cemetery to honor Senator LeRoy Percy. John Hereford Percy's black stone cenotaph for Don Carlos appears in *The Thanatos Syndrome* as the site where the cousin-protagonists reflect upon their common heritage of melancholy and death.

Not far from that site, at St. Joseph's Abbey, near Covington, Louisiana, lies the body of Walker Percy. He had died at home, May 10, 1990, surrounded by those he cared most about—Bunt, his daughters, his brothers Phinizy and LeRoy, and Shelby Foote. The writer's oldest friend had hastened down from Memphis when he heard the end was near. Walker's last years had been filled with pain from a spreading cancer and the treatments he had endured less for his sake than for the family's. Yet throughout the final ordeal he never lost his charm or wit. Walker always had given the impression that his visitor really mattered to him, and he found some way of making the stranger feel at ease.

Even when not feeling well, he thought of others, not himself. He called Cleanth Brooks, an old friend recently retired from the Yale Department of English. Cleanth's wife Edith, Percy heard, had been diagnosed as having cancer. The novelist offered to drive the Brookses on a tour of the historic inns of Connecticut. The autumn leaves were falling in an array of color, Percy reminded him. Alas, Cleanth had to decline the generous offer. Edith, who died in the fall 1986, was too ill for the exertion, but how much the suggestion meant to the grieving pair. At Brooks's request, a page proof copy of *The Thanatos Syndrome* arrived in the mail from Walker as a substitute, and Brooks read it aloud to his wife in their last days together.[87]

As Walker Percy would have appreciated, there was a final irony in the family's efforts to make sense the past. The genealogists' search for

Charles Percy's origins ended in irresolution and enigma, and the literary renditions of the past survive not as historical truth but as either transforming fiction or inspiring myth. Even the material emblems are not exactly what they seem to be. Just as there are no remains of Don Carlos beneath the tombstone in St. Francisville, so, too, the grieving sentry in the Greenville churchyard is not solid metal but, like all bronze castings, empty. According to Leon Koury, Will Percy's friend and a pupil of Malvina Hoffman, the sculptor did not craft the apparel that covers the Patriot. She simply took a suit of stage armor and made a mold; only the bleak face was sculpted.[88]

The story of the Percys, therefore, is typically American in its uncertain origins. But it also suggests something more about the nature of American class structure. The Percys belonged to the ruling element of their region. Because of their location in the South, however, they were never considered a part of a national elite—not like the Adams family, two of whose members served in the Presidency. The Percys' traditions ran deeper than those of most other families of their class, but they presided over a very small patch of America. The Delta was a sector riven with black people's poverty and scarred by the furies of nature—flood, drought, and pestilence. As a result its white rulers could never command the sympathies and support of other regions of the country. But if the family demonstrated any truth about the human condition it was that wealth and aristocratic bearing do not spare anyone from sorrow, defeat, or sense of personal failure. The Percys met these disappointments as best they could, even if the resources were merely silence, story-telling, legend-making, and reconstructing family trees. These were especially Southern devices. Historians can accept neither the policy of reticence nor the construction of tales at face value. The scholar must probe beneath the surface for signs of inner meaning and for the pain. By that means the strength and liveliness of creative minds like those of the Percys, can be revealed. The Percys were not perhaps noble in origin but they were—and are—in spirit. Both Will and Walker revealed how the family's tradition of creativity and constructive lives enlightened their times and overcame the sorrows that would have overwhelmed those less gifted.

Perhaps the first American Percy, the originator of all the difficulties and the successes, is laughing still wherever he is beyond the grave. For nearly two centuries trooper Charles has eluded detection. That state of affairs is unlikely ever to change. Nonetheless, the Percy family, which represents much that is best in American leadership and letters, will endure, as these pages have sought to verify. The family history illustrates that to overstress the melancholy of artists or even those with conventional careers serves unjustly to diminish their integrity and contribution to later generations. After all, as Herman Melville pointed out in *Moby-Dick*, "To trail the genealogies of these high mortal miseries . . . we must needs give in to this: That the gods themselves are not forever glad."[89]

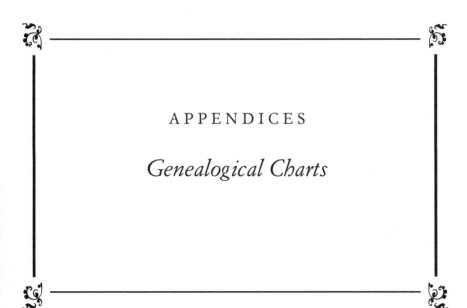

APPENDICES

Genealogical Charts

Descendants of Thomas George, Son of Charles Percy and Susannah Collins

Charles Percy
1740–1794

= *Susannah Collins*
1764–1803

= *Maria Pope*
1797–1847

Thomas George
1786–1841

┌───┐
│ Robert Henry 1831–1853; Ellis   │
│ Ware, Matilda Walker & Thomas   │
│ George died in childhood.   │
└───┘

Charles
Brown
1820–1850

= *Henrietta Mary
Ann Nicol*
1820–1848

Leroy
Pope
1825–1882

*Nannie I.
Armstrong*
1835–1897

= William
Alexander
1837–1888

John
Walker
1817–1864

= *Fannie*
1823–1894

May
1848–1876

= *J.S.
McNeily*

Fannie
1859–1882

= *A.
Downs
Pace*

Caroline
Yarborough

= William
Armstrong
1863–1912

*Lottie
Galloway
Morris*

2nd m.   1st m.

*Camille
Bourges*
1862–1929

= LeRoy
1861–
1929

Lady
1866–
1937

= *Charles
James
McKinney*

John
Walker
1864–1917

= *Mary
Pratt
DeBardeleben*

*Anne
Dent*

= William
Armstrong, Jr.
1906–1971

William
Alexander
1885–1942

LeRoy
1891–
1902

*Martha Susan
Phinizy*
1890–1932

= LeRoy Pratt
Percy
1889–1929

Matt
Murphy

= Ellen
1893–1968

William
Armstrong, III
1933–

*Mary
Bernice
Townsend*

= Walker
1916–1990

LeRoy
1917–

= *Sarah
Farish*

Billups
Phinizy
1921–

= *Jaye
Dobbs*

Ann
Boyd

Mary
Pratt

Direct descendants are in **bold**; all others are in *italic*.

Chief sourc: John Hereford Percy, *The Percy Family of Mississippi and Louisiana, 1776–1843* (Baton Rouge: priv. prnt., 1943).

These charts were created by Andrew K. Frank.

APPENDIX II (Selective) Descendants of Sarah, Eldest Daughter of Charles Percy & Susannah Collins

Nathaniel A. Ware (1780 or 1789–1853) = Sarah (1781–1836) [2nd m.]

Sarah (1781–1836) = John Ellis (?–1808) [1st m.]

Children:

- **Catherine Ann** (1816–1877) = *Robert Elisha Warfield* (?–1872)
- **Eleanor Percy** (1819–1849) = *William Henry Lee* (?–1784)
- **Thomas George** (1805–1838)
- **Mary Jane** ([c.1800]–1844) = *René LaRoche* (1795–1872)
- *Charles Adolphus Dahlgren* (1811–1888) = *Mary Malvina Routh* (?–1858) [1st m.]; = *Austin Mortimer* [2nd m.]; *John Adolphus*

Children of Catherine Ann & Robert Elisha Warfield:

- **Elinor Ware**
- **Mary Rose Percy**
- **Nathaniel Ware**

Catherine Sarah (Kate) = *Samuel Wragg Ferguson*

- **Sarah Anne Ellis** (1829–1879) = *Samuel Worthington Dorsey* (1811–1875)
- **Stephen Percy Ellis**
- **Inez** = *John Gordon* (divorce) [1st m.]; = *Edward Peckham* [2nd m.]
- **Thomas LaRoche Ellis** (1836–1862) = *Appolina Ingraham*

Mary [2nd m.]

APPENDIX III (Selective) The Southern Branch of the Robert Percy Line

Charles Percy = **Margaret Percy**
1740–1794   1745–1785[1]

Sarah
1767/8–1781[2]

Jane Middlemist Edinburgh = **Robert Percy**
1772–1831   1762–1819

Thomas Butler Percy = *Elizabeth Randolph*
1809–1851   1811–1874

Clarence Percy = *Annie Matilda Hereford*
1836–1909   1836–1898

John Bronaugh Hereford Percy = *Christine Dashiell Howell*
1870–1960   1874–1968

Annie Matilda Hereford Percy = *Oscar Menes Thompson*
1899–   1899–1990

William Heard Wright, Sr. = **Louisa Johnson Percy**
1900–1968   1903–1981

Oscar Menes Thompson, Jr. = *Laura Noland*
1927–   1927–

Mary Arwin Patrick = **William Heard Wright, Jr.**
1930–   1927–

Direct descendants are in **bold**: all others are in *italic*.

Chief sources: John Hereford Percy, *The Percy Family of Mississippi and Louisiana, 1776–1843* (Baton Rouge: priv. prnt., 1943) and B.B. Warfield, *The Warfields: Kentucky Branch* (Louisville: manuscript at Filson Club, 1882).

1 Date of burial, according to records at St. Giles-in-the-Fields, London.

2 Percy, *The Percy Family of Mississippi* gives date of death as 1780, but St. Giles records reveal the date above for her burial.

361

APPENDIX IV: (Selective)   The Northern Branch of the Robert Percy Line

Charles = **Margaret**
Percy   **Percy**
1740–1794   1745–1785

Sarah   **Robert** = *Jane*
1767/8–   **Percy**   *Middlemist*
1781   1762–1819   1772–1831

Margaret = *George*
Percy   *Washington*
1802–   *Sargent*
1865   1802–1864

Jane Percy = *William Butler*
Sargent   *Duncan*
1833–1905   1830–1912

Mary Butler *Jessie Percy*
Duncan   **Sargent**
1861–1922   1833–1905

Paul Dana = **Jane Percy**   *Warfield Theobald* = *William*
1852–1930   **Dana (Janet)**   *Longcope*   *Wilton*
                     1886–1974   1877–1953   *Phipps*

Barbara = *William*   *John M.* = **Mary Lee**   **Duncan**   **Christopher** = *Julia*
1916–   *Fenwick*   *Johansen*   **(Mellie)**   **Longcope**   1928–   *Coffin*
                  Keyser   1923–   1920–

Direct descendants are in **bold**; all others are in *italic*.
Chief source: John Hereford Percy, *The Percy Family of Mississippi and Louisiana, 1776–1843* (Baton Rouge: priv. prnt., 1943).

362

A Selected List
of Manuscript Collections

PRIVATE COLLECTIONS

"Autobiography," Charles Bell, Santa Fe, New Mexico.

The Rev. Joseph Stratton Buck Diary, typescript, in possession of Alma Carpenter, Natchez, Mississippi.

Robert Daniel MSS, in possession of Mrs. Robert Daniel, Sewanee, Tennessee.

Robert Craig Gilmore MSS, Lafayette, Louisiana.

Duncan Longcope and M. L. Johansen Collection, Cornhilll Farm, Lee, Massachusetts (Longcope-Johansen MSS).

Oscar M. Thompson and William H. Wright, Jr., Collection, Baton Rouge, Louisiana (Thompson-Wright MSS).

AMERICAN REPOSITORIES: LOCAL, COUNTY, STATE, AND REGIONAL

Adams County Courthouse, Natchez, Mississippi (ACC), Office of the Chancery Clerk (OCC): Spanish Records, Deed Books.

Alabama Department of Archives and History (ADAH): John Coffee MSS; John Williams Walker Family MSS; Richard Wilde Walker MSS; Madison County Tax List, 1811.

Filson Club, Louisville, Kentucky (FCL): Samuel and Orlando Brown Family Papers.

Historical Society of Delaware, Wilmington: Thomas Rodney MSS in H. F. Brown Collection.

Historical Society of Pennsylvania (HSP): Henry Gilpin MSS.

Henry E. Huntington Library, San Marino, California: Sargent Prentiss Knut Papers.

Huntsville City Library, Huntsville, Alabama (HCL): John Williams Walker MSS.

Maine Historical Society, Portland, (MHS): Charles E. Banks Collection; Joseph Williamson MSS.

Maryland Historical Society, Baltimore: Warfield Family materials.

Mississippi Department of Archives and History, Jackson, Mississippi (MDAH): Henry Waring (Harry) Ball Diary; J. F. H. Claiborne MSS, esp. George Poindexter materials; Archibald S. Coody MSS; Varina Davis MSS; Howell Family MSS; John Jones interviews; John Sharp Williams MSS; Percy Family MSS (PP); W. T. Walthall Papers; Subject Files; Superior Court of Chancery Records; and Territorial Court Records.

Museum of the Confederacy, Richmond, Virginia (MCR): Jefferson Davis MSS.

North Carolina Department of Archives and History, Raleigh: Will Books; Deed Books.

Rosenberg Library, Galveston, Texas: John L. Darragh MSS.

Tennessee State Archives, Nashville (TSA): Charles A. Dahlgren Papers; Charles Brown Percy Family Papers.

Tensas Parish Courthouse, Clerk's Office, St. Joseph, Louisiana: Deed Books.

Washington County Courthouse: Circuit Court Clerk's Office: Deed Books.

William Alexander Percy Memorial Library, Greenville, Mississippi: Oral History of Greenville Collection.

Wisconsin Historical Society, Madison (WHS): Oliver Pollock MSS in the Draper Collection.

NATIONAL REPOSITORIES

Library of Congress (LC): Society for the Propagation of the Gospel in Foreign Parts (SPG); Thomas Rodney Notebook; and copies of Colonial Office Papers.

National Archives, Fort Worth, Texas: Ellis v. Davis Case No. 8934.

National Archives, Washington, D.C. (NA): Department of the Interior MSS, Territorial Papers; Department of War MSS, Confederate Papers; and American Red Cross MSS.

UNIVERSITY AND PROFESSIONAL REPOSITORIES

Baker Library, Harvard University, Cambridge: Dun & Bradstreet Company Archives.

Barker Historical Center, University of Texas (BHC): James Campbell Wilkins MSS.

Jessie Ball DuPont Library, University of the South, Sewanee, Tennessee (USL): Alumni Files; Charlotte Gailor MSS; Leonidas L. Polk MSS; Hobart-Jefferys-Myers Collection.

Jean and Alexander Heard Library, Vanderbilt University, Nashville: Donald Davidson MSS.

Hill Memorial Library, Louisiana State University Libraries (H-LSU): Ware Family MSS; Ellis Family MSS; Lewis Baker interview with Brodie Crump; Janet Dana Longcope MSS.

Houghton Library, Harvard University, Cambridge: William Stanley Braithwaite MSS; Witter Bynner MSS; Robert Lowell MSS.

Howard-Tilton Library, Tulane University, New Orleans (H-TL): Jefferson Davis MSS in Kuntz Collection.

Library of the College of Physicians of Philadelphia (LCPP): René LaRoche MSS.

Pennsylvania Hospital Historic Library, Philadelphia: Admissions Book; Sarah Ware File.

Perkins Library, Duke University, Durham: Larkin Newby MSS.

Princeton University Archives, Princeton, New Jersey: Alumni Records.

University of Alabama Library, University (UAL): W. S. Hoole Special Collections: Jefferson Davis MSS.

University of Kentucky Library, Lexington (UKL): Samuel Brown MSS.

University of Mississippi Library: David L. Cohn MSS.

University of Southern Mississippi, Hattiesburg: Theodore G. Bilbo MSS.

Wilson Library, Southern Historical Collection, University of North Carolina, Chapel Hill (SHC): Sarah Dorsey Will with transcript of Charles A. Dahlgren interview in Philadelphia *Press*; Shelby Foote MSS; Walker Percy MSS.

FOREIGN REPOSITORIES

Glasgow City Archives, Mitchell Library, Glasgow, Scotland: John Dow Log Book.

Public Record Office, Dublin, Ireland: genealogical materials.

Public Record Office, Kew, London, U.K. (PRO): Admiralty (Adm), Ships' Logbooks; Auditor's Office (AO); Colonial Office (CO).

Provincial Archives of New Brunswick, Fredericton, Canada: Land Grants.

Public Archives of Nova Scotia (PANS), Canada: Rev. John Wiswall Journal.

John Rylands Library, University of Manchester, Manchester, England (UML): Stanley Family MSS.

St. Giles-in-the-Fields, St. Giles High Street, London: Burial Record, April 1762– June 1788.

Scottish Record Office, Sasines, Scotland: Lee, Tucker, & Co. MSS.

Notes

PREFACE

1. Entry for April 3, 1932, Henry Waring Ball Diary (hereafter Harry Ball Diary) Mississippi Department of Archives and History, Jackson.

2. See Simon Schama, *Dead Certainties (Unwarranted Speculations)* (New York: Alfred A. Knopf, 1991); Peter Novick, *That Noble Dream: The "Objectivity Question" and the American Historical Profession* (Cambridge: Cambridge University Press, 1988).

3. R. W. B. Lewis, *The Jameses: A Family Narrative* (New York: Farrar, Straus & Giroux, 1991); Peter Gay, *Freud: A Life for Our Time* (New York: W. W. Norton, 1988); Linda Wagner-Martin, *Sylvia Plath: A Biography* (New York: Simon and Schuster, 1987); Anne Stevenson, *Bitter Fame: A Life of Sylvia Plath* (Boston: Houghton Mifflin, 1989); Lawrence J. Friedman, *Menninger: The Family and the Clinic* (New York: Alfred A. Knopf, 1990); Robert V. Remini, *Henry Clay: Statesman for the Union* (New York: W. W. Norton, 1991); James C. Klotter, *The Breckinridges of Kentucky, 1760–1981* (Lexington: University Press of Kentucky, 1986); Paul C. Nagel, *The Lees of Virginia: Seven Generations of an American Family* (New York: Oxford University Press, 1990); Craig M. Simpson, *A Good Southerner: The Life of Henry A. Wise of Virginia* (Chapel Hill: University of North Carolina Press, 1985); Drew Gilpin Faust: *James Henry Hammond and the Old South: A Design for Mastery* (Baton Rouge: Louisiana State University Press, 1982); Darden Asbury Pyron, *Southern Daughter: The Life of Margaret Mitchell* (New York: Oxford University Press, 1991); Joel Williamson, *William Faulkner and Southern History* (New York: Oxford University Press, 1993).

4. Diane Wood Middlebrook, *Anne Sexton: A Biography* (Boston: Houghton Mifflin, 1991).

5. Jay Tolson, *Pilgrim in the Ruins: A Life of Walker Percy* (New York: Simon & Schuster, 1992).

6. See flyer for Jay Tolson, *Pilgrim in the Ruins: A Life of Walker Percy,* Simon & Schuster Publicity Department, 1992.

7. Quotations from Kay Redfield Jamison, *Touched with Fire: Manic-Depressive Illness and the Artistic Temperament* (New York: Oxford University Press, 1993), 192 and 192–232.

PROLOGUE

1. Cenotaph, Percy plot, St. James Episcopal Church Cemetery, Greenville, Miss.

2. See Josephine Haxton interview with Leon Zachary Koury, Sept. 4, 1978, p. 23, Oral History of Greenville Collection, William Alexander Percy Memorial Library, Greenville, Miss.

3. Malvina Hoffman, *Yesterday Is Tomorrow: A Personal History* (New York: Crown, 1965), 115–29, 376 (inaccurate date); Patricia O'Toole, *The Five of Hearts Club: An Intimate Portrait of Henry Adams and His Friends, 1880–1918* (New York: Clarkson Potter, 1990), 165–66; R. P. Blackmur, *Henry Adams,* ed. Veronica A. Makowsky (New York: Harcourt Brace Jovanovich, 1980), 339–43.

4. "The Evolution of Heroes' Honor in the Southern Literary Tradition," in Numan V. Bartley, ed., *The Evolution of Southern Culture* (Athens: University of Georgia Press, 1985), 108–30.

5. Charles T. Bunting interview, in Lewis A. Lawson and Victor A. Kramer, eds., *Conversations with Walker Percy* (Jackson: University Press of Mississippi, 1985), 53.

6. Walker Percy, "Foreword," in John Kennedy Toole, *A Confederacy of Dunces* (Baton Rouge: Louisiana State University Press, 1980), vi.

7. Walker Percy, "Questions They Never Asked Me," in Walker Percy, *Signposts in a Strange Land,* ed. Patrick Samway (New York: Farrar, Straus, Giroux, 1991), 397–423.

8. Robert Coles, *Walker Percy: An American Search* (Boston: Little, Brown, 1979).

9. John Hereford Percy, *The Percy Family of Louisiana and Mississippi, 1776–1943* (Baton Rouge, La.: prvt. prnt., 1943), 64, 65 (quotation).

10. James C. Klotter, *The Breckinridges of Kentucky, 1760–1981* (Lexington: University Press of Kentucky, 1986), ix.

11. Ibid.

12. Paul C. Nagel, *Descent from Glory: Four Generations of the John Adams Family* (New York: Oxford University Press, 1983); Paul C. Nagel, *The Lees of Virginia: Seven Generations of an American Family* (New York: Oxford University Press, 1990); Malcolm Bell, Jr., *Major Butler's Legacy: Five Generations of a Slaveholding Family* (Athens: University of Georgia Press, 1987). Klotter, *Breckinridges of Kentucky,* takes a more interpretive line than most others.

13. Lope de Vega quoted in Donald R. Larson, *The Honor Plays of Lope de Vega* (Cambridge: Harvard University Press, 1977), 5.

14. Bertram Wyatt-Brown, *Southern Honor: Ethics and Behavior in the Old South* (New York: Oxford University Press, 1982), 62–87.

15. Joan E. Cashin, *A Family Venture: Men & Women on the Southern Frontier* (New York: Oxford University Press, 1991), 9–20.

16. Jan Nordby Gretlund, "On the Porch with Marcus Aurelius: Walker Percy's Stoicism," in Jan Nordby Gretlund and Karl-Heinz Westarp, eds., *Walker Percy: Novelist and Philosopher* (Jackson: University Press of Mississippi, 1991), 75.

17. "Interview on *Worldnet*" (162) and Charlotte Hays interview, 1986, in Lewis A. Lawson and Victor A. Kramer, eds., *More Conversations with Walker Percy* (Jackson: University Press of Mississippi, 1993), 126; Gretlund, "On the Porch with Marcus Aurelius," 81; Lewis A. Lawson, "*The Moviegoer* and the Stoic Heritage," in

Duane J. Macmillan, ed., *The Stoic Strain in American Literature: Essays in Honour of Marston LaFrance* (Toronto: University of Toronto Press, 1979), 180–82.

18. Joseph L. Morrison, *W. J. Cash: Southern Prophet, A Biography and Reader* (New York: Alfred A. Knopf, 1967), 140; and Mary Cash Maury, "Suicide," and Maury to Morrison, Aug. 20, 1964, Joseph L. Morrison MSS, Southern Historical Collection, Wilson Library, University of North Carolina, Chapel Hill; Virginia Woolf to Vanessa Bell, March 23[?], 1941, in Nigel Nicholson and Joanne Trautman, eds., *The Letters of Virginia Woolf* (6 vols.; New York: Harcourt Brace Jovanovich, 1980), 6: 485; and Louise DeSalvo, *Virginia Woolf: The Impact of Childhood Sexual Abuse on Her Life and Work* (Boston: Beacon Press, 1989), 133. For an accurate reading of Woolf's psycho-neurological problems, see Thomas C. Caramagno, *The Flight of the Mind: Virginia Woolf's Art and Manic-Depressive Illness* (Berkeley: University of California Press, 1992).

19. Constance Fenimore Woolson, quoted in Joan Myers Weimer, ed., *Women Artists, Women Exiles: "Miss Grief" and Other Stories by Constance Fenimore Woolson* (New Brunswick, N.J.: Rutgers University Press, 1988), xviii, xxiii; and in Cheryl B. Torsney, *Constance Fenimore Woolson: The Grief of Artistry* (Athens: University of Georgia Press, 1989), 15–16.

20. Ted Hughes and Frances McCullough Hughes, eds., *The Journals of Sylvia Plath* (New York: Dial Press, 1982), Oct. 1, 1957, p. 177. See also, Anne Stevenson, *Bitter Fame: A Life of Sylvia Plath* (Boston: Houghton Mifflin, 1989), 114–15; Anthony Storr, *Churchill's Black Dog, Kafka's Mice and Other Phenomena of the Human Mind* (New York: Ballantine, 1988), 76.

21. Michael MacDonald and Terence R. Murphy, *Sleepless Souls: Suicide in Early Modern England* (Oxford: Clarendon Press, 1990), 15–17 (quotation, 15).

22. Geri Coppernoll Couchman, "Trying to Live with Suicide," *Newsweek,* Oct. 8, 1990, p. 12.

23. William Styron, "Why Primo Levi Need Not Have Died," New York *Times,* Dec. 19, 1988, p. 23.

24. Quotation, Ross Chambers, *The Writing of Melancholy: Modes of Opposition in Early French Modernism,* trans. Mary Seidman Trouille (Chicago: University of Chicago Press, 1993), 169; Donald A. Dewsbury, "Psychobiology," *American Psychologist* 46 (March 1991): 198–205.

25. Stanley W. Jackson, *Melancholia and Depression. From Hippocratic Times to Modern Times* (New Haven: Yale University Press, 1986), 394; Silvano Arieti and Jules Bemporad, *Severe and Mild Depression: The Psychotherapeutic Approach* (New York: Basic Books, 1978), 224–29; New York *Times,* July 20, 1993.

26. Walker Percy, interview with the author, June 14, 1987, Covington, La.

27. Sigmund Freud, *Totem and Taboo,* trans. James Strachey (New York: W. W. Norton, 1989), 76, 82.

28. Recent clinicians and theorists have effectively built upon Freudian ideas. John Bowlby and others emphasize the sense of abandonment that the early death of parents or surrogate parents and withdrawals of affection may have upon individuals too young to articulate their feelings of loss and inclined to blame themselves for events that deprived them of loved ones. See Gregory Zilborg, "Differential Diagnostic Types of Suicide," *Archives of Neurology and Psychiatry* 35 (1936): 270–91; John Bowlby, *Attachment and Loss* (3 vols.; New York: Basic Books, 1980); George H. Pollack, "On Siblings, Childhood Sibling Loss, and Creativity," in George Moraitis and George H. Pollack, eds., *Psychoanalytic Studies of Biogra-*

phy (Madison, Conn.: International Universities Press, 1987), 113–67; Sigmund Freud, "Mourning and Melancholia (1917)," in *Collected Papers of Sigmund Freud,* ed. Ernest Jones (21 vols.; London: Hogarth Press, 1948), 4: 152–70.

29. Paul Gilbert, *Depression: From Psychology to Brain State* (Hillsdale, N.J.: Lawrence Erlbaum Associates, 1984), 217–22.

30. Émile Durkheim, *Suicide, a Study in Sociology,* trans. John A. Spalding and George Simpson (New York: Free Press, 1951), 157–58.

31. Howard I. Kushner, *Self-destruction in the Promised Land: A Psychocultural Biology of American Suicide* (New Brunswick, N.J.: Rutgers University Press, 1989); Emil Kraepelin, *Manic-Depressive Insanity and Paranoia* (1921; reprint, New York: Arno Press, 1976), 165–84; Jackson, *Melancholia and Depression,* 270–73; Seymour S. Kety, et al., eds. *Genetics of Neurological and Psychiatric Disorders* (New York: Raven Press, 1983); Stephen Hodgkinson, et al., "Molecular Genetic Evidence for Heterogeneity in Manic Depression," *Nature* 325 (Feb. 1987): 805–6.

32. See Alice Miller, *The Drama of the Gifted Child: The Search for the True Self,* trans. Ruth Ward (New York: Basic Books, 1990), 42–43.

33. Percy on Cervantes, see interview, Oct. 9, 1988, Covington, La.; William Shakespeare, *Henry IV: The First Part,* Act II, Scene 3, ll. 41–111; Marvin Krims, "Shakespeare's Commentary on Phallocentricity: 'But Yet a Woman,' " paper, 9th International Conference in Literature and Psychology, Lisbon, July 3, 1992.

34. Juliana Schiesari, *The Gendering of Melancholia: Feminism, Psychoanalysis, and the Symbolics of Loss in Renaissance Literature* (Ithaca: Cornell University Press, 1992), 13, 14 (quotation).

35. See Durkheim, *Suicide,* table 29: 268, and 299.

36. Specialists like Murray Bowen argue that ofttimes families are doomed to repeat the distortions because they never face up to them but only repress and evade. See Michael E. Kerr, "Family Systems Theory and Therapy," in Alan S. Gurman and David P. Knishern, eds., *Handbook of Family Therapy* (New York: Brunner, Mazel, 1981), 226–64; Murray Bowen, *Family Therapy in Clinical Practice* (New York: Jason Aronson, 1978).

37. Elizabeth Stone, *Black Sheep and Kissing Cousins: How Our Family Stories Shape Us* (New York: Times Books, 1988), 90.

38. Arthur Koestler, *The Act of Creation* (1964; New York: Dell, 1975), 316–17 (first quotation). Chambers, *The Writing of Melancholy,* 169; Albert Rothenberg, *Creativity and Madness: New Findings and Old Stereotypes* (Baltimore: Johns Hopkins University Press, 1990), 47 (second quotation), and "Creativity, Articulation, and Psychotherapy," *Journal of the American Academy of Psychoanalysis* 11 (1983): 55–85.

39. Aristotle, *Problems,* Books XXII–XXXVIII, trans. W. S. Hett (2 vols.; Cambridge: Harvard University Press/London: Heinemann, 1953–57), 2: 155. The earliest example of suicidal melancholia is a text from the Middle Kingdom in Egypt (c. 2000–1740 B.C.). See D. Winton Thomas, ed., *Documents from Old Testament Times* (London: Thomas Nelson & Sons, 1958), 162–67.

40. Nancy Mairs, "When Bad Things Happen to Good Writers," New York *Times Book Review,* Feb. 21, 1993, pp. 1, ff.

41. Stone, *Black Sheep and Kissing Cousins,* 101.

42. Walker Percy, *The Last Gentleman* (New York: New American Library, 1968), 16.

43. Thomas J. Wentworth, quoted from Johnson J. Hooper, ed., *Wentworth's*

Reminiscences of the Creek, or Muskogee Indians (1859: Birmingham, Ala.: Birmingham Book Exchange, 1939), 73–74; I thank Joanna Shields for this entry.

Chapter One DEMONS OF CHARLES PERCY

1. James Smith to John Ellis, Nov. 26, 1800, in *Transcription of County Archives of Mississippi,* No. 2 Adams County (Natchez), Vol. I, Minutes of the Court of Quarter Sessions of the Peace, 1799, 1801, [mimeograph] Transcription of County Archives of Mississippi (Mississippi Historical Records Survey, Service Division, Works Project Administration, June 1942), 162. I am indebted to Christopher Morris for locating this document and to Terry Alford for calling attention to its existence.

2. Cash in Charlotte *News,* May 10, 1941, reprinted in Joseph L. Morrison, *W. J. Cash: Southern Prophet* (New York: Alfred A. Knopf, 1967), 291.

3. See Bernard Bailyn, *Voyagers to the West: A Passage in the Peopling of America on the Eve of the Revolution* (1986; New York: Vintage, 1988), 491; Eron Rowland, ed., *Life, Letters and Papers of William Dunbar of Elgin, Morayshire, Scotland, and Natchez, Mississippi, Pioneer Scientist of the Southern United States* (Jackson: Mississippi Historical Society, 1930), 9–10, 27, 28.

4. Charles Percy to Robert Percy, May 7, 1792, Duncan Longcope and M. L. Johansen Collection, Cornhill Farm, Lee, Mass. (hereafter Longcope-Johansen MSS). With the permission of the owners, I deposited photocopies of these papers at the Maine Historical Society, Portland, Maine. They may be found in the card catalogue with reference to Henry Mowat (see Chapter Two below).

5. James Simmons to John Manning, Jan. 7, 1859, quoted in Rosser H. Taylor, *Ante-Bellum South Carolina: A Social and Cultural History* (Chapel Hill: University of North Carolina Press, 1942), 25.; Bernard Bailyn, *The Peopling of British North America: An Introduction* (New York: Alfred A. Knopf, 1986), 129; Arthur H. DeRosier, Jr., "William Dunbar: A Product of the Eighteenth Century Scottish Renaissance," *Journal of Mississippi History* 28 (Aug. 1966): 185–227.

6. Mrs. Mary D. Butler to W. R. Percy, Minden, La., July 3 1913, Jane Percy Butler Duncan [Mrs William Butler Duncan], New York, to Clarence Percy, Baton Rouge, ca. Sept. or Oct. 1895, John Hereford Papers owned by Dr. Oscar M. Thompson and William H. Wright, Jr., Baton Rouge, (hereafter Thompson-Wright MSS). John Hereford Percy, *The Percy Family of Mississippi and Louisiana: 1776–1943* (Baton Rouge: priv. prnt., 1943), 5 (hereafter Percy, *Percy Family*). See also Hardy and Page to Dr. Edwin Freshfield, Feb. 13, 1896, Longcope-Johansen MSS; Frances Gerard, *Picturesque Dublin, Old and New* (London: Hutchinson, 1898), 257–92.

7. The undated, unsigned document is in Longcope-Johansen MSS.

8. See Clarence Percy to Harry Percy, Nov. 30, 1895, Thompson-Wright MSS; Robert Dow to Robert Percy, July 27, 1804, Longcope-Johansen MSS. On North Carolina Percys, Mary Best Bell, comp., *Colonial Bertie County North Carolina Deed Books A–H 1720–1757* (n.p.: Southern Historical Press, n.d.), 169; Alvaretta Kenan Register, comp., *State Census of North Carolina 1784–1787* (2nd rev. ed., Baltimore: Genealogical Publishing Co., 1983), 137; Percy, William 015 (Bute) 1776 100 Will Book 2/80, North Carolina Department of Archives and History,

Raleigh (hereafter NCDAH); and, on John, see Judith Dupree Ellison, comp., *Index and Abstracts of Deeds of Record of Pitt County, North Carolina Vol. 2 (1772–1801)* (South Miami, Fla.: Old South Historical Research, n.d.) (unpaginated): John Persey—(or) N-470; (ee) N-470; (or) O-246.

9. Y. Attema, *St. Eustatius: A Short History of the Island and Its Monuments* (Zutphen, Holland: De Walburg, 1976), 37–38.

10. Cecil Johnson, *British West Florida, 1763–1783* (New Haven: Yale University Press, 1943), 118; Garland Taylor, "Colonial Settlement and Early Revolutionary Activity in West Florida up to 1779," *Mississippi Valley Historical Review* 22 (Sept. 1935): 353–56; Johnson, "West Florida Revisited," *Journal of Mississippi History* 28 (May 1966): 124–25; and Johnson, "The Distribution of Land in British West Florida," *Louisiana Historical Quarterly* 16 (Winter 1933): 539–53; quotations from Robin F. A. Fabel, "An Eighteenth Colony: Dreams for Mississippi on the Eve of the Revolution," *Journal of Southern History* 59 (Nov. 1993): 647–72, 654n31 (quotations).

11. See Thomas W. Grimshaw, Registrar-General, Registration of Births, Deaths, and Marriages in Ireland, Charlemont House, Dublin, to Mrs. Paul Dana, Aug. 26, 1895, Longcope-Johansen MSS; Mary A. Peterson, "British West Florida: Abstracts of Land Petitions," *Louisiana Genealogical Register* 19 (Sept. 1972): 241–42; and Peterson, "British West Florida," *ibid.*, 18 (Dec. 1971): 318. See also Mrs. Dunbar Rowland, "Mississippi's Colonial Population and Land Grants," *Publications of the Mississippi Historical Society,* Centenary Series 1 (Jackson: Mississippi Historical Society, 1916): 418.

12. Petition of Charles Percy, Nov. 13, 1778, Colonial Office, America and West Indies, Series 5, petition No. 595, p. 527, Public Record Office, Kew (hereafter PRO); see also pp. 743–44, and Mary A. Petersen, "British West Florida Land Petitions," *Louisiana Genealogical Register* 19 (Sept. 1972): 242. A William Percy held land in Bute County, North Carolina, in this period, but his relationship to Charles is not known. See William Percy, Dec. 24, 1769, Bute County Deed Book 2, p. 260–70, and *ibid.,* 1776, Will Book 2, No. 100, p. 80, NCDAH.

13. See Charles Percy's Heirs, Dec. 27, 1879, Patent Certificate No. 117, Land Claim No. 3526, U.S. Land Office, Department of the Interior (hereafter DOI), National Archives, Washington; Laura S. D. Harrell, ed., "The Diary of Thomas Rodney, 1804," *Journal of Mississippi History* 7 (April 1945): 112–15; Percy, *Percy Family,* 5; Sargent Prentiss Knut to Mary D. Butler Dana, March 14, 1913, Longcope-Johansen MSS.

14. Charles Percy, land grant, Sept. 23, 1779, date of certification, CO 5/595, p. 527, PRO; see also, copy, May Wilson McBee, comp., *The Natchez Court Records, 1767–1805: Abstracts of Early Records,* 411 [from Deed Book C, p. 94, claim no. 594], and June 2, 1777, claim no. 595, ibid.]; Heirs of Charles Percy, July 15, 1880, U. S. Land Claim No. 3526; Levi Sholer, April 12, 1871, No. 4077; Mary Sholler under Wm Dortsch, April 12, 1871, Land Claim No. 4076, Louisiana, Private, Department of the Interior, RG 49, National Archives. His land plats may be found in Spanish Louisiana Land Surveys, microfilm, Reel 1, frames 60, 71(b), Reel 3, frames 34(b), 141(b) 239(b); Reel 4, frame 204, Natchez Records, Historic New Orleans Collection, New Orleans.

15. John Q. Anderson, "The Narrative of John Hutchins," *Journal of Mississippi History* 20 (Jan. 1958): 1–5.

16. See Forrest McDonald, *Alexander Hamilton: A Biography* (New York: W. W. Norton, 1982), 6–7.

17. Mary A. Peterson, comp., "Miscellaneous Records of Personae and Events of Interest," *Louisiana Genealogical Register* 31 (Dec. 1984): 309. Others appointed were Anthony Hutchins, Isaac Johnson, John Blommart, Thadeus Lyman, and William Hiorn, all prominent residents of the Natchez District. Light Townsend Cummins, *Spanish Observers and the American Revolution, 1775–1783* (Baton Rouge: Louisiana State University Press, 1991), 87–89.

18. J. F. H. Claiborne, *Mississippi as a Province, Territory and State with Biographical Notices of Eminent Citizens,* Vol. I (Jackson: Power & Barksdale, 1880 [1964]), 118; James Alton James, *Oliver Pollock: The Life and Times of an Unknown Patriot* (New York: Appleton-Century, 1937), 118; Robert V. Haynes, *The Natchez District and the American Revolution* (Jackson: University Press of Mississippi, 1976), 65.

19. Anderson, ed., "Narrative of John Hutchins," 9; Leland D. Baldwin, *The Keelboat Age on Western Waters* (Pittsburgh: University of Pittsburgh Press, 1941), 14; Mrs. Rowland Dunbar, ed., *Life, Letters and Papers of William Dunbar: of Elgin, Morayshire, Scotland and Natchez, Mississippi: Pioneer Scientist of the Southern United States* (Jackson: Mississippi Historical Society, 1930), entry for May 1, 1778, pp. 61–63; J. Barton Starr, *Tories, Dons, and Rebels, The American Revolution in British West Florida* (Gainesville: University Presses of Florida, 1976), 86–88.

20. Wilbur H. Siebert, "The Loyalists in West Florida and the Natchez District," *Mississippi Valley Historical Review* 2 (March 1916): 471; Peter Chester to Lord George Germain, May 7, 1778 C0/5-504:594, PRO; Martha Condray Searcy, *The Georgia-Florida Contest in the American Revolution, 1776–1778* (University: University of Alabama Press, 1985), 171; Starr, *Tories, Dons, and Rebels,* 87, 111, 111n71; Johnson, *British West Florida,* 209; Robert V. Haynes, "James Willing and the Planters of Natchez: The American Revolution Comes to the Southwest," *Journal of Mississippi History* 37 (Feb. 1975): 1–40.

21. Chester to Germain, May 7, 1778, C0\5-504:594, PRO (copies in Manuscripts Room, Library of Congress, hereafter LC). The military career of Charles Percy during the Seven Years' War and other matters regarding his early life, will appear in the final chapter of this work. *New York Journal,* June 22, 1778, and Oliver Pollock to George Rogers Clark, April 22, 1779, Dec. 22, 1779, Oliver Pollock MSS, Lyman Draper Collection, Series J, v. 49, p. 39, Wisconsin Historical Society, Madison (hereafter WHS); references kindly supplied by Professor Robert Rea.

22. See Jack D. L. Holmes, "French and Spanish Military Units in the 1781 Pensacola Campaign," in William S. Coker and Robert R. Rea, eds., *Anglo-Spanish Confrontation on the Gulf Coast During the American Revolution* (Pensacola: Gulf Coast History and Humanities Conference, 1982), 145. Holmes points out that various dates may be given for Spanish entry into the war.

23. Arthur P. Whittaker, *The Spanish-American Frontier, 1783–1795* (Boston: Houghton Mifflin, 1927), 174–80; Siebert, "Loyalists in West Florida," 475; Kenneth Scott, ed., "Britain Loses Natchez, 1779: An Unpublished Letter," *Journal of Mississippi History* 26 (Feb. 1964): 45–46; orig. "Address of the Inhabitants of Natchez to Lt. Col. Dickson," Oct. 4, 1779, C0\5-99, PRO.

24. Quoted in Johnson, *British West Florida*, 215.

25. See Baldwin, *Age of Keelboat*, 14; Eric Beerman, "José Solano and the Spanish Navy at the Siege of Pensacola," in Coker and Rea, eds., *Anglo-Spanish Confrontation*, 125–44.

26. John Caughey, "The Natchez Rebellion of 1781 and Its Aftermath," *Louisiana Historical Quarterly* 66 (Jan. 1933): 65. "An American" to Oliver Pollock, Dec. 2, 1781, Papers of the Continental Congress, 1774–1789, Item 50, Letters and Papers of Oliver Pollock, 1776–1785, 1792, microfilm #64, WHS.

27. Fabel, *Economy of British West Florida*, 174; Peterson, "British West Florida," *Louisiana Genealogical Register* 18 (Dec. 1971): 332–33; William S. Coker, "Luke Collins Senior of Opelousas: An Overview," *Louisiana History* 14 (Spring 1973): 137–55.

28. Daniel Clark, John Lovelace, Daniel Ogden, and David Lejeune to Don Manuel Gayoso de Lemos, Governor of Natchez, June 11, 1794, Spanish Records, Book C, p. 96, Office of the Chancery Clerk (hereafter OCC), Adams County Courthouse, Natchez, Miss. (hereafter ACC, Natchez). Rev. Donald J. Hebert, *Southwest Louisiana Records: Church and Civil Records of Settlers, Volume 1 (1756–1810)* (Eunice, La.: n.p., n.d.), 1: 450 and Certificates of Baptism for: "Susana Piercy," born, Sept. 26, 1783; "Sara Piercy," August, 1781[?], "Tomas Jorge Piercy," born, June 4, 1786; "Catalina Piercy," born, May 5, 1788, St. Landry Catholic Church, Opelousas, Louisiana. These were the only certificates forwarded to me from the church archives, but see Hebert (above) for "Carlos Piercy," born 1780, and baptized probably when "Susana" was, in 1783. In the birth dates for the children, there are discrepancies between the Spanish Records in Natchez and these certificates. In arranging the birth order, I have extrapolated from the Spanish Records in Natchez because, one may assume, Daniel Clark and friends did the more accurate job. In the 1780s and 1790s, the Catholic circuit-rider from Opelousas wrote down in his main registry the birth and baptismal dates from notes taken on his rounds. Another child named Sally appears in one document but nowhere else and may have been a eighth sibling who did not live to maturity. See Charles Percy to Robert Percy, May 7, 1792, Longcope-Johansen MSS.

29. Charles Percy to Robert Percy, May 7, 1792, Longcope-Johansen MSS. For the information about Charles Percy's appearance in the 1792 census and the state of the tobacco market, I am indebted to G. Douglas Inglis; see his letter to author, Nov. 5, 1993. Dr. Inglis, an historian now employed as a systems engineer, has developed a large database on Spanish Natchez from the records at the Archivo General de Indias near his home in Seville.

30. See Christopher Morris, *Becoming Southern: Vicksburg and Warren County, Mississippi 1770–1860* (New York: Oxford University Press, forthcoming), chap. 2.

31. Charles S. Sydnor, *A Gentleman of the Old Natchez Region: Benjamin L. C. Wailes* (Durham, N.C.: Duke University Press, 1938), 12–13; Charles Percy, Will, copy, in Subject File and Inventory list, Feb. 20, 1794, in *Robert Percy v. Charles Percy, Executors*, 1804, Series AA, Territorial Court, Record Group 6, Mississippi Department of Archives and History (hereafter MDAH). See also William B. Hamilton and William D. McCain, eds., "Wealth in the Natchez Region: Inventories of the Estate of Charles Percy, 1794 and 1804," *Journal of Mississippi History* 10 (Oct. 1948): 280–303.

32. "Carlos Percey," in Census for Natchez District, June 14, 1792, Archivo General de Indias, Papeles procedentes de las Isla de Cuba, legajo 2353, as kindly

reported to me by the late Jack D. Holmes, April 19, 1988. The total landholding in the household (some held in the name of Susannah and infant Thomas Percy) came to 7240 arpents. See *American State Papers: Documents Legislative and Executive, of the Congress of the United States, Public Lands,* Class VIII, Vol. I (Washington: Gales & Seaton, 1832), 615, 908, 866, 871, 888. See on measurement of arpent, Jack D. L. Holmes, "The Value of the Arpent in Spanish Louisiana and West Florida," *Louisiana History* 24 (Summer 1983): 314–20, and William S. Coker, "Spanish Regulation of the Natchez Indigo Industry, 1793–1794," *Technology and Culture* 13 (Jan. 1974):55–58.

33. Jack D. L. Holmes, "Indigo in Colonial Louisiana and the Floridas," *Louisiana History,* 8 (Fall 1967): 329–49; Charles Percy Inventory List of Feb. 20, 1794; Fortescue Cuming, "Sketches of a Tour to the Western Country through the States of Ohio and Kentucky; a Voyage down the Ohio and Mississippi Rivers, and a Trip through the Mississippi Territory, and Part of West Florida. Commenced at Philadelphia in the Winter of 1807, and Concluded in 1809," in Reuben G. Thwaites, ed., *Early Western Travels, 1748–1846* (32 vols.; Cleveland: A. H. Clark, 1904–07), 4: 320.

34. Jack D. L. Holmes, *Honor and Fidelity: The Louisiana Infantry Regiment and the Louisiana Militia Companies, 1766–1821* (Birmingham: n.p., 1965), 252; also in communication from Jack D. L. Holmes, April 19, 1988, to author; William Alexander Percy, *Lanterns on the Levee* (1941; Baton Rouge: Louisiana State University Press, 1973), 39–40; Coker, "Luke Collins," 142–43.

35. Quotation, Sarah Dorsey, *Lucia Dare,* reprinted in Mary Tardy [Ida Raymond pseud.], *Southland Writers: Biographical and Critical Sketches of the Living Female Writers of the South* (2 vols.; Philadelphia: Claxton, Remsen, & Haffelfinger, 1870), 1: 217; Charles Percy, Will, copy, Charles Percy, Inventory list, Feb. 20, 1794, in *Robert Percy v. Charles Percy, Executors,* 1804, John Holt Ingraham, *The South-West by a Yankee* (2 vols.; New York: Harper, 1835), 2: 97–98.

36. Robert Dow to Robert Percy, Feb. 12, 1794, in Percy, *Percy Family,* 51; Frederick K. Goodwin and Kay Redfield Jamison, *Manic-Depressive Illness* (New York: Oxford University Press, 1990), 39; Silvano Arieti and Jules Bemporad, *Severe and Mild Depression: The Psychotherapeutic Approach* (New York: Basic Books, 1978), 70–71.

37. Daniel Clark, statement before Congress, n.d., copy, Henry Gilpin MSS, Historical Society of Pennsylvania, Philadelphia (hereafter HSP).

38. See the colloquy of Senator Smith of Maryland and James Wilkinson, "Court of Enquiry, Washington Tuesday March 29 1808," Gilpin MSS, HSP; Daniel Clark, *Proofs of the Corruption of Gen. James Wilkinson and of His Connexion with Aaron Burr* (Philadelphia: Wm. Hall, Jr., and George W. Pierie, 1809), 6, 8–19, and statement before Congress, n.d., copy, Gilpin MSS, HSP.

39. Charles Percy to Robert Percy, May 7, 1792, Longcope-Johansen MSS; Clark, *Proofs of Corruption,* 15–22; Alexander DeConde, *This Affair of Louisiana* (New York: Scribner, 1976), 55–56; James Ripley Jacobs, *Tarnished Warrior, Major-General James Wilkinson* (New York: Macmillan, 1938), 135–37.

40. Joseph Collins, "Received from Gilbert Leonard six thousand, three hundred and thirty three dollars for the acc of General James Wilkinson. . . . ," n.d., copy, and Daniel Clark, statement before Congress, n.d., copy, Gilpin MSS, HSP.

41. Roster of Sept. 16, 1792, Natchez Cavalry Militia, Papeles procedentes de la Isla de Cuba, legajo 41, Archivo General de Indias, Sevilla, Spain. The reference

was kindly supplied by letter of Jack D. L. Holmes, Birmingham, Ala., April 7, 1990. See also, Jack D. L. Holmes, *Honor and Fidelity: The Louisiana Infantry Regiment and the Louisiana Militia Companies, 1766–1821* (Birmingham: n.p., 1965), 48–51, 252.

42. Francis Pousset to Gayoso, Jan. 31, 1794, Book C, p. 95, Spanish Records, OCC, ACC.

43. Francis Pousset to Gayoso, Jan. 31, 1794, Book C, p. 95, Spanish Records, OCC, ACC; see also McBee, *Natchez Court Records,* 98–99; Dow to Percy, Feb. 12, 1794, in Percy, *Percy Family,* 50.

44. Charles Percy to Robert Percy, May 7, 1792, Longcope-Johansen MSS; Robert Dow to Robert Percy, Feb. 12, 1794, in Percy, *Percy Family,* 51; Francis Pousset to Don Manuel Gayoso de Lemos, Jan. 31, 1794, and Charles Percy, Will, Jan. 22, 1794, Spanish Records, Book C, p. 95, OCC, ACC. See also McBee, *Natchez Court Records,* 111; Entries for Jan. 22, Aug. 24, 1802, in Nathaniel Evans, "Abstract of Disbursements for the Use and Account of Charles Wilkins: October 1, 1801–to October 31, 1802," in James Campbell Wilkins Papers, Barker Historical Center, University of Texas, Austin.

45. Pousset to Gayoso, Jan. 31, 1794, Book C, p. 95, Spanish Records, OCC, ACC; Hamilton and McCain, "Wealth in the Natchez Region," 290–91, ff.; quotation, Charles Percy to Robert Percy, May 7, 1792, Longcope-Johansen MSS.

46. Terry Alford, *Prince Among Slaves* (New York: Harcourt Brace Jovanovich, 1977), 40.

47. Charles Percy to Robert Percy, May 7, 1792, Longcope-Johansen MSS.

48. The above account is taken from Daniel Clark of Loftus-Cliffs, to Gayoso, March 15, 1794, Book F, pp. 246–48, Spanish Records, OCC, ACC.

49. "The King versus Zachariah Smith," Feb. 10, 1794, Book F, p. 243, Spanish Records, OCC, ACC.

50. Dow to Robert Percy, Feb. 12, 1794, in Percy, *Percy Family,* 50; Charles Percy to Robert Percy, May 7, 1792, Longcope-Johansen MSS.

51. See John E. Carr and Peter P. Vitaliano, "The Theoretical Implications of Converging Research on Depression and the Culture-Bound Syndromes," in Arthur Kleinman and Byron Good, eds., *Culture and Depression: Studies in the Anthropology and Cross-Cultural Psychiatry of Affect and Disorder* (Berkeley: University of California Press, 1985), 252–54; Arieti and Bemporad, *Severe and Mild Depression,* 59.

52. "King versus Smith," various depositions in petitioner's behalf, Feb. 10, 15, 18, 20, 27, 1794, pp. 244, Book F, Spanish Records, OCC, ACC.

53. See Percy, *Percy Family of Mississippi,* 63, 73; D. Clayton James, *Antebellum Natchez* (Baton Rouge: Louisiana State University Press, 1968), 17; Mrs. Sarah Anne Ellis Dorsey to J. F. H. Claiborne, June 13, 1877, Box 21, folder 12, Z 239, in Claiborne MSS, MDAH.

54. James Smith to John Ellis, Nov. 26, 1800, in *Mississippi Territory v. James Smith,* 161.

55. *Ibid.* Thomas Foster, Smith's wealthy brother-in-law, had to pay the largest share: the Foster family's biography may be found in Bertram Wyatt-Brown, *Southern Honor: Ethics and Behavior in the Old South* (New York: Oxford University Press, 1982), 320–23, 462–95.

Chapter Two SON OF TWO FATHERS

1. Quoted in Ray Palmer Baker, "The Poetry of Jacob Bailey, Loyalist," *New England Quarterly* 2 (Jan. 1929): 73.

2. Master's Log, H.M.S. *Canceaux,* Aug.–Nov. 1770, Admiralty Office 52 1183 (hereafter Adm), Public Record Office, Kew (hereafter PRO). See frontispiece map, P. Colquhoun, *A Treatise on the Commerce and Police of the River Thames* (London: Joseph Mawman, 1800); Robert Percy, Service Record, Reference 1500, PRO (copy made 9 June 1932) (hereafter RP Service Rec), Oscar M. Thompson–William H. Wright, Jr., Collection, Baton Rouge, La. (hereafter Thompson-Wright MSS); and Charles Percy to Robert Percy, May 7, 1792, Duncan Longcope-M. L. Johansen Collection, Cornhill Farm, Lee, Mass. (hereafter Longcope-Johansen MSS); Major Reginald Hargreaves, "Promotion from the Ranks," *Army Quarterly* 86 (1963): 201; Dudley Pope, *Life in Nelson's Navy* (Annapolis, Md.: Naval Institute Press, 1981), 64–65.

3. Glynn Christian, *Fragile Paradise: The Discovery of Fletcher Christian, Bounty Mutineer* (London: Hamish Hamilton, 1982), 47.

4. On psychological effects of shipboard conditions, see Jan Horbulewicz, "The Parameters of the Psychological Autonomy of Industrial Trawler Crews," in Peter H. Fricke, ed., *Seafarer & Community: Towards a Social Understanding of Seafaring* (London: Croom Helm, 1973), 67–84. On maritime homosexuality, see B. R. Burg, *Sodomy and the Perception of Evil: English Sea Rovers in the Seventeenth-Century Caribbean* (New York: New York University Press, 1983), xvi–xvi. But naval historian N. A. M. Rodger argues that the number of homosexual cases that appeared in the naval records was very small, given the size of the force. N. A. M. Rodger, *The Wooden World: An Anatomy of the Georgian Navy* (Annapolis: Naval Institute Press, 1986), 80–81.

5. For weather, see *Canceaux,* Log Book, Nov. 7–12, 1770, Adm/52/1183, PRO.

6. Rodger, *Wooden World,* 27–28, 68.

7. *Canceaux,* Log Book, Nov. 8, 1770, and Aug. 24, 1771, Adm 52/1637, and Master's Log, April 26, 1772, and Dec. 6, 1775, Adm 36/9661, PRO (copy, under title "Journal of the Proceedings of His Majesty's Ship, the Canceaux commencing the 18th May 1775, ending 1st June, 1776, Willm Hogg Master," in Charles E. Banks, Scrapbook, collection 1157, Maine Historical Society (hereafter MHS); Rev. Samuel Cole to Rev. Daniel Burton, Dec. 26, 1770, photostat, New Hampshire, 1640–1857, IV-G-1, Society for the Propagation of the Gospel in Foreign Parts MSS (hereafter SPG), Library of Congress (hereafter LC); claim of Capt. Henry Mowatt, Auditor's Office, 12/109, 214 (hereafter AO), PRO.

8. Earlier in the eighteenth century, a kinswoman had generously paid for the education of Henry Mowat's father, the Mowats being one of the leading families in Stromness, Orkney Islands. J. Storer Clouston, *The Family of Clouston* (Kirkwall, Orkney: Office of the "Orcadian," 1948), 98.

9. "Mowat's Complaint to Admiralty [n.d.]," typed copy, Joseph Williamson MSS, MHS; "Old Time Reminiscences: Letter from Elizabeth Oakes Smith," of Hollywood, N.C., newspaper clipping, n.d., Joseph Williamson, "Captain Mowatt," Portland *Advertiser,* Dec. 22, 1888, clipping, Mowat Scrapbook, Collection 1157, MHS; Molyneux Shuldham to Lord Sandwich, Jan. 13, 1776, in G. R. Barnes and J. H. Owen, eds., *The Private Papers of John, Earl of Sandwich: First Lord of*

the Admiralty, 1771–1782 (4 vols; London: Navy Records Society, 1932), 1: 106; see also, James P. Baxter, "A Lost Manuscript," containing "Manuscript Relation of the Services of Henry Mowat, R.N.," *Collections and Proceedings of the Maine Historical Society,* 2nd ser., 2 (Portland: MHS, 1891), 345–75, hereafter cited as "Services of Henry Mowat." The original materials are located in Joseph William-son, Collection 1157, MHS. Samuel Holland, Surveyor of Lands, agreed with Mo-wat's claim of navigational expertise. See Lt. William Fielding to Basil Fielding, Jan. 28, 1776, in Marion Balderston and David Syrett, eds., *The Lost War: Letters from British Officers During the American Revolution* (New York: Horizon Press, 1975), 64.

10. For the routines aboard smaller vessels like H.M.S. *Canceaux* and Percy's later ship *Albany,* see Rodger, *Wooden World,* 62–64; William Robinson, *Jack Nastyface: Memoirs of a Seaman* (1836; Annapolis: Naval Institute Press, 1973), 31, 32–38.

11. See RP Service Rec, Thompson-Wright MSS.

12. See the Rev. John Wiswall to Dr. McLean, Jan. 15, 1776, copy in the Rev. John Wiswall Journal, Public Archives of Nova Scotia (hereafter PANS); an enclo-sure, "Declaration of P. M. Morgan made at the request of Robert Dow relative to Charles Percy," July 21, 1804, in Robert Dow, New Orleans, to Robert Percy, July 27, 1804 (typed transcription; original was held by a "Thomas Percy," a kinsman of John Hereford Percy), (hereafter Morgan enclosure, July 27, 1804], Thompson-Wright MSS.

13. RP Service Rec, Thompson-Wright. MSS; HM Service Rec, Banks MSS, MHS.

14. Lords Commissioners, Admiralty, to Vice Adm. Molyneux Shuldham, April 4, 1776, in William Bell Clark, ed., *Naval Documents of the American Revolution* (9 vols., Washington; U. S. Government Printing Office, 1964–1986), 4: 1015–16; see also *ibid.,* 8: 34, 842; George Jackson to Vice Admiral Shuldham, Feb. 29, 1776, *The Despatches of Molyneux Shuldham, Vice Admiral of the Blue and Commander-in-Chief of His Britannic Majesty's Ships in North America, January–July, 1776* (New York: Naval Historical Society, 1913), 5: 105. Both *Albanys* are registered in J. J. Colledge, *Ships of the Royal Navy* (1969; Annapolis: Naval Insti-tute Press, 1987), 26. William B. Willcox, "Arbuthnot, Gambier, and Graves: 'Old Women' of the Navy," in George Athan Billias, ed., *George Washington's Oppo-nents: British Generals and Admirals in the American Revolution* (New York: Wil-liam Morrow, 1969), 263; Samuel Eliot Morison, *John Paul Jones: A Sailor's Biogra-phy* (1959; Boston: Little, Brown, 1959), 34–35, highly overrates the strength of the Royal Navy in American waters, given the tasks assigned.

15. Henry Mowat to Sir Henry Clinton, April 25, 1779, enclosure, Graves, Gen-eral Orders, Oct. 6, 1775, in *Report on American Manuscripts in the Royal Institute of Great Britain* (London: H.M. Stationery Office, 1904), 1: 16; also Mowat to Clinton, March 5, 1779, (transcription) Joseph Williamson MSS, MHS; Sloan, "New Ireland," 21; entry for July 29, 1779, in "Journal of the Attack of the Reb-els," in Nova Scotia *Gazette,* Halifax, Sept. 14, 1779, in *Collections of the Maine Historical Society* 7 (Bath: Maine Historical Society, 1876): 124; McLean and Bar-clay exchanges, June 22–26, 1779, in "British Headquarters (Carleton) Papers," *Report on American Manuscripts,* 1: 452–60. For the best account of the engage-ment from the American perspective, see Craig L. Symonds, "The American Naval Expedition to Penobscot, 1779," *Naval War College Review* 24 (April 1972): 64–

71. Joseph Williamson, *History of the City of Belfast in the State of Maine* (2 vols.; Portland, 1877–1913), 1: 181; Jack Coggins, *Ships and Seamen of the American Revolution: Vessels, Crews, Weapons, Gear, Naval Tactics, and Actions of the War for Independence* (Harrisburg, Pa.: Stackpole, 1969), 167–68; Mowat to Philip Stephens, Sept. 19, 1779, Adm Captains' Letters, PRO, (transcription), Williamson MSS, MHS; "Services of Henry Mowat," 364–65; William B. Willcox, ed., *The American Rebellion: Sir Henry Clinton's Narrative of His Campaigns, 1775–1782, with an Appendix of Original Documents* (New Haven: Yale University Press, 1954), 135–36; Sloan, "New Ireland," 75n65 and 76.

16. Grace Helen Mowat, *The Diverting History of a Loyalist Town: A Portrait of St. Andrews, New Brunswick* (Fredericton, N.B.: Brunswick Press, 1953), 26, 30–31; David Russell Jack, "The Caleff Family," *Acadiensis* 3 (July 1907): 269–70; 1783 entries, David Mowat, Cash Book, Loyalist Studies, microfilm, Reel #177, New Brunswick Museum, Fredericton; Archibald Gunn, letter, newspaper clipping, n.d., Banks Scrapbook, Collection 1157, MHS; E. Alfred Jones, *Loyalists of Massachusetts: Their Memorials, Petitions, and Claims* (London: St. Catherine Press, 1930), 71; John Calef, ed., *The Siege of Penobscot* (New York: Arno, 1971), 296–97, 319 (quotation); Collier to Lt. Michael Hyndman, Nov. 6, 1777, William James Morgan, ed., *Naval Documents of the American Revolution* (Washington, U.S. Government Printing Office, 1964–86), 7: 55–56.

17. John Knox Laughton, "Robert Digby," Sir Leslie Stephen and Sir Sidney Lee, eds., *The Dictionary of National Biography* (London: Oxford University Press, 1921–22), 5: 972. This volume of *Naval Documents* (Vol 7) is dated 1976 HM Service Rec, MHS; "Services of Henry Mowat," 369; Colledge, *Ships of the Royal Navy*, 322.

18. See George T. Bates, "A List of Cornwallis Settlers," entry for Oliver Mowat, Transport, *Merry Jacks*, supplied the author by Mrs. Dorothy Cooke of Halifax. RP Service Rec: Jan. 18, 1779 (midshipman), June 6, 1781 (master's mate), in Thompson-Wright MSS; "Memorandum for Walter Boyd, Esq.," Nov. 7, 1798, copy, Longcope-Johansen MSS; promotion dated Oct. 26, 1782, see *The Commissioned Sea Officers of the Royal Navy 1660–1815* (3 vols.; n.p. [1954]), 2: 650; see also, HM Service Rec, MHS; D. B. Bell, *Early Loyalist Saint John: The Origin of New Brunswick Politics, 1783–1786* (Fredericton: Priv. pub., 1983), 19; Jones, *Loyalists of Massachusetts*, 214–15.

19. Unfortunately the promotion papers have been lost, but see Henry Mowat to Robert Percy, London, Oct. 20, 1784, Mowat to Robert Percy, Oct. 20, 1784, Morgan enclosure, July 27, 1804, Longcope-Johansen MSS; RP Service Rec, April 22, 1783, Thompson-Wright MSS; Pope, *Life in Nelson's Navy*, 66;.

20. Colledge, *Ships of the Royal Navy*, 103–4; RP Service Rec, Thompson-Wright MSS.

21. John Adams quoted in Joseph Williamson, "The British Occupation of Penobscot During the Revolution," *Collections and Proceedings of the Maine Historical Society*, 2d ser., 1 (Portland: Maine: MHS, 1890): 397; see also 398–99; George Augustus Wheeler, *History of Castine, Penobscot, and Brooksville, Maine* (Bangor: Burr & Robinson, 1875), 275.

22. James Ryder Mowat to Commissioners, Loyalist Claims, March 24, 1784, AO/13/91, 512–14, PRO; David Russell Jack, "Robert and Miriam Pagan," *Acadiensis* 2 (Oct. 1902): 279, 284–85; Bailey to Morice, May 3 or 4, 1782, B-25, No. 259, transcript, SPG MSS, LC; Joseph Williamson, "The British Occupation of

Penobscot During the Revolution," *MHS Collections and Proceedings of the Maine Historical Society,* 2d ser., 1 (Portland: Maine Historical Society, 1890): 392, 395–400; Mowat, *Diverting History of a Loyalist Town,* 33.

23. John Masefield, *Sea Life in Nelson's Navy* (London: Methuen, 1937), 101–2; see Gregg and Corfield, Skinners Hall, to Mr. Wilby, Soho Square, received Dec. 9, 1798, which concerns the bonding of David and Henry Mowat for Robert Percy, issued on *Albany,* Longcope-Johansen MSS.

24. Rodger, *Wooden World,* 87–98; Robinson, *Jack Nastyface,* 151; Pope, *Nelson's Navy,* 233–34; Masefield, *Sea Life in Nelson's Navy,* 56.

25. Henry Mowat to Robert Percy, London, Oct. 20, 1784, Thompson-Wright MSS. See, for instance, E. Powell, "Memoranda," to Robert Percy, n.d., 1799; William Cowan to Robert Percy, July 22, 1799, Longcope-Johansen MSS; RP Service Rec, Thompson-Wright MSS.

26. J. C. Beaglehole, ed., *The Journals of Captain James Cook on His Voyages of Discovery. The Voyage of the Resolution and Discovery, 1776–1780* (4 vols.; Cambridge: Cambridge University Press, 1967), 1: 251n2; Gananath Obeyesekere, *The Apotheosis of Captain Cook: European Mythmaking in the Pacific* (Princeton: Princeton University Press, 1992), 39; Mowat to Percy, Oct. 20, 1784, Thompson-Wright MSS; "Services of Henry Mowat," 368.

27. See, for instance, E. Powell, "Memoranda," to Robert Percy, n.d., 1799; Cowan to Robert Percy, July 22, 1799, E. Powell to Percy, April 10, 1793, Longcope-Johansen MSS. Lee and his family were listed as residents of Castine as late as Nov. 1796. See Wheeler, *History of Castine,* 346.

28. See E. P[owell], London, to Robert Percy, c/o John Lee of Penobscot, April 10, 1793, Longcope-Johansen MSS. See also Roger Paul Nason, " 'Meritorious But Distressed Individuals': The Penobscot Loyalist Association and the Settlement of the Township of St. Andrews, New Brunswick, 1783–1821," M.A. thesis, University of New Brunswick, 1982, p. 6; Lee, Tucker, & Co., RD 4, 1006–8, Scottish Record Office, Sasines. Robert Pagan established in 1769 a branch of the Greenock, Scotland, firm of Lee, Tucker & Co., at Falmouth, Massachusetts (Maine). Their chief contract was the supply of timber for the Royal Navy. See AO/12/11, 71, 78, 93, PRO; also Jack, "Robert and Miriam Pagan," 280.

29. See Petition to Lord Lydney, Aug. 10, 1787, Thompson-Wright MSS; "Personal Notes: Dr. John Calef," in Calef, ed., *The Siege of Penobscot* (1781; New York: Arno Press, 1971), 297–98; "Dr. John Calef: Some Interesting Facts Concerning One of the Essex Loyalists," newspaper clipping, Mowat Scrapbook, Banks MSS, Collection 1157, MHS. See Gregg & Cornfield to Wilby, Dec. 9, 1798, Longcope-Johansen MSS; Sharon Dubeau to the author, Dec. 23, 1989; Sharon Dubeau, *New Brunswick Loyalists: A Bicentennial Tribute* (Agincourt, Ont.: Generation Press, 1983), 100; John Calef to Maurice Morgan, Nov. 20, 1782, *Report on American Manuscripts,* 229–30. Also living at St. Andrews was another Loyalist, James Percy, brick mason, but whether he was Robert's kinsman cannot be established. See David Russell Jack, "New Brunswick Loyalists of the War of the American Revolution," *New York Genealogical and Biographical Record* 39 (Jan. 1908): 15.

30. Henry Mowat to Robert Percy, Oct. 20, 1784, Longcope-Johansen MSS; Jones, *Loyalists of Massachusetts,* 303; Wiswall, Journal, June 24, Oct. 26, 1782, Jan. 17–June 2, 1783, PANS.

31. Enclosure, Patrick Morgan, July 21, 1804, in Robert Dow to Robert Percy,

July 27, 1804, Longcope-Johansen MSS; *Lowndes's London Directory for the Year 1784* (London: T. W. Lowndes, 1784), 114.

32. Hammersmith information comes from Morgan enclosure, July 27, 1804, Longcope-Johansen MSS. For Earl Street, see entry for Sarah Piercy, Aug. 24, 1781, Burial Record, April 1762–June 1788, Archival Safe, St. Giles-in-the-Fields, St. Giles High Street, London. Hardy and Page to Edwin Freshfield, Feb. 13, 1896, Longcope-Johansen MSS. "With regard to the burial of Mrs. Margaret Percy we should like to say the entry to our record "St Anne's W. stands for St Anne's *Westminster,* not St Anne's Soho," Hardy and Page wrote. In a phone conversation, the Rev. Gordon Taylor, current rector of St. Giles Church and city historian, July 18, 1991, explained to me how the entries in the parish record books should be interpreted.

33. Rodger, *Wooden World,* 252.

34. K. H. W. Shepherd, ed., *Survey of London: The Parish of St. James Westminster* (London: Athlone Press, 1960), 30: 543; Henry Mowat to Robert Percy, Oct. 20, 1784, Longcope-Johansen MSS.

35. Robert Percy, land grant petition, April 9, 1785, approved May 12, 1785, Land Grants, (microfilm), Provincial Archives of New Brunswick, Fredericton.

36. Rev. Gordon Taylor, "St. Giles-in-the-Fields: Its Part in History" (London: n.p. 1971), 8; Rowland Dobie, *The History of the United Parishes of St. Giles in the Fields and St. George Bloomsbury* (London: priv. prnt., 1829), 157. Entry for Sept. 9, 1783, Burial Records, April 1762–June 1788, St. Giles-in-the-Fields, London, has reference to a Jane Percy. A Jane Percy was the daughter of Henry Percy (b. 1725) of Seskind, County Wicklow, and never married. If she is the same Jane Percy, it is possible that she was a relation, since the signs point to this family as a possible source of Charles's roots, especially since the slum was inhabited by largely Irish immigrants. See "Abstracts of Wills," in *Registry of Deeds, Dublin,* #328, 139, a copy of which was kindly supplied by Malcolm Bell of Savannah.

37. Entry for Oct. 18, 1785, Burial Records, April 1762–June 1788, Archival Safe, St. Giles-in-the-Fields, St. Giles High Street, London.

38. Family tradition in the Orkneys claimed that Mowat soon would have been promoted to admiral's rank. A factor in his decision to remain in the Royal Navy was the failure of his effort to gain Crown compensation for the loss of New Hampshire lands. See Claim of Capt. Henry Mowatt, AO/12/109, 214, PRO, and Jones, *Loyalists of Massachusetts,* 73; Mowat to Percy, Oct. 20, 1784, Longcope-Johansen MSS; Clouston, *Family of Clouston,* 99.

39. See Henry Mowat to Robert Percy, Oct. 20, 1784; W. R. Percy to Mrs. Paul Dana, June 28, 1913, Longcope-Johansen MSS; John Fitzpatrick to Robert Dow, May 23, 1785, in Margaret Fisher Dalrymple, ed., *The Merchant of Manchac: The Letterbook of John Fitzpatrick, 1768–1790* (Baton Rouge: Louisiana State University Press, 1978), 416. On Dow's career, see Bertram Wallace Korn, *The Early Jews of New Orleans* (Waltham, Mass.: American Jewish Historical Society, 1969), 51–54. Dow married Angélica Montsanto, who belonged to a prominent Jewish family of New Orleans.

40. The sources for the interpretation of the Scottish connection are numerous. David S. Macmillan, "The 'New Men' in Action: Scottish Mercantile and Shipping Operations in the North American Colonies, 1760–1825," in David S. Macmillan, ed., *Canadian Business History: Selected Studies, 1497–1971* (Toronto: McClelland and Stewart, 1972), 63; Jack, "Robert and Miriam Pagan," 279–88; Jones, *Loyalists*

of Massachusetts, 215; Dow to Percy, April 27, 1802, Longcope-Johansen MSS,; Ian Charles Cargill Graham, *Colonists from Scotland: Emigration to North America, 1707–1783* (Ithaca: Cornell University Press, 1956), 189; John Dow to his wife, Dec. 2, 1762, March 24, 1764, and entries for July 3, Sept. 5, 1765, June 21, 1766, John Dow Log Book, Merchant Seaman of Saltcoats, 1764–66, microfilm TD 97, Glasgow City Archives, Mitchell Library, Glasgow, Scotland; A. M. Jackson, Principal Archivist, Mitchell Library, Glasgow, to author, Jan. 31, 1990. I am also indebted to Mrs. Isobel L. E. Couperwhite, archivist, Watt Library, Greenock, Scotland, for locating the following sources: *The Greenock Directory for 1815–1816* (Glasgow: Hutcheson and Brookman, 1828), 22, 34–35; *ibid., 1820,* 21, 32–33; *ibid., 1829,* 22, 36, *ibid., 1831–32,* 28, 40–41; *ibid., 1841–42,* 115, 138–39; and John F. and Sheila Mitchell, comps., *Monumental Inscriptions of Renfrewshire* (mimeograph, 1969), Nos. 107–09, esp. 106.

41. See Robert Dow to Robert Percy, July 27, 1804, Longcope-Johansen MSS.

42. Morgan enclosure, July 27, 1804, Longcope-Johansen MSS.

43. Charles Percy to Robert Percy, May 7, 1792 (quotations), also, Charles Percy to Robert Percy, May 7, 1792, Longcope-Johansen MSS; Robert Dow to Robert Percy, Feb. 18, 1798, in John Hereford Percy, *The Percy Family of Mississippi and Louisiana: 1776–1943* (Baton Rouge, La.: priv. prnt., 1943), 53.

44. Charles Percy to Robert Percy, May 7, 1792, Longcope-Johansen MSS.

45. *Ibid.*

46. Gayoso to Daniel Clark, [after June 11 and before June 15, 1794], Spanish Records, Book C, 98, OCC, ACC.

47. Susannah Percy to Don Manuel Gayoso de Lemos, June 15, 1794, Gayoso to Susannah Percy, July 4, 1794, Spanish Records, Book C, 98–99, OCC, ACC.

48. Clark to Gayoso, June 11, 1794, Book C, 96–97, and William Collins, John Newton, et al., to Gayoso, June 15, 1794, Book C, 99–100, Spanish Records, OCC, ACC.

49. Clark to Gayoso, June 11, 1794, Book C, 97, Spanish Records, OCC, ACC.

50. John Woodcock, Boy Estate, Jamaica, to Robert Percy, H.M.S. *Africa,* May 18, 1796, Longcope-Johansen MSS.

51. Susannah Percy to Gayoso, June 15, 1794, Spanish Records, 98–99, Book C, OCC, ACC. See also Judge Seth Lewis's summary on this point, in *Robert Percy v. Charles Percy's Heirs,* Thomas Rodney Notebook, LC.

52. Entry for Feb. 16, 1795, Book C, 252 ff., Spanish Records, OCC, ACC; William B. Hamilton and William D. McCain, "Wealth in the Natchez Region: Inventories of the Estate of Charles Percy, 1794 and 1804," *Journal of Mississippi History* 10 (Oct. 1948): 293; D. Clayton James, *Antebellum Natchez* (Baton Rouge: Louisiana State University Press, 1968), 15; see also "Analysis of Land Grants," in Clinton N. Howard, *The British Development of West Florida, 1763–1769* (Berkeley: University of California Press, 1947), 74–101.

53. This inference is drawn from the remarks of Dow to Percy, July 23, 1799, Thompson-Wright MSS.

54. E. P[owell] to Robert Percy, April 10, 1793, London to c/o John Lee of Penobscot, Longcope-Johansen MSS.

55. Copy, "Marriage Contract betwixt Thomas Middlemist, Vintner in Edinburg[,] and Jean Proudfoot dated 26th July 1762 and registered 30th November 1775," and P[owell] to Percy, April 10, 1793, Longcope-Johansen MSS; Percy, *Percy Family,* 9.

56. Dow to Robert Percy, July 23, 1799, and unidentified correspondent to "Mrs. Percy," June 23, 1801, Thompson-Wright MSS.

57. See RP Service Rec, Thompson-Wright MSS; Robert Percy to Evans Napon [*sic,* Napeau], Dec. 20, 1798, in Percy, *Percy Family,* 53–54; Robert Percy to Evans Napeau, March 27 1799, Adm 1/3065 and Percy and John Guyon to Napeau, March 24, April 4, 1799, Adm 1/3065, PRO.

58. Robert Percy to Evans Nopeon [*sic,* Napeau], Dec. 20, 1798, *Percy Family,* 53–54.

59. Dow to Percy, March 2, 1796, Thompson-Wright MSS.

60. Dow, Saltcoats, to Robert Percy, Dec. 23, 1801, Thompson-Wright MSS. For further information about Dow, see Robert Dow, 1820 Federal Census, Orleans County (New Orleans), M33-32, 82; Patent date, May 16, 1791, Register's Office, Oct. 1, 1808, Thomas H. Williams, Land Office West of the Pearl River, *Land Claims in the Mississippi Territory,* Register's Number 1735.

61. RP, Service Rec, Thompson-Wright MSS.

62. "Charter of the Schooner Bilboa," Sept. 8, 1802, in Percy, *Percy Family,* 7–8.

63. Robert Dow to Robert Percy, Dec. 23, 1801, *ibid.,* 55; Wilkinson to Daniel Clark, Dec. 15, 1803, Henry Gilpin MSS, HSP.

64. Deed of sale, Feb. 10, 1804, Archives of the Spanish Government of West Florida, VIII (1804), transcript, [trans. from the Spanish], 31–32, copy, St. Francisville, La., Courthouse; Percy, *Percy Family,* 8–9.

65. See Colledge, *Ships of the Royal Navy,* 292. On naval punishments aboard Percy's ships, see H.M.S. *Albany,* Log Book, March 25, May 17, May 20, Aug. 7, 1779, Adm 52/1552, PRO; also, H.M.S. *Robust,* Log Book, July 5, 1794, Adm 52/3126, PRO.

66. *Robust,* Log Book, April 23, 1794, Adm 52/3126, PRO.

67. *Albany,* Log Book, Feb. 5, 1777, Adm 52/1553, PRO.

68. *Ibid.,* April 25, 1779, Adm 52/1552, PRO.

69. *Robust,* Log Book, July 6, 1794, Adm 52/3126, PRO.

70. Bryan Nolan, "A Possible Perspective of Deprivations," in Fricke, ed., *Seafarer & Community,* 88–89.

71. "Transcript of Entries of Letters in Vice-Admiralty Court," March 21, 1777, in J. W. Morgan, ed., *Naval Documents of the American Revolution: American Theatre, Mar. 1, 1777–Apr. 30, 1777* (9 vols.; Washington: U.S. Government Printing Office, 1964–86), 8: 163.

72. Dow to Robert Percy, July 23, 1799, Thompson-Wright MSS; Percy, *Percy Family,* 5; Hamilton and McCain, "Wealth in the Natchez Region," 293.

73. *John Collins, Executor of Charles Percy, Esq. deceased vs. Robert Percy,* Dec. 22, 1804, and other documents, Mississippi Territory Court Records, Series AA, RG-6, MDAH.

74. Dow to Robert Percy, July 27, 1804 [transcript, letter since lost], Thompson-Wright MSS.

75. Morgan enclosure, July 27, 1804, Thompson-Wright MSS.

76. See William Baskerville Hamilton, *Anglo-American Law on the Frontier: Thomas Rodney & His Territorial Cases* (Durham: Duke University Press, 1953), entry for Nov. 27, 1807, 311: "a Document read respect[in]g R[obert] P[ercy] Legitimacy. &c.—Object[e]d by Mr H[arding] & S[hields] That this Instr[u]m[e]nt is not releavent [*sic*]—ackn[owledge]d on both Sides That none of The

heirs are disputed but [are] ackn[owledge]d in both bill and answer." The document could have been Patrick Morgan's statement which scarcely qualified as proof of a marriage.

77. Entry for Dec. 1, 1807, in Hamilton, *Rodney,* 314.

78. Percy, *Percy Family,* 9.

79. Hamilton and McCain, "Wealth in the Natchez Region," 295–96.

80. Robert Percy, agent for succession of Peter Walker, June 28, 1810, Court Records, see also XIII, 366–68, XV, 98, XVIII, 267–A, Spanish Archives, St. Francisville; Percy, *Percy Family,* 9.

81. Stanley Clisby Arthur, *The Story of the West Florida Rebellion* (St. Francisville, La.: St. Francisville *Democrat,* 1935), 90.

82. Arthur, *West Florida Rebellion,* passim; Isaac Cox, *The West Florida Controversy, 1798–1813: A Study in American Diplomacy* (Baltimore: Johns Hopkins University Press, 1918), 381–82.

83. W. H. Sparks, *The Memories of Fifty Years* (Philadelphia: Claxton, Remsen, and Haffelfinger, 1872), 324, 325.

84. See Stanley Clisby Arthur, ed. and comp., *Old Families of Louisiana* (Baton Rouge, Claitor's Publishing Division, 1971), 188; Elijah Smith to Samuel Brown, Nov. 26, 1819, Samuel and Orlando Brown Family Papers, Filson Club, Louisville (hereafter FCL).

85. Fortescue Cuming, "Sketches of a Tour to the Western Country," in Reuben G. Thwaites, ed., *Early Western Travels, 1748–1846* (32 vols.; Cleveland, A. H. Clark, 1904–07), 4: 335; Sparks, *Memories of Fifty Years,* 329–30.

86. Natchez *Mississippi Republican,* Nov. 19, 1819; Richard Butler, diary, quoted in Louise Butler, "West Feliciana: A Glimpse," *Louisiana Historical Quarterly* 7 (Jan. 1924): 96.

87. Adam Hodgson, *Letters from North America, Written During a Tour in the United States and Canada* (2 vols.; New York: G. P. Putnam & Son, 1869), 1: 169–85 (quotation, 185).

88. Charles S. Sydnor, *A Gentleman of the Old Natchez Region: Benjamin L. C. Wailes* (Durham: Duke University Press, 1938), 128–30.

89. Sparks, *Memories of Fifty Years,* 327.

90. Percy, *Percy Family,* 21–22.

91. Marriage announcement, Natchez *Ariel,* May 17, 1828.

92. Alice Ford, *John James Audubon: A Biography* (Norman: University of Oklahoma Press, 1964), 136, 154.

93. Quoted by Stanley Clisby Arthur, *Audubon: An Intimate Life of the American Woodsman* (New Orleans: Harmanson, 1937), 263.

94. Carolyn E. Delatte, *Lucy Audubon: A Biography* (Baton Rouge: Louisiana State University Press, 1982), 128–44 (quotation 139), 170–71; Maria R. Audubon, ed., *Audubon and His Journals* (2 vols.; New York: Dover, 1960) 1: 53.

95. Natchez *Mississippi Republican,* Nov. 30, 1819.

96. Elijah Smith to Samuel Brown, Nov. 26, 1819, Brown MSS, FCL.

Chapter Three BREVITY OF LIFE

1. Catherine Ann Warfield and Eleanor Percy Lee, *The Wife of Leon and Other Poems* (Cincinnati: E. Morgan & Co., 1845), 75.

2. William Alexander Percy, *Lanterns on the Levee: Recollections of a Planter's Son* (1941; Baton Rouge: Louisiana State University, 1973), 271 (hereafter Percy, *Lanterns*).

3. Huntsville *Democrat,* Oct. 9, 1841; "Judge Rodney's Docquet of Business Done out of Court at his Chambers," Thomas Rodney MSS, Historical Society of Delaware, Wilmington; Certificate of Baptism, "Susana (Susanne) Piercy," birth, Sept. 26, 1783, baptized Sept. 29, 1783, St. Landry Catholic Church, Opelousas, La.; John Williams Walker to James S. Walker, John Williams Walker MSS, Huntsville City Library, Huntsville, Ala. (hereafter Walker MSS, HCL).

4. Percy, *Lanterns,* 271; Thomas George Percy to John Williams Walker, Feb. 1, 1821, John Williams Walker Family Collection, Alabama Department of Archives and History, Montgomery (hereafter Walker MSS, ADAH).

5. Walker Percy, "Uncle Will's House," in Walker Percy, *Signposts in a Strange Land,* ed. Patrick Samway (New York: Farrar, Straus, Giroux, 1991), 64; Percy, *Lanterns,* 271.

6. Percy to Walker, Feb. 1, 1821, Walker MSS, ADAH.

7. Quoted in Morton Rothstein, " 'The Remotest Corner:' Natchez on the American Frontier," in Noel Polk, ed., *Natchez Before 1830* (Jackson: University Press of Mississippi, 1989), 105n12.

8. See Sarah Anne Ellis Dorsey to J. F. H. Claiborne, June 13, 1877, in J. F. H. Claiborne MSS, MDAH, Jackson; John Hereford Percy, *The Percy Family of Mississippi and Louisiana, 1776–1943* (Baton Rouge: priv. prnt., 1943), 43–44, 63 (hereafter Percy, *Percy Family*).

9. See William B. Hamilton and William D. McCain, eds., "Wealth in the Natchez Region: Inventories of the Estate of Charles Percy, 1794 and 1804," *Journal of Mississippi History* 10 (Oct. 1948): 297–98; Morton Rothstein, "The Changing Social Networks and Investment Behavior of a Slaveholding Elite in the Ante Bellum, South: Some Natchez 'Nabobs,' 1800–1860," in Sidney M. Greenfield, Arnold Strickon, and Robert T. Aubrey, eds., *Entrepreneurs in Cultural Context* (Albuquerque: University of New Mexico Press, 1979), 65–88, esp. 69; quotation, Mary T. Tardy [pseud. Ida Raymond], *Southland Writers: Biographical and Critical Sketches of the Female Writers of the South* (2 vols.; Philadelphia: Claxton, Remsen & Haffelfinger, 1870), 1: 26.

10. *Charles Percy Executors v. Robert Percy,* Mississippi Territorial Court Records, Court of Chancery, 1804 term, MDAH, Jackson. She died sometime before the November term. Percy, *Percy Family of Mississippi,* 5, claims that she died in 1803, but 1804 seems more likely.

11. Hamilton and William D. McCain, "Wealth in the Natchez Region," 29?; see entries for Jan. 22, Aug. 24, 1802 in Nathaniel Evans, "Abstract of Disbursements for the Use and Account of Charles Wilkins: October 1, 1801–to October 31, 1802," in Box 2E540, James Campbell Wilkins Papers, Barker Historical Center, University of Texas, Austin.

12. See Thomas George Percy, Alumni Record, Class of 1806, University Archives, Princeton University.

13. See Thomas Jefferson Wertenbaker, *Princeton, 1746–1896* (Princeton: Princeton University Press, 1946), 49, 118–32.

14. Hugh C. Bailey, *John Williams Walker: A Study of the Political, Social, and Cultural Life of the Old Southwest* (University: University of Alabama Press, 1964), 11–18.

15. Bailey, *Walker,* 33 (quotation), 33–35.

16. First quotation in Jay Tolson, *Pilgrim in the Ruins: A Life of Walker Percy* (New York: Simon & Schuster, 1992), 164; 2nd quotation in John W. Walker to James S. Walker, Oct. 23, 1808, Walker MSS, HCL.

17. Quoted in Bailey, *Walker,* 35, 36.

18. Hugh C. Bailey, "The Petersburg Youth of John Williams Walker," *Georgia Historical Quarterly* 43 (March 1959), 125; Walker to James S. Walker, Aug. 19, 1806, Walker MSS, HCL (quotation); Walker to Larkin Newby, May 4, June 30, 1803, Larkin Newby Collection, Perkins Library, Duke University, Durham (hereafter Newby MSS, DUL); Silvano Arieti and Jules Bemporad, *Severe and Mild Depression: The Psychotherapeutic Approach* (New York: Basic Books, 1978), 381–82.

19. Walker to Newby, May 4, 1808, Newby MSS, DUL; John W. Walker to James S. Walker May [?], 1808, Walker MSS, HCL.

20. Bayless E. Hardin, "Dr. Preston W. Brown, 1775–1826, His Family and Descendants," *Filson Club History Quarterly* 19 (Jan. 1945): 3–28; Bayless E. Hardin, "Dr. Samuel Brown, 1769–1830, His Family and Descendants," *ibid.* 26 (Jan. 1952): 7.

21. James M. Phalen, "Samuel Brown," in Allen Johnson and Dumas Malone, eds., *Dictionary of American Biography* (New York: Scribners, 1958), 2: 152–53; René LaRoche, "Samuel Brown, 1769–1830," in Samuel D. Gross, ed., *Lives of Eminent American Physicians and Surgeons of the Nineteenth Century* (Philadelphia: Lindsay & Blakiston, 1861), 231–46; Thomas Perkins Abernathy, *The Burr Conspiracy* (New York: Oxford University Press, 1954), 167.

22. Samuel Brown to Orlando Brown, Feb. 12, 1819, Samuel Brown Collection, University of Kentucky, Lexington (hereafter Brown MSS, UKL).

23. Declaration of David Lejeune, John Lovelace, and Daniel Ogden, in McBee, comp., *Natchez Court Records,* 99.

24. See Bertram Wyatt-Brown, *Southern Honor: Ethics and Behavior in the Old South* (New York: Oxford University Press, 1982), 382–87, 474–75.

25. Walker to Newby, Feb. 12, 1809, Newby MSS, DUL.

26. Walker to James S. Walker, April 21, 1809, Walker MSS, HCL.

27. Walker to James S. Walker, June 14, 1809, *ibid.*

28. J. Mills Thornton III, *Politics and Power in a Slave Society: Alabama, 1800–1860* (Baton Rouge: Louisiana State University Press, 1978), 8, 10; Walker to James S. Walker, Aug. 18, Dec. 19, 1805, Walker MSS, HCL. Both quotations are from Bailey, *John Williams Walker,* 31; John Williams Walker to Larkin Newby, Dec. 13, 1811, Newby MSS, DUL.

29. Entry for Jan. 1, 1812, in "John Williams Walker's 1810–1816 Account Book, Madison County, Mississippi Territory (later Alabama)," *Valley Leaves* (Huntsville, Ala.) (March 1972), 123.

30. Walker quoted in Thomas J. Taylor, "Early History of Madison County, and Incidentally of North Alabama," *Alabama Historical Quarterly* 1 (Summer 1930): 168.

31. Walker to Samuel Brown, May 20, 1810, Walker MSS, ADAH (quotation); entry for Thomas G. Percy, in the Madison County Tax List, 1811, ADAH.

32. Haynes, "Road to Statehood," 231.

33. Mack Buckley Swearingen, *The Early Life of George Poindexter: A Story of the First Southwest* (Chicago: University of Chicago Press, 1934), 19–21.

34. J. F. H. Claiborne, *Mississippi as a Province, Territory and State with Biographical Notices of Eminent Citizens,* Vol. I (Jackson: Power and Barksdale, 1880 [1964], 363 (all quotations); Swearingen, *Poindexter,* 27 (second quotation); 61 (first quotation).

35. Dunbar Rowland, *Courts, Judges, and Lawyers of Mississippi, 1798–1935* (Jackson: Hederman Bros., 1935), 35, 41.

36. D. Clayton James, *Antebellum Natchez* (Baton Rouge: Louisiana State University Press, 1968), 111; Swearingen, *Poindexter,* 66. Within twenty years, he was to be a millionaire, buying thousands of acres throughout the Southwest. In the 1830s his landholdings in Washington County, Mississippi, where the Percy family was later to settle, were alone worth over a quarter-million dollars. Swearingen, *Poindexter,* 70n17 (quotation).

37. See, for instance, Poindexter to "dear sir" June 27, 1815; W. J. Hamilton, statement, n.d., Poindexter material in Claiborne MSS, MDAH; Divorce papers, Mississippi Territorial Superior Court, Ser. A, vol. 24, MDAH; W. H. Sparks, *Memoirs of Fifty Years* (Philadelphia: Claxton, Remsen & Haffelfinger, 1870), 341–42. Claiborne, *Mississippi as a Province,* 1: 363–64 (quotation), 371n, in which Claiborne gallantly asserts her innocence (although evidence one way or the other is absent), and 376–79.

38. Claiborne, *Mississippi as a Province,* 1: 371–74, 379, 382n. See also Poindexter Subject File, MDAH; Duelling agreement, George Poindexter, Abijah Hunt, William C. Mead, and Ebenezer Bradish, June 8, 1811, William C. Mead to George Poindexter, July 19, 1816, Poindexter to Percy, July 3, 1815, Poindexter materials, in Claiborne MSS, MDAH.

39. Michael Grossberg, *Governing the Hearth: Law and the Family in Nineteenth-Century America* (Chapel Hill: University of North Carolina Press, 1985), 234–37; Wyatt-Brown, *Southern Honor,* 243–44; see Albert Poindexter to George Poindexter, Feb. 7, 1821, Lydia Carter Williams to George Poindexter, July 16, 1822, Poindexter materials, Claiborne MSS, MDAH; Pendergrast to Poindexter, Feb. 19, 1832, in Claiborne, *Mississippi as a Province, Territory and State,* 1: 384n.

40. Samuel Brown to Margaretta [his sister-in-law, wife of John Brown], Feb. 22, 1813, Samuel and Orlando Brown Family Papers, Filson Club Library, Louisville (hereafter Brown MSS, FCL).

41. John Frederick Dorman, *The Prestons of Smithfield and Greenfield in Virginia: Descendants of John and Elizabeth (Patton) Preston Through Five Generations* (Louisville: Filson Club, 1982), 45; Bayless E. Hardin, "The Brown Family of Liberty Hall," *Filson Club History Quarterly* 16 (April 1942): 81–82; and Hardin, "Dr. Samuel Brown," 7–12 On Brown's career, see Samuel Brown, "Article III," [November 10, 1800], in *The Medical Repository* 4 (1801): 223–25. LaRoche, "Samuel Brown," 231–46; Samuel Brown to James Brown, May 14, 1806, Brown MSS, UKL; entry for Samuel Brown, *National Cyclopædia of American Biography* (New York: James T. White Co., 1897), 4: 348–49; Niels Henry Sonne, *Liberal Kentucky, 1780–1828* (Lexington: University Press of Kentucky, 1939), 84; F. A. Michaux, *Travels to the West of the Alleghany [sic] Mountains* [London, 1805], in Reuben G. Thwaites, ed., *Early Western Travels, 1748–1846* (32 vols.; Cleveland: A. H. Clark, 1904–07), 3: 205–6.

42. Samuel Brown to Margaretta Brown, Dec. 27, 1812, in Hardin, "Dr. Samuel Brown," 8, and Samuel Brown to Margaretta Brown, Feb. 1, 1813, ibid., 9, and

see 12, 13; Brown to Margaretta Brown, Feb. 22, 1813, Brown MSS, FCL; Samuel Brown to John [?] Brown, Feb. [?], 1813, Brown MSS, UKL.

43. Brown to Margaretta Brown, March 1, June 13, 1813, Brown MSS, UKL; with reference to correspondence with James Brown, June 23, 1813, Brown MSS, FCL.

44. Edward Chambers Betts, *Early History of Huntsville, Alabama, 1804 to 1870* (Montgomery, 1916), 23–24; Anne Royall, *Sketches of History, Life and Manners in the United States* (New Haven: priv. prnt., 1826), 14.

45. "Letter XVII," Jan. 1, 1818, in Anne Newport Royall, *Letters from Alabama 1817–1822,* ed. Lucille Griffith (1830; rpt. ed., University: University of Alabama Press, 1969), 119 and also Pope quoted in "Letter L," June 8, 1822, p. 246; Walker to Brown, June 13, 1821, Brown MSS, FCL; Ruth Ketring Nuermberger, "The 'Royal Party' in Early Alabama Politics," *Alabama Review* 6 (April 1953): 83n8. Nuermberger's source is U.S. Census, 5th (1830), Population Schedules [Original MSS Returns], 77ff.

46. Thomas George Percy, Alumni Records, Princeton University; Percy to Walker, April 5, 1820, Dec. 18, 1820, Walker MSS, ADAH.

47. Thomas George Percy to John Williams Walker, Jan. 25, 1820, *ibid.*

48. Percy to Walker, Nov. 17, 1819 (quotation), Percy to Walker, Dec. 2, 1819, *ibid.*

49. Brown to Walker, Nov. 15, 1819, *ibid.*

50. Samuel Brown to Thomas George Percy, Nov. 16, 1820, *ibid.*

51. Taylor, "Early History of Madison County," 500.

52. Huntsville *Republican,* Aug. 17, 1817, Jan. 13, 1818; Larry Schweikart, *Banking in the American South from the Age of Jackson to Reconstruction* (Baton Rouge: Louisiana State University Press, 1987), 148.

53. Undeterred, the Royalists pushed through a substitute bill with different but completely innocuous provisions. The most significant change was to adjust the bank's name from Mechanics to Merchants. Bibb, however, was not fooled. He vetoed the new bill as well. See William H. Brantley, *Banking in Alabama, 1816– 1860.* Vol. I (Birmingham: priv. prnt., 1961), 1: 3–16.

54. *Ibid.,* 20.

55. Percy to Walker, Jan. 25, 1820, Walker Family MSS, ADAH; Pope to Crawford, June 21, 1820, *American State Papers, Finance,* III, 765; Brantley, *Banking in Alabama,* 23.

56. See Percy to Walker, Dec. 2, 1819, Jan. 18, 1820, Walker MSS, ADAH, and Walker to Newby, Jan. 2, 1820, Newby MSS, DUL. Percy's wealth is not easy to reconstruct, but his initial 1811 investment, probably paid in cash, had amounted to $12,144.60 for nearly the largest single bloc of land sold that year. In 1818, however, he had unwisely added to his estate some $2285 worth of town lots in the fast rising town of nearby Florence, Alabama. Next to former President James Madison, the largest investor in the town's development, Percy was the most heavily committed. See "List of Purchasers of lots in the town of Florence at the first sale held July 22, 1818," John Coffee MSS, ADAH. This document was supplied to me by Daniel Dupre of the University of North Carolina at Charlotte. Despite such difficulties, Percy's crops during the early years of the depression were enormous—140,000 pounds. Nathaniel Ware to Brown, Jan. 8, Dec. 15, 1820, Thomas G. Percy to Samuel Brown, Oct. 10, 1820, Brown MSS, FCL; Percy to Brown, Jan. 9, 1822, Brown MSS, FCL.

57. Percy to Walker, Feb. 1, 1821, Walker MSS, ADAH.

58. Percy to Walker, Feb. 29, 1820 (quotations), Jan. 15, 1821, *ibid.*

59. Brown to Walker, June 29, 1821, *ibid.*

60. Percy to Walker, July 13, 1821, Mary Jane Walker to Matilda Walker, July 30, to Walker, Aug. 7, 1821, *ibid.;* Steven M. Stowe, *Intimacy and Power in the Old South: Ritual in the Lives of the Planters* (Baltimore: Johns Hopkins University Press, 1987), 171, 177; Samuel Brown to Orlando Brown, June 19, 1822 (quotation), Brown MSS, FCL.

61. Percy to Brown, Nov. 24, 1821, Brown MSS, FCL.

62. Thomas George Percy to John Williams Walker, Nov. 7, Dec. 6, 1821, Percy to Walker, Nov. 21, enclosed in Percy to James S. Brown, Dec. 6, 1821, Walker MSS, ADAH.

63. Quoted in Bailey, *Walker,* 176.

64. Percy to Brown, Oct. 31, 1823, Brown MSS, FCL.

65. Percy to Richard Wilde Walker, July 18, 1841, Richard Wilde Walker Papers, ADAH.

66. Percy, *Lanterns,* 273.

Chapter Four PHILADELPHIA YEARS

1. Catherine Ann Warfield and Eleanor Percy Lee, "They Tell Me There's an Eastern Bird," in *The Indian Chamber and Other Poems* (New York: priv. prnt., 1846), 105.

2. Quotation, Harnett T. Kane, *Natchez on the Mississippi* (New York: Morrow, 1947), 255. See also a more elaborate and fanciful version in Kathryn Tucker Windham, *13 Mississippi Ghosts and Jeffrey* (Huntsville, Ala.: Strode Publishers, 1974), 63–71.

3. Windham, *13 Mississippi Ghosts,* 63–71. I thank Louis Parks of Ocala, Fla., a genealogist and former resident of Natchez, for this source and story; see also Kane, *Natchez,* 255.

4. T. E. B. Howarth, *Citizen King: The Life of Louis-Philippe, King of the French* (London: Eyre and Spottiswoode, 1961), 101.

5. Entry for Sept. 15, 1804, in Laura D. S. Harrell, ed., "Diary of Thomas Rodney, 1804," in *Journal of Mississippi History* 7 (April 1945): 115.

6. Samuel Brown to Margaretta Brown, March 1 (1st quotation) and Feb. 22, 1813 (2nd quotation), Samuel and Orlando Brown Family Papers, Filson Club, Louisville (hereafter Brown MSS, FCL).

7. Brown to Margaretta Brown, February 22, 1813, *Ibid.*

8. Juan Delavillabeuvre to Bernardo de Galvez, Dec. 12, 1779, in Anna Lewis, ed. and trans., "Fort Panmure, 1779," *Mississippi Valley Historical Review* 18 (March 1932): 545; see also Pierce Butler, *The Unhurried Years: Memories of the Old Natchez Region* (Baton Rouge: Louisiana State University Press, 1948), 1–16.

9. See entries for June 15, July 18, 1808, for instance, in Thomas Rodney Diary, March 14, 1806–09, in H. F. Brown Collection, Historical Society of Delaware, Wilmington.

10. Entry for Sept. 15, 1804, in Harrell, ed., "Diary of Thomas Rodney," 115.

11. See Dunbar Rowland, *Courts, Judges, and Lawyers of Mississippi, 1798–1935* (Jackson: Hederman Bros., 1935), 73–74.

12. Mary T. Tardy [pseud. Ida Raymond], *Southland Writers: Biographical and Critical Sketches of the Female Writers of the South* (2 vols.; Philadelphia: Claxton, Remsen & Haffelfinger, 1870), 2: 27.

13. John C. Calhoun to James Monroe, April 17, 1815 (quotation), David Holmes to President James Madison, Jan. 19, 1813, Microfilm 438, Roll no. 8, 10-19-3, Territorial Papers, National Archives, Washington (hereafter NA); Josiah Simpson to Secretary of State, March 28, 1815, Appointment Office Files, Department of State, NA.

14. Broadus Mitchell, "Nathaniel A. Ware," in Dumas Malone, ed., *Dictionary of American Biography* (20 vols.; New York: Scriber 1928–37), 19: 451 (hereafter *DAB*); William Diamond, "Nathaniel A. Ware, Economist," *Journal of Southern History* 5 (Nov. 1939), 503n4. "The Maryland & Kentucky [Warfield] Affiliations," 27, genealogical account, Maryland Historical Society, Baltimore. See also Simpson to Secretary of State, March 28, 1815, Appointment Office Files, Department of State, NA. An additional source is *Biographical and Historical Memoirs of Mississippi* (2 vols.; Chicago: Goodspeed, 1891), 1: 733.

15. See "Resolutions of Citizens of Wilkinson County, July 25, 1812," Clarence Edwin Carter, ed., *The Territorial Papers of the United States* (Washington, D.C.: U.S. Government Printing Office, 1938), 6: 302; Haynes, "Road to Statehood," 230.

16. David Holmes to President James Madison, Jan. 19, 1813, and election certification, by Thomas B. Read, Dec. 4, 1812, Microfilm 438, Roll no. 8, 10-19-3, Mississippi Territorial Papers, NA.

17. Nathaniel A. Ware to James Monroe, Secretary of State, Sept. 4, 1815, in Carter, ed., *Territorial Papers*, 6: 553–54; Ware to the Secretary of War, Sept. 18, 1815, *ibid.*, 6: 555, and 560n10; Mitchell, "Ware," *DAB*, 19: 451.

18. Ralph Regan, Daniel Greenleaf, et al., "Recommendation for B. R. Grayson for Legislative Council," Jan. 18, 1814, enclosure in William Lattimore to James Monroe, Feb. 14, 1814, in Carter, ed., *Territorial Papers*, 6: 422; entry for William Grayson, in *Biographical Dictionary of the American Congress, 1774–1927* (Washington, D.C.: U.S. Government Printing Office, 1928), 1030; Drew R. McCoy, "James Madison and Visions of American Nationality in the Confederation Period: A Regional Perspective," in Richard Beeman, Stephen Botein, and Edward C. Carter II, eds., *Beyond Confederation: Origins of the Constitution and American National Identity* (Chapel Hill: University of North Carolina Press, 1987), 244–45.

19. John Hereford Percy, *The Percy Family of Mississippi and Louisiana, 1776–1943* (Baton Rouge: prev prnt., 1943), 63, 64 (hereafter Percy, *Percy Family*); Diamond, "Nathaniel A. Ware," 501–26.

20. See Christopher C. Morris, *Becoming Southern: Vicksburg and Warren County, Mississippi 1770–1860* (New York: Oxford University Press, forthcoming), chap. 8.

21. Laura Mansnerus, "Disturbing Questions on the Darkest Side of Postpartum Blues," New York *Times*, Oct. 12, 1988, 17, 21; Silvano Arieti, "Psychoanalysis of Severe Depression: Theory and Therapy," *Journal of the American Academy of Psychoanalysis* 4 (July 1976): 327–45; G. Stern and L. Kruckman, "Multi-Disciplinary Perspectives on Post-Partum Depression: An Anthropological Critique," *Social Science & Medicine* 17 (1983): 1027–41; D. Pines, "Pregnancy and Motherhood: Interaction Between Fantasy and Reality," *British Journal of Medical Psychology* 45 (Dec. 1972): 333–43.

22. For the psychological literature on this point, see Stanley Cath, Alan Gurwitt, et al., *Father and Child* (Boston: Little, Brown, 1982); Erna Furman, *A Child's Parent Dies: Studies in Childhood Bereavement* (New Haven: Yale University Press, 1974); E. James Anthony and Cyrille Koupernik, eds., *The Child in His Family* (2 vols.; New York: Wiley, 1970); Michael Rutter, *Children of Sick Parents* (New York: Oxford University Press, 1966).

23. Entry, "No. 538, Admitted June 22, 1819, Sarah Ware, Disease: Insanity," Admissions Book, Pennsylvania Hospital Historic Library, Philadelphia: Status: Pay, [as opposed to a charity case], "Discharged by her husband March 7, 1820. Admitted, March 30, 1820, Discharged September 28, 1831, by her husband [Nathaniel A. Ware]."

24. Quotations from Charles S. Rosenberg, *The Care of Strangers: The Rise of America's Hospital System* (New York: Basic Books, 1987), 19, 33, 34; Gerald N. Grob, *Mental Illness in American Society, 1875–1940* (Princeton: Princeton University Press, 1983).

25. See Nancy Tomes, *A Generous Confidence: Thomas Story Kirkbride and the Art of Asylum-Keeping, 1840–1883* (Cambridge, Eng.: Cambridge University Press, 1984).

26. See Norman Dain, *Disordered Minds: The First Century of Eastern State Hospital in Williamsburg, Virginia, 1766–1866* (Williamsburg: Colonial Williamsburg Foundation, 1971), 76–80; Samuel Coates, hospital director from 1785 to 1825, personally interviewed the patients and some of his notes remain. For obvious reasons, however, he only recorded the handful of charity cases, many of whom suffered from delusions of grandeur. Sarah Ware's comments on her feelings were not preserved. See excerpts from Coates's diary in Thomas G. Worth and Frank Woodbury, *The History of the Pennsylvania Hospital, 1751–1895* (Philadelphia: Times Printing House, 1897), 139–46. The original diary at the hospital archives demonstrates the nature of patients' delusions.

27. Nathaniel Ware to The Managers of the Asylum, Philadelphia, March 16, 1824, Sarah Ware, Patients' Files, Historic Pennsylvania Hospital Library, Philadelphia.

28. Deposition, Sept. 17, 1821, before Isaac Dellahunty, J. P., Wilkinson County, in Nathaniel A. Ware, Subject File, MDAH; Robert Moore, Will, July 10, 1826, [recorded Nov. 14, 1929, Will Book 1, 429–30, Adams County Courthouse, a reference kindly provided by Professor Terry Alford; Thomas Butler to James C. Wilkins, Jan. 7, 1831, Box 2E457, Wilkins Papers, Natchez Trace Collection, Barker Historical Center, University of Texas, Austin.

29. Terry Alford, *Prince Among Slaves* (New York: Harcourt Brace Jovanovich, 1977), 85–111. On Foster's payment of the fine, see *Transcription of County Archives of Mississippi,* No. 2 Adams County (Natchez), Vol. I, Minutes of the Court of Quarter Sessions of the Peace, 1799, 1801, [Mimeograph] Transcription of County Archives of Mississippi (Mississippi Historical Records Survey, Service Division, Works Project Administration, June 1942), 161?.

30. Alford, *Prince Among Slaves,* 112–13 (quotation, 113); Bertram Wyatt-Brown, *Southern Honor: Ethics and Behavior in the Old South* (New York: Oxford University Press, 1982), 462–93; Bertram Wyatt-Brown, "The Mask of Obedience: Male Slave Psychology in the Old South," *American Historical Review* 93 (Dec. 1988): 1228–55.

31. Ware to Brown, Jan. 8, 1820, Brown MSS, FCL.

32. Nathaniel A. Ware, *Henry Belden, or, A True Narrative of Strange Adventures* (Cincinnati: priv. prnt., 1846).

33. Mitchell, "Ware," *DAB*, 22: 451.

34. See Canter Brown, Jr., "Peter Stephen Chazotte and the East Florida Coffee Land Association Expedition of 1821," unpublished paper, kindly provided by the author. See also Boston *Patriot and Daily Mercantile Advertiser*, February 9, 12, 14, 16, March 19, 1822, and letter, March 8, 1822.

35. John Mahon, *History of the Second Seminole War 1835–1842* (Gainesville: University of Florida Press, 1967), 102, 125, 135.

36. Nathaniel A. Ware to Samuel Brown, Dec. 30, 1821, Thomas George Percy to Brown, Feb. 15, 1822, Brown MSS, FCL.

37. Ware to Brown, Dec. 30, 1821, Brown MSS, FCL; Tardy, *Southland Writers*, 2: 28, 36.

38. Quotation, Ware to Brown, Dec. 30, 1821; Dec. 1, 1823, Brown MSS, FCL; Nathaniel A. Ware and Samuel R. Overton to the President [James Monroe], Aug. 24, to the Secretary of State [John Quincy Adams], Aug. 25, Oct. 21, to Philip P. Barbour [Speaker of the House], Nov. 24, 1822, Delegate Hernandez to the Vice President [Daniel Tompkins], Feb. 17, 1823, with enclosure, dated Dec. 27, 1823, in Clarence Edwin Carter, comp. and ed., *The Territorial Papers of the United States, The Territory of Florida 1821–1824* (Washington: U.S. Government Printing Office, 1956), 22: 428–29, 514–15, 552–53, 563–65, 619–23. Ware had resigned by May 1823, see Overton to James Monroe, May 8, 1823, *ibid.*, 678–79.

39. Percy to Walker, March 12, 1822, Walker MSS, ADAH.

40. Nathaniel A. Ware, *Notes on Political Economy, as Applicable to the United States* (New York: Leavitt, Trow, 1844); Diamond, "Ware," 508–25; Douglas R. Egerton, *Charles Fenton Mercer and the Trial of National Conservatism* (Jackson: University Press of Mississippi, 1989), 305.

41. Henry Austin to Samuel F. Austin, March 4, 1831, in Eugene D. Barker, ed., *The Austin Papers: Volume II. Annual Report of the American Historical Association for the Year 1922* (3 vols.; Washington: U.S. Government Printing Office, 1928), 2: 605.

42. Henry Austin to Stephen Austin, March 15, 1831, Barker, ed., *Austin Papers*, 2: 613–14, see also 2: 634; Stephen Austin to Ware, Aug. 26, 1831, 2: 690–91; Stephen Austin to Henry Austin, Jan. 7, 1836, in John H. Jenkins, ed., *The Papers of the Texas Revolution 1835–1836* (10 vols.; Austin: Presidial Press, 1973) 3: 429; T. Jefferson Chambers to Public, *ibid.*, 8: 181.

43. John Frederick Dorman, "The Prestons of Smithfield and Greenfield in Virginia: Descendants of John and Elizabeth (Patton) Preston Through Five Generations," *Filson Club Publications, Second Series, Number Three* (Louisville: Filson Club, 1982), 44.

44. Samuel Brown to Margaretta Brown, Feb. 22, 1813, Brown MSS, FCL.

45. Samuel Brown to Orlando Brown, Nov. 26, 1819, Brown MSS, UKL.

46. Elijah Smith to Samuel Brown, Oct. 29 (first quotation), Nov. 26, 1819 (second quotation); Walker to Brown, April 7, 1819, Richard Harlan to Brown, Oct. 23, 1819, Brown MSS, FCL.

47. René LaRoche to Brown, Dec. 8, 1823, Brown MSS, FCL. See Steven M. Stowe, *Intimacy and Power in the Old South: Ritual in the Lives of the Planters* (Baltimore: Johns Hopkins University Press, 1987), 171.

48. See Thomas P. Govan, *Nicholas Biddle: Nationalist and Public Banker,*

1786–1844 (Chicago: University of Chicago Press, 1959), 346–47; Townsend Ward, "The Germantown Road and Its Associations," *Pennsylvania Magazine of History and Biography* 6 (No. 3, 1882): 265.

49. Tardy, *Southland Writers,* 2: 28 (1st quotation); Tardy, *Female Writers of the South,* 20 (2nd quotation).

50. René LaRoche to Brown, Dec. 8, 1823, Brown MSS, FCL.

51. The wedding list included John Bell, Hugh Lenox Hodge, and Joseph Anthony Mathieu, all prominent physicians later in life. See Philadelphia *National Gazette,* July 2, 1824.

52. René LaRoche to Samuel Brown, Nov. 14, 1822, Dec. 8, 1823, Jan. 1, 1824, Brown MSS, FCL. René LaRoche, "Samuel Brown, 1760–1830," in Samuel D. Gross, *Lives of Eminent American Physicians and Surgeons of the Nineteenth Century* (Philadelphia: Lindsay & Blakiston, 1861), 231–46.

53. "Medical Jurisprudence," *American Medical Society Journal* 5 (1828): 454–59, and "History of a Case of Puerperal Convulsions," *North American Medical and Surgical Journal* 9 (April 1830): 368–72.

54. Percy to Brown, Jan. 9, 1821; Walker to Brown, June 13, 1821; Percy to Brown, Oct. 26, 1821, July 26, 1822, Brown MSS, FCL; Percy to Walker, June 12, 20, 29, July 2, 13, 1821, Maria Percy to Matilda Walker, May 29, 1821, Percy to Walker, July 2, 1821, Walker MSS, ADAH.

55. Richard Harlan to Brown, Oct. 23, 1819, Brown MSS, FCL.

56. Henry Miller to Samuel Brown, Nov. 22, 1819, *ibid.*

57. Mary Ann Jimenez, *Changing Faces of Madness: Early American Attitudes and Treatment of the Insane* (Hanover, N.H.: Brandeis University Press, 1987), 73, 72.

58. Maria Percy to Matilda Walker, May 29, 1821, Walker MSS, ADAH; Tardy, *Living Female Writers,* 19.

59. Ware to Brown, Jan. 8, Dec. 15, 1820, Percy to Brown, Oct. 20, 1820, Percy to Brown, May 8, 1822, Nathaniel Ware to Samuel Brown, Dec. 30, 1821, Brown MSS, FCL; Tardy, *Southland Writers,* 27.

60. Percy to Brown, May 8, 1822 (quotation), Ware to Brown, Dec. 15, 1820, Brown MSS, FCL.

61. Bayless E. Hardin, "Dr. Samuel Brown, 1769–1830: His Family and Descendants," *Filson Club History Quarterly* 26 (Jan. 1952): 25; Thomas G. Percy to Samuel Brown, Oct. 10, 1820, and Nathaniel Ware to Samuel Brown, Jan. 8, 1820, Samuel Brown to James Brown, May 7, 1829[?], Brown MSS, FCL.

62. Tardy, *Female Writers of the South,* 75; Tardy, *Southland Writers,* 2: 30–31, 217; Sarah A. Dorsey [pseud. Filia], *Agnes Graham: A Novel* (2 vols.; Philadelphia: Claxton, Remsen and Haffelfinger, 1869), 1: 51.

63. Sarah Percy's tombstone, dated 1835, Routh Cemetery, Homochitto Avenue, Natchez. See Entry for May 30, 1836, in William Ransom Hogan and Erwin Adams Davis, *William Johnson's Natchez: The Ante-Bellum Diary of a Free Negro* (Baton Rouge: Louisiana State University Press, 1951), 118.

64. Entry for May 30, 1836, *ibid.*; Petition to Edward Turner, Chancellor of Mississippi, filed Jan. 1839, in *Eleanor Percy Ware* vs. *Nathaniel A. Ware,* Case #1194, Superior Court of Chancery (Jackson), 1839, MDAH.

65. Hardin, "Dr. Samuel Brown," 6; Samuel Brown to Orlando [?] Brown, May 7, 1828 or 1829, Brown MSS, UKL. See entry for René LaRoche, in Walker L. Burrage, *Dictionary of American Medical Biography* (Boston: Milford House, 1928),

720–21; Certificate of election as president of the Philadelphia Medical Society, Feb. 7, 1859, LaRoche Papers, American Philosophical Society in the Historical Society of Pennsylvania; George Ord, Secretary, American Philosophical Society, Jan. 19, 1827, and William V. Harold to LaRoche, Oct. 31, 1828, René LaRoche MSS, Library of the College of Physicians of Philadelphia (hereafter LCPP); René LaRoche, "Account of Some Important Operations Recently Performed in Europe," [dated September 11, 1828], in *North American Medical and Surgical Journal* 7 (Jan. 1829): 15–25.

66. Tardy, *Southland Writers,* 2: 29, 38 (quotation). See Daniel Drake to René LaRoche, March 15, 1831, LaRoche MSS, LCPP.

67. Percy, *Percy Family,* 62; quotation, Tardy, *Southland Writers,* 2: 38, also, *idem, Living Female Writers,* 20; John Bell to René LaRoche, July 2, 1828, LaRoche MSS, LCPP.

Chapter Five   TWO SOUTHERN BRONTËS

1. Gail Godwin, *A Southern Family* (New York: Avon, 1987), 69.

2. Sometimes Catherine Ann Warfield spelled her first name Catharine. For consistency's sake, I use Catherine throughout the text. Some portions of this chapter were first published in Carol Bleser, ed., *In Joy and in Sorrow: Women, Family, and Marriage in the Victorian South, 1830–1900* (New York: Oxford University Press, 1991), 176–95.

3. S. G. M. to Eleanor Percy Ware, Feb. 8, 1845, Ware Family Papers (acquisition no. 1416), Hill Library, Louisiana State University, Baton Rouge (hereafter Ware MSS, H-LSU).

4. Mary T. Tardy, *The Living Female Writers of the South* (Philadelphia: Claxton, Remsen & Haffelfinger, 1872), 19 (quotations), 23, 24.

5. S. G. M. to Eleanor Percy Lee, Feb. 8, 1845, Ware MSS, H-LSU.

6. Tardy, *Living Female Writers of the South,* 20. See also, Mary T. Tardy [Ida Raymond, pseud.], *Southland Writers: Biographical and Critical Sketches of the Living Female Writers of the South* (2 vols.; Philadelphia: Claxton, Remsen & Haffelfinger, 1870), a first edition, marred by errors but sometimes containing information dropped from the second edition.)

7. Julia Deane Freeman [Mary Forrest], *Women of the South Distinguished in Literature Illustrated with Portraits on Steel* (New York: Derby & Jackson, 1861), 115.

8. Tardy, *Southland Writers,* 2: 30.

9. Lee to Warfield, June 22, 1843, Ware MSS, H-LSU.

10. B. B. Warfield, "The Warfields, the Kentucky Branch," (1882), 27, University of Kentucky Library, Lexington (hereafter UKL).

11. *Ibid.,* 17. In 1833, Mary Jane Warfield, Catherine's sister-in-law, married Cassius Marcellus Clay. Highly conscious of his honor, the Kentucky abolitionist and Lincoln's wartime minister to Russia was as belligerent as any Southern fire-eater. Their marriage, always strained, ended in the scandal of a divorce in 1878. The most noteworthy family descendant was Wallis Warfield, another divorcée. See Elizabeth M. Simpson, *Bluegrass Houses and Their Traditions* (Lexington: Transylvania Press, 1932), 105–13; Evelyn Ballenger, *Warfield Records* (Annapolis,

Md.: Thomas Ord Warfield, 1970), 335, 466–67; David L. Smiley, *Lion of White Hall: The Life of Cassius M. Clay* (Madison: University of Wisconsin Press, 1962), 31, 220–21; G. Glenn Clift, *Kentucky Marriages: 1797–1865* (Baltimore: Genealogical Publishing Company, 1966), 73.

12. Lee to Warfield, May 10, 1844, Ware MSS, H-LSU.

13. Quotation, Nathaniel Ware, indenture of Dec. 20, 1838, Deed Book G, 416, Circuit Court Clerk's Office, Washington County, Greenville, Miss.; see also *Eleanor Percy Ware Lee v. Nathaniel A. Ware, et al.*, July 24, 1838, and indenture in behalf of Catherine Warfield, Dec. 21, 1838, in *Eleanor P. Lee v. Ware, Nathaniel*, December 6, 1846, Case 1194, Superior Court of Chancery (Jackson), 1839, Mississippi Department of Archives and History, Jackson, Mississippi (hereafter MDAH).

14. Quotation, Nathaniel Ware, indenture of Dec. 20, 1838, Deed Book G, 415, Circuit Court Clerk's Office, Washington County, Greenville, Miss. The children were: Nathaniel Ware Warfield, b. Paris, April 24, 1834; Eleanor Percy Warfield, b. Louisville, Jan. 5, 1837; Thomas Percy Warfield, b. Lexington, Nov. 19, 1839; Mary Ross Warfield, b. Lexington, April 4, 1841; Catherine Sarah Warfield, b. Lexington, May 29, 1844; and Lloyd Elisha Warfield, b. Lexington, Dec. 16, 1847. Thomas Percy Warfield died on Dec. 15, 1872, unmarried. Catharine's husband Robert Elisha Warfield died in Oldham County, Kentucky, Aug. 10, 1872. See B. B. Warfield, "The Warfields: Kentucky Branch," UKL.

15. When sixteen, she flirted for two years with a Lt. George W. Chapman, a Philadelphian in the navy, assigned to U.S.S. *Peacock*. George W. Chapman to Eleanor Percy Ware, July 10, Dec. 4, 1835, June 22, 1837, Ware MSS, H-LSU.

16. *Biographical and Historical Memoirs of Mississippi* (Chicago: Goodspeed's, 1891), 1: 738.

17. Actually, he was something of an amateur historian of science, sharing an interest in botany and geology with his father-in-law. See H. Lee to "sir," Oct. 22, 29, 1836, in Sargent Prentiss Knut Papers, Henry E. Huntington Library, San Marino, Calif.

18. Eleanor Percy Ware [Lee?] to Henry William Lee, Thursday [?], [1840?], Ware MSS, H-LSU.

19. Lee to Ellen Ware, n.d., *ibid.*

20. Ellen Ware to Harry Lee, Sunday, n.d., *ibid.*

21. Nathaniel Ware to Thomas G. Ellis and Thomas George Percy, April 13, 1836, Deed Book Y, 107, Clerk's Office, Adams County Courthouse, Natchez, Miss.; *William Henry Lee et ux. vs. Nathaniel Ware et al.*, Dec. 8, 1846, Case #1194, State Superior Court of Chancery (Jackson), MDAH; Freeman, *Women of the South*, 151.

22. Lee to Warfield, June 22, 1843, Ware MSS, H-LSU.

23. *Ibid.*

24. William Beckford, *Vathek,* in Peter Fairclough, ed., *Three Gothic Novels* (1968; London: Penguin, 1986). William Patrick Day, *In the Circles of Fear and Desire: A Study of Gothic Fantasy* (Chicago: University of Chicago Press, 1985), 10; and Elizabeth McAndrew, *The Gothic Tradition in Fiction* (New York: Columbia University Press, 1979), 71–73, 129–30.

25. Catherine Ann Warfield, *Ferne Fleming: A Novel* (Philadelphia: T. B. Peterson and Brothers, 1877), 74. See also Catherine Ann Warfield, *Miriam Monfort: A Novel* (New York, D. Appleton & Co., 1873), 234.

26. Ware "To———," Poetry Notebook, 1830–1837, Ware MSS, H-LSU.

27. Eleanor Percy Lee, "Agatha," 18–19, *ibid.*

28. J. S. Hartin, "Eliza Ann DuPuy," in James E. Lloyd, ed., *Lives of Mississippi Authors* (Jackson; University Press of Mississippi, 1981), 147.

29. Nathaniel A. Ware, *Henry Belden: Or, a True Narrative of Strange Adventures* (Cincinnati: priv. pub., 1848). Broadus Mitchell, "Nathaniel A. Ware," in Dumas Malone, ed., *Dictionary of American Biography* (20 vols.; New York: Scribner, 1928–37), 19: 451.

30. See Freeman, *Women of the South,* 163–81; Joseph Blotner, *Faulkner: A Biography* (2 vols.; New York: Random House, 1974), 1: 15, 18; Joel Williamson, *William Faulkner and Southern History* (New York: Oxford University Press, 1993), 17, 55.

31. Nina Baym, "Rewriting the Scribbling Women," *Legacy* 2 (Fall 1985): 4.

32. Joseph Holt Ingraham, *The South-West by a Yankee* (2 vols.; New York: Harper & Brothers, 1835).

33. Ingraham's son Prentiss was a veritable fiction factory, writing one thousand novels and novellas. Edgar Legare Pennington, "The Ministry of Joseph Holt Ingraham in Mobile, Alabama," *Historical Magazine of the Protestant Episcopal Church* 26 (Dec. 1957): 344–60. Robert W. Weathersby, II, "Joseph Holt Ingraham," in Lloyd, *Lives of Mississippi Writers,* 247–52; and "Prentiss Ingraham," *ibid.,* 52–67; Warren G. French, "A Hundred Years of a Religious Bestseller," *Western Humanities Review* 10 (Winter 1955–56): 45–54.

34. Tardy, *Southland Writers,* 2: 105–14.

35. John Seely Hart, *A Manual of American Literature* (1873; New York: Johnson Reprint Co., 1969), 507.

36. Hartin, "Eliza Ann DuPuy," 147–51; Tardy, *Living Female Writers,* 29–31.

37. Mrs. Catherine A. Warfield and Mrs. Eleanor Percy Lee, "the Sisters of the West," in *The Indian Chamber, and Other Poems* (New York: priv. prnt., 1846).

38. "The Lake of Coeur Creve," *ibid.,* 49–50; see also "The Mammoth Legend," *ibid.,* 54–59.

39. Carolyn G. Heilbrun, *Writing a Woman's Life* (New York: W. W. Norton, 1988), 15.

40. Warfield and Lee, "Remorse," in Warfield and Lee, *Indian Chamber,* 65.

41. Quoted in Tardy, *Southland Writers,* 2: 41–42; see also, Catherine A. Warfield and Eleanor Percy Lee, *The Wife of Leon and Other Poems* (1843; Cincinnati: E. Morgan, 1845), 145–48. Like Warfield, Abraham Lincoln, the most familiar depressive of that era, wrote a poem in the same period (sometime between 1844 and 1846) which expressed similar sentiments. See Howard I. Kushner, *Self-destruction in the Promised Land: A Psychocultural Biology of Suicide* (New Brunswick, N.J.: Rutgers University Press, 1989), 141.

42. For quotation see note 1 above; Lila Abu-Lughod, *Veiled Sentiments: Honor and Poetry in a Bedouin Society* (Berkeley: University of California Press, 1986), and idem, "Honor and the Sentiments of Loss in a Bedouin Society," *American Ethnologist* 12 (May 1985): 245–61.

43. Warfield and Lee, *Wife of Leon,* 94–97.

44. Lee, Chevy Chase, to Warfield, May 10, 1844, *ibid.*

45. Lee to Harry Lee, July 8, 1849, *ibid.*

46. Tardy, *Southland Writers,* 2: 31; Tardy, *Living Female Writers.* 21.

47. Tardy, *Living Female Writers,* 21–22. See Catherine Ann Warfield to John L. Darragh, Oct. 23, Nov. 3, 1853, June 17, 1854, April 3, 1855 (quotation), May

2, 1855; Nathaniel Ware Warfield to Darragh, Oct. 16, 1853, inventory of the Estate of N. A. Ware, Jan. 5, 1854. On their dispute over the will, see John L. Darragh, demurrer, document 27-0106, dated March 1, 1854, and settlement, March 29, 1854 (document 27-0108), John L. Darragh MSS, Rosenberg Library, Galveston, Texas. The Clerk's Office in the courthouse in Galveston has records of Ware's purchases beginning in 1842, too numerous to cite here. Quotation, Tardy, *Southland Writers,* 2: 31.

48. Tardy, *Southland Writers,* 2: 27; [A Southern Lady] Catherine Ann Warfield, *The Household of Bouverie; or the Elixir of Gold* (2 vols.; New York: Derby & Jackson, 1860).

49. Christine Alexander, ed., *An Edition of the Early Writings of Charlotte Brontë. Volume One: The Glass Town Saga, 1826–1832* and *Volume Two: The Rise of Angria, 1833–1835* (Oxford: Blackwell/Shakespeare Head, 1987–91).

50. See Elizabeth Moss, *Domestic Novelists in the Old South: Defenders of Southern Culture* (Baton Rouge: Louisiana State University Press, 1992).

51. Tardy, *Living Female Writers,* 26.

52. Warfield, *Household of Bouverie,* 1: 16.

53. Charlotte Brontë, *Jane Eyre,* ed. Q. D. Leavis (New York: Penguin, 1966), 242.

54. Warfield, *Household of Bouverie,* 1: 255.

55. Quoted in Leavis, ed., introduction, Brontë, *Jane Eyre,* 7–8.

56. See Kushner, *Self-destruction in the Promised Land;* 141.

57. Poem quoted in Tardy, *Southland Writers,* 2: 38.

58. Warfield, *Household of Bouverie,* 1: 246–47.

59. Julia Dean Freeman [Mary Forrest], *Women of the South Distinguished in Literature* (New York: Derby & Jackson, 1861), 150.

60. Eleanor Percy Lee, "My Cousin Jane," in Warfield and Lee, *Indian Chamber,* 262.

61. S. G. M. to Lee, Feb. 8, 1845, Ware MSS, H-LSU.

62. See Charlotte Elizabeth Lewis, "Sarah Anne Dorsey: A Critical Estimate," unpublished M.A. thesis, Louisiana State University, 1940, pp. 1–5; this thesis, now outdated, offers the only critical evaluation of her work; J. B. Smallwood, "Dorsey, Sarah Anne Ellis (Mrs. Samuel W.): 1829–1879," in Lloyd, ed., *Lives of Mississippi Authors,* 137–40; Grant C. Knight, "Warfield, Catherine Ann Ware," in *DAB,* 10: 454–55; Freeman, *Women of the South,* 150–57.

63. Charlotte Brontë, *Villette* (1853; New York: Bantam Books, 1986), 154.

64. *Ibid.,* 219–20.

65. Catherine Ann Warfield, *The Romance of Beauseincourt: An Episode Extracted from the Retrospect of Miriam Monfort* (New York: G. W. Carleton, 1867).

66. Tardy, *Southland Writers,* 2: 36.

67. Warfield, *The Romance of Beauseincourt,* 109, 210.

68. *Ibid.,* 127, 130, 133.

69. Catherine Ann Warfield, *The Cardinal's Daughter: A Sequel to Ferne Fleming* (Philadelphia: T. B. Peterson & Bros., 1877), 148.

70. The novel was apparently written much earlier. See Tardy, *Southland Writers,* 2: 36.

71. Catherine Ann Warfield, *Hester Howard's Temptation: A Soul's Story* (Philadelphia: T. B. Peterson & Brothers, 1875), 107.

72. Tardy, *Southland Writers,* 39 (quotations); Edward L. Ayers, *The Promise of*

the New South: Life After Reconstruction (New York: Oxford University Press, 1992), 339–72.

Chapter Six SARAH DORSEY

1. "To S**** A** E****," in Catherine Ann Warfield and Eleanor Percy Lee, *The Indian Chamber, and Other Poems* (New York: prvt. prnt., 1846), 198–99.

2. See Thomas George Ellis tombstone, Routh cemetery, Homochitto Street, Natchez.

3. See Mary M. Dahlgren tombstone, Dahlgren plot, Natchez City Cemetery; Thomas G. Ellis and Job Routh, bondholders, for Mary M. Routh, May 14, 1828, Marriage Book 5, 134, Circuit Clerk's Office, Adams County Courthouse (hereafter CCO, ACC).

4. W. A. Evans, "Sarah Ann [*sic*] Ellis Dorsey, Donor of Beauvoir," *Journal of Mississippi History,* 6 (Jan.–Oct. 1944): 89. This amateurish paper is full of genealogical inaccuracies but is useful for some facts. Theodora Britton Marshall and Gladys Crail Evans, *They Found It in Natchez* (New Orleans: Pelican, 1939), 209–10. Professor Herschel Gower of Vanderbilt University has been unable to verify Job Routh's origins but suggests these possibilities. (Gower to author, May 26, 1992).

5. Job Routh tombstone, Routh cemetery; Heirs of Job Routh to Mary Ellis, March 24, 1837, Deed Book Z, 175, CCO, ACC.

6. (Quotation) C. G. H. [Charles G. Dahlgren], "Fort Panmure," Natchez *Democrat,* Jan. 24, 1886; Marshall and Evans, *They Found It in Natchez,* 209–10; David King Gleason, Mary Warren Miller, and Ronald W. Miller, *The Great Houses of Natchez* (Jackson: University Press of Mississippi, 1986), 25.

7. Mary T. Tardy, *The Living Female Writers of the South* (Philadelphia: Claxton, Remsen & Haffelfinger, 1872), 74; her tombstone gives her Christian name as Mary Malvina, but John Hereford Percy and the Routh Genealogy (copy, William Alexander Percy Library, Greenville) offer "Mary Magdeline." On the marriage contract, see "Destruction of Llangollen," Natchez *Democrat,* July 17, 1932; [Ida Raymond] Mary Tardy, *Southland Writers. Biographical and Critical Sketches of the Living Female Writers of the South* (2 vols.; Claxton, Remsen & Haffelfinger, 1870), 1: 205.

8. Quotations from Sarah A. Dorsey, *Recollections of Henry Watkins Allen* (New Orleans: M. Doolady, 1866), 41; Tardy, *Living Female Writers,* 74; Evans, "Sarah Ann Dorsey, Donor of Beauvoir," 97.

9. See entry for May 30, 1836, in William Ransom Hogan and Erwin Adams Davis, *William Johnson's Natchez: The Ante-Bellum Diary of a Free Negro* (Baton Rouge: Louisiana State University Press, 1951), 118; 1: 206 (quotation).

10. General Dahlgren interview, transcription, 1879, Philadelphia *Press,* with Sarah Dorsey's Will, #1513 (hereafter Dahlgren, Phila. *Press*), Southern Historical Collection, Wilson Library, University of North Carolina at Chapel Hill (hereafter SHC); Thomas George Ellis tombstone, Routh cemetery; John Hereford Percy, *The Percy Family of Louisiana and Mississippi, 1776–1943* (Baton Rouge: priv. prnt., 1943), 63 (hereafter Percy, *Percy Family*); Tardy, *Southland Writers,* 1: 205 (1st quotation) and 1: 206 (2nd quotation).

11. Entry for April 13, 1837, *Diary of William Johnson,* 173; Tardy, *Southland Writers,* 1: 205 (quotation); Charles G. Dahlgren and Mary M. Routh, Oct. 19, 1840, Marriage Book 6, 427, CCO, ACC.

12. See *Thomas G. Ellis v. James H. Steele,* March 15, 1836, pp. 31–32, Natchez, Record of Judgments (damaged) First Mississippi Judicial District, Basement, Adams County Courthouse, Natchez. Ellis owned a number of town lots, Deed Book Y, 214, CCO, ACC.

13. See marriage contract, Dahlgren and Mary M. Ellis, Oct. 19, 1840, Book C-C, 239, CCO, ACC. The document assures that she does not relinquish any control of the Thomas G. Ellis estate but has full powers to do with it as she wishes, assisted by John Routh and Dr. Elias Ogden. See also, Mary M. Dahlgren will, Jan. 16, 1858, Will Book 3, 109–10, CCO, ACC, and for Nov. 28, 1836, 149–50.

14. Eli Montgomery to John Routh and Elias Ogden, mortgage, May 20, 1841, Deed Book D-D, 13–14, also Charles G. Dahlgren and Mary M. Dahlgren, May 20, 1841, Deed Book, 15–17, Charles G. Dahlgren and Mary M. Routh, Nov. 28, 1842, Deed Book D-D, 473, and Charles G. Dahlgren to Buckner and Johnson, April 25, 1843, Chancery Clerk's Office, Deed Book D-D, 655–56, CCO, ACC.

15. Will of Mary M. Dahlgren, Jan. 16, 1858.

16. Charles F. Coan, "Dahlgren, John Adolphus Bernard," in Allen Johnson and Dumas Malone, eds., *Dictionary of American Biography* (20 vols.; New York: Scribner, 1959), 3: 29; Dahlgren, Phila. *Press,* SHC.

17. "John Adolf Dahlgren," *National Cylopædia of American Biography,* 3: 377–80; Madeleine Vinton Dahlgren, *Memoir of John A. Dahlgren, Rear-Admiral United States Navy* (Boston: James R. Osgood, 1882), 5–18; (*Historical and Biographical Memoirs of Mississippi:* (2 vols.; Chicago: Goodspeed's, 1891), 1: 611; Dahlgren, Phila. *Press,* SHC.

18. "Special Sketches, D.," *Historical and Biographical Memoirs of Mississippi,* 1: 611; clipping, Jackson, [Mississippi] *Clarion-Ledger,* enclosed in Douglas Walworth to Jefferson Davis, Jan. 3, 1889, Jefferson Davis Collection, Museum of the Confederacy, Richmond (hereafter Davis MSS, MCR). Professor Herschel Gower of Vanderbilt, who is writing his biography, fixes Charles A. Dahlgren's birthday on Aug. 13, 1811. See also D. Clayton James, *Antebellum Natchez* (Baton Rouge: Louisiana State University Press, 1968), 159; Ira Smith & Co., New York, to Charles G. Dahlgren, June 12, 1848[?], (form letter) March —, 1851, and similar documents in Charles G. Dahlgren, subject file, MDAH.

19. Entry for March 14, 1836, Hogan and Davis, eds., *Johnson's Natchez,* 108.

20. Entry for Nov. 28, 1836, *ibid.,* 149–50; Dahlgren, Phila. *Press,* SHC; Atlanta *Constitution* clipping, enclosed in Douglas Walworth to Jefferson Davis, Jan. 3, 1889, Davis MSS, MCR.

21. Will of Mary M. Dahlgren, Jan. 16, 1858.

22. Entry for March 4, 1858, Stratton Diary.

23. Entry for July 17, 1855, Diary of the Rev. Joseph Buck Stratton, copy of typescript kindly provided by Mrs. Alma Carpenter. See advertisement, Natchez *Daily Courier,* March 25, 1853, p. 3; see Dahlgren Charles G., U. S. Census, Mississippi, City of Natchez, 1860, microfilm. Charles G. Dahlgren to Alfred V. Davis, Jan. 4, 1859, remainder of land in Routhland (not given to Jefferson College) is conveyed for sum of $15,000 in cash and two promissory notes for $7500, Deed Book M-M, 126–7, CCO, ACC. The children of Charles Dahlgren by his first marriage were: Bernard Ulric; Charles; Austin Mortimer; John Adolph; and two

girls who died very young; by the second: Gustavus; Rowen; Edgar; Charles; Ira and John (twins); and Bernardina. See also property agreements made in Nashville and recorded on Dec. 16, 29, 1859, Deed Book M-M, 450, CCO, ACC; Atlanta *Constitution* clippings, n.d., and Jackson *Clarion-Ledger,* n.d., in Douglas Wadsworth to Jefferson Davis, Jan. 3, 1889, Davis MSS, MCR.

24. Dahlgren, Phila. *Press,* SHC.

25. Tardy, *Living Female Writers,* 29; Dahlgren, Phila. *Press,* SHC. It is quite possible that Dahlgren simply boasted of keeping her on; DuPuy herself simply mentioned Thomas G. Ellis as her employer.

26. See Lucy Leigh Bowie, "Madame Grelaud's French School," *Maryland Historical Magazine* 39 (June 1944): 141–48; R. A. Howell to Mrs. William B. Howell, Nov. 21, 1836, Howell Family Collection, MDAH; Eron Rowland and Mrs. Dunbar Rowland, *Varina Howell, Wife of Jefferson Davis* (2 vols.; New York: Macmillan, 1927), 1: 43. On the school's denominational affiliation, see *Stephen Percy Ellis vs. Jefferson Davis,* Equity Case No. 8934, RG 21, U.S. Circuit Courts, Entry #212, General Case Files, Eastern District of Louisiana, New Orleans—Circuit Court, 22, National Archives, Fort Worth, Texas (hereafter *Ellis vs. Davis*).

27. Dahlgren, Phila. *Press,* SHC.

28. Tardy, *Southland Writers,* 1: 206; *DeBow's Review,* new ser., 6 (May 1869): 415–27, and subsequent issues to 7 (Feb. 1870): 175–82; Dahlgren, Phila. *Press,* SHC.

29. See Mrs S. M. C. Ewen, "Biographical Notes," in [Vincenzo Botta, ed.], *Memoirs of Anne C. L. Botta* (New York: J. Selwin Tait & Sons, 1894), 1–3, 8; Anne Marie Dolan, "The Literary Salon in New York, 1840–1860," M.A. thesis, Columbia University, 1957, pp. 83–84.

30. Sarah Ellis to "Dear Miss [Charlotte] Lynch [Botta]," Oct. 22, 1852, reported in auction sale, Sarah Dorsey, subject file, MDAH.

31. Emerson quoted in Dolan, "Literary Salons," 96, 97; Ewen, "Biographical Notes," 14, 16; Anne Charlotte Lynch Botta, *Handbook of Universal Literature from the Best and Latest Authorities* (Boston and New York: Houghton Mifflin, 1902); Dolan, "Literary Salons," 89–90 (quotation), 91; entry for Vincenzo Botta, *DAB,* 1: 470.

32. See Alexander Nicolas DeMenil, *The Literature of the Louisiana Territory* (St. Louis: St. Louis News Co., 1904), 162; entry for Sarah Anne Dorsey, *National Cyclopædia of American Biography,* 3: 213; quotation, Eliza Quitman to Henry Quitman (son), March 6, 1849, John Quitman family letters, a reference from the files of Alma Carpenter of Natchez.

33. Identification of plantations comes from Sarah A Dorsey to Gilbert Livingston & Robert Livingston Thompson, lease, Dec. 18, 1875, Record Book H, 620–21, Clerk's Office, Tensas Parish Courthouse, St. Joseph, La.; Mary Alice Fontenot and Edith Ziegler, *The Tensas Story* (Grand Coteau, La.: n.p. n.d.), 7; Evans, "Dorsey: Donor of Beauvoir," 95. Roger W. Shugg, *Origins of Class Struggle in Louisiana: A Social History of White Farmers and Laborers during Slavery and After, 1840–1875* (Baton Rouge: Louisiana State University Press, 1939), 92; Brief, William Reed Mills, attorney, 2, in *Ellis vs. Davis;* Lewis, "Dorsey," 4.

34. Evans, "Dorsey: Donor of Beauvoir," 95; certificate of membership, Sept. 21, 1841, Sarah Dorsey MSS, MCR.

35. Jan. 19, 1853, Marriage Record Book 7, 146, CCO, ACC; Laura L. DeLap

in Sarah A. Dorsey, subject file, MDAH; Evans, "Dorsey," 101; C. G. Dahlgren, account with Bailey & Co., 136 Chesnut St., Philadelphia, Oct. 8, 1853, Charles G. Dahlgren, "Subject File," MDAH.

36. Dahlgren, Phila. *Press,* SHC.

37. Percy, *Percy Family,* 9; Dorothy Rice Guthrie, *Marriage Records: Concordia Parish, 1816–1916, Tensas Parish, 1850–1860* (n.p., n.d.), 8; Fontenot and Ziegler, *Tensas Story,* 2, 4–5, 7, 56; *Historical and Biographical Memoirs of Mississippi,* 2: 521–23.

38. In 1860 it was reported that the Rouths—John, John Knox, Stephen, and Calvin—produced a total of 3,787 bales of cotton. Locally, Sarah's uncle, John Routh, was known as the Cotton King. See Fontenot and Ziegler, *Tensas Story* 4–5; U. S. Census, Tensas Parish, Louisiana, 1860, see listings for John Knox Routh, who claimed $230,880 in real estate and $160,000 in personal property, and John Routh; John K. Routh, promissory note, to Samuel Dorsey, Oct. 21, 23, 1862, Dorsey MSS, MCR; *Historical and Biographical Memoirs of Mississippi,* 2: 523.

39. (Quotation) Dorsey, *Allen,* 166; Fontenot and Ziegler, *Tensas Story,* 88.

40. See, for instance, receipt, Koontz to Dahlgren, Dorsey & Ellis, Nov. 30, 1864, Dorsey MSS, MCR.

41. See Samuel W. Dorsey to Dahlgren, vouchers, n.d. [1854], Louisiana tax receipts, 185-, in Dahlgren, subject file, MDAH.

42. Tardy, *Southland Writers,* 1: 206.

43. Quoted in J. B. Smallwood, "Sarah Anne (Ellis) Dorsey (Mrs. Samuel W.): 1829–1879," in James B. Lloyd, ed., *Lives of Mississippi Authors, 1817–1967* (Jackson: University Press of Mississippi, 1981), 137.

44. Ewen, "Biographical Notes," 30.

45. Dorsey, *Allen,* 43.

46. I gratefully acknowledge the help of Patrick J. Geary, whose translation I adopted, and of Horace Gregory, trans., Ovid, *The Metamorphoses* (New York: Mentor, 1958), 63–64.

47. Lewis, "Dorsey," 4.

48. Fontenot and Ziegler, *Tensas Story,* 4.

49. See entry for July 22, 1855, for baptisms, and Jan. 11 and 14, 1857, for confirmation services, St. Joseph's [Episcopal] Church, Parish of Tensas, Diocese of Louisiana, Book I, 1855–88, Records of Parishioners, Communicants, Baptisms, Marriages, Confirmations, and Burials of the Parish of St. Joseph, La. The confirmed slaves' names were Dorcas Clark, Henrietta Kedman, William Fuller, and William Franklin.

50. Sarah Dorsey, Lease to Abraham Isaacs, Nov. 25, 1876, Book H, 787–89, Tensas Parish Records Office, St. Joseph, La.; Lewis, "Dorsey," 4, 5 (quotation), 8. See also, Mrs. Sarah W. Dorsey to G. L. and R. L. Thompson, Dec. 18, 1875, Notarial Records, Book H, 620–22, Tensas Parish Courthouse, St. Joseph, La. James W. Davidson, *The Living Writers of the South* (New York: Carleton, 1869), 154. In 1871, at the height of "Black Republican" Reconstruction, Sarah Dorsey gave the school and land, a 100-square-foot section of the old plantation garden, to Tensas Parish for the benefit of the freedmen.

51. Evans, "Dorsey," 98–99; Lewis, "Dorsey," 6.

52. Daniel Walker Howe, *The Political Culture of the American Whigs* (Chicago: University of Chicago Press, 1979).

53. See Ralph A. Wooster, *The Secession Conventions of the South* (Princeton: Princeton University Press, 1962), 108; see Dorsey's resolution on Jan. 23, in New Orleans *Times-Picayune,* Jan. 29, 1861.

54. *8th U. S. Census, 1860,* Louisiana—Tensas Parish, Reel 426, 8, shows no living children born to her. Dorsey, *Allen,* 65.

55. Dorsey, *Allen,* 70 (quotation); Dorsey to A. D. Mann, Aug. 4, 1878, Ellis Family MSS, Hill Memorial Library, Louisiana State University Libraries, Baton Rouge (hereafter LSUL); quotation in Tardy, *Southland Writers,* 1: 205.

56. See entries for June 4, Aug. 24, Oct. 31, 1849, March 9, May 7, Aug. 1, 1850, Aug. 1, 1851, April 5, 1852, Diary of Rev. Joseph Buck Stratton, D.D., Pastor, Presbyterian Church of Natchez, Miss., 1843–1903, copy in typescript, private possession. The original is located in the Louisiana and Lower Mississippi Valley Collection, LSUL.

57. See Joan Cashin, *A Family Venture: Men and Women on the Southern Frontier* (New York: Oxford University Press, 1991), 80, 94; Tardy, *Southland Writers,* 1: 208 (quotation).

58. Sarah A. Dorsey to the Rt. Rev. Leonidas L. Polk, Feb. 20, 1862, Leonidas L. Polk MSS, Jessie Ball DuPont Library, University of the South, Sewanee, Tennessee (hereafter USL).

59. Dorsey, *Allen,* 166–67. See also Jeffrey Alan Owens, "The Burning of Lake St. Joseph," *Louisiana History* 32 (Fall 1991): 393–415.

60. Tardy, *Southland Writers,* 1: 208.

61. *Ibid.,* 207; Bell I. Wiley, *Confederate Women* (Westport, Conn.: Greenwood), 79.

62. Evans, "Dorsey," 99; Ewen, "Biographical Notes," 17.

63. Vincent H. Cassidy, "Louisiana," in W. Buck Yearns, ed., *The Confederate Governors* (Athens: University of Georgia Press, 1985), 102; Dorsey, *Allen,* 30.

64. See Cassidy, "Louisiana," in Yearns, ed., *Confederate Governors,* 102–7 and 229; Dorsey, *Allen,* 284.

65. Dorsey, *Allen,* 56, 61.

66. See Nina Baym, "Women and the Republic: Emma Willard's Rhetoric of History," *American Quarterly* 43 (March 1991): 1–23.

67. Davidson, *Living Writers of the South,* 155; Mildred Lewis Rutherford, *The South in History and Literature: A Hand-Book of Southern Authors* (Athens, Ga.: Franklin Times, 1907), 359.

68. Tardy, *Southland Writers,* 1: 212.

69. Dorsey, *Allen,* 9, 10 (quotation), 11.

70. *Ibid.,* 10–12.

71. Dorsey to Stanley, Dec. 28, 1871, Oct. 29, 1872, English MS. 1094, R 84307, John Rylands University Library of Manchester.

72. Tardy, *Southland Writers,* 1: 220.

73. Rutherford, *The South in History and Literature,* 359.

Chapter Seven COLLISION OF MINDS

1. Dorsey to Stanley, Jan. 3, 1872, Ryl. English MS. 1094, R 84307, John Rylands University Library of Manchester (hereafter 1094, UML). See also Marcus

Cunliffe, "Notes on the Dorsey-Stanley Correspondence (1871–1873) in the John Rylands Library," *Bulletin of the John Rylands Library* 36 (1953–54): 360–85.

2. "President Davis and His Dog Traveler," *Confederate Veteran* 13 (April 1909): 173.

3. Dorsey to Stanley, Sept. 6, 1871, 1094, UML.

4. Entry for Edward John Stanley in J. R. H. Weaver, ed., *The Dictionary of National Biography, 1922–1930* (London: Oxford University Press, 1931), 18: 951–52; Nancy Mitford, ed., *The Stanleys of Alderley: Their Letters Between the Years 1851–1865* (London: Chapman & Hall, 1939), x–xii (quotation xi). After the death of two elder brothers, Edward Lyulph Stanley fell heir to three baronies: Alderley, Eddisbury, and Sheffield. In 1903 he took the title of Lord Sheffield.

5. Henrietta Maria Stanley to Edward Stanley, July 31, Aug. 3, 4, 7, (11 quotation), 12, 7–15, Nov. 9, 1851 (quotation, 24), in Mitford, ed., *The Stanleys of Alderley*, 11, 20.

6. Quotation, Henrietta Maria Stanley to Edward Stanley, Aug. 3, 1851, *ibid.*, 9; on the courtship, see the correspondence during the Airlie-Stanley courtship, *ibid.*, 7–18.

7. Dorsey to Stanley, Sept. 6, 1871, 1094, UML.

8. See Mitford, ed., *Stanleys of Alderley*, xiii–xiv; and Nancy Mitford, ed., *The Ladies of Alderley: Being the Letters Between Maria Josepha Lady Stanley of Alderley and Her Daughter-in-Law Henrietta Maria Stanley During the Years 1841–1850* (London: Hamish Hamilton, 1938), xxv; Lady Stanley to Maria Josepha Stanley, Feb. 2, 1855, in Mitford, ed., *Stanleys of Alderley*, 125 (quotation); Dorsey to Stanley, Sept. 13, 1872, 1094, UML.

9. Mitford, ed., *Stanleys of Alderley*, xiii and xviii (quotation); Mitford, ed., *Ladies of Alderley*, xxii; Naomi B. Levine, *Politics, Religion and Love: The Story of the Love Affair That Changed the Face of Politics in the British Empire* (New York: New York University Press, 1991), 105; Cunliffe, "Notes on the Dorsey-Stanley Correspondence," 360–85, esp. 365; Dorsey to Stanley, Sept. 6, 1871, 1094, UML.

10. Cunliffe, "Notes on Dorsey-Stanley Correspondence," 363.

11. Henrietta Maria Stanley to Lyulph Stanley, July 2, 1871, English MS. 1092, letter 104, UML.

12. Dorsey to Stanley, May 22, 1871, 1094, UML.

13. Cunliffe, "Notes on Dorsey-Stanley Correspondence," 363–65.

14. Robert K. Massie, *Dreadnought: Britain, Germany, and the Coming of the Great War* (New York: Random House, 1991), 578–80; Levine, *Politics, Religion and Love* 169–95, 262–69; Cunliffe, "Notes on Dorsey-Stanley Correspondence," 363, 378.

15. Russell quoted in Nicholas Griffin, ed., *The Selected Letters of Bertrand Russell. Vol. I The Private Years, 1884–1914* (Boston: Houghton Mifflin, 1992), 5; Henrietta Maria Stanley, *DNB*, 18: 952–53: Dorsey to Stanley, Jan. 3, 1872, 1094, UML.

16. See "Sarah Anne Dorsey," *National Cyclopædia of American Biography* 3: 213; quotation, in Lady Stanley to Lyulph Stanley, July 2, 1871, 1092, UML.

17. Quotation, Dorsey to Stanley, Nov. 5, 1871, 1094, UML. See Walter E. Houghton, *The Victorian Frame of Mind 1830–1870* (New Haven: Yale University Press, 1957), 48.

18. "Dover Beach," in Lionel Trilling, ed., *The Portable Arnold* (New York: Viking, 1949), 166. I owe this discussion to Eugene L. Williamson, "Words from

Westminster Abbey: Matthew Arnold and Arthur Stanley," *Studies in English Literature 1500–1900* 11 (Autumn 1971): 749–61, esp. 759–61.

19. Dorsey to Stanley, July 27, 1872 (first two quotations), Nov. 5, 1871 (last quotation), 1094, UML. Elizabeth Fox-Genovese, an expert on Evans, assures me that Sarah Dorsey's view was out of line with Evans's understanding of revelation and faith.

20. Mitford, ed., *Stanleys of Alderley,* xiii–xvii (quotation, xv); Algernon Stanley's comment quoted in Levine, *Religion, Politics and Love,* 106; Lady Stanley to Lyulph Stanley, Jan. 17, 1872 (quotation), 1092, UML; Levine, *Politics, Religion and Love,* 106.

21. Anna Harrietta Leonowens, *The Romance of the Harem,* ed. Susan Morgan (1868; Charlottesville: University Press of Virginia, 1991); *Life and Travel in India: Being Recollections of a Journey Before the Days of Railroads* (Philadelphia: Porter & Coates, 1884); *The English Governess at the Siamese Court: Being Recollections of Six Years in the Royal Palace at Bangkok* (Boston: Fields, Osgood, & Co., 1870); Anne H. Leonowens, "A Tribute," in [Botta, ed.], *Memoirs of Anne C. L. Botta,* 100–101; Dorsey to Stanley, Nov. 5, 1871, 1094, UML.

22. Leonowens, *Romance of the Harem,* ix–xxxix (quotation, xxx).

23. Dorsey to Stanley, March 22, 1871 (1st quotation), Dorsey to Stanley, Jan. 12, 1873 (2nd quotation), 1094, UML.

24. Dorsey to Stanley, Nov. 5, 1871, Feb. 21, 1872, 1094, UML.

25. Sarah A. Dorsey, *The Aryan Philosophy: Second Paper Prepared at the Request of the Academy of Sciences* (New Orleans: George Ellis and Brother, n.d.), 4.

26. *Ibid.,* 26.

27. John Stratton Hawley, "Naming Hinduism," *Wilson Quarterly* 15 (Summer 1991): 20–34, esp. 32.

28. Dorsey to Stanley, Dec. 28, 1871, 1094, UML.

29. Dorsey to Stanley, Feb. 21, 1872, 1094, UML.

30. Dorsey to Stanley, May 22, 1871, and Feb. 21 (quotation), Oct. 29, 1872, 1094, UML. See James Hinton, *Life in Nature* (New York: D. Appleton, 1872).

31. Dorsey to Stanley, Feb. 21, 1872, UML. See Francis Mark Mondimore, *Depression: The Mood Disease* (Baltimore: Johns Hopkins University Press, 1990), 116–17.

32. Quoted in A. Alvarez, *The Savage God: A Study of Suicide* (New York: Random House, 1972), 220.

33. Dorsey to Stanley, Nov. 5, 1871 (quotation), 1094, UML; John K. Routh, St. Joseph, May 25 and July 31, 1869 (quotation), Tensas Parish, La., Vol. 22, R.G. Dun & Company Archives, Baker Library, Harvard University.

34. Caleb Forshey to St. John Richardson Liddell, March 14, 1869, Liddell Family MSS, Hill Library, Louisiana State University Libraries, Baton Rouge (H-LSU).

35. Dorsey to Stanley, Nov. 5, 1871 (quotation), Oct. 29, 1872, 1094, UML.

36. Dorsey to Stanley, Jan. 12, 1871 (quotation), 1094, UML; Richard Nelson Current, *Those Terrible Carpetbaggers* (New York: Oxford University Press, 1988), 3–23, 242–49, 416 (quotation of anonymous lady).

37. Dorsey to Stanley, Nov. 5, 1871 (quotations); Henry Clay Warmoth, *War, Politics and Reconstruction: Stormy Days in Louisiana* (New York: Macmillan, 1930), 118; Dorsey to Stanley, Jan. 3, 1872, 1094, UML; Joe Gray Taylor, "Henry Clay Warmoth," in Joseph G. Dawson III, ed., *The Louisiana Governors: From*

Iberville to Edwards (Baton Rouge: Louisiana State University Press, 1990), 164–68.

38. Dorsey to Stanley, Jan. 12, Nov. 5, 1871, Oct. 29, 1872, 1094, UML; Current, *Carpetbaggers*, 278–79.

39. Dorsey to Stanley, Jan. 3, 1872, 1094, UML.

40. Dorsey to Stanley, July 27, Jan. 12, 1094, UML.

41. See Elizabeth R. Varon, "The Ladies Are Whigs: Lucy Barbour, Henry Clay, and Nineteenth-Century Virginia Politics," *Virginia Cavalcade* 42 (Autumn 1992): 72–83; Dorsey to Stanley, Sept. 13, 1872, 1094, UML.

42. Dorsey to Stanley, Nov. 5, 1871, Thomas P. Farrar to Sarah Dorsey, Jan. 3, 1872, 1094, UML.

43. Dorsey to Stanley, Jan. 3, 1872 (quotation), Oct. 29, 1872, April 8, 1872, 1094, UML.

44. See Emma Lydia Bolzau, "Almira Hart Lincoln Phelps: Her Life and Work," Ph.D. dissertation, University of Pennsylvania, 1936, pp. 122–26.

45. *Ibid.*, 137 (quotation), also 197; Patricia E. Haines, "The Patapsco Female Institute," undergraduate research paper, Goucher College, March 1966, Maryland Historical Society, Baltimore. See Sam Worthington, "Ante-Bellum Slave-Holding Aristocracy of Washington County," in William D. McCain and Charlotte Capers, eds., *Memoirs of Henry Tillinghast Ireys: Papers of the Washington County Historical Society 1910–1915* (Jackson: MDAH, 1954), 353; quotation, Dorsey to Stanley, Nov. 9, 1871, 1094, UML.

46. Dorsey to Stanley, Nov. 9, 1871, 1094, UML.

47. *Ibid.;* Dorsey to Stanley, Dec. 28, 1871, 1094, UML.

48. Dorsey to Stanley, Nov. 9, 1871, 1094, UML.

49. *Ibid.*

Chapter Eight   ENSHRINING THE LOST CAUSE

1. See Mary Forrest, pseud. [Julia Deane Freeman], *Women of the South Distinguished in Literature* (New York: Derby & Jackson, 1861), 149.

2. Dorsey to Stanley, Dec. 28, 1871, Ryl. Eng. MS 1094, R 84307, John Rylands University Library of Manchester (hereafter 1094, UML).

3. Dorsey to Stanley, Jan. 12, 1873, 1094, UML.

4. Entry for Edward Lyulph Stanley, in J. R. H. Weaver, ed., *The Dictionary of National Biography, 1922–1930* (London: Oxford University Press, 1931), 18: 805–7 (hereafter *DNB* (1922–1930)).

5. Dorsey to Stanley, Jan. 3, 1872, 1094, UML.

6. *Ibid.*

7. *Ibid.*

8. *DNB (1922–1930)*, 18: 805–7.

9. Dorsey to Stanley, Jan. 3, 1872, 1094, UML.

10. Virginia Woolf, *The Death of the Moth and Other Essays* (1942: New York: Harcourt Brace and Jovanovich, 1970), 235–42, esp. 235, 237.

11. Dorsey to Stanley, April 8, 1872, 1094, UML.

12. Helen Taylor, *Gender, Race, and Region in the Writings of Grace King, Ruth*

McEnery Stuart, and Kate Chopin (Baton Rouge: Louisiana State University Press, 1989); Edward L. Ayers, *The Promise of the New South: Life after Reconstruction* (New York: Oxford University Press, 1992), 339–72.

13. Sarah A. Dorsey, *Recollections of Henry Watkins Allen, Brigadier-General Confederate States Army Ex-Governor of Louisiana* (New York: M. Doolady, 1866), 13–14.

14. Fanny Kemble to Harriet St. Leger, Aug. 5, 1831, in *Records of a Girlhood* (New York: Henry Holt, 1879), 447.

15. "Dean Stanley on Charles Dickens," in *Speeches, Letters, and Sayings of Charles Dickens* (New York: Harper & Bros., 1870), 144–47.

16. Woolf, *Death of the Moth,* 241.

17. Dorsey to Stanley, Jan. 3, 1872, 1094, UML.

18. See Joseph Frazier Wall, *Andrew Carnegie* (1970; Pittsburgh: University of Pittsburgh Press, 1989), 362–64.

19. Dorsey to Stanley, Jan. 3, 1872, 1094, UML.

20. *Ibid.*

21. *Ibid.,* April 8, 1872.

22. *Ibid.,* July 27, 1872.

23. *Ibid.,* Sept. 6, 1871.

24. *Ibid.,* Sept. 13, 1872.

25. *Ibid.,* Oct. 29, 1872.

26. *Ibid.,* Jan. 12, 1873.

27. *Ibid.,* Jan. 3, 1873.

28. William C. Davis, *Jefferson Davis: The Man and His Hour* (New York: Harper Collins, 1991), 669.

29. W. A. Evans, "Jefferson Davis Shrine—Beauvoir House," *Journal of Mississippi History,* 3 (April 1941): 206–11. A. F. Johnston to Sarah A. Dorsey, deed, July 7, 1873, Deed Book 13, 376, Clerk's Office, Harrison County, Gulfport, as transcribed in *Mississippi Court Records from the May Wilson McBee Papers* (Baltimore: Genealogical Publishing Co., 1967), 75.

30. Sarah A. Dorsey to Major W. T. Walthall, May 1, 1877, W. T. Walthall Papers, MDAH.

31. Robert McElroy, *Jefferson Davis: The Unreal and the Real* (New York: Harper & Bros., 1937), 642; see also Sarah Dorsey to Colonel A. D. Mann, Aug. 4, 1878, Jefferson Davis MSS, Kuntz Collection, Howard-Tilton Library, Tulane University, New Orleans (hereafter Davis MSS, H-TL); Dorsey to Mann, April 25, 1878, Ellis Family Papers, H-LSU; quotation, recollections of Maud Walthall, typed transcription, Sarah Anne Dorsey, Subject File, MDAH.

32. See for instance, Dorsey to Caleb Goldsmith Forshey, May 9, 1877, Davis MSS, H-TL.

33. Dorsey to W. T. Walthall, Feb. 23, 1877, in Dunbar Rowland, ed., *Jefferson Davis: Constitutionalist, His Letters, Papers, and Speeches* (10 vols.; Jackson: MDAH, 1923), 8: 523; *ibid.,* March 14, 17, April 5, May 1, 3, June 21, 29, 1877, 7: 526–58.

34. W. C. Davis, *Jefferson Davis,* 9–10; 692 (quotation), and 691–96. My interpretation owes much to W. C. Davis's biography.

35. *Ibid.,* 375–78.

36. *Ibid.,* 671; *Stephen Percy Ellis, et al. vs. Jefferson Davis,* Equity Case No.

8934, RG21, U.S. District Courts, Entry #121—general case files—Eastern District of New Orleans—Circuit Court, 21, National Archives, Fort Worth, Texas (hereafter *Ellis vs. Davis*); Sarah Dorsey to W. T. Walthall, March 14, 17, April 3, 4, 5, May 1, 3, June 21, 29, 1877, in Rowland, ed., *Jefferson Davis,* 7: 523–59.

37. See Clement Eaton, *Jefferson Davis* (New York: Free Press, 1977), 102–4, 262–63; Shelby Foote, *The Civil War: A Narrative. Fort Sumter to Perryville* (3 vols.; New York: Random House, 1958), 1: 15, 122, 127; Varina Howell Davis, *Jefferson Davis, Ex-President of the Confederate States of America: A Memoir* (2 vols.; New York: Belford Co., 1890), 2: 161. On "neurasthenia," see Janet Oppenheim, *Shattered Nerves: Doctors, Patients, and Depression in Victorian England* (New York: Oxford University Press, 1991), 99–100.

38. V. Davis, *Jefferson Davis,* 2: 163; Paul D. Escott, *After Secession: Jefferson Davis and the Failure of Confederate Nationalism* (Baton Rouge: Louisiana State University Press, 1978), 260–63 (quotation, 261). See also, Clifford Dowdey, *Experiment in Rebellion* (Garden City, N.Y.: Doubleday, 1946), 32, 70, 143, 205, 304, 346, 359.

39. Austin Mortimer Dahlgren to Mrs. Charles A. Dahlgren, April 22, July 8, 1877, Charles A. Dahlgren Papers, Tennessee State Archives, Nashville (hereafter TSA).

40. Brief, William Reed Mills, attorney, 22, in *Ellis vs Davis; Ellis vs. Davis;* Sarah Dorsey to "My Dear Miss Betty," Feb. 10, 1877, copy, original in private hands, kindly supplied by Lynda Lasswell Crist, editor, Jefferson Davis Papers, Rice University, Houston, Texas; Hudson Strode, *Jefferson Davis: Tragic Hero, The Last Twenty-five Years, 1864–1889* (3 vols.; New York: Harcourt, Brace and World, 1955), 3: 422. See also Herschel Gower, "The Dahlgrens and Jefferson Davis," *Journal of Mississippi History* 55 (August 1993): 179–201.

41. *Historical and Biographical Memoirs of Mississippi* (2 vols.; Chicago: Goodspeed's, 1891), 1: 612; Mortimer Dahlgren to Mrs. Dahlgren, July 8, 1877, Dahlgren Papers, TSA.

42. See "Elk-Ridge History Remembered," in *Tensas Gazette* (St. Joseph, La.), April 15, 1987, clipping supplied by Mrs. Melba Fulton, St. Joseph. On confiscation, see Dahlgren, Phila. *Press,* SHC.

43. Burton Harrison to Constance Harrison, May 13, 1867, in *Recollections, Grave and Gay* (New York: Scribner 1911), 263; *Historical and Biographical Memoirs of Mississippi,* 1: 611–12.

44. Joan E. Cashin, "Varina Howell Davis (1826–1906)," in G. J. Barker-Benfield and Catherine Clinton, eds., *Portraits of American Women: From Settlement to the Present* (New York: St. Martin's Press, 1991), 271.

45. Margaret Davis Hayes to Varina Davis, June 9, 1877, Jefferson Davis MSS, W. S. Hoole Special Collections, University of Alabama Library (hereafter Jefferson Davis MSS, UAL); Strode, *Jefferson Davis,* 3: 428.

46. Quoted in W. C. Davis, *Jefferson Davis,* 672.

47. Mortimer Dahlgren to Mrs. Dahlgren, Dec. 28, 1877, Dahlgren Papers, TSA.

48. Varina Davis to Jefferson Davis, April 18, 1878, Davis MSS, H-TL; Strode, *Jefferson Davis,* 3: 429; see also, Isabel Ross, *First Lady of the South: The Life of Mrs. Jefferson Davis* (New York: Harper & Bros., 1958), 331.

49. See Cashin, "Varina Davis," 271.

50. Varina Davis to Miss Emily Virginia Mason, May 28, 1878, Varina Davis

MSS, MDAH; Dorsey to Mann, Aug. 4, 1878, Ellis MSS, H-LSU; McElroy, *Davis*, 650; Ross, *First Lady of the South*, 326, 328.

51. V. Davis, *Jefferson Davis*, 2: 827–28; Ross, *First Lady of the South*, 329, 330.

52. Escott, *After Secession*, 262; V. Davis, *Jefferson Davis*, 2: 163; Steven E. Woodworth, *Jefferson Davis and His Generals: The Failure of Confederate Command in the West* (Lawrence: Kansas University Press of Kansas, 1990), 315; Davis, *Jefferson Davis*, 84, 263–64.

53. W. C. Davis, *Jefferson Davis*, 666.

54. *Ellis vs. Davis*, also see Cashin, "Varina Davis," 274; New York *Herald*, Sept. 30, 1879.

55. Dorsey, Last Will in *Ellis vs. Davis*; also, *Ellis vs. Davis*, 8–9; recollections of Maud Walthall, typed transcription, Dorsey, Subject File, MDAH.

56. Dorsey to Stanley, Jan. 12, 1873, 1094, UML; J. B. Atlay, "Haliburton, Arthur Lawrence," Sir Sidney Lee, ed., *The Dictionary of National Biography Second Supplement.* (New York: Macmillan, 1912), 2: 186. George Clement Boase, "Haliburton, Thomas Chandler," Sir Leslie Stephen and Sir Sidney Lee, eds., *The Dictionary of National Biography* (London: Oxford University Press, 1921–22), 8: 927–29. *Davis vs.*

57. *Ellis vs. Davis*, 22.

58. Quoted in Tardy, *Living Female Writers*, 1: 216.

59. Petitions for opening and probating the will, July 10, 15, 1879, in *Ellis vs. Davis*; also see Succession of Sarah Dorsey to Jefferson Davis, July 29, 1879, Wills & Donations, Records Office, Tensas Parish Courthouse; see also Sarah Dorsey, Last Will & Testament, Jan. 4, 1878, Will Book 2, 212, copied from Will Book 20 of 2nd District Court, folios, 160–62, as transcribed in *Mississippi Court Records*, 77; Sarah A. Dorsey to Jefferson Davis, deed, Feb. 19, 1879, Deed Book 16, 328–29, Clerk's Office, Harrison County Courthouse, Gulfport, Miss., as transcribed in *Mississippi Court Records*, 75; see also Dorsey to Davis, March 20, 1879, annexed conditions, Deed Book 13, 131–32, *ibid.*

60. See Clement L. Walker to the Editor of the New York *Sun*, Aug. 25, 1879, reprint, in Davis MSS, H-TL.

61. McElroy, *Davis*, 655; M. M. Broadwell to Jefferson Davis, Aug. 11, 1880, Dunbar Rowland, *Jefferson Davis: Constitutionalist: His Letters, Papers and Speeches* (10 vols; Jackson: MDAH), 1923, 8: 484; Clement L. Walker to Editor of the New York *Sun*, Aug. 25, 1879, reprint, in Davis MSS, H-TL.

62. Quoted from *Ellis vs. Davis*, 16–17.

63. Dahlgren, Phila. *Press*, SHC.

64. V. Davis, *Jefferson Davis*, 2: 828; Dorsey, Sarah A. Dorsey, *Panola: A Tale of Louisiana* (Philadelphia: T. B. Peterson, 1877), 208.

65. See brief, *Ellis vs. Davis*, 9; also, New Orleans, *Daily Picayune*, Dec. 13, 1879; Breaux, Fenner, & Hall and E. H. Farrar, Demurrer of Defendant, Jan. 15, 1880, 5, *Ellis vs. Davis*.

66. Dahlgren, Phila. *Press*, SHC.

67. Quoted, *ibid.*

68. See Charles G. Dahlgren to A. G. Brown, Dec. 3, 1863, Letters Received by the Confederate Secretary of War, 1861–1865, Roll 90, Aug.–Dec. 1863, frames 380–81, War Department, NA, Washington; quotation in Harrison, *Recollections, Grave and Gay*, 273; Dahlgren, Phila. *Press*, SHC; W. B. Woods, judgment, March 8, 1880; appeal allowed, Sept. 17, 1880, in *Ellis vs. Davis*. Stephen Percy Ellis and

J. Adolphe Dahlgren dropped their names from the appeal to the Supreme Court which had had involved a $250 filing fee.

69. Varina Davis to the Rev. John A. Dorsey, April 3, 1889, Davis MSS, MDAH.

Chapter Nine   KNIGHT-ERRANT'S DEFEAT

1. William Alexander Percy, *Lanterns on the Levee: Recollections of a Planter's Son* (1941; Baton Rouge: Louisiana State University, 1973), 145 (hereafter Percy, *Lanterns*).

2. Lewis Baker interview with Brodie S. Crump, Nov. 3, 1976, pp. 34–36, Hill Memorial Library, Louisiana State University Libraries, Baton Rouge (hereafter H-LSU).

3. See Greenville *Times,* July 19, Nov. 8, 1878, July 15, 1885 (quotation).

4. Percy Bell, "A Child of the Delta" (chap. 6, p. 10), copy of an unpublished autobiography, kindly lent by Charles Bell, his son, a professor at St. John's College, Santa Fe, N.M.; Crump interview, 39–41, H-LSU; William F. Holmes, *The White Chief: James Kimble Vardaman* (Baton Rouge: Louisiana State University Press, 1970), 120, 204; Nannie Pitts McLemore, "James K. Vardaman: A Mississippi Progressive," *Journal of Mississippi History* 24 (Feb. 1967): 1–11; Harry Ball Diary, July 10, 1895, MDAH.

5. Quoted in James Cobb, *The Most Southern Place on Earth: The Mississippi Delta and the Roots of Regional Identity* (New York: Oxford University Press, 1992), 132.

6. James P. Coleman, "The Mississippi Constitution of 1890," in Richard Aubrey McLemore, ed., *A History of Mississippi* (2 vols.; Jackson: University & College Press of Mississippi, 1973), 2: 4; See (Miss) Willie D. Halsell, "The Bourbon Period in Mississippi Politics, 1875–1890," *Journal of Southern History* 11 (Nov. 1945): 532–33; quotation, Lee J. Langley, "Italians in the Cotton Fields," *Manufacturer's Record* 45 (April 7, 1904): 250.

7. Neil R. McMillen, *Dark Journey: Black Mississippians in the Age of Jim Crow* (Urbana: University of Illinois Press, 1989), 112, 113.

8. William F. Holmes, "William Alexander Percy and the Bourbon Era in the Yazoo-Mississippi Delta," *Mississippi Quarterly* 26 (Winter 1972–73): 85.

9. Percy, *Lanterns,* 144–45; LeRoy Percy, *Speech Made to the Legislative Caucus in Response to the Invitation to Speak Extended by the Caucus to the Candidates for the United States Senate* (n.p. [1910]), 7; Holmes, "William Alexander Percy and the Bourbon Era," 85.

10. George Coleman Obsorn, *John Sharp Williams: Planter-Statesman of the Deep South* (Baton Rouge: Louisiana State University Press, 1943), 311–20.

11. *Historical and Biographical Memoirs of Mississippi* (2 vols.; Chicago: Goodspeed's, 1891), 2: 581; Keating, *History of Washington County,* 35; Douglas Southall Freeman, *Lee's Lieutenants: A Study in Command* (3 vols.; New York: Scribner, 1944), 3: 280–81.

12. See Jackson, *Clarion-Ledger* [?], Oct. 26, 1930, newspaper clipping, William Alexander Percy Subject File, MDAH.

13. Walker Percy, *The Last Gentleman* (New York: New American Library, 1968), 210.

14. Percy, *Lanterns* 273.

15. Mississippi Legislature, *The Testimony in the Impeachment of Adelbert Ames as Governor of Mississippi* (Jackson, n.p., 1877); *ibid.* (1878), 4–6; Adelbert Ames, Subject File, clipping, MDAH; speech, Washington County Democratic Nominating Convention, in Greenville *Times,* July 12, 1879, July 15, 1885; Greenville *Times,* Oct. 9, 1875, Jan. 1, 1875, Aug. 23, 1884, Oct. 18, March 21, April 4, July 15, 1885; Keating, *History of Washington County,* 52; William Alexander Percy, Subject File, clippings, and clippings in Percy Family MSS (hereafter PP), MDAH; Walter Sillers, Sr., "Flood Control in Bolivar County, 1838–1924," *Journal of Mississippi History* 9 (Jan. 1947): 7, 9; Yazoo City, *Yazoo Herald,* June 30, 1882; Cobb, *The Most Southern Place on Earth,* 78–79, 95.

16. Percy, *Lanterns* 272–73.

17. Will of LeRoy Pope Percy, June 26, 1873, Will Book 1, 428, CoC, Wash.; Percy, *Lanterns* 272; Alice Wade and Katherine Branton, eds., *Early Records of Issaquena and Washington County 1827–1900* (2 vols.; Greenville: priv. prtn., 1977), 2: 79; Greenville *Times,* July 1, 1882.

18. Nannie Armstrong Percy to Lady Armstrong, Jan. 7, 1888, Armstrong Family MSS, Southern Historical Collection, Wilson Library, University of North Carolina, Chapel Hill (SHC).

19. Percy, *Lanterns* 29, 32; Nannie Armstrong Percy to Lady Armstrong, Jan. 7, 1888, Armstrong MSS, SHC.

20. Greenville *Times,* Jan. 28, 1888; Percy, *Last Gentleman,* 16; see Jackson, *Clarion-Ledger* [?], Oct. 26, 1930, newspaper clipping, William Alexander Percy Subject, File, MDAH.

21. John G. Jones interview, 1983, in Lewis Lawson and Victor A. Kramer, eds., *Conversations with Walker Percy* (Jackson: University Press of Mississippi, 1985), 250.

22. Percy, *Lanterns,* 57.

23. John Griffin Jones, "Interview with Joe Rice Dockery," Dec. 13, 1979, pp. 25–29, MDAH; see also LeRoy Percy to Will Dockery, Jan. 4, 1926, PP, MDAH.

24. McMillen, *Dark Journey,* 7.

25. W. J. Cash, *The Mind of the South* (1941; New York: Random House, 1991), especially, 252–53; McMillen, *Dark Journey,* 62, 224 (quotation).

26. Percy, *Lanterns,* 143.

27. Albert D. Kirwan, *Revolt of the Rednecks: Mississippi Politics, 1876–1925* (1951; New York: Harper, 1965), 162–77; William F. Holmes, "James K. Vardaman: From Bourbon to Agrarian Reformer," *Journal of Mississippi History* 31 (May 1969): 97–115.

28. Holmes, *The White Chief,* 200 (quotation), 203, 203n; New York *Times,* April 17, 1910.

29. New York *Times,* April 17, 1910; Percy, *Lanterns,* 145; Baker interview with Brodie S. Crump, Oct. 22, 1976, H-LSU; Robert B. Fulton, in New York *Times,* March 7, 1910; Holmes, *White Chief,* 168–76.

30. This scandal is fully treated in the forthcoming *The Literary Percys* to be published by the University of Georgia, the chapters having been presented as the Lamar Lectures at Mercer University in October 1993.

31. See Kirwan, *Revolt of the Rednecks,* 193. This account owes much to the story that Kirwan offered.

32. See William C. Sallis, "A Study of the Life and Times of LeRoy Percy,"

M.S. thesis, Mississippi State College, 1957, pp. 74–76; House of Representatives, *Inquiry into the Charge of Bribery*, 395; Vicksburg *Herald,* Feb. 23, 1910; Baker interview with Brodie S. Crump, Oct. 22, 1976 (quotation), H-LSU; Lewis Baker, *The Percys of Mississippi: Politics and Literature in the New South* (Baton Rouge: Louisiana State University Press, 1983), 44–45.

33. Sallis, "LeRoy Percy," 83 quoting Memphis *Commercial Appeal,* Feb. 23, 1910; Bowling, "Holding the Line," 29; George Coleman Osborn, *James Kimble Vardaman: Southern Commoner* (Jackson: Hederman Brothers, 1981), 117.

34. Sallis, "LeRoy Percy," 83, quoting Memphis *Commercial Appeal,* Feb. 23, 1910.

35. Percy, *Lanterns,* 145–46.

36. Greenville *Daily Democrat,* Feb. 26, 1910, clipping, Reel 8, PP, MDAH; New York *Times,* Feb. 23, 1910; Sallis, "LeRoy Percy," 86–94 (Solomon quoted, 94).

37. Lawson H. Bowling III, "Trying to Hold the Line: Mississippi Conservatives and the Senatorial Campaign of 1910–1911," Columbia University honors paper, 1981, p. 31, copy at MDAH; Jackson *Daily News,* Feb. 24, 1910; New York *Times,* Feb. 24, 1910; see also newspaper clippings, reel 8, PP, MDAH.

38. "Transcript of Testimony taken before the Grand Jury of Hinds County, Mississippi, beginning on the 22d day of March, A.D. 1910, in the matter of the charges of bribery and corruption in connection with the election of United States Senator by the Legislature," copy, in Theodore G. Bilbo Papers, University of Southern Mississippi, Hattiesburg (hereafter cited as "Transcript," Bilbo MSS), 116–17.

39. Sallis, "LeRoy Percy," 97; LeRoy Percy to Ben Exum, March 1, 1910 (quotation), Percy to Will Crump, Feb. 8, 1911, and W. A. Speakes to A. Y. Scott, Aug. 2, 1911, PP, MDAH.

40. New York *Times,* April 17, 1910.

41. Editorial in *The Issue,* March 5, 1910 (quotation).

42. Testimony of H. Vaughn Watkins, "Transcript," Bilbo MSS, 31, testimony of S. H. Johnson, 46, 50.

43. See "Transcript," Bilbo MSS, 33–44, 48, 78–79; Jackson *Clarion-Ledger,* Feb. 1, 2, 1910. Kirwan misidentifies Robinson as Walter W. Robertson: Kirwan, *Revolt of the Rednecks,* 196; cf. Baker, *The Percys of Mississippi,* 43; Holmes, *The White Chief,* 216–17.

44. "Transcript," Bilbo MSS, 173.

45. *Ibid.,* 69; see also, Mississippi Senate, *Investigation of the State of Mississippi of the Charges of Bribery in the Election of a United States Senator, Session 1910* (Nashville: Brandon, 1910), 207–31, 460–71.

46. Judge J. H. Potter, "Transcript," Bilbo MSS, 124; see also S. H. Johnson, 133–34.

47. "Transcript," Bilbo MSS, 192–200 (quotations, 195).

48. *Ibid.,* 111, 114, 116–17, 166; Holmes, *The White Chief,* 204 n27; Spight quoted in Memphis *Commercial Appeal,* March 30, 1910.

49. Percy, *Lanterns on the Levee,* 147.

50. "Transcript," Bilbo MSS, 189; Lorraine Catchings Dulaney, Subject File, and LeRoy Percy to John Sharp Williams, March 30, 1910 (quotation); Williams to Percy, March 30, 1910, Gerrard Harris to Williams, Jan. 25, 1916 (quotation), John Sharp Williams MSS, MDAH; Holmes, *The White Chief,* 154.

51. See New York *Times,* April 8, 10, 1910.

52. Bilbo testimony, "Transcript," Bilbo MSS, 83–84 (quotation, 84); see also, Mississippi Senate, *Investigation . . .,* 37, 49 (quotation).

53. "Transcript," Bilbo MSS, 86–87, 149, 154–56; A. Wigfall Green, *The Man Bilbo* (Baton Rouge: Louisiana State University Press, 1963), 32.

54. "Transcript," Bilbo MSS, 71–75, 94–96, 99–100, 104–5, 107–9, 158 (M. O'Byrne, quoted).

55. Mississippi Senate, *Investigation . . .,* 36–77 (esp. 42), 207–23, 227–31, 301–20, 460–63, 470–71. William D. McCain, "Theodore Gilmore Bilbo and the Mississippi Delta," *Journal of Mississippi History* 31 (Feb. 1969): 5; Kirwan, *Revolt of the Rednecks,* 203.

56. Holmes, *The White Chief,* 225n93, citing House of Representatives, *Inquiry into the Charge of Bribery in the Recent Senatorial Contest* (Jackson, Miss., 1910), 320–21; New York *Times,* April 3, 1910.

57. Quoted in Kirwan, *Revolt of the Rednecks,* 206; Mississippi Senate, *Investigation . . .,* 9–10.

58. The jurors later defended themselves from charges of bias by listing their political preferences, with six for Vardaman, four for Percy, and two for Alexander. Delta loyalties, however, undoubtedly played a role. Of course, feelings ran so high that probably an impartial jury could not have been drawn up anywhere in the state. See *Congressional Record* 48 (1911): 228.

59. "Senator Bilbo Turns on the Light," broadside (n.p.n.d.), PP, MDAH; author's interview with Shelby Foote, Memphis, Tenn., Aug. 16, 1987; Kirwan, *Revolt of the Rednecks,* 208; Allan A. Michie and Frank Ryhlick, *Dixie Demagogues* (New York: Vanguard Press, 1939), 93.

60. Baker interview with Crump, H-LSU; Memphis *Commercial Appeal,* Oct. 17, 1910; see also sundry clippings, March 1910–July 1911, PP, MDAH.

61. See Memphis *Commercial Appeal,* July 3, 1911; Larry Thomas Balsamo, "Theodore G. Bilbo and Mississippi Politics, 1877–1932," Ph.D. dissertation, University of Missouri, 1967, pp. 67–68, 74; Percy, *Lanterns,* 148.

62. Jackson *Clarion-Ledger,* Nov. 1, 1910.

63. H. Vaughn Watkins to A. S. Coody, April ?, 1910, Box 9, folder 160, Archibald S. Coody Papers, MDAH.

64. Holmes, *The White Chief,* 238–39; William Alexander Percy to LeRoy Percy, May 27, 1911, PP, MDAH.

65. F. O. Ingram interview, quoted in Sallis, "LeRoy Percy," 133; Bowling, "Trying to Hold the Line," 44–45; Jackson *News,* April 22, 1911.

66. Memphis *Commercial Appeal,* Feb. 26, 1910 (quotation); Stone quoted in Bowling, "Trying to Hold the Line," 59; clipping, n.d. [Aug. 1910], April 2[?], 1911, PP, MDAH.

67. William Alexander Percy to J. S. McNeilly, Aug. 25, 1910, and William Alexander Percy diary, Dec. 4, 1910, PP, MDAH. On the Sunnyside episode, see Jeannie M. Whayne, ed., *Shadows over Sunnyside: An Arkansas Plantation in Transition, 1830–1945* (Fayetteville: University of Arkansas Press, 1993), especially Bertram Wyatt-Brown, "LeRoy Percy and Sunnyside: Planter Mentality and Italian Peonage in the Mississippi Delta," 77–94.

68. Percy, *Lanterns,* 150; Brodie Crump interview, in Sallis, "LeRoy Percy," 127.

69. Jackson *News,* July 2, 1910.

70. Quoted in Kirwan, *Revolt of the Rednecks,* 220; Jackson *Clarion-Ledger,* July 7, 1910; Percy, *Lanterns on the Levee,* 150.

71. Kirwan, *Revolt of the Rednecks,* 221–22; Baker, *Percys of Mississippi,* 53; R. A. Meek to LeRoy Percy, Aug. 2, 1911, PP, MDAH.

72. Osborn, *Vardaman,* 138.

73. Charles G. Hamilton, "Mississippi Politics in the Progressive Era, 1904–1920," Ph.D. dissertation, Vanderbilt University, 1958, p. 225.

74. LeRoy Percy to Fred Sullens, July 5 [misdated, Aug. 5], 1911, PP, MDAH; Sargent Prentiss Knut to LeRoy Percy, Aug. 9, 1911, Nov. 26, 1912, Sargent Prentiss Knut Papers, Huntington Library, San Marino, Calif.

75. George Creel, "What Are You Going to Do About It? The Carnival of Corruption in Mississippi," *Cosmopolitan* 51 (Nov. 1911): 725–35.

76. Dickson quoted in Sallis, "LeRoy Percy," 143; Baker, *Percys of Mississippi,* 39–57.

77. LeRoy Percy to W. W. Cain, Nov. 19, 1912, PP, MDAH; Percy, *Lanterns,* 152.

Chapter Ten WILL PERCY: YEARS OF TESTING

1. William Alexander Percy, "Year's End," Percy Family MSS (hereafter PP, MDAH).

2. Hodding Carter, *Where Main Street Meets the River* (New York: Rinehart, 1953), 74; Lucas Myers, phone conversation, Aug. 31, 1992; Hortense Powdermaker, *Stranger and Friend: The Way of an Anthropologist* (New York: W. W. Norton, 1966), 141.

3. Jonathan Daniels, *A Southerner Discovers the South* (New York: Macmillan, 1938), 175; David L. Cohn, "Eighteenth-Century Chevalier," *Virginia Quarterly Review* 31 (Autumn 1955): 562–63; Walker Percy, "Introduction," in William Alexander Percy, *Lanterns on the Levee: Recollections of a Planter's Son* (1941; Baton Rouge: Louisiana State University, 1973), viii (hereafter Percy, *Lanterns*).

4. This fact was pointed out to me by Jay Tolson, editor of the *Woodrow Wilson Quarterly* and author of *Pilgrim in the Ruins: A Life of Walker Percy* (New York: Simon & Schuster, 1992).

5. Percy, *Lanterns,* 26.

6. *Ibid.,* 273.

7. *Ibid.,* 26–27, 79; "On Sunday Morning," in William Alexander Percy, *In April Once* (New Haven: Yale University Press, 1920), 70.

8. Percy, *Lanterns,* 27–28.

9. *Ibid.,* 27–34 and 46–55; quotation, Richard H. King, *A Southern Renaissance: The Cultural Awakening of the American South, 1930–1955* (New York: Oxford University Press, 1980), 90.

10. See Anon., "Will Percy's Book" (review of *Lanterns on the Levee*), Jackson *News,* March 23, 1941, clipping, PP, MDAH.

11. Percy, *Lanterns,* 57.

12. *Ibid.,* 141.

13. *Ibid.*

14. *Ibid.,* 79 (quotation); Percy, "On Sunday Morning," 70; James Joyce, *The Portrait of the Artist as a Young Man* (1916; New York: Viking Press, 1974).

15. *Percy, Lanterns,* 32 (1st quotation), 36 (2nd quotation), 45 (3rd quotation).

16. Walker Percy, *The Last Gentleman* (New York: Simon & Schuster, 1968), 210; Bertram Wyatt-Brown, *Southern Honor: Ethics and Behavior in the Old South* (New York: Oxford University Press, 1982), 51–52.

17. W. A. Percy to J. Dana, Oct. 2, 1915, Janet Dana Longcope Papers, Hill Memorial Library, Louisiana State University Libraries, Baton Rouge (hereafter Longcope MSS, H-LSU).

18. W. A. Percy to Lelia Bourges Warren, Feb. 3, 1893, transcribed in Hester Sharbrough Ware, "A Study of the Life and Works of William Alexander Percy," M.S. thesis, Mississippi State College, 1950, p. 13.

19. Lewis Baker, *The Percys of Mississippi: Politics and Literature in the New South* (Baton Rouge: Louisiana State University Press, 1983), 61; Ware, "William Alexander Percy," 17.

20. Percy, *Lanterns,* 77 (1st quotation), 86–91, 138–39 (2nd quotation); W. A. Percy to Carrie Stern, April 21, 1907, PP, MDAH.

21. Percy, *Lanterns,* 82 (quotations), and 77–88; King, *A Southern Renaissance,* 87.

22. Percy, *Lanterns,* 83; Tolson, *Pilgrim in the Ruins,* 67.

23. LeRoy Percy to B. L. Wiggins, June 30, 1900, LeRoy Percy, C '79, Alumni file, Jessie Ball DuPont Library Archives, University of the South, Sewanee, Tennessee; Billups Phinizy Spalding, "William Alexander Percy: His Philosophy of Life as Reflected in His Poetry," Ph.D. dissertation, University of Georgia, 1957, 20.

24. Percy, *Lanterns,* 93, 97.

25. *Ibid.,* 94; Matthew Arnold, "Dover Beach," in A. Dwight Culler, ed., *Poetry and Criticism of Matthew Arnold* (Boston: Houghton Mifflin, 1961), 162.

26. Baker, *Percys of Mississippi,* 61 (quotation).

27. Quotations from Camille Percy to W. A. Percy, Aug. 14, 1902, and LeRoy Percy to W. A. Percy, Aug. 14, 1902, LeRoy Percy to W. A[rmstrong] Percy (son of William Armstrong Percy) Feb. 18, 1919, PP, MDAH.

28. Percy, *Lanterns,* 125–26; William Alexander Percy, *Collected Poems* (New York: Alfred A. Knopf, 1943), 380.

29. Percy, *Lanterns,* 345; see also Baker, *Percys of Mississippi,* 61–63, in which the author sensitively discusses the impact of young LeRoy's death.

30. Roark Bradford, Foreword to Percy, *Collected Poems,* 5.

31. Percy, *Lanterns,* 95.

32. *Ibid.;* Joyce, *A Portrait of the Artist,* 252–53.

33. Percy, *Lanterns,* 106, 107.

34. W. A. Percy to Camille Percy, Dec. 22, 1904, Jan. 17, 28, Feb. 4 & 7, April 10, Aug. 11, Sept. 29, 1905, PP, MDAH.

35. Percy, *Lanterns,* 111 and 112 (quotations).

36. LeRoy Percy to W. A. Percy, July 16, 1907, PP, MDAH.

37. W. A. Percy to LeRoy Percy, Nov. 11, 1907, (1st quotation), *ibid.,* Jan. 14, 1906, and to Camille Percy, Feb. 13, 1906 (2nd quotation), and ibid., March 11, 1907, PP, MDAH.

38. B. Phinizy Percy interview with John Jones of the State Department of Archives and History Conducted in New Orleans on Coliseum Street, April 17, 1980, p. 17, MDAH; Silas Williams et al. to W. A. Percy, April 7, 1909, W. A. Percy to LeRoy Percy, March 8, 1909, PP, MDAH.

39. Percy, *Lanterns,* 120–21.

40. *Ibid.,* 125–26.

41. Page quoted in Fred Hobson, *Tell About the South: The Rage to Explain* (Baton Rouge: Louisiana State University Press, 1983), 162; W. J. Cash, *The Mind of the South* (1941; New York: Random House, 1991), 96; conversation with the late Leon S. Koury, Sept. 28, 1992.

42. Percy, *Lanterns,* 127–28.

43. W. A. Percy to LeRoy Percy, n.d. (1905); W. A. Percy to C. C. Moody, Aug. 23, 1910, PP, MDAH; and see Baker, *Percys of Mississippi,* 66.

44. W. A. Percy to Dr. John M. McBryde, July 29, 1910, PP, MDAH.

45. Percy, *Lanterns,* 151.

46. *Congressional Record* 48 (1911): 226–30; William Alexander Percy, *Enzio's Kingdom and Other Poems* (New Haven: Yale University Press, 1924), 127; "To a Mocking-Bird," in William Alexander Percy, *Sappho in Levkas and Other Poems* (New Haven: Yale University Press, 1915), 20–21; dating of the poem is ascertained from Percy to Bynner, Sunday, [n.d. 1912?], W. A. Percy to Witter Bynner, 1914–23 MSS, bms AM 1891.28 (385), Houghton Library, Harvard University.

47. Walker Percy, *The Moviegoer,* quoted in Mary Joan Lueckenbach, "William Alexander Percy: The Progeny of the 'Brooding Knight' " (M.A. thesis, University of Mississippi, 1973), 58.

48. Carter, *Where Main Street,* 70; W. A. Percy to J. Dana, Oct. 2, 1915, Longcope MSS, H-LSU.

49. See Percy, *Lanterns,* 337–43.

50. William Alexander Percy, "The Fifth Autumn," in PP, MDAH. Will Percy's autumnal gloom was characteristic of artists and writers with depressive tendencies. See Kay Redfield Jamison, *Touched by Fire: Manic-Depressive Illness and the Artistic Temperament* (New York: Free Press, 1993), 109–16, 129–44, 313–16.

Chapter Eleven AT WAR

1. William Alexander Percy, *Collected Poems* (New York: Alfred A. Knopf, 1943), 191.

2. William Alexander Percy, *Lanterns on the Levee: Recollections of a Planter's Son* (1941; Baton Rouge: Louisiana State University, 1973), 157 (hereafter Percy, *Lanterns*).

3. William Alexander Percy, *Sappho in Levkas and Other Poems* (New Haven: Yale University Press, 1915), 82.

4. Percy, *Lanterns,* 158–59, J. Dana to Will Percy, Dec. 30, 1914, Feb. 28, 1915, Nov. 2, 1915 (quotation), Percy Family MSS, (hereafter PP, MDAH); W. A. Percy to J. Dana, Nov. 20, 1914, Janet Dana Longcope Papers, Hill Memorial Library, Louisiana State University Libraries, Baton Rouge (hereafter Longcope MSS, H-LSU).

5. Janet Dana to Will Percy, Feb. 2, 1915, PP, MDAH.

6. *Ibid.,* June 9, 1915.

7. Ibid., Feb. 2, 1915, Sept. 23, 1915 (quotation); W. A. Percy to J. D. Longcope, Glen Cove, L.I., Sept. 3, 1916, Longcope MSS, H-LSU.

8. W. A. Percy to J. Dana, Oct. 2, 1915, Longcope MSS, H-LSU.

9. W. A. Percy to J. Dana, Oct. 2, 1915 (all quotations) Longcope MSS, H-LSU; J. Dana to W. A. Percy, Oct. 23, Nov. 2, 1915, PP, MDAH.

10. Percy, *Lanterns*, 161.

11. *Ibid.*, 160–67 (quotation, 161); certificate, Commission for Relief in Belgium, March 24, 1917; *Delta Light House* (Greenville, Miss.), July 7, 1917, clipping; W. A. Percy to Carrie Stern, Jan. 6, March 2, April 2, Dec. 10, 1917, PP, MDAH.

12. William Groom Leftwich to George G. Leftwich, Oct. 21, 1917; J. Longcope to W. A. Percy, Dec. 22, 1917, PP, MDAH; W. A. Percy to J. Longcope, July 7, 1917, Longcope MSS, H-LSU.

13. Percy, *Lanterns*, 169–83; LeRoy Percy, Greenville, (hereafter LeRoy Percy) to LeRoy Pratt Percy (Birmingham), Sept. 21, 1917, PP, MDAH.

14. Percy, *Lanterns*, 174, 177.

15. Quoted in Lewis Baker, *The Percys of Mississippi: Politics and Literature in the New South* (Baton Rouge: Louisiana State University Press, 1983), 81.

16. LeRoy Percy to W. A. Percy, Dec. 22, 29, 1917, PP, MDAH.

17. Sandra M. Gilbert and Susan Gubar, *No Man's Land: The Place of the Woman Writer in the Twentieth Century, Volume Two, Sex Changes* (2 vols.; New Haven: Yale University Press, 1989): 2: 6–7; Percy, *Lanterns*, 184.

18. Percy, *Lanterns*, 198.

19. William P. Jackson to Camille Percy, Jan. 5, 1919, J. Longcope to Will Percy, Jan. 5 [?], Jackson to W. A. Percy, May 10, 1919, Des Armées Françaises de L'Est, Ordre No. 13.320 'D' (Extrait), to W. A. Percy, Feb. 8, 1919, Hymans, Belgian Minister of Foreign Affairs, to W. A. Percy, May 6, 1919, General Order No. 2, HQ 74th Infantry Brigade, Jan. 30, 1919, Adjutant General of the Army to W. A. Percy, April 30, 1919, PP, MDAH; Percy, *Lanterns*, 223.

20. W. A. Percy to Camille Percy, Aug. 7, 1918, in Percy, draft of "Lanterns on the Levee," chap. 17, PP, MDAH.

21. W. A. Percy to Camille Percy, Sept. 13, to LeRoy Percy, Oct. 4, 1918 (also reprinted in newspaper, n.d.), PP, MDAH.

22. Morris Turner, "Twenty Years Ago—the Argonne," Cincinnati *Enquirer,* Oct. 6, 20, Nov. 3, 1938, clippings, and W. A. Percy to LeRoy Percy, Oct. 25, 1918, PP, MDAH.

23. W. A. Percy to LeRoy Percy, Nov. 15, 1918, PP, MDAH.

24. Percy, *Lanterns*, 198–200 (quotation 199); W. A. Percy to Camille Percy, Feb. 2, 1919, to Camille Percy, June 16, 1918 (newspaper clipping, n.p., n.d.), PP, MDAH.

25. W. A. Percy to LeRoy Percy, Oct. 4, 1918, PP, MDAH; *United States Army in the World War, 1917–1919: Military Operations of the American Expeditionary Force* (17 vols., 1948; Washington: Center for Military History, 1990), 9: 129–35; John Keegan, *The Face of Battle: A Study of Agincourt, Waterloo & the Somme* (1976; New York: Vintage, 1977), 206.

26. W. A. Percy to Camille Percy, Nov. 15, 1918, PP, MDAH.

27. William P. Jackson to Camille Percy, Jan. 5, 1919; see various certificates of military honors in Jan.–May, 1919, PP, MDAH.

28. W. A. Percy to Camille Percy, Jan. 25, 1919, PP, MDAH.

29. See LeRoy Percy to Senator John Sharp Williams, June 5, 1915, to Joseph W. Bailey, Aug. 10, 1915, to Theodore Roosevelt, Jan. 20, 1916, to J. M. Dickin-

son, May 22, 1916, to Ben G. Humphreys, May 26, 1917, to A. B. Blanton, June 16, 1917, Henry Cabot Lodge to LeRoy Percy, Oct. 12, 1918, PP, MDAH. LeRoy Percy was offered a post in the War Industries Board, but he could not sell his plantations as was required. See LeRoy Percy to H. M. Garwood, June 24, 1918, Edwin D. Parker to LeRoy Percy, July 2, 1918, PP, MDAH.

30. "Letters from the Front," an early version of *Lanterns* that omits this letter and the introductory material to his wartime correspondence, PP, MDAH.

31. W. A. Percy, "Chapter Seventeen: Letters to the Front," unpublished version of *Lanterns on the Levee,* PP, MDAH; the letter, however, did appear in the local newspaper, see undated clipping, *ibid.;* Percy, *Lanterns,* 201–24; Baker, *Percys of Mississippi,* 166.

32. Baker, *Percys of Mississippi,* 166.

33. See on parataxis, Judith Summerfield and Geoffrey Summerfield, *Texts and Contexts: A Contribution to the Theory and Practice of Teaching Composition* (New York: Random House, 1986), 147.

34. See W. A. Percy to LeRoy Percy, Oct. 25, 1918, quoted in Baker, *Percys of Mississippi,* 86–87 (I cannot find the original in the microfilm version of the Percy Family MSS); Percy, *Lanterns,* 156.

35. Percy, *Lanterns,* 216.

36. Percy to William Stanley Braithwaite, May 23, 1919, William Stanley Braithwaite MSS, bms Am 1444 (874), Houghton Library, Harvard University.

37. J. Longcope to W. A. Percy, April 8, 1919, Jan. 15, 1923, PP, MDAH.

38. T. C. Catchings to LeRoy Percy, June 2, 1922, PP, MDAH; Percy, *Lanterns,* 243.

39. Huger Jervey (105 East 21st Street, New York City) to W. A. Percy, Jan. 12, 1920, PP, MDAH.

40. See W. A. Percy to Major McKellar, May 4, to Ben Finney, Oct. 12, 1922 and other letters in folder "University of the South," 1922, for much correspondence on Sewanee affairs, and James M. Glass to W. A. Percy, June 155, 1920, PP, MDAH; Percy, *Lanterns,* 226.

41. See, for example, W. A. Percy to Camille Percy, June 24, July 4, 1924, Gerstle Mack to Camille Percy, July 3, 1924; Lindley Hubell to W. A. Percy, Sept. 22, 1924, LeRoy Percy to Caroline Percy, May 8, 1924, PP, MDAH; conversation by phone with Shelby Foote, Jan. 10, 1994.

42. Frederick W. Galbraith, Jr. to LeRoy Percy, n.d., PP, MDAH.

43. Percy, *Lanterns,* 225.

44. See Paul Fussell, *The Great War and Modern Memory* (New York: Oxford University Press, 1975), 283–86; Timothy d'Arch Smith, *Love in Earnest: Some Notes on the Lives and Writings of English "Uranian" Poets from 1889 to 1939* (London: Routledge & Kegan Paul, 1970).

45. Owen, quoted in Fussell, *The Great War and Modern Memory,* 276 (quotation), 284; Walter E. Houghton, *The Victorian Frame of Mind* (New Haven: Yale University Press, 1957), 287.

46. W. A. Percy to Camille Percy, June 16 or 17, 1909, PP, MDAH; John G. Jones interview, 1983, in Lewis Lawson and Victor A. Kramer, eds., *Conversations with Walker Percy* (Jackson: University Press of Mississippi, 1985), 255; Jean-Claude Lemagny, ed., *Taormina, Début de Siècle: Photographies du Baron de Gloeden* (Paris: Chêne, 1975), 5–11; Smith, *Love in Earnest,* 62–63; Robert

Hughes, "Art, Morals and Politics," *New York Review of Books,* April 23, 1992, p. 21; W. A. Percy to Braithwaite, Oct. 11, 1922, Braithwaite MSS, Houghton Library, Harvard University; see Percy, *Sappho in Levkas,* 45 and 61.

47. Constantine Fitzgibbon, *Norman Douglas: A Pictorial Record* (New York: McBride, 1953), 27; quotation from Frank Swinnerton, *The Georgian Scene: 1910–1935* (New York: n.p., n.d.), 138, quoted in Ralph D. Lindeman, *Norman Douglas* (New York: Twayne, 1965), 60.

48. A highly censorious account of Douglas is Richard Aldington, *Pinarman: Personal Recollections of Norman Douglas, Pino Orioli, and Charles Prentice* (London: Heinemann, 1954), 40, 83–84, 116–17, 134–35. See Norman Douglas, *Looking Back: An Autobiographical Excursion* (London: Chatto & Windus, 1934), 197; Lindeman, *Norman Douglas,* 60–61; Lewis Leary, *Norman Douglas* (New York: Columbia University Press, 1968), 10; Shelby Foote in conversation by phone, Jan. 10, 1994. Will Percy showed Foote an amusing communication from Douglas about 1940.

49. W. A. Percy to Camille Percy, Aug. 28, 1922, PP, MDAH.

50. See Lindeman, *Norman Douglas,* 61–62; H. M. Tomlinson, *Norman Douglas* (London: Hutchinson, 1952), 31–32; Norman Douglas, *Siren Land,* excerpted in D. M. Low, ed., *Norman Douglas: A Selection from the Works* (London: Chatto & Windus, Secker and Warburg, 1955), 61–63.

51. Percy, *Lanterns,* 320.

52. *Ibid.,* 320–21.

53. Tomlinson, *Norman Douglas,* 30 and 47; Norman Douglas, *Siren Land* (1911; London: Penguin, 1948), 193.

54. Lindeman, *Norman Douglas,* 61–65; William Alexander Percy, "Foreword," in Norman Douglas, *Beasts and Birds of the Greek Anthology* (New York: Jonathan Cape and Harrison Smith, 1929), ix–xv (quotations xi, xii); Smith, *Love in Earnest;* Ian Greenlees, *Norman Douglas* (London: Longmans, Green, 1957), 27–31 (quotation, 31), and Richard MacGillivray, *Norman Douglas* (Florence: G. Orioli, 1933), 93 (quotation); also see Will Percy to Donald Davidson, May 18, 1928, Donald Davidson MSS, Jean and Alexander Heard Library, Vanderbilt University, Nashville.

55. See Christopher Hairtree, "The Marginalia of Graham Greene," *Times Literary Supplement,* Aug. 14, 1992, pp. 11–12. Douglas was the uncle of Graham Greene, the English Catholic novelist, who was also subject to severe depression.

56. Quoted in Richard H. King, *A Southern Renaissance: The Cultural Awakening of the American South, 1930–1955* (New York: Oxford University Press, 1980), 89.

57. William Alexander Percy [A. W. Percy] in Edward Mark Slocum, ed., *Men and Boys* (New York: n.p., 1924), 81. Slocum, a native Tennessean, graduated from the University of Tennessee in 1901. The history of this anthology of poetry celebrating pederasty is given in Donald H. Mader, introduction, in the reprint published by Coltsfoot Press of New York, 1978, pp. xv–li.

58. W. A. Percy to Witter Bynner, [n.d., 1912?], W. A. Percy to Witter Bynner 1914–23, bms AM 1891.28 (385), Houghton Library, Harvard University.

59. See "To Lucrezia," 66–67, and "Sappho in Levkas," 12–28, and "Pan Rejected," 36 in Percy, *Collected Poems;* Percy, *Lanterns,* 340–41.

60. Percy, *Sappho in Levkas,* 2, 5, 64; Billups Phinizy Spalding, "William Alexander Percy: His Philosophy of Life as Reflected in His Poetry," M.A. thesis, University of Georgia, 1957, p. 33.

61. Percy, *Sappho in Levkas,* 2, 4, 7, 9 (quotation), 18, 19 (quotation).

62. William Stanley Braithwaite, in Boston *Transcript,* Jan. 22, 1916, clipping, PP, MDAH; O. W. Firkins, "Tale-Tellers and Lyrists," *Nation* 102 (May 25, 1916): 566; see also William Stanley Braithwaite, ed., *Anthology of Magazine Verse for 1914 and Year Book of American Poetry* (Boston: Small, Maynard, 1914), 180, 190.

63. H. M., "A Misguided Poet," *Poetry* (July 1917), 213, 214, 215; William Faulkner, *Early Poetry and Prose,* ed. Carvel Collins (Boston: Atlantic Monthly Press, 1962), 72.

64. Will Percy to Donald Davidson, May 31, 1930, Davidson MSS, Vanderbilt.

65. Percy, *Collected Poems,* 191–94; see clippings in PP, MDAH.

Chapter Twelve TERRORS OF KLAN AND FLOOD

1. William Alexander Percy, *Lanterns on the Levee: Recollections of a Planter's Son* (1941; Baton Rouge: Louisiana State University Press, 1973), 231 (hereafter Percy, *Lanterns*).

2. Augustus Benners to W. A. Percy, Sept. 14, 1937, David L. Cohn MSS, University of Mississippi Library Archives, Oxford (hereafter Cohn MSS, UML).

3. Percy, *Lanterns,* 231.

4. *Ibid.,* 229; LeRoy Percy to Lawrence E. McKeekin, Sept. 17, 1917, Percy Family MSS (hereafter PP, MDAH); LeRoy Percy to Sargent Prentiss Knut, Feb. 10, 1912, Sargent Prentiss Knut MSS, Huntington Library, San Marino, Calif. See also Knut to Percy, Feb. 12, 1912, *ibid.*

5. Percy, *Lanterns,* 229.

6. See, for instance, LeRoy Percy to LeRoy Pratt Percy, June 12; to Will Percy, June 8, 1923, PP, MDAH.

7. Recent Klan scholarship and interpretation are summed up by Leonard J. Moore, "Historical Interpretations of the 1920's Klan: The Traditional View and the Populist Revision," *Journal of Social History* 24 (Winter 1990): 341–57; Stanley Coben, *Rebellion Against Victorianism: The Impetus for Cultural Change in 1920s America* (New York: Oxford University Press, 1991), chap. 7; and Michael Kazin, "The Grass-Roots Right: New Histories of U. S. Conservatism in the Twentieth Century," *American Historical Review* 97 (Feb. 1992): 136–55.

8. See David M. Chalmers, *Hooded Americanism: The First Century of the Ku Klux Klan, 1865–1965* (Garden City, N.Y.: Doubleday, 1965), 2–4; and Mark E. Carnes, *Secret Ritual and Manhood in Victorian America* (New Haven: Yale University Press, 1989), 13–14.

9. Percy, *Lanterns,* 231; cf. transcription from Leland (Miss.) *Enterprise,* March 18, 1922, PP, MDAH.

10. Cohn to Hodding Carter, April 4, 1955, Cohn MSS, UML.

11. *Address to Hon. LeRoy Percy, Delivered at Peoples Theatre, Greenville, Mississippi, April 23 1923: Under Auspices of the Protestant Committee of Fifty Opposed to the Ku Klux Klan* (Greenville: n.p., n.d.), in PP, MDAH (hereafter, *Peoples Theatre*).

12. Vicksburg *Herald,* March 4, 1922, clipping, PP, MDAH.

13. The best source for Percy's speech is *Address by Senator LeRoy Percy, Greenville, Miss., March 18, 1922,* a pamphlet reprint from the Houston *Chronicle,* March 19, 1922, in PP, MDAH; but see also William Charles Sallis, "A Study of the Life and Times of LeRoy Percy," M.S. thesis, Mississippi State College, 1957, pp. 152–55; Lewis Baker, *The Percys of Mississippi: Politics and Literature in the New South* (Baton Rouge: Louisiana State University Press, 1983), 99; Percy, *Lanterns,* 233. On Klan anti-Jewish sentiment, see *Colonel Mayfield's Weekly* (Houston, Texas), April 1, 1922, clipping, PP, MDAH.

14. H. M. Garwood to LeRoy Percy, April 5, 1922, PP, MDAH.

15. Ellery Sedgwick to LeRoy Percy, telegram, April 7; Roy to Will Percy, April 8; LeRoy Percy to Sedgwick, April 8, 1922, telegram. PP, MDAH.

16. See LeRoy Percy, *Ku Klux Klan Unnecessary: An Extemporaneous Address to the Citizens of Washington County* (n.p., n.d.), another version of the March 1, 1922, confrontation with Joseph L. Camp, PP, MDAH.

17. See William J. McGinley, Supreme Secretary, Knights of Columbus, New Haven, Conn., to LeRoy Percy, June 2 1922; Leo C. Moran, Mattoon, Ill., to Percy, Aug. 21, 1922, LeRoy Percy to Carl A. Lewis, Worcester, Mass., Nov. 20, 1922, Clark Musgrove to LeRoy Percy, Feb. 25, 1924, PP, MDAH; Baker, *Percys of Mississippi,* 133.

18. Chalmers, *Hooded Americanism,* 62–63; see also *Sgt. Dalton's Weekly* (Winnfield, La.), Jan. 13, 1923; *Brann's Iconoclast* (Chicago, Ill.), 33 (Feb. 1923): 11–12. Clippings, PP, MDAH.

19. Alfred H. Stone, *As to Senator Percy: A Personal Word* (n.p., n.d.), 16–17, PP, MDAH; Percy, *People's Theatre,* PP, MDAH; William Ivy Hair, *The Kingfish and His Realm: The Life and Times of Huey P. Long* (Baton Rouge: Louisiana State University Press, 1991), 12–13, 129–32; *Sgt. Dalton's Weekly* (Winnfield, La.), January 13, 1923, *Brann's Iconoclast* (Chicago, Ill.), 33 (Feb. 1923), 11–12, copies, PP, MDAH.

20. John M. Parker to LeRoy Percy, May 17, 1923, PP, MDAH; on Skipworth's defiance of federal authority, see Hair, *Kingfish,* 133.

21. Matthew J. Schott, "John M. Parker," in Joseph G. Dawson III, ed., *The Louisiana Governors: From Iberville to Edwards* (Baton Rouge: Louisiana State University Press, 1990), 214–19; LeRoy Percy to Parker, Feb. 19, 1923; Patrick H. O'Donnell to Percy, Feb. 28, 1923; R. B. Nance to LeRoy Percy, Oct. 24, and Percy to Nance, Oct. 26, 1923; Chicago *Tolerance,* n.d. clipping, and *Tri-State American* (Memphis Tenn.), May 9, 1923, clipping; A. Stone, *As to Senator Percy,* 4, PP, MDAH.

22. LeRoy Percy to Editor, Memphis *Commercial Appeal,* May 19, 1923, PP, MDAH.

23. LeRoy Percy to William A[rmstrong] Percy (nephew), June 8, 1923, PP, MDAH.

24. LeRoy Percy to M. S. Waterman, trustee, Boston Club, New Orleans, Jan. 29, Feb. 13, 1923; A. B. Blakemore, president, Lake Arthur Club, New Orleans, to LeRoy Percy, Feb. 1, 1923; LeRoy Percy to Mrs. William A. Percy, Feb. 3, 1923; to Robert Trabue, New Orleans, Feb. 6, 1923; PP, MDAH.

25. LeRoy Percy to Ray Toombs, May 13, 1923, in Greenville, Miss., *Delta Democrat,* May 14, 1923.

26. Percy, *Lanterns,* 236; see Leland (Miss.) *Enterprise,* March 18, 1922, clip-

ping, PP, MDAH; W. A. Percy to Charlotte Gailor, May 16, 1923, Charlotte Gailor MSS, Jessie Ball DuPont Library, University of the South, Sewanee, Tennessee (hereafter Gailor MSS, USL).

27. Percy, *Lanterns,* 238–39; W. A. Percy to Elliott Cage, May 21, 1923; on Noel's allegiance, see LeRoy Percy to Will Percy, June 16, 1924, PP, MDAH.

28. LeRoy Percy to Alice D. Jenkins, July 21, 1922, PP, MDAH; W. A. Percy to Mrs. Anne K. Stokes, Oct. 21, 1924, quoted in Billups Phinizy Spalding, "William Alexander Percy: His Philosophy of Life as Reflected in His Poetry," M.A. thesis, University of Georgia, 1957, p. 42.

29. LeRoy Percy to LeRoy Pratt Percy, June 16, to Will Percy, June 16, 1924, to Judge J. M. Dickinson, June 17, 1924, LeRoy Percy to Lady Percy McKinney, Oct. 29, 1924; telegram, S. J. Smith to LeRoy Percy, May 28, 1928, William T. Wynn to LeRoy Percy, June 18, 1928, LeRoy Percy to William Armstrong Percy II, June 30, 1928, to Pat Harrison, Aug. 24, 1928, PP, MDAH.

30. Quotations, LeRoy Percy to J. Speed Elliott, March 28; to W. Percy McKinney, April 2, 1923; LeRoy Percy to Caroline Percy, May 8, 1924; PP, MDAH; Spalding, "Percy," 42.

31. [Anon.] Goodman, Miss., to LeRoy Percy, May 10, 1923, PP, MDAH; W. A. Percy to James T. Williams [Editor, Boston *Transcript*], July 5, 1922, James Thomas Williams Papers, Perkins Library, Duke University.

32. Mark Twain, *Life on the Mississippi* (1883; New York, 1965), 145, quoted in Pete Daniel, *Deep'n as They Come: The 1927 Mississippi River Flood* (New York: Oxford University Press, 1977), 6.

33. LeRoy Percy, in U.S. Congress, *Hearings Before the Committee on Flood Control of the Destructive Flood Waters of the United States,* 70th Cong., 1st sess., (1927) Part 1: 44 (hereafter *Flood Control Hearings*).

34. Entry for Sept. 5, 1890, Harry Ball Diary, MDAH.

35. LeRoy Percy to Mrs. Archie Barkley, Wayne, Pa., Oct. 12, 1927, PP, MDAH.

36. LeRoy Percy to Mrs. C. J. McKinney, Feb. 12, 1927, PP, MDAH.

37. See Daniel, *Deep'n as They Come;* Robert L. Brandfon, *Cotton Kingdom of the New South: A History of the Yazoo Mississippi Delta from Reconstruction to the Twentieth Century* (Cambridge, Mass.: Harvard University Press, 1967), 23 (quotation); Donald J. Lisio, *Hoover, Blacks, and Lily Whites: A Study of Southern Strategies* (Chapel Hill: University of North Carolina Press, 1985), 4.

38. *Flood Control Hearings,* 1: 44, 45.

39. Percy, *Lanterns,* 247–48.

40. Greenville *Delta Democrat-Times,* April 30, 1927; Percy Bell, "Child of the Delta," chap. 7, p. 11, unpublished MSS, copy kindly supplied by Charles Bell.

41. Percy, *Lanterns,* 250–51; WAP to Charlotte Gailor, June 27, 1924, Gailor MSS, USL; WAP to Gerstle Mack, May 15, 1927, PP, MDAH.

42. Percy to Mack, May 15, 1927, PP, MDAH; Mrs. E. R. Metcalfe to "Bessie" Bell, May 3, 1927, and Percy Bell to "Dear Folks," April 30, May 12 (quotation), 15, 1927, in Bell, "Child of the Delta"; Harry Ball diary, July 13, 1927, MDAH; Percy, *Lanterns,* 255.

43. *Ibid.,* 155.

44. Greenville *Delta Democrat-Times,* May 4, 1927; David L. Cohn, *Where I Was Born and Raised* (Boston: Houghton Mifflin, 1948), 49.

45. Percy Bell to "Dear Folks," April 30, 1927, in Bell, "Child of the Delta"; Percy, *Lanterns,* 257–58.

46. Richard King, *A Southern Renaissance: The Cultural Awakening of the American South, 1930–1955* (New York: Oxford University Press, 1980), 94; Pete Daniel, *The Shadow of Slavery: Peonage in the South, 1901–1969* (Urbana: University of Illinois Press, 1972), 157.

47. Quoted by Neil R. McMillen, *Dark Journey: Black Mississippians in the Age of Jim Crow* (Urbana: University of Illinois Press, 1989), 148.

48. Daniel, *Shadow of Slavery,* 149.

49. Lisio, *Hoover, Blacks, and Lily-Whites,* 3–20; Daniel, *Shadow of Slavery,* 157; Percy, *Lanterns,* 261–63; W. A. Percy to John Hope, Member, Hoover Committee, June 7, 1927, Box 135, folder 1051, R. R. Moten Papers, Hollis Burke Frissell Library, Tuskegee Institute, Tuskegee, Alabama.

50. Greenville *Delta Democrat-Times,* May 23, 1927.

51. Percy Bell to "Dear Folks," April 30, 1927, in Bell, "Child of the Delta."

52. A. L. Schafer and Richard W. Thrush, "Reconstruction Office Report for Mississippi, Tennessee and Kentucky," Mississippi River Valley Flood 3/30/27, Ky-Miss. Reconstruction Office, Box 737, Records of the American National Red Cross, 1917–1934, DR 224, National Archives, Washington.

53. Clipping, n.p., n.d., and W. A. Percy to Charlotte Gailor, Oct. 13, 1927, Gailor MSS, USL.

Chapter Thirteen   ACQUAINTANCE WITH GRIEF

1. Henry James, "The Beast in the Jungle," in *The Short Stories of Henry James,* ed. Clifton Fadiman (New York: Modern Library, 1945), 561–62.

2. U.S. Census: *Population, Eleventh Census,* 402.

3. Entry for April 24, 1888, Harry Ball diary, Mississippi Department of Archives and History (hereafter MDAH).

4. Charles T. Bunting interview, in Lewis A. Lawson and Victor A. Kramer, eds., *Conversations with Walker Percy* (Jackson: University Press of Mississippi, 1985), 54.

5. Birmingham *News,* Feb. 9, 1917: the paper reported that he went to Johns Hopkins Hospital but there is no record. Therefore it is likely that he entered Shepherd-Pratt.

6. Sallie B. Comer Lathrop, *The Comer Family Grows Up* (3 vols; Birmingham: Birmingham Printing Co., n.d.), 3: 38–39.

7. See Walker Percy, Subject File, University Archives, Jessie Ball DuPont Library, University of the South, Sewanee, Tennessee; see also Jay Tolson, *Pilgrim in the Ruins: A Life of Walker Percy* (New York: Simon & Schuster, 1992), 27.

8. Birmingham *News,* Feb. 9, 1917 On Walker Percy's brief political career, see Carl V. Harris, *Political Plower in Birmingham, 1871–1921* (Knoxville: University of Tennessee Press, 1977), 83–84; clipping (n.p.), March 30, 1910, in "Walker Percy," Subject File, ADAH; R. Ray Marshall, *Labor in the South* (Cambridge: Harvard University Press, 1967), 74, 213–14.

9. Quotation, Birmingham *News,* Feb. 9, 1917; Birmingham *Age-Herald,* Feb. 9, 1917, called it an accident.

10. LeRoy Percy to Mrs. Harriet Turner, Washington, D.C. Feb. 15, 1917, Percy Family MSS (hereafter PP, MDAH).

11. LeRoy Percy to Commanding Officer of Naval Air Station, Miami, Fla., May 24, 1918, PP, MDAH.

12. LeRoy Percy to Mrs. Caroline Percy, March 23 (quotation), Oct. 12, 1922, LeRoy Percy to Percy McKinney of Shop Engineering and Sales Co., Knoxville, telegram and also letter, Feb. 6, 1922, LeRoy Percy to Mrs. C. J. McKinney, Oct. 30, 1924, PP, MDAH.

13. LeRoy Percy to LeRoy Pratt Percy, Dec. 14, 1917, W. A. Percy to Camille Percy, Sept. 13, 1918, PP, MDAH.

14. LeRoy Pratt Percy to LeRoy Percy, March 29, 1922; LeRoy Percy to Mrs. W. A. Percy, Feb. 3, 1923. PP, MDAH.

15. Walker Percy to William A. Percy, Oct. 19, 1911, PP, MDAH.

16. LeRoy Pratt Percy to LeRoy Percy, March 11, 1922, PP, MDAH.

17. A. Leo Oberdorfer, of Beddow and Oberdorfer, Birmingham, to LeRoy Percy, March 29, 1922, PP, MDAH.

18. LeRoy Pratt Percy to LeRoy Percy, Feb. 17, May 18, 1923, PP, MDAH. The information about LeRoy Pratt Percy's records at the Phipps Clinic comes from Dr. Paul McHugh, head of the Department of Psychiatry, The Johns Hopkins University Hospital, Baltimore, through an interview on July 17, 1990. Dr. McHugh assured me that the thick folder, which I did not examine, had somatic information and little else.

19. Interview with Lee C. Bradley of Bradley, Arant, Rose and White, 1400 Park Place Tower, Birmingham, Aug. 13, 1987; interview with Walker Percy, June 17, 1987, Covington, La.; Tolson, *Pilgrim in the Ruins,* 34–35.

20. LeRoy Percy to Mrs. Archie Barkley, Wayne, Pa., Oct. 12, 1927, PP, MDAH.

21. Conversation with Dr. Paul McHugh, Director, Phipps Clinic, Johns Hopkins Hospital, June 10, 1990.

22. LeRoy Percy to Mrs. C. J. McKinney, Jan. 25, 1926, PP, MDAH; Tolson, *Pilgrim in the Ruins,* 44.

23. LeRoy Percy to Caroline Percy, Feb. 28, 1928, to Martha Susan Phinizy Percy, March 20, 1928; LeRoy Percy to LeRoy Pratt Percy, Oct. 13, W. A. Percy to Caroline Percy, Nov. 26, 1928; LeRoy Percy to W. A. Percy, Feb. 24, telegram, to LeRoy Pratt Percy, April 27, to Lady Percy (niece), May 3, 1929. PP, MDAH.

24. See Frederick Goodwin, M.D., quoted in New York *Times,* Jan. 5, 1993, B6.

25. Walker Percy, "Bourbon," *Esquire* (Dec. 1975), 149; Martha Susan Percy to LeRoy Percy, "Thursday night," n.d., PP, MDAH. See LeRoy Percy to LeRoy Pratt Percy, June 20, 1929, PP, MDAH.

26. Interview with Walker Percy, June 13, 1990; Cheryl B. Torsney, *Constance Fenimore Woolson: The Grief of Artistry* (Athens: University of Georgia Press, 1989), 1, 11, 20, 14–17; Leon Edel, *Henry James* (1960; New York: Penguin, 1977), 1: 603–11, 793; idem, *Henry James: The Master: 1901–1916* (New York, Avon, 1972), 135; Henry James, "The Beast in the Jungle (1903)," in *The Novels and Tales of Henry James* (New York: Scribner,, 1909).

27. Tolson, *Pilgrim in the Ruins,* 45.

28. Birmingham *News,* July 10, 1929; Tolson, *Pilgrim in the Ruins,* 45.

29. LeRoy Percy to Mattie Sue Percy, Aug. 13, 1929, PP, MDAH.

30. Interview with Mrs. A. K. Stokes, in William Charles Sallis, "A Study of the Life and Times of LeRoy Percy," M. S. thesis, Mississippi State College, 1957, p. 166; LeRoy Percy to Mrs. Anne K. Stokes, Aug. 12, telegram, to Mrs. LeRoy Pratt Percy, Aug. 13, to W. A. Percy, Aug. 17, telegram, Secretary to William Armstrong Percy (nephew), Oct. 19, 1929, quotation, John Sharp Williams to LeRoy Percy, Nov. 21, 1929—all PP, MDAH; Baker, *Percys of Mississippi,* 148–49.

31. Harris Dickson quoted in Jonathan Daniels, *A Southerner Discovers the South* (New York: Macmillan, 1938), 176.

32. *Ibid.;* William Alexander Percy, *Collected Poems* (New York: Alfred A. Knopf, 1943), 339.

33. J. D. Longcope to W. A. Percy, Dec. 19, 29, and n.d. [c. Nov.–Dec. 1929], PP, MDAH; W. A. Percy to Mrs. Archie Barkle, March 21, 1930, in Spalding, "William Alexander Percy," 109.

34. W. A. Percy to Mrs. Louise W. Montgomery, Sept. 6, 1938, to Mrs. George Roberts, Dec. 18, 1939, cited in Hudean Windham, "Percy's Reliques, New Style," M.A. thesis, George Peabody College for Teachers, 1939, cited in Spalding, "William Alexander Percy," 47 and 47 n98.

35. W. A. Percy, Jr., to LeRoy Percy, Oct. 4, 1924, PP, MDAH.

Chapter Fourteen   STOIC HONOR

1. Marcus Aurelius, *Meditations,* Book IV: 31, trans. George Long, in Robert Maynard Hutchins, ed., *Great Books of the Western World* (54 vols.; Chicago: Encyclopædia Britannica, 1952), 12: 266.

2. Carol Malone, "William Alexander Percy: Knight to His People, Ishmael to Himself, and Poet to the World," M.A. thesis, University of Mississippi, 1964, p. 19.

3. Lewis Baker, *The Percys of Mississippi: Politics and Literature in the New South* (Baton Rouge: Louisiana State University Press, 1983), 156.

4. Conversation with Leon S. Koury, Sept. 29, 1992; interview with Charles Bell, July 29, 1987, Montpelier, Vt.; see also Susan Snell, *Phil Stone of Oxford: A Vicarious Life* (Athens: University of Georgia Press, 1991), 7.

5. Baker, *Percys of Mississippi,* 25, 151; quotations, William Alexander Percy, *Lanterns on the Levee: Recollections of a Planter's Son* (1941; Baton Rouge: Louisiana State University Press, 1973), 270 (hereafter Percy, *Lanterns*).

6. Lewis Baker interview with Brodie S. Crump, Oct. 22, 1976, in Greenville, Special Collections, Hill Memorial Library, Louisiana State University Libraries, Baton Rouge (hereafter H-LSU).

7. Percy, *Lanterns,* 128.

8. Hodding Carter, "The Most Unforgettable Character I've Ever Met," *Reader's Digest* 61 (Aug. 1952): 22.

9. Memphis *Commercial Appeal,* May 21, 1939; interview with Mrs. Charles P. Williams, 1963, in Malone, "Percy," 70; Hodding Carter, *Where Main Street Meets the River* (New York: Harper, 1953), 76; "B. Phinizy Percy, interview by John Jones, transcript, April 17, 1980," MDAH.

10. William Alexander Percy, *Collected Poems* (New York: Alfred A. Knopf, 1943), 311–12; Percy, *Lanterns,* 281. Cf. Jay Tolson, *Pilgrim in the Ruins: A Life*

of Walker Percy (New York: Simon & Schuster, 1992), 96–97, 101–2; Raymond McClinton, "A Social-Economic Analysis of a Mississippi Delta Plantation," M.A. thesis, University of North Carolina, 1938, p. 20.

11. Lewellyn Lee Jordan, "A Biographical Sketch of David L. Cohn," M.A. thesis, University of Mississippi, 1963, p. 39.

12. Carter, *Where Main Street Meets the River,* 74 (quotation); Hodding Carter, *Southern Legacy* (Baton Rouge: Louisiana State University Press, 1950), 5–6; Jordan, "Cohn," 39.

13. Jordan, "Cohn," 40.

14. Entry for Aug. 22, 1931, Harry Ball Diary, MDAH.

15. David L. Cohn, "Hometown Revisited," *Tomorrow* 8 (Nov. 1947): 6.

16. Malone, "Percy," 70.

17. James C. Cobb, *The Most Southern Place on Earth: The Mississippi Delta and the Roots of Regional Identity* (New York: Oxford University Press, 1992), 132.

18. Entries for June 5, 1930, Jan. 25, 1933, Harry Ball Diary, MDAH.

19. Quotation, David L. Cohn, "The Eighteenth-Century Chevalier," *Virginia Quarterly Review* 31 (Autumn 1955): 574; Mrs. Louise E. Crump, interviewed, July 23, 1963, in Malone, "Percy," 44; W. A. Percy to Charlotte Gailor, April 22, 1941, Charlotte Gailor MSS, University Archives, Jessie Ball DuPont Library, Sewanee, Tennessee (hereafter Gailor MSS, USL).

20. Carter, *Where Main Street Meets the River,* 75–76; author's interview with Cynthia Ware, June 30, 1989, New Orleans; interview with Maury McGee of Leland and Sewanee, June 10, 1988, Sewanee.

21. Percy, *Lanterns,* 303–4; David L. Cohn, "Autobiography," 270, David L. Cohn MSS, University of Mississippi Library Archives, Oxford (hereafter Cohn MSS, UML); Baker, *Percys of Mississippi,* 156–57.

22. Interview with Ben Wasson in July 23, 1963, Malone, "William Alexander Percy," 47; author's interview with Cynthia Ware, June 30, 1989, New Orleans.

23. Entry for Feb. 19, 1931, Harry Ball Diary, MDAH.

24. See Cobb, *The Most Southern Place on Earth,* 189–92.

25. *Ibid.,* 155, 193.

26. Raymond McClinton, "A Social-Economic Analysis of a Mississippi Delta Plantation," M.A. thesis, University of North Carolina, 1938, pp. 9, 23–24, 37.

27. See Clinton, "A Social-Economic Analysis," 13.

28. Carter, *Where Main Street Meets the River,* 67–68; Jack Temple Kirby, *Rural Worlds Lost: The American South 1920–1960* (Baton Rouge: Louisiana State University Press, 1987), 136–37.

29. Carter, *Where Main Street Meets the River,* 67–68.

30. *Ibid.,* 68; author's interview with LeRoy Percy, Aug. 17, 1987, Greenville; Baker, *Percys of Mississippi,* 156.

31. "B. Phinizy Percy interview."

32. Carter, *Where Main Street Meets the River,* 77; Jonathan Daniels, *A Southerner Discovers the South* (New York: Macmillan, 1938), 174; Jones interview, 1983, in Lawson and Kramer, eds., *Conversations with Walker Percy,* 256.

33. Cohn, "Autobiography," 259–60, in Cohn MSS, UML.

34. *Ibid.*

35. *Ibid.,* 263, Cohn MSS, UML.

36. Percy, *Lanterns,* 27, 94, 49, 298; Hortense Powdermaker, *Stranger and Friend* (New York: W. W. Norton, 1966), 191–93.

37. Percy, *Lanterns*, 299.

38. *Ibid.*, 300–301.

39. Robert Staples, *Black Masculinity: The Black Male's Role in American Society* (San Francisco: The Black Scholar Press, 1982), 79–80.

40. Percy, *Lanterns on the Levee*, 301; John Dollard, *Caste and Class in a Southern Town* (Garden City, N.Y.: Doubleday, 1949).

41. See Bertram Wyatt-Brown, "The Mask of Obedience: Male Slave Psychology in the Old South," *American Historical Review* 93 (Dec. 1988): 1228–55.

42. Richard H. King, *A Southern Renaissance: The Cultural Awakening of the American South, 1930–1955* (New York: Oxford University Press, 1980), 88.

43. Clinton, "A Social-Economic Analysis," 16–17.

44. Percy, *Lanterns*, 289–90; conversation with the late Leon Koury, Sept. 29, 1992, interview with Mrs. Commodore, Boston; Baker, *Percys of Mississippi*, 156–57; Walker Percy, "Introduction," to *Lanterns*, xiii.

45. David L. Cohn, *Where I Was Born and Raised* (Cambridge, Mass.: Riverside Press, 1948), 271–72.

46. Daniels, *A Southerner Discovers the South*, 173; author's interview with LeRoy Percy, Aug. 17, 1987.

47. McClinton, "A Social-Economic Analysis."

48. Percy, *Lanterns*, 291.

49. *Ibid.*, 287; Tolson, *Pilgrim in the Ruins*, 88 (quotation).

50. Percy, *Lanterns*, 287.

51. *Ibid.*, 296.

52. *Ibid.*, 297.

Chapter Fifteen NEW DUTIES AND OLD MEMORIES

1. Quoted in *Delta Review* (Spring 1966), 42.

2. John Griffin Jones interview, 1983, in Lewis A. Lawson and Victor Kramer, eds., *Conversations with Walker Percy* (Jackson: University Press of Mississippi, 1985), 254.

3. Interview with Mrs. Charles (Donie) Allison, Birmingham, Aug. 7, 1988; Jay Tolson, *Pilgrim in the Ruins: A Life of Walker Percy* (New York: Simon & Schuster, 1992), 47.

4. Tolson, *Pilgrim in the Ruins*, 47–48; Walker Percy, "Introduction," in William Alexander Percy, *Lanterns on the Levee: Recollections of a Planter's Son* (1941; Baton Rouge: Louisiana State University, 1973), viii, ix (hereafter Percy, *Lanterns*).

5. David L. Cohn, "The Eighteenth-Century Chevalier," *Virginia Quarterly Review* 31 (Autumn 1955): 570; Walker Percy, "Uncle Will's House," in Walker Percy, *Signposts in a Strange Land*, ed. Patrick Samway (New York: Farrar, Straus & Giroux, 1991), 63–64.

6. "B. Phinizy Percy Interview with John Jones," of the State Department of Archives and History, New Orleans, April 17, 1980, typescript, pp. 2–3, MDAH.

7. Cohn, "The Eighteenth-Century Chevalier," 571.

8. Walker Percy, "Uncle Will's House," 63–64.

9. John Griffin Jones interview, in Lawson and Kramer, eds., *Conversations with Walker Percy*, 255.

10. Entries for April 7, 1931, April 3, 1932, Harry Ball Diary, MDAH; Adah

Williams quoted in Carol Malone, "William Alexander Percy: Knight to His People, Ishmael to Himself, and Poet to the World," M.A. thesis, University of Mississippi, 1964, p. 33; and Percy, *Lanterns,* 333.

11. Walker Percy, "Introduction," *Lanterns,* viii–ix.

12. Tolson, *Pilgrim in the Ruins,* 91–93.

13. "Interview with Walker Percy: Interviewed by John Jones, Done at Covington, Louisiana," typescript, p. 9, MDAH; see also interview by Jones, in Lawson and Kramer, eds., *Conversations with Walker Percy,* 254, 255.

14. Tolson, *Pilgrim in the Ruins,* 98.

15. This account is largely drawn from Tolson, *ibid.*

16. Entry for April 3, 1932, Harry Ball Diary, MDAH; Greenville *Delta Democrat-Times,* April 2, 1932.

17. "B. Phinizy Percy Interview with John Jones," typescript, pp. 1, 10, MDAH.

18. Interview with Shelby Foote, June 10, 1987, Memphis; interview with Phinizy Percy, July 17, 1989.

19. Interview by Jones, in Lawson and Kramer, eds., *Conversations with Walker Percy,* 258.

20. W. Kenneth Holditch, unpublished interview, May 13, 1980, 9, MDAH.

21. Author's interview with Charles Bell, July 29, 1987; Percy, "Uncle Will's House," 64.

22. Walker Percy, "Uncle Will's House," 64.

23. Interview by Jones, in Lawson and Kramer, eds., *Conversations with Walker Percy,* 256; Phil Stone to David L. Cohn, Dec. 24, 1940, D. Cohn MSS, UML.

24. Lewellyn Lee Jordan, "A Biographical Sketch of David L. Cohn," M. A. thesis, University of Mississippi, 1963, pp. 1–17, 38, 48; see Malcolm Bull, "Caught in the Crossfire," *Times Literary Supplement,* Sept. 25, 1992, pp. 20–21.

25. Hortense Powdermaker, *Stranger and Friend* (New York: W. W. Norton, 1966), 138–42.

26. Walker Percy, "Uncle Will's House," 65.

27. Interview by Jones, in Lawson and Kramer, eds., *Conversations with Walker Percy,* 261; "B. Phinizy Percy interview with Jones," p. 4, MDAH.

28. Jonathan Daniels, *A Southerner Discovers the South* (New York: Macmillan, 1938), 177; Jones interview, in Lawson and Kramer, eds., *Conversations with Walker Percy,* 256.

29. Jones interview, in Lawson and Kramer, eds., *Conversations with Walker Percy,* 256; Walker Percy, "Uncle Will's House," 50; interview with Walker Percy, June 15, 1987.

30. William Faulkner, *Early Prose and Poetry,* ed. Carvel Collins (Boston: Atlantic-Little, Brown, 1962), 71; Joseph Blotner, *Faulkner: A Biography* (2 vols.; New York: Random House, 1974), 1: 288–89, 323; Ashley Brown interview, 1967, in Lawson and Kramer, eds., *Conversations with Walker Percy,* 11; Percy, "Uncle Will's House," 50; Ben Wasson, *Count No 'Count: Flashbacks to Faulkner* (Jackson: University Press of Mississippi, 1983), 63.

31. See W. A. Percy to Charlotte Gailor, May 27, 1936, University Archives, Jessie Ball DuPont Library, University of the South, Sewanee, Tennessee (hereafter Gailor MSS, USL); interviews with LeRoy Pratt Percy and Ben Wasson, in Malone, "Percy," 128; Cohn, "Eighteenth-Century Chevalier," 575.

32. W. A. Percy to Charlotte Gailor, "Saturday," n.d., from Bacon's-by-the-Sea, Fort Walton, Fla., and Aug. 28, 1939, Gailor MSS, USL.

33. W. A. Percy to Harold A. Straus, Aug. 28, 1939, Gailor MSS, USL.

34. Alfred A. Knopf to W. A. Percy, Aug. 16, 1939, Gailor MSS, USL; conversation with Hunter Wyatt-Brown of Beaufort, S.C., Sept. 20, 1993 (at Jervey's request he also read Percy's manuscript at Jervey's Fifth Avenue apartment in 1938).

35. W. A. Percy to Huger Jervey, Sept. 19, 1940, Percy to Gailor, Sept. 19, 1940, Gailor MSS, USL.

36. W. A. Percy to Huger Jervey, Sept. 19, 1940, and Percy to Gailor, Sept. 19, 1940, Jan. 10, 1941 (quotation), USL.

37. W. A. Percy to Gailor, March 4, 1941, Gailor MSS, USL.

38. See Gilbert E. Govan, "Ellen Glasgow and the Pulitzer Prize," Chattanooga *Times,* May 10, 1942, in Gailor MSS, USL.

39. Lawrence Olson, in New York *Herald Tribune,* March 9, 1941; Herschel Brickell in New York *Times Book Review,* March 23, 1941, 5; Charles Poore, "Books of the Times," New York *Times,* May 30, 1941; all clippings in Gailor MSS, USL.

40. Quoted in Helen White and Redding S. Sugg, Jr., ed., *From the Mountain* (Memphis: Memphis State University Press, 1972), 16.

41. David McDowell, in David Madden, ed., *Remembering James Agee* (Baton Rouge: Louisiana State University Press, 1974), 96; Agee's review appeared in *Time,* March 24, 1941; Cash's review in the Charlotte *News,* May 10, 1941, is reprinted in Joseph L. Morrison, *W. J. Cash: Southern Prophet, A Biography and Reader* (New York: Alfred A. Knopf, 1967), 290–94. See Bertram Wyatt-Brown, "Creativity and Suffering in a Southern Writer: W. J. Cash," in Paul Escott, ed., *W. J. Cash and the Minds of the South* (Baton Rouge: Louisiana State University Press, 1992), 38–66, and idem, "Types of Depression in Three Southern Writers: Will Percy, W. J. Cash, and James Agee, the Class of '41," at the Ninth International Conference on Psychoanalysis and Literature, Lisbon, Portugal, July 5, 1992; Laurence Bergreen, *James Agee: A Life* (1984; New York: Penguin, 1985).

42. Fred Hobson, *Tell About the South: The Southern Rage to Explain* (Baton Rouge: Louisiana State University Press, 1983), 245.

43. Richard H. King, *A Southern Renaissance: The Cultural Awakening of the American South, 1930–1955* (New York: Oxford University Press, 1980), 87.

44. Percy, *Lanterns,* 74–75. Cathings helped to obstruct the processes of justice in the Sunnyside case against LeRoy Percy. See Randolph H. Boehm, "Mary Grace Quackenbos and the Federal Campaign Against Peonage," in Jeannie H. Whayne, ed., *Shadows over Sunnyside: An Arkansas Plantation in Transition, 1830–1945* (Fayetteville: University of Arkansas Press, 1993), 63; and Bertram Wyatt-Brown, "LeRoy Percy and Sunnyside: Planter Mentality and Italian Peonage in the Mississippi Delta," *ibid.,* 91.

45. Percy, *Lanterns,* 117, 118; Henry Adams as quoted in William R. Taylor, *Cavalier and Yankee: The Old South and American National Character* (Garden City, N.Y.: Doubleday, 1963), 218.

46. Percy, *Lanterns,* 115, 116.

47. Georges Gusdorf, "Conditions and Limits of Autobiography," in James Olney, ed. and trans., *Autobiography: Essays Theoretical and Critical* (Princeton: Princeton University Press, 1980), 39.

48. C. Vann Woodward, *Origins of the New South, 1877–1913* (Baton Rouge: Louisiana State University Press, 1951), 67.

49. Walker Percy, "Mississippi: The Fallen Paradise," in Percy, *Signposts,* ed. Samway, 48.

50. Walker Percy, "The Delta Factor," in *The Message in the Bottle: How Queer Man Is, How Queer Language Is, and What One Has to Do with the Other* (New York: Farrar, Straus & Giroux, 1975), 4; Percy, *Lanterns,* 223.

51. Interview with Walker Percy, June 15, 1987; Will Percy to Charlotte Gailor, Thurs., n.d. [from Johns Hopkins Hospital], Gailor MSS, USL; Charlotte Elliott, biographical folder, Elliott MSS, USL.

52. "B. Phinizy Percy interview," 14; Kathleen Moore Peacock, "William Alexander Percy: A Study in Southern Conservatism," M.A. thesis, Birmingham-Southern College, 1958, 75.

Chapter Sixteen   WALKER AND THE LEGACY OF "UNCLE WILL"

1. Walker Percy, *The Moviegoer* (1960; New York: Farrar, Straus & Giroux, 1973), 144.

2. Walker Percy, "Uncle Will," in Walker Percy, *Signposts in a Strange Land,* ed. Patrick Samway, (New York: Farrar, Straus & Giroux, 1991), 55, 62.

3. Shelby Foote, *The Civil War: A Narrative* (3 vols.; New York: Random House, 1958–74).

4. John Griffin Jones interview, 1979, in William C. Carter, ed., *Conversations with Shelby Foote* (Jackson: University Press of Mississippi, 1989), 157.

5. Interview with Shelby Foote, Aug. 16, 1989, Memphis, Tenn.; see Robert L. Phillips, Jr., *Shelby Foote: Novelist and Historian* (Jackson: University Press of Mississippi, 1992), 6–11 (quotation, 10).

6. Interview with Charles Bell, July 25, 1987; interview with Walker Percy, June 15, 1988; Jay Tolson, *Pilgrim in the Ruins: A Life of Walker Percy* (New York: Simon & Schuster, 1992), 38.

7. Charles G. Bell, *The Half Gods* (Boston: Houghton Mifflin, 1968); interview with Charles Bell, Montpelier, Vt., July 29, 1987.

8. Charles Bell interview, Montpelier, July 29, 1987; Percy Bell, Alumni files, Jessie Ball DuPont Library, University of the South, Sewanee, Tennessee (hereafter USL); conversation with Hunter Wyatt-Brown, Beaufort, S.C., May 14, 1992, and Ned Kirby-Smith, Sewanee, Nov. 13, 1992.

9. See Tolson, *Pilgrim in the Ruins,* 92–94, 100–01, 104–5.

10. Linda Whitney Hobson, "A Sign of the Apocalypse," *Horizon* 23 (Aug. 1980): 59.

11. J. Donald Crowley, introduction, in J. Donald Crowley and Sue Mitchell Crowley, eds., *Critical Essays on Walker Percy* (Boston: G. K. Hall, 1989), 3.

12. Jones, in Carter, ed., *Conversations with Shelby Foote,* 161.

13. Marcus Smith interview, in Lewis Lawson and Victor A. Kramer, eds., *Conversations with Walker Percy* (Jackson: University Press of Mississippi, 1985), 135–36.

14. Tolson, *Pilgrim in the Ruins,* 317.

15. Billups Phinizy Spalding, "William Alexander Percy: His Philosophy of Life

as Reflected in His Poetry," M.A. thesis, University of Georgia, 1957, 108; Will Percy quoted in William Delaney interview, 1977, in Lawson and Kramer, eds., *Conversations with Walker Percy,* 152.

16. Tolson, *Pilgrim in the Ruins,* 134; Shelby Foote, interview, Aug. 16, 1987, Memphis; Baldesar Castiglione, *The Book of the Courtier,* trans. Charles S. Singleton (New York: Doubleday, 1959), 43.

17. Copy, William Alexander Percy, Will, July 17, 1941, probated Jan. 27, 1942, Letters Testamentary Cause #12584, Executor's Book 2, p. 64, Clerk of Chancery Court, Washington County Court House, Greenville, Miss., and copy, Deed of Sale, Brinkwood property, to Captain Wendell F. Kline, USN, Sept. 19, 1950, William Alexander Percy Alumni file, Jessie Ball DuPont Memorial Library, USL. The Brinkwood property deeds are located in Deed Book 51, 78, indicating purchase April 1, 1925, and sale by Huger Wilkinson Jervey to Percy, Feb. 1, 1934, in Deed Book 58, 544, Office of the Register, Franklin County Court House, Winchester, Tennessee.

18. Tolson, *Pilgrim in the Ruins,* 145.

19. Phone interview with Mary Shepherd Quintard Wyatt-Brown, Beaufort, S.C., Nov. 11, 1992.

20. Interview, Mrs. Duval ("Boo" Sanborn) Cravens, Sewanee, June 30, 1987; interview, Mrs. William (Cynthia Sanborn Smith) Ware, New Orleans, Nov. 14, 1988; interview, Mrs. David (Betty Cocke) Wright, Bremo Bluffs, Va., Sept. 18, 1989; Margaret Myers Diary, 1936–41, passim, USL; phone interview with Mary Shepherd Quintard Wyatt-Brown, Nov. 11, 1992; Ann Waldron, *Close Connections: Caroline Gordon and the Southern Renaissance* (Knoxville: University of Tennessee Press, 1987), 207–15.

21. Phone interview with Mary Shepherd Quintard Wyatt-Brown, Nov. 11, 1992; and phone interview with Lady Thornton, July 4, 1993.

22. Interview with Walker Percy, Oct. 17, 1988, Covington, La.; Gilbert Schricke, "A Frenchman's Visit to Walker Percy," *Delta,* No. 13 (Nov. 1981): 23.

23. Samuel Greenberg, "Sullivan and Treatment," in Patrick Mullahy, ed., *The Contribution of Harry Stack Sullivan* (New York: Science House, 1967), 136–37; A. H. Chapman, *Harry Stack Sullivan: His Life and Work* (New York: G. P. Putnam's Sons, 1976), 45–53; John Griffin Jones interview, in Lawson and Kramer, eds., *Conversations with Walker Percy,* 256; Walker Percy, "A Doctor Talks with the South and Its Young Heroes," *National Observer,* Sept. 16, 1972, p. 14; quotations, Walker Percy, "Uncle Will's" House," in Percy, *Signposts in a Strange Land,* 50; Helen Swick Perry, *Psychiatrist of America: The Life of Harry Stack Sullivan* (Cambridge: Harvard University Press, 1982), 374.

24. Percy quoted in Jones, "Moralist of the South," 44.

25. Tolson, *Pilgrim in the Ruins,* 137–38; conversation with Alfred Kazin, Gainesville, Fla., April 19, 1987; Janet MacKenzie Rioch, "The Transference Phenomenon in Psychoanalytic Therapy," *Psychiatry* 6 (May 1943): 156.

26. Tolson, *Pilgrim in the Ruins,* 139.

27. Felix Brown, "Bereavement and Lack of a Parent in Childhood," in Elizabeth Miller, ed., *Foundations of Child Psychiatry* (London: Pergamon, 1968), 444, 451–54.

28. Walker Percy, *The Last Gentleman* (New York: New American Library, 1968), 32–38; quotation, Linda Whitney Hobson, "Sign of the Apocalypse," 59.

29. Rioch, "The Transference Phenomenon," 151.

30. *Ibid.,* 152.

31. See Anne G. Jones, review of Jay Tolson, *Pilgrim in the Ruins* in Boston *Globe,* Nov. 15, 1992.

32. Robert Coles, *Walker Percy: An American Search* (Boston: Little, Brown, 1979), 63.

33. Barbara King interview, 1974, in Lawson and Kramer, eds., *Conversations with Walker Percy,* 94.

34. Linda Hobson, "Study of Consciousness," 58.

35. Walker Percy, "The Coming Crisis in Psychiatry," *America* 96 (Jan. 5, 1957): 391.

36. Quotation, Sherry Turkle, "War Zone," a review of *Winnicott* by Adam Phillips in *London Review of Books,* Nov. 23, 1989, p. 13.

37. Jones review, Boston *Globe,* Nov. 15, 1992.

38. Percy, *Last Gentleman,* 143, 144.

39. Percy to Foote, Feb. 3, 1971, Walker Percy MSS, #4294, Southern Historical Collection, Wilson Library, University of North Carolina, Chapel Hill (hereafter SHC).

40. Percy, *Last Gentleman,* 222–23.

41. Tolson, *Pilgrim in the Ruins,* 162; Dannye Romine interview, in Lawson and Kramer, eds., *Conversations with Walker Percy,* 200–201.

42. "B. Phinizy Percy interview with John Jones of the State Department of Archives and History Conducted in New Orleans on Coliseum Street, 4-17-80," 14, typed transcript, MDAH; Kathleen Moore Peacock, "William Alexander Percy: A Study in Southern Conservatism," M.A. thesis, Birmingham-Southern College, 1958, p. 75.

43. Coles, *Walker Percy,* 65.

44. Foote quoted by Coles, *Walker Percy,* 66; quotation, Tolson, *Pilgrim in the Ruins,* 165; Walker Percy to Lt. (j.g.) E. T. P. Boone, Oct. 2, 1943, Percy Papers, #4294, SHC. Swiss quotation from Barbara Bates, *"Bargaining for Life" A Social History of Tuberculosis, 1876–1938* (Philadelphia: University of Pennsylvania Press, 1992), 41.

45. James Atlas, interview, Lawson and Kramer, eds., *Conversations with Walker Percy,* 185.

46. Coles, *Walker Percy,* 65.

47. Ralph Harper, *The Seventh Solitude: Metaphysical Homelessness in Kierkegaard, Dostoevsky, and Nietzsche* (Baltimore: Johns Hopkins University Press, 1965), 5.

48. Coles, *Walker Percy,* 67; Tolson, *Pilgrim in the Ruins,* 225, 236; Margaret Myers, June 23, 1945, Hobart-Jefferys-Myers Collection (hereafter Myers MSS, USL).

49. Linda Whitney Hobson, "Man vs. Malaise, in the Eyes of Louisiana's Walker Percy," *Louisiana Life* (July/Aug. 1983), 56.

50. Margaret Myers, diary, Dec. 2, 1942; Margaret Myers to Rosamond Myers, Nov. 20, 1939, and wartime correspondence with Rosamond Myers, Myers MSS, USL.

51. Entry for April 12, 1944, Margaret Myers, diary; Rosamond Myers to Margaret Myers, April 15, 1944, Nov. 24, 1945, *ibid.;* phone interview with Mary Shepherd Quintard Wyatt-Brown, Nov. 11, 1992; see also Tolson, *Pilgrim in the Ruins,* 189.

52. Margaret Myers, diary, Jan. 16, 1946; phone interview with Mary Shepherd Quintard Wyatt-Brown, Nov. 11, 1992, and with Lady Thornton, July 4, 1993.

53. Tolson, *Pilgrim in the Ruins,* 189.

54. Quoted by Waldron, *Close Connections,* 284.

55. Rosamond Myers and Peter Thornton (later knighted for his civil service work with the Board of Trade) were married on July 27, 1946. Tolson, *Pilgrim the Ruins,* 185–88.

56. Hobson, "Man vs. Malaise," 56;

57. Coles, *Walker Percy,* 66.

58. Bradley R. Dewey interview, 1974, in Lawson and Kramer, eds., *Conversations with Walker Percy,* 121.

59. See Shelby Foote to Walker Percy, Nov. 19, 1949, Shelby Foote MSS, #4038, SHC; Tolson, *Pilgrim in the Ruins,* 145.

60. Harriet Doar interview, 1962, in Lawson and Kramer, eds., *Conversations with Walker Percy,* 5; quotation from Walker Percy, Introduction, in Linda Whitney Hobson, *Walker Percy: A Comprehensive Descriptive Bibliography* (New Orleans: Faust Publishing Co., 1988), xviii.

61. Coles, *Walker Percy,* 72.

62. Hobson, "Sign of the Apocalypse," 59.

63. Harold Bloom, introduction, in Bloom, ed., *Thomas Mann* (New York: Chelsea House, 1986), 2.

64. See Ernst Pavel, *The Nightmare of Reason: The Life of Franz Kafka* (New York: Farrar, Straus & Giroux, 1984); Coles, *Walker Percy,* 66, 72, 187–88, 242; Robin Leary interview, in Lewis A. Lawson and Victor A. Kramer, eds., *More Conversations with Walker Percy* (Jackson: University Press of Mississippi, 1993), 63.

65. William Alexander Percy, *Collected Poems* (New York: Alfred A. Knopf, 1943), 212, 213, 250; *The Hymnal of the Protestant Episcopal Church in the United States of America* (New York: Church Pension Fund, 1940), No. 437. I am indebted to the Rev. Heather Cook of Bedford, New York, for bringing this hymn to my attention. William Alexander Percy to A. T. Molligen, Sept. 21, 1939, cited in Spalding, "William Alexander Percy," 101.

66. See Ralph C. Wood, *The Comedy of Redemption: Christian Faith and Comic Vision in Four American Novelists* (Notre Dame, Ind.: University of Notre Dame, Press, 1988), 137.

67. Tolson, *Pilgrim in the Ruins,* 204.

68. *Ibid.,* 171, 174–75, 198, 200.

69. Foote to Percy, Nov. 19, 1949, Foote MSS, #4038, SHC.

70. Bradley R. Dewey interview, in Lawson and Kramer, eds., *Conversations with Walker Percy,* 106.

71. Walker Percy, *The Message in the Bottle: How Queer Man Is, How Queer Language Is, and What One Has to Do with the Other* (New York: Farrar, Straus & Giroux, 1975), 292.

72. Noam Chomsky, "A Review of B. F. Skinner's *Verbal Behavior,*" *Language* 35 (1959): 25–58; and Chomsky, *Aspects of the Theory of Syntax* (Cambridge, Mass.: MIT Press, 1965).

73. See Ralph C. Wood, "The South as a Redemptive Place," unpublished paper; and Julia Kristeva, *Black Sun: Depression and Melancholia,* trans. Leon S. Roudiez (New York: Columbia University Press, 1989), 4.

74. Percy, *Message in the Bottle,* 83.

75. Tolson, *Pilgrim in the Ruins,* 317; Patricia Rice, "No Happily Ever After for Walker Percy's Characters," St. Louis *Post-Dispatch,* April 23, 1985, 3-D; Hobson, "Sign of the Apocalypse," 61; Jones interview, in Lawson and Kramer, eds., *Conversations with Walker Percy,* 240 (quotation).

Chapter Seventeen WALKER PERCY: THE MAKING OF A SOUTHERN NOVELIST

1. Walker Percy to Caroline Gordon, Aug. 30, 1974, in Jay Tolson, *Pilgrim in the Ruins: A Life of Walker Percy* (New York: Simon & Schuster, 1992), 393.

2. Lewis Lawson, *Following Percy: Essays on Walker Percy* (Troy, N.Y.: Whitston, 1988), 1.

3. Holmes Adams, "Writers of Greenville, Mississippi, 1915–1950," *Journal of Mississippi History* 32 (Fall 1970): 229–43.

4. Tolson, *Pilgrim in the Ruins,* 197, 209, 212–16.

5. *Ibid.,* 205–6, 246.

6. *Ibid.,* 57; Linda Whitney Hobson, "Man vs. Malaise, in the Eyes of Louisiana's Walker Percy," *Louisiana Life* (July/Aug. 1983), 57.

7. See Tolson, *Pilgrim in the Ruins,* 213.

8. "The Man on the Train," in Walker Percy, *The Message in the Bottle: How Queer Man Is, How Queer Language Is, and What One Has to Do with the Other* (New York: Farrar, Straus & Giroux, 1975), 83.

9. Bertram Wyatt-Brown, "Walker Percy: Autobiographical Fiction and the Aging Process," *Journal of Aging Studies* 3 (Jan. 1989): 81–89.

10. William Rodney Allen, *Walker Percy: A Southern Wayfarer* (Jackson: University Press of Mississippi, 1986), 5–6; Tolson, *Pilgrim in the Ruins,* 212–16.

11. Caroline Gordon to Robert Lowell, n.d., Robert Lowell Papers, Houghton Library, Harvard University. Margaret Myers, diary, Oct. 12, 1945, March 26, 1946, Myers-Jefferys-Hobart MSS, University Archives, Jessie Ball DuPont Library, University of the South, Sewanee, Tennessee (hereafter Myers MSS, USL); Ann Waldron, *Close Connections: Caroline Gordon and the Southern Renaissance* (Knoxville: University of Tennessee Press, 1987), 285.

12. Percy to Gordon, n.d., excerpted copy sent as enclosure in Gordon to Lowell, n.d. [1951], Lowell MSS, Houghton Library.

13. Tolson, *Pilgrim in the Ruins,* 38–39; also Percy excerpt, Gordon to Lowell, n.d., Lowell MSS, Houghton Library.

14. His photo still hangs in the club hallway. Tolson, *Pilgrim in the Ruins,* 36, 44.

15. *Ibid.,* 214.

16. Caroline Gordon to Walker Percy, Dec. 11, 1951, Percy MSS, SHC.

17. Gordon to Walker Percy, Dec. 11, 1951, *ibid.*

18. See Fred Kaplan, *Henry James, The Imagination of Genius: A Biography* (New York: Morrow, 1992), 456, 456–58, and entry for Feb. 5, 1895, in Leon Edel and Lyall H. Powers, eds., *The Complete Notebooks of Henry James* (New York: Oxford University Press, 1987), 113.

19. See Eva Kosofsky Sedgwick, "The Beast in the Closet: Henry James and the Writing of Homosexual Panic," in *The Epistemology of the Closet* (Berkeley: University of California Press, 1990), 182–212.

20. Tolson, *Pilgrim in the Ruins,* 214–16.

21. Gordon to Walker Percy, Nov. 25, 1952, Percy MSS, SHC.

22. Gordon to Walker Percy, Jan. 31 (quotation), and ca. Feb. 1953, Jack Wheelock to Walker Percy, Feb. 3, 1953, *ibid.*

23. See Nigel Hamilton, "A Case of Literary Fratricide: The Brüderzwist between Heinrich and Thomas Mann," in Norman Kiell, ed., *Blood Brothers: Siblings as Writers* (New York: International Universities Press, 1983), 49–72, esp. 60; Richard Winston, *Thomas Mann: The Making of an Artist, 1875–1911: From His Childhood to the Writing of Death in Venice* (New York: Simon & Schuster, 1981), 128–29; Nigel Hamilton, *The Brothers Mann: The Lives of Heinrich and Thomas Mann, 1871–1950 and 1875–1955* (New Haven: Yale University Press, 1978), 142–43.

24. See John C. Carr interview, 1971, in Lewis Lawson and Victor A. Kramer, eds., *Conversations with Walker Percy* (Jackson: University Press of Mississippi, 1985), 61.

25. E. M. Forster, *Commonplace Book,* ed. Philip Gardner (Stanford: Stanford University Press, 1985), 55.

26. Cf. Gary M. Ciuba, "Percy's Enchanted Mountain," in Jan Nordby Gretlund and Karl-Heinz Westarp, eds., *Walker Percy: Novelist and Philosopher* (Jackson: University Press of Mississippi, 1991), 19; Walker Percy, *The Gramercy Winner,* 251–52, Percy MSS, SHC, but the actual quotation comes from Tolson, *Pilgrim in the Ruins,* 232.

27. Walker Percy, *The Moviegoer* (New York: Alfred A. Knopf, 1961), 54.

28. Martin Luschei, "*The Moviegoer* as Dissolve," in Panthea Reid Broughton, ed., *The Art of Percy: Stratagems for Being* (Baton Rouge; Louisiana State University, 1979), 29.

29. Percy, *The Moviegoer,* 55, 200.

30. *Ibid.,* 25.

31. Walker Percy to Robert Daniel, Jan. 12, 1963, Robert Daniel papers, in the personal possession of Mrs. Robert Daniel, Sewanee, Tenn.; Robert Coles, *Walker Percy: An American Search* (Boston: Little, Brown, 1979), 144–45.

32. Quoted by Tolson, *Pilgrim in the Ruins,* 297; see also Martha Montello, "The Diagnostic 'I': Presenting the Case in *The Thanatos Syndrome,*" *New Orleans Review* 16 (Winter 1989): 32–36.

33. Walker Percy to Robert Daniel, March 19, 1962, Daniel papers; Ann Hurlburt, *The Interior Castle: The Art and Life of Jean Stafford* (New York: Alfred A. Knopf, 1992), 226, 326; see Robert Cubbage, "Novelist Walker Percy," *St. Anthony Messenger* 96 (Nov. 1988): 11.

34. Walker Percy, *The Last Gentleman* (New York: Farrar, Straus & Giroux, 1966), 217.

35. *Ibid.,* 150, 206.

36. *Ibid.,* 277.

37. *Ibid.,* 144.

38. *Ibid.,* 117–18.

39. *Ibid.,* 253–54.

40. *Ibid.,* 258–59; Baudelaire, quoted in Ross Chambers, *The Writing of Melancholy: Modes of Opposition in Early French Moderns,* trans. Mary Seidman Trouille (Chicago: University of Chicago Press, 1993), 156.

41. Percy, *The Last Gentleman,* 16.

42. Quoted in Tolson, *Pilgrim in the Ruins,* 332.

43. Walker Percy, "The Southern Moderate," *Commonweal* 67 (Dec. 13, 1957): 282.

44. Tolson, *Pilgrim in the Ruins,* 356; see also, Walker Percy, "Random Thoughts on Southern Literature, Southern Politics, and the American Future," *Georgia Review* 32 (Fall 1978): 499–511, esp. 503.

45. Percy to Foote, June 12, 1970, Percy MSS, SHC; Tolson, *Pilgrim in the Ruins,* 353.

46. Walker Percy, "A Southern View," *America* 97 (July 20, 1957): 428–29, quotation, 428; Percy to Foote, June 12, 1970, Percy MSS, SHC.

47. "Stoicism in the South," in Walker Percy, *Signposts in a Strange Land,* ed. Patrick Samway, (New York: Farrar, Straus & Giroux, 1991), 83–88 (quotation, 84).

48. Quoted in Tolson, *Pilgrim in the Ruins,* 390.

49. Walker Percy, "Introduction," *Lanterns on the Levee* (1973), xi, xii, xiii; Tolson, *Pilgrim in the Ruins,* 199.

50. Tolson, *Pilgrim in the Ruins,* 393.

51. Michael Kobre, "The Consolations of Fiction: Walker Percy's Dialogic Art," *New Orleans Review* 16 (Winter 1989): 45–53; Kiernan Quinlan, *The Last Catholic Novelist: Walker Percy in His Time* (forthcoming), 226.

52. See Quinlan, *The Last Catholic Novelist;* I thank the author for a chance to read his penetrating study in manuscript.

53. Tolson, *Pilgrim in the Ruins,* 396.

54. Walker Percy, *Lancelot* (New York: Farrar, Straus & Giroux, 1977), 3. Percy also expressed the same idea in *The Second Coming* when Will Barrett reflects upon Ed Barrett's suicide and declares that "nothing else had ever happened" in his life, thereby dismissing marriage, child-rearing, and career as rather meaningless. Walker Percy, *The Second Coming* (New York: Farrar, Straus & Giroux, 1980), 52.

55. See Lewis Baker, *The Percys of Mississippi: Politics and Literature in the New South* (Baton Rouge: Louisiana State University Press, 1983), 169; Coles, *Walker Percy,* 112.

56. John W. Draper, *The Humors and Shakespeare's Characters* (New York: AMS Press, 1965), 62–80; Percy, *Lanterns on the Levee,* 158.

57. Tolson, *Pilgrim in the Ruins,* 405–06.

58. Percy, *Lancelot,* 95–96.

59. Tolson, *Pilgrim in the Ruins,* 374.

60. Lewis A. Lawson, "The Fall of the House of Lamar," in Broughton, ed., *The Art of Walker Percy: Stratagems for Being,* 219–20; on suicide, see William Rodney Allen, "All the Names of Death: Walker Percy and Ernest Hemingway," *Mississippi Quarterly* 36 (Winter 1982–83): 3–19.

61. Percy, *Lancelot,* 213.

62. See Lawson, "Fall of House of Lamar," 239–40; Percy, *Lancelot,* 232–41.

63. Percy, *Lancelot,* 5, 14–15; see Lawson, "Fall of House of Lamar," 219–44.

64. Emma Jung and Marie-Louise von Franz, *The Grail Legend,* 2nd ed., trans. Andrea Dykes (Boston: Sigo Press, 1980), 111; Percy, *Lancelot,* 10 (quotation); John C. Carr interview, in Lawson and Kramer, eds., *Conversations with Walker Percy,* 64.

65. Interview, Nov. 17, 1989, Covington, La.

66. Percy, *Lanterns on the Levee,* 345, 348. See James B. McCarthy, *Death Anxiety: The Loss of the Self* (New York: Gardner Press, 1980), 37–40.

67. Percy, *Lancelot,* 256, 257.

68. See Tolson, *Pilgrim in the Ruins,* 42.

69. Percy, *The Second Coming,* 55.

70. Walker Percy, "Bourbon," *Esquire* (Dec. 1975), 149. In *The Moviegoer,* Walker Percy has Binx Bolling comment that he had inherited from his father "a deed to ten acres of a defunct duck club down in St. Bernard Parish, the only relic of my father's many enthusiasms" (p. 7). LeRoy Pratt Percy and the senator both belonged to such a club and loved to hunt there together. Percy, *The Second Coming,* 162. See *Hamlet,* I, v, 162–63.

71. Percy, *The Second Coming,* 360.

72. *Ibid.,* 302. I am indebted to Anne Wyatt-Brown for the reflections about the meaning of *The Second Coming* from an authorial perspective. Interestingly, Percy has Barrett muse that it should be called "Housman's" condition rather than the German physician's, in reference to "the disorder suffered by the poet who mourned dead Shropshire lads and rose-lipt maids and his own lost youth" sentiments that once again bring memories of Will Percy to the foreground.

Chapter Eighteen   THANATOS AND LINEAGE

1. F. R. Surtees, "The Lamente of Henry Percye," in Gerald Brenan, *A History of the House of Percy: From the Earliest Times down to the Present Century* (2 vols.; London: Freemantle & Co., 1902), 1: 233.

2. Phil McCombs, "Century of Thanatos: Walker Percy and His 'Subversive Message,' " [interview] *Southern Review* 24 (Autumn 1988): 822.

3. *Ibid.,* 820.

4. See Howard I. Kushner, "Suicide, Gender, and the Fear of Modernity in Nineteenth-Century Medical and Social Thought," *Journal of Social History* 26 (Spring 1993): 461–90; Michael MacDonald and Terence R. Murphy, *Sleepless Souls: Suicide in Early Modern England* (Oxford: Clarendon Press, 1990), 186–87, 188 (quotation).

5. Walker Percy, *The Message in the Bottle: How Queer Man Is, How Queer Language Is, and What One Has to Do with the Other* (New York: Farrar, Straus & Giroux, 1975), 109.

6. Quoted in Raymond Klibansky, Erwin Panofsky, and Fritz Saxl, *Saturn and Melancholy: Studies in the History of Natural Philosophy, Religion, and Art* (New York: Basic Books, 1964), 229.

7. Walker Percy to Shelby Foote, Nov. 8, 1977, Walker Percy MSS, Southern Historical Collection, Wilson Library, University of North Carolina, Chapel Hill (hereafter Walker Percy MSS, SHC).

8. Walker Percy, *Lost in the Cosmos: The Last Self-Help Book* (New York: Pocket Books, 1983), 75–76, 79–80.

9. Jay Tolson, *Pilgrim in the Ruins: A Life of Walker Percy* (New York: Simon & Schuster, 1992), 453–55, 484–89.

10. Percy, *The Message in the Bottle;* Anne Wyatt-Brown, "Another Model of an Aging Writer: Sarton's Politics of Old Age," in Anne M. Wyatt-Brown and

Janice Rossen, eds., *Aging and Gender in Literature: Studies in Creativity* (Charlottesville: University Press of Virginia, 1993), 53.

11. Walker Percy, *The Thanatos Syndrome* (New York: Farrar, Straus & Giroux, 1987), vii.

12. John Edward Hardy, *The Fiction of Walker Percy* (Urbana: University of Illinois Press, 1987), 229–31.

13. Percy, *Thanatos Syndrome,* 197; see also, *ibid.,* 265.

14. See William Rodney Allen, "Father Smith's Confession in *The Thanatos Syndrome,*" Jan Nordby Gretlund and Karl Heinz-Westarp, eds., *Walker Percy: Novelist and Philosopher* (Jackson: University Press of Mississippi, 1991), 195–96.

15. Percy, *Thanatos Syndrome,* 136.

16. Gary M. Ciuba, *Walker Percy: Books of Revelations* (Athens: University of Georgia Press, 1991), 270.

17. Percy, *Thanatos Syndrome,* 140.

18. Sarah A. Dorsey [Filia], *Agnes Graham: A Novel* (Philadelphia: Claxton, Remsen and Haffelfinger, 1869); Percy, *Thanatos Syndrome.*

19. See William Styron, *Darkness Visible, A Memoir of Madness* (New York: Random House, 1990), 32–33; Stanley W. Jackson, *Melancholia and Depression: From Hippocratic Times to Modern Times* (New Haven: Yale University Press, 1986), 105–6.

20. Percy to William L. Percy, c/o Dobbs and Wey, Atlanta, Ga., April 25, 1907, Percy MSS, Mississippi Department of Archives and History, Jackson (hereafter PP, MDAH); phone conversation with John Seymour Erwin, Sun City Center, Fla., Feb. 20, 1994; Jonathan Daniels, *A Southerner Discovers the South* (New York: Macmillan, 1938), 172. On Eustace Percy, see *Burke's Peerage* (1949), 1513.

21. William Alexander Percy, *Lanterns on the Levee: Recollections of a Planter's Son* (1941; Baton Rouge: Louisiana State University, 1973), 39 (hereafter, Percy, *Lanterns*).

22. Percy, *Lanterns,* 40; W. A. Percy to John Hereford Percy, March 3, 1941, O. M. Thompson and William Wright MSS, Baton Rouge (hereafter Thompson-Wright MSS).

23. John Hereford Percy to W. A. Percy, Feb. 28, 1941, copy, Robert Craig Gilmore Collection, Lafayette, Louisiana.

24. W. A. Percy to John Hereford Percy, March 3, 1941, Wright-Thompson MSS; a copy is located in the Gilmore MSS; see R. W. B. Lewis, *The Jameses: A Family Narrative* (New York: Farrar, Straus & Giroux, 1991), 586.

25. Percy, *Lanterns,* foreword.

26. Percy, *Lanterns,* 39. (Her name was Mary Butler Duncan Dana, according to her grandson Duncan Longcope. Note to author, March 10, 1993.)

27. Percy, *Lanterns,* 40.

28. Percy Ferguson to John Hereford Percy, Aug. 8, 1931, Percy to Clarence Percy, Jan. 24, 1905, Oscar M. Thompson and William H. Wright, Jr. Collection, Baton Rouge, Louisiana (hereafter Thompson-Wright MSS); William Alexander Percy to Mrs. William Butler Duncan, Dec. 18, 1904, Longcope-Johansen Collection, Cornhill Farm, Lee, Massachusetts, (hereafter Longcope-Johansen MSS); Edward Barrington de Fonblanque, *Annals of the House of Percy from the Conquest to the Opening of the Nineteenth Century* (2 vols.; London: Richard Clay & Sons, 1887), 2: Table X, 586.

29. Fonblanque, *Annals,* 2: 587–89; George Tate, *History of Alnwick* 1: 302–

06; G. R. Bartho, "The Percies and Alnwick Castle, 1557–1632," *Archeologica Aeliana,* 4th ser. 35 (1957): 51; William Armstrong Percy to Mrs. William Butler Duncan, n.d., Longcope-Johansen MSS.

30. See, for instance, Archie J. McMillan to Robert Craig Gilmore, Nov. 5, Dec. 4, 1980, Gilmore to Archie McMillan, Dec. 28, 1980, Jan. 13, 1981, Gilmore MSS.

31. Sargent Prentiss Knut, Metropolitan Club, Washington, D.C., to Mary Duncan Butler Dana, March 14, 1913, Longcope-Johansen MSS. Margaret S. Routh (1830–1910) was the widow of John Knox Routh, one of the wealthiest men of Adams County, sister-in-law of Senator Seargent S. Prentiss, and daughter of James Cadwallader and Jane Percy Williams, another wealthy couple. See obituary for Margaret Routh, copy from a Natchez newspaper, Aug. 19, 1910, in Longcope-Johansen MSS; John Hereford Percy, *The Percy Family of Mississippi and Louisiana, 1776–1943* (Baton Rouge: priv. prnt., 1943), 11 (hereafter Percy, *Percy Family*).

32. See Michael Kammen, *Mystic Chords of Memory: The Transformation of Tradition in American Culture* (New York: Alfred A. Knopf, 1991), 218; Gaines M. Foster, *Ghosts of the Confederacy: Defeat, the Lost Cause, and the Emergence of the New South, 1865 to 1913* (New York: Oxford University Press, 1987).

33. See, for instance, Leila Percy Hardy, Lynchburg, Va., to William R. Percy, Minden, La., Feb. 22, 1915, Harry Percy Veazie to Clarence Percy, Sept. 15, 1905, Clarence Percy to Harry Percy Veazie [copy], New Orleans, Oct. 18, 1905, Thompson-Wright MSS; Eustace Percy, Guildford, Eng., to Mrs. Violetta Percy Merritt, Denver, Colo., June 26, 1936, Dudley G. Dwyer, Consul-General, London, to Mrs. Merritt, June 30, 1936, Gilmore MSS.

34. Others involved were P. V. Stratton of Philadelphia, Mary I. Prentiss, Margaret Routh, and J. P. Howell of St. Francisville, Mrs. Appolina Ingraham Ellis of Philadelphia, and Margaret Percy McGehee of Natchez. See especially, Sargent Prentiss Knut to Mrs. Mary Duncan Butler Dana, March 14, 1913, and other correspondence in the Longcope-Johansen MSS.

35. Percy, *Percy Family,* 11–15.

36. Henry James, *The American* (1877; New York: Holt, Rinehart & Winston, 1949).

37. Morgan bought the house and land in 1909. See John Douglas Forbes, *J. P. Morgan, Jr., 1867–1943* (Charlottesville: University Press of Virginia, 1981), 68.

38. Percy, *Percy Family,* 15; "Alexander Duncan," in *The National Cyclopædia of American Biography* (New York: James T. White, 1907), 9: 559.

39. See "Paul Dana," in *The National Cyclopædia of American Biography* (New York: James T. White & Co., 1924), 8: 253; Allan Nevius, "Charles Anderson Dana," in Allen Johnson and Dumas Malone, eds., *Dictionary of American Biography* (New York: Scribner, 1959), 3: 49–52. Jane and William Butler Duncan's two sons became leading New York industrialists, one of them an early executive officer of General Electric in Schenectady, N.Y.; see Percy, *Percy Family of Mississippi,* 15.

40. Clarence Percy to Harry Percy, Nov. 30, 1895, Harry Percy to Clarence Percy, Dec. 5, 1895 and another, n.d.; Harry Veazie Percy to Clarence Percy, Sept. 15, 1905, June 22, 1913; W. Chaille Percy to Harry Percy, Aug. 22, 1895, Jane Percy Butler Duncan [Mrs William Butler Duncan] to Clarence Percy, ca. Sept. or Oct. 1895, Jan. 21, [?]; Jane Butler Dana to Clarence Percy, March/April ? 1900; Mary D. Butler Dana to John Hereford Percy, June 22, July 19, 28, 1913, to John

Hereford Percy, June 22, 1913, to W. R. Percy, July 3, 1913, Thompson-Wright MSS.

41. Harry Percy Veazie to Clarence Percy, Oct. 13, 1905, Thompson-Wright MSS.

42. Jane Percy Duncan to Clarence Percy, Jan. 21, ca. 1895, *ibid.,* April 16, 1900, Mary Dana to William R. Percy, Minden, Louisiana, n.d., Thompson-Wright MSS.

43. Jane Percy Butler Duncan [Mrs. William Butler Duncan] to Clarence Percy, ca. Sept. or Oct. 1895, and March–April, 1900 (quotation), Thompson-Wright MSS.

44. See, for instance, J. P. Russell to Jane Duncan, March 20, 1896, Longcope-Johansen MSS.

45. Jane Duncan to Clarence Percy, January 21, ca. 1895; (second quotation), *ibid.,* April 16, 1900, Thompson-Wright MSS.

46. Rowan Percy's information was reported in Jane Percy Prentiss (1843–1902) to Mrs. Paul Dana, Aug. 14, 1893, Longcope-Johansen MSS.

47. Clarence Percy to Harry Veazie Percy, Nov. 30, 1895, Thompson-Wright MSS.

48. Hardy Page, 21 Old Buildings, Lincolns Inn, London, to Edwin Freshfield, Feb. 13, 1896, Longcope-Johansen MSS. The Bible has since disappeared. John Hereford Percy to Stanley C. Arthur, June 11, 1931, Gilmore MSS. Perhaps this was the Robert Percy of Dublin whose daughter married into the Tennison family in 1764. C. M. Tennison, "Pedigree of Tenison," *Miscellanea Genealogica et Heraldica,* 4th ser. 4, Pt. 1 (Dec. 1904): 149.

49. See J. B. M. Frederick, *Lineage Book of the British Army: Mounted Corps and Infantry, 1660–1968* (Cornwallville, N.Y.: Hope Farm Press, 1969), viii; Frances St. Clair Vivian, "John Andre as a Young Officer: The Army in the Eighteenth Century and a Young Man's Impressions on First Joining His Regiment in the 1770s," *Army Historical Research* 50 (No. 162, 1950): 30–31.

50. Mary Butler Dana to Clarence Percy, n.d. [ca. 1909], Thompson-Wright MSS.

51. Clarence Percy to Harry Percy, Nov. 30, 1895; Harry Percy to Clarence Percy, Sept. 15, Dec. 5, 1895 (transcription); see also Jane P. Butler Duncan [Mrs. William Butler Duncan] to Clarence Percy, Nov. 1 [?], 1895, and March/April [?], 1900, and Mary Dana to W. R. Percy, July 3, 1913, Thompson-Wright MSS. On Alice Mary Percy, see Wills, Kilkenny, 1903, Ref t 10, p. 629, Public Record Office, Dublin, Ireland.

52. Brenan, *History of the House of Percy,* 2: "Genealogical Table of the Irish Percies," IV, appendix; also, Robert Percy Esquire, Snugborough, County Wicklow, Grant of Admon. 1750/51 Prerog. Gt. Bk. (Fol. 187B), died intestate, Elizabeth Shee, his daughter and next of kin, Feb. 23, 1750, Public Record Office, Dublin.

53. Jane Percy Butler Duncan to Clarence Percy, April 10, 1900, Thompson-Wright MSS. The first daughter was named for his wife Janes's mother, Jean Proudfoot.

54. Percy, *Percy Family,* 5.

55. Hardy and Page to Freshfield, Feb. 13, 1896, Longcope-Johansen MSS.

56. Hardy and Page to Edward Freshfield, Feb. 13, 1896, Longcope-Johansen

MSS. The law firm noted that out of 47 parishes in Kilkenny only five had record books so early as 1760. Robert Dow to Robert Percy, July 27, 1804, copy, Longcope-Johansen MSS, and original in Thompson-Wright MSS. I am indebted to Alma Carpenter of Natchez for showing why Robert Percy's case for his legitimacy was more fragile than it first might appear to the investigator. On John Hereford Percy's ignorance of this report, see, for example, Percy to the Rev. Samuel Hammond Stratham, Somerset, Eng., May 14, 1932;

57. See Merlin G. Butler, M.D., et al., "DAR Family Tree Genetics Project: Frequency of Genetic and Other Health Problems," *Daughters of the American Revolution Magazine* 124 (March 1990): 165–67, 184; A. E. H. Emery and D. L. Rimoin, eds., *Principles and Practices of Medical Genetics* (New York: Churchill Livingstone, 1983).

58. Brenan, *History of the House of Percy*, 2: Table IV, Appendix.

59. See James Percy, *The Case of James Percy, Claymant to the Earldom of Northumberland. . . .* (London, priv. prnt., 1685) and *idem, To the Right Honourable Lords Spiritual and Temporal in Parliament Assembled, the Humble Petition of James Percy: A True Pedegree to Prove the Claymant, James Percy . . . Is Cousin and Next Heir-Male to Joscelin Percy, the late and 11th Earl of Northumberland, Deceased* (London?: n.p., 1681?), 1–8; Nancy Valpy, "Elizabeth Percy," *British Heritage* 4 (April/May 1983): 22–31.

60. In some doggerel that quite incensed the duchess, James Percy had declared: "Resolved I am to spend my all/ Before a Percy's name shall fall." See *History of Alnwick*, 1: 303.

61. The eccentric Earl of Anglesea thought he had a good case and cast the only vote against the trunkmaker's harsh penalty. *A True Pedegree to prove the Claymant, James Percy, to be the Second Son of Henry Percy of Horton in the County of Northampton* (London: n.p., 1685), 1; Brenan, *History of the House of Percy* 2: 332–33; *History of Alnwick*, 1: 304–6; Craik, *Romance of the Peerage* 4: 319; Harry Percy of County Leitrim to W. Chaille Percy, Aug. 22, 1895, Thompson-Wright MSS, suggests that the Ulster Herald-at-Arms took seriously the claim that Charles belonged to the "trunkmaker" branch of the Percys.

62. See Fonblanque, *Annals of the House of Percy*, 2: 487.

63. Percy Ferguson to John Hereford Percy, Aug. 8, 1931, [partial copy], Gilmore MSS, original in Thompson-Wright MSS; Percy, *Percy Family*, 64.

64. On Henry Lord Percy (Hotspur), see Geoffrey H. White and Lord Howard de Walden, *The Complete Peerage* (London: St. Catherine Press, 1945), 10: 464; see "Sir Henry Percy," in Sir Leslie Stephen and Sir Sidney Lee, eds., *Dictionary of National Biography* (London: Oxford University Press, 1921–22 rprt.), 15: 840–44 (hereafter *DNB*). Merwyn E. James, "The Murder at Cocklodge 28th April 1489," *Durham University Journal*, n.s. 26 (vol. 57 o.s.; March 1965): 80–87.

65. John Skelton versified the Earl's device. One line ran: "Esperaunce in exaltation of honoure. /Nay it widderethe away lyke a floure." The Earl had the entire poem painted on his bedroom wall. Merwyn E. James, *Society, Politics and Culture: Studies in Early Modern England* (Cambridge: Cambridge University Press, 1986), 89–90.

66. Brenan, *History of the House of Percy*, 1: 172; Fonblanque, *Annals of the House of Percy*, 1: 476.

67. Fonblanque, *Annals of the House of Percy*, 1: 365, 370–71.

68. James, *Society, Politics and Culture,* 171; Doubleday, G. White, and de Walden, *The Complete Peerage,* 9: 721.

69. Fonblanque, *Annals of the House of Percy,* 1: 377–78; *DNB,* 15: 861 (quotation).

70. James, *Society, Politics and Culture,* 170–71; Fonblanque, *Annals of the House of Percy,* 1: 436, 436n2, 437–38.

71. See Arthur Kleinman and Byron Good, eds., *Culture and Depression: Studies in the Anthropology and Cross-Cultural Psychiatry of Affect and Disorder* (Berkeley: University of California 1985), 20; Brenan, *History of the House of Percy,* 1: 182, 198–83; Fonblanque, *Annals of the House of Percy,* 1: 380–81, 407–8, 436 n2, 455–56 (quotation, 455), 470–76. Thomas Hilton, one of the rebels in the Pilgrimage of Grace, had counted on the Earl's support; in exasperation for not gaining it he declared that Percy had elevated knaves to the rank of "gentlemen, to whom he had disposed much of his living . . . ." James, *Society, Politics and Culture,* 300–415.

72. Fonblanque, *Annals of the House of Percy,* 1: 454–55; James Gairdner, ed., *Letters and Papers, Foreign and Domestic, of the Reign of Henry VIII* (London: H.M. Stationery Office, 1885), 8: No. 166, 56 (quotation).

73. James, *Society, Politics, and Culture,* 174 n125, and James, 270–307; Fonblanque, *Annals of the House of Percy,* 1: 468–69, 2: 119 (quotation), 119 n5; "Thomas Percy," *DNB,* 15: 878–81; *Proclamation Against the Earl of Northumberland 24 November 1569* (1569; New York: Da Capo Press, 1971); M. M. Merrick, *Thomas Percy Seventh Earl* (London: Duckett, 1949), a filiopietistic account of a Catholic "martyr." He was beatified in 1895, see p. 113.

74. Fonblanque, *Annals of the House of Percy,* 2: 166–67, 168 and 168 n2; Brenan, *History of the House of Percy,* 2: 1–25.

75. Fonblanque accepts the verdict of suicide; Brenan, *History of the House of Percy,* 2: 25–29, speculates, but not convincingly, that he was murdered.

76. Brenan, *History of the House of Percy,* 2: 36; William Percy, a younger brother, was also severely distressed by the loss. Though an intellectual, he amounted to little, served time in the Tower for homicide, drank "nothing but ale," and died a pauper in Penny Farthing Street, Oxford; see Fonblanque, *Annals of the House of Percy,* 2: 365.

77. Brenan, *History of the House of Percy,* 2: 37 (quotation), 78.

78. *Ibid.,* 2: 39, 60, 97 (quotation), 206; Fonblanque, *Annals of the House of Percy,* 2: 242, 243 n3, 243–44, 332.

79. Brenan, *History of the House of Percy,* 2: 38; 191; Fonblanque, *Annals of the House of Percy,* 2: 177–345, 351.

80. Northumberland befriended the dejected Raleigh in a most generous way before the latter's eventual execution in 1618. The earl bribed the surly warden with ruby earrings for his daughter. Raleigh was soon transferred to less wretched quarters. Moreover, Northumberland housed Thomas Harriot, the greatest mathematician and astronomer of the day, in Brenan, *History of the House of Percy,* 2: 165 (quotation), 166.

81. *Ibid.,* 2: 168.

82. *Ibid.,* 2: 211, 220; Fonblanque, *Annals of the House of Percy,* 2: 406–7. See "Algernon Percy," *DNB,* 15: 834.

83. Fonblanque, *Annals of the House of Percy,* 2: 446.

84. James Gregg, ed., *The Diaries of a Duchess. Extracts from the Diaries of the First Duchess of Northumberland (1716–1776)* (New York: George H. Doran Co., 1927), foreword by the Duke of Northumberland, vi–vii; Peter Townsend, ed., *Burke's Genealogical and Heraldic History of the Knightage* (London: Burke's Peerage Ltd., 105th ed., 1970), 1999.

85. Percy Ferguson to John Hereford Percy, Mississippi City, Miss., to John Hereford Percy, Aug. 8, 1931; Mrs. W. T. Bolton, Biloxi, Miss., to Percy, Jan. 25, 1943, and Percy to Bolton, Feb. 3, 1943, Thompson-Wright MSS.

86. John Hereford Percy to W. A. Percy, March 13, 1941 [copy], Thompson-Wright MSS.

87. Interview with Cleanth Brooks, Aug. 12, 1993, Atlanta.

88. Interview with the late Leon Koury, Feb. 25, 1993, Greenville.

89. See Kay Redfield Jamison, *Touched with Fire: Manic-Depressive Illness and the Artistic Temperament* (New York: Free Press, 1993), 3, Melville quotation, 191.

Index